Management Information Systems

FOR THE INFORMATION AGE

FOURTH CANADIAN EDITION

Stephen Haag
DANIELS COLLEGE OF BUSINESS
UNIVERSITY OF DENVER

Maeve Cummings
COLLEGE OF BUSINESS
PITTSBURG STATE UNIVERSITY

Al Pilcher
SCHOOL OF BUSINESS
ALGONQUIN COLLEGE

Rob Riordan
SPROTT SCHOOL OF BUSINESS
CARLETON UNIVERSITY

McGraw-Hill
Ryerson

Toronto   Montréal   Boston   Burr Ridge, IL   Dubuque, IA   Madison, WI   New York   San Francisco
St. Louis   Bangkok   Bogotá   Caracas   Kuala Lumpur   Lisbon   London   Madrid   Mexico City
Milan   New Delhi   Santiago   Seoul   Singapore   Sydney   Taipei

Management Information Systems
Fourth Canadian Edition

ISBN-13: 978-0-07098533-9
ISBN-10: 0-07-098533-2

1 2 3 4 5 6 7 8 9 10   TCP   0 9

Printed and bound in Canada

Care has been taken to trace ownership of copyright material contained in this text; however, the publisher will welcome any information that enables them to rectify any reference or credit for subsequent editions.

Vice President, Editor-in-Chief: Joanna Cotton
Sponsoring Editor: Bruce McIntosh
Developmental Editor: Sarah Fulton
Marketing Manager: Cathie Lefebvre
Senior Developmental Editor: Suzanne Simpson
Senior Editorial Associate: Christine Lomas
Supervising Editor: Graeme Powell
Copy Editor: Karen Rolfe
Team Lead, Production: Paula Brown
Cover Design: Michelle Losier
Cover Image: © David C. Chen/Veer
Interior Design: Michelle Losier
Page Layout: ArtPlus Limited
Printer: Transcontinental Gagne

Library and Archives Canada Cataloguing in Publication Data

Management information systems / Stephen Haag ... [et al.].—4th Canadian ed.

Previous eds. published under title: Management information systems for the information age.
ISBN 978-0-07-098533-9

1. Management information systems—Textbooks. 2. Information technology—Management—Textbooks. I. Haag, Stephen II. Title: Management information systems for the information age.

T58.6.M34 2009   658.4'038011   C2008-906323-6

For Alexis; my new daughter
and special princess.
Stephen Haag

To the memory of Steve Lunce who was
a good friend and a good man.
Maeve Cummings

Thanks Jennie, Thomas, and Jake for letting
me experience this journey.
Al Pilcher

For all the marvellous students who have
allowed me to learn along with them.
Robert Riordan

AL PILCHER is a professor in the Bachelor of Applied Business e-Business Supply Chain Management Degree program at Algonquin College, Ottawa. He holds a Bachelor of Commerce in Information Systems and an M.B.A thesis option in Technology Management from the Sprott School of Business, Carleton University; his thesis topic was "Factors Affecting Mobile Data Technology Adoption by Canadian SME's." Al is certified as a Project Management Professional and as an SAP Consultant Certification Solution Architect ERP—Integration of Business Processes.

Before joining Algonquin full-time in December 2008, Al was a term instructor at the Sprott School of Business, teaching Management Information Systems. Prior to academics, Al was a two-time Canadian Olympian for Cross Country Skiing in the 1988 and 1992 Olympics. He stills holds the record of best Canadian male result at Nordic World Championships, finishing seventh in the 50 kilometres. Al also competed and placed nationally in the Canadian Road Race Cycling, Triathlon, and Duathlon Championships. An entrepreneur during his undergrad years, Al raised over $100,000, implemented several business plans, supported six agents, and developed proprietary software. Other accomplishments include leading camping trips, pilot's license, building a cedar log home, and owning a 1927 Model-T. But to date, his greatest personal accomplishment (besides his family) is getting his undergrad when he was 38 years old.

ROB RIORDAN is an instructor in Information Systems in the Sprott School of Business at Carleton University in Ottawa. He holds an Honours Bachelor of Arts degree in Sociology and a Master's Degree in Social Demography from the University of Western Ontario, where he also studied toward a Ph.D. in Epidemiology and Biostatistics in the Faculty of Medicine. Before quite finishing his studies, he accepted a position at Statistics Canada, where he worked for 15 years while teaching Information Systems on a contract basis at Carleton. At the height of the tech boom, Carleton wooed him to a full-time faculty position, where he has remained ever since.

Rob began his near-lifelong passion for information systems while an undergraduate, becoming somewhat of an expert in the use of SPSS on the venerable CDC Cyber mainframe. From there, he learned to program in FORTRAN on the Cyber and then in BASIC on the DEC VAX. Needing to support his burgeoning family, Rob took various programming and database management positions for research projects in epidemiology, demography, and sociology, along with analyst and project director positions for the Health Care Research Unit at Western.

Rob is the recipient of several teaching awards (and near awards), including the prestigious Teaching Achievement Award for 2009 at Carleton. He was also recipient of the Commerce Society Excellence in Teaching Award, the Teaching Excellence Award of the Carleton University Students Association, and twice a finalist for the National Capital Educator's Award. Rob also received a Professional Achievement Award from Carleton in 2002–2003. He lives with his wife Fara and two remaining at-home children (of four) near the beach in the Ottawa suburb of Britannia. He has two grandchildren living in Germany. He is an avid cyclist, clocking more than 5,000 kilometres a year including a solo cross-Ontario-and-back cycle trip every June. He fancies himself a poet.

STEPHEN HAAG is a professor of Information Technology and Electronic Commerce in the Daniels College of Business at the University of Denver. Previously, Stephen served as Chair of the Department of Information Technology and Electronic Commerce, Director of the Master of Science in Information Technology program, Director of the MBA program, and Associate Dean of Graduate Programs. Stephen holds a B.B.A. and M.B.A. from West Texas State University and a Ph.D. from the University of Texas at Arlington.

Stephen is the author/coauthor of numerous books including *Computing Concepts in Action* (a K-12 textbook), *Interactions: Teaching English as a Second Language* (with his mother and father), *Information Technology: Tomorrow's Advantage Today* (with Peter Keen), *Excelling in Finance, Business Driven Technology*, and more than 40 books within the I-Series. He has also written numerous articles appearing in such journals as *Communications of the ACM*, *Socio-Economic Planning Sciences*, the *International Journal of Systems Science*, *Managerial and Decision Economics*, *Applied Economics*, and the *Australian Journal of Management*. Stephen lives with his family in Highlands Ranch, Colorado.

MAEVE CUMMINGS is a professor of Information Systems at Pittsburg State University. She holds a B.S. in Mathematics and Computer Science and an M.B.A from Pittsburg State, and a Ph.D. in Information Systems from the University of Texas at Arlington. She has published in various journals including the *Journal of Global Information Management* and the *Journal of Computer Information Systems*. She serves on various editorial boards and is a coauthor of *Case Studies in Information Technology*, the concepts books of the *I-Series*, entitled *Computing Concepts and Information Systems Essentials*, now in its second edition. Maeve has been teaching for 25 years and lives in Pittsburg, Kansas, with her husband, Slim.

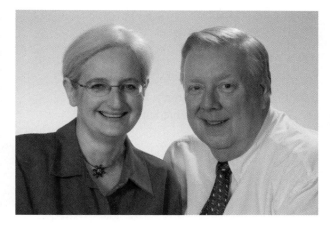

BRIEF TABLE OF CONTENTS

TABLE OF CONTENTS

EXTENDED LEARNING MODULE E
Online at www.mcgrawhill.ca/olc/haag
The World Wide Web and the Internet

EXTENDED LEARNING MODULE F
Online at www.mcgrawhill.ca/olc/haag
Designing Databases and
Entity-Relationship Diagramming

EXTENDED LEARNING MODULE G
Office 2007 Version
Online at www.mcgrawhill.ca/olc/haag
Implementing a Database with Microsoft Access

The fourth Canadian edition of *Management Information Systems for the Information Age* provides you the ultimate in flexibility to tailor content to the exact needs of your MIS or IT course. The nine chapters and twelve Extended Learning Modules may be presented in any sequence, and you may choose your own mix of technical and business/managerial topics.

The nine chapters form the core of material covering business and managerial topics, from strategic and competitive technology opportunities to the organization and management of information using databases and data warehouses. If you covered only the chapters and none of the modules, the focus of your course would be MIS from a business and managerial point of view.

The twelve Extended Learning Modules provide a technical glimpse into the world of IT, covering topics ranging from building a Web site, to computer crime and digital forensics, to how to use Microsoft Access. If you chose only the modules and none of the chapters, the focus of your course would be on the technical and hands-on aspects of IT.

You can easily select a course format that represents your own desired blend of topics. While you might not choose to cover the technologies of networks, for example, you might require your students to build a small database application. In that case, you would omit Module B (Network Basics) and spend more time on Module F (Designing Databases and Entity-Relationship Diagramming) and Module G (Implementing a Database with Microsoft Access).

On the next page, we've provided a table of the chapters and the modules. As you put your course together and choose the chapters and/or modules you want to cover, we suggest the following:

- Cover any or all of the chapters as suits your purposes.
- Cover any or all of the modules as suits your purposes.
- You may cover the modules in any order you wish.

Please note that your students will find Modules E, F, G, H, I, J, K, and L online at www.mcgrawhill.ca/olc/haag.

The unique organization of this text gives you complete flexibility to design your course as you see fit.

- Management focus—By focusing on the chapters, your class will take a managerial approach to MIS.
- Technical focus—If hands-on, technical skills are more important, focus your MIS course on the modules.

THE CHAPTERS	THE EXTENDED LEARNING MODULES
CHAPTER 1 The Information Age in Which You Live	**Extended Learning Module A** Computer Hardware and Software
CHAPTER 2 Major Business Initiatives	**Extended Learning Module B** Network Basics
CHAPTER 3 Databases and Data Warehouses	**Extended Learning Module C** Computer Crime and Digital Forensics
CHAPTER 4 Decision Support and Artificial Intelligence	**Extended Learning Module D** Careers in Business
CHAPTER 5 Electronic Commerce	**Extended Learning Module E*** The World Wide Web and the Internet
CHAPTER 6 Systems Development	**Extended Learning Module F*** Designing Databases and Entity-Relationship Diagramming
CHAPTER 7 Enterprise Infrastructure, Metrics, and Business Continuity Planning	**Extended Learning Module G*** **(Office 2007 Version)** Implementing a Database with Microsoft Access
CHAPTER 8 Protecting People and Information	**Extended Learning Module G*** **(Office 2003 Version)** Implementing a Database with Microsoft Access
CHAPTER 9 Emerging Trends and Technologies	**Extended Learning Module H*** **(Office 2007 Version)** Decision Analysis with Spreadsheet Software
	Extended Learning Module H* **(Office 2003 Version)** Decision Analysis with Spreadsheet Software
	Extended Learning Module I* Object-Oriented Technologies
	Extended Learning Module J* Building a Web Page with HTML
	Extended Learning Module K* Building an E-Portfolio
	Extended Learning Module L* Programming in Excel with VBA

* The complete text for Modules E, F, G, H, I, J, K, and L is on-line at **www.mcgrawhill.ca/olc/haag**.

Organization—The Haag Advantage

The separation of content between the chapters and the Extended Learning Modules is very simple. We can sum it up by saying:

- The chapters address what you want your students to **know**.
- The modules address what you want your students to **be able to do**.

Together, both combine to provide a well-balanced repository of important information aimed at developing a prospective business professional equipped with both foundational knowledge and application experience, ready to take on today's highly competitive job market.

Each chapter and module contains full pedagogical support:

- Student Learning Outcomes
- Summary
- Key Terms and Concepts
- Short-Answer Questions
- Assignments and Exercises

The chapters focus on the *business and managerial* applications of MIS and information technology.

The modules focus on giving your students real *hands-on-knowledge* they can apply in both their personal and professional experiences.

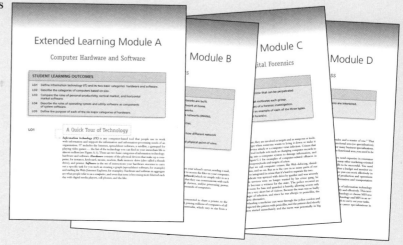

Pedagogy

Each chapter and module contains complete pedagogical support in the form of

STUDENT LEARNING OUTCOMES

LO1 Describe the key characteristics of a relational database.
LO2 List the five software components of a database management system.
LO3 Describe key characteristics of a data warehouse.
LO4 Describe four major types of data-mining tools in a data warehouse environment.
LO5 Describe business intelligence and its role in an organization.
LO6 List key considerations in information ownership in an organization.

Learning Outcomes and Summarized Learning Outcomes: Student learning outcomes open and close each chapter and module. We summarize the learning content by revisiting each student learning outcome: "Tell them what you're going to tell them, tell them, and then tell them what you told them."

OPENING CASE STUDY
Offsite Backup a Snug Fit for Adidas Canada

Adidas Canada's headquarters in Concorde, Ontario, just north of Toronto, supports a head office of about 120 staff; a high-tech distribution facility serving 4,000 retail outlets from Brantford, Ontario, with a staff of about 100; a 30-seat call centre in suburban Montreal; a small showroom in Burnaby, B.C.; about 50 sales reps flogging the Adidas and Taylor Made Golf lines across the country, and a fast-growing owned-retail arm operating 12 stores, with a flagship store still to open at Yonge and Dundas in Toronto.

These varied and far-flung operations generate a lot of data—and this data needs to be backed up. The Brantford warehouse is highly automated, and features insourced (see Chapter 8) software applications that provide supply chain and a myriad of both internal- and external-facing Web applications. With an IT staff of 13—most at head office but one each at the warehouse and call centre—it made sense to Adidas management to outsource the complicated process of maintaining current data backups to an

Opening Case Studies: Each chapter begins with an opening case study, highlighting how an organization has successfully implemented many of that chapter's concepts.

PERSPECTIVES

GOT MILK? THEY DO IN BRITISH COLUMBIA

The British Columbia Milk Marketing Board has the responsibility of collecting raw milk from farmers and transporting it to processing plants. The Marketing Board transfers payments from the processors to the farmers—to the tune of $17 million every two weeks. Milk is picked up from 350 farms per day by a fleet of 70 trucks, so that all 700 farms in the system see collection every other day. The milk goes to 26 processors across the vast province.

The paper-based system of record keeping was collapsing under its own weight. Upon pumping a farmer's milk into his truck, a driver recorded the number of litres collected on a four-part paper form and gave the farmer one copy. To fill a two-trailer truck, a driver collected milk from five farms and kept track, on paper, of how much milk came from each one. When the trailers were full of milk, the driver headed for the processing plant where a receipt for the quantity of milk was filled out. The truck then pro-

much time that there wasn't much left for the in-depth analysis necessary for the type of decision making that would have led to more effective use of resources.

The new decision support system handles data entry in real time. Each driver uses a handheld wireless scanning unit to send information to the central system. Each farm and processing plant has a unique bar code that the driver just has to scan. All that's left is to enter the volume of milk and add any comments like the temperature of the milk and so on. A wireless printer in the truck's cab can produce a printed copy of the transaction for the farmer or processing plant. The data is then sent over the cellular data network to the Marketing Board's Internet access point, and from there to the main computer for processing.

Quite apart from collecting data faster and more accurately, enabling more efficient decision making, the

Perspectives: Each chapter contains boxed features highlighting the application of chapter material, most often in a Canadian context.

CLOSING CASE STUDY 2
It's All About Customer Relations in the Financial Services Market

ScotiaMcLeod (www.scotiabank.com) is the investment arm of Scotiabank, one of Canada's largest financial organizations with over $280 billion in assets. ScotiaMcLeod's financial advisers specialize in helping individuals and small business customers plan financial solutions for trusts, estate planning, borrowing, and banking services. ScotiaMcLeod has more than 800 financial advisers working in 84 branches across the country. According to Chris Carter, associate director and branch manager for ScotiaMcLeod's North Vancouver office, the financial services sector is a people-driven business where customer service is critical to success. Chris wanted the ability to turn every customer interaction into an opportunity to provide services to his clients. He wanted to know if technology—specifically a customer relationship management (CRM) system—could help him promote a professional image and customer-oriented business philosophy at his

branch as a way of putting clients at ease and attracting prospective clients who are searching for financial advice.

Chris knew he needed to be proactive in order to keep existing clients happy and to build his base of new customers. Since his team of financial advisers contacts clients often and tracks accounts daily, he also knew that he would need a more effective CRM solution. "A client may be worth up to $50,000 for professional consulting and ongoing management fees," says Chris. "If customers are not tracked and followed up immediately we could easily lose them to another financial institution." Prior to implementing a complete CRM strategy, Chris and his team developed a rudimentary in-house system using a popular desktop database. Each call the team received was looked up and then manually recorded. "Our team was becoming frustrated with this technology as it was limiting them from reaching out to our customers in a more proactive

Closing Case Studies and Discussion Questions (chapters only)**:** To help your students apply what they have just learned, you'll find two closing case studies at the end of each chapter. Each case has a set of questions that are great for class discussion.

Key Terms and Concepts

Application generation subsystem, 75
Backup, 76
Business intelligence (BI), 63
Competitive intelligence (CI), 83
Data administration, 85
Data administration subsystem, 76
Database, 65
Database administration, 85
Database management system (DBMS), 70
Data definition subsystem, 71
Data dictionary, 66
Data manipulation subsystem, 72

Data mart, 81
Data-mining tool, 79
Data warehouse, 77
DBMS engine, 70
Digital dashboard, 84
Foreign key, 68
Integrity constraint, 68
Logical view, 70
Multidimensional analysis (MDA) tool, 80
On-line analytical processing (OLAP), 64
On-line transaction processing (OLTP), 64

Operational database, 64
Physical view, 70
Primary key, 66
Query-and-reporting tool, 79
Query-by-example (QBE) tool, 73
Recovery, 76
Relation, 65
Relational database, 65
Report generator, 73
Structured query language (SQL), 74
View, 72

Key Terms and Concepts: These include page numbers of where discussions of them are found.

End-of-Chapter Material

Short-Answer Questions: These questions target the key concepts from the chapter and provide a quick indicator of a student's grasp of the critical aspects of the material.

Assignments and Exercises: These problems are designed to give your students the chance to apply key concepts.

Discussion Questions: (chapters only) Challenging questions promote an atmosphere of critical thinking in your classroom.

EVEN MORE RESOURCES ON-LINE

Electronic Commerce Projects: Electronic commerce projects require your students to learn through Web exploration.

Group Projects: These require your students to use technology to solve a problem or take advantage of an opportunity.

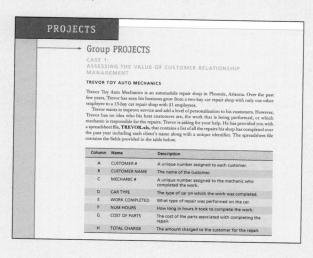

Changes to the Fourth Canadian Edition

The content changes for the Fourth Canadian Edition were driven by

- Haag's U.S. seventh edition of *Management Information Systems for the Information Age*
- Instructor feedback from the third Canadian edition
- Changes that have occurred in the business world
- Advances that have occurred in the technology area
- Changes made by our competitors.

As a group of authors and contributors working together, we carefully sifted through all the competitive scanning information we could gather to create a fourth Canadian Edition that builds on the success of the third Canadian and seventh U.S. edition.

Throughout the text, you'll find that all opening, closing, and perspectives cases are new or updated. You'll also find new or expanded coverage on the following essential IT topics:

- **Enterprise Resource Planning (ERP) Systems**—now appearing in Chapter 2 (as a system foundation for integrating CRM, SCM, and e-collaboration functions) and Chapter 7 as the enabling infrastructure of a service-oriented architecture framework.

- **Service-oriented Architecture (SoA)**—now appearing in Chapter 6 (as the architecture approach within which component-based development is undertaken) and Chapter 7 in creating an SoA-enabled ERP infrastructure.

- **Component-based Development**—now appearing in Chapter 6 as the "umbrella" for rapid application development (RAD), extreme programming (XP), and agile software development methodologies.

- **Web 2.0**—integrated throughout the text, especially in Extended Learning Module E and Chapter 9. Technologies include wikis, social networking sites, blogs, RSS feeds, and podcasting.

- **IT Metrics**—extensive coverage in Chapter 7 including specific metrics that focus on infrastructure-centric measures, call centre measures, and Web-centric measures.

- **Business Continuity Planning**—in-depth coverage of the business continuity planning development cycle, including risk assessment, requirement recovery documents, collocation facilities, hot and cold sites, and disaster recovery plans.

- **Service Level Agreements (SLAs)**—expanded coverage in Chapters 6 (outsourcing), 7 (call centres), and 9 (personal application service providers), including service level specifications and service level objectives.

- **9 Major E-Commerce Business Models**—every combination of "B" Business, "C" Consumer, and "G" Government with good illustrations and examples.

- **E-Business Trends**—now a part of Chapter 5, focusing on screenagers, digital immigrants, digital natives, mobile computing (and m-commerce), and the Long Tail.

- **IT Culture**—now appearing in Chapter 2 with two focuses: (1) the structural placement of the IT function—silo, matrix, and fully integrated; and (2) the philosophical approach to the acquisition, development, and use of IT (ranging from "wait and see" to supporting technology innovation failure).

Changes specific to each chapter/module include

- **Chapter 1** is no longer an introduction to the book. Now it jumps right into the integration of business strategy and information technology by covering Porter's Five Forces Model, Porter's three generic strategies, top line versus bottom line, the run-grow-transform (RGT) framework, and value-chain analysis. These major topics drive all our discussions of technology throughout the book.
- **Updated Chapter 2**—expanded coverage of e-collaboration and new content on IT culture and enterprise resource planning (ERP) systems
- **Updated Chapter 3**—Updated Access 2007 coverage, business intelligence revisited, and information ownership updated
- **Updated Chapter 4**—New content on multi-agent systems and agent-based modelling
- **Updated Chapter 5**—Less coverage of electronic government and new content on e-business trends
- **Updated Chapter 6**—New content on component-based development (CBD), service-oriented architectures (SoA), and service level agreements (SLAs).
- **Updated Chapter 7**—Expanded coverage of ERP systems and new content on IT success metrics and business continuity planning.
- **Updated Chapter 8**—Expanded coverage of Canadian privacy issues
- **Updated Chapter 9**—including the addition of such topics as haptic interfaces and nanotechnology.

Overall, you'll find exciting new content on the following topics (and many more):

- Ad-supported e-commerce model
- Blogs
- Business continuity planning
- Call centre success metrics
- Component-based development (CBD)
- Crowdsourcing
- Digital immigrants
- Digital natives
- Drones
- GIGO
- Infrastructure-centric metrics
- Intrusion prevention systems
- Invisible backlog
- IT culture
- Location mashups
- The Long Tail
- Mashups
- Microsoft Windows Vista
- Nanotechnology
- Near Field Communication
- Open-source information Botnets
- Path-to-profitability (P2P)
- Pharming
- Podcasting
- Porter's three generic strategies
- Predictive analytics
- Redacting
- Requirement recovery document
- Rootkit
- RSS feeds
- Screenagers
- Service level agreements
- Service-oriented architecture
- Technology innovation failure
- Web 2.0
- Web-centric success metrics
- Wiki
- Zombie

Instructor Supplements and Support

We realize that no text is complete without a well-rounded and value-added support package. Our support package is designed to ease your teaching burden by providing you with a Web site full of valuable information, more than 2,000 test bank questions, easy-to-use test generating software, an Instructor's Manual that walks you through each chapter and module and provides value-added teaching notes and suggestions, as well as PowerPoint presentations.

ONLINE LEARNING CENTRE (OLC)

WWW.MCGRAWHILL.CA/OLC/HAAG

As in previous editions, the OLC for the fourth Canadian edition contains a wealth of valuable information and supplements for both the instructor and the student.

- **Electronic commerce projects** require your students to learn through Web exploration.
- **Group projects** require students to use technology to solve a problem or take advantage of an opportunity. Make use of these for take-home assignments, or long in-class group discussions.
- **Additional cases:** Even more MIS cases are available for you to choose from, to keep each class new and exciting for your students, and to allow those with different backgrounds and knowledge to benefit from various scenarios.
- **Videos:** Downloadable from the OLC, videos will help engage your students and help you illustrate the text material.
- **Instructor's Manual:** The Instructor's Manual will help you prepare for your class presentations. In its new format, you will find a separate box for each PowerPoint slide. In that box, you will find an overview of the slide and a list of key points to cover. This enables you to prepare your class presentation by working solely with the Instructor's Manual because you also see the PowerPoint slide presentations. We've also provided embedded links within each Instructor's Manual document to the various in-text pedagogical elements. The Instructor's Manual is downloadable at www.mcgrawhill.ca/olc/haag.
- **Computerized Test Bank:** For each chapter and module, there are approximately 125 multiple-choice, true/false, and fill-in-the-blank questions aimed at challenging the minds of your students. McGraw-Hill's EZ Test is a flexible and easy-to-use electronic testing program. The program allows instructors to create tests from book-specific items. It accommodates a wide range of question types and instructors may add their own questions. Multiple versions of the test can be created and any test can be exported for use with course management systems such as WebCT or BlackBoard. EZ Test Online is a new service and gives you a place to easily administer your EZ Test–created exams and quizzes online. The program is available for Windows and Macintosh environments. To get to EZ Test, go to the Online Learning Centre at www.mcgrawhill.ca/olc/haag.
- **Microsoft PowerPoint® Presentations:** The PowerPoint presentations are ready for you to use in class. In preparing to use these, you simply work through the Instructor's Manual, which includes thumbnails of each slide and important points to cover. Of course, we realize that you'll probably want to customize some of the presentations. So, we've made available to you most of the images and photos in the text. You can find these on the text's Web site at www.mcgrawhill.ca/olc/haag.

Superior Service

Service takes on a whole new meaning with McGraw-Hill Ryerson and *Management Information Systems*, Fourth Canadian Edition. More than just bringing you the text, we have raised the bar for innovation and educational research. These investments in learning and the academic community have helped us understand the needs of students and educators across the country, and allowed us to foster the growth of integrated learning.

ILEARNING SALES SPECIALIST

Your Integrated Learning Sales Specialist is a McGraw-Hill Ryerson representative who has the experience, product knowledge, training, and support to help you assess and integrate any of our products, technology, and services into your course for optimum teaching and learning performance. Whether it's using our test bank software, helping students improve their grades, or putting your entire course online, your iLearning Sales Specialist is there to help you do it.

TEACHING, TECHNOLOGY, AND LEARNING CONFERENCE SERIES

The educational environment has changed tremendously in recent years, and McGraw-Hill Ryerson continues to be committed to helping you acquire the skills you need to succeed in this new milieu. Our innovative Teaching, Technology, and Learning Conference Series brings faculty together from across Canada with 3M Teaching Excellence award winners to share teaching and learn best practices in a collaborative and stimulating environment. Pre-conference workshops on general topics, such as teaching large classes and technology integration, are also offered. We will also work with you at your own institution to customize workshops that best suit the needs of your faculty at your institution.

PRIMIS ONLINE

Primis Online gives you access to our resources in the best medium for your students: printed textbooks or electronic e-books. You can create customized learning tools from the more than 350,000 pages of content available at our online database at www.mhhe.com/primis.

COURSESMART

CourseSmart brings together thousands of textbooks across hundreds of courses in an eTextbook format, providing unique benefits to students and faculty. By purchasing an eTextbook, students can save up to 50 percent off the cost of a print textbook, reduce their impact on the environment, and gain access to powerful Web tools for learning including full text search, notes and highlighting, and e-mail tools for sharing notes between classmates. For faculty, CourseSmart provides instant access to review and compare textbooks and course materials in their discipline area without the time, cost, and environmental impact of mailing print examination copies. For further details contact your iLearning Sales Specialist or go to www.coursesmart.com.

Student Support and Supplements

ONLINE LEARNING CENTRE RESOURCES FOR THE STUDENT

WWW.MCGRAWHILL.CA/OLC/HAAG

For a wealth of questions, cases, terms and projects, visit www.mcgrawhill.ca/olc/haag. Here, for each chapter and module, you will find:

- **Multiple-Choice and True/False Quizzes** for each chapter,
- **Glossary** containing key terms from the text,
- **Web links**—if applicable to the text, cases, or problem material—are posted,
- **Electronic commerce projects** requiring Web exploration,
- **Group projects** that ask you to use technology to solve a problem or take advantage of an opportunity,
- **Additional cases**—even more MIS cases are available for you to choose from to illustrate the concepts in the text.

As we present our Fourth Canadian Edition of this text, we remember how things began and the people who have helped us along the way. There are so many to thank. Starting with our families, who have generously donated their time to pick up the slack for two authors in the process of making this text not only comprehensive, factual and up to date, but significantly Canadian in tone and content. Thus we thank Jennie Pilcher and Fara Riordan. Next come the fabulous people at McGraw-Hill Ryerson in Whitby, without whose constant prodding, praise, and penchant for perfection this book would still be languishing on someone's to-do list. Specifically, we thank Colleen Henderson, our original sponsoring editor; Suzanne Simpson Millar, Senior Developmental Editor; Sarah Fulton, Developmental Editor, who returned to us in the final stages after starting her family with a beautiful daughter; Rhondda McNabb, Senior Sponsoring Editor; Graeme Powell, Supervising Editor/Design Coordinator; Bruce McIntosh, our ultimate Sponsoring Editor; and the incredibly eagle-eyed freelance editor Karen Rolfe, whose diligent work on the final drafts saved us from immeasurable embarrassment. To everyone at McGraw-Hill Ryerson, a very humble thank you.

Last, but certainly not least, we offer our gratitude to the reviewers who took on a thankless job that paid only a fraction of its true worth. We had the best. They include

Lloyd Ash
Mount Royal College

Todd Boyle
St. Francis Xavier University

Christine Brown
Ryerson University

James Clark
University of Lethbridge

Brian Detlor
McMaster University

John Fraser
University of Waterloo

Mary Furey
Memorial University of Newfoundland

Bob Goldstein
University of British Columbia

Nija Hope
University of Toronto

Terry Huston
University of Victoria

Yonghua Ji
University of Alberta

Saroj Koul
Acadia University

Brenda Lang
Mount Royal College

Francisco Moro
University of Windsor

Joram Ngwenya
Athabasca University

Shauna Roch
Fanshawe College

Ken Sekhon
Camosun College

Trent Tucker
Wilfrid Laurier University

Management Information Systems

FOR THE INFORMATION AGE

Chapter 1

The Information Age in Which You Live

Changing the Face of Business

LEARNING OUTCOMES

LO1 Define management information systems (MIS) and describe the three important organizational resources within it.

LO2 Describe how to use Porter's Five Forces Model to evaluate the relative attractiveness of and competitive pressures in an industry.

LO3 Compare and contrast Porter's three generic strategies; top line versus bottom line; and the run-grow-transform framework as approaches to the development of business strategy.

LO4 Describe the role of value chain analysis in identifying value-added and value-reducing processes.

LO5 List three major types of Enterprise Systems (ES) and describe how they can create value for an organization.

OPENING CASE STUDY
Identity Theft—Crime of the Information Age

Information systems are everywhere. We are entering an age of ubiquitous computing. We are no longer tethered to a machine plugged into a wall; we can get computing virtually anywhere. While this may seem like a good thing, nothing is free. We are also now more vulnerable than ever to the effects of criminal activity. If you think you don't need to pay attention to information systems and the computing that is going on around us everywhere, consider the following:

Thousands of Canadians have fallen victim to identity theft. PhoneBusters, a national anti-fraud call centre jointly operated by the Ontario Provincial Police and the Royal Canadian Mounted Police, reported 32,125 Canadian identity-theft victims amounting to a loss of just over $43 million between 2004 and 2006.[1] On the Internet you can find sites such as CardingWorld.cc, Dumps International, and TalkCash.net that sell such information and much more, including malware, software that can be used to infiltrate the identity management systems of organizations and steal personal information. A site called Dumps International appears to provide Canadian credit cards for sale ranging between $40 for a standard credit card up to $100 for the platinum card. These sites typically stay in existence for only about six months or so before having to change their names to elude law enforcement. Trend Micro, a global leader in network antivirus and Internet content security, has cited what people are willing to pay for data, such as

- $78–$294: billing data including account number, address, birth date, etc.
- $147: driver's license number
- $147: birth certificate
- $6–$24: credit card number with security code and expiration date
- $6: PayPal logon and password.

Therefore, identity theft should be high on your personal priority list. From an organizational point of view, identity management and the protection of identity information are usually at the top of the priority list. Unfortunately, hackers have found ways to steal identity information; they may spoof or phish you into giving away your personal information and they may unleash malware (the generalized term for malicious software such as viruses, worms, and Trojan horses) on organizational identity management systems to steal millions of identities. On January 17, 2007, TJX Cos., the U.S. parent firm of Canadian retailers Winners and HomeSense, reported the infiltration of its identity management systems, which may eventually affect over 40 million customers worldwide, 2 million of them being Canadian Visa card holders.

By some accounts, the black market for identity information is now a billion-dollar-a-year industry. Transactions occur daily with the buying and selling of identities, credit card information, and even brokerage accounts. One man stole numerous online brokerage accounts and used them to employ the old "pump-and-dump" stock scam. With his legitimate personal account he bought many shares of a penny stock. He then used the accounts he'd stolen to buy more shares of the same stock, which raised the price significantly. He then sold the shares in his legitimate personal account for a tidy profit of $82,000. We can tell you this story only because he got caught.

In today's digital world, computers can be used for all sorts of nefarious scams; they can also be used in many wonderful and legal ways—to increase profit, to reduce costs, to increase product and service quality, to reach suppliers and customers all over the world, and to benefit society in general. This book focuses on helping you learn to use technology for the sustained competitive advantage of your organization and for your personal productivity. Along the way, however, we will talk about the bad uses of technology and inform you of steps you can take to avoid being a victim of cyber crimes.[2]

Questions

1. Have you, a friend, or a family member been a victim of identity theft? If so, tell the story to your class.

2. How often do you buy your credit report? Did you know you get one for free annually?

3. Is technology good or bad?

Introduction

You live in the "digital age." You live, work, learn, play, drive, network, eat, and shop in a digital world. The influence of technology permeates everything you do. The average North American relies daily on hundreds of computers. Every part of your life depends on technology. Your TV, iPod, DVD player, car, and cell phone are all technology enabled and—more importantly—not "able" without technology. Technology is so pervasive in your life it is often considered "invasive." Here's a wild statistic: According to a worldwide survey conducted by *Time* magazine in 2005, 14 percent of cell phone users stated they had stopped having sex to take a phone call.[3] Hmmm ... The real unanswered question is whether cell phones have led to more or less personal intimacy. Cell technology has clearly led to an explosion of hitherto impossible personal communication (witness the number of cell phones pressed firmly to ears of shoppers in a mall, for example, and the number of text messages exchanged). While this intimacy is not experienced in person, it is, nonetheless, experienced. The jury is still out ...

Your generation, specifically, the cohort of people born in the mid-to-late 1980s and very early 1990s, was born into a digital age unimaginable to those born in cohorts before yours. In the early 1990s, few people as yet had ever heard of the Internet, "surfing" was a term identified only as a water sport, and Microsoft was not the dominant software publisher for word processing, spreadsheet, presentation, or database management systems (DBMS—considered in depth in Chapter 3 and Extended Learning Module [ELM] F) applications. Viruses were seen only under a microscope, worms were used for fishing, and "spam" was just a canned meat. But all this changed in your first years on earth.

As you moved through your early teens, e-commerce exploded and then quickly imploded, transforming overnight Internet millionaires into overnight Internet paupers. You are probably more than familiar with unique and interesting IT terms such as podcasting, wiki, avatars, emoticons, spoofing, acorns, and phishing (now with a completely different kind of bait). Technology has been so much a part of your life that you may consider it more of a necessity than a convenience.

Generations of people before you witnessed the evolution and revolution of many other technologies, such as automobile and air travel, radio, television, and the telephone. Your generation has been at the centre of the digital revolution. Perhaps more than any technology before, digital technologies such as computers and the Internet have radically transformed the very fabric of society.

The reach of digital technologies is vast and wide. Technology touches your personal life every day. Equally so, digital technologies have dramatically altered the competitive landscape of business. Fifty of the *Fortune* top 500 companies in 2006 (that's one in every 10) were digital technology companies such as Cisco Systems, Hewlett-Packard, and Dell. Amazon.com ranked 272 on the *Fortune* list and eBay ranked 458—both of these companies have been around for only about 10 years.[4] In Extended Learning Module D (Careers in Business) we take an in-depth look at how Information Systems can be crucial in various careers in business. IT is everywhere. Pay close attention.

Technology companies are by no means the only ones interested in using technology effectively in the workplace. Every business you can name wrestles with management information systems on a daily basis. Broadly, *management information systems* (MIS) is both a business discipline that deals with the use of information technology (IT)—or computers, computer technology, or simply technology—and an academic field of study. Technology is so important to modern organizations because we are in the information age, a time when knowledge is power. Today, more than ever, businesses and organizations in every sector need information, information technology, and the overarching MIS function to massage, assimilate, and distribute information and knowledge to create and sustain a competitive advantage and/or to deliver vital services.

As businesses approach the acquisition and use of technology, they do so very differently from you in your personal life. You find a cool piece of technology and quickly calculate in your head if you have enough money to purchase it. You may not get everything you want, such as a large hard disk or a really fast processor, but you can usually buy the personal technology you need. Businesses are different; they carefully scrutinize their technology purchases, seeking to find and justify a competitive advantage and a return on a big investment. Businesses ask questions such as:

1. Can this technology help streamline and lower the cost of our business processes while not sacrificing the quality we deliver to our customers?

2. Can this technology enable us to reach larger markets of customers, understand our customers better so we can deliver more tailored products and services to them, and/or help us design and develop products that are better than those of our competitors?

3. Can this technology enable us to innovate our business operations and move into completely new markets?

This book's goal is to introduce you to the fast-paced and ever-changing dynamics of information technology, focusing specifically on (1) how you—as an individual—can use technology to increase your productivity and (2) how organizations can use technology to increase profit, expand market share, serve the needs of society, eliminate time and location boundaries, and engage in a host of other worthy activities. We deliver on the first goal—increasing your personal productivity—through the use of our Extended Learning Modules (ELMs), which typically are hands-on, "can-do" explorations of technology such as how to use the decision support features in Excel (ELM H Decision Analysis with Spreadsheet Software), build a Web site (ELM E The World Wide Web and the Internet), and design and use a database and database management system ELM F and G (Designing Databases and Entity-Relationship Diagramming, and Implementing a Database with Microsoft Access).

We deliver on the second goal—explaining organizational uses of technology—in the book's chapters. We'll start in this very first chapter by stating that *business strategy drives technology decisions, not the reverse*. This is a "refinement approach" that moves from the big picture (the industry in which your business operates) to the details (the technologies you should choose). So, you start with the bigger view of your industry and continually refine your analysis until you arrive at the technologies you should use (see Figure 1.1 on the next page).

The steps are as follows:

1. Assess the state of competition and industry pressures affecting your organization.

2. Determine business strategies critical to successfully addressing those competitive and industry pressures.

3. Identify important business processes that support your chosen business strategies.

4. Finally, align technology tools with those important business processes.

So, you first need to understand the industry in which your business operates and the competitive forces affecting that industry. Decisions regarding business strategies, business processes, and finally technology, follow. Your organization must perform these steps in this order. If you don't understand the competitive nature of your industry, you can't determine business strategies that ensure success. If you don't then identify the most important business processes to support those business strategies, you will undoubtedly implement the wrong technologies and doom your organization to failure. It is our goal in this first chapter to help you through the first two steps above. The remaining chapters focus on further refinement of business strategies and the identification of important business processes—and the technology tools that support them.

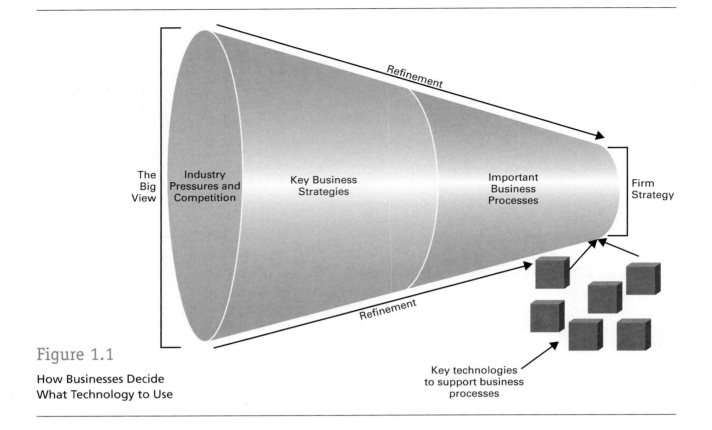

Figure 1.1

How Businesses Decide
What Technology to Use

LO1

Management Information Systems

Just like finance, accounting, marketing, and many others, management information systems is a business function vitally important to the success of your organization. Formally, we define management information systems as follows:

- *Management Information Systems (MIS)* deals with the planning for, and development, management, and use of information technology tools to help people perform all tasks related to information processing and management.

So, MIS deals with the coordination and use of three very important organizational resources—information, people, and information technology. Stated another way, *people* use *information technology* to work with *information*. To do so, they are involved in MIS. Ideally, of course, people use technology to support the goals and objectives of the organization as driven by competitive pressures and determined by appropriate business strategies. MIS helps them to do this.

INFORMATION AS A KEY RESOURCE

As stated above, we are in the information age, a time when knowledge is power. But what *are* information and knowledge? Let's first define *data, information,* and *business intelligence* and give an example to understand them better. Finally, we'll discuss the elusive term *knowledge*.

- **Data** are raw facts that describe a particular phenomenon such as the current temperature, the price of a movie rental, or your age. (Actually, the term *data* is plural; *datum* is singular.)

- **Information** is data that have a particular meaning within a specific context. The current temperature becomes information if you're deciding what to wear; in deciding what to wear, the data describing the price of a movie rental are not pertinent information.

- **Business intelligence (BI)** *is* collective information—about your customers, your competitors, your business partners, your competitive environment, and your own internal operations—that gives you the ability to make effective, important, and often strategic business decisions.

Consider Figure 1.2. In the left image is a single Excel cell containing the number 21; let's assume that's your age. That is a piece of data—some sort of fact that describes the amount of time you have been alive. Now let's create a list of customers for a business that contains the age of each customer (the right portion of Figure 1.2). This is potential *information* since your business can use it. Notice that you can create an average, find the ages of the youngest and oldest customers, and build a frequency distribution of customers by age.

In an Excel cell, you can store a single piece of data. Here, the cell contains the number 21, which we're assuming to be your age.

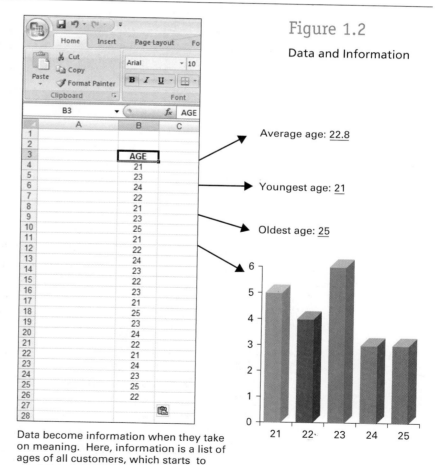

Data become information when they take on meaning. Here, information is a list of ages of all customers, which starts to provide insight into your customers.

Figure 1.2
Data and Information

Now, look at Figure 1.3. There you'll see an Excel workbook containing many pieces of information for each customer. This is *business intelligence* (often referred to simply as BI). What does this mean? Take a careful look at some of the columns of information. For each customer, we know the preferred salesperson. We can also see the number of coupons each customer has used. Now we can start to derive more meaningful information—business intelligence. We can compare how men and women use coupons. We can derive the customer average age by preferred salesperson.

Notice how data, information, and business intelligence all build on each other. Information is a more complete picture of multiple data points; in our example, an age was a single piece of data while information was the collective ages of all customers. Business intelligence extends that information to include gender behaviour, the use of coupons, preferred salespersons, and total purchases. And *knowledge* builds upon all of those. You acquire knowledge in a business or field through practice over time using information and intelligence. You will understand better what we mean by knowledge as we go along.

Knowledge is a broad term that can describe many things; (1) it can provide contextual explanation for business intelligence; (2) it can point toward actions to take to affect business intelligence; (3) it can include intellectual assets such as patents and trademarks; and (4) it includes organizational know-how for things such as best practices.

Consider our example in Figures 1.2 and 1.3. Knowledge can provide context by explaining the reason that more women than men use coupons is that the majority of coupons are placed in women's magazines. You would derive this sort of knowledge by having the business intelligence in Figure 1.3 and at the same time having access to the marketing strategies. Given the business intelligence in the figure, the knowledge

Figure 1.3

Business Intelligence

When you start to combine multiple sets of information, you can generate a considerable amount of business intelligence. Business intelligence helps you make effective strategic business decisions.

of individuals in the organization would help them make use of it. Knowledge would address what marketing strategy, for instance, should be undertaken to get more customers on Plan B to increase total purchases.

The *quality* of intelligence and knowledge is obviously critical. We'll talk next about the quality of these assets. Then we'll discuss other characteristics of information. (In the following discussion, we'll be using the term *information* generically to refer to all intellectual assets—data, information, business intelligence, and knowledge because the term *information* is also used by business people and academics alike in this way.)

DEFINING INFORMATION QUALITY Information exhibits high quality only if it is pertinent, relevant, and useful to you. Unfortunately, in today's information age, information is not exactly at a premium; you are bombarded daily with information, much of which is not really important to you in any way. Below are some information attributes that help define its quality:

- **Timeliness**—First, do you have access to information *when you need it?* If you're preparing to make a stock trade, for example, you need access to the price of the stock right now. Second, does the information describe the time period or periods you're considering? A snapshot of sales today may be what is relevant. Or for some important decisions, you really need other information as well—sales yesterday, sales for the week, today's sales compared to the same day last week, today's sales compared to the same day last year, and so on.

- **Location**—Information is of no value to you if you can't access it. Ideally, your location or the information's location should not matter. IT can definitely create information quality through technologies that support telecommuting, workplace virtualization, mobile e-commerce, and so on, so you can access information at or from any location.

- **Form**—First, is the information in a form that is most useful to or usable by you— audio, text, video, animation, graphical, or other? Depending on the situation, the quality of information is defined by its form and your ability to make use of it. Second, is the information free of errors? Think of information as you would a physical product. If you have a defective product, it lacks quality in that you cannot use it. Information is the same. This is the concept of ***garbage-in garbage-out (GIGO)***. If the information coming into your decision-making process is in bad form (i.e., garbage-in), you'll more than likely make a poor decision (i.e., garbage-out).

- **Validity**—Validity is closely related to the second aspect of form above. Validity addresses the credibility of information. Information is all over the Internet, but does it come from a credible source? Much of the information on the Internet has not gone through any sort of quality control or verification process before being published, so its validity is subject to legitimate question.

CONSIDERING INFORMATION FROM AN ORGANIZATIONAL PERSPECTIVE Organizations must treat information as any other resource or asset. It must be organized, managed, and disseminated effectively for the information to exhibit quality. Within an organization, information flows in four basic directions (see Figure 1.4 on the next page):

1. **Upward.** Upward information flows describe the current state of the organization based on its daily transactions. When a sale occurs, for example, that information originates at the lowest level of the organization and is passed upward through the various levels. Along the way, the information takes on a finer level of *granularity*. ***Information granularity*** refers to the extent of detail within the information. At lower organizational levels, information exhibits fine granularity

Figure 1.4

An Organization, Its
Information Flows, and
Information Granularity

because people need to work with information in great detail. At the upper
organizational levels, information becomes coarser because it is summarized
or aggregated in some way. That is, strategic managers need sales by year, for
example, as opposed to knowing the detail of every single transaction.

2. **Downward.** Strategies, goals, and directives that originate at a higher level are
   passed to lower levels in downward information flows. The upper level of an
   organization develops strategies; the middle levels of an organization convert
   those strategies into tactics; and the lower levels of an organization deal with the
   operational details.

3. **Horizontal.** Information flows horizontally between functional business units
   and work teams. The goal here is to eliminate the old dilemma of "the right
   hand not knowing what the left hand is doing." All units of your organization
   need to inform other units of their processes and be informed by the other units
   regarding their processes. In general, everyone in a company needs to know
   everything relevant in a business sense (personal and sensitive data not included).

4. **Outward/inward.** Information is communicated from and to customers, suppliers,
   distributors, and other partners for the purpose of doing business. These flows of
   information are really what electronic commerce is all about. Today, no organization
   is an island, and outward/inward flows can yield a competitive advantage.

Another organizational perspective on information concerns what information
describes. Information is internal or external, objective or subjective, and various combinations of these.

- *Internal information* describes specific operational aspects of an organization.
- *External information* describes the environment surrounding the organization.
- *Objective information* quantifiably describes something that is known.
- *Subjective information* attempts to describe something that is unknown.

Consider a bank that faces the decision about what interest rate to offer on a daily
interest savings account. That bank will use internal information (how many customers
have such accounts), external information (what rate other banks are offering), objective information (what is today's prime interest rate), and subjective information (what

OVERCOMING LANGUAGE BARRIERS ON THE INTERNET

The Internet is certainly a disruptive innovation (an innovation that unexpectedly displaces an established technology—in this case the telephone and other synchronous communications technologies[5]) that has eliminated geographical and location barriers. With almost one-sixth of the world's population having access to the Internet, "location, location, location" in the physical world is becoming less and less and less important.

However, we now have new issues to deal with, notably a language barrier. What happens if you connect to a site that offers information in a language you don't understand? How can you send an e-mail to someone who doesn't speak English? One solution is language translation software, and one company leading the way in the development of language translation software is SYSTRAN. General Motors of Canada uses the English–French translation capability of SYSTRAN to produce literature within the Canadian market.

SYSTRAN offers a suite of software tools that enables you to translate about 3,700 words per minute for e-mail, Web page, and pdf content, as well as display Asian fonts. Most of SYSTRAN's software products are also available as plug-ins for Microsoft Outlook, Word, Excel, and PowerPoint.

Is it perfect? Not according to SYSTRAN's disclaimer. It states specifics about what its products will do, then encourages you to carefully review any translation before making it a part of your business communications.

Indeed, when Kentucky Fried Chicken wanted to translate its slogan "Finger-lickin good" into Chinese, it came out as "Eat your fingers off." Product names are another example. When General Motors tried to sell the Chevy Nova in South America, people didn't buy it because *No va* means "it won't go" in Spanish. (Neither of those two companies were using language translation software provided by SYSTRAN.)

Experiment with this. Connect to SYSTRAN's Web site at www.systransoft.com. Type in a phrase and choose the language into which you would like it translated.[6]

the prime interest rate is expected to be in the future). Actually, the rate other banks are offering is not only external information (it describes the environment surrounding the organization) but also objective information (it is quantifiably known). Information usually has more than one aspect to it.

PEOPLE AS A KEY RESOURCE IN MIS

The single most important resource in any organization is its people. People set goals, carry out tasks, make decisions, serve customers, and, in the case of IT specialists, provide a stable and reliable technology environment so the organization can run smoothly and gain a competitive advantage in the marketplace. So, this discussion is all about *you*.

In business, your most valuable asset is *not* technology but rather your *mind*. IT is simply a set of tools that help you work with and process information. It's really a mind support tool set. Technology such as spreadsheet software can help you quickly create a high-quality and revealing graph. But it can't tell you whether you should build a bar or a pie graph, and it can't help you determine whether you should show sales by territory or sales by salesperson. Those are *your* tasks, and that's why your business curriculum includes classes in human resource management, accounting, finance, marketing, and perhaps production and operations management.

Nonetheless, technology is an important set of tools for you. Technology can help you be more efficient and can help you dissect and better understand problems and opportunities. So, it's as important for you to learn how to use your technology tool set as it is important that you understand the information to which you're applying your technology tools.

TECHNOLOGY LITERACY   A *technology-literate knowledge worker* knows how and when to apply technology. The "how" aspect includes knowing which technology to purchase, how to exploit the many benefits of application software, and what technology infrastructure is required to get businesses connected to each other, just to name a few. From your personal perspective, we've provided ELMs in this text to help you become a technology-literate knowledge worker.

We encourage you to read all the ELMs, especially ELM D (Careers in Business). That module covers career opportunities in a variety of business disciplines including finance, marketing, accounting, management, and many others. Reading ELM D (Careers in Business) will help prepare you for whatever career you choose. You'll find a discussion there of key technologies for each business discipline that will help you succeed in your career.

A technology-literate knowledge worker also knows "when" to apply technology. Unfortunately, in many cases, people and organizations blindly decide to use technology in a desperate effort to solve a business problem. Technology is not a panacea. You can't simply apply technology to any given process and expect that process instantly to become more efficient and effective. Look at it this way—if you apply technology to a process that doesn't work correctly, then you'll only be doing things wrong millions of times faster. There are cases when technology is not the solution. Being a technology-literate knowledge worker will help you determine when and when not to apply technology.

INFORMATION LITERACY   An *information-literate knowledge worker*

- Can define what information is needed
- Knows how and where to obtain information
- Understands the information once it is received (i.e., can transform the information into business intelligence)
- Can act appropriately based on the information to help the organization achieve the greatest advantage.

Consider a real-life example of an information-literate knowledge worker. Several years ago, a manager of a retail store received some interesting information: diaper sales on Friday evenings accounted for a larger than expected percentage of total sales of that item for the week. Most people learning this would have immediately jumped to a strategy that ensured diapers were always well stocked on Friday evenings, or to run a special on diapers Friday evenings to increase sales even further; but not our information-literate knowledge worker. She first looked at the information and decided that she needed more information in order to create business intelligence. She simply needed to know more before she could act.

She decided the business intelligence she needed was *why* diaper sales spiked on Friday evenings and *who* was buying the diapers. That intelligence was not stored within the computer system, so she stationed an employee in the diaper aisle on Friday evening to record any information pertinent to the situation (i.e., she knew how and where to obtain the information). The store manager learned that young businessmen purchased the most diapers on Friday evenings—obviously stocking up for the weekend on their way home from work. The manager's response was to stock premium domestic and imported beer near the diapers. Since then, Friday evening has been a big sales time not only for diapers but also for premium beer.

There are a couple of important lessons you can learn from this story. First, as we've stated, technology is not a panacea. Although a computer system generated the initial report detailing the sales of diapers on Friday evenings, our retail store manager did not make any further use of technology to design and implement her innovative and highly effective solution. Second, this story can help you distinguish between information and business intelligence. In this case, the information was the sales of diapers on Friday evening. The business intelligence, however, included

- *Who* was making diaper purchases on Friday evening
- *Why* those people were purchasing diapers on Friday evening
- *What* complementary product(s) those people might also want or need. (This last point might also illustrate the manager's special *knowledge*.)

As a good rule of thumb, when you receive information and need to make a decision based on it, ask yourself questions that start with *who*, *what*, *when*, *why*, *where*, and *how*. Answers to those questions will help you create business intelligence and make better decisions.

YOUR ETHICAL RESPONSIBILITIES   Your roles as a technology-literate and information-literate knowledge worker extend far beyond using technology and business intelligence to gain a competitive advantage in the marketplace for your organization. You must also consider your social responsibilities: This is where ethics become important. ***Ethics*** are the principles and standards that guide our behaviour toward other people. Your ethics have consequences for you just as laws do. But ethics are different from laws. Laws either clearly require or prohibit an action. Ethics are more subjective, more a matter of personal or cultural interpretation. Thus, ethical decision making can be complex. A decision or an action in some cases might have—or be expected to have—an outcome that is actually right or wrong according to different people's ethics. Consider the following examples of actions:

1. Copying software you purchase, making copies for your friends, and *charging them* for the copies
2. Making an extra backup of your software just in case both the copy you are using and the primary backup fail for some reason
3. Giving out the phone numbers of your friends and family, without their permission, to a telecom provider of some sort of calling plan so you can receive a discount.

Each of these examples is either ethically (according to you or some people) or legally (according to the government) incorrect or both. In the second example, you might be ethically okay in making an extra backup copy (because you didn't share it with anyone), but according to some software licenses you're prohibited by law from making more than one backup copy. What do you think about the first and third examples? Illegal? Unethical? Both?

To help you better understand the relationship between ethical acts and legal acts, consider Figure 1.5. The graph is composed of four quadrants, and the complexity of ethical decisions about behaviour is suggested by quadrant III (legal but unethical). Do any of the three examples above fall in quadrant III? Perhaps you can think of some other actions that although legal might still be unethical (how about gossiping?). You always want your actions to remain in quadrant I. If all your actions fall into that quadrant, you'll always be acting both legally and ethically and thus in a socially responsible way. Clearly, technology has further increased the complexity of ethics in our society because of the speed and casual ease with which people can access, distribute, and use information.

Being socially and ethically responsible in the information age involves not only the actions you initiate yourself but also what you do to protect

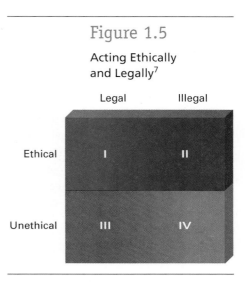

Figure 1.5

Acting Ethically and Legally[7]

E-LEARNING: NOT JUST FOR SCHOOL

To become effective in your use of information, you can use technology to learn—not only about what information means, but also basically how to perform your work responsibilities better. Brink's Home Security, the largest international security network with over 200 branches in Canada and the United States, recently implemented an e-learning management system to help (1) train its 2,600 employees, (2) increase customer retention, (3) improve profits, and (4) reduce employee turnover.

Many of Brink's field personnel work nights and weekends, installing home security systems. For them, instructor-led classes in a central location (Brink's operates in more than 52 countries) simply didn't work.

The new e-learning management system helps managers develop customized on-line training modules and allows field personnel to access those modules 24 hours per day, seven days per week. The system even provides skills assessment and other forms of evaluation.

The total investment in the system for Brink's was US$300,000. Brink's expects to save US$500,000 in the first three years as a result of replacing instructor-led classes with the e-learning modules. Brink's has already noticed that its better-trained field personnel have improved profit margins and increased customer retention.[8]

yourself and your organization against the actions of others—that is, protecting yourself and your organization against cyber crimes. There are many types of cyber crimes—such as promulgating viruses or worms, committing identity theft, and engaging in Web defacing—performed by a variety of hackers such as black-hat hackers and cyberterrorists, and it is your responsibility to guard against them. It might even be considered an ethical lapse not to do so. We cannot stress enough how important it is for you to protect yourself and your organization's assets in cyberspace. We'll talk more about these issues in Chapter 8 (Protecting People and Information) and ELM C (Computer Crime and Digital Forensics).

INFORMATION TECHNOLOGY AS A KEY RESOURCE IN MIS

The third key resource for management information systems (MIS) is ***information technology (IT)***, any computer-based tool that people use to work with information and support the information and information-processing needs of an organization. IT includes a cell phone or PDA that you use to obtain stock quotes, your home computer that you use to write term papers, large networks that businesses use to connect to one another, and the Internet, which almost one in every six people in the world currently has access to.

KEY TECHNOLOGY CATEGORIES   One simple—yet effective—way to categorize technology is as either *hardware* or *software* (see Figure 1.6). ***Hardware*** is the physical devices that make up a computer. ***Software*** is the set of instructions that your hardware executes to carry out a specific task for you. So, your PDA is the actual hardware; and it contains software that you use to maintain your calendar, update your address book, check your e-mail, watch videos, obtain stock market quotes, and so on.

All hardware technology falls into one of the following six basic categories:

1. An ***input device*** is a tool you use to enter information and commands. Input devices include such tools as keyboard, mouse, touch screen, game controller, and bar code reader.

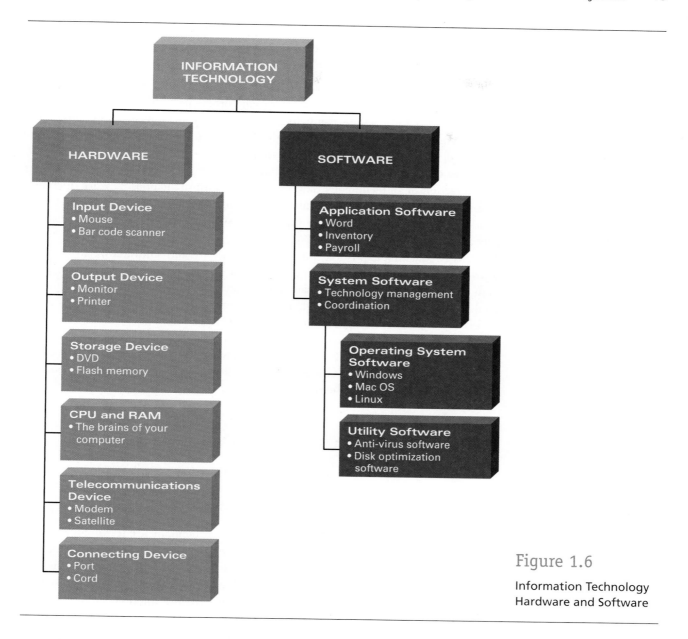

Figure 1.6

Information Technology
Hardware and Software

2. An **output device** is a tool you use to see, hear, or otherwise recognize the results of your information-processing requests. Output devices include such tools as printer, monitor, and speakers.

3. A **storage device** is a tool you use to store information for use at a later time. Storage devices include such tools as USB keys, flash memory cards, and DVDs.

4. The **central processing unit (CPU)** is the hardware that interprets and executes the system and application software instructions and coordinates the operation of all the hardware. **RAM**, or **random access memory**, is a temporary holding area for the information you're working with as well as the system and application software instructions that the CPU currently needs.

5. A **telecommunications device** is a tool you use to send information to and receive it from another person or computer in a network. If you connect to the Internet using a modem, the modem is a telecommunications device.

6. *Connecting devices* include such things as a USB port into which you connect a printer, connector cables to connect your printer to the USB port, and internal connecting devices on the motherboard.

There are two main types of software: *application* and *system*. **Application software** is the software that enables you to solve specific problems and perform specific tasks. Microsoft Word, for example, can help you write term papers. From an organizational point of view, payroll software, collaborative software, and inventory management software are all examples of application software.

System software handles tasks specific to technology management and coordinates the interaction of all technology devices. System software includes network operating system software, drivers for your printer and scanner, operating system software such as Windows Vista and Mac OS, and utility software such as anti-virus software, uninstaller software, and file security software.

If this is your first exposure to technology hardware and software, we suggest you explore ELM A (Computer Hardware and Software).

As we have seen, MIS really is all about three key organizational resources—the people involved, the information they need, and the information technology that helps them. MIS is about getting the right technology and the right information into the hands of the right people at the right time. To meet the technology and information needs of your organization, you must understand the industry in which you operate, build the appropriate business strategies, and then identify the important business processes that support the strategies. Finally, you select the right technologies.

LO2

Porter's Five Forces Model: Assessing the State of the Competition

Businesses should never "throw technology" at a problem, or use technology just for the sake of technology. On the contrary, businesses engage in discussion and strategic decision making to determine how technology can best support their efforts, which are quite different for each business. As you learn about the field of management information systems and the use of information technology, your foremost question should be: How do businesses decide which technologies to use and when? As we stated earlier, organizations determine which technology to use and when to use it by following a process such as

1. Assess the state of competition and industry pressures affecting your organization.
2. Determine business strategies critical to success in meeting those competitive and industry pressures.
3. Identify important business processes that support your chosen business strategies.
4. Align technology tools with the important business processes.

In this section we'll examine the first step—understanding the competitive forces within an industry. We'll do so by exploring the use of Porter's Five Forces Model. In the remaining two sections of the chapter, we'll cover several useful models for developing business strategy, the second step above, and then finally we'll cover value chain analysis as a tool for identifying important business processes. Throughout the entire book, we'll introduce you to technology and discuss its importance for supporting business processes.

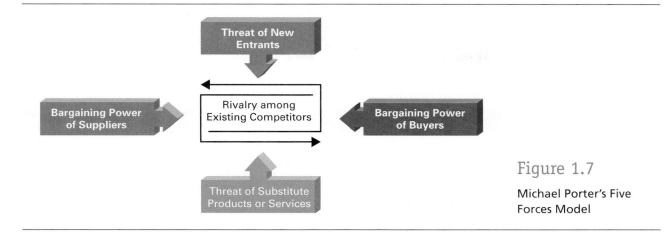

Figure 1.7

Michael Porter's Five Forces Model

Michael Porter's framework—called the Five Forces Model—has long been accepted as a useful tool for business people to use when thinking about business strategy and the impact of IT.[9] The ***Five Forces Model*** helps business people understand the relative attractiveness of an industry and the industry's competitive pressures in terms of the following five forces (see Figure 1.7):

1. Buyer power
2. Supplier power
3. Threat of substitute products or services
4. Threat of new entrants
5. Rivalry among existing competitors.

BUYER POWER

Buyer power in the Five Forces Model is high when buyers have many choices from which to buy, and low when their choices are few. Providers of products and services in a particular industry wish to reduce buyer power. They create a competitive advantage by making it more attractive for customers to buy from them than from their competition. Below are a few of the many companies using IT–enabled processes to reduce buyer power.

- zip.ca—Canada's largest online DVD rental service allows you to set up your movie list. After you watch a movie and return it, zip.ca will send you the next movie on your list.
- Air Canada—Enrol in the Aeroplan program. As you travel on Air Canada (or its many partners such as German airline Lufthansa), you accumulate miles for free air travel, upgrades, and hotel stays. Programs like this one, which reward customers based on the amount of business they do with a particular organization, are called ***loyalty programs***.
- Apple iTunes—Create an iTunes account and buy and download whatever music you want. Then, you can organize and manage your music, move it to your iPod, and burn CDs.
- Dell—Completely customize your computer purchase. It will be delivered to your doorstep within a few business days.

What's interesting about each of these examples (as well as all the others you can think of) is that the competitors in those industries have responded by creating similar programs. This simply means that no competitive advantage is ever permanent. A ***competitive*** *advantage* is providing a product or service in a way that customers value more than what the competition is able to do. zip.ca was the first to offer movie rentals within Canada (in partnership with Rogers Video) using the Internet as the primary platform. Therefore, it had *first-mover advantage*, a significant impact on gaining market share by being the first to market with a competitive advantage. However, others soon followed with similar offerings, thus nullifying that competitive advantage. Every major airline has a loyalty program similar to that of Air Canada. There are many places on the Internet where you can buy and download music. And almost every major computer vendor allows you to customize your computer purchase. The lesson learned here—and for all strategies that result in a competitive advantage—is that a competitive advantage is only temporary and your organization must constantly innovate to find new competitive advantages.

SUPPLIER POWER

Supplier power in the Five Forces Model is high when buyers have few choices from which to buy, and low when their choices are many. Supplier power is the opposite of buyer power: As a supplier organization in an industry, you want buyer power to be low and your supplier power to be high.

In a typical supply chain (see Figure 1.8), your organization will probably be both a supplier (to customer organizations) and a buyer, or customer (of other supplier organizations). As a customer of other supplier organizations, you want to increase your buyer power. As a supplier to other organizations, you want to increase your supplier power, thus reducing your customer's buyer power.

In the quest for increasing supplier power, organizations use many tools at their disposal, not just IT. Companies obtain patents and trademarks to minimize the extent to which products and services can be duplicated and offered by other organizations. The De Beers Group for many years has fought fiercely to tightly control the supply and distribution of diamonds. OPEC (the Organization of the Petroleum Exporting Countries) has organized 13 oil-producing nations to better control the distribution of the world's most popular energy resource (reportedly to ensure the stabilization of oil prices).

THREAT OF SUBSTITUTE PRODUCTS OR SERVICES

The *threat of substitute products or services* in the Five Forces Model is high when there are many alternatives to a product or service, and low when there are few alternatives from which to choose. Ideally, your organization would like to be a supplier organization in a market in which there are few substitutes for the products and services you offer. Of course, that's seldom possible in any market today, but you can still create a competitive advantage by increasing *switching costs*. **Switching costs** are costs that make customers reluctant to switch to another product or service supplier. A switching cost does not necessarily have to be an actual monetary cost.

Figure 1.8

Evaluating Buyer and Supplier Power for Your Organization

As you buy products at amazon.ca over time, for example, Amazon develops a unique profile of your shopping and purchasing habits through such techniques as collaborative filtering. When you visit Amazon, products are offered to you that have been tailored to your profile. This is possible only through the use of sophisticated technologies. If you choose to do your shopping elsewhere, there is a switching cost of sorts because the new site you visit will not have a profile of you or a record of your past purchases. (This is an effective variant of a loyalty program.) So Amazon has reduced the threat of substitute products and services, in a market in which there are many substitutes, by tailoring offerings to you, by creating a "cost" to you to switch to another online retailer.

Switching costs can of course be real monetary costs, too. You've probably been introduced to a switching cost when you signed up for the services of a cell phone provider. All the options and plans sound really great. But there is a serious switching cost in that most cell phone providers require you to sign a long-term contract (as long as two or three years) in order to receive a free phone or unlimited night and weekend calling minutes. The very successful substitute to this has been prepaid cards and, more recently, disposable cell phones that contain a certain number of minutes for your use.

THREAT OF NEW ENTRANTS

The ***threat of new entrants*** in the Five Forces Model is high when it is easy for new competitors to enter a market, and low when there are significant entry barriers to entering a market. An ***entry barrier*** is a product or service feature that customers have come to expect from organizations in a particular industry and that must be offered by an entering organization to compete and survive. Such barriers are erected, and overcome, and then new ones are created again. This is that vicious business cycle of build a competitive advantage, enjoy first-mover advantage, and then watch your competition develop similar initiatives— thereby nullifying your competitive advantage.

For example, if you're thinking of starting a bank, you must offer your customers an array of IT–enabled services, including ATM use, on-line bill paying and account monitoring, and the like. These are significant IT–based entry barriers to entering the banking market because you must offer them for free (or a very small fee). If you consider our previous example of cell phone providers, a significant entry barrier in the past had to do with your phone number. Previously, if you wanted to change cell phone providers, you couldn't take your telephone number with you (i.e., you had to get a new cell phone number). This created a significant entry barrier because new cell phone providers entering the industry were mainly limited to obtaining new customers who did not currently have a cell phone. But that has all changed with *LNP*, *Local Number Portability*, your ability to take your cell phone number with you to a new provider.

RIVALRY AMONG EXISTING COMPETITORS

The ***rivalry among existing competitors*** in the Five Forces Model is high when competition is fierce in a market, and low when competition is more complacent. Simply put, competition is more intense in some industries than in others, although the overall trend is toward increased competition in just about every industry. Rarely can you identify an industry that exhibits complacent competition. (One example might be mortician and burial services. Because of the nature of the services offered, you don't see mortician and burial service organizations actively advertising on TV, offering reduced rates, and so on.)

The retail grocery industry in Canada is intensely competitive. While Loblaw, Metro, and Safeway compete in many different ways, essentially they try to beat or match the competition on price. For example, most have loyalty programs that give shoppers special discounts and privileges. In this way, stores gather valuable business intelligence on customer buying habits that help the chains craft pricing, advertising, and coupon strategies.

COMPARING THE E-COMMERCE ACTIVITIES OF DIFFERENT GOVERNMENTS—A NEW KIND OF COMPETITION

Most people don't think that the government has any competitors but it does in many ways. Think about Income Security programs (Old Age Security and Canada Pension Plan), Canada's health insurance plans, and other types of programs that compete with for-profit companies offering retirement programs, health care insurance, prescription medication policies, and so on. Governments even compete with each other, after a fashion, to see who's doing the best job of serving their citizenry.

For example, according to a report presented by the United Nations, the U.S. government ranks first overall in the aggregated categories of number of computers per 100 citizens, number of Internet hosts per 1,000 citizens, percentage of population on-line, number of telephone lines per 100 citizens, and an information access index (the ease with which government information can be found.) That's pretty impressive.

However, according to a second report released by Accenture, the government of Canada ranked first in overall citizen satisfaction with the provision of e-government services. Categories in that report included e-government customer relationship management activities, maturity level of delivering services electronically, number of multichannel service delivery options, and extent to which the government shares information with its citizens. So, while the United States has the best infrastructure in place for e-government activities, Canada seems to be the best at determining what its citizens want and need. By the way, the United States ranked third in the Accenture study.

E-government is a major force and player on the Internet. According to Nielsen Net Ratings, the U.S. government ranked sixth among the most popularly visited sites, behind Microsoft, Time Warner (AOL), Yahoo!, Google, and eBay but ahead of Lycos, Walt Disney, RealNetworks, Amazon, and Ask.[10, 11, 12]

Since margins are quite low in the grocery retail market, grocers build efficiencies into their supply chains, connecting with their suppliers in IT-enabled information partnerships. Communicating with suppliers over telecommunications networks rather than using paper-based systems makes the procurement process much faster, cheaper, and more accurate. That equates to lower prices for customers—and increased rivalry among existing competitors.

As you can see, Porter's Five Forces Model is extremely useful in helping you better understand the positioning of your organization within its industry and in helping you better understand the competitive forces affecting your organization. With this knowledge in mind, your organization's second task is to develop specific business strategies to remain competitive and profitable.

LO3

Porter's Three Generic Strategies: Building Business Strategy

The development of business strategies is a vast and wide discipline. There are literally hundreds of methods and approaches to the development of business strategy. There are even more books on the subject. (One such book with a particularly innovative approach is *Blue Ocean Strategy* by Kim and Mauborgne. Be sure to put it on your wish list of business books to read.) Here, we'll focus on Michael Porter's three generic strategies and two other approaches.

Figure 1.9

Michael Porter's Three Generic Strategies

Michael Porter identified three approaches or strategies to beating the competition in any industry (see Figure 1.9). They are

1. Overall cost leadership
2. Differentiation
3. Focus

OVERALL COST LEADERSHIP

Overall cost leadership is defined by Porter as offering the same or better quality product or service at a price that is lower than any competitor is able to offer. Examples of organizations focusing on overall cost leadership are numerous and change almost daily, with the most well-known example being Walmart. Walmart's slogans of "Always Low Prices, Always" and "We Sell for Less, Every Day" accurately describe the strategy of overall cost leadership. For everything from women's lingerie to car batteries, Walmart's focus is on offering the same products as the competition but at a lower price. Walmart relies on an IT–enabled tight supply chain management system to squeeze out every penny possible from the procurement, distribution, and warehousing of its products. The company uses sophisticated business intelligence systems to predict what customers will want and when.

Dell works in a similar fashion. Its sell-source-ship model of customizing computer purchases revolutionized the industry. Automobile makers Hyundai and Kia similarly attempt to sell reliable low-cost vehicles to a wide audience, in contrast to Hummer and Mercedes-Benz, which have no overall cost leadership strategy. The large grocery retail chains we identified earlier such as Loblaw, Safeway, and Metro essentially compete on price, often offering loss leaders just to get customers in the store. A ***loss leader*** is a product sold at or below cost to entice customers into a store in the hope that they will also buy more profitable products. Loss leaders are often placed in the back of the store so customers will have to walk by products with higher profit margins.

IT can be a particularly effective tool if your organization chooses an overall cost leadership strategy. IT can tighten supply chain systems, help you capture and assimilate customer information to better understand buying patterns in an effort to better predict product inventory and shelf placement, and make it easy (efficient) for customers to order your products through Web-enabled e-commerce systems.

DIFFERENTIATION

Differentiation is defined by Porter as offering a product or service that is perceived as being "unique" in the marketplace. GM's Chevrolet Motor Division is trying to be just that with its Volt, a totally electric concept vehicle that GM promises to bring to production by 2010. GM and Chevrolet are positioning themselves as the ultimate green vehicle manufacturer—thus different from all others. Another example could unfold in the recent purchase of Canada's venerable Hudson's Bay Company by the owners of the upscale US chains Fortunoff and Lord & Taylor. While plans are preliminary, news as of the July 2008 purchase was that NRDC (the new owners of HBC) planned to embed Fortunoff and Lord & Taylor stores within existing HBC outlets, creating a wholly different shopping experience. Clearly there is a niche in this area between the moderately upscale HBC and the next step up in retail in Canada (Harry Rosen and Holt Renfrew, for example).[13]

Apple Computer also focuses on differentiation as a business strategy. Apple computers not only look different, but also have a different screen interface and focus more on non-textual information processing such as photos, music, and videos than do any of the competition.

Both Audi and Michelin have successfully created a differentiation strategy based on safety. To be sure, differentiation is not about being different based on lower price— that's the strategy of overall cost leadership—but the two are interrelated. While many people are willing to pay extra for grocery products at an upscale food market, they are not willing to pay too much extra. Organizations focusing on differentiation must still be concerned about price in relation to the competition.

FOCUS

Focus as a strategy is usually defined as focusing on offering products and services (1) to a particular market segment or buyer group, (2) within a segment of a product line, and/or (3) to a specific geographic market. Focus is the opposite of attempting to be "all things to all people." Many restaurants focus on only a certain type of food—Mediterranean, Mexican, Chinese, and so forth. Stores such as Bulk Barn, Canada's largest bulk food retailer, focus on allowing customers to buy non-packaged perishable items in any quantity. Many doctors focus on only a particular type of medical help—oncology, paediatrics, and so on; similarly, many law offices focus on a particular legal venue—worker's compensation, living trusts, patents and trademarks.

As with the other generic strategies defined by Porter, focus cannot be practised in isolation. If your organization chooses a particular buyer group on which to focus, you can bet that other competitors will do so as well, so you'll also have to compete on price (overall cost leadership) and/or differentiation, too.

TWO INTERESTING AND COMPLEMENTARY STRATEGY FRAMEWORKS

Besides Porter's three generic strategies, there are numerous other strategy frameworks. Most people tend to use more than one as each provides another perspective from which to make decisions regarding the best business strategy given the competitive pressures of the industry. Here, we'll briefly look at two other frameworks; you'll easily see they are both different from and similar to Porter's three generic strategies (and each other).

TOP LINE VERSUS BOTTOM LINE   A typical income statement for a business has two main parts: (1) revenues and (2) expenses (see Figure 1.10). Revenues are monies your organization receives from selling its products and services while expenses are the costs it incurs providing those products and services. From a strategy point of view, you can focus on the "top line" (revenues) or the "bottom line" (expenses).

When focusing on the top line, your strategy is to *increase revenues*, which can be achieved any number of ways—reaching new customer segments, offering new products, cross-selling related services, offering complementary products, just to name a few. Conversely, when focusing on the bottom line, your strategy is to *minimize your expenses* in making your products or providing your services, which can be achieved in a number of ways as well—optimizing manufacturing processes, decreasing transportation costs, reducing the costs of human capital, minimizing errors in a process, again to name just a few. A bottom-line strategy is similar to Porter's strategy of overall cost leadership. And a top-line strategy is analogous to either or both differentiation and focus as defined by Porter. You will never focus solely on one to the neglect of the other; rather, you will focus on some combination of the two, since they are means to the same end (greater profitability).

From an IT point of view, you must form a business strategy that addresses the role of IT in affecting both the top line and bottom line, though not necessarily equally. For example, you could use technology to implement a **customer self-service system** on the Web. A customer self-service system is an extension of a transaction processing system that places technology in the hands of an organization's customers and allows them to process their own transactions. (A **transaction processing system** or **TPS** is a system that processes transactions within an organization.) On-line banking and ATMs are examples of self-service systems. With these, bank customers have the ability to do their banking from anywhere at any time.

In the United States, on-line banking and ATMs have allowed banks to reduce the costs associated with the delivery of many types of services. Thus, they support a bottom-line strategy. Financial institutions also use these IT–enabled systems to attract new customers.

INCOME STATEMENT

Sales:

_____ $_____
_____ $_____
_____ $_____
Total Sales $_____

Top Line
Reach new customers, offer new products, cross-sell services, offer complementary products

Expenses:
Cost of Goods Sold $_____
Admin Expense $_____
Payroll $_____

Total Expenses $_____

Bottom Line
Optimize manufacturing processes, decrease transportation costs, reduce cost of human capital, minimize errors in a process

Figure 1.10

Business Strategy: Top Line versus Bottom Line

CREATING SYNERGY AMONG TOP LINE AND BOTTOM LINE

Top-line and bottom-line initiatives are different means to the same end: increased net profit. Top-line initiatives achieve that end by focusing on increasing revenue while bottom-line initiatives achieve that end by focusing on decreasing costs. What you really hope to find is a technology-supported initiative that will allow you to do both—simultaneously increase revenues and decrease costs. That's what Ottawa's Lee Valley Tools, among many other leading retailers, was able to do. Lee Valley Tools is a manufacturing and multi-channel retail company specializing in woodworking and gardening tools and equipment, as well as woodworking hardware and gifts. Its research, development, and manufactur-

ing arm, Veritas Tools, has developed, patented, and currently manufactures innovative tools, including numerous wood planes, marking gauges, and other measuring tools, as well as router tables and sharpening systems. A Lee Valley subsidiary, Canica Design, invents, patents, and manufactures highly advanced medical instruments including scalpels and an innovative wound-closure system.

Using integrated order management software such as that provided by CommercialWare, Lee Valley Tools and others are able to cut error rates in manual data entry and verification as well as simultaneously increase sales performance.[14]

Oddly, U.S. citizens and institutions have lagged considerably behind Canada and other industrialized countries in their use of automated payment systems (such as Interac). Though processing costs are considerably lower vis-à-vis the paper system of cheques, the United States has been slow to adopt the technology.[15] Many financial institutions now also offer various products such as stamps for sale through ATMs. Again, this is an example of using IT to focus on the top line, increasing revenues, by selling new products.

As you learn about various technologies in this book, ask yourself

1. How can I apply these technologies in a business environment to help my organization implement a top-line strategy (i.e., increase revenues)?

2. How can I apply these technologies in a business environment to help my organization implement a bottom-line strategy (i.e., minimize expenses)?

RUN-GROW-TRANSFORM FRAMEWORK A helpful conceptual framework for viewing the bigger organizational picture and determining the use of IT in it is the *run-grow-transform (RGT) framework*, an approach in which you allocate in terms of percentages how you will spend your IT dollars on various types of business strategies. For example, if you're interested only in "business-as-usual" but cheaper and faster than the competition, you would focus a great percentage of your IT dollars on a "run" strategy. If you wanted to transform your business in some way, you would allocate a certain percentage of your IT dollars to a "transformation" strategy. The following are the aspects of the RGT framework:

- *Run*—optimize the execution of activities and processes already in place. Seek organizational growth through offering products and services faster and cheaper than the competition.
- *Grow*—increase market reach and product and service offerings; expand market share; and so on. Seek organizational growth by taking market share from the competition (i.e., get a bigger piece of the pie).

- *Transform*—innovate business processes and/or products and services in a completely new way, move into seemingly different markets, and so on. Seek organizational growth through new and different means.

As you can see, the RGT framework is similar in many ways to both Porter's three generic strategies and a top-line versus bottom-line approach as follows:

- Run = overall cost leadership = bottom line
- Grow = focus and differentiation = top line
- Transform = (new) differentiation = top line (when the focus is innovation)

The application of the RGT framework is often best considered with an eye to the maturity of the organization and the maturity of the industry (see Figure 1.11). A new venture start-up, for example, will often focus more of its efforts on the grow aspect, while a mature organization—with a well-defined and successful line of products and services—in a mature industry will often focus more of its efforts on the run aspect. In the latter instance, the organization may already be a market leader and want to ensure and sustain its competitive advantage through price and cost optimization.

Regardless of maturity, however, all organizations must focus on the *transformation* aspect. In the business world, as is often said, if you're standing still, you're falling

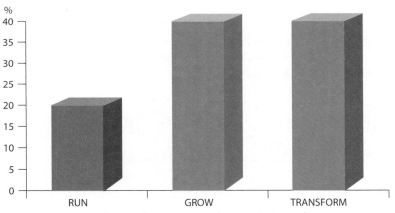

A new venture start-up focusing less on running the organization and more on growing and transforming the organization.

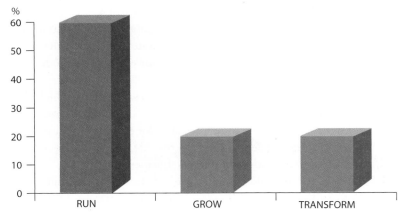

A mature organization within a mature industry focusing mainly on efficiently running the organization.

Figure 1.11

Illustrations of the Run-Grow-Transform (RGT) Framework

behind. It's a simple fact—your competition is always trying to do something better than you are. Therefore, your organization must constantly seek to evolve and, in most cases, to transform itself. Many times, your organization can take a proactive approach to using technology to transform itself. Below are just a few of the many examples of organizations that have focused on transformation.

- ePost—In 1999, Canada Post launched The Electronic Post Office™ service, ePost, the world's first universally available e-billing solution. While the value of being able to receive, view, pay, and store bills online is a major driver of Electronic Bill Presentment and Payment (EBPP) services, Canada Post envisions a time when all types of critical and sensitive documents will be securely delivered online.

- eBay—The world's most popular online auction site, eBay acquired PayPal a few years ago and began offering payment services to its buyers and sellers. In 2003, it began offering its own MasterCard credit card (a great example of transformation), with its "Anything Points" program offering eBay members the ability to buy products and pay for seller services with points accumulated from using a credit card.

- General Motors (GM)—Many people believe that GM's core competency is the production of automobiles. While that may be true, a major portion of its revenue comes from the financing of automobiles (and other big-ticket items such as homes). Its financing business segment (GMAC) is now more profitable than the actual manufacturing and selling of automobiles. GM doesn't want you to pay cash for a car—it wants you to finance the purchase through GMAC.

Like these examples, your organization too must constantly seek to transform itself. The highly competitive business environment necessitates this focus on evolving toward ever greater competitive advantage. IT can help.

LO4

Identifying Important Business Processes: Value Chain Analysis

Thus far, you've learned how to (1) understand your organization within the context of its industry and competitive pressures and (2) define your organization's major strategy for effectively competing using three approaches—Porter's three generic strategies, top line versus bottom line, and the run-grow-transform framework. Now, your organization is at a point "where the rubber meets the road" with respect to how technology will be used in a positive way to affect various processes in support of your strategy. A helpful tool is *value chain analysis*. **Value chain analysis** is a systematic approach to assessing and improving the value of business processes within your organization to further increase its competitive strengths.

A **value chain** is the chain or series of business processes, each of which adds value to your organization's products or services for customers. A **business process** is a standardized set of activities that accomplishes a specific task; for instance, processing a customer order, delivering the customer order, service after the sale, and so on. Overall, value chain analysis helps your organization identify valuable business processes.

Figure 1.12 depicts the typical components of a value chain. The chain of **primary value processes** along the bottom half takes in the raw materials and makes, delivers, markets, and sells, and services your organization's products or services.

- *Inbound logistics*—receiving and warehousing raw materials and distributing those raw materials to manufacturing as needed.

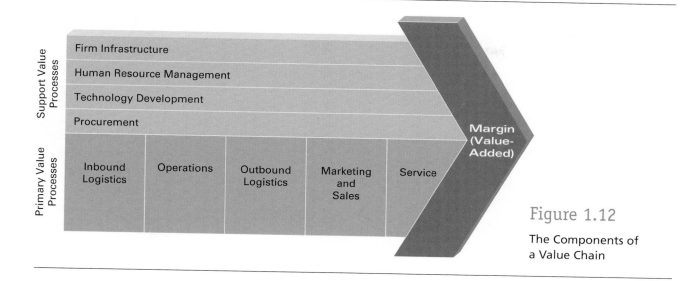

Figure 1.12

The Components of a Value Chain

- *Operations*—processing raw materials into finished products and services.
- *Outbound logistics*—warehousing and distributing finished products and services.
- *Marketing and sales*—identifying customer needs and generating sales.
- *Service*—supporting customers after the sale of products and services.

Support value processes along the top half of the chain—firm infrastructure (culture, structure, control systems, accounting, legal, and so on), human resource management, technology development, and procurement (purchasing of raw materials)—support the primary value processes. Your organization requires these support value processes to ensure the smooth operation of the primary value processes.

Your organization's margin or profit depends on how well you perform both the primary value processes and support value processes. That is, the amount that your customers are willing to pay (defining the value your customers place on your products and services) must exceed the cost of the processes in the value chain. This concept is similar to top-line and bottom-line strategies in that your success (profit) depends on the revenue from customers (top line) exceeding the costs of your operations (bottom line).

You may never have heard of the Robert Talbott Company of Carmel Valley, California, but if you know what a necktie is, you can get the gist of the analysis that follows.[16] Talbott is a premier necktie manufacturer in the United States. Talbott traditionally shunned the use of technology; for example, all of its tie orders were written on paper forms. That used to work fine, because Talbott always ensured value-added by utilizing high-quality workmanship, unique designs, and fine fabrics. However, in today's fast-changing consumer market, customers want constantly updated styles and more of them. Talbott now creates four neckwear lines for Nordstrom each year with up to 300 designs per line.

How might a value chain analysis help Talbott in its operations? It could do so by identifying both value-added and value-reducing processes within its value chain. Let's look at the identification of value-added processes first.

IDENTIFYING PROCESSES THAT ADD VALUE

Talbott should first construct a survey instrument for its customers and ask which of the processes (both primary and support) within the value chain add the most value. This type of survey is often in a format in which a customer must assign a total of 100 points

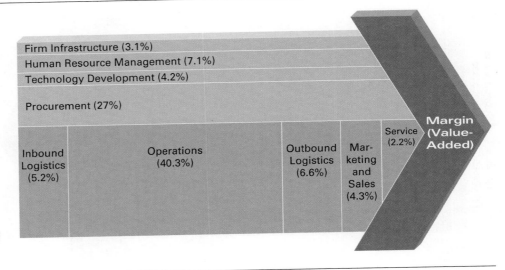

Figure 1.13

The Value-Added View of
a Necktie Manufacturer

across all the processes. Then, by summing all the responses and creating a percentage of total for each process, Talbott can determine which processes add the most value. Figure 1.13 depicts one possible customer survey result. Notice how the processes in the figure are sized to depict the value that customers attribute to each process. The largest value-added source is the high-quality manufacturing process (operations). Still, a close second is the purchasing procurement process that provides access to high-quality silks and other fabrics. As these processes are the ones that are most visible to customers, they will quickly add even more value when supported by IT. Therefore, Talbott has created a computer-aided design system to reduce the time it takes to create and manufacture new ties. It could also further strengthen its quality-control systems to ensure that the procurement of raw materials results in the highest quality of silks and other fabrics.

IDENTIFYING PROCESSES THAT REDUCE VALUE

After identifying value-added processes, it's important to identify those processes that reduce value for the customers. To do this, Talbott creates a second part to its survey instrument. In this part, Talbott asks customers to assign 100 points across all processes according to which processes reduce value. Then, by once again summing all the responses and creating a percentage of total for each process, Talbott can determine which processes reduce value the most.

Talbott identified the marketing and sales process as the process that reduced value the most, as shown in Figure 1.14. It found that sales were lost because salespeople were promising neckties that were out of stock. Customers were beginning to lose faith in Talbott's ability to deliver high-quality ties. They saw this process failure as one that reduced Talbott's value to them as customers.

To correct its marketing and sales process deficiencies, Talbott implemented a new IT system to get timely product information to the sales force. Using laptop computers, the sales force now carries product line information on the road with them. They place orders over their computers from their hotel rooms and receive inventory updates at the same time. As a result, neckties that customers want are on the shelves on a timely basis and customers have new faith in an old friend who now adds more value than ever.

Evaluating value chains is particularly effective because it forces your organization to gather and analyze quantifiable information from your customers. It eliminates much of

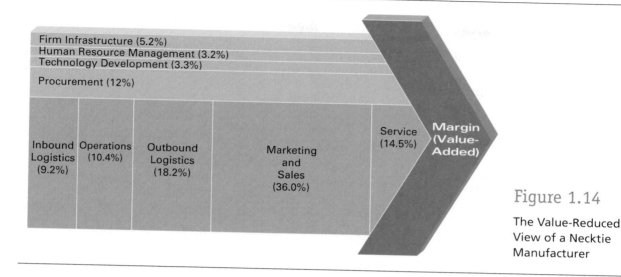

Firm Infrastructure (5.2%)
Human Resource Management (3.2%)
Technology Development (3.3%)

Procurement (12%)

| Inbound Logistics (9.2%) | Operations (10.4%) | Outbound Logistics (18.2%) | Marketing and Sales (36.0%) | Service (14.5%) | Margin (Value-Added) |

Figure 1.14

The Value-Reduced View of a Necktie Manufacturer

the "flying by the seat of your pants" in making decisions. And as you begin to quantify important information, you can build a better return-on-investment case for the acquisition, development, and use of IT to further add value to your processes and reduce ineffectiveness.

To briefly summarize our main points in this chapter, MIS is all about people using technology to work with information as they support the organization in its quest for a competitive advantage. You can't blindly apply technology; you must carefully select technology within the context of the competitive pressures of your industry, the business strategies that you choose, and the important business processes you identify.

Introduction to Enterprise Systems

LO5

To manage today's complex global business environments, organizations rely on enterprise systems (ES). The aim of an ES is to ensure that information can be shared across all functional levels and management hierarchies. ES help eliminate the problem of information fragmentation caused by multiple information systems in an organization.

Most businesses are moving away from home-grown solutions to ES. ES are incredibly complex, general-purpose software packages with capabilities to support a wide variety of companies and industries. As a result, they must be configured to support the organizational structures and business processes of the particular company to efficiently and effectively manage a firm's business processes. Unless a company uses it to become more efficient and effective in delivering goods and services to its customers, the ES will be only a drain on company resources.

Major solutions provided by ES include

- enterprise resource planning (ERP).
- customer relationship management (CRM).
- supply chain management (SCM).

These types of systems will be discussed throughout the text. The major business solutions comprise components (for example, sales & distribution, materials management, accounts payable, human resources, production, project system, marketing resource management, sales planning & forecasting, supplier network, and business warehouse) that allow organizations to select only those they require to meet their business requirements. It is important to note that all components are dependent on the financial and control components, making these the fundamental core of ES. All of the business solutions and selected components sit on top of one or more databases; it is the ES that controls and manages the database. Sometimes the ES and database are purchased from different vendors.

Summary: LEARNING OUTCOMES *REVISITED*

LO1 **Define management information systems (MIS) and describe the three important organizational resources within it.** *Management Information Systems (MIS)* deal with the planning for, development, management, and use of information technology tools to help people perform all tasks related to information processing and management. People, as an organizational resource within MIS, are the most important of the three. To be successful in their use of technology, people must be both *information-literate* and *technology-literate*. Information in various forms goes by many names such as *data*, *business intelligence*, and *knowledge*. All are intellectual assets but exhibit subtle differences. *Information* is data that has meaning within a specific context. *Information technology (IT)* is any computer-based tool that people use to work with information and support the information and information-processing needs of an organization.

LO2 **Describe how to use Porter's Five Forces Model to evaluate the relative attractiveness of and competitive pressures in an industry.** Porter's *Five Forces Model* focuses on industry analysis according to five forces: (1) *buyer power*—high when buyers have many choices and low when choices are few; (2) *supplier power*—high when buyers have few choices and high when choices are many; (3) *threat of substitute products and services*—high when many alternative are available and low when alternatives are few; (4) *threat of new entrants*—high when it is easy to get into a market and low when it is difficult to get into a market; and (5) *rivalry among existing competitors*—high when competition is fierce and low when competition is more complacent.

LO3 **Compare and contrast Porter's three generic strategies; top line versus bottom line; and the run-grow-transform framework as approaches to the development of business strategy.** Porter's *three generic strategies* are (1) *overall cost leadership*—the same or better quality products at a price less than that of the competition; (2) *differentiation*—a product or service that is perceived as being "unique;" and (3) *focus*—products or services for a particular buyer group, within a segment of a product line, and/or a specific geographic market. A *top-line* strategy focuses on increasing revenues by increasing market share, cross-selling complementary products, etc. A *bottom-line* strategy focuses on decreasing costs by optimizing processes, reducing errors, etc. Finally, the *RGT framework* requires that you allocate in terms of percentages how you will spend your IT dollars among running the organization, growing the organization, and transforming the organization.

LO4 **Describe the role of value chain analysis in identifying value-added and value-reducing processes.** *Value chain analysis* is a systematic approach to assessing and improving the value of business processes within your organization to further increase its competitive strengths. Value chain analysis allows you to gather customer data and quantifiably assess the extent to which different processes add value and reduce value, thus identifying those processes that would benefit from IT support.

LO5 **List three major types of enterprise systems (ES) and describe how they can create value for an organization.** We consider ES an umbrella, comprising several major system types in use within organizations of all kinds. These include enterprise resource planning (ERP), customer relationship management (CRM), and supply chain management (SCM) systems. Each provides an incredibly rich, complex, and powerful toolset, which must first be configured and tuned to match the business process of the individual organization. Without such individual fine-tuning and optimization, ES provide nothing more than a drain on organizational resources.

CLOSING CASE STUDY 1
Exploring Your Space at MySpace.com

While being interviewed by *The Hollywood Reporter* concerning MySpace, Rupert Murdoch stated, "In a sense, we say we've got 30 million portals." In early 2008, MySpace.com had more than 110 million active monthly users around the world. According to comScore, it ranked third in page views among all domains.[17]

Social networking sites are an interesting phenomenon on the Web. In a sense, eBay (www.ebay.ca) is a social networking site that supports the gathering of consumer buyers and sellers. Epinions.com (www.epinions.com) is a social networking site enabling consumers to share product reviews. Wikipedia (www.wikipedia.org) is a social networking site focusing on the development of free open-source information and content.

In MySpace.ca, you create and maintain your own "portal," a sort of personal Web site. In that portal, you create a personal page about yourself, sharing just about any information you care to. You can include photos, create a blog about a topic of interest, and establish relationships with other people in chat rooms.

Beyond just personal social networking, MySpace is becoming the space for many types of businesses. Most notably, musicians and bands are using MySpace to post and sell music. Over 660,000 musicians and bands maintain user profiles on MySpace. And those musicians aren't just limited to fledgling "wannabes." Madonna pursued an aggressive campaign at MySpace for her album *Confessions on a Dance Floor*. Madonna even posted her own confessions on MySpace, describing how she loves to go through people's bags while they're not looking (and other questionable acts). Other MySpace users can watch Madonna's videos, and even copy and paste them into their own profile sections.

Television shows and movies are also jumping into MySpace. TV shows like *Family Guy*, *The Man Show*, and *Kitchen Confidential* have a MySpace presence. Popular movies like *Walk the Line* and *Saw II* have their own space.

Book publishers spend extensive time reading and reviewing self-print books written on MySpace. Many people have found MySpace to be an excellent venue for self-publishing a book, getting people to read it, and getting publishers to take a look at their manuscripts. Many book publishers have profiles on MySpace and encourage authors to submit books and manuscripts there.

Of course, there is also a dark side to MySpace. Recently, a man created a MySpace portal and used it to attract underage girls for the purpose to committing sexual acts with them. He was caught but not before making contact with several potential victims.[18, 19]

Finally, with the introduction of legislation in Canada that prohibits the distribution of copyrighted material (Bill C-61 in June 2008), sites such as MySpace and YouTube also become targets for those monitoring copyright infractions. Whether this will have a chilling effect on Web 2.0 sharing is yet to be seen.

Questions

1. Visit MySpace (www.myspace.com). What process do you go through to create your own personal portal? Do you have to pay a fee? What information do you have to provide MySpace to create a personal portal?

2. Search for a "friend" on MySpace. How do you do this? What are the search criteria you can use?

3. Peruse the various blogs on MySpace. What seem to be the dominant blog topics? Did you find any blogs that are of questionable social value (according to your own ethics)? If so, what were the topics?

4. Search for your favourite garage band or perhaps a popular well-known band. What content were you able to find? Could you view a music video? If so, could you view the entire video or just a segment of it?

5. In your opinion, why have social networking sites grown in popularity? Do you have a MySpace profile? If so, why did you create it?

6. According to one account, MySpace is designed to be "unedited and democratic." But as you read above, MySpace has been used by pedophiles to attract young children. Should MySpace be completely uncontrolled and unedited? Does MySpace have a societal obligation to censor questionable content? In your view, what does "questionable content" mean?

7. Will Canada's Bill C-61 put a damper on the "democratization" of digital media? Review the legislation on-line (search for it) and decide whether you side with the government (balances the rights of copyright holders and consumers) or with the bill's critics (who state that it will lead to a police state). This is heady and controversial stuff. How do you feel about such legislation? Does it make Canada a groundbreaker or a laggard in terms of the digital revolution? Will it deter you from downloading and sharing copyrighted media? Why or why not? What would you do if you were caught breaking the law in this way?

CLOSING CASE STUDY 2
Is the World Dumping Data on You?

It goes by many terms—information overload, analysis paralysis, data dumping, and so on. You know what we're talking about. It is indeed great to live in the information age with a plethora of digital technologies at your fingertips giving you access almost instantly to massive amounts of information. But is all of that information really useful? Do you find yourself spending hours on end searching through that vast amount of information to find exactly what you need? Are search engines really good at helping you quickly locate the precise information you need?

Those are very important questions in the business world. Time is money, and time spent looking for the right information is wasted time and therefore an increased cost, resulting in a decrease in profits. An Accenture study of 1,009 managers at U.S. and U.K. companies with annual revenues exceeding $500 million in revenues revealed the following startling facts:

- IT managers spend 30 percent of their time trying to find information relevant to their jobs.

- 42 percent say they are bombarded by too much information.

- 44 percent complain that other departments don't share data.

- 39 percent can't figure out which information is current.

- 38 percent often receive duplicate data.

- 21 percent don't understand the value of the information once they receive it.

- 84 percent say they store information on hard drives or e-mail, and don't share data that might be relevant to others.

- Only 16 percent state that they use collaborative tools—essential tools for sharing information.[20]

Information is a critical and valuable resource to any organization. It can easily be shared and used by many people, unlike other resources such as money. Knowing the right information about your competitors, your own internal operations, and your customers can yield a significant competitive advantage in the marketplace.

From a personal point of view, having the right information is essential as well. It will help you pick the right classes to take and when. It can make you more efficient and effective in writing term papers. It can help you with your taxes, plan your retirement, and determine which car best fits within your budget and meets your needs.[21]

Questions

1. Critically evaluate the bulleted list of information-related items in this case study. How is each contradictory to the notion of being an information-literate knowledge worker?

2. Consider again Figure 1.1 on page 6 and the steps we presented in the chapter for determining which technologies are most appropriate in an organization. Why is this process so important? During *each* of the four steps in that decision process, what information should be derived and used in the next step?

3. Again, considering the four steps in determining which technologies are most appropriate in an organization, for the information you identified as crucial to be derived during each step in Question 2, which of that information is internal, external, objective, or subjective information? Which information is some combination of internal, external, objective, or subjective?

4. Is it ethical for people in an organization to withhold information and not share it with other employees? If so, under what circumstances would it be acceptable not to share certain types of information with other employees? What can organizations do to encourage their employees to share information?

5. What about your personal life at your school? How easy is it to find the following information on your school's Web site?
   - The course description for the classes you are currently taking.
   - A list of classes you need to take to complete your degree.
   - The requirements you must meet to qualify for various types of government-supported loan programs.
   - The process you go through to apply for graduation.

6. Overall, how would you rate your school's Web site in terms of providing the information you need? How would you rate your school's Web site in terms of allowing you to process your own transactions, such as signing up for a class, scheduling time with an adviser, and so on?

www.mcgrawhill.ca/olc/haag

Key Terms and Concepts

Application software, 16
Business intelligence (BI), 7
Business process, 26
Buyer power, 17
Central processing unit (CPU), 15
Competitive advantage, 17
Customer-self service system, 23
Data, 7
Differentiation, 22
Entry barrier, 19
Ethics, 13
External information, 10
First-mover advantage, 18
Five Forces Model, 17
Focus, 22
Garbage-in garbage-out (GIGO), 9
Hardware, 14
Information, 7
Information granularity, 9

Information-literate knowledge worker, 12
Information technology (IT), 14
Input device, 14
Internal information, 10
Knowledge, 8
Loss leader, 21
Loyalty program, 17
Management information systems (MIS), 6
Objective information, 10
Output device, 15
Overall cost leadership, 21
Primary value processes, 26
RAM (random access memory), 15
Rivalry among existing competitors, 19
Run-grow-transform (RGT) framework, 24

Software, 14
Storage device, 15
Subjective information, 10
Supplier power, 18
Support value processes, 27
Switching cost, 18
System software, 16
Technology-literate knowledge worker, 12
Telecommunications device, 15
Threat of new entrants, 19
Threat of substitute products or services, 18
Transaction processing system (TPS), 23
Value chain, 26
Value chain analysis, 26

Short-Answer Questions

1. What is the relationship between management information systems (MIS) and information technology (IT)?
2. What four steps should an organization follow in determining which technologies to use?
3. What are some relationships among data, information, business intelligence (BI), and knowledge?
4. How does the granularity of information change as it moves from lower to upper organizational levels?
5. What is the difference between a technology-literate knowledge worker and an information-literate knowledge worker?
6. How do ethics differ from laws?
7. What role does the Five Forces Model play in decision making?
8. Why are competitive advantages never permanent?
9. What are the three generic strategies according to Michael Porter?
10. How are Porter's three generic strategies, a top-line versus bottom-line approach, and the RGT framework similar?
11. Why is value chain analysis so useful to companies?

Assignments and Exercises

1. **USING PORTER TO EVALUATE THE MOVIE RENTAL INDUSTRY** One hotly contested and highly competitive industry is the movie rental business. You can rent videos from local video rental stores, you can order pay-per-view from the comfort of your own home, and you can rent videos from the Web at such sites as zip.ca. Using Porter's Five Forces Model, evaluate the relative attractiveness of entering the movie rental business. Is buyer power low or high? Is supplier power low or high? Which substitute products and services are perceived as threats? Can new entrants easily enter the market? What are the barriers to entry? What is the level of rivalry among existing competitors? What is your overall view of the movie rental industry? Is it a good or bad industry to enter?

2. **REVIEWING THE 100 BEST COMPANIES TO WORK FOR** Each year *Fortune* devotes an issue to the top 100 best companies to work for. Find the most recent issue of *Fortune* that does this. First, develop a numerical summary that describes the 100 companies in terms of their respective industries. Which industries are the most dominant? Pick one of the more dominant industries (preferably one in which you would like to work) and choose a specific highlighted company. Prepare a short class presentation on why that company is among the 100 best to work for.

3. **YOUR SCHOOL'S VALUE CHAIN** Develop a value chain for your school. You don't have to gather information to construct the value chain, but you do have to determine which processes are support value processes and which processes are primary value processes. Draw your value chain according to Figure 1.12 on page 27. Finally, list the three most important processes to you as a student and provide a short explanation of why they are the most important to you.

4. **BUSINESS STRATEGY FOR ENTERING THE CELL PHONE SERVICE INDUSTRY** Assume that you run a start-up and have decided to enter the cell phone service industry. Which of the three generic strategies would you choose as your primary business strategy—overall cost leadership, differentiation, or focus? Explain your choice by elaborating on the product and service features you would offer to lure customers from the competition.

5. **RESEARCHING YOUR CAREER AND INFORMATION TECHNOLOGY** To position yourself in the best possible way to succeed in the business world, you need to start researching your career right now. Here, we would like you to focus on the IT skills your career requires. First, consider what career you want to have. Second, visit monster.ca (www.monster.ca) and search for jobs that relate to your career. Read through several of the job postings and determine what IT skills you need to acquire.

Discussion Questions

1. The three key resources in management information systems (MIS) are information, information technology, and people. Which of these three resources is the most important? Why? The least important? Why?

2. We often say that hardware is the *physical* interface to a technology system while software is the *intellectual* interface. How is your hardware your physical interface to your computer? How is your software your intellectual interface to your computer? Do you see technology progressing to the point that we may no longer distinguish between hardware and software and thus no longer perceive differing physical and intellectual interfaces?

3. In a group of three to four students, consider eBay in the context of Porter's Five Forces Model. How does eBay reduce the threat of new entrants? If necessary, you may want to explore eBay's site (www.ebay.ca) and determine the role of buyer and seller ratings, its integration with PayPal, and how it helps buyers and sellers resolve disputes.

4. In this chapter, we discussed the use of loyalty programs in the travel industry as a mechanism for reducing buyer power. What is another industry that also uses loyalty programs to reduce buyer power? How does that industry use loyalty programs to do so?

5. As an information-literate knowledge worker for a local distributor of imported foods and spices, you've been asked to prepare a customer mailing list that will be sold to international cuisine restaurants in your area. If you do so, will you be acting ethically? Suppose you don't consider the proposal ethical. What will you do if your boss threatens to fire you if you don't prepare the list? Do you believe you would have any legal recourse if you didn't prepare the list and were subsequently fired?

Chapter 2

Major Business Initiatives

Gaining Competitive Advantage with IT

LEARNING OUTCOMES

LO1 Describe supply chain management (SCM) systems and their strategic and competitive opportunities.

LO2 Describe customer relationship management (CRM) systems and their strategic and competitive opportunities.

LO3 Define e-collaboration and describe its strategic and competitive opportunities.

LO4 Discuss the impact IT culture has on technology choices and their implementations within an organization.

LO5 Explain the significance of enterprise resource planning (ERP) software to the integration of functional software systems.

OPENING CASE STUDY:
A Smack—A Group of Jellyfish or Social Commerce Shopping?

A *smack* is actually both. It is the term for a group of jellyfish (just like a group of crows is called a *murder*), and it's also the term Mark McGuire uses to describe how customers shop on his social commerce site, that is, *smack shopping*. Mark is the CEO of Jellyfish.com (www.jellyfish.com), a Web site that provides for collaborative shopping by groups of customers to get the best deals. Jellyfish was acquired by Microsoft in fall 2007.

Jellyfish is actually a reverse auction site. A seller of a given product—say 100 Apple iPods—posts those items for sale on Jellyfish with a zero percent discount at the beginning of the auction. As the auction continues, the discount begins to go up. As a buyer, you can choose to buy at any time at a given discount percentage. The longer you wait, the higher the percentage discount you receive. But be careful, because none of the buyers ever knows how many of the iPods the seller has. So, if you wait, hoping that the percentage discount will rise to 75, the seller may have already sold his or her lot for a discount rate of 50 percent or less.

And 50 percent isn't that unreasonable. Smack shoppers have purchased Apple iPods for 41 percent off, Microsoft Xboxes for 46 percent off, and TiVo DVRs for a 23 percent discount.

Jellyfish supports other collaborative and social networking tools that also benefit buyers. A live chat board lets buyers interact with each other. Smacks (groups) of buyers on the chat board will attempt to dissuade other buyers from buying too early, letting everyone profit from increasing discounts. As you might guess, many of these buyers then resell the items on other traditional auction sites such as eBay.

The whole concept of *social commerce shopping* seems to be catching on. Jellyfish has more than 100,000 participants (both buyers and sellers) on a monthly basis. In the first five months of operation, the users of Jellyfish quintupled. As Mark describes it, smacking is turning marketing into entertainment. "We call it the Internet's first live shopping game show," says Mark.

Social commerce shopping certainly doesn't represent any new advance in technology, but rather a new and innovative way of *using* technology to reach customers. Customers in this case are both sellers (wanting to unload a lot of product) and buyers (seeking the best deals). In this chapter, we'll look at how organizations can use technology in support of major business initiatives such as supply chain management (for companies providing products and services), customer relationship management (for companies wanting to know everything about their customers), and e-collaboration.[1]

Questions

1. Do you use a live auction site like eBay? How does it differ from Jellyfish?

2. Visit jellyfish.com. What is the process of becoming a participant?

3. What sort of products would be best suited for a reverse auction format?

Introduction

In almost any study you care to read, research shows that as competition intensifies in an industry, companies must develop innovative products, services, and business processes to compete and survive. Further, most of these studies point to the use of information technology as a way to help companies separate from the competition and develop a significant competitive advantage. In Chapter 1, we explored how a company can use tools such as Porter's Five Forces Model and Porter's three generic strategies, top-line versus bottom-line initiatives, and the run-grow-transform framework to develop business strategy to address the ever-intensifying competitive environment. In this chapter, we focus on three of the most important IT implementations of business processes to support those business strategies:

- Supply chain management
- Customer relationship management
- E-collaboration.

As a company implements one of more of these IT–based systems, it must carefully consider its own internal IT culture and, just as importantly, how it will integrate these systems throughout the company using *Enterprise Resource Planning* software. After examining the three IT implementations above, we'll also explore IT culture and enterprise resource planning software.

LO1

Supply Chain Management

Dell's supply chain management system is the envy of the industry. Its direct customer model gives the company a huge advantage over any competitor using the traditional model of selling through retailers. Traditional computer manufacturers build computers and ship them to wholesalers, distributors, or retailers. Although Dell is in the process of evolving its business model by allowing value-added resellers and retail partners to sell its products, the direct customer model remains the foundation of Dell's strategy.[2] In the traditional model, computers sit in a warehouse or on the retailers' shelves until somebody comes in and buys them. If you took a look at a typical distribution chain, you would see that there are too many computers in inventory. A ***distribution chain*** is simply the path a product or service follows from the originator of the product or service to the end consumer. Holding onto inventory in a distribution chain costs money, because whoever owns the inventory has to pay for the operation of a warehouse or stores while waiting for someone to buy it. In the retailing of computers, not only does excess inventory cost money to hold, but also the computers themselves can become obsolete, requiring retailers to slash prices in an effort to sell older models before the newer ones arrive. Many such retailers use sites like jellyfish.com (from the opening case study) to dump old and obsolete inventory.

Dell's model is different. When Dell sells computers directly from its Web site, there is no inventory in its distribution chain. Dell has enhanced its *supply chain* as well. It uses i2 supply chain management software to send orders for parts to suppliers every two hours, enabling it to manufacture and deliver exactly what its customers want with little or no inventory in its supply chain.[3]

Supply chain management (SCM) involves planning, implementing, and controlling/monitoring the supply chain in order to increase efficiency. Supply chain management controls the movement and storage of raw materials, work-in-process inventory, and finished goods from suppliers through producers to consumers. Supply chain management (SCM) can also involve supply chain management software, which automates and manages supplier relationships and other crucial business processes.

The supply chain is sometimes referred to as the extended enterprise, which can be seen as a loosely coupled (sometimes informal and easy-to-break alliances), purpose-formed network of organizations involved in providing products and/or services to the marketplace. Industry consultant James P. Farnell writes, "Alternatively referred to as a 'supply chain' or a 'value chain,' the extended enterprise describes the trading relationships among a community of participants involved with provisioning a set of goods and service offerings. The extended enterprise associated with "McDonald's," for example, includes not only McDonald's Corporation, but also franchisees and joint venture partners of McDonald's Corporation, the 3PL's [Third-party logistics providers] that deliver food and materials to McDonald's restaurants, the advertising agencies that produce and distribute McDonald's advertising, the suppliers of McDonald's food ingredients, kitchen equipment, building services, utilities, and other goods and services, the designers of Happy Meal toys, and others. In this example, McDonald's Corporation has organized local purchasing cooperatives, made up of representatives of local McDonald's franchisees and McDonald's stores, which determine how the local stores will source local advertising, food ingredients and other materials."[4]

For a company the size of General Motors, with operations all over the world and tens of thousands of suppliers, supply chain management and IT–based supply chain management systems are critical to ensure the smooth flow of parts to GM factories. ***Supply*** *chain management (SCM)* tracks inventory and information among business processes and across companies. A *supply chain management (SCM) system* is an IT system that supports supply chain management activities by automating the tracking of inventory and information among business processes and across companies.

Most large manufacturing companies use *just-in-time* manufacturing processes, which ensure that the right parts are available as products in process move down the assembly line. *Just-in-time (JIT)* is a method for producing or delivering a product or service just at the time the customer wants it. For retailers such as Future Shop, Best Buy, and Staples, this means that products customers want to buy are on the shelves when the customers walk by. Supply chain management (SCM) systems also focus on ensuring that the right number of parts or products are available; not too many and not too few. Too many products on hand means that too much money is tied up in inventory and also increases the risk of obsolescence. Too few products on hand is not a good thing either, because it could force an assembly line to shut down or, in the case of retailers, lose sales because an item is not in stock when a customer is ready to buy.

Consider snow blowers in Québec in November. If a store like Rona has too many, it may not be able to sell them all early in the snowy season when most customers buy them. Snow blowers are large and bulky and also cost a considerable sum of money. Having too many is an expensive proposition for Rona. Likewise, if Rona has too few snow blowers on hand and runs out early in the snowy season, a customer looking for a snow blower won't wait for new Rona inventory; instead, the customer will go to Canadian Tire or some other retailer.

Companies with suppliers around the globe often employ inter-modal transportation. *Inter-modal transportation* is the use of multiple channels of transportation—railway, truck, boat, and so on—to move products from origin to destination (see Figure 2.1). This further complicates the logistics of SCM because companies are required to carefully schedule, monitor, and track parts and supplies as they move among different modes of transportation. Consider that a given train may be carrying 50 or more truck trailers that will each eventually be connected to different trucks. Even purely domestic supply chains often employ inter-modal transportation such as railway lines and carrier trucks.

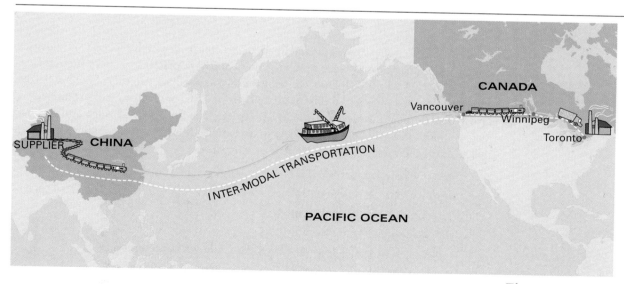

Figure 2.1

Inter-Modal Transportation

STRATEGIC AND COMPETITIVE OPPORTUNITIES WITH SCM

Overall, a tight supply chain management system focuses on squeezing every penny possible out of the supply chain process. Thus, the primary focus of supply chain management may be described in terms of our discussion in Chapter 1 as:

- Overall cost leadership (from Porter's three generic strategies)
- Bottom-line initiative (cost reduction)
- Running the organization (run-grow-transform framework).

Of course, lower costs in the supply chain lead to lower prices to consumers, which in turn can increase market share and top-line revenue. A well-designed supply chain management system helps your organization by optimizing the following specific supply chain activities:

- *Fulfillment*—ensuring that the right quantity of parts for production or products for sale arrive at the right time
- *Logistics*—keeping the cost of transporting materials as low as possible consistent with safe and reliable delivery
- *Production*—ensuring that production lines function smoothly because high-quality parts are available when needed
- *Revenue and profit*—ensuring that no sales are lost because shelves are empty
- *Cost and price*—keeping the cost of purchased parts and prices of products at acceptable levels.

Cooperation among supply chain partners for mutual success is another hallmark of modern supply chain management systems. For example, many manufacturing companies share product concepts with suppliers early in the product development cycle. This lets suppliers contribute their ideas about how to make high-quality parts at a lower cost. Such an arrangement is enabled through IT and is usually referred to as an ***information partnership***—two or more companies cooperating by integrating their IT systems, thereby providing customers with the best of what each can offer.

IT SUPPORT FOR SUPPLY CHAIN MANAGEMENT

While the SCM market was pioneered by specialist companies such as i2 and Manugistics, it is now dominated by enterprise management software (ERP) providers such as SAP, Oracle-Siebel, SSA Global, and Microsoft (more on ERP later in this chapter). If your career choice takes you into industries that focus on the manufacturing of products and/or the distribution and use of those products (such as hospitality, resort, and tourism management), you will have a great deal to do with SCM software. To learn more about this area, we encourage you to visit the following sites:

- Supply Chain Knowledge Base—http://supplychain.ittoolbox.com
- Supply Chain Management Review—www.scmr.com
- i2 Technologies—www.i2.com
- CIO Magazine—www.cio.com
- About.com: Logistics/Supply Chain —http://logistics.about.com
- Oracle-Siebel Supply Chain—www.oracle.com/applications/scm

STAPLES MAKES A BET ON ITS SUPPLY CHAIN MANAGEMENT SYSTEM

If you were running a highly successful retail operation, would you guarantee the availability of your fastest moving inventory or play it safe and guarantee only the availability of your slowest moving inventory that is seldom purchased? If you chose the latter, you'd be like many retailers, who play it safe, but you would be beaten by some of the competition such as Staples. Staples makes an in-stock guarantee to its customers for its fast-selling lines of ink-jet and toner cartridges, both of which Staples relies on heavily for revenue. (In Canada, Staples will give you a $5 coupon toward a compatible Staples brand ink-jet or toner cartridge or the out-of-stock cartridge.) If you live in the United States and a cartridge is not in stock, Staples will ship it to your home with no delivery fee the next business day. It will also include a $10 coupon you can use the next time you purchase the same toner cartridge. Now that's an ambitious guarantee—Staples will deliver an out-of-stock item the next business day and give you $10 off your next purchase of the same item!

Staples's computer systems are linked with those of shipping companies such as UPS, a form of an information partnership. If an item is out of stock, the Staples systems find the item at another store and immediately sends UPS a request for package pickup and delivery. That's the way Staples can guarantee the next-day delivery.

Staples can make the guarantee because of its tight supply chain management system. Through its inventory monitoring function, Staples's SCM system carefully tracks the daily sales of its hottest items. When inventory starts to run low, the Staples SCM system sends an electronic order for more toner and/or inkjet cartridges to the likes of HP. The product arrives in a timely manner to ensure shelf placement in light of forecasted demand.

While most retailers will offer you a rain cheque and perhaps even help you find the out-of-stock product at another nearby store, Staples simply asks you to go home and wait for the next-business-day arrival of your product (and a $10 coupon). That's a considerable assurance of Staples's IT–based supply chain management system.[5]

Customer Relationship Management

LO2

Wells Fargo Bank's customer relationship management system tracks and analyzes every transaction made by its 10 million retail customers at its branches, at its ATMs, and through its Web-based on-line banking systems. Wells Fargo, headquartered in the United States but with over 150 branches in 10 provinces across Canada, has become so good at predicting customer behaviour that it knows what customers need even before many of them realize they need it. Wells Fargo's CRM system collects every customer transaction and combines it with personal information provided by the customer. The system is able to provide tailored offerings that will appeal to individual customers (a competitive rate line of credit, for example) at just the right time. As a result, Wells Fargo sells four more banking products or services per customer than the industry average of 2.2.[6]

Acquiring customers and then retaining them are the basic objectives of any organization, and thus, *customer relationship management* systems have become one of the hottest IT systems in business today. A *customer relationship management (CRM) system* uses information about customers to gain insights into their needs, wants, and behaviours in order to serve them better. Customers interact with companies in many ways, and each interaction should be easy, enjoyable, and error free. *Multi-channel service delivery* is the term that describes a company's offering multiple ways in which customers can interact with it. E-mail, fax, phone, and the Web are all ways in which most companies interact with their customers. A fundamental goal of a CRM system, then, is the management and tracking of all these interactions. The communications within the various channels must be organized and carefully recorded for each customer. If that doesn't happen, then your experience with the company may be less than optimal and you may choose to change companies or perhaps return the product for a refund. It's not uncommon for a customer to change companies after having a negative experience. Thus, the overriding goal of CRM is to limit such negative interactions and provide customers with positive experiences (even delightful ones).

CRM systems (see Figure 2.2) typically include such functions as

- Sales force automation
- Customer service and support
- Marketing campaign management and analysis.

It's important to note that CRM is not just the software. It is a total business objective that encompasses many different aspects of a business including software, hardware, services, support, and strategic business goals. The CRM system you adopt should support all these functions and should also be designed to provide the organization with detailed customer information. In many cases, companies begin with a sales force automation application and then progress to the other two functions. ***Sales force automation (SFA)*** systems automatically track all the steps in the sales process, including contact management, sales lead tracking, sales forecasting and order management, and product knowledge.

Some basic SFA systems perform sales lead tracking, or listing potential customers for the sales team to contact. They also perform contact management, tracking all the times a salesperson contacts a potential customer, what was discussed, and the next steps. More sophisticated SFA systems perform detailed analysis of the market and customers, and can even offer product configuration tools to enable customers to configure their own products. Some of the more robust CRM systems and methods, such as at General Motors (see Figure 2.3), focus on creating repeat customers. It is far more expensive to acquire a new customer than it is to retain an existing customer, especially in the automotive retail industry.

Figure 2.2

Customer Relationship
Management (CRM) System

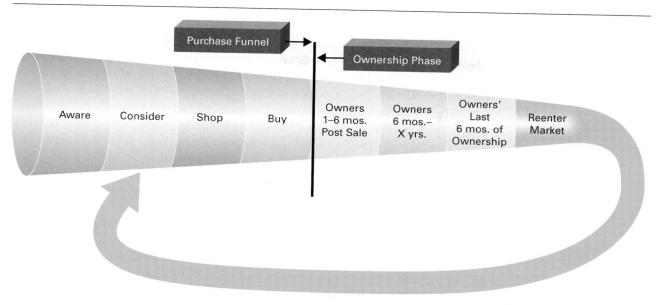

Figure 2.3

General Motors
Purchase Funnel[7]

STRATEGIC AND COMPETITIVE OPPORTUNITIES WITH CRM

Overall, a well-designed customer relationship management system focuses on increasing revenue by providing delightful experiences for the customer in a variety of ways—tailored product and service offerings, seamless interaction, product knowledge, and so on. Thus, the primary focus of customer relationship management is

- Differentiation and focus (Porter's three generic strategies)
- Top-line initiative (revenue enhancement)
- Growing the organization (run-grow-transform framework).

Of course, customers are willing to pay only so much for these "delightful" interactions and product selections, so your organization must have a tight supply chain management system in place to ensure an acceptable price.

One of the rewards of CRM is competitive advantage through superior performance in CRM functions; in particular:

- Devising more effective marketing campaigns based on more precise knowledge of customer needs and wants
- Assuring that the sales process is efficiently managed
- Providing superior after-sale service and support, for example, through well-run call centres.

All the classic goals of CRM—treating customers better, understanding their needs and wants, tailoring offerings in response—are likely to result in buyers choosing your product or service instead of the competition's. Predicting the amount by which the CRM–enabled organization will gain market share, however, can be difficult. But, certainly, it is something that can be measured after the fact, thus allowing your organization to understand the true results of better CRM in terms of customers' buying decisions.

IT SUPPORT FOR CUSTOMER RELATIONSHIP MANAGEMENT

Figure 2.4 shows a sample CRM system infrastructure. The ***front-office systems*** are the primary interface to customers and sales channels; they send all the customer information they collect to the database. The ***back-office systems*** are used to fulfill and support customer orders, and they also send all their customer information to the database. The CRM system analyzes and distributes the customer information and provides the organization with a complete view of each customer's experience with the business. A typical back-office function, such as order fulfillment, would have direct ties to the supply chain management system, creating synergy between the customer relationship management system and the supply chain management system.

There are many CRM systems available for purchase today. Some of the bigger providers of these packages are Clarify, Oracle-Siebel, and SAP. Oracle-Siebel and SalesForce.com are two of the most prominent sales force automation (SFA) software providers. salesforce.com was the first company to offer CRM using an ASP (application service provider, which hosts its software on a Web server and allows customer organizations to use the software via the Internet) model, and others have since followed suit. For additional CRM resources, we encourage you to visit the following:

- Oracle-Siebel Systems—www.oracle.com/siebel
- salesforce.com—www.salesforce.com
- MyCustomer.com—www.mycustomer.com
- CRMToday—www.crm2day.com
- CRM Knowledge Base—http://crm.ittoolbox.com
- destinationCRM.com—www.destinationcrm.com

Figure 2.4

A Sample CRM System
Infrastructure

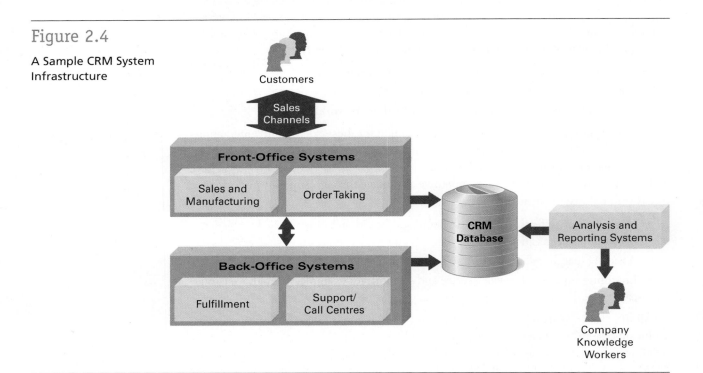

APC CREATES A WORLDWIDE PROTECTION PRESENCE WITH CUSTOMER RELATIONSHIP MANAGEMENT

"We want to know as much information about customers as we can possibly get … It's not only about being a supplier but a trusted business partner and adviser for customers to solve real business problems," explains Brian Belliveau, CIO of American Power Conversion (APC). APC's customers include those who purchase surge protection for high-end items such as home PCs and flat-screen TVs and also other businesses wanting to protect expensive computers and data centres from frying during thunderstorms.

APC's ships products around the world to over 160 countries. In 2005, 52 percent of APC's revenues were in North and Central America; 30 percent in Europe, the Middle East, and Africa; and 18 percent in Asia.

APC established a CRM initiative called the *Customer Loyalty Framework*. Using CRM technology provided by such companies as Oracle-Siebel, APC identifies each and every touch point with customers, failed transactions, and what is needed to elevate customer satisfaction. APC has developed an automated credit approval process and expects the new function to yield $8 million in benefits over a three-year period.

Now, all employee bonuses are tied to customer satisfaction. As Belliveau explains it, "All employee bonuses are tied back to customer satisfaction. If customers aren't happy and the satisfaction numbers are going down, everybody gets a piece of that. And if the numbers are doing better, we get a piece of that, too."[8, 9]

E-Collaboration

LO3

Almost everything you do in an organization will be performed in a team environment. So, improving team collaboration greatly increases your organization's productivity and competitive advantage. Broadly defined, *e-collaboration* is the use of technology to support

1. Work activities with integrated collaboration environments
2. Knowledge management with knowledge management systems
3. Social networking with social networking systems
4. Learning with e-learning tools
5. Informal collaboration to support open-source information.

WORK ACTIVITIES WITH INTEGRATED COLLABORATION ENVIRONMENTS

For support of work activities you'll find *integrated collaboration environments (ICEs),* environments in which virtual teams do their work. *Virtual teams* are teams whose members are located in varied geographical locations and whose work is supported by specialized ICE software or by more basic collaboration systems. A collaboration system is software designed specifically to improve the performance of teams by supporting the sharing and flow of information. More and more, virtual teams are composed of people from your company's information partnerships as well, as we discussed earlier in the context of supply chain management systems.

Many companies first use e-mail and then move on to ICEs that incorporate more advanced features such as giving employees access to each other's calendars, group scheduling software, imaging software, and the following:

- *Workflow systems* facilitate the automation and management of business processes. A *workflow* defines all the steps or business rules, from beginning to end, required for a business process. For example, all the steps to process a loan application in a bank could be enabled by a workflow system with the necessary documents updated and passed from employee to employee as electronic documents (complete with electronic signatures).

- *Document management systems* manage a document through all the stages of its processing. They are similar to workflow systems except that the focus is more on document storage and retrieval.

KNOWLEDGE MANAGEMENT WITH KNOWLEDGE MANAGEMENT SYSTEMS

We introduced you to the notion of *knowledge* in Chapter 1. A *knowledge management (KM) system* is an IT system that supports the capturing, organizing, and dissemination of knowledge (i.e., know-how) throughout the organization. The objective of KM systems is to be sure that a company's knowledge of facts, sources of information, solutions, patents, trademarks, and best-practice processes are available to all of its employees whenever needed. For example, consulting firms make very effective use of KM systems by ensuring that consultants working on a new project can see and read what other consultants have done on similar types of projects. The idea is that there is both efficiency and effectiveness on an organization-wide basis if consultants don't have to continually "reinvent the wheel" when faced with a challenge similar to a challenge faced on another project. A significant challenge for organizations that outsource some or all of their information systems development and management activities is presented by the reality that outside contractors, not the host organization, create the knowledge and benefit from the experience. Thus succession (movement of knowledge and expertise from departing to arriving employees) becomes a difficult process. A carefully planned and diligently maintained KM system is crucial in this context.

SOCIAL NETWORKING WITH SOCIAL NETWORKING SYSTEMS

Most likely, you're familiar with some very popular social networking sites such as MySpace and Facebook. A *social networking site* is a site on which you post information about yourself, create a network of friends, read about other people, share content such as photos and videos, and communicate with other people. In the business world, social networks take on a different meaning and are referred to by the term *social networking system*. A *social networking system* is an IT system that links you to people you know and, from there, to people your contacts know. For example, if a salesperson at your company wants an introduction to an influential executive at another company, a social networking system could find out if someone in your company has good enough connections to arrange an introduction. This is exactly the kind of question that could get a quick reply from the right kind of social networking system.

Business-focused social networking systems, such as LinkedIn (www.linkedin.com), have been slower in subscriber growth than general-population sites such as MySpace and Google's Orkut. Nonetheless, business-focused social networking systems are gaining in acceptance, use, and profitability.

LEARNING WITH E-LEARNING TOOLS

Also in the area of e-collaboration we find *e-learning tools.* E-learning tools are IT–enabled systems that facilitate learning. You've probably worked with an e-learning tool such as WebCT or Blackboard (previously competitors, they merged operations in early 2005). These tools primarily focus on educational environments such as schools. But an important part of your career is ongoing learning and you will find numerous organizations that provide e-learning tools so their employees can learn on the job, in virtual classrooms, or in self-study environments 24/365.

INFORMAL COLLABORATION TO SUPPORT OPEN-SOURCE INFORMATION

Integrated collaboration environments (ICEs), knowledge management systems, and e-learning tools are vitally important organizational resources. We say "organizational" here in reference to an actual organization such as a company or your school. There are also many informal organizations, such as a network of friends on MySpace, supported by social networking systems. Even more informally, groups of people may want to share information on specific ideas and topics. While you can do this with a blog or within a social networking system, many people are now gathering around *wikis.*

A *wiki* is a Web site that allows you—as a visitor—to create, edit, change, and often eliminate content—or *open-source information.* **Open-source information** is content that is publicly available (in a broad sense), free of charge, and most often updateable by anyone. The most popular and well-known wiki is Wikipedia (www.wikipedia.org). Millions of people use Wikipedia as a reference site and a large percentage of those people then participate in no predefined manner in the development, editing, and review of the content (hence, *open-source* information). Thus, wikis support very informal collaboration as opposed to the more formal collaboration that would take place in an organization when a team is working on a project. This is not to say that open-source (user-contributed) information resources such as Wikipedia are not without their drawbacks, as illustrated by the controversy that erupted over an employee who misrepresented his credentials, falsely lending credibility to his Wikipedia contributions. While on-line resources are by no means alone in their potential exposure to fraudulent claims, the ease with which fraud can be committed on-line, coupled with the pervasiveness of such information, should lead to a healthy skepticism regarding the value of such information. *Caveat emptor*!

STRATEGIC AND COMPETITIVE OPPORTUNITIES WITH E-COLLABORATION

The payoffs from collaboration can be huge. For example, while oil and gas exploration companies usually form joint ventures on large projects, they often do not collaborate on purchases of high-dollar-value commodities for the project. A recent survey estimated that the industry could realize up to $7 billion in annual savings by using collaborative technologies and seeking more collaborative preferred provider relationships.[10]

There are many examples of knowledge management systems successfully adding value. For example, in making the case for a knowledge system at Hewlett-Packard (HP), John Doyle, former head of HP Labs, is credited with saying, "If only HP knew what HP knows."[11] He meant there was a huge amount of valuable knowledge in the brains and files (both paper and computer) of HP employees. If HP knew what knowledge was there, and it was shared and accessible to others, it could be useful in solving critical problems, or could lead to ideas for new products and services. Finally, social networking systems

Figure 2.5

A Few E-Collaboration
Systems

Type	Basic Functions	Example	Web Site
Collaboration	Real-time collaboration and conferencing	LiveMeeting	www.microsoft.com
Workflow	Business process management	Metastorm	www.metastorm.com
Document management	Enterprise content management	FileNet (IBM)	www.filenet.com
Peer to peer	Desktop and mobile collaboration	Groove (Microsoft)	www.groove.net
Knowledge management	Knowledge capture, organization, location, and reuse	IBM Knowledge Discovery	http://www01.ibm .com/software/lotus/ category/team/

and e-learning tools promise to forever change the face of business with respect to finding and making new contacts and facilitating learning. These types of e-collaboration tools are relatively new to business, but they already offer great efficiencies and effectiveness.

IT SUPPORT FOR E-COLLABORATION

There are literally scores of different e-collaboration software vendors and tools on the market today. Figure 2.5 provides a list of just a very few. The broad integrated collaboration environment market is dominated by the likes of IBM/Lotus, Microsoft, and Novell. There are many knowledge management systems available today with no clear-cut market leader. Social networking systems that are business focused are still relatively new but include LinkedIn (www.linkedin.com), Spoke (www.spoke.com), and Tribe.net (canada.tribe.net/welcome). A quick search of Google yielded over 300,000 Web sites for exploring e-collaboration and supporting IT–based e-collaboration tools.

LO4

IT Culture—An Organizational Perspective

How your organization chooses its technologies and their implementation to support major business initiatives (and, for that matter, simple and mundane day-to-day processing activities) depends greatly on its IT culture. *IT culture* refers to how the IT function is placed structurally within an organization and the organization's philosophical approach to the development, deployment, and use of IT. As you can see, IT culture has two primary aspects:

1. The structuring of the IT function
2. The organization's philosophy as to the use of IT.

IT CULTURE—STRUCTURING THE IT FUNCTION

Structurally, your organization can place the IT function in any number of ways, with these three being the most common (see Figure 2.6):

1. Top-down silo
2. Matrix
3. Fully integrated throughout the organization.

CONSTELLATION ENERGY: CONNECT. INTERACT. TRANSFORM.

Constellation Energy is a company that supplies electricity and natural gas to Alberta, Ontario, and Quebec. When Beth Perlman joined Constellation Energy as its CIO in 2002, she noticed that employees didn't seem to communicate with each other—not necessarily around the water cooler or at lunch, but rather concerning vitally important documents, information, and knowledge. She immediately acquired and implemented a suite of standardized collaboration tools for everyone to use. The suite includes Microsoft Live Meeting for information sharing, SharePoint for document collaboration, and Windows Messenger for instant messaging. Just a year later the results were astounding.

Through Live Meeting, for example, the company held more than 10,000 hours of meetings, saving the company $41 per attendee and gaining an average of 98 minutes in productivity per employee. Constellation's

"Connect. Interact. Transform." initiative has literally been enabled through the use of technology. And although initially Beth didn't think many employees would take advantage of document collaboration through SharePoint, she now believes that just about everyone is doing so. Take Kevin Hadlock, Constellation Energy's director of investor relations, for example. Because of SharePoint's deployment, Kevin can now spend more time analyzing data for earnings releases because he spends hundreds of fewer hours collecting the documents that go into the releases. For his analyst presentations, Kevin now claims to spend at least one week less in preparation because of SharePoint.

Collaboration tools can yield great benefits in the business environment. They don't have to be fancy or hard to use—they simply need to support people in their sharing of information.[12]

In a *top-down silo* approach (the structure in the upper left of Figure 2.6 on the next page), your organization would create a department or IT function devoted exclusively to everything related to technology—budgeting, project management, capacity, processing, and so on. Such an approach exhibits a strong "command and control" management style. All other functions (e.g., marketing, finance, etc.) must go through the IT department for approval of new projects, the generation of ad hoc reports, support functions, and the like.

In a *matrix* approach (the structure in the upper right of Figure 2.6), you will still find a separate IT department or function, but the goal here is to maintain IT personnel within the IT department but matrix them across the other functions. In this instance, IT considerations such as budgeting, project management, processing, and the like are done in concert with significant input from the other functions. While control still rests with the IT function or branch, everything becomes more collaborative across the organization.

In a *fully integrated* approach (the structure in the bottom of Figure 2.6 on the next page), many IT personnel are now located within the other functional units, although there is still usually a separate IT department or function. Moreover, these integrated IT people have their own budget, can approve department projects, and can initiate the end-user development of smaller projects, ad hoc reports, and so on.

In Figure 2.6, you'll notice a number of acronyms that may be new to you; these are significant and important strategic IT functions within an organization. They include

- *CIO (chief information officer)*—responsible for overseeing every aspect of an organization's information resource
- *CTO (chief technology officer)*—responsible for overseeing both the underlying IT infrastructure within an organization and the user-facing technologies (such as CRM systems)

Figure 2.6

IT Culture—Structuring the IT Functions

- **CSO (chief security officer)**—responsible for the technical aspects of ensuring the security of information such as the development and use of firewalls, intranets, extranets, and anti-virus software
- **CPO (chief privacy officer)**—responsible for ensuring that information is used in an ethical way and that only the right people have access to certain types of information such as financial records, payroll, and health care information.

All of these functions have in recent years joined the ranks of strategic management such as CFO (chief financial officer) and CEO (chief executive officer).

IT CULTURE—PHILOSOPHICAL APPROACH TO IT

The placement of the IT function within an organization is greatly influenced by the organization's philosophy as to the development, deployment, and use of IT. In Figure 2.7, you can see two axes. The horizontal axis provides a spectrum of philosophy ranging from organizations that are early adopters of IT to organizations that "wait and see" whether emerging

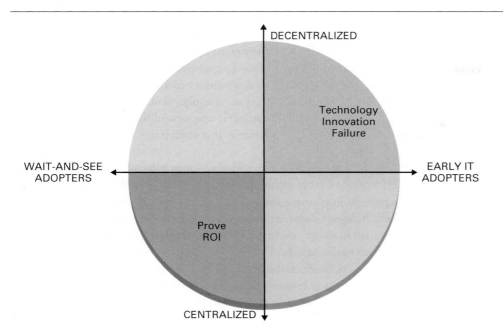

Figure 2.7

IT Culture—Philosophical Approach to IT

technologies prove themselves before adopting them. Along the vertical axis, structural placement of the IT function ranges from greatly decentralized ("fully integrated" in our previous discussion) to greatly centralized ("top-down silo" in our previous discussion).

Decentralized early adopters of technology (top right quadrant in Figure 2.7) empower employees throughout the organization to try new and emerging technologies in the hope of finding a few that can provide significant competitive advantage. These organizations support and encourage **technology innovation failure,** a reward system for trying new technologies even if they prove to be unsuccessful. At the opposite extreme are centralized, wait-and-see organizations (bottom left quadrant in Figure 2.7) that require the demonstration of significant **proven ROI** (return on investment) before first adopting a new technology within the IT function and then deploying that technology to the rest of the organization.

Is any particular IT structure or philosophical approach better than another? The answer is definitely yes, depending on a number of factors. Companies looking for significant growth in an emerging industry would probably emphasize being a decentralized early adopter, while companies in a mature industry with little possibility for increasing market share would not. Overall, the IT culture within your organization should match its overall culture and be developed keeping in mind the industry in which your organization competes.

Enterprise Resource Planning— Bringing IT Together

LO5

To this point, we've considered major business initiatives such as supply chain management, customer relationship management, and e-collaboration individually, focusing on the key strengths and advantages of each. But in the business world, you will deal with the issue of integrating them and making them work together. Consider supply chain and customer relationship management. They must work together, sharing information. To create tight supply chains that provide the right products and services at exactly the right time, you must know what customers want and when they want it (the province of customer relationship management). That brings us to enterprise resource planning systems, an example of enterprise software. An ***enterprise resource planning (ERP) system*** is a collection of integrated software for business management, accounting, finance, human resources management, project management, inventory management, service and maintenance, transportation, e-business, and—yes—supply chain management, customer relationship management, and e-collaboration. It may sound like a long list (and it is), but the central notion behind an ERP system is that it includes all technology systems and software in your organization.

In Figure 2.8, an ERP system allows transparent integration of functions, providing flows of information among all areas within the enterprise in a consistently visible manner. ERPs allow companies to implement a single integrated system to replace their *legacy* information systems. A ***legacy information system (LIS)*** represents a massive, long-term business investment in a software system with a single focus; such systems are often brittle (picky and difficult to debug), slow, and non-extensible (do not allow functionality to be added). ERP systems are configurable information systems packages that seamlessly integrate all the information processes in the company within and across all functional areas—financial, accounting, human resources, supply chain, and customer information. The result is (1) integrated information across the board (data, information, and business intelligence), (2) one suite of applications, and (3) a unified interface across the entire enterprise. An ERP system is required to have the following characteristics:

- Modular design comprising many distinct business functions such as finance, manufacturing, and distribution
- A centralized database that organizes and manages information

Figure 2.8

Overview of ERP System

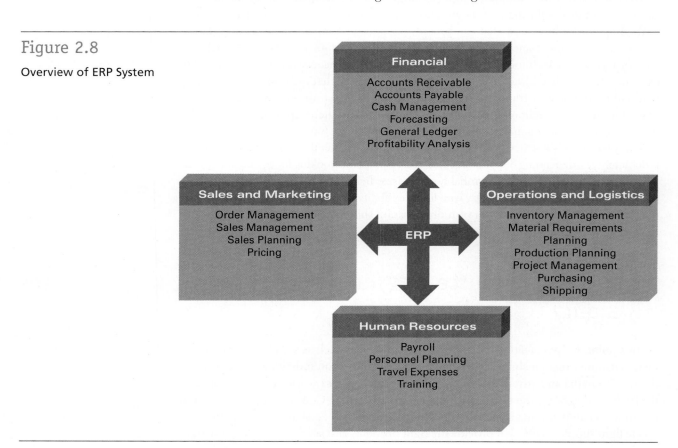

- Integrated functions that provide seamless information flow among them
- Flexible best practices
- Functions that work in real time
- Internet-enabled.[13]

Different ERP vendors provide ERP systems with some degree of specialty, but the core functions are almost the same for all of them (see Figure 2.9). Some of the core ERP functions found in the successful ERP systems are the following:

- Accounting
- Financials
- Manufacturing
- Production
- Transportation
- Sales and distribution
- Human resources
- Supply chain
- Customer relationship
- E-business.

ERP systems will not improve organizations' functionalities overnight. The high expectation of achieving cost savings (bottom-line initiative) and service improvements (leading to top-line revenue increases) is very much dependent on how well the chosen ERP system fits the organizational functionalities and how well the tailoring and configuration

Figure 2.9

ERP Vendors

Vendor/Web Address	ERP Specialties/Characteristics	Target Market
SAP www.sap.com	Customer relationship management, financial management, human resource management, and supply chain management	Large business
Oracle www.oracle.com	Financial management, human resource management, and supply chain management	Large business
Infor www.ssaglobal.com	Customer relationship management, financial management, human resource management, and supply chain management	Large business
Microsoft Dynamics www.microsoft.com/dynamics	Financial management, distribution, manufacturing, project accounting, human resource management, and business analytics	Small-to-medium business
SAP www.sap.com/solutions/sme/businessone	Automate operations, such as sales, finance, purchasing, inventory and manufacturing	Small business

process of the system matches with the business culture, the IT culture, the strategy, and the structure of the organization. Overall, an ERP system is expected to improve both back-office and front-office functions simultaneously. Organizations choose and deploy ERP systems for many different benefits and reasons. In many cases the calculation of return on investment (ROI) is weighted against the many benefits expected.

It may be a challenge for you to wrap your brain around the concept of an ERP system without first-hand experience in using one. Consider your school for example, which to a greater or lesser degree, has some form of an ERP system. When you register for classes, for instance, you may not be able to do so because of outstanding parking tickets, overdue library books, an unpaid tuition balance, or a host of other reasons. And if you can register for classes, when you receive your tuition bill, it already includes allowances for government loans, scholarships, and the like. This is all possible because your school's individual IT systems—which each handle a different function such as registration, parking, tuition financials, and loans and scholarships—are tied together in the form of an ERP system. Businesses in the private sector (and some public-sector ones as well) attempt to do the same thing on a grander scale (see Figure 2.10). These organizations integrate predictions of customer demands (customer relationship management) into an ERP system to drive other functions such as finance, manufacturing, inventory, transportation, and distribution (with the latter four being an integral part of supply chain management). Organizations even attempt to predict the acquisition of human resource talent in light of existing human resource attrition and the need for increased human resource capacity based on predicted customer demands.

Everything in business is related to everything else in business. An effective customer relationship management system that accurately predicts product and service demand is of no use to your organization if that information is not seamlessly electronically flowed to a supply chain management system. Further, that CRM system is of no value if the SCM system doesn't effectively monitor the quality and shipping timeliness of suppliers to identify any weaknesses. Conversely, the best SCM system is no value to your organization if you don't have a CRM system that tracks the right information about your customers.

Figure 2.10

The Integration within an ERP System

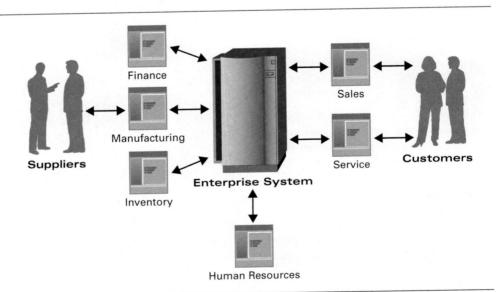

INVITE FEDEX INTO YOUR ERP

As you know from Chapter 1, competitive advantages can be fleeting and are at best only temporary. A few years ago, FedEx rolled out a customer-integrated Web package tracking system that gave it a substantial competitive advantage for about a year. The other package carriers then followed with similar systems and FedEx's competitive advantage was nullified.

FedEx's latest innovation through IT promises to be even better. Its new offering is called *Ship Manager*, a complete computer system that FedEx will install on your organization's Web site. Ship Manager allows you to easily weigh packages, calculate shipping, and print shipping labels. Of course, it will also automatically notify FedEx that you have a package ready to ship.

But it doesn't stop there. Ship Manager can then tie seamlessly into your ERP back-office systems, providing data to your customer billing, inventory, and warehouse operations functions. For example, the FedEx shipping number and expected arrival date for a specific package can flow directly into a customer purchase record. If that customer calls, your organization can quickly provide the shipping number and also the expected arrival date.

With Ship Manager, FedEx hopes to create a sustainable competitive advantage. Because Ship Manager integrates with your ERP system to provide the automated flow of information, why would you consider ever switching carriers? We'll have to see how the likes of UPS respond to FedEx's latest IT–based innovation.[14]

Summary: STUDENT LEARNING OUTCOMES *REVISITED*

LO1 Describe supply chain management (SCM) systems and their strategic and competitive opportunities. A *supply chain management (SCM) system* is an IT system that supports supply chain management by automating the tracking of inventory and information among business processes and across companies. Strategic and competitive opportunities for SCM systems include

- Overall cost leadership (Porter), bottom-line initiative (cost reduction), and running the organization (RGT framework)
- Fulfillment—right quantity of parts or products at the right time
- Logistics—low cost of transporting materials
- Production—ensuring production lines run smoothly
- Revenue and profit—no sales are lost
- Cost and price—keeping part costs down and product prices at acceptable levels.

LO2 Describe customer relationship management (CRM) systems and their strategic and competitive opportunities. A *customer relationship management (CRM) system* uses information about customers to gain insights into their needs, wants, and behaviours in order to serve them better. Strategic and competitive opportunities for CRM systems include

- Differentiation and focus (Porter), top-line initiative (revenue enhancement), and growing the organization (RGT framework)
- Devising more effective marketing campaigns
- Assuring the sales process is efficiently managed
- Providing superior after-sale service and support

LO3 Define e-collaboration and describe its strategic and competitive opportunities. *E-collaboration* is the use of technology to support

- Work activities with *integrated collaboration environments (ICEs),* as well as *workflow systems* and *document management systems*

www.mcgrawhill.ca/olc/haag

- Knowledge management with **knowledge management systems**
- Social networking with **social networking systems**
- Learning with e-learning tools
- Informal collaboration to support **open-source information.**

LO4 **Discuss the impact IT culture has on technology choices and their implementations within an organization.** *IT culture* has two aspects. First is the structural placement of the IT function within the organization: *top-down silo* for a command-and-control approach to technology choices and their implementations; *matrix* for a more collaborative approach; and *fully integrated* for truly empowering employees to make technology choices and implementations. The second aspect of IT culture is the philosophy of an organization toward IT, ranging from early adopters, who aggressively pursue emerging technologies hoping to find some good ones, to wait-and-see cultures that demand proven ROI before adopting a technology.

LO5 **Explain the significance of enterprise resource planning (ERP) software to the integration of functional software systems.** An *enterprise resource planning (ERP) system* is a collection of integrated software for business management, accounting, finance, project management, SCM, e-collaboration, and a host of other business functions. The basic goal of an ERP system is to provide (1) integrated information (data, information, and business intelligence); (2) one suite of applications; and (3) a unified interface across the enterprise. An ERP system replaces legacy systems and seamlessly integrates all functional software systems within an organization.

CLOSING CASE STUDY 1
Is ERP the Answer for a Company That Hasn't Made a Profit in Six Years?

Sun Microsystems lived and operated in a dream world throughout most of the 1990s, realizing significant revenue mainly from its line of server computers. Then, along came the dot-com implosion around 2000 and a new entrant into the market, Dell Computer. Dell had previously focused most of its efforts on providing customized personal computers. Its growth strategy was to take its famous and world-renowned sell-source-ship model into the server market. And that hurt Sun probably more so than the dot-com implosion.

In fact, Sun had negative profits for five years and in its 2006 fiscal year it posted a loss of $864 million.

Previously, Sun did what many computer vendors did. It received unfinished products from manufacturers, stored them in warehouses, and configured them according to customer needs once a customer placed an order. As Eugene McCabe, executive VP of worldwide operations for Sun, explained it, "We knew we had to make some changes." And Sun did, with the rollout of the One Touch Supply Chain effort in 2004, in which products are sent directly from manufacturers to customers. This alone has cut in half the time between when you order a computer from Sun and when you receive it. As Eugene summarized it, "What we wanted to do is take that step out of the supply chain." That step was Sun itself—now when you order a computer from Sun, it never sees, handles, or warehouses it. Sun's logistics expenses have been reduced by more than $20 million annually, which helps alleviate the financial losses the company has been experiencing.

According to Robert Worrall, Sun's CIO, who has been with the company for 16 years, "We live and die by the supply chain and the demand cycle." So much so that Robert estimated that 20 percent of the company's IT staff spends part of its time devoted to demand planning and supply chain systems. Those staff are now focused on One Touch Supply Chain. The infrastructure of that initiative is ERP applications from Oracle, supply chain management software from Manugistics, and demand planning software from i2 Technologies.

When you order a Sun server, One Touch Supply Chain determines which manufacturer can best fulfill your order and electronically transmits your order information to the manufacturer. The manufacturer assembles, configures, and tests your system before sending it directly to you. This increased efficiency in the supply chain has enabled Sun to deliver products to customers within the promised time 95 percent of the time, up from 85 percent. The manufacturers even tap into Sun's order-processing system and generate a customer invoice and shipping order for you.

Equally important, Sun has been able to close distribution centres in Asia, Europe, and the United States, creating valuable cost savings. It has also significantly cut inventory costs.[15]

Questions

1. In reference to Porter's Five Forces Model from Chapter 1, how was Sun affected by Dell Computer? Do you think Dell had a similar impact on other computer vendors in the same server market? Why or why not?

2. How closely does Sun's supply chain now mirror that of Dell? Is it wise to "mimic" a competitor so closely? Should Blockbuster in Canada follow the model of Zip.ca? How are they similar? What could Blockbuster do to its video rental model that might appeal to Canadians?

3. In this case study, we explained that Sun is now using software from multiple vendors—ERP from Oracle, supply chain management from Manugistics, and demand planning from i2 Technologies. Can this collection of software truly be an integrated, seamless, unified-interface, all-encompassing ERP system? How do you believe organizations get different pieces of software from different vendors to "talk to" each other?

4. What are the advantages of Sun's customer relationship management? How can it use the information it gathers on customers and their ordering habits to create a competitive advantage?

5. How has Sun created an information partnership with its supplier manufacturers? How has this information partnership created efficiencies in the supply chain?

CLOSING CASE STUDY 2
It's All About Customer Relations in the Financial Services Market

ScotiaMcLeod (www.scotiabank.com) is the investment arm of Scotiabank, one of Canada's largest financial organizations with over $280 billion in assets. ScotiaMcLeod's financial advisers specialize in helping individuals and small business customers plan financial solutions for trusts, estate planning, borrowing, and banking services. ScotiaMcLeod has more than 800 financial advisers working in 84 branches across the country. According to Chris Carter, associate director and branch manager for ScotiaMcLeod's North Vancouver office, the financial services sector is a people-driven business where customer service is critical to success. Chris wanted the ability to turn every customer interaction into an opportunity to provide services to his clients. He wanted to know if technology—specifically a customer relationship management (CRM) system—could help him promote a professional image and customer-oriented business philosophy at his branch as a way of putting clients at ease and attracting prospective clients who are searching for financial advice.

Chris knew he needed to be proactive in order to keep existing clients happy and to build his base of new customers. Since his team of financial advisers contacts clients often and tracks accounts daily, he also knew that he would need a more effective CRM solution. "A client may be worth up to $50,000 for professional consulting and ongoing management fees," says Chris. "If customers are not tracked and followed up immediately we could easily lose them to another financial institution." Prior to implementing a complete CRM strategy, Chris and his team developed a rudimentary in-house system using a popular desktop database. Each call the team received was looked up and then manually recorded. "Our team was becoming frustrated with this technology as it was limiting them from reaching out to our customers in a more proactive way and giving them the type of quality attention for which ScotiaMcLeod is known," says Chris.

As Chris and his team started learning more about their customer's preferences and behaviours, he realized he needed a comprehensive CRM strategy to retain key customers in order to build and maintain solid relationships with his clients, and provide his team with the appropriate tools to help them achieve their goals, "With our CRM system in place, we all have access to a single, unified system," said Chris. "We're already seeing the results of our marketing efforts as we can now direct the right message to the right customers and prospects at the right time." Using Maximizer Enterprise from the highly successful Vancouver-based CRM provider, the ScotiaMcLeod office can more easily determine certain characteristics of their best customers, which is helping staff develop comprehensive profiles of their most likely prospects and even establish themselves in new territories.

"Financial services is an incredibly complex and competitive industry where expectations are high and customer loyalty can be hard to retain if you're not giving customers what they want," Chris says. "It's similar to other selling situations in which your level of professionalism is dictated by the quality of information you have on hand. When you have good, up-to-date information that your front-line team can access quickly, you have a better chance of anticipating your customers' needs. Using technology to improve the overall customer experience gives the client a good indication of how organized your company is and shows the competency of the individuals and management team at your firm. When we can anticipate the needs of our customers and make informed suggestions to help them meet their financial goals, not only are they more likely to stay with us, they are also likely to refer more business to us. When this happens we know our CRM program is paying off."[16]

Questions

1. How are ScotiaMcLeod's efforts an excellent example of the implementation of customer relationship management? In what ways has ScotiaMcLeod developed significant knowledge and insight into the wants and needs of its customers?

2. With respect to the use of information technology, is ScotiaMcLeod focusing on a top-line or bottom-line initiative? Perhaps a combination of both? Justify your answer. Within the context of the RGT framework (described in Chapter 1), what is ScotiaMcLeod's principal's focus?

3. Within the context of Porter's three generic strategies, is ScotiaMcLeod mainly focusing on overall cost leadership, differentiation, or focus? Pick only one and justify your answer.

4. ScotiaMcLeod really offers only services to customers; that is, it has no physical products to sell. How would ScotiaMcLeod make effective use of an ERP system, while not needing modules such as manufacturing, transportation, and logistics? As more and more companies focus on only service offerings, do you see a need for a *service* ERP that targets companies like ScotiaMcLeod?

5. If you were to consider the financial services needs of a customer over his or her entire lifetime (after post-secondary education), what specific information would you want to know about a customer? We identified information such as age, marital and family status, salary, and benefits. What five other information "milestones" would you want to track?

Key Terms and Concepts

Back-office system, 44
Chief information officer (CIO), 49
Chief privacy officer (CPO), 50
Chief security officer (CSO), 50
Chief technology officer (CTO), 49
Customer relationship
  management (CRM) system, 41
Distribution chain, 38
Document management system, 46
E-collaboration, 45
Enterprise resource planning (ERP)
  system, 52

Front-office system, 44
Information partnership, 40
Integrated collaboration
  environment (ICE), 45
Inter-modal transportation, 39
IT culture, 48
Just-in-time, 39
Knowledge management (KM)
  system, 46
Legacy information system (LIS), 52
Multi-channel service delivery, 41
Open-source information, 47
Proven ROI, 51

Sales force automation (SFA)
  systems, 42
Social networking site, 46
Social networking system, 46
Supply chain management
  (SCM), 38
Supply chain management (SCM)
  system, 39
Technology innovation failure, 51
Virtual team, 45
Wiki, 47
Workflow, 46
Workflow system, 46

Short-Answer Questions

1. Why is the traditional buy-hold-sell inventory model an expensive and potentially risky one?
2. What is the role of a supply chain management (SCM) system?
3. How does SCM fit into Porter's three generic strategies?
4. What are the typical functions in a CRM system?
5. How does CRM fit into the RGT framework?
6. What is the difference between front-office and back-office systems?
7. For what five things does e-collaboration provide support?
8. What is the difference between a social network site and a social networking system?
9. What is open-source information?
10. What are the three most common ways in which the IT function can be placed within an organization?
11. How are the structuring of the IT function and the philosophical approach to IT interrelated?
12. What is an enterprise resource planning (ERP) system?

Assignments and Exercises

1. **COLLABORATION WORK** In a group of three or more students, collaborate on a project to make a list of your group's most popular music CDs. Then, classify the CDs into musical genres such as pop, classical, and so on. All communication about your project must be electronic (but not by voice or video phone). You can use e-mail, set up a Web site, use a chat room, use instant messaging, or use a collaboration e-room, if your school has that facility. Print out a copy of all correspondence on the project and put the correspondence together in a folder in chronological order.

Was this task very different from collaborating face to face with your partners? In which ways was it better? In which ways was it worse? What additional problems or advantages would you expect if people you were working with were in a different hemisphere?

2. **WALMART'S SCM SYSTEM** Walmart is famous for its low prices, and you may have experienced its low prices first-hand. At least, you have probably seen its motto, "Always Low Prices, Always." One of the biggest reasons Walmart is able to sell at prices lower than almost everyone else is that it has a superefficient

supply chain. Its IT–enabled supply chain management system is the envy of the industry because it drives excess time and unnecessary costs out of the supply chain. So, because Walmart can buy low, it sells low. As a matter of fact, if your company wants to sell items to Walmart for it to sell in its stores, you will have to do business with it electronically. If your company can't do that, Walmart won't buy anything from you. Log on to Walmart's Web site (www.walmart.ca), search for supplier information, and find out Walmart's requirements for its suppliers to do business with it electronically. Prepare a brief summary of its requirements for presentation in class.

3. **REAL-WORLD APPLICATIONS** In the chapter we mentioned that many CRM installations have been less than successful. On the other hand, there are many satisfied users of CRM applications. On the Internet find at least three examples of companies that are getting real business benefits from their CRM systems. Prepare a report on the results they are getting and the ways they achieved them. One place to start your search is at www.searchcrm.com. Other good sources are the Web sites of CRM application software vendors Oracle-Siebel and Salesforce.com (www.oracle.com/siebel and www.salesforce.com). At least one of your examples must be from a site other than the three mentioned.

4. **ERP FOR THE SMALL BUSINESS** Most major ERP vendors have been focusing on selling multimillion-dollar installations of their software to very large organizations. That is shifting in focus somewhat as ERP vendors realize that the small-to-medium-size business market is probably just as large. Search the Internet for ERP vendors that focus on small-to-medium-size businesses. Also search for open-source ERP software. Prepare a short report for class presentation and offer the vendors that you found and their Web site addresses.

5. **IT CULTURE** Interview someone working in the business world: a friend, a family member, or simply someone you know. Explain to him or her the three most common ways of structurally placing the IT function within an organization. Also, explain to him or her the range of philosophical approaches to the development, deployment, and use of IT in an organization. Finally, show the person Figure 2.8 on page 52. Ask him or her to point out on that figure where his or her organization would be located. Understand the justification for the decision. Make a short presentation to the class. If necessary, you can omit the company name but do provide its characteristics.

Discussion Questions

1. Do you think your school would benefit from installing a CRM system? How might it benefit you as a student? How could it benefit your school?

2. Spoke is e-collaboration software that examines all employees' e-mail contact lists searching for people at potential customer sites who may be known to employees. Do you think a company has an ethical obligation to notify employees it is going to use Spoke, or (because it will search only computer files on company-owned computers) is it none of the employees' business?

3. In the run-grow-transform (RGT) framework, the third component is transformation, or enabling your organization to operate in entirely new ways. Of the three major business IT applications we discussed in this chapter (supply chain management, customer relationship management, and e-collaboration), which one(s) do you believe most support organizational transformation? Justify your answer.

4. Think about IT culture and its two main aspects—(1) the structural placement of the IT function within an organization and (2) the philosophical approach to the development, deployment, and use of IT. In terms of changing and transforming an organization, which of these two would present the greatest challenge? Justify your answer. Of the three types of structural placement of the IT function within an organization that we described, which do you believe is most common? Justify your answer.

5. We noted that it is extremely difficult to measure the success of a CRM system prior to its implementation and use. Why do you believe this is so? What can organizations do to develop measures of success before implementing a CRM system?

Chapter 3

Databases and Data Warehouses
Building Business Intelligence

STUDENT LEARNING OUTCOMES

LO1 Describe the key characteristics of a relational database.

LO2 List the five software components of a database management system.

LO3 Describe key characteristics of a data warehouse.

LO4 Describe four major types of data-mining tools in a data warehouse environment.

LO5 Describe business intelligence and its role in an organization.

LO6 List key considerations in information ownership in an organization.

OPENING CASE STUDY:
Can Companies Keep Your Personal Information Private and Secure?

Without a doubt, databases are one of the most important IT tools that organizations use today. Databases are large repositories of very detailed information. When a transaction occurs, a sale for example, a database stores every detail of the transaction including your credit card number and other personal information, which products you purchased, what discount you received, the shipping schedule for your products, and so on.

Organizations must carefully manage their databases. This management function includes properly organizing the information in these information repositories in the most efficient way, ensuring that no erroneous information ever enters the databases, and—most importantly—protecting the information from theft and loss.

Information is a valuable commodity, and, sadly, there are people who want to steal valuable information. Much of that information is personal information. When someone steals your personal information (not necessarily by taking it from you but rather stealing it from a company you do business with), you can become a victim of identity theft. Consider this shortlist of organizations that have lost information and the huge potential numbers of customers affected:

- Passport Canada (December 2006)
- TJX—Winners and Home Sense (2003 to December 2006)
- Newfoundland and Labrador Provincial Public Health Laboratory (November 2007)
- Canadian Imperial Bank of Commerce (CIBC) (January 2007)
- Brock University (September 2006).

Potentially the most staggering information loss was that reported by TJX Company Limited, a leading off-price retailer of apparel and home fashions in the United States, Canada, and worldwide. TJX announced that it had suffered an unauthorized intrusion into its computer system that handles most of the company's credit card, debit card, cheque, and merchandise return transactions for the United States, Canada, Puerto Rico, the United Kingdom, and Ireland. Over 40 million customers worldwide were affected.

All organizations rely on a variety of technologies to analyze, manage, and securely store information. At the very heart of every organization are databases that store vast amounts of transaction information. This information is often very personal to large numbers of individuals, and all organizations have the responsibility to keep that information secure from predators. This chapter focuses on those large repositories of information (both databases and data warehouses) and the tools organizations use to manage and secure that information.[1,2]

Questions

1. Have you been a victim of identity theft? If so, what happened?

2. What can you do to protect yourself from identity theft?

3. How many organizations have your credit card number?

Introduction

As we've discussed in the first two chapters, you and your organization need more than just data and information. You need **business intelligence (BI)**—collective information about your customers, your competitors, your business partners, your competitive environment, and your own internal operations—that gives you the ability to make effective, important, and often strategic business decisions. Business intelligence enables your organization to extract the true meaning of information so that you can take creative and powerful steps to ensure a competitive advantage. Many such actions by your organization support some or all the initiatives we discussed in Chapter 2—customer relationship management, supply chain management, and collaboration, to name just a few.

Of course, to create business intelligence, you need both data and *information* (we'll commonly refer to both as *information* in this chapter). Business intelligence doesn't just magically appear. You must first gather and organize all your information. Then, you need the right IT tools to define and analyze various relationships within the information. In short, knowledge workers such as you use IT tools to create business intelligence from information. The technology, by itself, won't do it for you. However, technology such as databases, database management systems, data warehouses, and data-mining tools can definitely help you build and use business intelligence.

Figure 3.1

Building Business
Intelligence

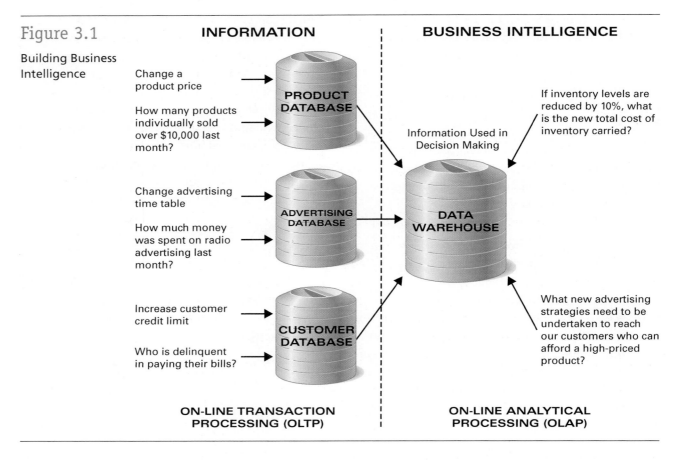

INFORMATION | BUSINESS INTELLIGENCE

Change a product price

How many products individually sold over $10,000 last month?

PRODUCT DATABASE

Change advertising time table

How much money was spent on radio advertising last month?

ADVERTISING DATABASE

Increase customer credit limit

Who is delinquent in paying their bills?

CUSTOMER DATABASE

Information Used in Decision Making

DATA WAREHOUSE

If inventory levels are reduced by 10%, what is the new total cost of inventory carried?

What new advertising strategies need to be undertaken to reach our customers who can afford a high-priced product?

ON-LINE TRANSACTION PROCESSING (OLTP) | **ON-LINE ANALYTICAL PROCESSING (OLAP)**

As you begin working with these IT tools (which we'll discuss in great detail throughout this chapter), you'll be performing the two types of information processing: on-line transaction processing and on-line analytical processing. ***On-line transaction processing (OLTP)*** is the gathering of input information, processing of that information, and updating of existing information to reflect the gathered and processed information. Databases and DBMSs (database management systems) are the technology tools that directly support OLTP. Databases that support OLTP are most often referred to as ***operational databases.*** Inside these operational databases is valuable information that forms the basis for business intelligence.

As you can see in Figure 3.1, you can also query operational databases to gather basic forms of business intelligence, such as how many products individually sold over $10,000 last month and how much money was spent last month on radio advertising. While the results of these queries may be helpful, you really need to combine product and advertising information (with several other types of information including customer demographics) to perform on-line analytical processing.

On-line analytical processing (OLAP) is the manipulation of information to support decision making. At Australian P&C Direct, one of the world's largest companies in the insurance market, OLAP within a data warehouse is a must. P&C has created a data warehouse that supports its customer relationship management activities, cross-selling strategies, and marketing campaigns. By creating a data warehouse with customer information (including census data and lifestyle codes), its wide array of insurance and financial products, and its marketing campaign information, P&C agents can view all the products a given customer has purchased and more accurately determine cross-selling opportunities and what marketing campaigns a given customer is likely to respond to.[3]

A data warehouse is, in fact, a special form of a database that contains information gathered from operational databases for the purpose of supporting decision-making tasks. When you build a data warehouse and use data-mining tools to manipulate the data warehouse's information, your single goal is to create business intelligence. So, data warehouses support only OLAP; they do not at all support OLTP. As you can see in Figure 3.1, you can perform more in-depth queries to gather business intelligence from a data warehouse than you can with a single database. For example, "What new advertising strategies need to be undertaken to reach our customers who can afford a high-priced product?" is a query that would require information from multiple databases. Data warehouses better support creating that type of business intelligence than do databases.

As this chapter unfolds, we'll look specifically at (1) databases and database management systems, (2) data warehouses and data-mining tools, and (3) the whole notion of business intelligence. Databases today are the foundation for organizing and managing information, and database management systems provide the tools you use to work with a database. Databases are the heart and soul of any organization because they organize and manage all of the organization's information resources. Data warehouses are relatively new technologies that help you organize and manage business intelligence, and data-mining tools help you extract that vitally important business intelligence.

As we first look at databases and database management systems in this chapter, we'll be exploring their use by Solomon Enterprises in support of customer relationship management and order processing. Solomon Enterprises specializes in providing concrete to commercial builders and individual homeowners in the greater Toronto area. Solomon tracks detailed information on its concrete types, customers, raw materials, raw materials' suppliers, trucks, and employees. It uses a database to organize and manage all this information. As we discuss Solomon Enterprises and its use of a database, we'll focus mostly on CRM and ordering processing. In ELM F (Designing Databases and Entity-Relationship Diagramming), we'll look at how to design the supply chain management side of Solomon's database.

The Relational Database Model

LO1

For organizing and storing basic and transaction-oriented information (that is eventually used to create business intelligence), businesses today use databases. There are actually four primary models for creating a database. The object-oriented database model is the newest and holds great promise; we'll talk more about the entire object-oriented genre in ELM I (Object-Oriented Technologies). Right now, let's focus on the most popular database model: the relational database model.

As a generic definition, we would say that any **database** is a collection of information that you organize and access according to the logical structure of that information. In reference to a **relational database**, we say that it uses a series of logically related two-dimensional tables or files to store information in the form of a database. The term **relation** often describes each two-dimensional table or file in the relational model (hence its name *relational* database model). A relational database is actually composed of two distinct parts: (1) the information itself, stored in a series of two-dimensional tables, files, or relations (people use these three terms interchangeably) and (2) the logical structure of that information. Let's look at a portion of Solomon's database to further explore the characteristics of the relational database model.

COLLECTIONS OF INFORMATION

In Figure 3.2, we've created a view of a portion of Solomon's database. Notice that it contains five files (also, again, called tables or relations): *Order, Customer, Concrete Type, Employee,* and *Truck.* (It will contain many more as we develop it completely in ELM F [Designing Databases and Entity-Relationship Diagramming].) These files are all related for numerous reasons—customers make orders, employees drive trucks, an order has a concrete type, and so on. And you need all these files to manage your customer relationships and process orders.

Within each file, you can see specific pieces of information (or *attributes*). For example, the *Order* file contains *Order Number, Order Date, Customer Number, Delivery Address, Concrete Type, Amount* (this is given in cubic metres), *Truck Number,* and *Driver ID.* In the *Customer* file, you can see specific information including *Customer Number, Customer Name, Customer Phone,* and *Customer Primary Contact.* These are all important pieces of information that Solomon's database should contain. Moreover, Solomon needs all this information (and probably much more) to effectively process orders and manage customer relationships.

CREATED WITH LOGICAL STRUCTURES

Using the relational database model, you organize and access information according to its logical structure, not its physical position. So, you don't really care in which row of the *Employee* file Allison Smithson appears. You really need to know only that Allison's *Employee ID* is 984568756 or, for that matter, that her name is Allison Smithson. In the relational database model, a ***data dictionary*** contains the logical structure for the information in a database. When you create a database, you first create its data dictionary. The data dictionary contains important information (or logical properties) about your information. For example, the data dictionary entry for *Customer Phone* in the *Customer* file would require 10 digits. The data dictionary entry for *Date of Hire* in the *Employee* file would require a month, day, and year.

This is quite different from other ways of organizing information. For example, if you want to access information in a certain cell in most spreadsheet applications, you must know its physical location—row number and column character. With a relational database, however, you need only know the field name of the column of information (for example, *Amount*) and its logical row, not its physical row. As a result, in Solomon's database example, you could easily change the amount for an order, without having to know where that information is physically stored (by row or column).

And with spreadsheet software, you can immediately begin typing in information, creating column headings, and providing formatting. While newer versions of popular desktop database systems (such as Microsoft Access for Office 2007) will allow you to approximate the low-overhead approach to design that is possible using spreadsheets, you should resist the temptation to just start typing Before you start adding information to a database, you must clearly define the characteristics of each field by creating a data dictionary. Thus you must first carefully plan the design of your database.

LOGICAL TIES WITHIN THE INFORMATION

In a relational database, you must create ties or relationships in the information that show how the files relate to each other. Before you can create these relationships among files, you must first specify the primary key of each file. A ***primary key*** is a field (or group of fields in some cases) that uniquely describes (or identifies) each record. In Solomon's database, *Order Number* is the primary key for the *Order* file and *Customer Number* is the primary key for the *Customer* file. That is to say, every order in the *Order* file must have a unique *Order Number* and every customer in the *Customer* file must have a unique *Customer Number.*

ORDER FILE

Order Number	Order Date	Customer Number	Delivery Address	Concrete Type	Amount	Truck Number	Driver ID
100000	9/1/2004	1234	55 Smith Lane	1	8	111	123456789
100001	9/1/2004	3456	2122 Bloor E.	1	3	222	785934444
100002	9/2/2004	1234	55 Smith Lane	5	6	222	435296657
100003	9/3/2004	4567	1333 Burr Ridge	2	4	333	435296657
100004	9/4/2004	4567	1333 Burr Ridge	2	8	222	785934444
100005	9/4/2004	5678	1222 Westminster	1	4	222	785934444
100006	9/5/2004	1234	222 East Hampton	1	4	111	123456789
100007	9/6/2004	2345	9 W. Charles	2	5	333	785934444
100008	9/6/2004	6789	4532 Lane Circle	1	8	222	785934444
100009	9/7/2004	1234	987 Furlong	3	8	111	123456789
100010	9/9/2004	6789	4532 Lance Circle	2	7	222	435296657
100011	9/9/2004	4567	3500 Tomahawk	5	6	222	785934444

CUSTOMER FILE

Customer Number	Customer Name	Customer Phone	Customer Primary Contact
1234	Smelding Homes	3333333333	Bill Johnson
2345	Home Builders Superior	3334444444	Marcus Connolly
3456	Mark Akey	3335555555	Mark Akey
4567	Triple A Homes	3336666666	Janielle Smith
5678	Sheryl Williamson	3337777777	Sheryl Williamson
6789	Home Makers	3338888888	John Yu

CONCRETE TYPE FILE

Concrete Type	Type Description
1	Home foundation and walkways
2	Commercial foundation and infrastructure
3	Premier speckled (concrete with pea-size smooth gravel aggregate)
4	Premier marble (concrete with crushed marble aggregate)
5	Premier shell (concrete with shell aggregate)

EMPLOYEE FILE

Employee ID	Employee Last Name	Employee First Name	Date of Hire
123456789	Johnson	Emilio	2/1/1985
435296657	Evaraz	Antonio	3/3/1992
785934444	Robertson	John	6/1/1999
984568756	Smithson	Allison	4/1/1997

TRUCK FILE

Truck Number	Truck Type	Date of Purchase
111	Ford	6/17/1999
222	Ford	12/24/2001
333	Chevy	1/1/2002

Figure 3.2

A Portion of Solomon Enterprises' Database for Customer Relationship Management and Ordering Processing

Figure 3.3

Creating Logical Ties
with Primary and
Foreign Keys

When you define that a specific field in a file is the primary key, you're also stating as well that the field cannot be blank. That is, you cannot enter the information for a new employee in the *Employee* file and leave the *Employee ID* field blank. If that were possible, you could potentially have two employees with identical primary keys (blank), which is not possible in a database environment. You must be able to uniquely and discretely identify and isolate each record (employee) in a relation (employee table).

Again, this is quite different from working with spreadsheets. Using a spreadsheet, it would be almost impossible to ensure that each field in a given column is unique. This reinforces the notion that, while spreadsheets work with information according to physical location, databases work with information logically and regardless of physical location.

If you look back at Figure 3.2, you can see that *Customer Number* appears in both the *Customer* and *Order* tables. This implies a logical relationship between the two tables and is an example of a foreign key. A **foreign key** is a primary key from one table that appears in another table. Now look at Figure 3.3. In it, we've provided the logical relationships among all five tables. Notice, for example, that *Truck Number* is the primary key for the *Truck* table. It also appears in the *Order* table. This enables Solomon to track which trucks were used to deliver the various orders. So, *Truck Number* is the primary key in the *Truck* table and is also a foreign key that appears in the *Order* table. There are other examples of foreign keys as well in Figure 3.3.

Foreign keys are essential in the relational database model. Without them, you have no way of creating logical ties among the various files. As you might guess, we use these relationships extensively to create business intelligence because they enable us to track the logical relationships within many types of information.

WITH BUILT-IN INTEGRITY CONSTRAINTS

By defining the logical structure of information in a relational database, you're also developing **integrity constraints**—rules that help ensure the quality of the information. Integrity can in part be defined as the state of being whole, entire, or undiminished. As such, one can think of a requirement of organizational data that it be complete and that it contain the characteristics required to turn it into information. Thus, data must make sense in the context in which it is collected, and must make sense in combination with other data being collected in the same context. For example, by stating that *Customer Number* is the primary key of the *Customer* file and a foreign key in the *Order* file, you're saying (1) that no two customers can have the same *Customer Number* and (2) that a *Customer Number* that is entered into the *Order* file must have a matching *Customer*

THOMPSONFLY (FORMERLY BRITANNIA AIRWAYS) FLIES HIGH WITH A CONTENT MANAGEMENT DATABASE

Airlines fly millions of passengers around the globe each year. That creates a lot of paperwork—too much, in fact. According to John Gough, Thompsonfly's E-Business Program Manager, "[Thompsonfly] had over 120 forms related to the flight. We urgently needed to rationalize the amount of paperwork we were generating and the efficiency of our databases processes around the paperwork."

To create a competitive advantage and reduce the paperwork involved, Thompsonfly implemented a content management database (a special kind of database) solution provided by Open Text Corporation (www.opentext.com). Headquartered in Waterloo, Ontario, Open Text started as a little spin-off company from the University of Waterloo and became the market leader in Enterprise Content Management solutions. A content management database tracks and organizes information such as

1. Departure and destination times and locations of flight crews and passengers

2. Capacity utilization information for flight crews and baggage handlers

3. Customer relationship management information for flight attendants.

The new system goes far beyond just an operational database that manages and organizes transaction information. It provides each crew member with a single log-in and point of access through a Web portal. The new system provides automated workflow capabilities to ensure that the right employees receive and process the necessary information in the least amount of time. It even provides forums in which all employees can record and discuss ideas for making flights better and more comfortable for passengers.

So, the new system supports both bottom-line efforts (i.e., optimizing information processing to reduce costs) and top-line initiatives (such as customer relationship management), giving Thompsonfly the ability to grow and nurture relationships with its most frequent flyers.[4]

Number in the *Customer* file. So, as Solomon creates a new order and enters a *Customer Number* in the *Order* file, the database management system must find a corresponding and identical *Customer Number* in the *Customer* file. This makes perfect sense. You cannot create an order for a customer who does not exist. Similarly, one would not want to allow a negative number for a customer's age, or a selection other than M or F for gender. These are simple examples of integrity constraints. More complex rules can also be modelled, such as if a client is under 10 years of age, for example, the client should not have a graduate degree as his or her highest level of educational attainment. In this situation, there is a high probability that either the age or the education data (or perhaps both) are incorrect. When complex data patterns are encountered, software might be programmed to send up a flag to force a manual check by an analyst or data integrity worker. Surely you can imagine many other situations where combinations of data would be suspect and organizations would be advised to do detailed data verification.[5]

Consumer Reports has rated Ritz-Carlton first among luxury hotels. Why? It's simple: Ritz-Carlton has created a powerful guest preference database to provide customized, personal, and high-level service to guests of any of its hotels. For example, if you leave a message at a Ritz-Carlton front desk that you want the bed turned down at 9 P.M., prefer no chocolate mints on your pillow, and want to participate in the 7 A.M. aerobics class, that information is passed along to the floor maid (and others) and is also stored in the guest preference database. By assigning to you a unique customer ID that creates logical ties to your various preferences, Ritz-Carlton transfers your information to all of its other hotels. The next time you stay in a Ritz-Carlton hotel, in Vancouver for example, your information is already there, and the hotel staff immediately knows of your preferences.

For the management at Ritz-Carlton, achieving customer loyalty starts first with knowing each customer individually (the concept of customer relationship management). That includes your exercise habits, what you most commonly consume from the snack bar in your room, how many towels you use daily, and whether you like a chocolate on your pillow. To store and organize all this information, Ritz-Carlton uses a relational database, and employees use it to meet your needs (or whims).

LO2

Database Management System Tools

When working with word processing software, you create and edit a document. When working with spreadsheet software, you create and edit a workbook. The same is true in a database environment. A database is equivalent to a document or a workbook because they all contain information. And while word processing and spreadsheet are the software tools you use to work with documents and workbooks, you use database management system software to work with databases. A *database management system (DBMS)* helps you to specify the logical organization for a database and to access and use the information within a database. A DBMS contains five important software components (see Figure 3.4):

1. DBMS engine
2. Data definition subsystem
3. Data manipulation subsystem
4. Application generation subsystem
5. Data administration subsystem.

The DBMS engine is perhaps the most important, yet seldom recognized, component of a DBMS. The *DBMS engine* accepts logical requests from the various other DBMS subsystems, converts them into their physical equivalent, and actually accesses the database and data dictionary as they exist on a storage device. Again, the distinction between logical and physical is important in a database environment. The *physical view* of information deals with how information is physically arranged, stored, and accessed on some type of storage device such as a hard disk. The *logical view* of information, on the other hand, focuses on how you as a knowledge worker need to arrange and access information to meet your particular business needs.

Databases and DBMSs provide two great advantages in separating the logical from the physical view of information. First, the DBMS engine handles the physical tasks so you, as a database user, can concentrate solely on your logical information needs. Second, although there is only one physical view of information, there may be numerous knowledge workers who have different logical views of the information in a database. That is, according to what business tasks they need to perform, different knowledge workers logically view information in different ways. The DBMS engine can process virtually any logical information view or request into its physical equivalent. In addition, databases allow for the important principle of program/data independence. Many different tools can connect to and use data stored in a database. Thus a database can simply act as a repository for data, while allowing many different tools, functions, and software vendors to access the data in a known format. A well-known implementation of this principle is

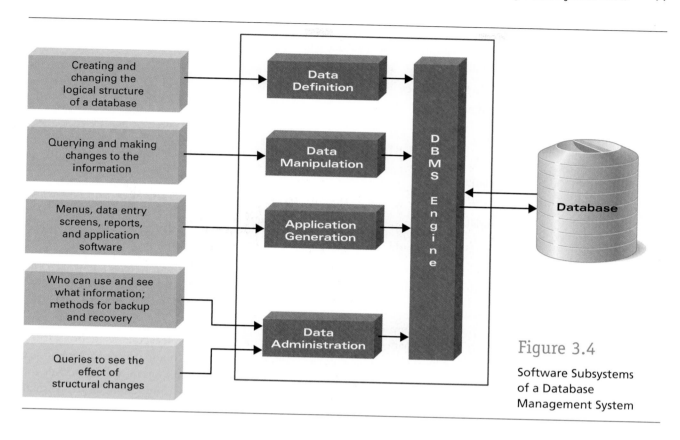

Figure 3.4

Software Subsystems
of a Database
Management System

the Microsoft ODBC (Open Database Connectivity) protocol, which allows MS Excel, for example, to read, manipulate, and update data stored in an MS Access database. There are many, many vendors that take advantage of ODBC to read and write data stored in Microsoft's various software tools, and vice versa.

DATA DEFINITION SUBSYSTEM

The *data definition subsystem* of a DBMS helps you create and maintain the data dictionary and define the structure of the files in a database.

When you create a database, you must first use the data definition subsystem to create the data dictionary and define the structure of the files. This is very different from using something like spreadsheet software. When you create a workbook, you can immediately begin typing in information and creating formulas and functions. As mentioned, while some popular desktop databases allow great flexibility in use, it is highly recommended that you first define its logical structure before you begin entering data. Typing in the information is the easy part: Defining the logical structure is more difficult. ELM F (Designing Databases and Entity-Relationship Diagramming) takes you through the process of defining the logical structure for the supply chain management (SCM) side of Solomon Enterprises' database. We definitely recommend that you read that module—knowing how to define the correct structure of a database can be a substantial career opportunity.

If you ever find that a certain table needs another piece of information, you have to use the data definition subsystem (the design view) to add a new field in the data dictionary. Likewise, if you want to delete a given field for all the records in a table, you must use the data definition subsystem to do so.

As you create the data dictionary, you're essentially defining the logical properties of the information that the database will contain. Logical structures of information include the following:

Logical Properties	Examples
Field name	*Customer Number, Order Date*
Type	Alphabetic, numeric, date, time, etc.
Format	Is an area code required for a phone number?
Default value	If no *Order Date* is entered, the default is today's date.
Validation rule	Can *Amount* exceed 8?
Is an entry required?	Must you enter *Delivery Address* for an order or can it be blank?
Can there be duplicates?	Primary keys cannot be duplicates; but what about order amounts or invoice totals?

These are all important logical properties to a lesser or greater extent depending on the type of information you're describing. For example, a typical concrete delivery truck can hold at most eight cubic metres of concrete. Further, Solomon may not accept orders for less than four cubic metres of concrete. Therefore, an important validation rule for *Amount* in the *Order* file is "must be greater than or equal to 4 and cannot be greater than 8." (Unless, of course, it was large enough to require more than one truck. We will leave this issue for a more advanced treatment, probably available in a database course at your institution). These are examples of business rules that can be enforced through the logical design of the database. Thus careful and rigorous design is vital.

DATA MANIPULATION SUBSYSTEM

The *data manipulation subsystem* of a DBMS helps you add, change, and delete information in a database and query it for valuable information. Software tools within the data manipulation subsystem are most often the primary interface between you as a user and the information contained in a database. So, while the DBMS engine handles your information requests from a physical point of view, it is the data manipulation tools within a DBMS that allow you to specify your logical information requirements. Those logical information requirements are then used by the DBMS engine to access the information you need from a physical point of view.

In most DBMSs, you'll find a variety of data manipulation tools, including views, report generators, query-by-example tools, and structured query language (SQL).

VIEWS   A *view* allows you to see the contents of a database file, make whatever changes you want, perform simple sorting, and query to find the location of specific information. Views essentially provide each file in the form of a spreadsheet workbook. The screen in Figure 3.5 shows a view in Microsoft Access for the *Order* file in Solomon's database. At this point, you can click on any specific field and change its contents. You could also point at an entire record and click on the Cut icon (the scissors) to remove a record. If you want to add a record, simply click in the *Order Number* field of the first blank record and begin typing. You can also perform a variety of other functions such as sorting, searching, spell checking, and hiding columns.

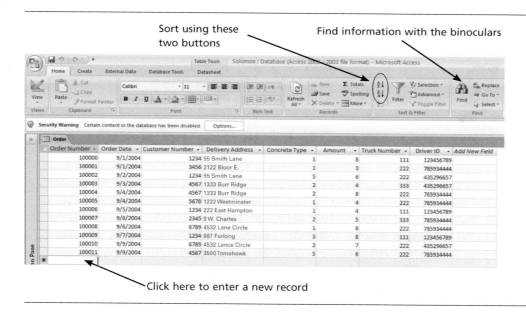

Figure 3.5

A View in Microsoft Access

REPORT GENERATORS *Report generators* help you quickly define formats of reports and what information you want to see in a report. Once you define a report, you can view it on the screen or print it. Figure 3.6 shows two intermediate screens in Microsoft Access. The first allows you to specify which fields of information are to appear in a report. We have chosen to include *Customer Number, Order Number, Order Date,* and *Amount* from the *Order* file. The second allows you to choose from a set of predefined report formats. Following a simple and easy-to-use set of screens (including the two in Figure 3.6), we went on to specify that sorting should take place by *Customer Number* and that the name of the report should be "Customer and Amount Report." The completed report is also shown in Figure 3.6 on the next page. Notice that it displays only those fields we requested, that it's sorted by *Customer Number,* and that the title is "Customer and Amount Report."

A nice feature about report generators is that you can save a report format that you use frequently. For example, if you think you'll use the report in Figure 3.6 often, you can save it by giving it a unique name. Later, you can request that report and your DBMS will generate it, using the most up-to-date information in the database. You can also choose from a variety of report formats (we chose a simple one for our illustration). And you can choose report formats that create intermediate subtotals and grand totals, which can include counts, sums, averages, and the like.

QUERY-BY-EXAMPLE TOOLS *Query-by-example (QBE) tools* help you graphically design the answer to a question. Suppose for example that Janielle Smith from Triple A Homes (*Customer Number* 4567) has called and ordered a delivery of concrete. Although she can't remember the name of the driver, she would like to have the driver that comes out the most often to deliver concrete to Triple A Homes. Solomon's task, from a customer relationship management point of view, is to go through all the orders and determine which employee most often delivers concrete to Triple A Homes. The task may seem simple considering that Solomon currently has very few orders in its database. However, can you imagine trying to answer that question if there were thousands of orders in Solomon's database? It would not be fun.

Fortunately, QBE tools can help you answer this question and perform many other queries in a matter of seconds. In Figure 3.7 on page 75, you can see a QBE screen that formulates the answer to the question. When you perform a QBE, you (1) identify the

Figure 3.6

Using a Report
Generator

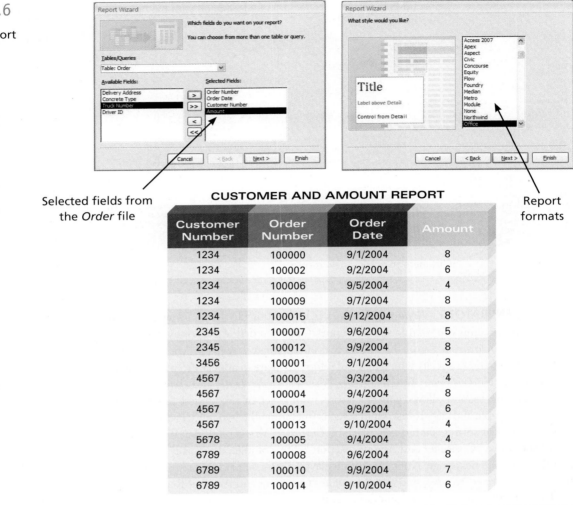

Selected fields from
the *Order* file

Report
formats

CUSTOMER AND AMOUNT REPORT

Customer Number	Order Number	Order Date	Amount
1234	100000	9/1/2004	8
1234	100002	9/2/2004	6
1234	100006	9/5/2004	4
1234	100009	9/7/2004	8
1234	100015	9/12/2004	8
2345	100007	9/6/2004	5
2345	100012	9/9/2004	8
3456	100001	9/1/2004	3
4567	100003	9/3/2004	4
4567	100004	9/4/2004	8
4567	100011	9/9/2004	6
4567	100013	9/10/2004	4
5678	100005	9/4/2004	4
6789	100008	9/6/2004	8
6789	100010	9/9/2004	7
6789	100014	9/10/2004	6

files in which the needed information is located, (2) drag any necessary fields from the identified files to the QBE grid, and (3) specify selection criteria.

For the names of employees who have delivered concrete to Triple A Homes, we identified the two files of *Order* and *Employee*. Second, we dragged *Customer Number* from the *Order* file to the QBE grid and dragged *Employee Last Name* and *Employee First Name* from the *Employee* file to the QBE grid. Finally, we specified in the Criteria box that we wanted to view only the orders for *Customer Number* 4567 (Triple A Homes). Access did the rest and provided the information in Figure 3.7.

QBEs rely heavily on the logical relationships within a database to find information. For example, *Order Number* 100004 has the *Customer Number* of 4567 (Triple A Homes). So, the QBE tool took the *Driver ID* from the *Order* file for that order and found a match in the *Employee* file. When it found a match, it presented the *Employee Last Name* and *Employee First Name* (John Robertson). Without the logical relationships being correctly defined, this QBE query would not have worked properly.

STRUCTURED QUERY LANGUAGE *Structured query language (SQL)* is a standardized fourth-generation query language found in most DBMSs. SQL (pronounced see-quill) performs the same function as QBE, except that you perform the query by

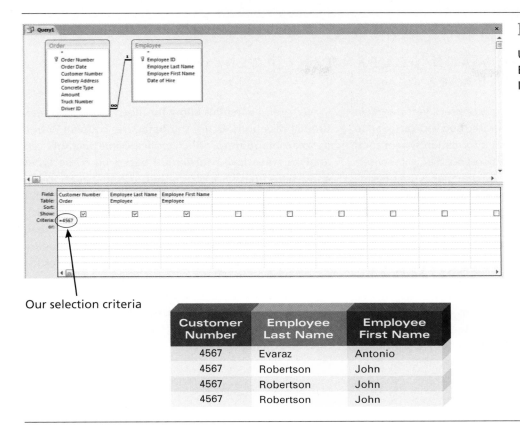

Figure 3.7

Using a Query-by-Example to Find Information

Our selection criteria

Customer Number	Employee Last Name	Employee First Name
4567	Evaraz	Antonio
4567	Robertson	John
4567	Robertson	John
4567	Robertson	John

creating a statement instead of pointing, clicking, and dragging. The basic form of a SQL statement of the type we are implying above is

SELECT ... FROM ... WHERE ...

After the SELECT, you list the fields of information you want; after the FROM, you specify what logical relationships to use; and after the WHERE, you specify any selection criteria. Thoroughly introducing you to the syntax of building SQL statements is outside the scope of this text and would easily require almost 100 pages of material. But you should be aware that SQL does exist. If you're majoring in IT or MIS, you'll undoubtedly take a course that provides a comprehensive introduction to SQL.

APPLICATION GENERATION SUBSYSTEM

The *application generation subsystem* of a DBMS contains facilities to help you develop transaction-intensive applications. These types of applications usually require that you perform a detailed series of tasks to process a transaction. Application generation subsystem facilities include tools for creating visually appealing and easy-to-use data entry screens, programming languages specific to a particular DBMS, and interfaces to commonly used programming languages that are independent of any DBMS.

As with SQL, application generation facilities are most often used by IT specialists. We recommend that knowledge workers leave application generation to IT specialists as much as possible. You need to focus on views, report generators, and QBE tools. These will help you find information in a database and perform queries so you can start to build and use business intelligence.

SERVING CITIZENS AND GOVERNMENT AGENCIES WITH A GIS DATABASE

Databases typically serve a variety of users. Versaterm, an Ottawa-based provider of integrated and vertical (a range of products for the same client) information system tools for the police, fire, and EMS (emergency medical services) market, provides a GIS–based tool that makes use of existing data supplied by the client to model its jurisdiction. Police, fire, and EMS vehicles can easily and seamlessly access municipal maps at varying levels of resolution. Maps, or portions of maps, from a high-level perspective (jurisdictions, beats, etc.) down to individual buildings can be displayed and they can be overlaid with symbols depicting things such as roadblocks, stakeouts, officer locations, emergency vehicles, or any other object with special meaning. The GIS maps, often provided by the municipality, can be used for various other purposes as well, but the data are invaluable for emergency services.

Versaterm's systems allow for much more than real-time applications. Using the database, coupled with a desktop mapping product, police crime analysts can analyze statistical information based on crime types and where they were committed. This information can be displayed both on maps and in reports. Using this feature, queries such as "rank the number, by district, of Break & Enters with violence perpetrated between January 1st and March 31st" are possible. Responses are easily obtained with a few keystrokes and the results can be displayed on a map and/or report.

Jurisdictions from Halifax to BC, from the RCMP to the Royal Newfoundland Constabulary, and dozens in between are currently using such systems to manage their emergency services.[6]

DATA ADMINISTRATION SUBSYSTEM

The **data administration subsystem** of a DBMS helps you manage the overall database environment by providing facilities for backup and recovery, security management, query optimization, concurrency control, and change management. The data administration subsystem is most often used by a data administrator or database administrator—someone responsible for assuring that the database (and data warehouse) environment meets the entire information needs of an organization:

- *Backup and recovery facilities*—provide a way for you to (1) periodically back up information and (2) restart or recover a database and its information in case of a failure. A **backup** is simply a copy of the information stored on a computer. **Recovery** is the process of reinstalling the backup information in the event the information was lost. In Chapter 7, we talk specifically about how to develop plans and strategies in the event of some sort of failure. We call this business continuity planning or disaster recovery planning.

- *Security management facilities*—allow you to control who has access to what information and what type of access those people have. Always remember **CRUD**—**C**reate, **R**ead, **U**pdate, and **D**elete. Identifying who can perform those functions on database information is vitally important.

- *Query optimization facilities*—often take queries from users (in the form of SQL statements or QBEs) and restructure them to minimize response times. Basically, these facilities find the "shortest route" to the information you want so you don't have to.

- *Reorganization facilities*—continually maintain statistics concerning how the DBMS engine physically accesses information and reorganizes how information is physically stored. For example, if you frequently access a table by a specific order, the reorganization facilities may maintain the records in that pre-sorted order by creating an index that maintains the sorted order in that table.

- *Concurrency control facilities*—ensure the validity of database updates when multiple users attempt to access and change the same information. Consider your school's on-line registration system. What if you and another student try to register for a class with only one seat remaining—at exactly the same time? Who gets enrolled in the class? What happens to the person who does not get his or her desired class schedule?
- *Change management facilities*—allow you to assess the impact of proposed structural changes to a database. For example, if you decide to add a character identifier to a numeric truck number, you can use the change management facilities to see how many files would be affected.

All these—backup and recovery, security management, query optimization, reorganization, concurrency control, and change management—are vitally important facilities in any DBMS and thus any database environment. As a user and knowledge worker, you probably won't deal with these facilities specifically as far as setting them up and maintaining them is concerned. But how they're set up and maintained will affect what you can do. So knowing that they exist and understanding their purpose are important.

Data Warehouses

Suppose as a manager at Also Shoes, you wanted to know the total revenues generated from the sale of shoes last month. That's a simple query, which you could easily implement using either SQL or a QBE tool. But what if you wanted to know, "By actual versus budgeted, how many size 8 shoes in black did we sell last month in the Pacific and Prairie regions, compared with the same month over the last five years?" That task seems almost impossible, even with the aid of technology. If you were actually able to build a QBE query for it, you would probably bring the organization's operational database environment to its knees.

This example illustrates the two primary reasons so many organizations are opting to build data warehouses. First, while operational databases may have the needed information, the information is not organized in a way that lends itself to building business intelligence within the database or using various data manipulation tools. Second, if you could build such a query, your operational databases, which are probably already supporting the processing of hundreds of transactions per second, would seriously suffer in performance when you hit the Start button to perform the query.

To support such intriguing, necessary, and complex queries to create business intelligence, many organizations are building data warehouses and providing data-mining tools. A data warehouse is simply the next step (beyond databases) in the progression of building business intelligence. And data-mining tools are the tools you use to mine a data warehouse and extrapolate the business intelligence you need to make a decision, solve a problem, or capitalize on an opportunity to create a competitive advantage.

WHAT IS A DATA WAREHOUSE?

A *data warehouse* is a logical collection of information—gathered from many different operational databases—used to create business intelligence that supports business analysis activities and decision-making tasks. Sounds simple enough on the surface, but data warehouses represent a fundamentally different way of thinking about organizing and managing information in an organization. Consider these key features of a data warehouse, detailed in the sections that follow.

Figure 3.8

A Multidimensional
Data Warehouse with
Information from Multiple
Operational Databases

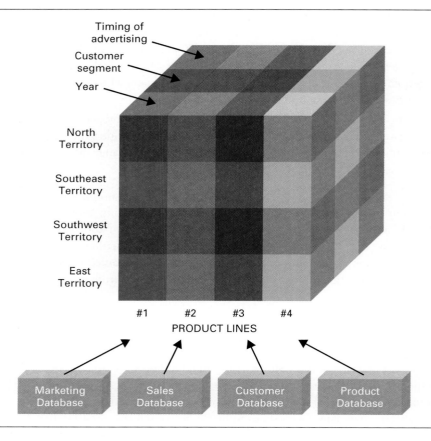

DATA WAREHOUSES ARE MULTIDIMENSIONAL   In the relational database model, information is represented in a series of two-dimensional files or tables. Not so in a data warehouse—most data warehouses are multidimensional, meaning that they contain layers of columns and rows. For this reason, most data warehouses are really *multidimensional databases*. The layers in a data warehouse represent information according to different dimensions. This multidimensional representation of information is referred to as a *hypercube*.

In Figure 3.8, you can see a hypercube that represents product information by product line and region (columns and rows), by year (the first layer), by customer segment (the second layer), and by the timing of advertising media (the third layer). Using this hypercube, you can easily ask *According to customer segment A, what percentage of total sales for product line 1 in the southwest territory occurred immediately after a radio advertising blitz?* The information you would receive from that query constitutes business intelligence.

Any specific *subcube* within the larger hypercube can contain a variety of summarized information gathered from the various operational databases. For example, the front, top and leftmost subcube contains information for the North territory, by year, for product line 1. So, it could contain totals, average, counts, and distributions summarizing in some way that information. Of course, what it contains is specified at design time by knowledge workers according to their needs.

DATA WAREHOUSES SUPPORT DECISION MAKING, NOT TRANSACTION PROCESSING   In an organization, most databases are transaction-oriented. That is, most databases support on-line transaction processing (OLTP) and, therefore, are

As in a DBMS, a data warehouse system
has an engine responsible for converting your
logical requests into their physical equivalent.

Figure 3.9

The Data Miner's Tool Set

operational databases. Data warehouses are not transaction-oriented: They exist to support decision-making tasks in your organization. Therefore, data warehouses support only on-line analytical processing (OLAP).

As we just stated, the subcubes within a data warehouse contain summarized information. So, while a data warehouse may contain the total sales for a year by product line, it does not contain a list of each individual sale to each individual customer for a given product line. Therefore, you simply cannot process transactions with a data warehouse. Instead, you process transactions with your operational databases and then use the information contained within the operational databases to build the summary information in a data warehouse.

Data Mining

LO4

WHAT ARE DATA-MINING TOOLS?

Data-mining tools are the software tools you use to query information in a data warehouse. These data-mining tools support the concept of OLAP—the manipulation of information to support decision-making tasks. Data-mining tools include query-and-reporting tools, intelligent agents, multidimensional analysis tools, and statistical tools (see Figure 3.9). Essentially, data-mining tools are to data warehouse users what data manipulation subsystem tools are to database users.

QUERY-AND-REPORTING TOOLS ***Query-and-reporting tools*** are similar to QBE tools, SQL, and report generators in the typical database environment. In fact, most data warehousing environments support simple and easy-to-use data manipulation subsystem tools such as QBE, SQL, and report generators. Most often, data warehouse users use these types of tools to generate simple queries and reports.

INTELLIGENT AGENTS Intelligent agents utilize various artificial intelligence tools such as neural networks and fuzzy logic to form the basis of "information discovery" and building business intelligence in OLAP. For example, Wall Street analyst Murray Riggiero uses OLAP software called Data/Logic, which incorporates neural networks to generate rules for his highly successful stock and bond trading system.[7] Other OLAP tools, such as Data Engine, incorporate fuzzy logic to analyze real-time technical processes.

CREDIT SCORING WITH SAS AT CANADA'S LAURENTIAN BANK

Data mining has an untold number of applications that can help all types of businesses make better decisions. In the financial services industry, Canada's Laurentian Bank has turned to SAS (www.sas.com), the leading provider of statistical tools, to create a credit scoring model to approve loans for snowmobiles, ATVs, boats, RVs, and motorcycles.

According to Sylvain Fortier, senior manager for Retail Risk Management at Laurentian Bank, "Our objective was to improve our use of the technological tools available for data exploitation and analysis that we needed to develop a scorecard internally. We wanted to develop a flexible system that would help us learn about our customers and business through the loan process." The system, called SAS Credit Scoring, develops a credit risk scorecard for each loan applicant based on a variety of information, including socioeconomic data, and determines the risk level of the applicant in the form of a score.

In just a few short months, the bank realized a 33 percent return on investment and expects to reduce losses on automotive loans by 8 percent.[8]

Intelligent agents represent the growing convergence of various IT tools for working with information. Previously, intelligent agents were considered only within the context of artificial intelligence and were seldom thought to be a part of the data organizing and managing functions in an organization. Today, you can find intelligent agents being used not only for OLAP in a data warehouse environment but also for searching for information on the Web. In Chapter 4, we'll explore artificial intelligence techniques such as intelligent agents.

MULTIDIMENSIONAL ANALYSIS TOOLS *Multidimensional analysis (MDA) tools* are slice-and-dice techniques that allow you to view multidimensional information from different perspectives. Within the context of a data warehouse, we refer to this process as "turning the cube." That is, you're essentially turning the cube to view information from different perspectives.

This turning of the cube allows you to quickly see information in different subcubes. If you refer back to the data warehouse in Figure 3.8 (on page 78), you'll notice that information by customer segment and timing of advertising is actually hidden. Using MDA tools, you can easily bring this to the front of the data warehouse for viewing. What you've essentially done is to slice the cube vertically by layer and bring some of the background layers to the front. As you do this, the values of the information are not affected.

STATISTICAL TOOLS Statistical tools help you apply various mathematical models to the information stored in a data warehouse to discover new information. For example, you can perform a time-series analysis to project future trends. You can also perform a regression analysis to determine the effect of one variable on another.

Sega of America, one of the largest publishers of video games, uses a data warehouse and statistical tools to effectively distribute its advertising budget of more than US$50 million a year.[9, 10] Using its data warehouse, product line specialists and marketing strategists "drill" into trends of each retail store chain. Their goal is to find buying trends that will help them better determine which advertising strategies are working best (and at what time of the year) and how to reallocate advertising resources by media, territory, and time. Sega definitely benefits from its data warehouse, and so do retailers such as Toys Я Us, Walmart, and Sears—all good examples of customer relationship management through technology.

To learn more about today's best data warehousing and data-mining tools, visit the Web site that supports this text at www.mcgrawhill.ca/olc/haag.

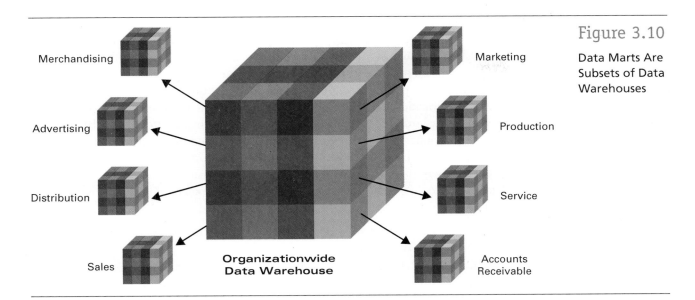

Figure 3.10

Data Marts Are Subsets of Data Warehouses

DATA MARTS: SMALLER DATA WAREHOUSES

Data warehouses are often perceived as organization-wide, containing summaries of all the information that an organization tracks. However, some people need access to only a portion of that data warehouse information as opposed to all of it. In this case, an organization can create one or more data marts. A ***data mart*** is a subset of a data warehouse in which only a focused portion of the data warehouse information is kept (see Figure 3.10).

Lands' End first created an organization-wide data warehouse for everyone to use, but soon found that there can be "too much of a good thing."[11] In fact, many Lands' End employees wouldn't use the data warehouse because it was simply too big, too complicated, and included information they didn't need. So, Lands' End created several smaller data marts. For example, Lands' End created a data mart just for the merchandising department. That data mart contains only merchandising-specific information and not any information, for instance, that would be unique to the finance department.

Because of the smaller, more manageable data marts, knowledge workers at Lands' End are making better use of information. If some of your employees don't need access to organization-wide data warehouse information, consider building a smaller data mart for their particular needs.

If you do choose to build smaller data marts for your employees, the data-mining tools are the same. That is, data marts support the use of query-and-reporting tools, intelligent agents, multidimensional analysis tools, and statistical tools. This yields efficiency in an organization with respect to training. Once you've trained your employees to use any or all data-mining tools, they can apply them to an organization-wide data warehouse or smaller data marts.

DATA MINING AS A CAREER OPPORTUNITY

Data mining represents a substantial career opportunity for you, no matter your career choice. In the business world, you'll face numerous situations in which you need business intelligence to make the right and most effective decisions.

Fortunately, you don't have to be an IT expert to perform data mining. As you'll learn in ELM H (Decision Analysis with Spreadsheet Software), you can actually use a spreadsheet tool such as Microsoft Excel to build a three-dimensional cube similar to the one in Figure 3.8 (on page 78). You can then use Excel's other decision support features to build a graph, perform a regression analysis, and "turn the cube" by bringing new layers of information forward. You can do the same with Microsoft Access, by building a three-dimensional cube (i.e., data warehouse) of information stored in a database. We definitely recommend that you learn to use these tools and then note your proficiency in your e-portfolio (discussed in ELM K [Building an E-Portfolio]).

Beyond personal productivity tools, you should consider learning how to use some data-mining tools specific to the data warehouse environment. Some of the more popular ones include

- Query and Analysis and Enterprise Analytic tools in Business Objects (www.businessobjects.com)
- Business Intelligence and Information Access tools in SAS (www.sas.com)
- ReportNet, PowerPlay, Visualizer, NoticeCast, and DecisionStream tools in Cognos (www.cognos.com)
- PowerAnalyzer tools in Informatica (www.informatica.com).

There are many, many others. You should have a look at your school's catalogue of courses in data mining—you may find them offered in the technology department, statistics department, and other departments. We recommend that at the very least you become acquainted with the following: SAS (the leading vendor in statistical software), Cognos (the Ottawa-based market leader in data warehousing and data-mining tools—recently acquired by IBM), and Informatica (the second-leading vendor in data warehousing and data-mining tools).

IMPORTANT CONSIDERATIONS IN USING A DATA WAREHOUSE

As is true with all types of technology, you can't simply implement a data warehouse and use data-mining tools just because they're a "hot" set of technologies and expect automatically to increase your efficiency and effectiveness. Always let your business needs drive your technology decisions. You have to need the technology and the technology has to fit your needs. With respect to data warehouse and data-mining tools, consider your answers to the following questions.

1. **Do you need a data warehouse?** Although great IT tools, they are not necessarily the best technologies for all businesses because (1) they are expensive, (2) they may not be necessary since some businesses can easily extract all the business intelligence they need from databases, and (3) they require extensive and often expensive support.

2. **Do all your employees need an entire data warehouse?** If not, consider building data marts.

3. **How up to date must the information be?** To create a data warehouse, you take "snapshots" of database information and load it into a data warehouse. If crucial information changes every second, this may not be possible.

4. **What data-mining tools do you need?** User needs should always drive the answer to this question. Whichever you choose, training will be key. If your users can fully exploit all the features of their chosen data-mining tools, your entire organization will reap the benefits.

Business Intelligence Revisited

Business intelligence is one of the hottest topics and markets today. The entire BI market (both hardware and software) is in the range of $50 billion annually with double-digit growth expected for the next several years. When *InformationWeek* asked 300 business technology managers about their immediate project plans, 44 percent identified data warehouses and 43 percent identified data-mining tools.[12]

"We were desperate to get good information quickly," explained Joel Taylor, director of IS for FiberMark North America, a manufacturer of specialty packaging and paper, which could not easily retrieve business intelligence from its expensive transaction processing systems. To address this problem, Taylor spent less than $75,000 on QlikView—BI software from QlikTech (www.qliktech.com). FiberMark's 29 salespeople, who previously printed 1,000-page monthly sales reports, now print on the average only four pages and it's exactly the four pages of business intelligence they need. The $75,000 investment paid for itself in nine months in saved paper and related costs alone. Of course, the real benefit is that salespeople and executives can get the specific, up-to-date BI they want anytime they want it.[13]

FiberMark is one of thousands of success stories related to business intelligence. (Of course, an equal number have probably not met with as much success, sometimes because they did not adequately identify which technology they needed.) The objective of BI is to improve the timeliness and quality of the input for decision making by helping knowledge workers to understand the

- Capabilities available in the organization
- State of the art, trends, and future directions in the markets
- Technological, demographic, economic, political, social, and regulatory environments in which the organization competes (remember Porter's Five Forces Model)
- Actions of competitors and the implications of these actions.[14]

As illustrated in Figure 3.11, BI encompasses both internal and external information. Some business people treat competitive intelligence as a specialized branch of business intelligence. ***Competitive intelligence (CI)*** is business intelligence focused on the external competitive environment. There is even an organization for people who specialize in competitive intelligence called the Society for Competitive Intelligence Professionals (SCIP, at www.scip.org).

A survey of the strategic uses of business intelligence by the Gartner Group found that such uses were ranked by firms in the following order of importance:

1. Corporate performance management
2. Optimizing customer relations, monitoring business activity, and traditional decision support
3. Packaged stand-alone BI applications for specific operations or strategies
4. Management reporting of business intelligence.[15]

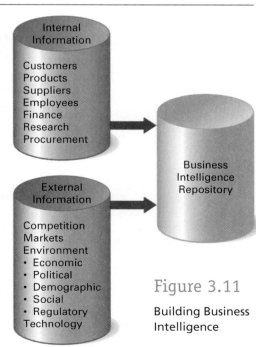

Figure 3.11

Building Business Intelligence

Figure 3.12

Sample Digital Dashboard

As we have stressed, one of the primary purposes of BI is to improve the timeliness and quality of input to the decision process. Companies with well-designed BI systems available to their managers find that their managers make better decisions on a variety of business issues. Higher quality managerial decision making lets companies gain an advantage over their competitors that operate without the benefit of BI systems. BI systems provide managers with actionable information and knowledge

- At the right time
- In the right location
- In the right form.[16]

One particularly interesting feature of many BI software packages is a *digital dashboard*. A **digital dashboard** displays key information gathered from several sources on a computer screen in a format tailored to the needs and wants of an individual knowledge worker (see Figure 3.12). Digital dashboards can provide up-to-the-minute snapshots of any type of information and can often help you identify trends that may represent opportunities or that may be problems.

LO6

Information Ownership

Your organization will be successful, in part, because of your ability to organize and manage information in a way that best moves the organization toward its goals. As we close this chapter, let's look at the notion of *information ownership* and what it means.

STRATEGIC MANAGEMENT SUPPORT

As we discussed in Chapter 2, an organization's *IT culture* defines how the organization structures and views both the IT department and information responsibilities within it. Starting with vitally important roles such as CPO (chief privacy officer), CSO (chief security officer), CIO (chief information officer), and CTO (chief technology officer), organizations work down through the organization defining additional positions of

SUPPORTING HEALTH CARE WITH ELECTRONIC MEDICAL RECORDS

Health care costs are rising. In spite of low-cost generic prescription medications and the like, it's simply becoming more and more expensive to provide quality health care. But there is another factor weighing on rising health care costs and it is technology related. The costs associated with storing, organizing, and managing health care information are skyrocketing. In Canada, there are 2,000 health care transactions every minute. In 2006, there were 440 million laboratory tests, 382 million prescriptions, 322 million office-based physician visits, 35 million diagnostic images, and 2.8 million in-patient hospitalizations. Every one of these transactions required documentation and information exchange. Canada Health Infoway, a federally funded, independent, not-for-profit organization, is a catalyst for collaborative change to accelerate the use of electronic information systems and the electronic health record (EHR). An EHR is a secure and private lifetime record of an individual's health and care history, available electronically to authorized health care providers. It is designed to tie together the output of a number of information systems. Some of these systems are in use today, while others are in development. For example, a number of projects are underway across Canada to develop systems that form the essential building blocks of an EHR, such as digital imaging, summaries of drug prescriptions, and lab test results.

The United States is a different story; there are no well-defined standards for what an EHR should look like. As a result, almost every health care provider and insurer stores medical records in different formats, making it almost impossible to share information between companies. This has everyone scared—so much so that the U.S. government has created a panel, the Health Information Technology Standards Panel, and charged it with selecting a single standard for the health care industry to adopt. But therein lies another problem; there are dozens of major competing vendors creating electronic health record systems that sell software incompatible with their competitors'. To select the electronic standard being used by only one or a few health care companies would mean that all others have to change their systems, and that would be expensive.

Nonetheless, the standard electronic health record is imperative. With it in place, health care costs can drop because of the ease, speed, and efficiency with which organizations will be able to organize and manage information in a database.[17, 18]

responsibility with respect to the management of information and IT. Two of those functions are data administration and database administration.

Data administration is the function in an organization that plans for, oversees the development of, and monitors the information resource. This function must be completely in tune with the strategic direction of the organization to assure that all information requirements can be and are being met. *Database administration* is the function in an organization that is responsible for the more technical and operational aspects of managing the information contained in organizational information repositories (databases, data warehouses, and data marts). Database administration functions include defining and organizing database structures and contents, developing security procedures (in concert with the CSO), and approving and monitoring the development of database and database applications.

In large organizations, both of these administrative functions are usually handled by steering committees rather than by a single individual. These steering committees are responsible for their respective functions and for reporting to the CIO.

SHARING INFORMATION WITH RESPONSIBILITY

Information sharing in your organization means that anyone—regardless of title or department—can access and use whatever information he or she needs. But information sharing brings to light an important question: Does anyone in your organization *own* the information? In other words, if everyone shares the information, who is ultimately responsible for providing the information and assuring the quality of the information? Information ownership is a key consideration in today's information-based business environment. Someone must accept full responsibility for providing specific pieces of information and ensuring the quality of that information. If you find the wrong information is stored in the organization's data warehouse, you must be able to determine the source of the problem and whose responsibility it is.

INFORMATION CLEANLINESS

Information "cleanliness" (an aspect of information ownership) is an important topic today and will be for many years. Have you ever received the same piece of advertising mail (snail mail, that is) multiple times from the same company on the same day? Many people have, and it's an example of "unclean" information. The reason may be that your name may appear twice in a database, once with your middle initial and once without it. Or your name may appear twice in a database with two different spellings of your last name.

In all popular business-oriented DBMSs, such as Oracle, you can find utilities to help you "clean" your information. In the case of having your information twice in a database with two different spellings of your last name, the utility would probably determine that the two records actually belong to the same person (you) because of the identical nature of other associated information such as your address and phone number. Always remember GIGO—garbage in, garbage out (from Chapter 1). If bad information—such as duplicate records for the same customer—goes into the decision-making process, you can rest assured that the decision outcome will not be optimal.

Summary: STUDENT LEARNING OUTCOMES *REVISITED*

LO1 Describe the key characteristics of a relational database. The *relational database* model uses a series of logically related two-dimensional tables or files to store information in the form of a database. Relational databases

- Are a collection of information—Composed of many files or tables of information that are related to each other
- Contain logical structures—You care only about the logical information and not about how it's physically stored or where it's physically located

- Have logical ties among the information—All the files in a database are related in that some *primary keys* of certain files appear as *foreign keys* in others
- Possess built-in *integrity constraints*—When creating the data dictionary for a database, you can specify rules by which the information must be entered (e.g., not blank, etc.).

LO2 List the five software components of a database management system. The five software components of a database management system include

- *DBMS engine*—Accepts logical requests from the various other DBMS subsystems, converts them into their physical equivalent, and actually accesses the database and data dictionary as they exist on a storage device
- *Data definition subsystem*—Helps you create and maintain the data dictionary and define the structure of the files in a database
- *Data manipulation subsystem*—Helps you add, change, and delete information in a database and query it for valuable information
- *Application generation subsystem*—Contains facilities to help you develop transaction-intensive applications
- *Data administration subsystem*—Helps you manage the overall database environment by providing facilities for backup and recovery, security management, query optimization, concurrency control, and change management.

LO3 Describe the key characteristics of a data warehouse. A data warehouse

- Is multidimensional—While databases store information in two-dimensional tables, data warehouses include layers to represent information according to different dimensions
- Supports decision making—Because they contain summarized information, data warehouses support business activities and decision-making tasks, not transaction processing.

LO4 Define the four major types of data-mining tools in a data warehouse environment. The four major types of data-mining tools in a data warehouse environment include

- *Query-and-reporting tools*—Similar to QBE tools, SQL, and report generators in the typical database environment

- *Intelligent agents*—Utilize various artificial intelligence tools such as neural networks and fuzzy logic to form the basis of "information discovery" and building business intelligence in OLAP
- *Multidimensional analysis (MDA) tools*—Slice-and-dice techniques that allow you to view multidimensional information from different perspectives
- Statistical tools—Help you apply various mathematical models to the information stored in a data warehouse to discover new information.

LO5 Describe business intelligence and its role in an organization. *Business intelligence* is collective information—about your customers, your competitors, your partners, your competitive environment, and your own internal operations—that gives you the ability to make effective, important, and often strategic business decisions. Business intelligence is much more than just a list of your products or to whom you've sold them. It might combine your product information with your advertising strategy information and customer demographics, for instance, to help you determine the effectiveness of various advertising media on demographic groups segmented by location.

LO6 List key considerations in information ownership in an organization. Key considerations in information ownership in an organization include

- Strategic management support
- The sharing of information with responsibility
- Information cleanliness.

CLOSING CASE STUDY 1
Ben & Jerry's, Bigelow Teas, and Business Intelligence

Organizations want information. Organizations need information. However, information must be in an organized format that supports the creation of business intelligence. Otherwise, according to Rebecca Wettemann, vice president of Research at Nucleus Research, "It's like having a bank account with millions of dollars in it but no ATM card. If you can't get it [business intelligence] and can't make it work for you, then it is not really useful."

In support of creating and using business intelligence, companies have focused much of their spending efforts on business intelligence software and data-mining tools. According to a Merrill Lynch survey in 2003, business intelligence software and data-mining tools were at the top of the technology spending list of CIOs. And according to A.G. Edwards, the market for that type of software was expected to grow from $4.7 billion in 2003 to $7.5 billion in 2006.

Consider two companies—Ben & Jerry's and Bigelow Teas—and their approach to creating and using business intelligence.

BEN & JERRY'S

Ben & Jerry's, located in Waterbury, Vermont, produces 190,000 pints of ice cream and frozen yogurt daily and ships to over 50,000 grocery stores in the United States, Canada, and 11 other countries. Every single pint is meticulously tracked, first by being entered into an Oracle database. With that information carefully organized, Ben & Jerry's uses a sophisticated data-mining tool set from a company called Business Objects, a unit of German enterprise resource planning software giant SAP AG.

For example, sales people can easily monitor sales to determine how much ground Cherry Garcia Frozen Yogurt is gaining on Cherry Garcia Ice Cream, the company's number-one selling product. The consumer affairs staff can even correlate each of the several hundred calls and e-mails received each week to the exact pint of ice cream. If complaints are consistent concerning a specific batch, the consumer affairs staff can drill down to the supplier who provided the ingredients such as milk or eggs.

In one particular instance, Ben & Jerry's received a large number of complaints that its Cherry Garcia Ice Cream didn't have enough cherries. The complaints were coming in from all over the country, so it wasn't a regional problem. Employees continued drilling through business intelligence with Business Objects and determined that the manufacturing process (from the supplies of raw materials to the mixing) was satisfactory and had no anomalies. Eventually the problem was determined to be that the ice cream box for Cherry Garcia Ice Cream had on it a photo of frozen yogurt, a product with more cherries than the ice cream. Simply changing the photo on the box solved the problem.

BIGELOW TEAS

Bigelow Teas provides over 50 varieties of flavoured, traditional, iced, decaffeinated, and herbal teas. Over the past 50 years, Bigelow Teas has relied on business intelligence to determine the success of each individual tea, and today is no different.

Although it may not seem like it, bringing a new tea to the market is a risky endeavour. It could fail in every way or it could simply cannibalize the sales of an existing tea, neither of which makes business sense. Employees at Bigelow Teas pore over consumer, sales, marketing, and finance business intelligence to ensure that they are making the right decisions in all aspects of the business.

To help facilitate the creation and use of business intelligence, Bigelow Teas turned to the Andrews Consulting Group and Business Objects. Prior to using Business Objects, Bigelow employees had a difficult time finding and using the right information. As Melanie Dower, project leader at Bigelow Teas, describes it, "Our existing end-user reporting tool wasn't user-friendly, so users simply weren't using it. Most users were unable to create their own reports, so we looked for a solution that offered self-serve business intelligence (BI) to free up IT resources." Business Objects is both easy to learn and easy to use because it looks like Microsoft Excel. Explains Dower, "Enterprise 6 [of Business Objects] looks and feels like Microsoft Excel, which speeds up the learning curve for our end-users."

With Business Objects, Bigelow employees can access and view business intelligence in real time, more accurately predict sales forecasts based on shipment levels, identify where to increase sales efforts before it's too late, and even compare current consumer, sales, and marketing information with similar types of information up to five years old.

Gourmet coffees exploded onto the consumer market in the late 1990s and gourmet teas quickly followed. Bigelow Teas is riding this wave of success with success of its own because of its use of business intelligence.[19, 20, 21]

Questions

1. Ben & Jerry's tracks a wealth of information on each pint of ice cream and frozen yogurt. If you were to design Ben & Jerry's data warehouse, what dimensions of information would you include? As you develop your list of dimensions, consider every facet of Ben & Jerry's business operations, from supply chain management to retail store monitoring.

2. Databases are the underlying technology that allows Ben & Jerry's to track ice cream and frozen yogurt information. Based on your knowledge of databases, what sort of tables or files of information would Ben & Jerry's need in its database? What would be the primary keys for each of those? What would be the foreign keys among those to create the necessary relationships?

3. According to the discussion of Bigelow Teas, part of the success of Business Objects comes from its look and feel of being similar to Microsoft Excel. Why do you believe this is true? When introducing employees to enterprise-wide BI tools such as Business Objects, why is it an advantage to have the BI tool look like and work like personal productivity software tools? Why was a similar look and feel to spreadsheet software more important than word processing or presentation software?

4. How could Bigelow Teas open up its business intelligence information to its suppliers and resellers? What benefits would Bigelow Teas gain by keeping its suppliers and resellers more informed with business intelligence? What types of business intelligence would Bigelow Teas want to exclude its suppliers and resellers from seeing? Why?

5. Neil Hastie, CIO at TruServe Corporation, once described most decision making in all types of businesses as "a lot of by-guess and by-golly, a lot of by-gut, and a whole lot of paper reports." That statement is not kind to managers in general or to IT specialists charged with providing the right people with the right technology to make the right decisions. What's the key to turning Hastie's statement into a positive one? Is it training? It is providing timely information access? Is it providing everyone with a wide assortment of data-mining tools? Other solutions? Perhaps it's a combination of several answers?

CLOSING CASE STUDY 2
Mining Dining Data

Restaurants and fast-food chains rely heavily on business intelligence to make important decisions. Casinos do as well. Some of the leading restaurants, fast-food chains, and casinos using data warehouses include AFC Enterprises (operator and franchiser of more than 3,300 Church's Chicken, Popeye's Chicken and Biscuits, Seattle Coffee Company, Cinnabon, and Torrefazione outlets worldwide); Red Robin International (a 170-unit casual-dining chain); Geest (a 22-site U.K. retailer); Pizzeria Uno; and Einstein/Noah Bagel (operator of 428 Einstein's and 111 Noah's New York Bagel stores).

AFC ENTERPRISES

AFC Enterprises cultivates a loyal clientele by slicing and dicing its data warehouse to strategically configure promotions and tailor menus to suit local preferences. AFC's data warehouse helps it better understand its core customers and maximize its overall profitability. AFC tracks customer-specific information from name and address to order history and frequency of visits. This enables AFC to determine exactly which customers are likely to respond to a given promotion on a given day of the week.

AFC also uses its data warehouse to anticipate and manipulate customer behaviour. For example, AFC can use its data warehouse to determine that coffee is added to the tab 65 percent of the time when a particular dessert is ordered and 85 percent of the time when that dessert is offered as a promotional item. Knowing that, AFC can run more promotions for certain desserts figuring that customers will respond by ordering more desserts and especially more coffee (coffee is a high-margin item in the restaurant business).

RED ROBIN INTERNATIONAL

Red Robin's terabyte-size data warehouse tracks hundreds of thousands of point-of-sale (POS) transactions, involving millions of menu items and more than 1.5 million invoices. As Howard Jenkins, Red Robin's vice president of Information Systems, explains it, "With data mining in place, we can ask ourselves, 'If we put the items with high margins in the middle of the menu, do we sell more versus putting it at the top or bottom, [and if so], to whom and where?' We can also tell if something cannibalizes the sale of other items and can give the marketing department an almost instant picture of how promotions are being sold and used."

The placement of items on a menu is strategic business, just as the placement of promotional items in a grocery store can mean increased sales for one item and reduced sales for another. The job of finding the right mix is definitely suited to mining a data warehouse.

Using Cognos Business Intelligence, Red Robin now has measurable results of promotion and menu changes, makes better and more timely decisions, and has realized seven-figure savings in operational costs.

KEEPING GEEST AT THE TOP OF THE FOOD CHAIN

Geest, which has 22 sites across the United Kingdom, has been a powerhouse in the retail industry since the 1930s, specializing in providing freshly prepared food and produce for retail brands. Geest already had the data it needed, such as costs, quantity, and source. However, it was missing the means to turn this data into information that in turn could be used for management decision making, reporting, and company streamlining across the entire organization. The company turned to Cognos PowerPlay in an effort to improve the information-gathering process. Cognos PowerPlay was an immediate hit. The entire installation from start to finish took six months, and PowerPlay

was up and running on time and on budget. Its success could probably be traced to the fact that the team, in order to get quick results, started with a deliberately simple spec. Now what used to take two weeks—pulling together disparate information from all over the company—literally takes 30 minutes.

PIZZERIA UNO

Pizzeria Uno uses its data warehouse to apply the 80/20 rule—a rule that states that 20 percent of your customers provide 80 percent of your revenue. These are your very best customers. So Pizzeria Uno can determine which 20 percent of its customers contribute to 80 percent of its sales and adjust menus and promotions to suit top-patron preferences. These changes can often lead to converting some of the 80 percent non-top customers to the more profitable 20 percent.

EINSTEIN/NOAH BAGEL

Einstein/Noah Bagel uses its data warehouse in real time to maximize cross-selling opportunities. For example, if data warehouse information reveals that a manager in a given store might be missing a cross-selling opportunity on a particular day, an e-mail is automatically sent out to alert managers to the opportunity. Salespeople can then respond by offering the cross- selling opportunity ("How about a cup of hot chocolate with that bagel since it's so cold outside?") to the next customer.[22, 23, 24, 25, 26]

Questions

1. Consider the issue of timely information with respect to the businesses discussed in the case. Which of the businesses must have the most up-to-date information in its data warehouse? Which business can have the most out-of-date information in its data warehouse and still be effective? Rank the five businesses discussed with a 1 for the one that needs the most up-to-date information and a 5 for the one that is least sensitive to timeliness of information. Be prepared to justify your rankings.

2. Geest tracks a wealth of information about its customers' preferences. If you were to design Geest's data warehouse, what dimensions of information would you include?

3. AFC Enterprises includes information in its data warehouse such as customer name and

address. Where does it (or could it) gather such information? Think carefully about this, because customers seldom provide their names and addresses when ordering fast food at a Church's or Popeye's. Is AFC gathering information in an ethical fashion? Why or why not?

4. Visit a local grocery store and walk down the breakfast cereal aisle. You should notice something very specific about the positioning of the various breakfast cereals. What is it? On the basis of what information do you think grocery stores determine cereal placement? Could they have determined that information from a data warehouse or from some other source? If another source, what might that source be?

5. Suppose you're opening a pizza parlour in the town where you live. It will be a "take and bake" pizza parlor in which you make pizzas for customers but do not cook them. Customers buy the pizzas uncooked and take them home for baking. You will have no predefined pizza types but will make each pizza to the customer's specifications. What sort of data warehouse would you need to predict the use of toppings by time of day and by day of the week? What would your dimensions of information be? If you wanted to increase the requests for a new topping (such as mandarin oranges), what information would you hope to find in your data warehouse that would enable you to do so?

Key Terms and Concepts

Application generation subsystem, 75
Backup, 76
Business intelligence (BI), 63
Competitive intelligence (CI), 83
Data administration, 85
Data administration subsystem, 76
Database, 65
Database administration, 85
Database management system (DBMS), 70
Data definition subsystem, 71
Data dictionary, 66
Data manipulation subsystem, 72

Data mart, 81
Data-mining tool, 79
Data warehouse, 77
DBMS engine, 70
Digital dashboard, 84
Foreign key, 68
Integrity constraint, 68
Logical view, 70
Multidimensional analysis (MDA) tool, 80
On-line analytical processing (OLAP), 64
On-line transaction processing (OLTP), 64

Operational database, 64
Physical view, 70
Primary key, 66
Query-and-reporting tool, 79
Query-by-example (QBE) tool, 73
Recovery, 76
Relation, 65
Relational database, 65
Report generator, 73
Structured query language (SQL), 74
View, 72

Short-Answer Questions

1. What is business intelligence? Why is it more than just information?
2. What is on-line transaction processing (OLTP)?
3. What is on-line analytical processing (OLAP)?
4. What is the most popular database model?
5. How are primary and foreign keys different?
6. What are the five important software components of a database management system?

7. How are QBE tools and SQL similar? How are they different?
8. What is a data warehouse? How does it differ from a database?
9. What are the four major types of data-mining tools?
10. What is a data mart? How is it similar to a data warehouse?

Assignments and Exercises

1. **FINDING "HACKED" DATABASES** *The Happy Hacker* (www.happyhacker.org) is a Web site devoted to "hacking"—breaking into computer systems. When people hack into a system, they often go after information in databases. There, they can find credit card information, and other private and sensitive information. Sometimes they can even find designs of yet-to-be-released products and other strategic information about a company. Connect to *The Happy Hacker* Web site and find an article that discusses a database that was hacked. Prepare a short report for your class detailing the incident.

2. **DEFINING QUERIES FOR A DVD RENTAL STORE** Consider your local DVD rental store. It certainly has an operational database to support its on-line transaction processing (OLTP). The operational database supports such things as adding new customers, renting DVDs (obviously), ordering DVDs, and a host of other activities. Now, assume that the DVD rental store also uses that same database for on-line analytical processing (OLAP) in the form of creating queries to extract meaningful information. If you were the manager of the DVD rental store, what kinds of queries would you build? What answers are you hoping to find?

3. **CREATING A QUERY** On the Web site that supports this text (www.mcgrawhill.ca/olc/ haag, choose ELM G [Implementing a Database with Microsoft Access]), we've provided the database (in Microsoft Access) we illustrated in this chapter. Connect to the text's Web site and download that database. Now, create three queries using the QBE tool. The first one should extract information from only one table (your choice). The second one should extract information found in at least two tables. The third should include some sort of selection criteria. How easy or difficult was it to perform these three queries? Would you say that a DBMS is just as easy to use as something like word processing or spreadsheet software? Why or why not? (By the way, ELM G [Implementing a Database with Microsoft Access] takes you through the step-by-step process of creating a query in Access.)

4. **CAREER OPPORTUNITIES IN YOUR MAJOR** Knowledge workers throughout the business world are building their own desktop databases (often called end-user databases or knowledge worker databases). To do so, they must understand both how to design a database and how to use a desktop DBMS such as Microsoft Access or FileMaker (made by FileMaker, a division of Apple Inc.). The ability to design a database and use a desktop DBMS offers you a great career advantage. Research your chosen major by looking at job postings (the Web is the best place to start). How many of those jobs want you to have some database knowledge? Do they list a specific DBMS package? What's your take—should you expand your education and learn more about databases and DBMSs? Why or why not?

5. **SALARIES FOR DATABASE ADMINISTRATORS** Database administrators (DBAs) are among the highest paid professionals in the information technology field. Many people work for 10 to 20 years to get a promotion to DBA. Connect to monster.ca (www.monster.ca) or another job database of your choice and search for DBA job openings. As you do, select all locations and job categories and then use "DBA" as the keyword search criteria. How many DBA job postings did you find? In what industries were some of the DBA job openings? Read through a couple of the job postings. What was the listed salary range (if any)? What sort of qualifications were listed?

6. **HOW UP TO DATE SHOULD DATA WAREHOUSE INFORMATION BE?** Information timeliness is a must in a data warehouse—old and obsolete information leads to poor decision making. Below is a list of decision-making processes that people go through for different business environments. For each, specify whether the information in the data warehouse should be updated monthly, weekly, daily, or by the minute. Be prepared to justify your decision.

   a. To adjust classes sizes in a university registration environment
   b. To alert people to changes in weather conditions

c. To predict scores of professional hockey games

d. To adjust radio advertisements in light of demographic changes

e. To monitor the success of a new product line in the clothing retail industry

f. To adjust production levels of food in a cafeteria

g. To switch jobs to various printers in a network

h. To adjust interest rates in a bank

i. To adjust forecasted demands of tires in an auto parts store.

Discussion Questions

1. Databases and data warehouses clearly make it easier for people to access all kinds of information. This will lead to great debates in the area of privacy. Should organizations be left to police themselves with respect to providing access to information or should the government impose privacy legislation? Answer this question with respect to (1) customer information shared by organizations, (2) employee information shared within a specific organization, and (3) business information available to customers.

2. Business intelligence sounds like a fancy term with a lot of competitive advantage potentially rolled into it. What sort of business intelligence does your school need? Specifically, what business intelligence would it need to predict enrolments in the coming years? What business intelligence would it need to determine what curricula to offer? Do you think your school gathers and uses this kind of business intelligence? Why or why not?

3. Consider your school's registration database that enforces the following integrity constraint: to enrol in a given class, the student must have completed or currently be enrolled in the listed prerequisite (if any). Your school, in fact, probably does have that integrity constraint in place. How can you get around that integrity constraint and enrol in a class for which you are not taking nor have completed the prerequisite? Is this an instance of when you should be able to override an integrity constraint? What are the downsides to being able to do so?

4. In this chapter, we listed the five important software components of a DBMS: the DBMS engine, the data definition, data manipulation, application generation, and data administration subsystems. Which of those are most and least important to users of a database? Which of those are most and least important to technology specialists who develop data applications? Which of those are most and least important to the chief information officer (CIO)? Justify each of your responses.

5. Some people used to believe that data warehouses would quickly replace databases for both on-line transaction processing (OLTP) and on-line analytical processing (OLAP). Of course, they were wrong. Why can data warehouses not replace databases and become "operational data warehouses"? How radically would data warehouses (and their data-mining tools) have to change to become a viable replacement for databases? Would they then essentially become databases that simply supported OLAP? Why or why not?

6. Consider that you work in the human resources management department of a local business and that many of your friends work there. Although you don't personally generate payroll cheques, you still have the ability to look up anyone's pay. Would you check on your friends to see if they're earning more money than you? For that matter, would you look up their pay just out of simple curiosity, knowing that you would never do anything with the information or share it with anyone else? Why or why not? What if people working at Canada Revenue Agency just curiously looked up the reported incomes of hockey stars and other high-profile public figures? Is this acceptable? Why or why not?

7. In spite of the need for "clean" information, many organizations have databases with duplicate records for you. You've probably experienced the consequences of this by receiving two identical pieces of junk mail from the same company. One record in the database may have your middle initial while the other doesn't, or there is some other type of minor discrepancy. Why would some organizations intentionally *not* go through a process of cleaning their database information?

Chapter 4

Decision Support and Artificial Intelligence

Brainpower for Your Business

STUDENT LEARNING OUTCOMES

LO1 Compare and contrast decision support systems and geographic information systems.

LO2 Understand expert systems and describe the types of problems to which they apply.

LO3 Understand neural networks and fuzzy logic and the use of these AI tools.

LO4 Define genetic algorithms and list some concepts upon which they are based and the types of problems they solve.

LO5 Describe four types of agent-based technologies.

OPENING CASE STUDY:
Visualizing Information in Map Form Can Aid in Decision Making

What do shuttle debris, trees, and icebergs have in common? They can all be mapped and managed using a geographic information system (GIS). A GIS allows you to see information spatially. If you've ever explored our world using Google Earth (earth.google.com), then you're familiar with a GIS. Being able to visualize the physical location of objects and their proximity to each other greatly aids the decision-making process.

On February 1, 2003, after 16 days of intensive research conducted while orbiting the earth, the space shuttle *Columbia* headed home. But something went terribly wrong; the shuttle exploded over East Texas and arrived on earth in small pieces. To figure out what had happened, it was necessary to gather the pieces and try to reconstruct the sequence of events that led to the disaster. The exact location of the pieces of debris was key, as researchers and scientists worked backward from that information to determine how and why the shuttle had exploded. Teams of people used GPS (global positioning system) gear to mark the exact location of each piece of debris as they came across it.

Water transit is vital to Canada's economy. Each year, ships face many challenges travelling the waters of the Arctic Ocean, the Gulf of St. Lawrence, and the Labrador Sea. Ice floes and icebergs obstruct shipping lanes, delaying transit and creating hazards for both the ships and those on board. These environmental conditions have caused some of history's more famous maritime disasters—most notably the sinking of the *Titanic* off the coast of Newfoundland in April 1912. Consequently, the Canadian government places a premium on studying and understanding the dynamics of sea ice formation and drift. The Ice and Marine Services Branch (IMSB), a branch of the Meteorological Service of Canada, provides the Canadian Coast Guard (CCG) and the United States Coast Guard, through partnership with the National Ice Centre in Washington, with accurate and timely reports of sea ice conditions for the east coast of Canada and the Canadian Arctic. To fulfill its mandate, the IMSB depends on integrated GIS and supporting information technologies for the acquisition and efficient processing of data from satellites, airborne radars, ice/weather models, and other data sources.

The city of Chattanooga, Tennessee, has created a GIS that maps the location of the 6,000 trees in and around its business district, along with details on each tree that include its species, tree-pit dimensions, irrigation status, and trunk diameter. This information is very helpful when working out a maintenance plan to keep the trees healthy. For example, the size of a tree determines how many pruning hours it will need. Having an accurate map of tree location by species allows the city to plan for future foliage. The city doesn't want to have more than 10 percent of any one species in such a small area since any insect infestation or disease that takes hold on one tree could spread more easily and potentially eliminate the whole tree population.[1]

Questions

1. Do you use Web-based map services to get directions and find the location of buildings? If so, why?

2. In what ways could real estate agents take advantage of the features of a GIS?

3. How could GIS software benefit a bank wanting to determine the optimal placements for ATMs?

Introduction

Decision making is crucial to business. Using all forms of intellectual assets—basic data to information to business intelligence to knowledge—decision makers in the business world ponder "make-or-break" decisions. Some are responding to changes in customer demographics (customer relationship management); others are considering the trade-offs of using low-cost suppliers as compared to higher-cost suppliers that deliver fewer defective products in faster time (supply chain management); still others are attempting to determine the best overall strategy for the organization. Does the organization position itself for overall cost leadership, differentiation, or focus? How does the organization combat an abundance of e-commerce businesses on the Web offering the same products and services (i.e., buyer power)? In this chapter, we'll investigate the tools that IT can provide to help you transform business information into business intelligence and make good decisions. According to *Management Review*, the big winners in tomorrow's business race will be those organizations that are "big of brain and small of mass."[2]

In business, decision making has four distinct phases, as proposed by Herbert Simon (see Figure 4.1).[3] These four phases are

1. *Intelligence* (find what to fix): Find or recognize a problem, need, or opportunity (also called the diagnostic phase of decision making). The intelligence phase involves detecting and interpreting signs that indicate a situation needs your attention. These "signs" come in many forms: consistent customer requests for new product features, the threat of new competition, declining sales, rising costs, an offer from a company to handle your distribution needs, and so on.

2. *Design* (find fixes): Consider possible ways of solving the problem, filling the need, or taking advantage of the opportunity. In this phase, you develop all the possible solutions you can.

3. *Choice* (pick a fix): Examine and weigh the merits of each solution, estimate the consequences of each, and choose the best one (which may be to do nothing at all). The "best" solution may depend on such factors as cost, ease of implementation, staffing requirements, and timing. This is the prescriptive phase of decision making—it's the stage at which a course of action is prescribed.

4. *Implementation* (apply the fix): Carry out the chosen solution, monitor the results, and make adjustments as necessary. Simply implementing a solution is seldom enough. Your chosen solution will always need fine-tuning, especially for complex problems or changing environments.

This four-phase process is not necessarily linear: You'll often find it useful or necessary to cycle back to an earlier phase. When choosing an alternative in the choice phase, for example, you might become aware of another possible solution. Then you would go back to the design phase, include the newly found solution, return to the choice phase, and compare the new solution to the others you generated.

A second model of decision making, also proposed by Simon, is *satisficing*, which differs from the four-phase process. **Satisficing** is making a choice that meets your needs

Figure 4.1

Four Phases of Decision Making

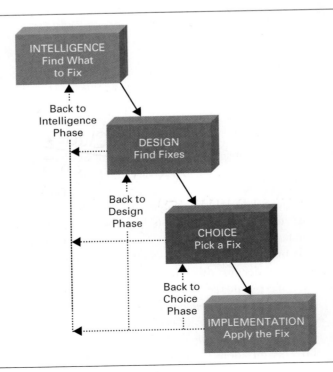

and is satisfactory without necessarily being the best possible choice available. The term is a combination of the words "satisfied" and "suffice."

Organizations in the private and public sectors are "satisficing" all the time in setting goals such as "fair price" or "reasonable profit." There's a fundamental difference between setting a goal of "high growth" and one of "maximum growth." "Maximum growth" is an optimizing strategy while "high growth" is a satisficing strategy. Usually a term like "high growth" is precisely defined. It may be 3 percent or 30 percent, but the idea is that when you reach that level, you can declare success.

In both business and your personal life, you'll face decisions that are some combination of four main types of decisions (see Figure 4.2): The first type is a ***structured decision***, which involves processing a certain kind of information in a specified way so that you will always get the right answer. No "feel" or intuition is necessary. These are the kinds of decisions you can program—if you use a certain set of inputs and process them in a precise way, you'll arrive at the correct result. Calculating gross pay for hourly workers is an example. You can easily automate these types of structured decisions with IT.

On the other hand, a ***nonstructured decision*** is one for which there may be several "right" answers, and there is no precise way to get a right answer. No rules or criteria exist that guarantee you a good solution. Deciding whether to introduce a new product line, employ a new marketing campaign, or change the corporate image are all examples of decisions with nonstructured elements. In reality, most decisions fall somewhere between structured and unstructured; for example, choosing a job. Structured elements of choosing a job include consideration of such things as salary and signing bonus. Unstructured elements of such a decision include things like the potential for advancement.

Another type of decision regards frequency with which the decision is made. A ***recurring decision*** is one that happens repeatedly, and often periodically, whether weekly, monthly, quarterly, or yearly. Deciding how much inventory to carry and deciding at what price to sell the inventory are recurring decisions. A ***nonrecurring***, or ***ad hoc***, ***decision*** is one that you make infrequently (perhaps only once), and you may even have different criteria for determining the best solution each time. Company mergers or deciding where to

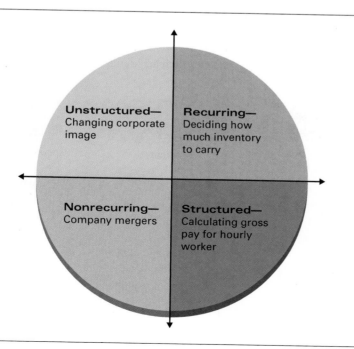

Figure 4.2

Categorizing Decisions by Type

Unstructured— Changing corporate image

Recurring— Deciding how much inventory to carry

Nonrecurring— Company mergers

Structured— Calculating gross pay for hourly worker

build a distribution centre are examples of nonrecurring or ad hoc decisions (although, the general trend in business today is for companies to consider mergers on a more consistent basis).

LO1

Decision Support Systems

In Chapter 3, you saw how data mining can help you make business decisions by giving you the ability to slice and dice your way through massive amounts of information. Actually, a data warehouse with data-mining tools is a form of decision support. A ***decision support system (DSS)*** is a highly flexible and interactive IT system that is designed to support decision making when the problem is not structured. A DSS is an alliance between you (the decision maker) and specialized support provided by IT (see Figure 4.3). IT brings speed, vast amounts of information, and sophisticated processing capabilities to help you create information useful in making a decision. You bring know-how in the form of your experience, intuition, judgment, and knowledge of the relevant factors. IT provides great power, but you—as the decision maker—must know what kinds of questions to ask of the information and how to process the information to get those questions answered. In fact, the primary objective of a DSS is to improve your effectiveness as a decision maker by providing you with assistance that will complement your insights. This union of your know-how and IT power helps you generate business intelligence so that you can quickly respond to changes in the marketplace and manage resources in the most effective and efficient ways possible. Following are some examples of the varied applications of DSSs:

- A national insurance company uses a DSS to analyze its risk exposure when insuring drivers with histories of driving under the influence. The DSS revealed that married male homeowners in their forties with one DUI conviction were rarely repeat offenders. By lowering its rates to this group the company increased its market share without increasing its risk exposure.[4]
- Burlington Northern and Santa Fe (BNSF) railroad regularly tests the rails its trains ride on to prevent accidents. Worn out or defective rails result in hundreds of derailments every year, so it's important to address the problem. Using a decision support system to schedule rail testing, BNSF decreased its rail-caused derailments by 33 percent in 2000, while the other three large U.S. railroad companies had a 16 percent rise in such accidents.[5]

Figure 4.3

The Alliance between You and a Decision Support System

What You Bring	Advantages of a DSS	What IT Brings
Experience	Increased productivity	Speed
Intuition	Increased understanding	Information
Judgment	Increased speed	Processing capabilities
Knowledge	Increased flexibility	
	Reduced problem complexity	
	Reduced cost	

- Customer relationship management (CRM), as you saw in Chapter 2, is an important part of any successful company's strategy. Decision support is an important part of CRM. Retail brokerage companies on Wall Street and Bay Street analyze customers' behaviours and goals with decision support systems, alerting brokers of opportunities and when possible problems begin.[6]

COMPONENTS OF A DECISION SUPPORT SYSTEM

DSSs vary greatly in application and complexity, but they all share specific features. A typical DSS has three components (see below and Figure 4.4 on the next page): model management, data management, and user interface management.

Before we look at these three components individually, let's get a quick overview of how they work together: When you begin your analysis, you tell the DSS, using the user interface management component, which model (in the model management component) to use on what information (in the data management component). The model requests the information from the data management component, analyzes that information, and sends the result to the user interface management component, which in turn passes the results back to you. Here's an example of a decision support system at Lands' End clothing business (Lands' End is owned by giant U.S. retailer Sears).

- *Model management*—The DSS at Lands' End has to have models to analyze information. The models create new information that decision makers need to plan product lines and inventory levels. For example, Lands' End uses a statistical model called regression analysis to determine trends in customer buying patterns and forecasting models to predict sales levels.
- *Data management*—The DSS's data management component stores Lands' End's customer and product information. In addition to this organizational information, the company also needs external information, such as demographic information and industry and style trend information.
- *User interface management*—A user interface enables Lands' End decision makers to access information and specify the models they want to use to create the information they need.

Now we'll examine the three DSS components in more general terms.

MODEL MANAGEMENT COMPONENT   The *model management* component consists of both the DSS models and the DSS model management system. A model is a representation of some event, fact, or situation. Businesses use models to represent variables and their relationships. For example, you would use a statistical modelling technique called analysis of variance (ANOVA) to determine whether newspaper, television, and billboard advertising are equally effective in increasing sales. DSSs help in various decision-making situations by using models that allow you to analyze information in many different ways. The models you use in a DSS depend on the decision you're making and, consequently, the kind of analysis you require. For example, you would use what-if analysis to see what effect the change of one or more variables will have on other variables, or optimization to find the most profitable solution given operating restrictions and limited resources. You can use spreadsheet software such as Excel to create a simple DSS for what-if analysis.

The model management system stores and maintains the DSS's models. Its function of managing models is similar to that of a database management system. The model management component can't select the best model for you to use for a particular problem—that requires your expertise—but it can help you create and manipulate models quickly and easily.

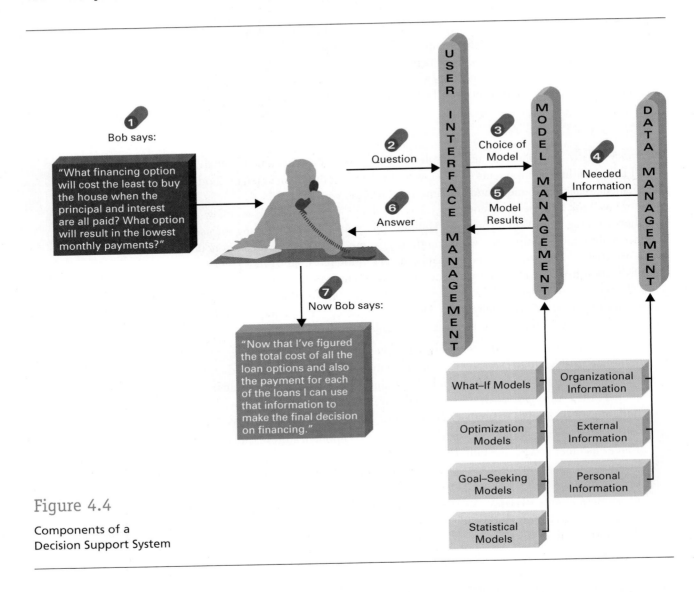

Figure 4.4

Components of a
Decision Support System

DATA MANAGEMENT COMPONENT   The *data management* component performs the function of storing and maintaining the information that you want your DSS to use. The data management component, therefore, consists of both the DSS information and the DSS database management system. The information you use in your DSS comes from one or more of three sources:

1. *Organizational information*—You may want to use virtually any information available in the organization for your DSS. You can design your DSS to access this information directly from your company's databases and data warehouses.

2. *External information*—Some decisions require input from external sources of information. Various branches of the federal government, Toronto Stock Exchange (TSX), and the Internet, to mention just a few, can provide additional information for use with a DSS.

3. *Personal information*—You can incorporate your own insights and experience— your personal information—into your DSS.

GOT MILK? THEY DO IN BRITISH COLUMBIA

The British Columbia Milk Marketing Board has the responsibility of collecting raw milk from farmers and transporting it to processing plants. The Marketing Board transfers payments from the processors to the farmers—to the tune of $17 million every two weeks. Milk is picked up from 350 farms per day by a fleet of 70 trucks, so that all 700 farms in the system see collection every other day. The milk goes to 26 processors across the vast province.

The paper-based system of record keeping was collapsing under its own weight. Upon pumping a farmer's milk into his truck, a driver recorded the number of litres collected on a four-part paper form and gave the farmer one copy. To fill a two-trailer truck, a driver collected milk from five farms and kept track, on paper, of how much milk came from each one. When the trailers were full of milk, the driver headed for the processing plant where a receipt for the quantity of milk was filled out. The truck then proceeded to the next farm and repeated the process.

Each day's work generated 350 producer slips from the farms and about 70 truck slips used to keep track of payments to the truck companies. To enter and process all this information, even using a computer, took many hours each day, especially with the problems of slips that truck drivers lost or forgot to turn over, and data-entering mistakes that had to be investigated. The cost of the paper system was about $100,000 per year. The basic accounting of incoming milk and outgoing payments took so much time that there wasn't much left for the in-depth analysis necessary for the type of decision making that would have led to more effective use of resources.

The new decision support system handles data entry in real time. Each driver uses a handheld wireless scanning unit to send information to the central system. Each farm and processing plant has a unique bar code that the driver just has to scan. All that's left is to enter the volume of milk and add any comments like the temperature of the milk and so on. A wireless printer in the truck's cab can produce a printed copy of the transaction for the farmer or processing plant. The data is then sent over the cellular data network to the Marketing Board's Internet access point, and from there to the main computer for processing.

Quite apart from collecting data faster and more accurately, enabling more efficient decision making, the IT system allows the British Columbia Milk Marketing Board to quickly identify any farm that was the source of a substandard shipment so that corrective action can be taken immediately. And it's not just management that benefits from the decision support aspect of the new system. IT also supplies drivers with useful information, such as how much space is left in each trailer and how a load should be divided between trailers. The new decision support system not only brings costs down but also increases profits.[7]

USER INTERFACE MANAGEMENT COMPONENT   The *user interface management* component allows you to communicate with the DSS. It consists of the user interface and the user interface management system. This is the component that allows you to combine your know-how with the storage and processing capabilities of the computer. The user interface is the part of the system you see; through it you enter information, commands, and models. If you have a DSS with a poorly designed user interface—if it's too rigid or too cumbersome to use—you simply won't use it, no matter what its capabilities. The best user interface uses your terminology and methods and is flexible, consistent, simple, and adaptable. In this vein, we would be remiss to not mention Digital Dashboards, a software tool that amalgamates user-configurable indicator data from various sources into an easy-to-digest display of the environment. Think of the dashboard in a car and how it provides various metrics for very different dimensions (speed, engine temperature, revolutions per minute, oil pressure, turn indicators, high-beam indicator, etc.) that together paint a picture of the motoring environment. The same metaphor can be applied to business metrics such as sales, demand, material price, consumer income, competitors' sales, etc. to create a digital picture of the essential elements of an enterprise. Such software tools are invaluable and are used in a decision support role by many organizations.

GEOGRAPHIC INFORMATION SYSTEMS

In 1992, Hurricane Andrew attacked the east coast of the United States, leaving devastation throughout several states. One of the places hardest hit was Miami, Florida, where the hurricane came on land, smashing businesses and private buildings and causing billions of dollars in damage. Reporters at the *Miami Herald* believed that not all the damage was due to Andrew. They hypothesized that at least some of the harm was a result of shoddy construction of homes built after 1980.

Four months after Hurricane Andrew, the paper ran a series of reports and used geographic information system maps to make its point. A *geographic information system (GIS)* is a decision support system designed specifically to analyze spatial information. Spatial information is any information that can be shown in map form, such as roads, the distribution of the caribou population, sewer systems, or the path of a hurricane.

The *Miami Herald* plotted the arrival point of the hurricane where winds were strongest and charted the progress of Andrew inland, where it lost some of its initial punch. Then the reporters plotted the damaged houses with one dot representing 10 homes. These dots were colour-coded to show level of damage—blue showed 10 repairable homes and orange dots represented 10 destroyed homes. When the two maps were laid over each other, it was clear that the wind strength did not match up with damage as it should have. That is, the reporters showed that Hurricane Andrew alone was not responsible for all the devastation. The net result was that building codes in Dade County were tightened so that contractors had to use more nails and install stronger windows, doors, and shutters on homes. The *Miami Herald* received the Pulitzer Prize for its investigative work.

Businesses use GIS software to analyze information, generate business intelligence, and make decisions. GIS is a powerful combination of database and graphics technology. There is virtually no limit to the sort of information you can plot with a GIS, including the placement of roads, the course of rivers, income levels, health conditions, areas of high or low crime, and so on. Of course, you can do this with paper maps, too. The strength of an electronic GIS is its ability to get to layer information with a mouse click.

Canada was the first country in the world to have a computerized GIS. Dr. Roger Tomlinson joined the Canadian government in 1962 to develop this new technology. Tomlinson, a recipient of the prestigious Order of Canada for his pioneering work on geographic information systems, is widely considered to be the "father of GIS." He conceived and developed GIS as an application to be used by the Canada Land Inventory. Scientists, academics, and practitioners in the areas of land use, sustainability, and urban management from around the world have consulted with this Canadian visionary.[8, 9]

Figure 4.5 is a map of the Denver area shown using the real estate search function in Zillow (www.zillow.com). On the left-hand side you can see the layers (or types of information) that can be shown on the map—homes for sale, homes recently sold, and so on. The map itself is colour-coded to show the estimated dollars per square foot for residential areas. Colour shadings of red through maroon are in the US$500 to $700 per square foot range and variations of blue are in the US$0 to $200 per square foot range.

This is an example of the feature of GIS software that represents information thematically (i.e., in map or theme form). With themes, you can show the layers in combination as the *Miami Herald* reporters did for Hurricane Andrew. You can represent either sta-

Note the colour coding by square footage price

Legends of information

Figure 4.5

Square Footage Costs in Denver according to Zillow

tistical information, for instance, the average salary of homeowners, or point information, such as the location of a bank's customers.

When businesses use GIS software to generate maps showing information of interest to them, we call it *business geography*. You can find a wealth of information to incorporate into your GIS from various sources. For example, Statistics Canada has a vast database of demographic and employment information. Both of these would be statistical information. In the private sector, many research companies would be happy to sell you consumer habit information.

Studies show that the way in which information is presented significantly impacts the effectiveness and efficiency of the decision-making process. Here are other examples of GISs in use:

- Toronto's ambulances use GPS for dispatching. Vehicle position information is sent to the Communications Centre to ensure fast response to critical medical emergencies. The radio system processes up to 80,000 data calls daily, consisting of remote and host-originated individual calls with an average duration of one second. The same system is used to transfer vehicle status messages.

- During the bovine spongiform encephalopathy (BSE, or more commonly, mad cow disease) outbreak in 2003 it became clear that a national tracking system of cattle, from birth on, was needed to help keep the beef supply—and the people who consume it—safe. It took Canadian and American officials days to track down animals that might have been linked to a single case of BSE in Alberta. During 2003, only 87 cattle and 15 calves were at risk of being susceptible to BSE, but over 400 were slaughtered because officials did not have complete enough records on the movement of these animals. To correct that problem, a tracking system was developed to log every producer, sales barn, feed yard, and processing facility through which each animal passes. This is a gargantuan task since every year tens of millions of cattle travel from one part of North America to another. This tracking system combines RFID (radio frequency identification; see Chapter 9) tags on the ears of cattle, GPS, GIS, and a wireless network to track each animal's movements and transmit the information to a national database.[10]

LOCATION MASHUP = GIS + THE INFORMATION YOU WANT

Broadly defined, a *mashup* is a combination of content from more than one source. Due in large part to the technologies of Web 2.0 (see ELM E [The World Wide Web and the Internet]), people produce and post mashups of all kinds—music mashups (a single song using parts of numerous other songs), video mashups (just like a music mashup but using video), and even location mashups. A *location mashup* is a geographic information system (GIS) that displays a particular geographic area and then overlays content according to the user's desires. For example, at www.gawker.com/stalker, you can view a mashup showing the latest travels and locations of celebrities such as Madonna.

Location mashups are actually quite easy to create using many new and emerging tools including Pipes (by Yahoo!), GeoCommons (by FortiusOne), and GeoIQ (also by FortiusOne). Many of them come with location data that you can instantly add to a GIS map to create a location mashup. GeoIQ, for example, includes a wealth of data such as the location of spammers by street address and incidents of the West Nile virus.

Location mashups are not limited to personal use; many businesses use them. Google, British Petroleum, UPS, Best Buy, Century 21, Chrysler LLC, FedEx, Ford, General Motors, H&R Block, and Starbucks are among the many businesses exploiting the capabilities of location mashups. Some use them for internal efficiency and decision-making efforts (e.g., BP can now provide updated weather patterns to employees in the Gulf of Mexico), while others use them in the form of a customer-facing technology (e.g., Starbucks' location mashup helps customers find their next caffeine fix).[11]

DSSs and GISs are IT systems that augment business brainpower. IT can further expand business brainpower by means of *artificial intelligence (AI)*—the science of making machines imitate human thinking and behaviour. Financial analysts use a variety of artificial intelligence systems to manage assets, invest in the stock market, and perform other financial operations. Hospitals use artificial intelligence in many capacities, from scheduling staff, to assigning beds to patients, to diagnosing and treating illness. Many government agencies, including CRA and the Canadian Armed Forces, use artificial intelligence. Credit card companies use artificial intelligence to detect credit card fraud, and insurance companies use artificial intelligence to spot fraudulent claims. Artificial intelligence lends itself to tasks as diverse as airline ticket pricing, food preparation, oil exploration, and child protection. It is widely used in the insurance, meteorology, engineering, and aerospace industries. The AI systems that businesses use most can be classified into the following major categories:

1. Expert systems
2. Neural networks (and fuzzy logic)
3. Genetic algorithms
4. Intelligent agents (or agent-based technologies).

LO2

Expert Systems

In business, people are valuable because they perform important business tasks. Many business tasks require expertise, and people often carry this expertise in their heads—often that's the only place it can be found in the organization. AI can provide you with an expert system that can capture expertise, thus making it available to those who are not experts so that they can use it, either to solve a problem or to learn how to solve a problem.

An **expert system**, also called a **knowledge-based system**, is an artificial intelligence system that applies reasoning capabilities to reach a conclusion. Expert systems are excellent for diagnostic and prescriptive problems. Diagnostic problems are those requiring an answer to the question, "What's wrong?" and correspond to the intelligence phase of decision making. Prescriptive problems are those that require an answer to the question, "What to do?" and correspond to the choice phase of decision making.

An expert system is usually built for a specific application area called a *domain*. You can find expert systems in the following domains, among others:

- *Accounting*—for auditing, tax planning, management consulting, and training
- *Medicine*—to prescribe antibiotics where many considerations must be taken into account (such as the patient's medical history, the source of the infection, and the price of available drugs)
- *Process control*—to control offset lithographic printing, for example
- *Human resource management*—to help personnel managers determine whether they are in compliance with an array of federal employment laws
- *Financial management*—to identify delinquency-prone accounts in the loan departments of banks
- *Production*—to guide the manufacture of all sorts of products, such as aircraft parts
- *Forestry management*—to help with harvesting timber on forest lands.

A DSS sometimes incorporates expert systems, but an expert system is fundamentally different from a DSS. To use a DSS, you must have considerable knowledge or expertise about the situation with which you're dealing. As you saw earlier in this chapter, a DSS assists you in making decisions. That means that you must know how to reason through the problem. You must know which questions to ask, how to get the answers, and how to proceed to the next step. When you use an expert system, however, the know-how is in the system—you need provide the expert system only with the facts and symptoms of the problem for which you need an answer. The know-how, or expertise, that actually solves the problem came from someone else—an expert in the field. What does it mean to have expertise? When someone has expertise in a given subject, that person not only knows a lot of facts about the topic but also can apply that knowledge to analyze and make judgments about related topics. It's this human expertise that an expert system captures.

Let's look at a very simple expert system that would tell a driver what to do when approaching a traffic light. Dealing with traffic lights is an example of the type of problem to which an expert system is well suited. It is a recurring problem, and to solve it you follow a well-defined set of steps. You've probably gone through the following mental question-and-answer session hundreds of times without even realizing it (see Figure 4.6 on the next page).

When you approach a green traffic light, you proceed through. If the light is red, you need to stop. If you're unable to stop, and if traffic is approaching from either side, you'll surely be in trouble. Similarly, if the light is yellow, you may be able to make it through the intersection before the light turns red. If not, you will again be faced with the problem of approaching traffic.

WHAT EXPERT SYSTEMS CAN AND CAN'T DO

An expert system uses IT to capture and apply human expertise. For problems with clear rules and procedures, expert systems work very well and can provide your company with great advantages. An expert system can

- Handle massive amounts of information
- Reduce errors

Rule	Symptom or Fact	Yes	No	Explanation
1	Is the light green?	Go through the intersection.	Go to Rule 2.	Should be safe if light is green. If not, need more information.
2	Is the light red?	Go to Rule 4.	Go to Rule 3.	Should stop, may not be able to.
3	Is the light likely to change to red before you get through the intersection?	Go to Rule 4.	Go through the intersection.	Will reach this point only if light is yellow; then you'll have two choices.
4	Can you stop before entering the intersection?	Stop.	Go to Rule 5.	Should stop, but there may be a problem if you can't.
5	Is traffic approaching from either side?	Prepare to crash.	Go through the intersection.	Unless the intersection is clear of traffic, you're likely to crash.

Is the light green (Yes/No)?   No.

Is the light red (Yes/No)?   No.

Is the light likely to change to red before you get through the intersection (Yes/No)?   Why?

Will reach this point only if light is yellow, then you'll have two choices.

Is the light likely to change to red before you get through the intersection (Yes/No)?   No.

Conclusion: Go through the intersection.

Figure 4.6

Traffic Light Expert System Rules

- Aggregate information from various sources
- Improve customer service
- Provide consistency in decision making
- Provide new information
- Decrease personnel time spent on tasks
- Reduce cost.

You can run into trouble, however, in building and using an expert system. Difficulties can include the following:

1. Transferring domain expertise to the expert system is sometimes difficult because domain experts cannot always explain how they know what they know. Often experts are not aware of their complete reasoning processes. Experience has given them a "feel" for the problem, and they just "know."

2. Even if the domain expert can explain the whole reasoning process, automating that process may be impossible. The process may be too complex, requiring an excessive number of rules, or it may be too vague or imprecise. In using an expert system, keep in mind that it can solve only the problems for which it was designed. It cannot deal with inconsistency or a newly encountered problem situation. An expert system can't learn from previous experience and can't apply previously acquired expertise to new problems the way humans can.

3. An expert system has no common sense or judgment. One of the early expert systems built into an F-16 fighter plane allowed the pilot to retract the landing gear while the plane was still on the ground and to jettison bombs while the plane was flying upside down.

Neural Networks and Fuzzy Logic

LO3

Suppose you see a breed of dog you've never encountered before. Would you know it's a dog? For that matter, would you know it's an animal? Probably so. You know, because you've learned by example. You've seen lots of living things, have learned to classify them, and so can recognize a dog when you see one. A neural network simulates this human ability to classify things without taking prescribed steps leading to the solution. A **neural network** (often called an **artificial neural network** or **ANN**) is an artificial intelligence system that is capable of finding and differentiating patterns. Your brain has learned to consider many factors in combination to recognize and differentiate objects. This is also the case with a neural network. A neural network can learn by example and can adapt to new concepts and knowledge. Neural networks are widely used for visual pattern and speech recognition systems. If you've used a PDA that deciphered your handwriting, it was probably a neural network that analyzed the characters you wrote.[12]

Neural networks are useful in a variety of situations. For example, bomb detection systems in Canadian and U.S. airports use neural networks that sense trace elements in the air that may indicate the presence of explosives. The Chicago Police Department uses neural networks to identify corruption within its ranks.[13] In medicine, neural networks check 50 million electrocardiograms per year, check for drug interactions, and detect anomalies in tissue samples that may signify the onset of cancer and other diseases. Neural networks can detect heart attacks and even differentiate between the subtly different symptoms of heart attacks in men and women.[14, 15, 16] In business, neural networks are very popular for securities trading, fraud detection, real estate appraisal, evaluating loan applications, and target marketing, to mention a few. Neural networks are used to control machinery, adjust temperature settings, and identify malfunctioning machinery.

Neural networks are most useful for identification, classification, and prediction when a vast amount of information is available. By examining hundreds, or even thousands of examples, a neural network detects important relationships and patterns in the information. For example, if you provide a neural network with the details of numerous credit card transactions and tell it which ones are fraudulent, eventually it will learn to identify suspicious transaction patterns.

Here are some examples of the uses of neural networks:

- Citibank uses neural networks to find opportunities in financial markets.[17] By carefully examining historical stock market data with neural network software, Citibank financial managers learn of interesting coincidences or small anomalies (called market inefficiencies). For example, it could be that whenever IBM stock goes up, so does Unisys stock. Or it might be that a U.S. Treasury note is selling for 1 cent less in Japan than it is in the United States. These snippets of information can make a big difference to Citibank's bottom line in a very competitive financial market.

- A large Canadian bank used neural networks to examine the relative branch efficiency as well as to make short-term efficiency predictions.[18]

- In Westminster, California, a community of 87,000 people, police use neural network software to fight crime. With crime reports as input, the system detects and maps local crime patterns. Police say that with this system they can better predict crime trends, improve patrol assignments, and develop better crime-prevention programs.[19]

- Fingerhut, the mail order company based in Minnesota, has 6 million people on its customer list. To determine which customers were and were not likely to order from its catalogue, Fingerhut recently switched to neural network software. The company finds that the new software is more effective and expects to generate millions of dollars by fine-tuning its mailing lists.[20]

- Fraud detection is one of the areas in which neural networks are used the most. Visa, MasterCard, and many other credit card companies use a neural network to spot peculiarities in individual accounts. MasterCard estimates neural networks save the company $50 million annually.[21]

- Many U.S. health insurance companies along with other carriers use neural network software to identify fraud. The system searches for patterns in billing charges, laboratory tests, and frequency of office visits. A claim for which the diagnosis was a sprained ankle but included an electrocardiogram would be flagged for the account manager.[22]

- FleetBoston Financial Corporation uses a neural network to watch transactions with customers. The neural network can detect patterns that may indicate a customer's growing dissatisfaction with the company. The neural network looks for signs like decreases in the number of transactions or in the account balance of one of Fleet's high-value customers.[23]

All of the above situations have pattern recognition in common. They all require identification and/or classification, which may then be used to predict a finding or outcome. Neural networks are often called predictive systems since they can see patterns in huge volumes of information.

Neural networks have many advantages. For example, neural networks can

- Learn and adjust to new circumstances on their own
- Lend themselves to massive parallel processing
- Function without complete or well-structured information
- Cope with huge volumes of information with many dependent variables
- Analyze nonlinear relationships in information (they've been called fancy regression analysis systems).

The biggest problem with neural networks to date has been the fact that the hidden layers are "hidden." That is, you can't see how the neural network is learning and how the "neurons" are interacting. Newer neural networks no longer hide the middle layers. With these systems you can manually adjust the weights or connections, giving you more flexibility and control.

FUZZY LOGIC

Fuzzy logic is a way of reaching conclusions based on ambiguous or vague information. Humans tend to make decisions based on approximate information, since not every type of information can be separated into mutually exclusive categories. For example, you might consider –20 degrees Celsius to be very cold, 0 degrees to be cold, 15 degrees to be warm, 25 degrees to be hot, and 35 to be very hot, but you can't really specify exact degree values that would separate these categories of warmth (or lack of it). Compounding the problem is the fact that somebody else might experience it differently; subjectively, a temperature some people consider warm others would judge to be hot—or cool. Thus,

HOW PROFITABLE WOULD A NEURAL NETWORK SAY YOU ARE?

Would your banker give you an A, B, or C? What about your supermarket? You know you're being graded in your classes, but did you know that you're also being graded by businesses?

Special treatment for certain customers is not new. Airline customers who fly first class have always received preferential treatment, even when flights were cancelled or delayed. You won't find them napping on a stone floor with their backpacks as pillows. This makes business sense to the airlines, since these are the customers who are most profitable.

Although companies have always offered preferential treatment to their more profitable customers, the speed and capacity of computers today are making the segmenting of customers possible to a degree unheard of just a few years ago. Part of the reason for this is neural networks. Using neural network software, busi-

nesses now have the ability to look for patterns in their customer information and classify customers according to how they affect the company's bottom line and thus to gauge whether it's worth the trouble of making them happy.

Banks are using software that categorizes people into red, green, and yellow classes depending on the customer's history and value to the bank. Customers who are green might get better credit card rates than customers who are red and are judged to add less to the bank's bottom line.

Say you called the bank that issued you your credit card and said that you didn't want to pay the annual fee anymore. The bank could look at your credit card activity and decide whether it's more profitable to the bank to waive your fee rather than risk your not using the credit card anymore.[24,25]

---

you need a way to translate an approximate or vague judgment into something that a computer, requiring a precise assignment of numbers to all events, can handle. This is the type of situation in which fuzzy logic is very effective.

Fuzzy logic is a mathematical method of handling imprecise or subjective information. The basic approach is to assign values between 0 and 1 to vague or ambiguous information. The higher the value, the closer it is to 1. For example, you might assign the value of 0.8 to the value "hot" (with 1 being hottest). Then you would construct rules and processes, called *algorithms*, to describe the interdependence among variables. A fuzzy logic algorithm is a set of steps that relate variables representing inexact information or personal perceptions.

Fuzzy logic and neural networks are often combined to express complicated and subjective concepts in a form that makes it possible to simplify the problem and to apply rules. The rules are executed with a level of certainty. This is similar to, but not the same as, confidence levels in statistics. In statistics, probability is used to estimate the likelihood of an outcome, whereas fuzzy logic describes the data point itself while incorporating subjective perception.

In the business world, fuzzy logic has been applied to financial analysis, the pharmaceutical industry, the wood processing and metal cutting industries, the manufacture of antilock brakes, and washing machines that determine by themselves how much water to use or how long to wash. (They wash until the water is "clean.") In accounting and finance, for example, fuzzy logic allows you to analyze information with subjective financial values (say, on an important intangible resource like goodwill) that are very important considerations in economic analyses.

Fuzzy logic is used by Google to find answers to your search terms, which makes sense, since your perception of a topic often influences how you phrase your query, hence determining the relevance of the Web pages that Google delivers.

LO4

Genetic Algorithms

Have you ever wondered how chefs around the world create recipes for great-tasting foods? For example, how did the Chinese discover that cashew nuts and chicken taste good when combined? How did Mexican chefs arrive at combining tomatoes, onions, cilantro, and other spices to create pica de gallo? All those great recipes came about through *evolutionary processes*. Someone decided to put together a few ingredients and taste the result. Undoubtedly, many of those combinations resulted in unpalatable concoctions that were quickly discarded. Others were tasty enough to warrant further experimentation of combinations.

Today significant research in AI is devoted to creating software capable of following a similar trial-and-error process, leading to the evolution of a good result. Such a software system is called a genetic algorithm. A **genetic algorithm** is an artificial intelligence system that mimics the evolutionary, survival-of-the-fittest process to generate increasingly better solutions to a problem. In other words, a genetic algorithm is an optimizing system: It finds the combination of inputs that give the best outputs.

Here's an example. Suppose you were trying to decide what to put into your stock portfolio. You have countless stocks to choose from but a limited amount of money to invest. You might decide that you'd like to start with 20 stocks and you want a portfolio growth rate of 7.5 percent.

Probably you'd start by examining historic information on the stocks. You would take some number of stocks and combine them, 20 at a time, to see what happens with each grouping. If you wanted to choose from a pool of 30 stocks, you would have to examine 30,045,015 different combinations. For a 40-stock pool, the number of combinations rises to 137,846,500,000. It would be an impossibly time-consuming, not to mention numbingly tedious, task to look at this many combinations and evaluate your overall return for each one. This is just the sort of repetitive number-crunching task at which computers excel, however.

So, instead of a pencil, paper, and calculator, you might use a genetic algorithm. You could input the appropriate information on the stocks, including the number of years the company has been in business, the performance of the stock over the last five years, price to earnings ratios, and other information.

You would also have to tell the genetic algorithm your exact "success" criteria. For example, you might use a growth rate in the company over the last year of at least 10 percent, a presence in the marketplace going back at least three years, a connection to the computer industry, and so forth. The genetic algorithm would simply combine and recombine stocks, eliminating any combinations that don't fit your criteria and continuing to the next iteration with the acceptable combinations—those that give an aggregate growth rate of at least 7.5 percent while aiming for as high a growth rate as possible.

Genetic algorithms use three concepts of evolution:

1. *Selection*—or survival of the fittest. The key to selection is to give preference to better outcomes.

2. *Crossover*—or combining portions of good outcomes in the hope of creating an even better outcome.

3. *Mutation*—or randomly trying combinations and evaluating the success (or failure) of the outcome.

Genetic algorithms are best suited to decision-making environments in which thousands, or perhaps millions, of solutions are possible. Genetic algorithms can find and evaluate solutions intelligently and can get through many more possibilities more thoroughly and quickly than can a human. As you might imagine, businesses face decision-making environments for all sorts of problems like engineering design, computer graphics, strategies for game playing—anything, in fact, that requires optimization techniques. Here are some other examples.

- Genetic algorithms are used by business executives to help them decide which combination of projects a firm should invest in, taking complicated tax considerations into account.[26]

- They're used by investment companies to help in trading choices and decisions.[27]

- In any garment that you buy, the fabric alone accounts for between 35 percent and 40 percent of the selling price. So, when cutting out the fabric to make the garment, it's important that there be as little waste as possible. Genetic algorithms are used to solve this problem of laying out the pieces of the garment and cutting fabric in a way that leaves as little waste as possible.[28]

- US West uses a genetic algorithm to determine the optimal configuration of fibre-optic cable in a network that may include as many as 100,000 connection points. By using selection, crossover, and mutation, the genetic algorithm can generate and evaluate millions of cable configurations and select the one that uses the least amount of cable. At US West, this process used to take an experienced design engineer almost two months. US West's genetic algorithm can solve the problem in two days and saves the company $1 million to $10 million each time it's used.[29]

Genetic algorithms are good for these types of problems because they use selection, crossover, and mutation as methods of exploring countless solutions and the respective worth of each.

You have to tell the genetic algorithm what constitutes a "good" solution. That could be low cost or high return, among other factors, since many potential solutions are useless or absurd. If you created a genetic algorithm to make bread, for example, it might try to boil flour to create moistness. That obviously won't work, so the genetic algorithm would simply throw away that solution and try something else. Other solutions would eventually be good, and some of them would even be wonderful. According to David Goldbert, a genetic algorithm pioneer at the University of Illinois at Urbana–Champaign, evolution is the oldest and most powerful algorithm there is, and "three billion years of evolution can't be wrong!"[30]

Intelligent Agents

LO5

Do you have a favourite restaurant? Is there someone there who knows you and remembers that you like Italian dressing, but not croutons, on your salad; and ice cream and a slice of cheddar cheese with your apple pie? Does this person familiar with your tastes put a glass of diet cola on your favourite table when you come in the door? If so, he or she has the qualities that artificial intelligence scientists are working on incorporating into intelligent agents. An ***intelligent agent*** is software that assists you, or acts on your behalf, in performing repetitive computer-related tasks. Future intelligent agents will most likely be autonomous, acting independently, and will learn and adapt to changing circumstances.

You may not realize it, but you're probably already familiar with a primitive type of intelligent agent—the shifty-eyed paper clip that popped up in some older versions of Microsoft Word. For example, if your document looked as if it was going to be a business letter—that is, you type in a date, name, and address—the animated paper clip offered (what some considered helpful) suggestions on how to proceed.

You can find hundreds of intelligent agents, or bots, for a wide variety of tasks. The BotSpot and SmartBot Web sites at www.botspot.com and www.smartbots.com are good places to get an idea of the many different types of agents available.

Essentially there are four types of intelligent agents:

- Information agents (including buyer agents or shopping bots)
- Monitoring-and-surveillance agents
- Data-mining agents
- User or personal agents.

INFORMATION AGENTS

Information agents are intelligent agents that search for information of some kind and bring it back. The best known information agents are buyer agents. A *buyer agent*, also known as a *shopping bot*, is an intelligent agent on a Web site that helps you, the customer, find products and services that you need. Buyer agents work very efficiently for commodity items such as CDs, books, electronic components, and other one-size-fits-all products. Amazon.com uses intelligent technology to show you a list of books or other products that you might like. The Web site classifies you into a category of people with similar tastes and, based on that category, presents you with a list of products that Amazon hopes you will find appealing enough to buy.

Shopping bots make money by selling advertising space, from special promotions in cooperation with merchants, or by charging click-through fees, which are payments to the site that provided the link to the merchant site. Some shopping bots give preference to certain sites for a financial consideration. The people who run shopping bot sites have two, sometimes competing, objectives. They want to present as many listings as possible to the consumer in the most useful way, but they also want to make money doing it.

Both the Google and Ask Web sites use information agents to find information—and not just when you request it. The URL server at Google sends thousands of Googlebots out to surf the Web sites of all the sites in Google's index. They copy individual pages, at the rate of more than 100 per second, to Google's repository, where the Google software indexes them. This means that when you perform a Google search, the search engine builds a list of all the pages that have the keywords you specify and presents them to you in PageRank order. Google's PageRanking process sorts the pages in order of links pointing to each page. That is, the more links on the Web that point to a Web site, the higher that Web site will be in the list.[31]

Government sites have information agents you can use to get the information you need. Canada has a system called the Canadian Socio-Economic Information Management system (CANSIM) that is a time-series database containing chronological series. CANSIM is Statistics Canada's key database profiling Canada's population, labour, health, income, trade, education, manufacturing, investments, and more. The United States has a system called FERRET (Federal Electronic Research and Review Extraction Tool) that was developed jointly by the Census Bureau and the Bureau of Labor Statistics. With FERRET you can find information on employment, health care, education, race and ethnicity, health insurance, housing, income and poverty, aging, and marriage and family. Other types of information agents include intelligent agents that scan Web pages and highlight relevant text for you, and still others that can assemble customized news reports. There are several versions of these. A CNN Custom News bot will gather news from CNN on the topics you want to read about—and only those topics.

INTELLIGENT AGENTS RUN EXPERIMENTS ABOARD SPACECRAFT

We all know that NASA sends various types of craft into space for a variety of purposes. We've heard of the Hubble telescope that has been sending back terrific pictures for years. A lesser known but similarly spectacular observation craft—although in this case its mission is to observe the earth—is the Earth Observing-1 (or simply EO1) satellite.

During 2004, NASA uploaded intelligent agent software to EO1 to run experiments and even the spacecraft itself. One of EO1's tasks was to avoid wasting fuel without disrupting the onboard experiments or otherwise compromising the mission. This was a job that used to be handled by ground control, but now the people at mission headquarters are free to concentrate on tasks other than routine maintenance while the agents do the job in space.

EO1 was launched in 2001 on a one-year mission to observe the earth from space. It was part of NASA's New Millennium Program mission and was originally intended as a pilot project to test new space technologies. It's still going strong collecting and sending back to us valuable information about our earth with about 20 times more detail than any previous Earth-observing satellites. The information that EO1 sends back encompasses all manner of happenings on Earth, like the spread of forest and bush fires, the impact of cattle grazing in South America, the state of the rain forest, and the spread of harmful plant species.

The beauty of incorporating intelligent agents into the spacecraft is that they can learn and adapt to changing and unexpected conditions. NASA's software engineers have designed these agents to achieve certain goals rather than to react to prespecified situations, making them able to handle complex interactions. Since the software can "learn" and function autonomously, it can react to unexpected situations, allowing scientists to conduct more complex and interesting research on board.[32]

MONITORING-AND-SURVEILLANCE AGENTS

Monitoring-and-surveillance agents (also called *predictive agents*) are intelligent agents that constantly observe and report on some entity of interest; a network or manufacturing equipment, for example. NASA's Jet Propulsion Laboratory has an agent that monitors inventory, planning, and the ordering of scheduled equipment to keep costs down.[33] Other monitoring-and-surveillance agents work on the manufacturing shop floor, finding equipment problems and locating other machinery that can perform the same job.

Monitoring-and-surveillance agents are often used to monitor complex computer networks. Allstate Insurance has a network with 2,000 computers. The company uses a network monitoring agent from Computer Associates called Neugent that watches its huge networks 24 hours a day. Every five seconds, the agent measures 1,200 data points and can predict a system crash 45 minutes before it happens. Neugent combines intelligent agent technology with neural network technology to look for patterns of activity or problems. The neural network part can learn what conditions predict a downturn in network efficiency or a slowing in network traffic. Neugent also watches for electronic attacks and can detect them early so that they can be stopped.

Another type of monitoring-and-surveillance agent is one that works on computer networks keeping track of the configuration of each computer connected to the network. It tracks and updates the central configuration database when anything on any computer changes, like the number or type of disk drives. An important task in managing networks is prioritizing traffic and shaping bandwidth. That means sending enough network capacity or bandwidth to the most important tasks versus those that are secondary. At a university, for example, processing end-of-semester grades might take precedence.

Some other types of monitoring-and-surveillance agents include

- Agents that watch your competition and bring back price changes and special-offer information
- Agents that monitor Internet sites, discussion groups, mailing lists, and so on, for stock manipulation, insider training, and rumours that might affect stock prices
- Agents that monitor sites for updated information on the topic of your choice
- Agents that watch particular products and bring back price or term changes
- Agents that monitor auction sites for products or prices that you want

DATA-MINING AGENTS

A *data-mining agent* operates in a data warehouse where its task is discovering information. A data warehouse brings together information from lots of different sources. Data mining is the process of looking through the data warehouse to find information that you can use to take action—such as ways to increase sales or to keep customers who are considering defecting. Data mining is so called because you have to sift through a lot of information for the gold nuggets that will affect the bottom line (or top line). This sort of nugget spotting is similar to what the RCMP and CSIS do when they bring together little bits of information from diverse sources and use the overall pattern to spot trouble brewing.

As you learned in Chapter 3, database queries answer questions like "How much did we spend on transportation in March of this year?" Multidimensional analysis is the next step in complexity and answers questions like "How much did we spend on transportation in the Maritime Region during March of the last five years?" Data mining goes deeper and may suggest questions you may not even have thought to ask, such as the retail manager we mentioned in Chapter 1 who thought "What else do young men buy on Friday afternoons when they come in to buy diapers?"[34]

One of the most common types of data mining is classification, which finds patterns in information and categorizes items into those classes. You may remember that this is just what neural networks do best. So, not surprisingly, neural networks are part of many data-mining tools. And data-mining agents are another integral part, since these intelligent agents search for information in a data warehouse.

A data-mining agent may detect a major shift in a trend or a key indicator. It can also detect the presence of new information and alert you. Volkswagen uses an intelligent agent system that acts as an early-warning system about market conditions. If conditions become such that the assumptions underlying the company's strategy are no longer true, the intelligent agent alerts managers.[35] For example, the intelligent agent might see a problem in some part of the country that is about to or will shortly cause payments to slow down. Having that information early lets managers formulate a plan to protect themselves.

USER AGENTS

User agents (sometimes called *personal agents*) are intelligent agents that take action on your behalf. In this category belong those intelligent agents that already perform, or will shortly perform, the following tasks:

- Check your e-mail, sort it according to priority (your priority), and alert you when good stuff comes through—like post-secondary acceptance letters.
- Play computer games as your opponent or patrol game areas for you.
- Fill out forms on the Web automatically for you. They even store your information for future reference.
- "Discuss" topics with you from your deepest fears to your favourite sports.

One expanding application of intelligent agent technology is in automating business functions. For example, Mission Hockey (a division of Mission.ITECH Hockey), a company that manufacturers and distributes in-line and ice hockey skates and other gear, uses software from Sweden called Movex that has a user-agent component. Movex will search the Internet or a company intranet or extranet to negotiate and make deals with suppliers and distributors. In this case, the intelligent agent is incorporated into an enterprise resource planning system. Enterprise resource planning (or ERP) is a very important concept in today's business world. The term refers to a method of getting and keeping an overview on every part of the business (a bird's-eye view, so to speak), so that production, development, selling, and servicing of goods and services will be coordinated to contribute to the company's goals and objectives. We discussed ERPs in Chapter 2 and will explore them further in Chapter 7.

MULTI-AGENT SYSTEMS AND AGENT-BASED MODELLING

What do cargo transport systems, book distribution centres, the video game market, a flu epidemic, and an ant colony have in common? They are all complex adaptive systems and thus share some common characteristics. By observing parts of the ecosystem, like ant or bee colonies, artificial intelligence scientists can use hardware and software models that incorporate insect characteristics and behaviour to (1) learn how people-based systems behave; (2) predict how they will behave under a given set of circumstances; and (3) improve human systems to make them more efficient and effective. This concept of learning from ecosystems and adapting their characteristics to human and organizational situations is called **biomimicry**.

In the last few years, AI research has made much progress in modelling complex organizations as a whole with the help of multi-agent systems. In a **multi-agent system**, groups of intelligent agents have the ability to work independently and to interact with each other. **Agent-based modelling** is a way of simulating human organizations using multiple intelligent agents, each of which follows a set of simple rules and can adapt to changing conditions.

Agent-based modelling systems are being used to model stock market fluctuations, predict the escape routes that people seek in a burning building, estimate the effects of interest rates on consumers with different types of debt, and anticipate how changes in conditions will affect the supply chain, to name just a few. See Figure 4.7 for examples of companies that have used agent-based modelling to their advantage.

Figure 4.7

Companies That Use
Agent-Based Modelling[36]

- Air Canada—to optimize cargo routing

- Procter & Gamble—to overhaul its handling of what the company calls its "supply network" of 5 billion consumers in 140 countries

- Air Liquide America—to reduce production and distribution costs of liquefied industrial gases

- Merck & Co.—to find more efficient ways of distributing anti-AIDS drugs in Africa

- Ford Motor Co.—to build a model of consumer preferences and find the best balance between production costs and customers' demands

- Edison Chouest Offshore LLC—to find the best way to deploy its service and supply vessels in the Gulf of Mexico

ANT COLONIES AND SWARM INTELLIGENCE

The ant ecosystem is one of the most widely used types of simulations in business problems. If you've ever tried to remove ants from your home, you know how determined and effective ant colonies are. Individual ants are autonomous, acting and reacting independently. (If you drop a crumb into the middle of a group of ants, they'll all scatter in different directions.) However, ants are unusual insects in that they are social. (Less than 2 percent of insects are social, with termites being the only other entirely social species, although some types of bees and wasps are, too.) The term "social" implies that all the members of a colony work together to establish and maintain a global system that's efficient and stable. So, even though the ants are autonomous, each ant contributes to the system as a whole. Ants have been on Earth for 40 million years, compared to the relatively short human occupation of 100 thousand years, and their extraordinary evolutionary success is the result of ants' collective behaviour, known as swarm intelligence.

Swarm (collective) intelligence is the collective behaviour of groups of simple agents that are capable of devising solutions to problems as they arise, eventually leading to coherent global patterns.[37] That is to say, complex collective behaviour can result from the individuals in the system consistently following a small number of simple rules. Swarm intelligence allows the creation and maintenance of systems that have the following four characteristics:

1. *Flexibility*, so that the system can respond to changes, both large and small, in the environment around it. In an ant colony, for example, if you move the food, the ants will find it again very quickly.

2. *Robustness*, so that even if some individual members of the system don't succeed, the work gets done. For example, if you remove some of the ants, others will step in and continue the work.

3. *Decentralization*, in that each individual has a relatively simple job to do and performs that job without supervision. In the ant colony there are forager ants, soldier ants that protect the nest, queens that produce the new generations, ants that take care of and feed the cocoons, and so on.

4. *Self-organization*, in that the methods of problem solving are not prescribed from a central authority, but rather are developed as problem-solving strategies by the individuals in the group that are responsible for the completion of the work. For example, if an ant finds a food morsel that's too large for one ant to carry, others come to help and they run around changing positions until they have the morsel balanced well enough that they can carry it off. See the Web site at web.mac.com/camazine/Camazine/Greeting_page.html for other examples of self-organization in nature.[38]

So, how are the workings of ant colonies related to information technology in modern business? Swarm intelligence gives us a way to examine collective systems where groups of individuals have certain goals, solve problems, and make decisions without centralized control or a common plan.

A comparison of the activities of forager ants and those of the cargo-handling arm of Southwest Airlines affords a striking example of the similarities between ecosystems and human organizations, which we will consider shortly. There are some uncanny parallels that surprised Southwest's management. First, though, let's ponder the ants.

Forager ants have the sole responsibility of providing food to the colony. They don't form committees and discuss strategies or look to a central authority for direction; they just find food and bring it back to the nest, and in doing so they follow a simple procedure.

Say two ants (A and B) leave the same point to search for food. Ant A finds food first because ant B has to traverse around several rocks before finding food (i.e., Ant A found a shorter route to the food). Having found a food source, Ant A returns to the nest by the same route, leaving behind a trail of pheromones (a biological bread crumb trail) so that it will know what path to take next time and so will the other ants. The first ant that returns "lays the trail" first so that's the one that other ants take. Then the other ants strengthen the pheromone trail on their return journey by leaving their own pheromone tracks along the path Ant A found.

Meanwhile, Ant B arrives back at the nest after the shorter path has already been established. The other ants that are already on the move don't change their route. The pheromone trail on the unused path (that left by ant B) evaporates after a certain length of time so that it's effectively deleted from the system as a desirable route to food. The approach is straightforward but effective, and can be expressed in the following rules:

- Rule 1: Follow the trail if one exists; otherwise, create one.
- Rule 2: Find food.
- Rule 3: Return to the nest, making a pheromone trail.

If changes occur (say, for example, that the food source is removed), the ants cease returning to the place where the food used to be, and the trail disappears. Then the process begins again, and proceeds relentlessly, with forager ants finding a new food source and creating pheromone corridors that lead the way.

The problem that the ants have just solved is one of the oldest problems that humans (as well as ants) have faced. It's known as "the shortest path problem" or the "travelling salesman problem." Anyone who schedules drop-off and pick-up routes for delivery trucks, or schedules jobs on the factory floor, or even colours maps, making sure that no two adjacent components have the same colour, has had to find a solution to the same type of problem.

Taking their cue from nature, AI researchers built sets of small robots and incorporated software that allowed the robots to follow rules and interact with each other in the same basic ways as the ants. They also dispensed with the physical forms altogether, creating virtual ants in the form of small autonomous blocks of code that we call intelligent agents. And each code block could follow certain rules, interact, and adapt. These virtual ants were then arranged into multi-agent systems that were further refined into agent-based models. Enter Southwest Airlines as a case in point.

Even though cargo is a small part of Southwest's business, it was causing management headaches and bottlenecks at busy airports. Southwest consulted with swarm intelligence experts, who used a virtual model of foraging ants to simulate the cargo-handling process. And that was how Southwest managers discovered, to their surprise, that there were actually better ways to handle cargo than to put it on the first plane flying in the right direction. Surprisingly, the computer's swarm intelligence model showed that it might actually be better to leave cargo on a plane heading in the wrong direction. For example, cargo headed from Chicago to Boston would be better left on a plane going from Chicago to Atlanta and then reloaded onto a flight to Boston, requiring less unloading and reloading. Following the ant model, Southwest decreased its cargo transfer rates by 80 percent, reduced the workload of cargo employees by 20 percent, and also found that there was spare cargo space on flights that were previously full, enabling the company to accept more business. The overall gain to Southwest was in excess of $10 million per year.[39]

The future will see many more uses of intelligent agents. It's a pretty safe bet that these applications will include swarm intelligence and agent-based modelling. Already, swarm intelligence is being implemented widely for scheduling, resource allocation, and routing. Other applications in the early stages include networks that have self-organizing components and robots that assemble themselves. There must be many, many more that have not yet been dreamt of. Some people believe that intelligent agents will replace many of the other types of simulations in the future since swarm intelligence supports individuality, flexibility, and entities that can adapt quickly and effectively in a fast-changing business environment.

Summary: STUDENT LEARNING OUTCOMES *REVISITED*

LO1 Compare and contrast decision support systems and geographic information systems. A *decision support system (DSS)* is a highly flexible and interactive IT system that is designed to support decision making when the problem is not structured. A *geographic information system (GIS)* is a decision support system designed specifically to analyze spatial information. So they both are designed to support decision-making efforts. While traditional DSSs mainly use text and numeric data, GISs represent many types of information in spatial or map form.

LO2 Understand expert systems and describe the types of problems to which they apply. An *expert system* (or *knowledge-based system*) is an artificial intelligence system that applies reasoning capabilities to reach a conclusion. A rule-based expert system asks the user questions and, based on the answers, asks other questions until it has enough information to make a decision or a recommendation. Expert systems are good for diagnostic (what's wrong) and prescriptive problems (what to do). For example, you could use an expert system to diagnose illness or to figure out why a machine is malfunctioning. And you could use an expert system to determine what to do about the problem.

LO3 Understand neural networks and fuzzy logic and the uses of these AI tools. A neural network (also called an *artificial neural network* or *ANN*) is an artificial intelligence system that is capable of finding and differentiating patterns. Neural networks are good for finding commonalities in situations that have many variables. *Fuzzy logic* is a mathematical method of handling imprecise or subjective information. It is used to represent relative terms such as "hot" and "cold" so that a computer can use them in processing.

LO4 Define genetic algorithms and list some concepts on which they are based and the types of problems they solve. A *genetic algorithm* is an artificial intelligence system that mimics the evolutionary, survival-of-the-fittest process to generate increasingly better solutions to a problem. Genetic algorithms use the principles of *selection*, *crossover*, and *mutation* from evolution theory. These systems are best suited to problems where hundreds or thousands of solutions are possible and you need an optimum solution.

LO5 Describe the four types of agent-based technologies. An *intelligent agent* is software that assists you, or acts on your behalf, in performing repetitive computer-related tasks.

- *Information agents*, the most common of which are *buyer agents* (or *shopping bots*), search the Web for products and services.
- *Monitoring-and-surveillance agents* (or *predictive agents*) track conditions, perhaps on a network, and signal changes or troublesome conditions.
- *Data-mining agents* search data warehouses to discover information.
- *User agents* (or *personal agents*) take action for you, particularly in repetitive tasks like sorting e-mail.

Two emerging variants within agent-based technologies are (1) *multi-agent systems*, groups of intelligent agents that have the ability to work independently and to interact with each other, and (2) *agent-based modelling*, a way of simulating human organizations using multiple intelligent agents, each of which follows a set of simple rules and can adapt to changing conditions. Both are based on *biomimicry*, learning from ecosystems and adapting their characteristics to human and organizational situations.

CLOSING CASE STUDY 1
Crystal Ball, Clairvoyant, Fortune Telling ...
Can Predictive Analytics Deliver the Future?

In the Tom Cruise movie *Minority Report* police were able to accurately predict a crime, its location, and the criminal in advance of the event in time to send police to prevent the crime from occurring. Science fiction at its best, eh? Actually, that's somewhat of a reality now through predictive analytics.

Predictive analytics encompasses a variety of decision tools and techniques—such as data mining, statistics, neural networks, decision trees, and Bayesian networks—to analyze current and historical data and make predictions about the likelihood of the occurrence of future events. In business, predictive models exploit patterns founds in historical and transactional data to identify risks and opportunities. Models capture relationships among many factors to allow assessment of risk or potential associated with a particular set of conditions, guiding decision making for candidate transactions.

Along the lines of *Minority Report*, police in Richmond, Virginia, are using predictive analytics to determine the likelihood (probability) that a particular type of crime will occur in a specific neighbourhood at a specific time. Using the system, the mobile task force of 30 officers is deployed to the areas with the greatest likelihood of crimes occurring. According to Richmond Police Chief, Rodney Moore, "Based on the predictive models, we deploy them [the mobile task force] almost every three or four hours." Sixteen fugitives have been arrested directly as a result of the system's prediction of the next time and location of a crime. Moreover, in the first week of May 2006, no homicides occurred, compared to three in the same week of the previous year.

The predictive analytics system uses large databases that contain information on past calls to police, arrests, crime logs, current weather data, and local festivals and sporting and other events. From an IT point of view, the system is a combination of software—SPSS's Clementine predictive analysis software and reporting and visualization tools from Information Builder—and decision support and predictive models developed by RTI International.

The Richmond police afford just one of many examples of the use of predictive analytics. Some others include the following:

- SaskTel, a Saskatchewan-based telecommunications firm, uses a marketing automation tool from analytics software vendor SAS Institute Inc. to improve its customer contact and retention initiatives. The tool will enable SaskTel to quickly and effectively create and support marketing campaign strategies for its high-speed Internet and digital TV service bundles.

- FedEx uses a predictive analytics system that delivers accurate results significantly more often than would be expected based on chance alone. The system predicts how customers will respond to new services and price changes. It also predicts which customers will no longer use FedEx as a result of a price increase and how much additional revenue the company will generate from proposed drop-box locations.

- Marks & Spencer recently found that its stock and market share was declining. While the British retailer was focused on operational efficiencies, it wasn't tuned into what customers wanted. After looking at purchase data and applying business analytics, it was able to come up with 11 different customer clusters and tailor its marketing efforts toward each cluster. The result has been increased revenue, increased customer satisfaction, and better stock performance.

- HSBC Financial has embraced the movement toward plotting consumer behaviour patterns before loans fall delinquent, a trend emerging in risk management and collections work, fields that too often had counted on treating problem loans when it was too late to cure them. Risk management today is more about science than art and instincts. The Canadian arm of HSBC is based in Toronto, Ontario, and uses predictive analytics technology to identify high- and low-credit risks during the application process. The idea is to set corresponding credit limits and interest rates. Once an account is on the books, HSBC applies its modelling techniques while gathering real-time behavioural data. Accounts that look like they are becoming delinquent

www.mcgrawhill.ca/olc/haag

are flagged so that the marketing department avoids cross-, and other upsell opportunities that could increase HSBC's risk exposure.

The future of predictive analytics is very bright. Sales of predictive analytics software are expected to reach $3 billion by 2008. Moreover, businesses are beginning to build predictive analytics into mainstream, operational applications—such as CRM, SCM, and inventory management—which will further increase their use. But a huge number of customers are still using spreadsheets, gut instinct or the "backs of envelopes" to analyze their data. One reason to use business analytics is flawed data. For example, if an application asks for a customer's birthday as a required field, some customers will simply type in "11/11/11" if they don't want to provide that information to the company. This could lead company execs to think that many of their customers are seniors, which could result in an ineffective marketing campaign.[40, 41, 42, 43]

Questions

1. Many predictive analytic models are based on neural network technologies. What is the role of neural networks in predictive analytics? How can neural networks help predict the likelihood of future events?

2. What if the Richmond police began to add demographic data to their predictive analytics system to further attempt to determine the type of person (by demographic) who would in all likelihood commit a crime? Is predicting the type of person who would commit a crime by demographic data (ethnicity, gender, income level, and so on) good or bad?

3. In the movie *Gattaca* predictive analytics were used to determine the most successful career for a person. Based on DNA information, the system determined whether or not an individual was able to advance through an educational track to become something like an engineer or if the person should complete only a lower level of education and become a janitor. The government then acted on the system's recommendations and placed people in various career tracks. Is this a good or bad use of technology? How is this different from the variety of personal tests you can take that inform you of your aptitude for different careers?

4. What role can geographic information systems (GISs) play in the use of predictive analytics? As you answer this question, specifically reference FedEx's use of predictive analytics to (1) determine which customers will not respond positively to a price increase and (2) project additional revenues from proposed drop-box locations.

5. The U.S. Department of Defense (DoD) and the Pacific Northwest National Laboratory are combining predictive analytics with visualization technologies to predict the probability that a terrorist attack will occur. For example, suspected terrorists caught on security cameras who loiter too long in a given place might signal their intent to carry out a terrorist attack. How can this type of predictive analytics be used in an airport? At what other buildings and structures might this be used?

CLOSING CASE STUDY 2
Closing the Great Health Care Divide with Pattern Recognition and Data-Mining Technologies

In today's world, people, cultures, and nations are distinguished by which side of the *"great divides"* they are on. There are the financial and economic divides, which differentiate between the haves and have-nots with respect to wealth, income, and prosperity. There are the educational divides that distinguish among people on the basis of their access to education and according to whether a post-secondary degree is achieved. There is a "great digital divide," on either side of which are those who have or do not have access to technology.

Worldwide—and certainly in the United States—is a health care divide between those who can and cannot afford good health care. With health care costs spiralling out of control, the health care divide is widening and the population with access to affordable health care is shrinking. Therefore, many health care providers and technology providers such as IBM, the Mayo Clinic, and the Cleveland Clinic are collaborating on IT–enabled strategies to reduce the cost of health care while providing better health care than ever before.

IBM and the Mayo Clinic are collaborating on cost-efficient ways to provide customized medical treatments to individual patients, such as choosing the right chemotherapy treatment for a specific patient given his or her unique genetic makeup, by applying pattern recognition and data-mining technologies to the electronic medical records of some 4.4 million patients.

In the first phase of the project, IBM and the Mayo Clinic worked together to consolidate into one database all patients' medical records from numerous separate systems—including digitized (electronic) patient files, lab results, X-rays, and electrocardiograms—and from all of Mayo's hospitals in Arizona, Florida, and Minnesota. In the second phase, IBM and the Mayo Clinic are applying pattern recognition, data-mining technologies, and other decision support tools to help health care providers determine the best therapies for each patient. The goal of the decision support system is to find patterns relating to how well different types of patients respond to certain types of therapies. The system sifts through patient information concerning age, medical history, and genetics to find patterns that suggest the best treatments.

For example, the Mayo Clinic recently began using a new chemotherapy treatment for lung cancer that produced disappointing results, despite all the positive research findings. The decision support system, however, was able to determine that a small percentage of patients, all with the same genetic pattern, did respond positively to the therapy, which is now targeted for only those individuals matching that genetic profile.

Similarly, IBM and the Cleveland Clinic are working on a decision support system to identify patients most susceptible to abdominal aortic aneurysms. The presence of aneurysms often results In no symptoms until the aneurysm is about to rupture, and the survival rate of the rupture is less than 50 percent.

According to Dr. Kenneth Ouriel, chairman of the Division of Surgery and the Department of Vascular Surgery at the Cleveland Clinic, "If we can predict what patients are at risk for these ruptures, we can identify the patients who need surgery or other treatments." To identify such patients, the system evaluates a wealth of information including lab, genetic, imaging, and drug history and how different factors contribute to risks as well as to treatment outcomes.[44, 45, 46]

Questions

1. In the case study, we referred to the systems being developed and used as *decision support systems*. However, we also identified various artificial intelligence (AI) technologies. How can a decision support system incorporate and use AI technologies such as pattern recognition?

2. At the Mayo Clinic, patients are given opt-in and opt-out rights concerning whether or not their information is used in the system that determines the most appropriate therapies given the specific patient profile. So far, 95 percent of the patients have opted to have their information included in the system. (This is the notion of *opting in*.) Why do you believe that 5 percent of the patients have opted out? Would you opt in or opt out in this case? Provide your reasoning.

3. In this case, demographic information such as ethnicity, gender, and age greatly impacts the quality of the decision support and analysis. The same could be argued for the predictive analytics system used by the Richmond police in this chapter's first case study. Why would some people find it acceptable to use such demographic data in this case (for medical purposes) and not in the first case (for predicting crime, its location, and its timing)?

4. One of the most popular and widely used application areas for expert systems is medicine. What role could an expert system play in helping the Cleveland Clinic identify patients susceptible to abdominal aortic aneurysms? What sort of rules would the expert system include?

5. How might a monitoring-and-surveillance agent be used for patients in a medical environment? How can health care providers take advantage of the capabilities of an information agent to stay abreast of the latest medical trends and treatments?

www.mcgrawhill.ca/olc/haag

Key Terms and Concepts

Agent-based modelling, 115
Artificial intelligence (AI), 104
Artificial neural network, 107
Biomimicry, 115
Buyer agent (shopping bot), 112
Choice, 96
Crossover, 110
Data management, 100
Data-mining agent, 114
Decision support system (DSS), 98
Design, 96
Expert system (knowledge-based system), 105
Fuzzy logic, 109

Genetic algorithm, 110
Geographic information system (GIS), 102
Implementation, 96
Information agent, 112
Intelligence, 96
Intelligent agent, 111
Location mashup, 104
Mashup, 104
Model management, 99
Monitoring-and-surveillance agent (predictive agent), 113
Multi-agent system, 115

Mutation, 110
Neural network (artificial neural network, ANN), 107
Nonrecurring (ad hoc) decision, 97
Nonstructured decision, 97
Predictive analytics, 119
Recurring decision, 97
Satisficing, 96
Selection, 110
Structured decision, 97
Swarm (collective) intelligence, 116
User agent (personal agent), 114
User interface management, 101

Short-Answer Questions

1. What are the four types of decisions discussed in this chapter? Give an example of each.
2. What are the four steps in making a decision?
3. What is a DSS? Describe its components.
4. What is a geographic information system used for?
5. How is information represented in a geographic information system?
6. What is artificial intelligence? Name the artificial intelligence systems used widely in business.

7. What are the advantages of an expert system?
8. What sort of problems is an expert system used for?
9. How does a neural network work?
10. What three concepts of evolution are used by the genetic algorithm?
11. What are intelligent agents? What tasks can they perform?
12. What is a multi-agent system?
13. What do monitoring-and-surveillance agents do?

Assignments and Exercises

1. **MAKE A GIS** Make a GIS-type map using transparencies. Draw a map of your campus on one plastic transparency sheet. You can use software or felt-tip pens to do the actual drawing of the map. Next, use a second sheet as an overlay and mark on it what classes you have taken in what buildings. Take a third sheet and enter the type of classroom you had the course in (e.g., auditorium, lab, small, medium, large room). Make a fourth layer with special facilities, like a computer lab or a biology lab, and so on. What problems did you encounter while designing your GIS? What other information would you like to see in a real GIS of this type? Would this handmade GIS be helpful for new students? What layers would you keep for general use? What layers would you keep for sentimental value when your post-secondary days are over?

2. **CHOOSE A FINANCING OPTION** Using a spreadsheet (like Excel, for example) evaluate your options for a $20,000 car. Compare the payments (use the $pmt function in Excel), the total amount of interest, and the total you'll pay for the car under the following four options:

a. 3 years at 0 percent interest
b. 2 years at 1.99 percent annual percent rate (APR)
c. 4 years at 5 percent APR
d. 6 years at 6 percent APR

What other considerations would you take into account if you were going to buy a new car? Are there considerations other than the interest rate and the other parts that can be calculated? What are they? How is a car different from other purchases, such as CDs or TV sets or computers?

3. **WHICH SOFTWARE WOULD YOU USE?** Which type or types of computer-aided decision support software would you use for each of the situations in the list below? Note why you think each of your choices is appropriate. The decision support alternatives are

- Decision support system
- Geographic information system
- Expert system
- Neural network
- Genetic algorithm
- Intelligent agent

4. **WHAT SHOULD THE MUSIC STORE OWNER DO?** A music store owner wants to have enough of the hottest CDs in stock so that people who come in to buy a particular CD won't be disappointed—and the store won't lose the profit. CDs that are not sold within a certain length of time go onto the sale table where they may have to be sold at cost, if they sell at all.

The owner wants to design a decision support system to predict how many copies she should purchase and what information she will need. List some of the considerations that would go into such a system. Here are a couple to start you off: (1) the population of the target market; (2) sales for particular types of music in similar markets.

Problem	Type of Decision Support
You and another marketing executive on a different continent want to develop a new pricing structure for products.	
You want to predict when customers are about to take their business elsewhere.	
You want to fill out a short tax form.	
You want to determine the fastest route for package delivery to 23 different addresses in a city.	
You want to decide where to spend advertising dollars (TV, radio, newspaper, direct mail, e-mail).	
You want to keep track of competitors' prices for comparable goods and services.	

Discussion Questions

1. Some experts claim that if a business gets 52 percent of its decisions right, it will be successful. Would using a decision support system guarantee better results? Why or why not? What does the quality of any decision depend on? Do you think it matters what type of decisions are included in this 52 percent? For example, would getting the right type of paper clips be as influential a decision as deciding where to locate the business? Can you think of a situation where the type of paper clip matters a great deal?

2. Consider the topic of data warehouses in Chapter 3. In the future, AI systems will be increasingly applied to data warehouse processing. Which AI systems do you think might be helpful? For which tasks or situations might they best be applied? Do you think that AI systems will someday play a greater role in the design of databases and data warehouses? Why or why not?

3. Consider the differences and similarities among the four AI techniques discussed in this chapter.

Name some problems that might be amenable to more than one type of AI system. Say you sell baseballs from your Web site. What types of AI systems could you use to generate information that would be useful to you in deciding what direction to take your company in the future? If you were pretty successful at selling baseballs, would you expect to have the amount of information on customers that, say, Walmart has? Why or why not?

4. AI systems are relatively new approaches to solving business problems. What are the difficulties with new IT approaches in general? For each of the systems we discussed, identify some advantages and disadvantages of AI systems over traditional business processes. Say you were selling specialty teas and had both click-and-mortar stores. Would you use the same type of AI systems for each part of your business? In what way would you use them or why would you not? Is there a place for decision support and artificial intelligence techniques in small specialty businesses? In what way would decision support add value? Can you think of how a DSS or an AI system would be value reducing (in terms of the value chain concept we discussed in Chapter 1)? What do you see as the major differences between running a mammoth concern and a small specialty business?

5. Neural networks recognize and categorize patterns. If someone were to have a neural network that could scan information on all aspects of your life, where would that neural network potentially be able to find information about you? Consider confidential (doctor's office) as well as publicly available (provincial ministry of transportation) information.

6. What type of AI systems could your school use to help with registration? Intelligent agents find vast amounts of information very quickly. Neural networks can classify patterns instantaneously. What sorts of information might your school administration be able to generate using these (or other AI systems) with all of its student data?

7. For which activities that are part of post-secondary life could you use agent-based modelling to simulate what happens? Describe three such scenarios.

Chapter 5

Electronic Commerce
Strategies for the New Economy

STUDENT LEARNING OUTCOMES

LO1 Describe the major e-commerce business models.

LO2 Identify the differences and similarities among customers and their perceived value of products and services in the B2B and B2C e-commerce business models.

LO3 Compare and contrast the development of a marketing mix for customers in the B2B and B2C e-commerce business models.

LO4 Summarize ways of moving money in the world of e-commerce, and related issues.

LO5 Discuss major trends that are impacting both the e-commerce business world and society in general.

OPENING CASE STUDY
Will You Talk to Your Wallet?

The payment process is set to become a lot less painful. Forget loonies and toonies; you might soon be able to purchase your favourite snack or soft drink by simply waving your cellphone near a reader—an example of so-called "contactless" payment.

In commerce, especially e-commerce, one of the biggest stumbling blocks is getting customers to complete a transaction. On-line merchants pay particular attention to things such as abandoned shopping carts (filled by shop-

pers in the virtual store but never "wheeled" through the checkout) since such metrics can signal problems with the shopping experience, particularly with ease of payment. Thus if one of the barriers to closing a deal is the payment mechanism, then making it as easy as possible to pay is an important step to making mobile commerce (m-commerce) an accepted method of doing business. Enter the cell phone. Ubiquitous, small, efficient, accepted, and trusted. What better way to nudge suspicious

Canadians toward completing electronic transactions than to use something that's already in the pocket or purse of many shoppers?

To reduce transaction phobia, one of the industry's major challenges will be convincing Canadians that committing to a deal that doesn't require a signature or a PIN is, in fact, safe and secure. Canadians were early adopters and embracers of debit card technology (our rates still exceed those in the United States, for example) but with mobile payment, Canadians are showing some restraint. The technology grabbed hold in Asia before it was accepted here. When interviewed for a *Globe and Mail* article in 2007, Anne Koski, head of payments innovation at the Royal Bank of Canada's cards division, reported that Asia's early adoption of the technology was likely due to both geography and population demographics there.

"If you think about environments in Japan, Korea, places where you've got large populations in relatively small geographic spaces, then there's obviously a benefit to the merchant in making the payments process as fast as possible," she said. One place that such population density seems to come into play in Canada is around the ever-popular coffee chain, Tim Hortons. Despite the potential for creating snarled lineups of disgruntled customers, the chain announced a deal with MasterCard in summer 2007 using its PayPass contactless technology. As of late 2008, the system is still in use; something must have clicked.

In November 2007, RBC announced a partnership with Visa Canada to test contactless technology on cellphones, and began testing the concept at a lab in its head office. Ms Koski is hoping that by early 2009 the technology could be in customers' hands. "To do that, we would absolutely have to work with the telcos," she said. The top three wireless telcos in Canada are Bell, Rogers and Telus. While none is involved in the project, they all do belong to a joint venture called Wireless Payment Services (WPS) and are working on protocols and procedures to allow standardized wireless payments. Rob Burbach, a senior financial analyst with IDC Canada, said that for such a contactless payment system to be successful in Canada, numerous stakeholders, including the banks, telcos, phone manufacturers, and merchants would have get onboard.

VISA conducted a customer survey and found that more than half of respondents would be interested in using a phone with these types of mobile payment capabilities—not surprisingly, the majority of these are younger people, who, statistics show, carry their cell phones with them all the time—perhaps even more than their wallets. The technology uses Near Field Communication (NFC), in which contactless chips embedded in mobile phones allow customers to make purchases just as they would with a contactless device such as those that have been in use at Shell, Esso and Petro-Canada service stations for some time.

Other companies using PayPass and competing technology Tap & Go include Loblaw, Pioneer Petroleum, Cineplex Odeon Theatres, and, soon, Mcdonald's.[1, 2, 3, 4, 5]

How shopping by cellphone works:

1. An RFID chip-enabled phone is brought close to an RFID reader.

2. The RFID reader reads information from the cellphone's NFC chip and sends it to the Point of Sale (POS) application.

3. A POS validates the associated credit card info and sends it for authorization to the bank.

4. The back-office server forwards the transaction to the processor for authorization.

5. The processor validates the transaction, performs fraud check, and forwards to the card association for authorization.

6. The issuing bank authorizes purchase if valid and is within the credit limit, then returns the authorization code.

In this chapter, we'll explore the world of e-commerce, and we'll continue to introduce you to many considerations that you must take into account to be successful in e-commerce. Commerce will always be commerce—the buying and selling of products and services. But the "e" in e-commerce presents new challenges and opportunities.

Questions

1. What do you think of the explanation for the differential adoption rates of contactless payment solutions? Does demographics explain it all? Does culture play a role?

2. What do you think about the security of such systems? Would a $25 transaction limit satisfy your fear of fraud and theft?

3. What might places such as Tim Hortons do in order to make it easier to use such technology? What have you seen already that has addressed the issue of payment line delays?

4. What other applications for contactless payment systems can you envision?

Introduction

The new economy introduced by the World Wide Web has certainly been interesting. It has caused an entrepreneurial frenzy unlike anything the world has ever seen. Fortunes have been made and lost. Dot-com millionaires and billionaires were literally created overnight—many became dot-bomb paupers in about the same amount of time.

What fuelled this frenzy and is still doing so today? It's electronic commerce enabled by information technology. *Electronic commerce (e-commerce)* is commerce, but it is commerce accelerated and enhanced by IT, particularly Internet. E-commerce enables customers, consumers, and companies to form powerful new relationships that would not be possible without the enabling technologies. E-commerce breaks down business barriers such as time, geography, language, currency, and culture. In a few short hours, you can set up shop on the Internet and be instantly accessible to millions of consumers worldwide.

Is there a catch? The answer is both no and yes. It's "no" because it doesn't take much effort to create your own e-commerce Web site. It's "yes" because you still have to follow sound business fundamentals and principles to be successful. Let's not forget that fundamentally it's still all about commerce, businesses and people buying and selling products and services. E-commerce is no "silver bullet," as some entrepreneurs have found out to their chagrin.

In short, you must have a clear path-to-profitability. A *path-to-profitability (P2P)* is a formal business plan that outlines key business issues such as customer targets (by demographic, industry, etc.), marketing strategies, operations strategies (e.g., procurement, production, transportation, and logistics), and projected targets for income statement and balance sheet items. That is to say, running an e-commerce operation is no different from running a traditional bricks-and-mortar business. You must identify your customers, determine how to reach them with a compelling story, and so on. The major error that most dot-com businesses made in the late 1990s—and they are no longer in existence today—is that they never developed a clear *path-to-profitability*. Many had no experience with fulfillment—they could *attract* customers alright—but couldn't keep their own side of the agreement; they couldn't deliver. A crucial aspect of success in this era was whether or not the enterprise had a bricks-and-mortar presence beforehand. Many of those that did, survived. Too many of those that didn't, failed.

Figure 5.1

Nine Major E-Commerce
Business Models

SUPPLY
Business originating from ...

	BUSINESS	CONSUMER	GOVERNMENT
BUSINESS	B2B	C2B	G2B
CONSUMER	B2C	C2C	G2C
GOVERNMENT	B2G	C2G	G2G

DEMAND
And selling to ...

LO1

E-Commerce Business Models

As illustrated in Figure 5.1, there are nine major e-commerce business models. While we focus the majority of this chapter on business to business (B2B) e-commerce and business to consumer (B2C) e-commerce (both in the e-commerce private sector), let's start by exploring each e-commerce business model.

BUSINESS TO BUSINESS (B2B) E-COMMERCE

Business to business (B2B) e-commerce occurs when a business sells products and services to customers that are primarily other businesses. So, for example, when Gates Corporation, one of the world's largest manufacturers of industrial and automotive belts, sells belts, hoses, and other rubber and synthetic products to General Motors or any other manufacturer that needs those parts, this is B2B e-commerce. B2B e-commerce is where all the money is right now in the e-commerce world. It's not the flashy consumer-oriented businesses you read about and see every day such as eBay, MySpace, and so on. It's the many behind-the-scenes interactions that businesses engage in ultimately to support interacting with you as a customer, such as Gates selling a hose to General Motors for a car that you eventually buy. Another example is First Data Corporation. First Data is a payments infrastructure provider that many businesses use. When you pay with a credit card at most major stores, your credit card authorization and verification is handled by First Data for the store. You may not have even heard of First Data, but it is one of the top 250 largest corporations in the United States.

As you can see in Figure 5.2 (on the next page), businesses are taking full advantage of e-commerce by creating and using B2B e-marketplaces. *B2B e-marketplaces* are virtual marketplaces in which businesses buy from and sell products to each other, share information (as in information partnerships from Chapter 2), and perform other important activities. B2B e-marketplaces represent one of the fastest-growing trends in the B2B

Figure 5.2

Business-to-Business
and Business-to-Consumer
E-Commerce Business Models

e-commerce model. Businesses are increasingly aware that they must create supply chain management systems, drive down costs, create information partnerships with other businesses, and even collaborate with other businesses on new product and service offerings. B2B e-marketplaces offer tremendous efficiencies to businesses for performing all of these tasks.

BUSINESS TO CONSUMER (B2C) E-COMMERCE

Business to consumer (B2C) e-commerce occurs when a business sells products and services to customers who are primarily individuals. You are no doubt familiar with this model of e-commerce. If you've ever ordered a book on Chapters Web site (www.chapters.indigo.ca), purchased a CD from Future Shop on-line (www.futureshop.ca), or ordered a movie from zip.ca (www.zip.ca), you've participated in B2C e-commerce.

B2C e-commerce garners most of the attention these days in the popular media. B2C e-commerce is the model that fuelled the early growth of e-commerce in the 1990s. B2C e-commerce is very much a cut-throat environment, no matter what the product and service. Amazon, one of the most well-known B2C businesses, faces stiff competition from hundreds of other e-commerce businesses selling books, movies, music, clothing, computers, consumer electronics, health and beauty products, and home and garden products.

As you can see in Figure 5.2, the B2C e-commerce business model is very different from the B2B e-commerce business model. Consumers interact directly with businesses via the Web. Consumers surf around the Web evaluating products and services at numerous separate e-commerce sites until they eventually choose one site from which to make a purchase. And while businesses prefer to enter into long-term partnerships with other businesses in B2B e-commerce, consumers are fickle and purchase the same types of products and services from many different sites.

BUSINESS TO GOVERNMENT (B2G) E-COMMERCE

Business to government (B2G) e-commerce occurs when a business sells products and services to a government entity. Lockheed Martin, for example, generates almost 80 percent of its revenue by providing products and services to the U.S. Department of Defense (DoD).[6] Lockheed Martin sells tactical aircraft, aeronautical research equipment, commercial satellites, government satellites, strategic missiles, naval systems, and IT equipment and services to the U.S. federal government, much of it procured and managed through e-channels.

The Government of Canada spends about $20 billion a year on goods and services. The Government Electronic Tendering Service, through MERX (www.merx.com), is the Government of Canada's tool for advertising government procurement opportunities. Once bids have been received, Public Works and Government Services Canada (PWGSC) and government departments work together to evaluate the bids based on predetermined criteria, and the supplier that offers the best value wins the contract. PWGSC uses MERX to advertise most requirements for printing services, goods and services, communications services, construction and leasing services, and architectural and engineering consulting services.

CONSUMER TO BUSINESS (C2B) E-COMMERCE

Consumer to business (C2B) e-commerce occurs when an individual sells products and services to a business. The C2B e-commerce business model is a true inversion of the B2C e-commerce business model. In the B2C e-commerce business model, demand is driven by the consumer and supply is driven by the business. In C2B it is inverted; the consumer drives supply and the business drives demand.[7] Many people have mistakenly lumped such sites as Priceline.com (www.priceline.com) into the C2B category. At Priceline.com you, as a consumer, can set your price for items such as airlines tickets and hotel rooms, but you (as a consumer) still provide the demand and the airline or hotel still provides the supply.

A good example of a true C2B e-commerce business model is offered by Fotolia (www.fotolia.com). There, as an individual, you can post your photos and videos for sale to businesses. Businesses search through the photo and video archives, and, if they choose yours, will pay you a royalty fee to use the photo or video.

Affiliate programs are another good example of the C2B e-commerce business model. Through an affiliate program relationship with Amazon, for example, you can post links on your personal Web site to Amazon for products and services it sells. If a visitor to your site clicks on one of those links and eventually buys the product or service from Amazon, Amazon will pay you a commission fee, which is usually some small percentage of the sale. With this arrangement, you are selling advertising space to Amazon on your Web site; hence, it is an example of the C2B e-commerce business model.

Currently, the C2B e-commerce business model represents only a fraction of the total revenues in the e-commerce space, but it is expected to grow as businesses realize that individuals are more than just consumers of products and services. Blogging, for example, can easily become a C2B e-commerce business model, if you know what you're doing.

CONSUMER TO CONSUMER (C2C) E-COMMERCE

Consumer to consumer (C2C) e-commerce occurs when an individual sells products and services to another individual. C2C e-commerce usually takes place through an intermediary organization, such as eBay. eBay is a hybrid of both a B2C e-commerce site and a C2C e-commerce site. It is a B2C e-commerce site because it sells a service to you, that of giving you the ability to interact in the auctioning of items. (You pay eBay only if you're the seller, not the buyer.) And it is really an intermediary supporting your engagement in a C2C e-commerce business model. That is, you use eBay to sell products and services to other consumers, and you use eBay to buy products and services from other consumers.

Many C2C Web sites don't really support any sort of e-commerce (i.e., money exchanging hands for products and services). Rather, they facilitate the gathering of people with common interests and something to share. Kazaa (www.kazaa.com) is an example of such a site because it brings together people who want to share mainly MP3 music files. Blogs might also fall into the category of C2C, as they support people sharing and discussing common interests. Many of these types of sites are *ad supported*, meaning that they derive their revenue by selling advertising space, much like the concept of an affiliate program.

CONSUMER TO GOVERNMENT (C2G) E-COMMERCE

Consumer to government (C2G) e-commerce occurs when an individual sells products and services to a government entity. This is very similar to the C2B e-commerce business model, except that the buying partner is a government entity, not a business. The C2G market is quite small, and, to say the least, unremarkable. In this context, part of the issue is that the Canadian government does not engage in buying products and services from individuals. For example, you must register in the Supplier Registration Information (SRI) service as a potential supplier to the Government of Canada. An important feature of SRI is the Procurement Business Number (PBN) created using your Canada Revenue Agency (CRA) Business Number.

GOVERNMENT TO BUSINESS (G2B) E-COMMERCE

Government to business (G2B) e-commerce occurs when a government entity sells products and services to businesses. There are several good examples within this e-commerce business model.

The first is the Canada Small Business Financing (CSBF) Program (http://strategis. ic.gc.ca/epic/site/csbfp-pfpec.nsf/en/home). The program's objectives are to streamline loan administration to small-and medium-size enterprises that would be unable to get financing on their own. It does this by encouraging financial institutions to make their financing available to small businesses. Under the program, a small business must apply for a loan at a financial institution (bank, credit union, or *caisse populaire*) of its choice. If the loan is granted by the financial institution, the federal government will reimburse 85 percent of the lender's losses in the event of default.

Another example is government-surplus auctions. At all levels of government—local, provincial/territorial, and federal—many entities sell off government surplus, often to individuals but sometimes to only registered businesses. For example, British Columbia holds frequent auctions, called Asset Investment Recovery (AIR) to sell off surplus assets, such as art, boats, computers, and office furniture.

Some branches of government also sell information to businesses wanting to perform research. While much of the information gathered by Statistics Canada is freely and publicly available, a business can buy more detailed information (none of it sensitive, of course).

GOVERNMENT TO CONSUMER (G2C) E-COMMERCE

Government to consumer (G2C) e-commerce refers to the electronic commerce activities performed between a government and its citizens or consumers, including paying taxes, registering vehicles, providing information and services, and so on. This particular model of e-commerce does not often fit well within the supply-and-demand notion. In the B2C model for example, Amazon has the supply of books, movies, and other products, and you—as a consumer—provide the demand. In the G2C model, a government often provides citizens with the ability to interact with it electronically to achieve efficiencies. Paying your taxes is an example. You can file your taxes electronically and receive your refund (or pay additional taxes) electronically. The notion of supply and demand isn't particularly applicable in this case.

In many instances, you can expect the Canadian government (and provincial/territorial governments) to do this to such an extent that it is no longer a click-and-mortar enterprise but rather a click-and-order enterprise. *Click-and-mortar* refers to an organization that has a presence in the physical world such as a building you can visit and also a presence in the virtual world of the Internet, while *click-and-order* (also known as *pure play*) refers to an organization that has a presence in the virtual world but no presence in the physical world. One such example is buying, holding, and redeeming Canadian savings bonds (CSB). The Government of Canada (www.csb.gc.ca/eng/bonds_buy.asp) allows individuals to set up an account, buy savings bonds, check the maturation status and redeemable value of the bonds, and even redeem the bonds, all electronically. In the United States, the federal government is aggressively moving in the direction of this being the only way you can buy, sell, and redeem savings bonds.

GOVERNMENT TO GOVERNMENT (G2G) E-COMMERCE

Government to government (G2G) e-commerce refers to the electronic commerce activities performed within a nation's government. (It might also refer to the electronic commerce activities performed between two or more nations' governments including providing foreign aid.)

Vertical government integration refers to electronic integration of agencies, activities, and processes up and down federal, provincial/territorial, and local government levels. For example, if a manufacturing operation will be creating landfills of waste and pumping sanitized fluids into rivers and streams, it must meet the *Canadian Environmental Protection Act* (CEPA), 1999. As each level of government has powers to protect the environment, the CEPA allows close cooperation among the federal, provincial, territorial, and aboriginal governments. Thus, those levels requiring CEPA standards would integrate their IT systems to share information about that manufacturing operation. Another example here falls in the education arena. At all levels of government, there must be information sharing concerning K–12 education standards, test results, and the like.

Horizontal government integration refers to the electronic integration of agencies, activities, and processes across a specific level of government. For example, at the federal level, the CEPA may work with Health Canada to develop standards for food processing plants that emit gases into the atmosphere as a result of their operations. The CEPA and Health Canada share this information horizontally to ensure that each food processing plant is meeting both sets of guidelines (i.e., CEPA guidelines and Health Canada guidelines). Another good example here is that of the armed forces and Veterans Affairs Canada. As a member of the armed forces moves from active service to retired personnel (through retirement, injury, etc.), a large amount of information must be communicated to Veterans Affairs, including vitally important medical information.

That ends our overview of the nine e-commerce business models. Although conceptually distinct, in practice each overlaps with one or more of the other models. The question for you now is how to execute on the e-commerce model in which your business operates. We'll focus specifically on B2B and B2C e-commerce, since that is where you'll most likely be working. We will explore three e-commerce *critical success factors*: (1) understand your business, products, services, and customers; (2) find and establish relationships with customers; (3) move money easily and securely.

Understand Your Business, Products, Services, and Customers

To gain a competitive advantage and be successful in any business, you must clearly define the nature of your products and services, know who your target customers are, and understand how your customers perceive the use of your products and services in their business activities (for the B2B model) or in their personal lives (for the B2C model). To create sound business strategies you have to understand the value that your customers place on your products and services.

There are many worthwhile business activities. But as important as writing a mission statement and producing glitzy marketing brochures may be, what must come first is an objective, very down-to-earth understanding of what your business does. The reality is that you can't be all things to all customers. You must answer two questions: (1) Who are your target customers? and (2) What is the value of your products and services as perceived by your customers? Let's look at each in turn.

WHO ARE YOUR CUSTOMERS?

Just as in a bricks-and-mortar business, in the e-commerce world you focus your efforts on selling to other businesses, to individual end-consumers, or to some combination of the two. If you were in a business like Gates Corporation, which produces mostly rubber and synthetic products primarily for sale to the automotive industry and manufacturers of products such as boats and bicycles, you would focus almost exclusively on the B2B e-commerce model, with other businesses as your target customers. If, however, you were selling résumé writing and job placement services to individuals looking for careers, your customers would be B2C individual end-consumers. Finally, you might be like Monster.ca (www.monster.ca), which provides an electronic marketplace catering to both individuals looking for careers and businesses looking for employees. If you were in a business like Monster's, your customer mix would include both end-consumers and businesses and you'd need to carefully consider both groups of customers, their needs, and the value to them of the products and services you sell.

Many businesses in the travel industry, American Express for example, cater to both businesses and end-consumers. As an individual consumer, you might work with American Express to plan and pay for a vacation. At the same time, many businesses use the services of American Express to handle all their business travel needs.

Whatever the nature of your business, you must know who your customers are. In the world of e-commerce, that means clearly distinguishing between end-consumers (B2C) and other businesses (B2B), even if you target both. As you will see throughout this chapter, individual end-consumers and other businesses have dramatically different needs.

WHAT IS THE VALUE OF YOUR PRODUCTS AND SERVICES AS PERCEIVED BY YOUR CUSTOMERS?

If a customer orders a product or service from your organization, it is because that customer perceives some value in what you provide—the customer either *wants* or *needs* your product or service. When we examine wants and needs, the distinctions between end-consumers and businesses as customers become increasingly important and clearly evident. Let's look at product/service categories needed by each customer group in turn.

B2C: CONVENIENCE VERSUS SPECIALTY   In many respects, you can differentiate between *convenience* and specialty merchandise (or services) on the basis of price and consumers' frequency of purchase. To end-consumers, convenience merchandise is typically lower priced but something they often need, usually frequently. Non-perishable food items such as breakfast cereals are a good example. From organizations such as Canada Grocer (www.canadagrocer.ca) you can easily order food items and have them delivered to your home within seven business days by Canada Post. Consumers might pay more for these low-priced items in order to have them "conveniently."

Specialty merchandise might be such things as home sound systems, computers, name-brand clothing, furniture, and the like. For consumers, these are higher-priced (than convenience merchandise) items, are typically ordered on a less-frequent basis, and often require some sort of customization or feature specification. For specialty merchandise, consumers will spend more time "shopping around," not only to find the best deal in terms of price but also because value for these items is perceived in terms of customization, warranty, service, and other after-sales features.

B2C: COMMODITY-LIKE AND DIGITAL   In B2C e-commerce, as a general rule, the best merchandise to sell is either commodity-like, digital, or a combination of the two. This enables you to minimize your internal costs, but requires that you be innovative in how you offer your merchandise and attract consumers to your site.

Commodity-like merchandise, to your customers, is the same regardless of where they purchase it, and it is similar to convenience items in that respect. Books are a good example. No matter where you buy a particular book, it is the same. As a business, you compete in a commodity-like environment on the basis of

- Price
- Ease of ordering
- Ease and speed of delivery
- Your return policy.

Figure 5.3

B2C and B2B Products and Services

Business to Consumer (B2C)	Business to Business (B2B)
• **Convenience**—low priced but something needed on a frequent basis	• **Maintenance, repair, and operations (MRO) materials**—necessary items that do not relate directly to the company's primary business activities
• **Specialty**—higher priced, ordered on a less frequent basis, and often requiring customization	• **Direct materials**—materials used in production in a manufacturing company or placed on the shelf for sale in a retail environment
• **Commodity-like**—the same no matter where you buy it	
• **Digital**—the best of all because of low cost of inventory and shipping	

Of course, commodity-like business environments are typically easy to enter (i.e., they have low barriers to entry) and thus buyer power is high (from Porter's Five Forces Model in Chapter 1). Your organization's goals in this type of environment would have to include (1) minimizing price to the end-consumer and (2) minimizing your internal costs by creating a tight supply chain management system (from Chapter 2). You also want to create a "sticky" Web site that not only attracts consumers but also encourages them to return to your site again and again.

Digital merchandise offerings are also important in the B2C e-commerce model. The goal here is to eliminate shipping costs by delivering the digital product over the Internet once a consumer has made a purchase. Music is a good example. Apple's iTunes Web site (www.apple.com/itunes/store) allows you to select exactly the song you want, pay for it, and then download it from the Internet. Apple can offer each song for just 99 cents because it has no physical delivery costs and no physical inventory. As this example illustrates, digital products are also advantageous (to the business and to the consumer) because they are customizable. That is, customers don't have to purchase an entire music CD—they can pick only the song or songs they want.

B2C: MASS CUSTOMIZATION   End-consumers are often interested in customizing their purchases. In the B2C e-commerce model this need gives rise to the concept of *mass customization*—the ability of an organization to give its customers the opportunity to tailor its product or service to the customer's specifications. Customization can be appropriate and is a key competitive advantage regardless of other customer value perceptions. For example, Dell (www.dell.ca) is well regarded in its market especially for being the best at allowing consumers to customize a computer purchase. Clothing sites allow you to select from among various styles, colours, and sizes of clothing to fit your needs.

In a B2C environment, you're potentially dealing with millions of different consumers, each with unique tastes and needs. You must support the concept of mass customization.

B2B: MRO VERSUS DIRECT   *Maintenance, repair, and operations (MRO) materials* (also called *indirect materials*) are materials that are necessary for running a modern corporation, but do not relate to the company's primary business activities. MRO materials include everything from ballpoint pens to three-ring binders, repair parts for equipment, and lubricating oils. Thus, B2B MRO materials are similar to convenience and commodity-like items in the B2C e-commerce model.

In their purchases of these materials, however, business customers (B2B) are very different from end-consumers (B2C) in many ways. For example, because of its volume of MRO materials purchases, a business can bargain with suppliers for a discount (end-consumers in the B2C e-commerce model usually don't have this ability). Many businesses may band together to create even more volume and thus demand an even higher discount from a supplier. This practice is known as *demand aggregation*—the combining of purchase requests from multiple buyers into a single large order, which justifies a discount from the business. If your organization is a supplier of MRO materials in the B2B e-commerce model, you will compete mostly on price (including discounts), delivery, and ease of ordering.

Direct materials are materials that are used in production in a manufacturing company or are placed on the shelf for sale in a retail environment. So, as opposed to MRO materials, direct materials relate to a company's primary business activities. It is critically important that the customer business receives exactly what is needed in terms of quality, quantity, and the timing of delivery of direct materials.

For direct materials acquisition, some businesses participate in a reverse auction (through an electronic marketplace). A *reverse auction* is the process in which a buyer posts its interest in buying a certain quantity of items with notations concerning quality, specification, and delivery timing, and sellers compete for the business by submitting successively lower bids until there is only one seller left. Reverse auctions create tremendous "power" for the buyer because multiple sellers are competing for the same business.

B2B: HORIZONTAL VERSUS VERTICAL   As a supplier to other businesses, you also need to understand whether you are selling in a horizontal or vertical e-marketplace (see Figure 5.4 on the next page). An *electronic marketplace (e-marketplace)* is an interactive business providing a central market space where multiple buyers and suppliers can engage in e-commerce and/or other e-commerce business activities. E-marketplaces feature a variety of implementations including value-added network providers (which we'll discuss later in the chapter), horizontal e-marketplaces, and vertical e-marketplaces. A *horizontal e-marketplace* is an electronic marketplace that connects buyers and sellers across many industries, primarily for MRO materials commerce. Again, MRO materials include a broad range of both products and services including office supplies, travel, shipping, and some financial services. Because horizontal e-marketplaces support MRO materials commerce, much of our previous discussion on B2B e-commerce for MRO materials holds true here.

A *vertical e-marketplace* is an electronic marketplace that connects buyers and sellers in a given industry (e.g., oil and gas, textiles, and retail). Compuware-Covisint Canada (www.covisint.com) is a good example. Covisint provides a B2B e-marketplace in the automotive industry where buyers and sellers specific to that industry conduct commerce in products and services, share mission-critical information for the development of products and parts, collaborate on new ideas, and deploy infrastructure applications that enable the seamless communication of each other's proprietary IT systems.

To summarize, we offer some ideas to consider regarding e-commerce that will help you in understanding the nature of your business, products, services, and customers.

- **Business to Consumer**
  - There are greatly varying customer demographics, lifestyles, wants, and needs.
  - Distinction of products and services is by convenience versus specialty.
  - E-commerce works best for commodity-like and digital products and services.
  - Mass customization adds value in some instances.
- **Business to Business**
  - Distinction of products and services is by maintenance, repair, and operations (MRO) materials versus direct materials.
  - Demand aggregation and negotiation capabilities are enhanced for businesses as customers (buyer power).
  - E-marketplaces connect buyers and sellers through horizontal e-marketplaces (primarily for MRO materials) and vertical e-marketplaces (specific to a given industry).

A GLOBAL PARTNERSHIP TO CREATE GLOBAL PARTNERING OPPORTUNITIES

In March 2004, Business Commerce Limited, the Hong Kong subsidiary of Global eXchange Services (GXS), and ChinaECNet announced a new business partnership to establish a B2B electronic marketplace named "e-Hub." e-Hub connects China-based electronics manufacturers with other China-based manufacturers and international customers and suppliers as well.

ChinaECNet is China's leading digital media and e-commerce network, focused mainly on the electronic manufacturing industry. It represents a joint venture between the China Center for Industry Information Development, Avnet Inc., and Global Techmart.

Global eXchange Services provides one of the largest B2B e-commerce business networks in the world, supporting over 1 billion transactions annually among over 100,000 trading partners. Its goal is to automate business-critical procurement and supply chain processes.

e-Hub provides buyers and sellers with a standards-based transaction environment that supports more efficient and effective sourcing, purchasing, and tracking of inventory. According to Gou Zhongwen, vice minister of China's Ministry of Information Industry,

"Strengthening the electronics supply chain and material information management is an important step toward utilizing advanced information technology to reform and improve the manufacturing supply and distribution of electronics enterprises." As Wayne Chao, chairman and CEO of ChinaECNet, further explains, "We anticipate that the e-Hub will be China's premier procurement and logistic data exchange platform to connect Chinese electronics OEMs with other Chinese manufacturers of all sizes, and, as importantly, with international customers and suppliers. This will greatly help the Chinese OEM market improve material management efficiency and overcome the challenges caused by the rapid globalization of the Chinese electronics industry."

Sometimes, you build partnerships with other businesses specifically so you can support e-commerce activities among other businesses that also want to build partnerships. In the case of Global eXchange Services and ChinaECNet, their partnership will enable other businesses to create partnerships.[8,9]

Figure 5.4

Horizontal and Vertical B2B Electronic Marketplace

Vertical Marketplaces

Oil and gas | Textiles | Retail

Horizontal Marketplaces

Office supplies

Travel services

Financial services

LO3

Developing Marketing Mixes for Customers

You can't make a sale until you find and reach customers and establish a relationship with them. This is *marketing*. Special features of and technical considerations about marketing and creating customer relationships in e-commerce can create a competitive advantage for you.

BUSINESS TO CONSUMER

With almost 1.3 billion people on the Internet, you'd think it would be easy to find and attract customers to your B2C e-commerce site. But that's not necessarily true because all your competition is trying to do the same thing—drive customers to their Web sites and encourage them to make a purchase.

First, you need to determine your appropriate *marketing mix*—the set of marketing tools that your organization will use to pursue its marketing objectives in reaching and attracting potential customers. In B2C e-commerce, your marketing mix will probably include some or all of the following: registering with search engines, on-line ads, viral marketing, and affiliate programs.

Many Web surfers use *search engines* to find information and products and services. While most search engines will include your site for free, for an additional fee, sites like Google and Yahoo will guarantee that your site appears in the top portion of a search list.

On-line ads (often called *banner ads*) are small advertisements that appear on other sites (see Figure 5.5). Variations of on-line ads include pop-up and pop-under ads. A *pop-up ad* is a small Web page containing an advertisement that appears on your screen outside the current Web site loaded into your browser. A *pop-under ad* is a form of a pop-up

---

Figure 5.5

Banner ads at FoxSports.com

Banner ad for Vonage

Banner ad for a loan lending company

ad that you do not see until you close your current browser window. A word of caution here: Most people don't mind banner ads because they appear as a part of the site they're visiting. However, most people consider pop-up and pop-under ads to be very annoying.

Viral marketing encourages users of a product or service supplied by a B2C e-commerce business to encourage friends to join in as well. Blue Mountain Arts (www.bluemountain.com) is a good example. When you use Blue Mountain to send an e-birthday card (or some other type of card), the intended recipient will receive an e-mail directing him or her to Blue Mountain's site. Once the recipient views the card, Blue Mountain provides a link so that person can send you a card in return. Of course, Blue Mountain charges for each card sent, so it makes money both ways.

An *affiliate program* is an arrangement made between two e-commerce sites that directs viewers from one site to the other. Amazon.com is the most well-known creator of an affiliate program (this service is available only in the United States). If you become an Amazon associate, your e-commerce Web site directs viewers to Amazon's site for certain purchases. If a sale results, Amazon pays you a fee, which is usually a percentage of the sale (see Figure 5.6 on page 139). Likewise, you can pay another site to direct traffic to yours, which may be through an on-line ad. In some instances, affiliate programs create relationships such that a payment is made for each click-through. A *click-through* is a count of the number of people who visit one site, click on an ad, and are taken to the site of the advertiser.

In general, you want your marketing mix to drive as many potential customers as possible to have a look at your B2C e-commerce offerings. From there, however, you need to focus on your conversion rate. A *conversion rate* is the percentage of potential customers who visit your site who actually buy something. So, while total views or "hits" to your e-commerce Web site are important, obviously even more so is your conversion rate.

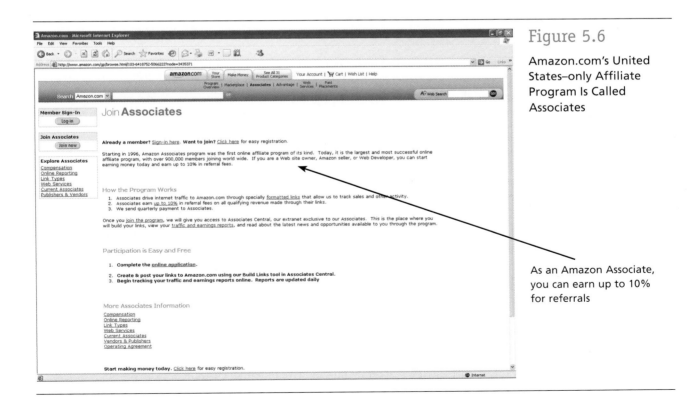

Figure 5.6

Amazon.com's United States–only Affiliate Program Is Called Associates

As an Amazon Associate, you can earn up to 10% for referrals

PERSPECTIVES

TOTING THE E-COMMERCE LINE WITH EBAGS

For a true e-commerce success story you don't have to look any further than eBags (www.ebags.com). While many pure-play e-commerce Web sites have fallen by the wayside, eBags is not only surviving, but also thriving. It is the world's leading on-line provider of bags and accessories for all lifestyles. With 500 brands and over 30,000 products, eBags has sold more than 6.8 million bags since its launch in March 1999. It carries a complete line of premium and popular brands, including Samsonite, JanSport, The North Face, Liz Claiborne, and Adidas. You can buy anything from backpacks and carry-ons to computer cases and handbags at extremely competitive prices from its Web site.

eBags has received several awards for excellence in on-line retailing, among them:

- Circle of Excellence Platinum Award, Bizrate.com
- Web Site of the Year, *Catalog Age Magazine*
- Email Marketer of the Year, ClickZ.MessageMedia
- Marketer of the Year, Colorado AMA
- Rocky Mountain Portal Award

- Gold Peak Catalog, Colorado AMA
- Entrepreneur of the Year—Rocky Mountain Region, Ernst and Young
- E-Commerce Initiative Award of Merit, Colorado Software and Internet Association
- Best of Show, eTravel World Awards
- 50 Essential Web Sites, *Condé Naste Traveler*
- Internet Retailer's Best of the Web

A good part of the reason for eBags's success is its commitment to providing each customer with superior service, 24 hours a day, 365 days a year. eBags provides customers with the ability to contact customer service representatives for personal assistance by telephone or e-mail, and also provides convenient, real-time UPS order tracking.

According to Jon Nordmark, CEO of eBags.com, "From a customer perspective, we've spent a great deal of time developing pioneering ways to guide our shoppers to the bags and accessories that enhance their lifestyles through function and fashion."[10,11]

BUSINESS TO BUSINESS

Finding and attracting customers to your B2B e-commerce site is much different. Businesses—customers in the B2B model—don't usually find products and services by surfing the Web or using search engines. Instead, business customers prefer to actively participate in e-marketplaces to find suppliers. Within an e-marketplace, an organization can participate in a reverse auction to find a supplier, as we discussed earlier.

Moreover, an organization can search an e-marketplace for suitable suppliers and then enter into negotiations outside the e-marketplace. This happens for organizations needing to purchase millions of dollars in inventory, parts, or raw materials, and it occurs for organizations wanting to establish a long-term relationship with just one supplier.

Relationships among businesses in B2B are very important. These relationships, characterized by trust and continuity, extend into the IT realm. In the B2B e-commerce business model, you must provide a level of integration of your IT systems with those of your business partners. Once a formal business relationship has been established, the goal is to use IT to streamline the ordering and procurement processes to create tight supply chain management systems and drive down cost, so your IT systems have to work closely together.

To summarize, some ideas about marketing, or finding customers and creating relationships with them, in e-commerce are

- **Business to Consumer**
  - Design the marketing mix to drive potential customers to a Web site.
  - Register with a search engine; use on-line ads, viral marketing, and affiliate programs.
  - Use conversion rates to measure success.

- **Business to Business**
  - Businesses participate in e-marketplaces—business customers don't surf the Web, so e-marketplaces need your attention; don't use a broad and generic marketing mix
  - Formal establishment of business relationships is based on trust and continuity.
  - Some level of IT system integration between you and your customer is required.
  - Negotiate on-line for pricing, quality, specifications, and delivery timing.

Move Money Easily and Securely

LO4

In the world of e-commerce, you must create IT systems that enable your customers (other businesses or end-consumers) to pay electronically, easily, and securely for their purchases. Of course, you can still accept credit cards as the form of payment just like in the bricks-and-mortar world, but credit card payments are really an electronic form of payment.

BUSINESS-TO-CONSUMER PAYMENT SYSTEMS

Your customers in the business to consumer e-commerce model will most often pay for products and services using credit cards, financial cybermediaries, electronic cheques, electronic bill presentment and payment (EBPP), or smart cards.

- *Credit cards*—use an accepted and supported card. Type in your number, expiry date and for some cards, the verification number (the final three digits) on the back of the card. The drawback is you are exposing your credit card number to the business.
- *Financial cybermediary*—an Internet-based company that makes it easy for one person to pay another person or organization over the Internet. PayPal (www.paypal.com) is the best-known example of a financial cybermediary (see Figure 5.7). You create a PayPal account by logging on to the PayPal Web site and providing it with personal, credit card, and banking information.

Figure 5.7

PayPal Is the Most Well-Known Financial Cybermediary

Sometimes, PayPal is free

PAYING BILLS ON-LINE

epost is Canada Post's *free* electronic bill presentment service, which helps you to manage your bills and other financial documents, safely and securely, *on-line*. epost, a world's first, has provided an universally available e-billing solution within the trusted Canada Post brand since 1999. With epost you can conveniently add, view, pay and manage over 200 types of bills and financial documents like phone, credit card, and tax receipts through your on-line banking Web site or epost.ca. The advantages to this service are

- Bills have been consolidated into one secure centralized location.
- You can conveniently sort by date, company, or other options.
- You can avoid late charges with reminders and delivery notifications.
- You can view your bills through on-line banking by connecting to epost.

Mailers are the companies and organizations that send bills, pay stubs, tax receipts, and other financial documents to your epost box™.

When you add Mailers to your epost box you are choosing to receive your existing paper mail in an electronic form. There are almost 100 mailers and over 200 documents to choose from, including

- Major bank credit card companies
- Major retailers
- Utility companies
- Telecom companies
- Payroll companies.

To add Mailers you need to fill out a registration form for each Mailer, including your account number (if applicable) and other relevant information that may be required. Once Mailers have been added, associated mail items will arrive in your epost box at the start of the next billing cycle.

epost is continually increasing the number of available Mailers.

While the value of being able to receive, view, pay, and store bills on-line is a major driver of Electronic Bill Presentment and Payment (EBPP) services, Canada Post envisions a time when all types of critical or sensitive documents will be securely delivered on-line.[12]

When you want to send money, you go to the PayPal site and enter the amount of money you want to send and provide information for either the person or organization you want to send the money to. You can also accumulate money in your personal PayPal account by accepting money from other people. You can transfer the money to one of your banking accounts, use it for other purposes, send the funds to someone else, or just leave it there for awhile.

- *Electronic cheque*—a mechanism for sending money from your chequing or savings account to another person or organization. There are many implementations of electronic cheques, with the most prominent being on-line banking.

- *Electronic Bill Presentment and Payment (EBPP)*—a system that sends bills (usually to end-consumers) over the Internet and provides an easy-to-use mechanism (such as clicking on a button) to pay for them if the amount looks correct. EBPP systems are available through local banks or on-line services such as CheckFree (http://quicken.intuit.com) and Quicken (www.quicken.com/banking_and_credit).

- *Smart card*—plastic card the size of a credit card that contains an embedded chip on which digital information can be stored and updated. The chip contains information about how much money you have. When you swipe your card to pay for a purchase, the swiping device deducts the purchase amount from the amount you have stored on the chip. Some debit cards are implementations of the smart card concept.

The entire payment process encompasses more than accepting a form of payment. It also includes determining the shipping address for your customer. You can create a competitive advantage by having a way of asking each customer only once for his or her delivery information and storing it, thus creating a switching cost because when your customer makes another purchase, you can simply ask him or her to verify the delivery information and not have to provide it all over again. One implementation of this is called a digital wallet. A **digital wallet** is both software and information—the software provides security for the transaction and the information includes payment information (for example, the credit card number and expiration date) and delivery information. Digital wallets can be stored either on the client side or the server side. A *client-side digital wallet* is one that you create and keep on your computer; you can then use it at a variety of e-commerce Web sites. Most browsers such as Internet Explorer support your ability to create this type of digital wallet. A *server-side digital wallet* (sometimes referred to as a *thin wallet*) is one that an organization creates for and about you and maintains on its server. Many credit card issuers use this type of digital wallet to verify your credit card transactions.

All of this is significant because your customers in the B2C e-commerce model exhibit some common characteristics when paying for your products and services.

- They tend to make numerous purchases for small amounts.
- They pay for each transaction individually.
- You must validate each transaction.

BUSINESS-TO-BUSINESS PAYMENT SYSTEMS

Payments for products and services in the business-to-business e-commerce model are usually much different from those in the business-to-consumer e-commerce model. In B2B e-commerce, your customers tend to make very large purchases and will not pay using a credit card or a financial cybermediary such as PayPal. Instead, other businesses will want to pay (1) through financial EDI and (2) often in large, aggregated amounts encompassing many purchases.

ELECTRONIC DATA INTERCHANGE   In the B2B model, another business wants to order products and services from your organization via electronic data interchange. *Electronic data interchange (EDI)* is the direct computer-to-computer transfer of transaction information contained in standard business documents, such as invoices and purchase orders, in a standard format. Benefits of EDI include eliminating the costs of paper, printing, and postage; minimizing data entry, as orders are not manually entered into the supplier's information system; and fast and efficient ordering. Large companies may require suppliers to use EDI, and therefore may pay EDI costs for small suppliers. This would help lock supplier and buyer in a long-term relationship (this is an advantage as long as both parties remain satisfied). Your organization can implement EDI–facilitated transactions in many ways; one of the more prominent is a B2B e-marketplace that supports EDI through a value-added network. Global eXchange Services (GXS at www.gxs.com) is one such B2B e-marketplace. (We introduced you to GXS in the Perspectives on page 137).

GXS, formerly known as General Electric (GE) Information Services, supports one of the largest B2B e-marketplaces in the world with more than 100,000 trading businesses processing 1 billion transactions annually, and accounting for over $1 trillion in products and services. GXS focuses on providing value-added network capabilities primarily to

Figure 5.8

How Value-Added
Network Providers
Support EDI

supply chain management activities. Figure 5.8 illustrates how General Motors, Ford, and Gates Corporation might use GXS's services to support electronic data interchange. In this case, General Motors and Ford would submit orders to Gates through GXS's value-added network (VAN). The VAN supports electronic catalogues (from which orders are placed), EDI-based transactions (the actual orders), security measures such as encryption (which we'll discuss in a moment), and EDI mail boxes (similar to your personal e-mail box). When GM sends an order, for example, to Gates, the order waits in Gates's EDI mail box for processing. Once the order is processed, Gates sends an order confirmation back through the VAN to GM's mail box.

FINANCIAL ELECTRONIC DATA INTERCHANGE   Thereafter, at some predetermined time, Gates would create an invoice totalling many of the orders and purchases from GM. That invoice would be sent through the VAN much like the orders themselves. When the invoice is accepted and approved by GM, GM would make a financial EDI payment to Gates. *Financial EDI (financial electronic data interchange)* is an electronic process used primarily within the business-to-business e-commerce model for the payment of purchases. The actual reconciliation of the funds may occur through a bank or an automated clearing house (ACH) support site such as National Cash Management System (www.ach-eft-ncms.com).

As you can see, B2B transactions among businesses are much more involved and complex than B2C transactions between a business and an end-consumer such as yourself. Most notably, business-to-business transactions require a level of system integration between the businesses. Considering our previous example in Figure 5.8, Gates's order fulfillment and processing systems would have to be integrated with similar systems at GM and Ford. That is to say, Gates's order fulfillment and processing systems would have to be able to accept and process EDI–based and standardized electronic order records. GM and Ford would have to have similar systems to create EDI–based and standardized electronic order records. In doing so, costs for order processing among all businesses are minimized as the orders can be handled electronically, without paper and without much human intervention.

SECURITY: THE PERVASIVE CONCERN

Whether your customers are other businesses or end-consumers, they are all greatly concerned about the security of their transactions. This includes all aspects of electronic information, but focuses mainly on the information associated with payments (e.g., a credit card number) and the payments themselves, that is, the "electronic money." Here, you need to consider such issues as encryption, Secure Sockets Layers, and Secure Electronic Transactions. This is by no means an exhaustive list but rather representative of the broad field of security relating to electronic commerce.

ENCRYPTION   *Encryption* scrambles the contents of a file so that you can't read it without having the right decryption key. Encryption can be achieved in many ways: by scrambling letters in a known way, replacing letters with other letters or perhaps numbers, and other ways.

Some encryption technologies use multiple keys. In this instance, you would be using *public key encryption (PKE)*—an encryption system that uses two keys: a public key that everyone can have and a private key for only the recipient (see Figure 5.9 on the next page). When implementing security using multiple keys, your organization provides the public key to all its customers (end-consumers and other businesses). The customers use the public key to encrypt their information and send it through the Internet. When it arrives at its destination, your organization uses the private key to unscramble the encrypted information.

SECURE SOCKETS LAYERS   *A Secure Sockets Layer (SSL)* (1) creates a secure and private connection between a Web client computer and a Web server computer, (2) encrypts the information, and (3) then sends the information over the Internet. SSLs do provide good security for transferring information and are used widely by B2C e-commerce Web sites. As an end-consumer, you can tell your information is being transferred via SSL if you see either (1) the Web site address starts with https:// (notice the inclusion of the "s") as opposed to just http:// or (2) the presence of a lock icon in the bottom portion of your Web browser window (see Figure 5.10 on the next page).

Figure 5.9

Public Key Encryption
(PKE) System

SECURE ELECTRONIC TRANSACTIONS   A *Secure Electronic Transaction (SET)* is a transmission security method that ensures transactions are *legitimate* as well as secure. Much like an SSL, an SET encrypts information before sending it over the Internet. Taking it one step further, an SET enables you, as a merchant, to verify a customer's identity by securely transmitting credit card information to the business that issued the credit card for verification. SETs are endorsed by major e-commerce players including MasterCard, American Express, Visa, Netscape, and Microsoft.

To summarize,

- **Business to Consumer**
  - Methods include credit cards, financial cybermediaries, electronic cheques, Electronic Bill Presentment and Payment (EBPP), smart cards, and digital wallets.

Figure 5.10

Secure Sockets Layer
(SSL) on a Web Site

The "s" in https:// and the
lock icon denote a Secure
Sockets Layer (SSL).

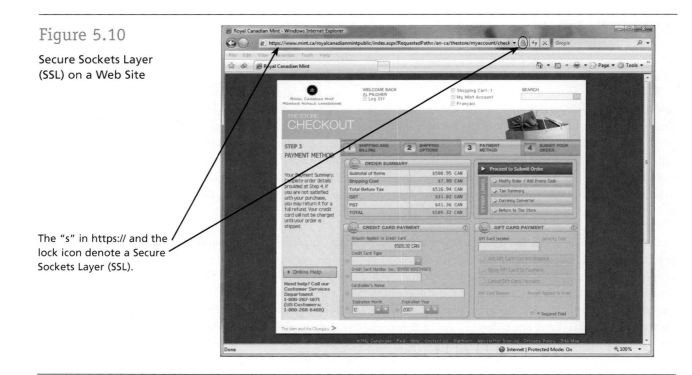

- Consumers make numerous individual purchases for small amounts that must each be validated.
- **Business to Business**
  - The use of electronic data interchange (EDI) facilitates the ordering process.
  - Use value-added network providers for EDI and financial EDI.
  - Use financial EDI for payment of purchases.
- **Both Business to Consumer and Business to Business**
  - Security is an overriding concern.
  - Security is provided by the use of encryption, Secure Sockets Layers (SSLs), and Secure Electronic Transactions (SETs).

E-Business Trends

LO5

If you look out over the e-business horizon, you can see many trends. In fact, we could write an entire book on e-business trends, but three seem particularly interesting right now.

YOUTH

Never before has the business world seen such an influence as that brought on by today's young people, and—yes—we are talking about you. Young people ages 6 to 24 are eagerly and aggressively adopting almost every new technology and new implementations of technology that hit the marketplaces. Even though you may be a 20-something, your generation is now appropriately called *screenagers*, because you spend so much time in front of a screen—TV, computer, IM, cell phone, iPod, etc. You are also called *digital natives*, a group of people ushered into this world alongside the digital revolution. This book's authors' generation (the one before you), is called *digital immigrants* because we were born and raised in a time prior to the digital society in which we now live. Here are some interesting Canadian statistics about *you*. Young Canadians in a Wired World—Phase II (YCWW II) was a comprehensive study looking at Canadian kids' on-line behaviours, attitudes, and opinions. (The study involved 5,200 children and youth from grades 4 to 11, in French- and English-language schools, in every province and territory.) YCWW II (2001–2005) research provides a snapshot of the kinds of technologies kids are using, the ways in which those technologies shape their social experiences, the challenges young people encounter on-line, and the impact of parental involvement on kids' behaviour. It also highlights some key changes that have taken place since the baseline research in 2001. Take a poll to see how representative your class is of these statistics:

- Ninety-four percent of young people say they go on-line from home, compared with 79 percent in 2001. Sixty-one percent report having high-speed access.
- Thirty-seven percent have their own Internet-connected computer.
- Points of access include more than computers. Twenty-three percent of students report having their own cell phone, 44 percent of which have Internet capability. Fifty-six percent of students' cell phones have text messaging and 17 percent have cameras.
- Eighty-six percent of students report that they have e-mail accounts, compared with 71 percent in 2001. Seventy-two percent of these are free Web-based accounts such as Hotmail.
- Of the 21 percent of students who report meeting an Internet friend offline, 72 percent say it was a good experience.

- Fifty-eight percent say they enjoy using the Internet for their schoolwork; 47 percent feel it makes no difference to the quality of their work.
- Fifty-nine percent say they have assumed a different identify on the web. Of those students, 17 percent say they pretended to be someone else.
- Forty-four percent of students are being bullied. Among those who report being bullied, 74 percent were bullied at school and 27 percent over the Internet.
- Sixty-six percent say they would like to learn "How to protect your privacy on the Net" in school. Half of students say they "sometimes" (44 percent) or "always" (5 percent) read privacy policies on the Web sites they visit.
- Ninety percent of students' top 50 Web sites have registration procedures in which visitors are asked to submit personal information. Almost one-third of young people say they would give their real name and address to sign up for a free e-mail account (30 percent) or to create an on-line profile on a site like MSN (27 percent). Nineteen percent would give this information to enter an on-line contest.[13]

Of course, many of these statistics may seem unremarkable to you. After all, technology has been an important part of your entire life. But to the business world, those statistics tell an interesting story.

You have become the target audience for much of today's advertising either about technology or through the use of technology. Marketers are flocking to sites like MySpace to catch your attention. Every cell phone provider is developing features that are screenager-centric—circles of friends (calling minutes don't accrue against these), improved instant messaging capabilities, video, etc. Yours is a generation that has embraced technology and is the future of any technology revolution. You are also one of the fastest-growing demographic groups being targeted for identity theft.

M-COMMERCE

Mobile computing is a broad general term describing your ability to use technology to wirelessly connect to and use centrally located information and/or application software. Mobile computing is all about wireless connectivity. For example, *m-commerce (wireless e-commerce)* describes electronic commerce conducted over a wireless device such as a cell phone, PDA, or notebook, giving you the ability to purchase and download music, buy and sell stocks, check weather forecasts, read your e-mail, and a host of other functions.

The future is definitely wireless, no matter what the technology application. And e-commerce businesses are quickly pursuing the recasting of their Web site e-commerce capabilities to fit on the small screen of a cell phone or digital media player. Just as many businesses are implementing *push technologies*, an environment in which businesses and organizations come to you via technology with information, services, and product offerings based on your profile. Right now, for the most part, the Web is *pull*—you go to a Web site and request information, services, and products. In a *push* environment, cell phone providers may use the GPS chip in your cell phone to determine where you are and push advertising to your cell phone for businesses in the same vicinity.

According to the latest statistics, 34 percent of Internet users have accessed the Internet wirelessly, and 25 percent of Internet users have a cell phone with wireless capabilities.[14] Also, of the total Internet user population, 34.6 million use purely mobile devices (cell phones and the like) to access the Internet.[15] Already, you can begin to see the trend toward mobile computing, the precursor to m-commerce. And although m-commerce is still in its infancy, global m-commerce market is expected to reach US$88 billion by 2009, largely driven by mobile entertainment. Revenues from mobile gaming are estimated to reach US$9.6 billion by 2011.[16]

In terms of remote computing, portability and mobility carry particular significance. Portability refers to the ease with which you can carry around your technology. Thus it refers to the size, shape, and weight of your technology. Mobility, on the other hand, is much broader and encompasses what you have the ability to do with your technology while carrying it around. To achieve maximum portability and mobility we would need *completely wireless communications*, or so-called *ubiquitous computing*.

Such a rich computing environment would allow for tremendous expansion of m-commerce along several dimensions. For example, location-based services (LBS) are important from the end-user application perspective as they allow you to consume traffic and weather information (e.g., driving directions, wireless advertising, and store location, etc.) *where you are*. From a systems developer and vendor perspective, LBS offer the opportunity to provide mapping, routing (directions), GPS navigation (real-time, turn-by-turn navigation), proximity searches, destination guides, tracking such as E-911 (emergency services), vehicle telematics (remote monitoring and diagnostics of the "health" of trucks, trains, and ships), moveable assets (such as rented or leased equipment) as well as friend or buddy finders. Finally, location-based billing, advertising, etc. are possible, allowing cell phone providers (as an example) to charge a customer one rate when the phone is used in a business locations and another when it's used elsewhere. If the system knows where you are, almost anything is possible.

This is a long list of potential uses, but why is this important? Why should you care? The answer is that you are probably already using such a computing metaphor in your day-to-day life. This kind of *untethered access*—where YOU are and not where the MACHINE is—is sometimes referred to as cloud computing (the cloud being the Internet) and is something akin to the ASP (application service provider) metaphor of computing that we talk about in Chapter 6. There are security implications implied by this *compute-everywhere* model, and we are continually putting ourselves at the mercy of those who provide such services since we are depending on them not only to provide the computing service for us (such as a spreadsheet or a supply chain application or a word processor) but also storing our data on their servers. So they have all the software and all our data. It's a compelling model as it allows us to be untethered and mobile and wander around with little devices and connect anywhere. But it's also a fundamental shift in the way we compute—both personal and in the organization. It bears scrutiny.

Such advances in m-commerce will allow for more and better mobile identity and payment since handheld devices such as your cell phone have an identity (SIM [Subscriber Identity Module]) card that securely stores the *service-subscriber key* used to identify a mobile phone. That's how your cell phone provider knows to whom to charge a call. It knows who you are and, within a certain margin, exactly where you are when your phone is with you. This is an interesting dilemma however, as you are not your cell phone and vice versa. You can well be somewhere without your phone at any time. And others can have your phone, either by you lending it to them or through other, not as cooperative, means. But authentication (is it you who is using the device or someone else?) can be reinforced by smart cards and biometrics such as voice or fingerprint (see Chapter 8). Note that once the sticky process of determining who is using the device is successfully resolved, your cell phone has an already has a built-in payment mechanism— your cell phone invoice and payment system! The question is whether it will become universally accepted.

Chances are good that it will. Look at the trends. Respected technology blogger David Houle (who blogs at www.evolutionshift.com/blog) wrote in February 2008 that the number of cell phone subscribers (including multiple subscriptions—the few who have more than one cell phone subscription) will exceed the number of nonsubscribers sometime during 2008. He writes that "I believe that this dynamic is moving us to a singularity in connectivity. We are literally erasing time and distance from human communication. If one had the appropriate calling plan from a cellular carrier and one had the phone numbers of the 3 billion people who have cell phones one could immediately connect with that many people at any time, wherever they are. That potential, that growing possibility is unlike anything that has ever existed in human history. In the short time since 1985, humanity has gone from place-based phone connectivity for hundreds of millions to mobile connectivity for billions."[17]

With improved means of delivering richer content (such as Enhanced SMS, Premium SMS and the greater penetration of MMS), both in terms of multimedia and data services and with improved billing and payment mechanisms, will come richer content and thus increasing consumer adoption. Once security concerns are addressed, new groups of mobile phone users will become comfortable using expanded m-commerce offerings and new delivery and billing mechanisms. This will lead to increasing adoption of mobile content delivery and m-commerce services by enterprises, including banks, media companies, travel and transportation companies, small and medium-sized businesses of all sorts, as well as others. These might include enhanced security through the monitoring of physical assets such as home, factory, store, installation, terminal, etc. as well as child-care workers, pets, children, guests, and perhaps even your partner or spouse. Imagine the possibilities and the implications.

What are the m-commerce challenges? It is estimated that somewhere between 70 and 80 percent of attempts to put invoice transactions on consumer phone bills are successful. Twenty to 30 percent fail for a broad variety of reasons. This is a big problem! If the enterprise receives payment for m-commerce transactions only 70 percent of the time, that digs deep into the top line. The reliability needs to approach 100%.

What happened to the first wave of e-commerce enterprises? Most e-commerce pioneers failed because they did not follow sound business principles, they had no path to profitability (P2P), and they had no basic commerce experience—they did not understand *fulfillment*. They understood development and marketing but they had no experience getting the goods into their supply chain or out to their customers. In short, they lacked a well-thought-out business plan and rode a wave of hype. Many floundered. Many drowned. Many lessons were learned.

In the face of some spectacular flameouts, B2B e-commerce, which predated the boom, survived and even flourished, as we have illustrated throughout this chapter. The rebirth of e-commerce has seen tremendous surges in C2C e-commerce and *e-government*. We believe, with increased portability and mobility, C2C e-commerce will occur over cell phones, PDAs, and other similar devices. This will represent a further revolution or paradigm shift in computing where commerce will be conducted between individuals with no organizational intermediaries at all. You may not even need an ISP to set up your own shop on your cell phone. It's right around the corner.

THE LONG TAIL

Finally, let's talk about the Long Tail. Think about Amazon, zip.ca, and Rhapsody (a competitor of iTunes). In purely financial terms, how would you describe their paths-to-profitability? For Rhapsody, you might say that it has no physical store, no unsold inventory that must be eventually dumped at a loss, and so on. You would, in fact, be partially correct. And you might similarly describe Amazon and zip.ca—no stores to manage, fewer employees, etc. Again, you would be partially correct. But the real key to their success lies in the Long Tail.

The *Long Tail*—first offered by Chris Anderson, editor-in-chief of *Wired* Magazine, as a way of explaining e-commerce profitability—actually refers to the tail of a sales curve

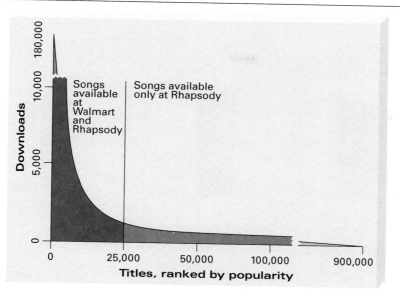

Figure 5.11

The Long Tail

Source: Anderson, Chris, *The Long Tail*, 2006, Hyperion, New York, p. 25.

(see Figure 5.11 on the next page).[18, 19] Figure 5.11 shows music song titles, ranked by popularity, for Walmart and Rhapsody (www.rhapsody.com). You see that a typical Wal-mart store stocks about 25,000 songs. Because of the cost of shelf placement in a retailing environment, that's about all Walmart can carry and make a profit. However, because everything is digital and retail shelf placement costs are irrelevant, Rhapsody carries 1.5 million tracks. Moreover, a full 40 percent of Rhapsody's total sales come from songs in the Long Tail of the sales distribution. Hence, the notion of the Long Tail.

E-commerce businesses that can reach the audience in the Long Tail can do so without the typical bricks-and-mortar retail costs and expenses. This is real *mass customization*, of which we spoke earlier, and also goes by the terms *slivercasting* (as opposed to *broadcasting*) and *massclusivity* (a combination of *mass production* and *exclusivity*). In Figure 5.12, we've provided inventory and sales data for Rhapsody, zip.ca, and Amazon. Notice that zip.ca generates 21 percent of its total sales from the Long Tail, and Amazon generates 25 percent of its total sales from the Long Tail.

Long Tail represents an entirely new business model and requires new business thinking. Traditional business thinking looks at sales in terms of economies of scale, seeking to sell as many of one item as possible to offset fixed costs (such as shelf placement costs). The Long Tail model is quite different. Because fixed costs are so minimal, Rhapsody and iTunes can afford to sell only one or two downloads of a given song and still make a profit. Walmart can't do that. In fact, Walmart will carry only music CDs for which it believes sales will be at least four or five. So, it doesn't carry niche products, whereas Rhapsody and iTunes do. The same is true for zip.ca. While a typical Blockbuster rental store carries only 3,000 movie DVDs, zip.ca carries over 72,000. Likewise, while a typical Chapters bookstore carries only 100,000 books, strictly online sellers such as Amazon have over 3.7 million book titles in inventory.

This is a significant trend in the world of e-business. Some older, more traditional bricks-and-mortar financial and inventory models no longer apply. A new way of thinking is required. It is this sort of thinking that a younger generation like you can embrace and act on.

Figure 5.12

The Long-Tail Economics for Rhapsody, Zip.ca, and Amazon

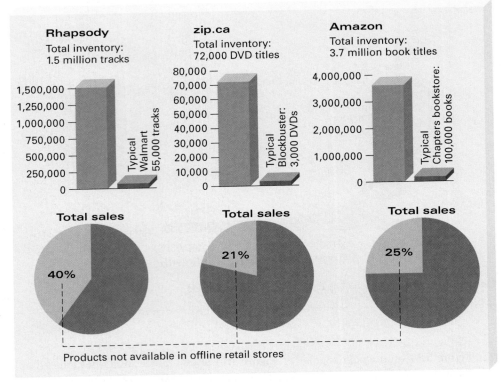

Source: 1. Anderson, Chris, *The Long Tail*, 2006, Hyperion, New York, p. 23.
2. zip.ca

Summary: STUDENT LEARNING OUTCOMES *REVISITED*

LO1   Describe the nine major e-commerce business models. The nine major e-commerce business models are

- *Business to business (B2B) e-commerce*—businesses selling products and services to other businesses
- *Business-to-consumer (B2C) e-commerce*—businesses selling products and services to individual consumers
- *Consumer-to-business (C2B) e-commerce*—individuals selling products and services to businesses
- *Consumer-to-consumer (C2C) e-commerce*—individuals selling products and services to other individuals
- *Business-to-government (B2G) e-commerce*—businesses selling products and services to a government entity

- *Consumer-to-government (C2G) e-commerce*—individuals selling products and services to a government entity
- *Government-to-business (G2B) e-commerce*—the government selling products and services to businesses
- *Government-to-consumer (G2C) e-commerce*—government selling products and services to individuals
- *Government-to-government (G2G) e-commerce*—e-commerce activities within a single government or among two or more governments.

LO2   Identify the differences and similarities among customers and their perceived value of products and services in the B2B and B2C e-commerce business models. Customers in the B2C e-commerce business model are end-consumers. They (1) exhibit greatly varying demographics, lifestyles,

DOES EVERY SOLUTION POSE A NEW PROBLEM?
CELL PHONES AND YOUR HEALTH

How much time do you spend talking on your cell phone each day? How long do you spend, on average, on any one call? Do you have a "friends" package that allows unlimited text and talk with a circle of friends (even if one of them is your brother)? Would you stick your head in a running microwave? While the jury is still out on the long-term health effects of cellular technology, there is no shortage of press on the potential harm,. Perhaps because cell phones are so pervasive (not necessarily in Canada, which has a fairly low adoption rate, relatively speaking), they are in the news.

In mid-July 2008, CBC News posted the following on its Web site. It's a balanced article, giving voice to both sides. We present it here as food for thought. Is every solution a possible problem? Time will tell.

Toronto's department of public health is advising teenagers and young children to limit their use of cellphones to avoid potential health risks. The advisory—believed to be the first of its kind in Canada—warns that because of possible side effects from radio frequencies, children under eight should use a cellphone only in emergencies and teenagers should limit calls to less than 10 minutes. "Teach them the ways to use a cellphone responsibly—to make shorter calls, to use other modes of communication; if it's possible,

use a landline," said Loren Vanderlinden, a health department supervisor and the report's author.

In an interview with the *Toronto Star*, Vanderlinden said scientists were dismissive of any risk years ago. But with more studies, she said, a pattern is emerging that suggests people who have used their cellphones for a long period of time are at greater risk of certain kinds of brain tumours. Eight years ago, a government inquiry in Britain concluded cellphones shouldn't be marketed to children under 16 because so little was known about the long-term health risks. But according to Health Canada, there is no firm evidence that cellphones pose health risks. "Health Canada currently sees no scientific reason to consider the use of cellphones as unsafe," the agency wrote. "Health Canada is basing this conclusion upon the bulk of scientific evidence from … studies that have been carried out worldwide, including at our laboratory."

The Canadian Wireless Telecommunications Association, which represents Canada's cellphone industry, also said there is no need for anyone, including children, to change their cellphone habits. "The state of the science right now from leading health agencies, including the World Health Organization, is that cell phone use—as set out in the guidelines—is that these devices are safe," said Marc Choma, a spokesman for the organization. "And that is the state of the science worldwide."[20]

---

wants, and needs; (2) distinguish products and services by convenience versus specialty; (3) often shop for commodity-like and digital products; and (4) sometimes require a level of mass customization to get exactly what they want. Customers in the B2B e-commerce business model are other businesses. They (1) distinguish products and services by *maintenance*, *repair, and operations (MRO) materials* versus *direct materials*; (2) aggregate demand to create negotiations for volume discounts on large purchases; and (3) most often perform e-commerce activities within an e-marketplace.

LO3 **Compare and contrast the development of a marketing mix for customers in the B2B and B2C e-commerce business models.**

A *marketing mix* is the set of marketing tools that your organization uses to pursue its marketing objectives in reaching and attracting potential customers. In B2B e-commerce, marketing mixes do not usually include broad and generic strategies that reach all potential businesses. Instead, marketing often occurs in the context of an e-marketplace. Once a contact has been made between businesses, the development of the relationship is still formal and often includes negotiations for pricing, quality, specifications, and delivery timing.

In B2C e-commerce, a marketing mix will include some or all of the following:

• Registering your site with a search engine.

- **On-line ads** (small advertisements that appear on other sites), including **pop-up ads** (small Web pages containing an advertisement that appear on your screen outside the current Web site loaded into your browser) and **pop-under ads** (a form of a pop-up ad that you do not see until you close your current browser session).

- **Viral marketing**, which encourages users of a product or service supplied by a B2C e-commerce business to encourage friends to join in as well.

- **Affiliate program**, which is an arrangement made between two e-commerce sites that directs viewers from one site to the other.

LO4 **Summarize ways of moving money in the world of e-commerce and related issues.** B2C e-commerce payment systems most commonly include credit cards, **financial cybermediaries** (such as PayPal), **electronic cheques** (with on-line banking being an implementation), **Electronic Bill Presentment and Payment (EBPP)**, **smart cards** (credit cards with an embedded computer chip on which digital information can be stored

and updated), and **digital wallets** (software and instructions for completing a transaction). In the B2B e-commerce business model, financial EDI is the norm. **Financial EDI** is an electronic process used primarily in the business-to-business e-commerce business model for the payment of purchases. Security for the electronic transfer of funds is an overriding concern. Techniques such as **encryption**, **public key encryption (PKE)**, **Secure Sockets Layers (SSLs)**, and **Secure Electronic Transactions (SETs)** all address this issue of security.

LO5 **Discuss some major trends that are impacting both the e-commerce business world and society in general.** Major trends include younger people (**digital natives** or **screenagers**) quickly embracing new technology developments and new innovative uses of technology; **m-commerce**—electronic commerce conducted over a wireless device such as a cell phone, PDA, or notebook computer; the **Long Tail model**—the tail of a sales curve that traditional businesses ignore but from which e-commerce businesses profit.

CLOSING CASE STUDY 1
When You're Big, You Can Be Your Own B2B e-Marketplace

Business-to-business (B2B) e-marketplaces are the growing trend in the B2B e-commerce business model. Businesses from all industries and countries can gather, perform commerce functions, share mission-critical information, and deploy infrastructure applications that allow those organizations to tie their internal systems to each other.

But some companies—the largest ones—don't have to play in the generic B2B e-marketplaces. Instead, they can build their own and literally require that their suppliers participate. Once such company is Volkswagen AG. Its B2B e-marketplace is called VWgroupsupply.com (www.vwgroupsupply.com).

Volkswagen AG offers eight brands of automobiles—Volkswagen (passenger), Volkswagen Commercial Vehicles, Audi, Bentley, Bugatti, Lamborghini, Seat, and Skoda. In 2003, Volkswagen spent almost 60 billion euros, or approximately US$77 billion, on components,

automotive parts, and MRO materials for its manufacturing operations. When you spend that much money with your suppliers, you can open and run your own B2B e-marketplace.

VWgroupsupply.com handles 90 percent of Volkswagen global purchases. Almost all requests for quotes, contract negotiations, catalogue updating and buying, purchase-order management, vehicle program management, and payments are handled electronically and on-line through VWgroupsupply.com.

Gains in efficiency and productivity, coupled with material costs reductions, have been tremendous. The cost savings alone generated over the last three years were more than 100 million euros, or approximately US$127 million.

Volkswagen requires that each of its 5,500 suppliers use VWgroupsupply.com for any interactions. Suppliers place product and pricing catalogues on the system, respond to requests for quotes, and collaborate with Volkswagen engineers on new product designs, all in the safe and secure environment of Volkswagen's proprietary B2B e-marketplace.

By requiring its suppliers to interact with Volkswagen in the e-marketplace, purchasing agents no longer have to spend valuable time searching for information and pricing. Volkswagen has, in essence, created a system that brings the necessary information to the purchasing agents. This new system within VWgroupsupply.com is called iPAD, or Internal Purchasing Agent Desk.

Prior to the implementation of iPAD, purchasing agents entering a purchase order for a vehicle front module had to use numerous separate systems to complete the process. They had to retrieve information from a supplier system and its database, query information in Volkswagen's internal parts information system, obtain information from a request-for-quotes database, enter information into a contract-negotiation transcript system, and interact with several other systems and databases. In all, the purchasing agent had to log into and use seven separate systems. Analysis revealed that Volkswagen purchasing agents were spending 70 percent of their time finding, retrieving, analyzing, validating, and moving information. This took away valuable time from such tasks as negotiating better prices with suppliers.

Using a form of an integrated collaboration environment, or ICE, which we discussed in Chapter 2, purchasing agents now participate in a simple three-step process. First, iPAD captures and sends a business event to the purchasing agent, such as the need to order vehicle front modules. Second, iPAD attaches to that communication other necessary information such as information about potential suppliers, their costs, and other forms of analysis and descriptive information. Finally, iPAD sends the corresponding business processes and work flows to be completed electronically.

It works much like a digital dashboard, which we also introduced you to in Chapter 2. When purchasing agents log onto the iPAD portal in the morning, they receive a customized Web page with announcements, business alerts, analyses, and digital workflows to be completed. The purchasing agents can set out immediately to complete the tasks for the day, without having to spend 70 percent of their time finding, retrieving, and analyzing information. iPAD even customizes the Web page according to the purchasing agent's native language, something very necessary for a global manufacturer of automobiles with more than 2,000 purchasing agents worldwide.[21, 22]

Questions

1. Volkswagen operates its own proprietary B2B e-marketplace in which its suppliers participate. What are the disadvantages to Volkswagen of not using a generic B2B e-marketplace with even more suppliers? What are the advantages to Volkswagen of developing and using its own proprietary B2B e-marketplace?

2. When Volkswagen needs a new part design, it uses VWsupplygroup.com to get its suppliers involved in the design process early. This creates a tremendous amount of interorganizational collaboration. What are the advantages to the suppliers and to Volkswagen in doing so?

3. How is Volkswagen's VWgroupsupply.com B2B e-marketplace an example of a vertical e-marketplace implementation? How is it an example of a horizontal e-marketplace implementation? Why is it necessary that Volkswagen combine both of these e-marketplaces into one e-marketplace? What would be the drawbacks to creating two different e-marketplaces—one for suppliers of direct materials and one for suppliers of MRO materials?

4. To make effective purchasing decisions, Volkswagen's purchasing agents need business intelligence. What kind of business intelligence does iPAD provide to purchasing agents for carrying out their tasks? What additional kinds of business intelligence not discussed in this case could Volkswagen's purchasing agents take advantage of to make more effective decisions?

5. iPAD manages the workflow for purchasing agents. Describe how iPAD manages this process including information provided, steps to be executed, and the presentation of information.

www.mcgrawhill.ca/olc/haag

CLOSING CASE STUDY 2
E-Business Trend: Far-East E-Commerce Explosion

MySpace has 200 million registered users but only 23 percent of the U.S. 20-something group are among those 92 million. On the other hand, Cyworld, the South Korean version of MySpace, boasts only 20 million users but 90 percent of the South Korean 20-somethings use Cyworld.

Cyworld ("cy" is Korean for "relationship") is an interesting blend of a social networking site, blogging site, Flickr (a photo-sharing Web site at www.flickr.com), and videogame-like avatars. Unlike the text-heavy bulky sites like MySpace, Facebook, Friendster, and Yahoo 360, Cyworld lets a user create an avatar called a mini-me. You can dress up the mini-me according to your mood on any particular day and even change hair styles. From your personal space, called a mini-room (which you can also decorate to your tastes), you can send out your mini-me to visit other people.

Cyworld is free to use, just like most other social networking sites, but it generates revenue by having users pay for virtual furniture and wall art for their mini-rooms and also to accessorize themselves in their virtual mini-mes. This may seem like an odd way to generate revenue, but Cyworld generates $7.78 annually per user while MySpace generates only $2.17 annually per user.

The creators of Cyworld are not content with owning the South Korean social networking market. Recently, Cyworld launched in Japan, Taiwan, Vietnam, Germany, and China (where it already has 1.5 million users). Moreover, Cyworld spent almost a year "Americanizing" its site and launched it in the United States, going head to head with MySpace and the other popular social networking sites aimed at the 20-something group ("digital natives" and "screenagers").

Another Asian entrant into the hotly contested e-commerce space is TaoBao (www.taobao.com), China's main competitor to eBay. If you visit, Taobao's Web site, it's in Chinese but the look and feel are similar to eBay. But don't get the idea that Taobao is copying everything that eBay is doing. On a recent trip to China, eBay CEO Meg Whitman learned that Taobao was allowing buyers and sellers to instant message through the Taobao auction system. Whitman came home and declared that eBay needed to do the same.

In the Chinese Consumer to Consumer auction space, eBay China holds a 29.1 percent market share. Taobao owns a remarkable 67.3 percent. If Taobao ever comes to the United States, it will give eBay a run for its money until the final gavel falls.[23, 24, 25]

Questions

1. According to Porter's Five Forces Model (from Chapter 1), how would you characterize the competitive space in which Cyworld and MySpace operate according to buyer power, supplier power, threat of substitute products or services, threat of new entrants, and rivalry among existing competitors? Pick one of Porter's Five Forces and describe what Cyworld has undertaken to shift that force in a positive way in its direction.

2. In our discussions of customers and their perceptions of value, we noted that customers tend to categorize products and services as either convenience or specialty. How would you characterize the products and services on Consumer to Consumer e-commerce auction sites such as Taobao and eBay—convenience, specialty, or perhaps a combination of the two? Justify your answer.

3. What sort of payment options does eBay provide? You may have to visit eBay's site to learn this information. If Taobao were to enter the U.S. market, would it have to offer similar payment options? Discuss whether eBay's current payment options would pose a barrier to entry for Taobao. Finally, describe possible innovations in eBay's payments mechanism that could either bolster current entry barriers for eBay's competitors or provide a competitive advantage for eBay, or both.

4. Privacy is an overriding concern today on the Internet. At sites like Cyworld and MySpace, some people often divulge too much information such as a full name, a phone number, and even an address. From an ethical point of view, do you believe that social networking sites have an obligation to protect users from cyber stalkers? If you believe the answer is no, justify your answer. If you believe the answer is yes, describe what steps can be undertaken to protect users.

5. One key to consumer retention is creating a "sticky" Web site. Review the virtual environments for both Cyworld and MySpace. Which do you think is more "sticky" and better retains consumers? What is your definition of "sticky"?

Key Terms and Concepts

Short-Answer Questions

1. What is electronic commerce?
2. How can you use a B2B e-marketplace to reduce your dependence on a particular supplier?
3. How do convenience and specialty items differ in the B2C e-commerce business model?
4. Why do commodity-like and digital items sell well in the B2C e-commerce business model?
5. What is mass customization?
6. How does a reverse auction work?
7. How are vertical and horizontal e-marketplaces different?
8. What can a marketing mix include for a B2C e-commerce business?
9. What are the major types of B2C e-commerce payment systems?
10. What is the difference between a client-side digital wallet and a server-side digital wallet?
11. How are Secure Sockets Layers (SSLs) and Secure Electronic Transactions (SETs) different? How are they the same?

Assignments and Exercises

1. **YOUR PROVINCIAL AND LOCAL GOVERNMENT E-COMMERCE ACTIVITIES** Visit the Web sites for your provincial and local governments. Do some looking around and make a list of what services, information deliveries, and transaction processing they offer that you previously could handle only by visiting a physical building. How are these different from and similar to comparable e-government activities now offered by the Canadian government?

2. **DEALING WITH THE GREAT DIGITAL DIVIDE** The "great digital divide" is a term coined to address the concerns of many people that the world is becoming one marked by "haves" and "have nots" with respect to technology—that is, the traditional notion of a "less-developed country" is now also being defined by the extent to which a country has access to and uses technology. Find out what, if anything, the United Nations is doing about this issue and express an opinion on whether or not you believe its efforts will be successful. Determine if there are organizations such as private companies or foundations that have the digital divide high on their agendas. For any such organizations you find, evaluate their efforts and express an opinion as to whether or not they will be successful. Finally, search for a less-developed country that is making significant local efforts to deal with the digital divide. If you can't find one, prepare a list of the countries you reviewed and briefly describe the conditions in one of them with respect to technology.

3. **RESEARCHING A BUSINESS TO BUSINESS E-MARKETPLACE** Biz2Biz (www.biz2biz. com/Marketplace) is a B2B e-marketplace. Connect to its site and do some looking around. What sort of marketing services does it provide through its Biz2BizCommunication program? What sort of services does it provide for creating and maintaining an electronic catalogue? If you owned a business and wanted to join, what process would you have to go through? How much does it cost your organization to join Biz2Biz? What buyer tools does Biz2Biz provide its membership?

4. **DEVELOPING M-COMMERCE SCENARIOS FOR GPS CELL PHONES** Soon, cell phones will be equipped with GPS chips that enable users to be located to within a geographical location about the size of a tennis court. The primary purpose for installing GPS chips in phones is to enable emergency services to locate a cell phone user. For example, if you dial an emergency assistance number (911 in Canada) from your home now, it is possible for a computer system to use your home telephone number to access a database and obtain your address. This is very useful in situations in which you are unable to give address information to the emergency operator for some reason. The problem with trying to do the same thing with present-day cell phones is that you could be calling from anywhere. GPS-enabled cell phones are intended to overcome that problem.

   As you might imagine, marketers have been monitoring this development with great interest because GPS-phones will support m-commerce. When the new cell phones become available, marketers visualize scenarios in which they will know who you are (by your telephone number) and where you are (by the GPS chip). One possible way they could use this information, for example, is to give you a call when you are walking past their shop in the mall to let you know of a special sale on items they know you would be interested in buying. Of course, retailers would have to possess IT systems that would permit them to craft such personalized offers, and you would have had to give them permission to call you.

   Find out what at least three e-commerce marketers are saying about personalized marketing using GPS-equipped cell phones and prepare an analysis of how the phones will be likely to be used when the technology is widely available.

5. **FINDING THE MOST POPULAR B2C E-COMMERCE SITES** Connect to the Web and do some research to find the most popular B2C e-commerce Web sites in terms of number of hits or views per month. What are the sites? Which of the sites in some way or another support the concept of an e-marketplace where end-consumers can gather?

Discussion Questions

1. In what ways can shopping over the Internet be more convenient for consumers? In what ways can it be less convenient? List at least five products you would have no hesitation buying over the Internet, five products you might want to think about a bit before buying, and five products you would never consider buying over the Internet. Justify your reasons in each case.

2. In your opinion, according to Porter's Five Forces Model (refer to Chapter 1), has competition increased or decreased overall as a result of the Internet and e-commerce? Specifically address each of the five forces in Porter's model.

3. Under what circumstances would it be appropriate to consider using viral marketing? See if you can think of an organization with an on-line presence that could benefit from viral marketing but is not currently using it. It could be your school, for example, or it could be an organization you are involved with. How would you suggest the organization go about using viral marketing in order for it to achieve the desired results? What are some of the other marketing techniques available for an e-commerce Web site to use? Why is it important to consider a mix of techniques rather than just relying on a single one?

4. Describe the services provided by value-added networks that make it easier for companies to exchange EDI transactions with each other. What are the pros and cons of using value-added networks for B2B e-commerce? Why don't more companies use the Internet for EDI since it is much cheaper than using a value-added network? Assume that you work for a telecommunications company that operates a value-added network (Bell Canada or Telus). What sort of strategies would you encourage your company to explore to deal with the possibility of losing considerable amounts of revenues as your customers leave you in favour of using other Internet-based services?

5. In this chapter, we've identified differences between end-consumers and businesses as customers. Review those differences and then list the three you consider most significant. Discuss those three. For the differences that you did not choose as the three most important, be prepared to justify your decision.

6. In this chapter, we discussed using such technologies as B2B e-marketplaces to create tighter supply chain management, thereby driving out costs. If you refer back to Chapter 2, you'll recall that another major business initiative is customer relationship management (CRM). How can B2C e-commerce businesses use the Internet to further enhance their CRM initiatives? How can B2B e-commerce businesses use the Internet to further enhance their CRM initiatives? Does it become easier or harder to maintain relationships with customers as businesses move toward more electronic commerce? Why?

Chapter 6

Systems Development

Phases, Tools, and Techniques

STUDENT LEARNING OUTCOMES

LO1 Define the traditional systems development life cycle (SDLC) and describe the seven major phases within it.

LO2 Compare and contrast the various component-based development methodologies.

LO3 Describe the self-sourcing process as an alternative to the traditional systems development life cycle.

LO4 Discuss the importance of prototypes and prototyping within any systems development methodology.

LO5 Describe the outsourcing environment and how outsourcing works.

OPENING CASE STUDY
Saving Lives through Systems Development and Integration

The Centers for Disease Control and Prevention (CDC) in Atlanta, Georgia, tracks a wealth of information on everything from antimicrobial-resistant infections in hospitals to influenza outbreaks to terrorist biochemical attacks. Unfortunately, not all of that information is kept in an accessible manner for everyone who needs it and for every application software environment that needs to draw from it.

With offices all over the country interacting with literally hundreds of state and local agencies, the CDC has volumes of information siloed on disparate servers and application software incapable of easily communicating with other application software. The CDC's IT initiative is to bring all this information together within a service-oriented architecture (SoA). An SoA is a holistic perspective of information and application software that focuses on ease of integration across all information repositories, application software, and hardware platforms.

While most businesses in the private sector use IT metrics such as ROI (return on investment), conversion rates, and click-through to measure the worth of a system, the CDC does so in terms of human life. For example, the CDC's BioSense initiative could provide early warning and critical information during an influenza pandemic. That system needs to be integrated with those of pharmacies dispensing medications. In the early stages of an influenza outbreak, sales of acetaminophen might alert government officials to the threat even before people start showing up at hospitals.

The scope of the CDC's integration initiative is almost incomprehensible. The interrelationships and interactions in the natural, living world are complicated and astronomical in number. Food-borne illnesses, adverse drug reactions, hospital infections, and even U.S. Environmental Protection Agency (EPA) estimates of bacteria in rivers and stagnant ponds all relate to each other in some way. Most of these have their own dedicated IT systems for data gathering and analysis that must be integrated for the CDC so that its Public Health Information Network initiative can provide the right information to researchers and health care professionals across the United States and around the world.

Systems development and the integration of all systems throughout an organization are of paramount importance in today's business world.

It doesn't matter if you're trying to thwart an influenza pandemic or selling clothing on the Internet. You need integrated systems and accessible information to make the best decisions possible. Systems development is the focus of this chapter—how organizations go about the process of systems development, various methodologies for systems development, and how you, as an end-user, can (and must) participate in the systems development process, and often, build systems for yourself. We live in a digital economy, and IT systems don't just magically appear. They must be thoughtfully and rigorously developed.[1]

Questions

1. All computers use a common binary base language. That being true, why is it so difficult to get computer systems to easily communicate with each other?

2. In systems development, prototyping is used to build a model of a proposed system. How have you used prototyping in your personal life to build something?

3. Outsourcing—going to another country for systems development—is big business. Why would the CDC *not* want to pursue outsourcing?

Introduction

Billions of dollars are spent each year on the acquisition, design, development, implementation, and maintenance of information systems. The ongoing need for safe, secure, and reliable systems solutions is a consequence of companies' increasing dependence on information technology to provide services and develop products, administer daily activities, and perform short- and long-term management functions.

Systems developers must ensure that all the business's needs and requirements are met when developing information systems, establish uniform privacy and security practices for system users, and develop acceptable implementation strategies for the new systems. This chapter focuses on the many factors that must come together to develop a successful information system.

You have three primary choices as to who will build your system (see Figure 6.1 on the next page). First, you can choose *insourcing*, which involves in-house IT specialists within your organization to develop the system. Second, you can choose *self-sourcing* (also called **end-user development**), which is the development and support of IT systems by end-users (knowledge workers) with little or no help from IT specialists. Third, you can choose **outsourcing**, which is the delegation of specific work to a third party for a specified length of time, at a specified cost, and at a specified level of service.

As we introduce you to the systems development life cycle in the next section, we'll focus on insourcing and how the overall process works, key activities within each phase, roles you may play as an end-user or knowledge worker, and opportunities you can capitalize on to ensure that your systems development effort is a success.

LO1

Insourcing and the Systems Development Life Cycle

The **systems development life cycle (SDLC)** is a structured, step-by-step approach for developing information systems. It includes seven key phases and numerous activities within each. This version of the SDLC is also referred to as a **waterfall methodology**— a sequential, activity-based process in which one phase of the SDLC is followed by another, from planning through maintenance (see Figure 6.2).

There are literally hundreds of different activities associated with each phase of the SDLC. Typical activities include determining budgets, gathering business requirements, designing models, writing detailed user documentation, and project management. The activities you, as an end-user, perform during each systems development project will vary depending on the type of system you're building and the tools you use to build it. Since we can't possibly cover them all in this brief introduction, we have chosen a few of the more important SDLC activities that you might perform on a systems development project as an end-user.

PHASE 1: PLANNING

During the **planning phase** of the SDLC, you create a solid plan for developing your information system. The following are the three primary activities performed during the planning phase.

1. *Define the system to be developed:* You must identify and select the system for development or determine which system is required to support the strategic goals of your organization. Organizations typically track all the proposed systems and prioritize them based on business impact or critical success factors. A **critical success factor (CSF)** is simply a factor critical to your organization's success. This process allows your organization to strategically decide which systems to build.

Figure 6.1

Insourcing, Self-sourcing, and Outsourcing

Insourcing

IT Specialists Within Your Organization

Self-sourcing

Knowledge Workers

Outsourcing

Another Organization

■ Figure 6.2

The Systems
Development Life
Cycle (SDLC), Phases
and Activities, and the
Waterfall Methodology

SDLC Phase	Activities
1. Planning	• Define the system to be developed • Set the project scope • Develop the project plan including tasks, resources, and timeframes
2. Analysis	• Gather the business requirements for the system • Prioritize the business requirements
3. Design	• Design the technical architecture required to support the system • Design system models
4. Development	• Build the technical architecture • Build the database and programs
5. Testing	• Write the test conditions • Perform the testing of the system
6. Implementation	• Write detailed user documentation • Provide training for the system users
7. Maintenance	• Build a help desk to support the system users • Provide an environment to support system changes

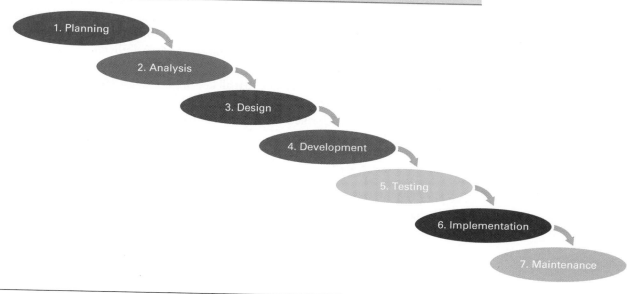

2. *Set the project scope:* You must define the project's scope and create a project scope document for your systems development effort. The project scope clearly defines the high-level requirements. Scope is often referred to as the 10,000-foot view of the system or the most basic definition of the system. A ***project scope document*** is a written document of the project scope and is usually no longer than a paragraph. Project scoping is important for many reasons; most importantly

Figure 6.3

A Sample Project Plan

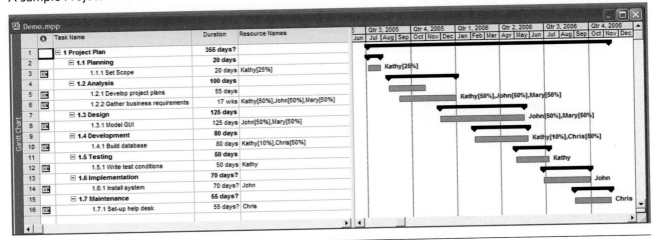

it helps you avoid *scope creep* and *feature creep*. **Scope creep** occurs when the scope of the project increases beyond its original intentions. **Feature creep** occurs when developers (and end-users) add extra features that were not part of the initial requirements.

3. *Develop the project plan*: You must develop a detailed project plan for your entire systems development effort. The **project plan** defines the *what*, *when*, and *who* questions of systems development including all activities to be performed; the individuals, or resources, who will perform the activities; and the time required to complete each activity. The project plan is the guiding force behind ensuring the on-time delivery of a complete and successful information system. Figure 6.3 provides a sample project plan. A **project manager** is an individual who is an expert in project planning and management, defines and develops the project plan, and tracks the plan to ensure that all key project milestones are completed on time. **Project milestones** represent key dates by which you need a certain group of activities performed. Either of the two creeps alluded to above can throw off a project plan.

PHASE 2: ANALYSIS

Once your organization has decided which system to develop, you can move into the analysis phase. It's worthwhile to point out at this juncture that Analysis answers the "what" questions (what is required?) and Design answers the "how" questions (how will we provide what is required?). The **analysis phase** of the SDLC involves end-users and IT specialists working together to gather, understand, and document the business requirements for the proposed system. The following are the two primary activities you'll perform during the analysis phase.

1. *Gathering the business requirements*: **Business requirements** are the detailed set of end-user requests that the system must meet to be successful. The business requirements drive the entire system. A sample business requirement might state, "The CRM system must track all customer inquiries by product, region, and sales representative." The business requirement states what the system must do from the business perspective. Gathering business requirements is similar to

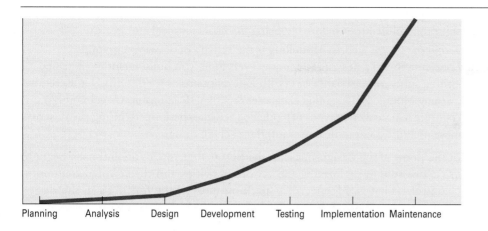

Planning   Analysis   Design   Development   Testing   Implementation   Maintenance

Figure 6.4

The Cost of Finding Errors

performing an investigation. You must talk to everyone who has a claim in using the new system to find out what is required. An extremely useful way to gather business requirements is to perform a joint application development session. During a ***joint application development (JAD)*** session users and IT specialists meet, sometimes for several days, to define and review the business requirements for the system.

2. *Prioritize the business requirements*: Once you define all the business requirements, you prioritize them in order of business importance and place them in a formal comprehensive document, the ***requirements definition document***. The users receive the requirements definition document for their sign-off. ***Sign-off*** comprises the users' actual signatures indicating they approve all the business requirements. Typically, one of the first major milestones in the project plan is the users' sign-off on business requirements.

One of the key things to think about when you are reviewing business requirements is the cost to the company of fixing errors if the business requirements are unclear or inaccurate. An error found during the analysis phase is relatively inexpensive to fix; typically, all you have to do is change a Word document. An error found during later phases, however, is incredibly expensive to fix because you have to change the actual system. Figure 6.4 displays how the cost to fix an error grows exponentially the later the error is found in the SDLC.

PHASE 3: DESIGN

The primary goal of the ***design phase*** of the SDLC is to build a technical blueprint of how the proposed system will work. During the analysis phase, end-users and IT specialists work together to develop the business requirements for the proposed system from a logical point of view. That is, during analysis you document business requirements without respect to technology or the technical infrastructure that will support the system. As you move into design, the project team turns its attention to the system from a physical or technical point of view. You take the business requirements generated during the analysis phase and define the supporting technical architecture in the design phase. The following are the primary activities you'll perform during the design phase.

1. *Design the technical architecture*: The ***technical architecture*** defines the hardware, software, and telecommunications equipment required to run the system. Most systems run on a computer network with each employee having a workstation and the application software running on a server. The telecommunications requirements encompass access to the Internet and the ability for end-users

to connect remotely to the server. You typically explore several different technical architectures before choosing the final technical architecture.

2. *Design the system models*: Modelling is the activity of drawing a graphical representation of a design. You model everything you build including screens, reports, software, and databases (with E-R diagrams as we described in Extended Learning Module F [Designing Databases & TITY-Relationship Diagramming]). There are many different types of modelling activities performed during the design phase including a graphical user interface screen design.

It is at the point of the design phase in the SDLC that you, as an end-user, begin to take a less active role in performing the various activities and divert your attention to "quality control." That is, IT specialists perform most of the functions in the design through maintenance phases. It is your responsibility to review their work, for example, verifying that the models of the screens, reports, software, and databases encapsulate all of the business requirements.

PHASE 4: DEVELOPMENT

During the ***development phase*** of the SDLC, you take all your detailed design documents from the design phase and transform them into an actual system. This phase marks the point at which you go from physical design to physical implementation. Again, IT specialists are responsible for completing most of the activities in the development phase. The following are the two main activities performed during the development phase.

1. *Build the technical architecture*: For you to build your system, you must first build the platform on which the system will operate. In the development phase, you purchase and implement equipment necessary to support the technical architecture you designed during the design phase (servers, networks, etc.).

2. *Build the database and programs*: Once the technical architecture is built, you initiate and complete creation of supporting databases and writing of software required for the system. These tasks are usually undertaken by IT specialists, and it may take months or even years to design and create the databases and write all the software.

PHASE 5: TESTING

The ***testing phase*** of the SDLC verifies that the system works and meets all the business requirements defined in the analysis phase. Testing is critical. The following are the primary activities you'll perform during the testing phase.

1. *Write the test conditions*: You must have detailed test conditions to perform an exhaustive test. ***Test conditions*** are the detailed steps the system must perform along with the expected results of each step. The tester will execute each test condition and compare the expected results with the actual results to verify that the system functions correctly. Each time the actual result is different from the expected result, a "bug" is generated, and the system goes back to development for a "bug fix." A typical systems development effort has hundreds or thousands of test conditions. You must execute and verify all of these test conditions to ensure that the entire system functions correctly.

2. *Perform the testing of the system*: You must perform many different types of tests when you begin testing your new system. A few of the more common tests include

   • ***Unit testing***—tests individual units or pieces of code for a system.

- *System testing*—verifies that the units or pieces of code written for a system function correctly when integrated into the total system.
- *Integration testing*—verifies that separate systems can work together.
- *User acceptance testing (UAT)*—determines if the system satisfies the business requirements and enables users to perform their jobs correctly.
- *Risk-based testing*—ranks the functions or features of a system that are most prone to failure, and tests them first.
- *Volume testing*—it's quite possible to test whether a system can do one calculation correctly, but can it do a million such calculations in three seconds, for example? Or access 100,000 database records in time to answer a time-sensitive question? This is the purpose of volume testing.
- *Stress (or load) testing*—the ability of a system to maintain a certain level of performance under unusual (unfavourable) circumstances. Such things as system crashes, output metrics, and others can be compared against accepted benchmarks.
- *Regression testing*—often, errors that have already been fixed reappear later in the design process. This can occur for a variety of reasons, but regression testing is designed to catch such re-emergence.

PHASE 6: IMPLEMENTATION

During the *implementation phase* of the SDLC you distribute the system to all the users and they begin using the system to perform their everyday jobs. The following are the two primary activities you'll perform during the implementation phase.

1. *Write detailed user documentation*: When you install the system, you must also provide employees with *user documentation* that highlights how to use the system. Users find it extremely frustrating to have a new system without documentation.

2. *Provide training for the system users*: You must also provide training for the users who will use the new system. You can provide several different types of training; two of the most popular are on-line training and workshop training. *On-line training* runs over the Internet or off a CD or DVD. Employees perform the training at any time, on their own computers, at their own pace. This type of training is convenient because they can set their own schedule to undergo the training. *Workshop training* is held in a classroom environment and is led by an instructor. Workshop training is most suitable for difficult systems for which employees need one-on-one time with an individual instructor.

You also need to choose the implementation method that best suits your organization, project, and employees to ensure a successful implementation. When you implement the new system, you have four implementation methods you can choose from:

1. *Parallel implementation* uses both the old and new systems until you're sure that the new system performs correctly.

2. *Plunge implementation* discards the old system completely and immediately uses the new system.

3. *Pilot implementation* has only a small group of people using the new system until you know it works correctly; then the remaining people are added to the system.

4. *Phased implementation* installs the new system in phases (e.g., accounts receivable, then accounts payable) until you're sure it works correctly; then the remaining phases of the new system are implemented.

FEDEX BELIEVES TESTING DOESN'T DELIVER

Testing is a critical step in any systems development effort. Just ask the people at FedEx. FedEx believes so strongly in testing, and that current testing methodologies are antiquated and don't work, that it has commissioned the University of Memphis to research and study software testing and develop a new methodology that will deliver real results.

Called *Systems Testing Excellence Program*, the University of Memphis faculty and students in the FedEx Institute of Technology program at the university will attempt to develop testing methodologies that ensure that applications are of the highest quality while doing so in a shorter period of time than current

testing methodologies. Using current methodologies, software code is written and turned over to a testing group; testers look for bugs and send those back to the development team. The development team must then assess the bug and determine if in fact it is a bug or if it results from an incorrect business requirement specification. Whatever the case, FedEx doesn't believe current testing methodologies work. According to Dave Miller, vice president of IT at FedEx, "We sort of believe that testing as a discipline has probably not kept up pace."

University students who stand out during the project may potentially be hired by FedEx to continue their work in the testing field.[2]

PHASE 7: MAINTENANCE

Maintaining the system is the final phase of any systems development effort. Interestingly, the maintenance phase is usually of the longest duration; the first six phases might take a few months to a few years, but the maintenance phase might last 20 years. During the ***maintenance phase*** of the SDLC, you monitor and support the new system to ensure that it continues to meet the business goals. Once a system is in place, it must change as your business changes. Constantly monitoring and supporting the new system involves making minor changes (for example, new reports or information retrieval) and reviewing the system to be sure that it continues to move your organization toward its strategic goals. The following are the two primary activities you'll perform during the maintenance phase.

1. *Build a help desk to support the system users*: One of the best ways to support users is to create a ***help desk***. A help desk is a group of people who respond to users' questions. Typically, users have a phone number for the help desk they call whenever they have issues or questions about the system. Providing a help desk is a terrific way to provide comprehensive support for users using new systems.

2. *Provide an environment to support system changes*: As changes arise in the business environment, you must react to those changes by assessing their impact on the system. It might well be that the system needs to be adapted or updated to meet the ever-changing needs of the business environment. If so, you must modify the system to support the new business environment.

LO2

Component-Based Development

The systems development life cycle you just read about is one of the oldest software development methodologies. In design and development (as well as the other phases), the SDLC takes a very singular view of the system under consideration and focuses solely on its development. That is, the SDLC does not really allow the development team to look around a software library and find existing code that can be reused for the new system under consideration, and this has some tremendous disadvantages. Most notably, all software is written from scratch each time it is needed for each application. For example, there are probably many applications in the typical organization that have some sort of customer view screen and the ability to update a customer's information. However, within the traditional SDLC, the software that supports the customer view screen and the ability to update the information would be written each time for each application.

This has given rise to the notion of component-based development. *Component-based development (CBD)* is a general approach to systems development that focuses on building small self-contained blocks of code (components) that can be reused across a variety of applications within an organization. The goal here, for example, is to write the customer view screen and updating software only once, place it in a library of software components, and then allow software development teams to plug that component (rather like the notion of *plug-and-play*) into whatever system needs to be developed.

Component-based development dramatically changes the systems development life cycle. It requires teams to (1) look through the software library for reusable code that already exists and (2) build new software in the form of components that can be reused later in other software development projects. In this approach, you can find new systems development methodologies being used including *rapid application development*, *extreme programming*, and *agile*.

In this context, it's worthwhile to relate another important technology paradigm (service-oriented architecture or SoA) to component-based development. SoAs are explained in more depth in the next chapter, but we can spend a moment here making sense of this technology in the current context. The philosophy behind SoAs suggests in part that business processes can be decomposed into their most granular tasks, and software implementations can then be created to exploit the similarities between such granular processes, thereby allowing many organizations under the same management umbrella—such as a federal government—to take advantage of the same atomic process.

This principle can be generalized to a wider audience, however, when considering the similarity between process across industries (and not just in a vertical sense such as is seen with governments). Any organization that requires shipping, for example, can purchase (or pay a fee) to a shipping expert (such as FedEx or Purolator) to embed and use its service software in the host's systems. Thus the host, whose expertise might be manufacturing, need not create a system to handle shipping when a perfectly good one is available for a fee from a service provider such as FedEx.

The same logic can be extended to much smaller units of service. If you want to embed a service in a personal Web site that provides the current temperature where you live, why not use The Weather Network? And if you want to calculate the BMI (Body Mass Index) of a visitor to your site, why not purchase, for a tiny fee each time it is accessed, a web-based service whose job it is to do that calculation? Why reinvent the wheel? Components and a service-oriented architecture can clearly lighten your application creation load.

RAPID APPLICATION DEVELOPMENT METHODOLOGY

The *rapid application development (RAD)* (also called *rapid prototyping*) *methodology* emphasizes extensive user involvement in the rapid and evolutionary construction of working prototypes of a system to accelerate the systems development process (see Figure 6.5 on the next page).

The fundamentals of RAD include

1. Perform the planning and analysis phases in a similar manner as if you were using the traditional systems development life cycle.

Figure 6.5

The Rapid Application Development (RAD) Methodology

2. Review the software library to determine if components already exist that can be used as part of the new system.

3. Create prototypes (i.e., working models of software components) that look and act like aspects of the desired system. Design, develop, and test the prototypes until they become fully functional software components.

4. Integrate the software components from the previous two steps and test them as a complete system.

5. Implement the new system, following many of the guidelines found in the traditional SDLC.

6. Provide ongoing support and maintenance.

Overall, you want to actively involve end-users in the analysis phase and in the iterative approach to the design, development, and testing of new software components. This end-user involvement and the use of prototyping tend to greatly accelerate the collecting of business requirements and the development of the software (i.e., software components). Moreover, if you can find reusable software components in the software library, the acceleration of the overall process is even greater. Prototyping is an essential part of the RAD methodology and we'll discuss it in more detail in a later section.

EXTREME PROGRAMMING METHODOLOGY

The *extreme programming (XP) methodology* breaks a project into tiny phases, and developers cannot continue on to the next phase until the current phase is complete. XP is a lot like a jigsaw puzzle; there are many small pieces (i.e., software components). Individually, the pieces make no sense, but when they are combined together an organization can gain visibility into the entire system. The primary difference between the traditional SDLC and XP methodologies is that XP divides its phases into iterations (see Figure 6.6). Although not shown in Figure 6.6, the XP methodology, much like the RAD methodology, does rely heavily on reusing existing software components contained in a software library.

Microsoft Corporation developed Internet Explorer and Netscape Communications Corporation developed Communicator using extreme programming. Both companies

PERSPECTIVES

MERCEDES-BENZ: BUILT-TO-ORDER TRUCKS FROM BUILT-TO-ORDER SOFTWARE

"Which driver's cabs and radios are available for a 24-tonne rig?" In the past, such a question would have cost Mercedes-Benz dealers a lot of time leafing through big manuals. Today, the Mercedes-Benz Web site offers orientation to the multitude of equipment variations with the Mercedes-Benz customer advisory system (MBKS), developed by CAS Software AG.

The on-line program, called Truck Online Configurator (TOC), required much more development time than simply displaying the finished on-line systems for the automobile and transporter divisions with other data and image material. The TOC was given a completely new user guide that orients itself on the different demands of the Web site visitors in three ways: through technical features, trade solution, and transport task. For example, interested customers are able to compile their own vehicle preference by entering the required technical details, such as the type of drive, wheelbase, or engine performance needed. Or an interested customer can select by trade solution or transport task (where he or she simply tells the TOC that a truck is

required for the transportation of frozen foods, for example) and a list of suitable models is offered.

CAS had only five months in which to realize this complex and extensive application, from the definition of the specialist requirements, to the technical specifications, right up to the development, testing, and installation of the software. This tight deadline required a risk-driven project management, which meant that individual phases of the project would overlap. While a few developers, together with the project managers of Mercedes-Benz, were clarifying the technical requirements of the individual functions, other parts of the TOC were already being implemented.

The CAS solution was virtually tailor-made for this project. The finished programs run in an extremely fast and stable manner. These were the central, technical requirements of Mercedes-Benz for the TOC: the company wanted an application that boasts maximum availability with minimum response times.

Thanks to using the rapid application development (RAD) process, CAS was capable of very quickly creating a high-quality application.[3]

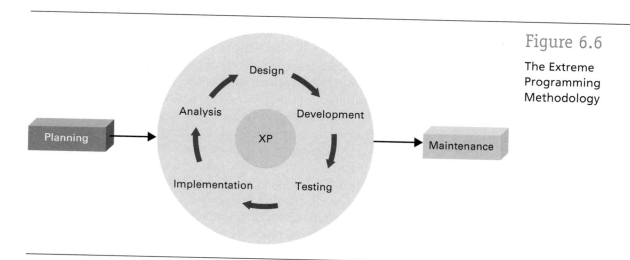

Figure 6.6

The Extreme Programming Methodology

did a nightly compilation (called a *build*) of the entire project, bringing together all the current components. They established release dates and expended considerable effort to involve customers in each release. The extreme programming approach allowed both Microsoft and Netscape to manage millions of lines of code as specifications changed and evolved over time. Most importantly, both companies frequently held user design reviews and strategy sessions to solicit and incorporate user feedback.[4]

XP is a significant departure from traditional software development methodologies, and many organizations in different industries have developed successful software using it. One of the reasons for XP's success is that it stresses customer satisfaction. XP empowers developers to respond to changing customer and business requirements, even late in the systems development life cycle, and emphasizes teamwork. Managers, customers, and developers are all part of a team dedicated to delivering quality software. XP implements a simple, yet effective, way to enable group style development. The XP methodology supports quickly being able to respond to changing requirements and technology.

AGILE METHODOLOGY

The *agile methodology*, a form of XP, aims for customer satisfaction through early and continuous delivery of useful software components. Agile is similar to XP but with less focus on team coding and more on limiting project scope. An agile project sets a minimum number of requirements and turns them into a deliverable product. Agile means what it sounds like: fast and efficient; small and nimble; lower cost; fewer features; shorter projects.

The Agile Alliance, a group of software developers, has made its mission to improve software development processes. Its manifesto includes the following tenets

- Satisfy the customer through early and continuous delivery of valuable software.
- Welcome changing requirements, even late in development.
- Business people and developers must work together daily throughout the project.
- Build projects around motivated individuals. Give them the environment and support they need, and trust them to get the job done.
- The best architectures, requirements, and designs emerge from self-organizing teams.
- At regular intervals, the team reflects on how to become more effective, then tunes and adjusts its behaviour accordingly.[5]

SERVICE-ORIENTED ARCHITECTURE—AN ARCHITECTURE PERSPECTIVE

Regardless which component-based methodology your organization chooses to use as its software development approach, it will most likely be employing a software architecture perspective called a *service-oriented architecture*. A *service-oriented architecture (SOA or SoA)* is a software architecture perspective that focuses on the development, use, and reuse of small self-contained blocks of code (called *services*) to meet all the application software needs of an organization. These *services* within the SoA architecture perspective are exactly the same as *components* in any of the component-based development methodologies.

An SoA is a high-level, holistic organizational approach to how your organization views and acts on all its software needs. If adopted, your organization would, in essence, be saying that all software will be developed and managed as a series of reusable services (blocks of code). From within your SoA perspective, you would then choose from among the different component-based development methodologies that support the concept of reusable services (i.e., components) for the development of specific systems. Those development methodologies would not include the traditional SDLC, but rather the approaches we just covered—RAD, XP, and agile.

CGI is a Canadian outsourcing, systems integration, and consulting company heavily involved in assisting clients to prepare for the inevitable shift to SoA. While reaping the early benefits of the move to SoA, CGI offers a combination of skilled expertise and evolutionary planning and implementation services to a worldwide clientele.[6]

SoAs are growing rapidly in business importance and we'll cover this topic further in Chapter 7.

CANADIAN GOVERNMENT AND SOA

One very compelling definition of a service is that it is something that doesn't exist until it's consumed. From this perspective, a taxi ride or a haircut are the same as a bank loan or a government grant. While the mechanism to deliver the service might well exist, the actual service is not found on a shelf at the local store, but rather requires the cooperation of a provider and a consumer in order for it to exist in a tangible way. Governments are enormous providers of services for the consumption of their citizenry.

The Government of Canada (GoC) has become a leader in embracing the concept of, and realizing value from, a Service-oriented Architecture (SoA). Many government departments, agencies, and programs provide service to Canadians. Examples of such services include providing a grant, delivering advice to entrepreneurs, providing information to immigrants, and a whole range of other tangible outputs that provider and consumer deem to be of value. According to the Treasury Board of Canada, "This makes service a very important and reusable building block for planning and designing government programs that achieve desired outcomes." The defining principle of SoA from a GoC perspective is that SoA represents a paradigm (a model or a pattern or a way of understanding something) for classifying and exploiting service delivery that, while possibly under the control of different departments or ministries, can be managed such that the federal government can appear to act and behave as one.

An excellent example is provided in understanding the origins of the RGBB (Receiver General Buy Button). The Receiver General for Canada (who as the Minister of Public Works and Government Services [PWGSC]) is responsible for, among many other things, collecting payments from Canadians (or others) who must pay a fee for a particular GoC product or service. Imagine the many, many Web sites that provide a mechanism for such payment. Now imagine if each such department were to undertake the development of a unique mechanism for transferring funds from clients to the Receiver General. Each time a customer arrived at a different GoC site, he or she would be met with a different look and feel and rules for payment. Cries of

"Why can't you standardize this process?" would be raised. Standardization is exactly what an SoA can help to implement. According to the Receiver General, the RGBB (which appears on various Web sites as a button with the caption "Buy" on it) specified the elements of the common business process (transferring funds) and elevated it to the level of a shared business service. Thus PWGSC was able to offer a standard approach to collecting fees on-line via credit cards without each department having to reinvent the wheel to do so.

In the Information Systems world, an organization's needs are typically met by either building or buying computer applications and systems. In this sense, if complex systems can be decomposed into small discrete units that mirror or model common business processes, then a Service-oriented Architecture can be employed in order to maximize the applicability of such systems.

If a haircut can be made to look like a taxi ride from the perspective of the systems that are required to manage the service, then barbers and taxi drivers can use the same system components to manage their business process. That's the value of SoA and that's the benefit reaped by the Government of Canada in implementing their version of SoA.[7, 8, 9]

There are challenges to SoA that need to be examined as well. The list would likely include

- Security—when an application needs to be open to interacting to other systems, whether in-house or over the Internet cloud, security concerns need to be raised.

- Testing—the methodology and implementation techniques surrounding SoA are not nearly as mature as with other methods (even those of component-based development). Thus the testing toolkit is not nearly as complete or rich.

- Management—when a system issues and receives potentially thousands (or more) of messages from distributed services, the issue of managing all this information is paramount. As the technology matures, more and more robust techniques will surely emerge.

LO3

Self-Sourcing (End-User Development)

What we want to look at now is how you, as a knowledge worker and end-user, can go about developing your own systems, which we call *self-sourcing* or *end-user development*. Recall that self-sourcing (end-user development) is the development and support of IT systems by end-users (knowledge workers) with little or no help from IT specialists. End-users are individuals who will use a system. Although they skilled are in their own domain, they are not IT or computer experts, and yet they know very well what they want from a system and are capable of developing such systems. Applications developed by end-users support a wide range of decision-making activities and contribute to business processing in a wide range of tasks. Although certainly not on the level of enterprise-wide enterprise resource planning systems, applications developed by end-users are an important source for the organization's portfolio of information systems. The major tools for self-sourcing have been, and continue to be, spreadsheets and database management systems and Web development.

Rapidly gaining in acceptance is the idea that self-sourcing can be a potent source of stress *relief* rather than a cause of stress. Rather than combating the trend toward end-user application development, IT staff should leverage it to offload solution building to end-users. IT then frees its own scarce resources for complex, visible, infrastructure management tasks. A successful strategy for self-sourcing relies on two keys: (1) knowing which applications are good candidates and (2) providing end-users with the right tools. After working through the self-sourcing process, we'll revisit the two keys.

THE SELF-SOURCING PROCESS

You can probably create many of the small end-user computing systems in a matter of hours, such as customizing reports, creating macros, building queries, and interfacing a letter in a word processing package with a customer database to create individualized mailings. More complicated systems, such as a student registration system or an employee payroll system, require that you follow some formal process (from among those discussed above) during development.

In Figure 6.7, we've illustrated the self-sourcing process. As you can see, the self-sourcing process is similar to the phases in the SDLC. However, you should notice that the self-sourcing process encompasses prototyping (model building, steps 3 through 6), which we'll cover thoroughly in the next section. This is key—when you develop a system for yourself, you will most often go through the process of prototyping, continually building on and refining your model or prototype until the system is complete. As you consider the key tasks in self-sourcing in Figure 6.8, we alert you to several important issues.

ALIGNING YOUR SELF-SOURCING EFFORTS WITH ORGANIZATIONAL GOALS

When you first begin planning a system, you must consider it in light of your organization's goals. If you're considering developing a system for yourself that is counterintuitive to your organization's goals, then you should abandon it immediately. You also have to consider how you spend your time building systems carefully, since you are busy and your time is valuable. It's important to remember that building a system takes time—*your* time.

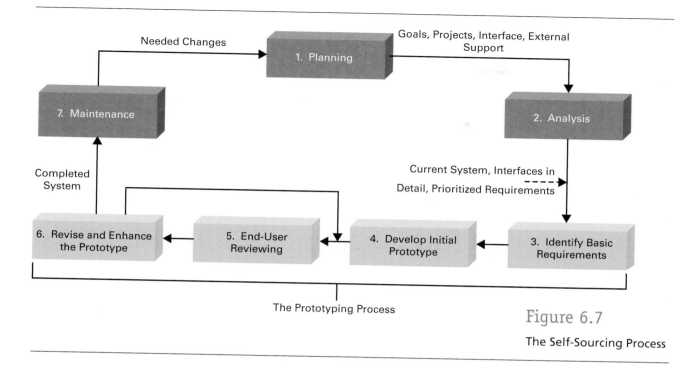

Figure 6.7

The Self-Sourcing Process

Figure 6.8

Key Tasks in Self-Sourcing

KEY TASKS IN SELF-SOURCING

Planning
- Define system goals in light of organizational goals.
- Create a project plan.
- Identify any systems that require an interface.
- Determine what type of external support you will require.

Analysis
- Study and model the current system.
- Understand the interfaces in detail.
- Define and prioritize your requirements.

Support
- Completely document the system.
- Provide ongoing support.

DETERMINING WHAT EXTERNAL SUPPORT YOU WILL REQUIRE Some self-sourcing projects may involve support from IT specialists within your organization. These may be located within the IT department, as is the case when the IT function is located within its own area (i.e., top-down silo or matrix structure). They may also be located within your department, as is the case when the IT function is fully integrated across all units. Your in-house IT specialists are a valuable resource during the self-sourcing process; be sure to include them in the planning phase. The chances of building a successful system increase greatly when you have both end-users and IT specialists working together.

DOCUMENTING THE SYSTEM ONCE COMPLETE Even if you're developing a system just for yourself, you still need to document how it works. When you get promoted or move on, other people will probably use the system you developed and might even make changes to it. For this reason, you must document how your system works from a technical point of view as well as create an easy-to-read user's manual.

PROVIDE ONGOING SUPPORT   When you develop a system through self-sourcing, you must be prepared to provide your own support and maintenance. Since you are the primary owner and developer of the system, you're solely responsible for ensuring the system continues to function properly and continues to meet all the changing business requirements. You must also be prepared to support other end-users who use your system, as they will be counting on you to help them learn and understand the system you developed. The systems development process doesn't end with implementation: It continues on a daily basis with support and maintenance.

THE ADVANTAGES OF SELF-SOURCING

- *Improves requirements determination*—During insourcing, end-users tell IT specialists what they want. In self-sourcing, end-users essentially tell themselves what they want. Potentially, this greatly improves the chances of thoroughly understanding and capturing all the business requirements and thus the prospect of success for the new system.
- *Increases end-user participation and sense of ownership*—No matter what you do, if you do it yourself, you always take more pride in the result. The same is true when developing an IT system through self-sourcing. If end-users know that they own the system because they developed it and now support it, they are more apt to participate actively in its development and have a greater sense of ownership, resulting in a better product.
- *Increases speed of systems development*—Many small systems do not lend themselves well to insourcing and the traditional SDLC. These smaller systems may suffer from "analysis paralysis" because they don't require a structured step-by-step approach to their development. In fact, insourcing may be slower than self-sourcing for smaller projects.
- *Reduces the invisible backlog*—No organization has all the resources to develop every system that end-users need. If end-users can take on the development of some of the smaller systems, the end result is the reduction of the backlog of systems that the organization needs to develop. The ***invisible backlog*** is the list of all systems that an organization needs to develop but—because of the prioritization of systems development needs—never get funded because of the lack of organizational resources.

POTENTIAL PITFALLS AND RISKS OF SELF-SOURCING

- *Inadequate end-user expertise leads to inadequately developed systems*—Many self-sourcing systems are never completed because end-users lack the real expertise with IT tools to develop a complete and fully working system. This might seem like no big deal, since the system couldn't have been that important if the people who needed it never finished developing it. But that's not true. If end-users devote time to the self-sourcing process and never complete the system, that time is wasted.
- *Lack of organizational focus creates "privatized" IT systems*—Many self-sourcing projects are done outside the IT systems plan for an organization, meaning there may be many private IT systems that do not interface with other systems and that contained uncontrolled and duplicated information. Such systems serve no meaningful purpose in an organization and can lead to only more problems.

- *Insufficient analysis of design alternatives leads to sub-par IT systems*—Some end-users jump to immediate conclusions about the hardware and software they should use without carefully analyzing all the possible alternatives. If this happens, end-users may develop systems whose components are inefficient.
- *Lack of documentation and external support leads to short-lived systems*—When end-users develop a system, they often forgo documentation of how the system works and fail to realize that they can expect little or no support from IT specialists. All systems—no matter who develops them—must change over time. End-users must realize that anticipating those changes is their responsibility and making those changes will be easier if they document their system well.
- *Lack of consideration for security leads to potential gaps in protection*—When end-users create their own systems, they often take for granted their access to data. Thus they tend to build in access to critical resources without considering that they might have role-based access to such resources that others might not have. End-users also often think of security measures as a nuisance, and ignore (or are ignorant of) the implications of security breaches.

WHICH APPLICATIONS FOR IT TO OFFLOAD

The following checklist helps IT staff to determine which applications are in IT's domain and which are good candidates for self-sourcing. IT delivers maximum value to the enterprise by focusing on high-cost, high-return applications with the following characteristics:

- Infrastructure-related
- Mission-critical ES such as ERP, CRM, SCM, as well as business intelligence and e-business systems
- Support large numbers of concurrent users, for example, call centre applications.

Other applications may be good candidates for self-sourcing.

THE RIGHT TOOL FOR THE JOB

Requirements for self-sourcing tools and enterprise development tools (for IT specialists) are quite different. Ease of use is paramount for self-sourcing development tools. That's because end-users are not skilled programmers and might use the development tools so infrequently that they can forget commands that aren't intuitive. Therefore, end-users must have development tools that

- *Are easy to use*—This is essential for rapid, low-cost development. For application programs, specific characteristics of ease-of-use include simple data entry, error checking for values in lists and ranges, easy report generation (e.g., drag and drop), and ease of Web publishing.
- *Support multiple platforms*—To minimize support requirements, end-users should select one or two development tools that run on the range of hardware platforms and operating systems within the organization.
- *Offer low cost of ownership*—Cost factors include not only the tool's purchase price, but also training time, speed of application development, and required skill level.
- *Support a wide range of data types*—By its very nature, data is dynamic. Therefore, the toolset should support all the features normally found in database management system products.

LO4

Prototyping

Prototyping is the process of building a model that demonstrates the features of a proposed product, service, or system. A **prototype**, then, is simply a model of a proposed product, service, or system. If you think about it, people prototype all the time. Automobile manufacturers build prototypes of cars to demonstrate and test safety features, aerodynamics, and comfort. Building contractors construct models of homes and other structures to show layouts and fire exits.

In systems development, prototyping can be an invaluable tool for you. Prototyping is an iterative process in which you build a model from basic business requirements, have users review the prototype and suggest changes, and further refine and enhance the prototype to include suggestions. Prototyping is a dynamic process that allows end-users to see, work with, and evaluate a model and suggest changes to that model to increase the likelihood of success of the proposed system. Prototyping is an invaluable tool in the component-based development methodologies (RAD, XP, and agile), self-sourcing, and insourcing.

You can use prototyping to perform a variety of functions in the systems development process:

- *Gathering requirements*: Prototyping is a great requirements- gathering tool. You start by simply prototyping the basic system requirements. Then you allow end-users to add more requirements (information and processes) as you revise the prototype.
- *Helping determine requirements*: In many systems development projects, end-users aren't sure what they really want. They simply know that the current system doesn't meet their needs. In this instance, you can use prototyping to help end-users determine their exact requirements.
- *Proving that a system is technically feasible*: Let's face it, there are some things to which you cannot apply technology. And knowing whether you can is often unclear when defining the scope of the proposed system. If you're uncertain about whether something can be done, prototype it first. A prototype you use to prove the technical feasibility of a proposed system is a **proof-of-concept prototype**.
- *Selling the idea of a proposed system*: Many people resist changes in IT. The current system seems to work fine, and they see no reason to go through the process of developing and learning to use a new system. In this case, you have to convince them that the proposed system will be better than the current one. Because prototyping is relatively fast, you won't have to invest a lot of time to develop a prototype that can convince people of the worth of the proposed system. A prototype you use to convince people of the worth of a proposed system is a **selling prototype**.

THE PROTOTYPING PROCESS

Prototyping is an excellent tool in systems development. Most often, IT specialists (insourcing) use prototyping in the SDLC to form a technical system blueprint. In self-sourcing, however, you can often continue to refine the prototype until it becomes the final system. The prototyping process for either case is almost the same up to a point; only the result differs. Figure 6.9 illustrates the difference between insourcing and self-sourcing prototyping. Regardless of who does the prototyping, the prototyping process involves four steps:

- *Identify basic requirements*: During the first step, you gather the basic requirements for a proposed system. These basic requirements include input and output

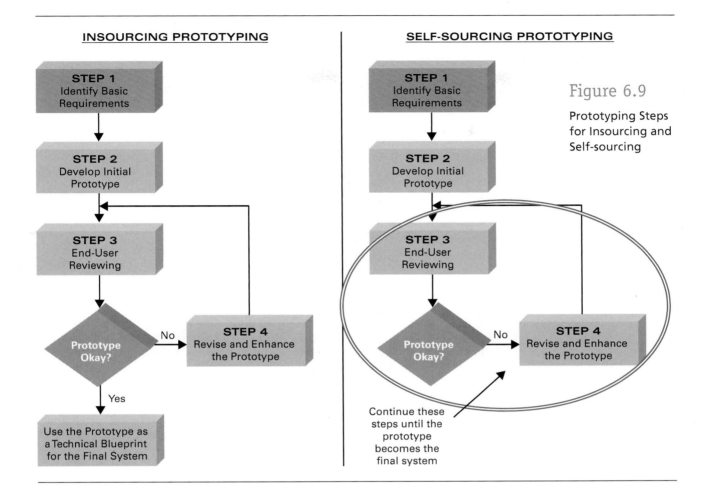

Figure 6.9

Prototyping Steps for Insourcing and Self-sourcing

information desired and, perhaps, some simple processes. At this point, you're typically unconcerned with editing rules, security issues, or end-of-period processing (for example, producing T4s for a payroll system at the end of the year).

- *Develop initial prototype*: Having identified the basic requirements, you then set out to develop an initial prototype. Most often, your initial prototype will include only user interfaces, such as data entry screens and reports.

- *End-user reviewing*: Step 3 starts the truly iterative process of prototyping. When end-users first initiate this step, they evaluate the prototype and suggest changes or additions. In subsequent returns to step 3 (after step 4), they evaluate new versions of the prototype. It's important to involve as many end-users as possible during this iterative process. This will help resolve any discrepancies in such areas as terminology and operational processes.

- *Revise and enhance the prototype*: The final sequential step in the prototyping process is to revise and enhance the prototype according to any end-user suggestions. In this step, you make changes to the current prototype and add any new requirements. Next, you return to step 3 and have the end-users review the new prototype; then step 4 again, and so on.

For either insourcing or self-sourcing, you continue the iterative processes of steps 3 and 4 until end-users are happy with the prototype. What happens to the prototype after that, however, differs.

During self-sourcing, you're most likely to use the targeted application software package or application development tool to develop the prototype. This simply means that you can continually refine the prototype until it becomes the final working system. For example, if you choose to develop a simple CRM application using Microsoft Access, you can prototype many of the operational features using Microsoft Access development tools. Because you develop these prototypes using the targeted application development environment, your prototype can eventually become the final system. This also holds true for component-based development methodologies.

That process is not necessarily the same when insourcing and using the traditional SDLC. Most often, IT specialists develop prototypes using special prototyping development tools. Many of these tools don't support the creation of a final system—you simply use them to build prototypes. Therefore, the finished prototype becomes a blueprint or technical design for the final system. In the appropriate stages of the SDLC, IT specialists will implement the prototype in another application development environment better suited to the development of production systems.

THE ADVANTAGES OF PROTOTYPING

- *Encourages active end-user participation*—First and foremost, prototyping encourages end-users to actively participate in the development process. As opposed to interviewing and reviewing documentation, prototyping allows end-users to see and work with models of a proposed system.
- *Helps resolve discrepancies among end-users*—During the prototyping process, many end-users participate in defining the requirements for and reviewing the prototype. The word many is key. If several end-users participate in prototyping, you'll find it's much easier to resolve any discrepancies the end-users may encounter.
- *Gives end-users a feel for the final system*—Prototyping, especially for user interfaces, provides a feel for how the final system will look and work. When end-users understand the look and feel of the final system, they are more likely to see its potential for success.
- *Helps determine technical feasibility*—Proof-of-concept prototypes are great for determining the technical feasibility of a proposed system.
- *Helps sell the idea of a proposed system*—Finally, selling prototypes can help break down resistance barriers. Many people don't want new systems because the old ones seem to work just fine, and they're afraid the new system won't meet their expectations and work properly. If you provide them with a working prototype that proves the new system will be successful, they will be more inclined to buy into it.

THE DISADVANTAGES OF PROTOTYPING

- *Leads people to believe the final system will follow shortly*—When a prototype is complete, many people believe that the final system will follow shortly. After all, they've seen the system at work in the form of a prototype—how long can it take to bring the system into production? Unfortunately, it may take months or even years. End-users need to understand that the prototype is only a model, not the final system missing only a few simple bells and whistles. Thus some apparent speed advantages of prototyping are in fact an artefact of the developer leaving out (or for inclusion later) code that is risky, or difficult to build or test. Thus the apparent advantage is actually a false economy—but one that could be avoided by carefully using risk-based testing (see the section on testing in this chapter).

THE KEY TO PROTOTYPING MAY BE IN VISUALIZATION

Using high-fidelity prototyping and simulation, software developers are now able to greatly accelerate the already fast and efficient process of prototyping. These sorts of visual definition capabilities can be found in prototyping products published by the likes of Compuware, Borland, and Serena. According to Forrester analyst Carey Schwaber, these tools "let you construct upfront a fairly accurate simulation of what the application's going to look like down the road. Instead of describing what you want, you work with a business analyst or usability engineer to construct it. It serves as a visual contract between business and development."

According to Ron Beck, director of software development at Bally Technologies, his company has had great success using Serena's Composer, a definition modelling and prototyping tool. Bally offers many IT–related products to the casino and gaming industry. One such product is Bally's latest enterprise accounting product. According to Beck, Composer has greatly reduced the time it takes to map casino-specific processes to the accounting software. In a short amount of time, it gives users an understanding of how the accounting software will handle functions unique to the gaming industry.

As Beck explains it, "We used to waste so much time on mapping requirements due to lack of communication. Now we're able to model the interface and interactions between systems and users to see what works."[10]

- *Gives no indication of performance under operational conditions*—Prototypes seldom take all operational conditions into consideration. This problem surfaced at the Department of Motor Vehicles in a state on the East Coast. During prototyping, the system, which handled motor vehicle and driver registration for the entire state, worked fine for 20 workstations at two locations. When the system was finally installed for all locations (which included more than 1,200 workstations), the system spent all its time just managing communication traffic; it had absolutely no time to complete any transaction. This is potentially the most significant drawback to prototyping. You must prototype operational conditions as well as interfaces and processes.

- *Leads the project team to forgo proper testing and documentation*—You must thoroughly test and document all new systems. Unfortunately, many people believe they can forgo testing and documentation when using prototyping. After all, they've tested the prototype; why not use the prototype as the documentation for the system? Don't make that mistake.

Outsourcing

LO5

The third choice as to who will build your IT systems—beyond insourcing (in-house IT specialists) and self-sourcing (end-users)—is outsourcing. Outsourcing is the delegation of specific work to a third party for a specified length of time, at a specified cost, and at a specified level of service. With competitive pressures to cut costs and reduce time to market, many organizations are looking to outsource their IT systems development (not to mention ongoing operation, maintenance, and support). The Outsourcing Research Council recently completed a study indicating that human resources (HR) is the top outsourcing area for many companies. Fifty percent of the companies surveyed said they were already outsourcing some or all of their payroll processing and another 38 percent said they were considering it.[11]

Energizer, the world's largest manufacturer of batteries and flashlights, outsourced its HR operations to ADP, one of the top HR outsourcing companies. Energizer currently has more than 3,500 employees and 2,000 retired employees who all require multiple HR IT–related services. ADP provides Energizer with centralized call centres, transaction-processing services, and Web-based employee self-service systems. Energizer's vice president of human resources, Peter Conrad, stated, "ADP was clearly the most capable, and offered the kind of one-stop shopping our company was looking for." For several of the systems provided by ADP employee usage topped over 80 percent in the first six months the systems were active.[12]

The main reasons behind the rapid growth of the outsourcing industry include the following:

- *Globalization*: As markets open worldwide, competition heats up. Companies may engage outsourcing service providers to deliver international services. And outsourcing service providers may be located throughout the globe.

- *The Internet*: Barriers to entry, such as the lack of capital, are dramatically reduced in the world of e-business. New competitors enter the market daily.

- *Growing economy and low unemployment rate*: Building a competitive workforce domestically is much harder and more expensive.

- *Technology*: Technology is advancing at such an accelerated rate that companies often lack the resources, workforce, or expertise to keep up.

- *Deregulation*: As private industries such as telecommunications and energy deregulate, markets open and competition increases.

IT outsourcing today represents a significant opportunity for your organization to capitalize on the intellectual resources of other organizations by having them take over and perform certain business functions in which they have more expertise than IT specialists in your company. Information technology outsourcing enables organizations to keep up with market and technology advances with less strain on human and financial resources and more assurance that the IT infrastructure will keep pace with evolving business practices. IT outsourcing for software development can take one of four forms (see Figure 6.10):

1. Purchase existing software.
2. Purchase existing software and pay the publisher to make certain modifications.
3. Purchase existing software and pay the publisher for the right to make modifications yourself.
4. Outsourcing the development of an entirely new and unique system for which no software exists.

In these instances, we're not talking about personal productivity software you can buy at a local computer store. We're talking about large software packages that may cost millions of dollars. For example, every organization has to track financial information, and there are several different systems they can purchase that help them perform this activity. Have you ever heard of Oracle Financials? This is a great system your organization can buy that tracks all organizational financial information. If Oracle Financials is exactly what you need (i.e., it meets all your business requirements), then you act on option 1. If it meets most of your needs, you can act on either option 2 or 3. However, if you have a need for a unique suite of software that doesn't exist in the commercial market, you need to act on option 4. Let's explore that process.

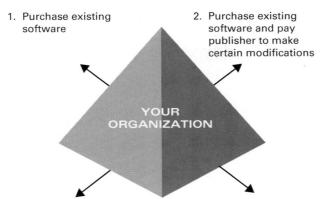

Figure 6.10

Major Forms of Outsourcing Systems Development

1. Purchase existing software

2. Purchase existing software and pay publisher to make certain modifications

YOUR ORGANIZATION

4. Outsource the development of an entirely new and unique system for which no software exists

3. Purchase software and pay publisher for the right to make modifications yourself

THE OUTSOURCING PROCESS

The outsourcing process is both similar to and quite different from the systems development life cycle. It's different in that you turn over much of the design, development, testing, implementation, and maintenance steps to another organization. It's similar in that your organization begins with planning and defining the project scope (see Figure 6.11 on the next page). It's during one of these first two phases of the process that your organization may come to understand that it needs a particular system but cannot develop it in-house. If so, that proposed system can be outsourced. That is step 3, of the process, in Figure 6.10, the selection of a target system for outsourcing. Below, we briefly describe the remaining steps in the outsourcing process, starting with step 4 in Figure 6.11.

ESTABLISH LOGICAL REQUIREMENTS   Regardless of your choice of insourcing or outsourcing, you must still perform the analysis phase—especially the primary activity of gathering the business requirements for the proposed system. Remember that identification of the business requirements drives the entire systems development effort; if the business requirements are not accurate or complete, there is no way the system will be successful. If you choose to outsource, part of gathering the business requirements becomes step 5, your request for proposal.

DEVELOP A REQUEST FOR PROPOSAL (RFP)   Outsourcing involves telling another organization what you want. What you want is essentially the logical requirements for a proposed system, and you convey that information by developing a request for proposal. A *request for proposal (RFP)* is a formal document that describes in excruciating detail your logical requirements for a proposed system and invites outsourcing organizations (which we'll refer to as vendors) to submit bids for its development. An RFP is one of the two most important documents in the outsourcing process. (The other is a service level agreement.) For systems of great size, your organization may create an RFP that's hundreds of pages long and requires months of work to complete.

It's vitally important that you take all the time you need to create a complete and thorough RFP. Eventually, your RFP will become the foundation for a legal and binding contract into which your organization and the vendor will enter. At a minimum, an RFP

Figure 6.11

The Outsourcing Process

includes key information such as an overview of your organization, underlying business processes that the proposed system will support, a request for a detailed development time frame, and a request for a statement of detailed outsourcing costs.

All this information is vitally important to both your organization and the vendors. For your organization, the ability to develop a complete and thorough RFP means that you completely understand what you have and what you want. For the vendors, a complete and thorough RFP makes it easier to propose a system that will meet most, if not all, of your needs.

EVALUATE RFP RETURNS AND SELECT A VENDOR   Your next activity in outsourcing (step 6 in Figure 6.11) is to evaluate the RFP returns and choose a vendor. You perform this evaluation of the RFP returns according to a scoring mechanism you identified in the RFP. This is not a simple process. No two vendors will ever provide RFP returns in the same format, and the RFP returns you receive are usually longer than the RFP itself.

CREATE A SERVICE LEVEL AGREEMENT (SLA)   Once you've chosen a vendor, a lengthy legal process follows. Outsourcing is serious business, and serious business between two organizations almost always requires a lot of negotiating and the use of lawyers. Eventually, your organization has to enter into a legal and binding contract that very explicitly states the features of the proposed system, the exact system costs, the time frame for development, acceptance criteria, criteria for breaking the contract for non-performance or non-compliance, and post-development metrics for activities such as maintenance, support, operational performances, and so on. This legal and binding contract is often called a service level agreement, which we'll discuss in more detail after explaining the remaining steps in the outsourcing process.

TEST AND ACCEPT THE SOLUTION   As with all systems, testing and accepting the solution are crucial. Once a vendor installs the new system, it's up to you and your organization to test the entire system before accepting it. You'll need to develop detailed test plans and test conditions that test the entire system. This alone may involve months of running and testing the new system while continuing to operate the old one (the parallel method).

When you "accept" a solution, you're saying that the system performs to your expectations and that the vendor has met its contractual obligations thus far according to the service level agreement. Accepting a solution involves granting your sign-off on the system, which releases the vendor from any further development efforts or modifications to the system.

MONITOR AND RE-EVALUATE   Just like the systems you develop using the SDLC, systems you obtain through outsourcing need constant monitoring and re-evaluation. In outsourcing, you also have to reassess your working relationship with the vendor. Is the vendor providing maintenance when you need it and according to the service level agreement? Does the system really perform the stated functions? Do month-end and year-end processes work according to your desires? Does the vendor provide acceptable support if something goes wrong? These are all important questions that affect the ultimate success of your outsourcing efforts.

THE SERVICE LEVEL AGREEMENT

When you contract the services of an outsourcing organization (i.e., vendor), you will most likely do so using a service level agreement. Broadly, a ***service level agreement (SLA)*** is a formal contractually obligated agreement between two parties. Within different environments, an SLA takes on different meanings. In the context of systems development, an SLA defines the work to be done, the time frame, the metrics that will be used to measure the success of the systems development effort, and the costs. Most SLAs are business oriented and void of detailed technical specifications. Technical specifications are included in a supporting document (similar to a contract addendum) called a ***service level specification (SLS)*** or ***service level objective (SLO)***.

If the vendor further agrees to provide post-development maintenance and support, then the SLA outlines in detail the terms of the maintenance and support activities, their costs, and—again—key metrics by which the success of those activities will be measured. The metrics you include in an SLA are the real key, and we'll describe and define such metrics in Chapter 7 when discussing how to create quantifiable measures of the value of an IT system.

Here's an example of a simplified service level agreement for an Internet Access and Hosting Service (see Figure 6.12).

- Overview
- General definitions
- Service level principles
- Service covered by this agreement
   a. Dial access services
   b. Dedicated access services
   c. Internet hosting services
- Internet access and hosting service level agreement
   a. Service availability
   b. Mean time to restore
- Provisioning on time delivery
- Excluded items

Figure 6.12

Sample Service Level Agreement

GEOPOLITICAL OUTSOURCING OPTIONS

In a geopolitical sense, furthermore, there are three types of outsourcing:

1. ***Onshore outsourcing*** is the process of engaging another company in the same country for services. Much of the current jargon relating to outsourcing is based on the United States as the reference point. Thus, "onshore" outsourcing typically means contracting a U.S. company to provide business services.

2. ***Nearshore outsourcing*** is contracting an outsourcing arrangement with a company in a nearby country. Often, this country will share a border with the native country. Again, this term is often used with the United States as the frame of reference. In this case, nearshore outsourcing will take place in either Canada or in Mexico, usually.

3. ***Offshore outsourcing*** is contracting with a company that is geographically far away. For many companies, certain IT services, such as application development, maintenance, and help desk support, fall within the category of functions that are ideal for *offshore* outsourcing.

Although onshore and nearshore outsourcing are important forms in the outsourcing industry, when outsourcing is spoken about nowadays, it is usually offshore outsourcing that is being referenced.

OFFSHORE OUTSOURCING   From a humble beginning as a mere cost-cutting concept, offshore outsourcing has gradually moved ahead and established itself as a successful business model by rendering not only cost-effective but also sophisticated and highly efficient quality services. According to International Data Corporation (IDC), U.S.-based companies tripled their offshore outsourcing spending from $5.5 billion in 2000 to more than $17.6 billion in 2005. The offshore outsourcing trend has overcome all barriers of political turmoil, language problems, and culture differences, and has proved that no matter in which part of the world your outsourcer resides, what really matters is industry-standard, high-quality service together with decisive cost advantage.[13]

What of the Canadian perspective? Are Canadians considered players in this huge trend? Yes and no. The Canadian and U.S. experiences differ in both form and content. While Canadians are the target of U.S. outsourcing, it is increasingly apparent that one of our big advantages was the low dollar, vis-à-vis the U.S. currency. When it is economical to do so, U.S. interests will outsource to Canada. While the case of Dell Computer's scaling back and closing of Canadian call centres in Ottawa and elsewhere cannot be wholly explained by the rise of the loonie (as the company has faced stiff competition in its segment from U.S. rivals such as HP), it is clear that Canada's outsourcing fortunes rise and fall in tandem with the dollar.

On the other hand, as major outsourcing nations such as China and India are joined by the Philippines, Poland, Hungary, Brazil, and Mexico, players such as Canada's SITEL (controlled by the Toronto-based private equity firm ONEX) are becoming major players in the management and provision of outsourcing. So Canada does play on both sides of the field in this important area.[14]

What types of functions or projects make good candidates for offshore outsourcing? Data conversions and system migrations with well-defined requirements and specifications and minimal end-user interaction with the development team are typical projects taken offshore. Naturally, the company must be willing to allow its application code to be located offsite during development. Application development projects are also good offshore candidates. From a SDLC perspective, offshore work is most beneficial in the

■ Figure 6.13

Typical Salary Ranges for
Computer Programmers

Country	Salary Range per Year ($US)
China	$5,168–9,302
India	$6,201–10,338
Philippines	$6,719–11,371
Russia	$7,236–13,439
Ireland	$21,709–28,946
Canada	$37,000–73,000 ($CDN)
United States	$62,027–93,042

development and testing phases where end-user interaction is limited, and the task is well defined. For stable applications, most maintenance activities can be performed remotely so application maintenance is also a good candidate for offshore outsourcing. With the right communication infrastructure and a clear understanding of your company's business language requirements, call centre or help desk functions can also be moved offshore.

THE ADVANTAGES AND DISADVANTAGES OF OUTSOURCING

Making the decision to outsource may be critical one way or the other to your organization's success. Thus far in our discussion of outsourcing, we've alluded to some advantages and disadvantages of outsourcing. Following is a summary of the major advantages and disadvantages of outsourcing the systems development process, in order to help you make the important outsourcing decision.

ADVANTAGES   Your organization may benefit from outsourcing because outsourcing allows you to

- *Focus on unique core competencies*: By outsourcing systems development efforts that support non-critical business functions, your organization can focus on developing systems that support important, unique core competencies.
- *Exploit the intellect of another organization*: Outsourcing allows your organization to obtain intellectual capital by purchasing it from another organization. Often you won't be able to find individuals with all the expertise required to develop a system. Outsourcing allows you to find those individuals with the expertise you need to get your system developed and implemented.
- *Better predict future costs*: When you outsource a function, whether systems development or some other business function, you know the exact costs.
- *Acquire leading-edge technology*: Outsourcing allows your organization to acquire leading-edge technology without having to acquire technical expertise and bear the inherent risks of choosing the wrong technology.
- *Reduce costs*: Outsourcing is often seen as a money saver for organizations. Reducing costs is one of the important reasons organizations outsource.
- *Improve performance accountability*: Outsourcing involves delegating work to another organization at a specified level of service. Your organization can use this specified level of service to guarantee that it gets exactly what it wants from the vendor.

DISADVANTAGES   Outsourcing may *not* be a beneficial option for you because it

- *Reduces technical know-how for future innovation*: Outsourcing is a way of exploiting the intellect of another organization, so it can also mean that your organization will no longer possess that expertise internally. If you outsource because you don't have the necessary technical expertise today, you'll probably have to outsource for the same reason tomorrow.
- *Reduces degree of control*: Outsourcing means giving up control. No matter what you choose to outsource, you are in some way giving up control over that function.
- *Increases vulnerability of your strategic information*: Outsourcing systems development involves telling another organization what information you use and how you use that information. In doing so, you could be giving away strategic information and secrets.
- *Increases dependency on other organizations*: As soon as you start outsourcing, you immediately begin depending on another organization to perform many of your business functions.

Summary: STUDENT LEARNING OUTCOMES *REVISITED*

LO1 Define the traditional systems development life cycle (SDLC) and describe the seven major phases within it. The *systems development life cycle (SDLC)* is a structured step-by-step approach for developing information systems. The seven major phases within it include

- *Planning*—creating a solid plan for developing your information system
- *Analysis*—gathering, understanding, and documenting the business requirements
- *Design*—building a technical blueprint of how the proposed system will work
- *Development*—taking all the design documents and transforming them into an actual system
- *Testing*—verifying that the system works and meets all the business requirements
- *Implementation*—distributing and using the new system
- *Maintenance*—monitoring and supporting the new system.

LO2 Compare and contrast the various component-based development methodologies. Component-based methodologies (CBD) include

- *Rapid application development (RAD or rapid prototyping)*—extensive user involvement in the rapid and evolutionary construction of working prototypes of a system to accelerate the systems development process.
- *Extreme programming (XP)*—breaks a project into tiny phases, with each phase focusing on a small aspect of the system that eventually becomes a component or small software module.
- *Agile*—aims for customer satisfaction through early and continuous delivery of useful software components.

LO3 Describe the self-sourcing process as an alternative to the traditional systems development life cycle. *Self-sourcing (end-user development)* is the development and support of IT systems by end-users with little or no help from IT specialists. While the traditional SDLC uses in-house IT specialists to develop a system, self-sourcing has the user developing his or her own system. The user typically prototypes the system using the targeted application software environment and can thus continually refine and enhance the prototype until it becomes the final working system.

LO4 **Discuss the importance of prototypes and prototyping within any systems development methodology.** *Prototyping* is the process of building a model (i.e., *prototype*) that demonstrates the features of a proposed product, service, or system. Prototyping can be used effectively to gather requirements, help determine requirements when they are unknown, prove that a system is technically feasible (*proof-of-concept prototype*), and sell the idea of a proposed system (*selling prototype*).

LO5 **Describe the outsourcing environment and how outsourcing works.** *Outsourcing* is the delegation of specific work to a third party for a specified length of time, at a specified cost, and at a specified level of service. Outsourcing is growing today because of globalization, the Internet, a growing economy and low unemployment rate, technology, and deregulation. Everything from food service to payroll services to call centres is being outsourced. In the outsourcing process, you target a system for outsourcing and build a *request for proposal (RFP)* that invites vendors to bid for its development. You choose a vendor and enter into an agreement called a *service level agreement (SLA)* that states exactly what the vendor will do. In the end, you test and accept the solution from the vendor and begin using the system.

CLOSING CASE STUDY 1
Getting on the Right Track at General Motors

"Our data tells us that the vehicle owners that don't have a satisfactory dealership repair experience are only half as likely to buy that model car again." Think about the ramifications of that statement. If a vehicle owner has a poor experience with something as simple as an oil change, that person is only half as likely to spend $30,000 or more on that model of car again. That is quite the return on investment (ROI) for providing a good experience for an oil change that costs about $50.

Bryan Burkhardt, global director of retail inventory management for General Motors (GM) service and parts operations, made the above statement. Bryan very clearly understands the relationship between after-sales and service and retaining the loyalty of a customer. Unfortunately, left to their own devices, most parts managers at any of GM's 7,000 North American dealerships overstock too many of the more commonly sold parts and seldom have those on hand that are infrequently purchased. As Bryan explains, there is "not enough breadth of parts, but way too much depth on the ones they do have."

That "not enough breadth of parts" means that GM repair shops have been providing customers with

a satisfactory repair experience only 67 percent of the time. Bryan and his team set out to change that and implemented a new inventory management system, upping the satisfactory repair experience to 96 percent of the time. The new inventory management system is a centralized, Web-based system that tracks inventory levels in real time. If the quantity on hand for any part ever falls below 5, the system notifies the parts manager and automatically routes an order for parts replenishment to one of 16 national parts distribution centres. The system can even accommodate regional differences and keep more of certain parts on hand for dealerships in a given region, such as more snow tires for dealerships in the north during the fall and winter. All told, the system tracks over 500,000 GM parts from 4,000 different suppliers.

One of the biggest challenges facing Bryan and his team is that each of the dealerships is allowed to choose its own dealership management system, resulting in the use of 28 different systems. So far, the new centralized inventory management system has been certified to work with only six of those systems. Because of the increase in productivity and inventory efficiencies, GM is working with the new inventory management system to provide certification for more of the dealership-centric systems in the hope that all systems will be certified and all dealerships converted to the new inventory management system. As the new inventory management system is certified to work with another dealership management system, GM pilots the system with a few of the dealerships interested in making the conversion. When the system is determined to work correctly, the remaining dealerships are encouraged to make the conversion.

The new inventory management system is yielding both efficiency and effectiveness. From an efficiency point of view, the new system improves inventory turnover by about 11 percent. It also reduces the time parts managers spend on reviewing inventory and ordering parts from 90 minutes per day to just 10 to 15 minutes per day.

But the most important results are being realized in the area of effectiveness, that is, customer-centric measures such as satisfaction. As Bryan explains it, "At heart, it's about enhancing the ownership experience." After all, providing a satisfactory repair experience doubles the chances that the automobile owner will buy that same model again. In short, customer retention is key.[15]

Questions

1. In implementing the new inventory management system and converting existing users (dealerships) to it, what sort of implementation method is GM using? In your opinion, why is this the most appropriate method? If you had to choose a different implementation method, what would it be and why?

2. Why do you believe that General Motors has allowed its 7,000 North American dealerships to choose different dealership management systems? What are the advantages to allowing this freedom of choice? What are the disadvantages to such an approach?

3. The new inventory management system provides a satisfactory repair experience 96 percent of the time, up from 67 percent. While that increase is both strong and good, is 96 percent really that good? Why or why not? What quantitative approach would you use to justify system enhancements to improve the 96 percent to 98 percent? To 100 percent?

4. If you refer back to Chapter 4 and decision support systems, how would you characterize the decision-making process of determining how many parts to keep on hand? Is that mainly a recurring decision or a non-recurring decision? Is that mainly a structured decision or a non-structured decision? For both the latter questions, justify your answers.

5. The new inventory management system reduces the overall costs of parts inventory and, at the same time, increases customer satisfaction. How is this an example of a bottom-line initiative? How is this an example of a top-line initiative? If necessary, refer back to Chapter 1.

CLOSING CASE STUDY 2
Should an Organization Outsource Security?

It may seem like an odd question, one that gets an immediate "no," but think again. Many businesses realize that they do not possess the expertise, time, or money to detect, identify, isolate, and stop the hundreds of hackers, viruses, worms, and other malcontents that daily bombard most IT systems. Moreover, most organizations wouldn't identify "security" as a unique core competency, so there is some argument for outsourcing it. The following statistics come from a survey performed by InformationWeek/Accenture Global Information Security. They identify the percentage of respondents who use an outsourcer for some form of security.

- Firewall management—29 percent
- Intrusion detection management—25 percent
- Messaging protection—18 percent
- Security strategy development—15 percent
- Security governance—11 percent
- End device security—11 percent.

The numbers show that many companies are willing to outsource IT–related security. But under what conditions might this decision cause a problem?

Consider the U.S. *Patriot Act*, for example. In general, the act specifies that if data are on U.S. soil then they can be requisitioned by the U.S. federal government for security purposes, and it is not necessary to inform the owner of such data that they are being scrutinized. Why do Canadians care?

Canadians care because if we outsource to a U.S.–based company, that company is still subject to the act even when doing business with Canadians. Our privacy, therefore, is potentially at risk of being violated. Canadian organizations would do well to make the distinction between security (*which involves availability, confidentiality,* and *integrity*) and privacy (which involves the use to which data can be put as well as consent and disclosure). While data might well be secure, it might not be private if outsourced to foreign interests.

With this caveat in mind, what are the important dimensions an organization's CIO must consider when seeking to outsource to a Managed Security Service Provider (MSSP)? First, a carefully executed vendor selection process, resulting in an airtight service level agreement is crucial. Next, a CIO would be well

advised to remember that 80 percent or more of security breaches occur as a result of the actions of insiders (employees and contractors) rather than outsiders. Thus one would need to consider whether the service being outsourced is capable of reacting to internal as well as external threats.

In Canada, major IT service providers, resellers, and integrators, as well as the major telcos such as Bell, Primus, Allstream, AT&T, and Telus, all offer flavours and varieties of MSSP. The choice is not always a simple one.[16, 17]

Questions

1. If you were developing a new system using the traditional systems development life cycle (SDLC), at what point would you need to identify that you needed to outsource some aspect of IT security?

2. In reference to the first question, how would you continue with the in-house systems development effort and, at the same time, carry on the process of outsourcing IT security with another company?

3. If the management and storage of sensitive health data, for example, were to be outsourced to a U.S.–based company, would it be subject to the *Patriot Act* and be potentially disclosable? Research this topic.

4. Turning over IT security to an outside organization is tantamount to giving another organization complete access to all your systems and information. What stipulations would you include in a service level agreement with an IT security outsourcer to ensure that it didn't exploit the openness of your systems and steal strategic and sensitive information?

5. Do some research on the Web for Canadian companies that specialize in IT security outsourcing (besides Primus, Allstream, AT&T, Telus, and Bell). Whom did you find? Do they seem to be reputable? Do they include a list of clients you can contact for references?

Key Terms and Concepts

Agile methodology, 172
Analysis phase, 164
Business requirement, 164
Component-based development
(CBD), 169
Critical success factor (CSF), 162
Design phase, 165
Development phase, 166
Extreme programming (XP)
methodology, 170
Feature creep, 164
Help desk, 168
Implementation phase, 167
Insourcing, 161
Integration testing, 167
Invisible backlog, 176
Joint application development
(JAD), 165
Maintenance phase, 168
Nearshore outsourcing, 186
Offshore outsourcing, 186
On-line training, 167
Onshore outsourcing, 186

Outsourcing, 162
Parallel implementation, 167
Phased implementation, 167
Pilot implementation, 167
Planning phase, 162
Plunge implementation, 167
Project manager, 164
Project milestone, 164
Project plan, 164
Project scope document, 163
Proof-of-concept prototype, 178
Prototype, 178
Prototyping, 178
Rapid application development
(RAD) (rapid prototyping)
methodology, 169
Regression testing, 167
Request for proposal (RFP), 183
Requirements definition
document, 165
Risk-based testing, 167
Scope creep, 164

Self-sourcing (end-user
development), 161
Selling prototype, 178
Service level agreement (SLA), 185
Service level objective (SLO), 185
Service level specification (SLS), 185
Service-oriented architecture
(SOA or SoA), 172
Sign-off, 165
Stress (or load) testing, 167
Systems development life cycle
(SDLC), 162
System testing, 167
Technical architecture, 165
Test condition, 166
Testing phase, 166
Unit testing, 166
User acceptance testing (UAT), 167
User documentation, 167
Volume testing, 167
Waterfall methodology, 162
Workshop training, 167

Short-Answer Questions

1. Who are the three primary groups of people who undertake the systems development process?
2. What is the systems development life cycle?
3. What are scope creep and feature creep?
4. How do the four implementation methods differ?
5. What is component-based development?
6. How are component-based development and a service-oriented architecture related?
7. Why do organizations prototype?
8. What are the advantages of self-sourcing?
9. What is the difference between a selling prototype and a proof-of-concept prototype?
10. What is the role of a service level agreement (SLA) in outsourcing?
11. What are the three geopolitical forms of outsourcing?

Assignments and Exercises

1. **REQUEST FOR PROPOSAL** A request for proposal (RFP) is a formal document that describes in detail your logical requirements for a proposed system and invites outsourcing organizations to submit bids for its development. Research the Web and find three RFP examples. Briefly explain in a one-page document what each RFP has in common and how each RFP is different.

2. **MAKING THE WHO DECISION** Complete the table below by answering yes, no, or maybe in the columns of insource, self-source, and outsource for each systems development condition listed on the left.

	INSOURCE	SELF-SOURCE	OUTSOURCE
The system will support a unique core competency			
Cost is an overriding consideration			
Time to market is critical			
You possess the necessary expertise			
Organizational control of the system is critical			
The system will support a common business function			
Gaining and having technical expertise is part of your strategic plan			
The system will support only a very few users			

3. **YOUR RESPONSIBILITIES DURING EACH STEP IN THE SDLC** During insourcing, you have many responsibilities because you're a business process expert, liaison to the customer, quality control analyst, and manager of other people. According to which step of the SDLC you're in, your responsibilities may increase or decrease. In the table below, determine the extent to which you participate in each SDLC step according to your four responsibilities. For each row you should number the SDLC steps 1 through 7, with a 1 identifying the step in which your responsibility is the greatest and a 7 identifying the step in which your responsibility is the least.

	SDLC STEP						
	PLANNING	ANALYSIS	DESIGN	DEVELOPMENT	TESTING	IMPLEMENTATION	MAINTENANCE
Business process expert							
Liaison to the customer							
Quality control analyst							
Manager of other people							

4. **CONSTRUCTION AND THE SDLC** The systems development life cycle is often compared to the activities in the construction industry. Fill in the following chart listing some of the activities performed in building a house and how they relate to the different SDLC steps.

SDLC	Activities for Building a Home
Planning	
Analysis	
Design	
Development	
Testing	
Implementation	
Maintenance	

Discussion Questions

1. Why is it important to develop a logical model of a proposed system before generating a technical architecture? What potential problems would arise if you didn't develop a logical model and went straight to developing the technical design?

2. If you view systems development as a question-and-answer session, another question you could ask is, "Why do organizations develop IT systems?" Consider what you believe to be the five most important reasons organizations develop IT systems. How do these reasons relate to topics in the first five chapters of this book?

3. Your company has just decided to implement a new financial system. Your company's financial needs are almost the same as those of all the other companies in your industry. Would you recommend that your company purchase an existing system or build a custom system? Would you recommend your company use end-user development or outsource the new system?

4. There are seven phases in the systems development life cycle. Which one do you think is the hardest? Which one do you think is the easiest? Which one do you think is the most important? Which one do you think is the least important? If you had to skip one of the phases, which one would it be and why?

5. You are talking with another student who is complaining about having to learn about the systems development life cycle, because he is not going to work in an IT department. Would you agree with this student? What would you say to him to convince him that learning about the systems development life cycle is important no matter where he works?

6. A company typically has many systems it wants to build, but unfortunately it usually doesn't have the resources to build all the systems. How does a company decide which systems to build?

7. People often think that a system is complete once it is implemented. Is this true? What happens after a system is implemented? What can you do to ensure the system continues to meet the knowledge workers' needs?

Chapter 7

Enterprise Infrastructure, Metrics, and Business Continuity Planning

Building and Sustaining the Dynamic Enterprise

STUDENT LEARNING OUTCOMES

LO1 Describe how a service-oriented architecture can be used as a philosophical approach to help the organization of the future meet all its IT–related needs.

LO2 Define and describe the various hardware and software infrastructure considerations in an organization.

LO3 Compare and contrast commonly used metrics for assessing the success of IT systems and IT–related initiatives.

LO4 Describe business continuity planning (BCP) and its phases.

OPENING CASE STUDY
Offsite Backup a Snug Fit for Adidas Canada

Adidas Canada's headquarters in Concorde, Ontario, just north of Toronto, supports a head office of about 120 staff; a high-tech distribution facility serving 4,000 retail outlets from Brantford, Ontario, with a staff of about 100; a 30-seat call centre in suburban Montreal; a small showroom in Burnaby, B.C.; about 50 sales reps flogging the Adidas and Taylor Made Golf lines across the country, and a fast-growing owned-retail arm operating 12 stores, with a flagship store still to open at Yonge and Dundas in Toronto.

These varied and far-flung operations generate a lot of data—and this data needs to be backed up. The Brantford warehouse is highly automated, and features insourced (see Chapter 8) software applications that provide supply chain and a myriad of both internal- and external-facing Web applications. With an IT staff of 13—most at head office but one each at the warehouse and call centre—it made sense to Adidas management to outsource the complicated process of maintaining current data backups to an external supplier. Around 2004, the company outsourced its backup management to Toronto-based Storagepipe.

While Adidas decided on the Internet as the connection method to Storagepipe's data centre, the option of a dedicated connection is also available to Storagepipe's customers. While security is not an issue over the SSL-encrypted Internet connection, the choice comes down to cost and quality of service.

Large amounts of data require a sizeable Internet connection and, as Internet traffic tends to be more expensive, an organization will end up paying more for the use of the "free" Internet infrastructure than it would with the same amount of traffic run through a direct connection. But new and so-called *burstable Internet pipes* (whereby clients pay only for the traffic they generate rather than for the capacity to use it) are available at quite reasonable cost.

If a customer does not want its data sent over the Internet, even when encrypted, it can opt for a local or wide area network equivalent—a direct connection.

Adidas backs up its data through Storagepipe on a daily, weekly and monthly schedule. It does its own inhouse backup at year-end.

Because of growth at Adidas, the original business case numbers for the outsourcing are outdated, but the company isn't necessarily preoccupied with cost-effectiveness. Rather, it pays for piece of mind; the knowledge that it can go about its core business, the business of athletics, in the secure knowledge that the company is covered in case of a disaster.[1]

Questions

1. Adidas's agreement with StoragePipe is part of a "business continuity plan." Offsite storage provides a measure of protection for the company's crucial data and information. What sort of "personal continuity plan" do you have for your car, apartment, and other important parts of your life?

2. Are bricks-and-mortar businesses or click-and-order businesses more susceptible to disasters and other interruptions? Justify your answer.

3. When was the last time you were dealing with a company and someone said, "I'm sorry but our computer systems are down right now, so I can't help you"? How did that make you feel? How did you react?

Introduction

In Chapter 6, we introduced you to the concept of a service-oriented architecture within the context of systems development. A *service-oriented architecture (SOA or SoA)* is a software architecture perspective that focuses on the development, use, and reuse of small self-contained blocks of code (called *services*) to meet many or even all the application software needs of an organization. Thus new applications build on past solutions organically using established building blocks. If SoA is adopted, the organization is saying that instead of bringing in brand new systems, all its software will be developed from reusable units of code. SoA is a high-level, holistic organizational approach to how an organization views and acts on all its software needs.

By way of illustration, let's move away from software development—and IT in general— for just a moment and consider the concept of your organization adopting a service-oriented architecture perspective for *everything* it does, such that those self-contained building-blocks of code (services) apply not just to software but also to people, processes, departments and units, operations, and best practices. What would that look like? With a service-oriented architecture philosophy, your organization would

- Be a lean, agile organization that takes advantage of every resource in the most efficient and effective way
- React quickly in a proactive way to perceived changes in the market, competition, and customer demographics, wants, and desires
- Respond quickly to and adapt to new advances in technology
- Transform its processes, structure, and HR initiatives to match a changing and dynamic workforce.

In short, SoA would enable your organization to become the organization of the future, bound by very few structural constraints, able to change on a moment's notice, always looking for and capitalizing on the next great competitive advantage.

Of course this is a book about how organizations use technology, so exploring a service-oriented architecture approach to things like HR or changing customer demographics is beyond our scope. So, let's refocus on IT, referring to Figure 7.1, which outlines how an SoA perspective enables your organization to respond more adeptly to customers, end-users, software development, information needs, and hardware requirements.

CUSTOMERS

An IT–enabled SoA philosophy allows your organization to provide customers with multichannel service delivery options and customizable products and services. Customers should be able to *plug-and-play* into any communications channel with your organization, such as fax, the Web, face-to-face contact, phone call, and so on. Regardless of the communications channel, the experience should be the same—a consistent and high-quality interaction with your organization. From the perspective of a sales manager at an auto dealership, for example, every single inquiry to the dealership, no matter how it is received, should be replied to with the same speed, accuracy, and attention to detail that an in-person request would generate. Price, availability, financing options and vehicle feature information would be accurate.

Customers should also be able to interact with IT systems that allow them to customize and personalize products and services. By simply "plugging in" their desires and wants, your organization should respond with unique and individually tailored offerings that satisfy and delight the customer. We spoke about the concept of mass customization (*slivercasting* and *exclusivity*) in Chapter 5. Keeping with our auto dealer example, customers should be afforded the opportunity to input their wants and desires for vehicle features without having to specify a vehicle and then check the feature list against their own wish list. The system should do the work.

END-USERS

An SoA philosophy requires that your organization view its end-users of IT (i.e., employees within the organization) just as it does external customers. This is mainly achieved through a fully integrated enterprise resource planning (ERP) system that meets every application software and information need of each and every employee. The ERP system should support transparent interoperability across multiple vendors and within ERP modules provided by the same vendor. Because ERP systems are so vitally important to today's integrated and agile organization, we'll further discuss them in an upcoming section in this chapter.

End-users should as well be able to take advantage of multichannel service delivery. In this case, end-users (employees) should be able to access computing and information resources

Figure 7.1

A Service-Oriented
Architecture (SoA)
Philosophy

THE FOCUS	NOTES
CUSTOMERS	• Multichannel service delivery • Consistent, high-quality interactions regardless of the venue • Customizable product and service capabilities
END-USERS	• Fully integrated ERP system • Interoperability among vendors • Interoperability of modules by the same vendor • Mobile computing (access to information and software regardless of location and device)
SOFTWARE DEVELOPMENT	• SoA as a framework • RAD, XP, and agile as development methodologies • Exciting new deployments like Web 2.0
INFORMATION NEEDS	• End-users with access to all types of information • Integrated information, business intelligence, and knowledge • Data warehouses • Standard information formats • Integrity controls • No duplicate information
HARDWARE REQUIREMENTS	• Integration of different technologies and technology platforms • Large storage capacity • Focus on logical, not physical • Safe and secure telecommunications platform

regardless of where they are (the notion of *mobile computing* from Chapter 5). And regardless of the IT device in hand (laptop, desktop, PDA, Web-enabled cell phone), employees should enjoy access to a full range of application software services and information.

SOFTWARE DEVELOPMENT

Organizations today can choose among numerous software development methodologies that focus on the production and reuse of blocks of code to speed the process of software development—rapid application development (RAD), extreme programming (XP), and agile methodology are among them. Each of these is discussed in Chapter 6.

If you delve into the nitty-gritty of software development, you'll find infrastructure platforms that support a service-oriented architecture approach. Some of these include Ajax (**A**synchronous **J**ava**S**cript and **XML**), SOAP (**S**ervice **O**riented **A**rchitecture **P**rotocol), WSDL (**W**eb **S**ervices **D**escription **L**anguage), UDDI (**U**niversal **D**escription, **D**iscovery, and **I**ntegration), and CORBA (**C**ommon **O**bject **R**equest **B**roker **A**rchitecture). Many of these platforms support the Web 2.0 applications—such as wikis, blogs, and mash-ups—that we discussed in Extended Learning Module E (The World Wide Web and the Internet) and Chapter 4.

INFORMATION NEEDS

A service-oriented architecture philosophy leverages the most vitally important organizational resource—information. End-users need access to all types of information on a moment's notice, regardless of where that information is located (or where the end-user is located). People throughout your organization need access to information, business intelligence, and knowledge that supports their **decision**-making efforts. In Chapter 3 we illustrate that data warehouses are built by combining information from multiple sources. These data warehouses are of paramount importance to good decision making.

For those reasons and many more, an SoA approach to information requires that

- Information be in a standard format no matter where it exists
- Strict and rigorous integrity control mechanisms are in place to ensure the completeness, accuracy, and validity of the information
- No duplicate information exists in disparate silos anywhere in your organization
- Any kind of information from any source (even external) can be quickly and easily coupled with other information.

HARDWARE REQUIREMENTS

Finally, a service-oriented architecture philosophy must pervade all choices in the realm of hardware. Organizations should be free to choose different technologies and different technology platforms and integrate them seamlessly (i.e., plug-and-play). Powerful storage area networks should have the capacity to store all your information needs. And you should not have to care where within these networks information is stored; your access to the information should be simple and easy.

Your telecommunications platform should be safe and secure and, at the same time, enable you to access a network, either wired or wireless, using the same steps or procedures. You should never have to look at the back of your computer to determine if you need to log on using a wired protocol or a wireless protocol.

That is what a service-oriented architecture philosophy is all about. Of course, the question now becomes how you implement such a philosophy. That's what the remainder of this chapter is about, specifically

1. Hardware and software infrastructure
2. Metrics for determining success
3. Measures to ensure consistent, uninterrupted success.

LO2

Hardware and Software Infrastructure

Generally, *infrastructure* is a relative term meaning "the structure beneath a structure." This definition implies different layers of structure, which provide support or services. An IT infrastructure is the implementation of an architecture—in our discussion here, a service-oriented architecture. In a city, the infrastructure includes its streets and street lighting, hospitals, schools, utility lines running above and below the ground, and so on. We all depend on this public infrastructure to make lives of communities, cities, and people safe and prosperous. In a corporation, the IT infrastructure includes the hardware, software (such as ES software), and information that (1) ensure the components work together and (2) enable people, business processes, and customers to interact and perform their tasks (see Figure 7.2).

ENTERPRISE RESOURCE PLANNING (ERP) REVISITED

ERP systems are big business; the ERP market is at the top of the IT spending list. For instance, the U.S. federal government will spend $7.7 billion on ERP products and services in fiscal year 2009, up 37 percent from 2004 spending of $5.6 billion. More than 60 percent of the Fortune 1000 companies have installed or are in the process of implementing ERP systems to support their business activities. The packages implemented by the Fortune 1000 companies run well over the IT budgets for most small-to-medium-size enterprises (SME), and ERP vendors are targeting this untapped market for smaller firms by offering simple, cheaper, preconfigured solutions easy to install within budget and time constraints. For instance, Microsoft now offers an ERP solution (called *Microsoft Dynamics*) geared toward the small-to-medium-size company.[2, 3] SAP has three products geared toward the SME market. SAP Business One, one of these three products, focuses on companies that require between 1 and 50 users. A typical cost for this product ranges from $15,000 to $400,000.

The dominating ERP software suppliers are SAP, Oracle, Infor, and Microsoft (see Figure 2.9 on page 53). Together they control more than 70 percent of the multibillion-dollar global market. Each vendor, for historical reasons, has a specialty in one particular

Figure 7.2

Infrastructure

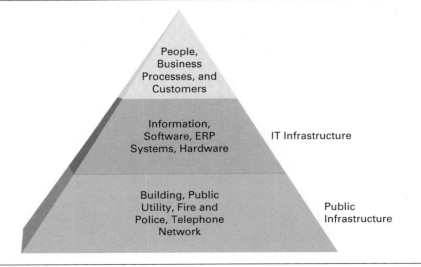

module area such as SAP in logistics, Oracle in financials, Infor in manufacturing, and Microsoft in retail management.

There are also about 50 established and a few more newly emerging smaller and mid-size ERP vendors including third-party developers competing for the very lucrative ERP market. Figure 7.3 displays a list of some other top ERP companies and their Web sites. There is stiff competition, and overlapping products are difficult to differentiate. The vendors are continuously updating their products and adding new technology-based features. Long-term vision, commitment to service and support, specialty features, experience, and financial strength for research and development are considered the major vendor qualities for product selection and implementation.

The ERP market has been growing at a rate of more than 30 percent per year and most forecasts predict more of the same. The growth of the ERP market has been boosted by both business and technical factors. With respect to business, the most cited reason is globalization, which has fostered mergers and stimulated the creation of big corporations with high information requirements that the former individual information systems were not able to fulfill. Another factor is general market maturity in developed countries, which has fostered competition among all companies and increased the power of consumers, thus forcing enterprises to upgrade the efficiency of their business processes. Finally, advances in information and communication technologies have made the development of ERP systems possible by allowing the database centralization to integrate with a distributed ERP environment.

A technical reason for ERP growth has been the introduction of the European Union (EU) currency, the euro, since most of the information systems in the EU zone were not able to handle multiple currencies.

THE EVOLUTION OF ERP SYSTEMS   ERP systems replace "islands of information and processes" with a single, packaged software solution that integrates all the traditional enterprise management functions such as financials, human resources, and manufacturing and logistics. Knowing the history and evolution of ERP is essential to understanding its current application and its future developments. To help give you a better perspective, let's review the evolution of ERP systems (also see Figure 7.4).

The early stage of ERP was carried out in the 1970s through a system called *Materials Requirement Planning (MRP)*. The focus of the MRP software was on internal production planning, calculating time requirements components, procurement, and materials planning. The MRP software did not focus on any type of service orientation, but, rather, was developed to provide the right materials at the right time.

Figure 7.3

Additional ERP Vendors and Their Web Addresses

Additional ERP Vendors and Their Web Addresses	
Invensys www.invensys.com	Cincom www.cincom.com
Visibility www.visibility.com	Verticent www.verticent.com
i2 www.i2.com	NetSuite www.netsuite.com
QAD www.qad.com	Epicor www.epicor.com
IFS www.ifsab.com	SYSPRO www.syspro.com
Exact www.exactamerica.com	
Open Source ERP Vendors and Their Web Addresses	
Compiere www.compiere.com	Openbravo http://www.openbravo.com
OpenERP http://www.tinyerp.org	Opentaps http://www.opentaps.org

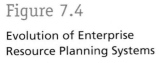

Figure 7.4

Evolution of Enterprise
Resource Planning Systems

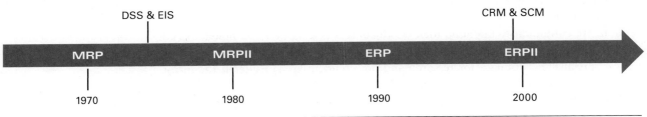

MRP, or "little MRP," represented a huge step forward in the planning process. For the first time, based on a schedule of what was going to be produced, which was supported by a list of materials that were needed for that finished item, the computer could calculate the total needed and compare it to what was already on hand or committed to arrive. This comparison could suggest an activity—to place an order, cancel orders that were already placed, or simply move the timing of these existing orders. The real significance of MRP was that, for the first time, management was able to answer the question "when?"

The next generation of these systems was introduced by the early 1980s under the name *Manufacturing Resources Planning or MRPII*. MRPII did not mean that MRP was done incorrectly the first time, but rather that it had evolved. MRPII closed the loop with the accounting and financial management systems. MRPII systems crossed the boundaries of the production functionality and started serving as decision support systems (DSS) as well as executive information systems (EIS—in the modern day many people refer to implementations of these as *digital dashboards*).

For the first time, a company could have an integrated business system that provided visibility for the requirements of material and capacity. Good information leads to good decisions, and therefore these integrated IT systems provided a competitive advantage.

By the time each functional area of a company had developed its own software program, the need for tightly integrating them became obvious. The next major shift during the late 1980s and early 1990s was that "time to market" was becoming increasingly short. Lead times expected by the market continued to shorten and customers were no longer satisfied with the service level that was considered world class only a few years earlier.

The need to develop a tightly integrated system that would use data stored in common databases and would be used enterprise wide became the highest priority for IT professionals. No longer was it tolerable to submit a request to the IT department and wait several months to obtain this critical information. This common-database, company-wide integrated system appeared at the beginning of the 1990s and was named *enterprise resource planning (ERP)*.

ERP encompasses all the resource planning for the enterprise including product design, warehousing, material planning, capacity planning, and communication systems. ERP systems help companies become leaner and more agile by integrating the basic transaction programs for all departments, allowing quick access to timely information.

ERP systems have evolved into what is now commonly referred to as *ERPII*. During the last few years, the functional perimeter of ERPII systems has begun an expansion into its adjacent markets, such as supply chain management (SCM), customer relationship management (CRM), data warehousing/business intelligence (DWBI), and e-business. The major ERP vendors have been busy developing, acquiring, and/or bundling new functionality so that their packages go beyond the traditional realms of finance, materials planning, and human resources.

ERP AND A SERVICE-ORIENTED ARCHITECTURE   Two of the primary goals of an ERP system within a service-oriented architecture are

1. Provide interoperability within an ERP vendor and for modules among different ERP vendors.
2. Hide the underlying IT infrastructure of information and hardware from end-users and customers.

In the first instance, ***interoperability*** refers to the capability of two or more computing components to share information and other resources, even if they are made by different manufacturers. In the top layer of Figure 7.5, you can see the software infrastructure of an ERP system. Let's assume it's provided by SSA Global, a leading publisher of ERP software. Notice that you see all the typical software modules present—accounting, distribution, supply chain, and the like.

However, two modules have been replaced in Figure 7.5—the HR component by in-house developed software and data analytics by Cognos BI and reporting software. This is the concept of interoperability. Your organization chooses the best ERP solution on the market that meets most of its needs. Within the chosen ERP suite, you can replace software modules with in-house developed software and software modules from other vendors (and software developed through outsourcing for that matter). Long after implementation, you can add other modules and plug them directly into your ERP solution as well. This is the concept of *sustainable interoperability*.

In the lower portion of Figure 7.5, you can see the implementation of the second goal of an ERP system, that is, hide the underlying IT infrastructure of information and hardware from end-users and customers. The ERP system—specifically screens, reports, and the like—are the *customer-facing aspect of the system*. The physical structure and location of information should not be of concern to you as an end-user, nor should the physical hardware infrastructure matter.

ERP ADVANTAGES AND DISADVANTAGES   Finally, although the benefits that an effective and SoA-enabled ERP system can provide are huge, and we have focused on many of those advantages throughout our discussions of ERP, unfortunately, your organization will need to overcome certain problems and disadvantages associated with ERP systems. While we expect these disadvantages to lessen in the coming years, they are important factors to consider when investing in ERP. The advantages and disadvantages of ERP are listed below. You'll notice that many of the advantages have a corresponding disadvantage. This simply means that overall the reaction is mixed to the perceived success of ERP implementations.

Advantages	Disadvantages
• Centralize database	
• Reliable information access	• Time consuming
• Avoid data and operations redundancy	• Expensive
• Delivery and cycle time reduction	• Lack of conformity of modules
• Cost reduction	• Vendor dependence
• Easy adaptability	• Too many features, too much complexity
• Improved scalability	• Questionable scalability and global reach
• Global reach	• Not enough extended ERP capability
• E-business support	

Figure 7.5

An ERP Infrastructure

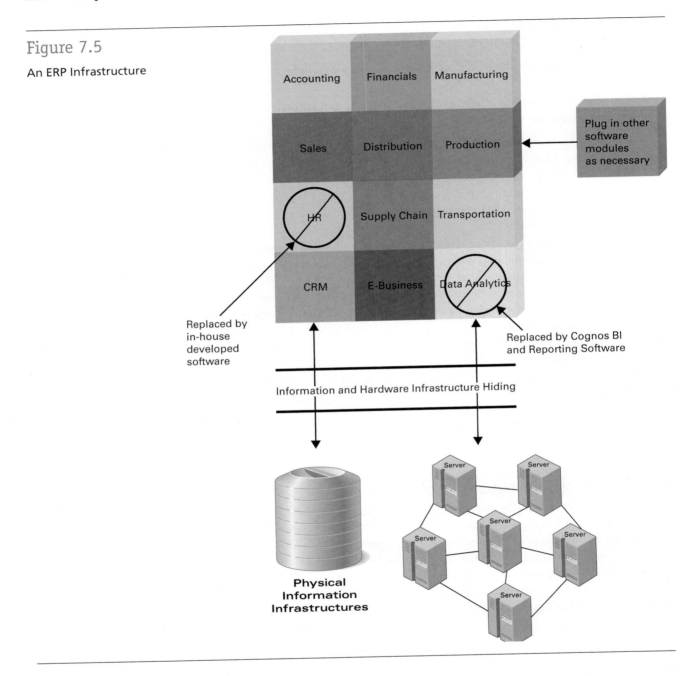

SUPPORTING NETWORK INFRASTRUCTURES

The fundamental underlying infrastructure for any IT environment is a network, two or more computers sharing information, software, peripheral devices, and processing power. Network infrastructure is such a wide and vast field that volumes have been written on the subject and many schools (primarily within the computer science department) offer entire programs and majors in IT networks. Our discussion here focuses on only the five major types of network infrastructures.

DECENTRALIZED INFRASTRUCTURE *A decentralized infrastructure* involves little or no sharing of IT and other resources such as information. Generally, this infrastructure

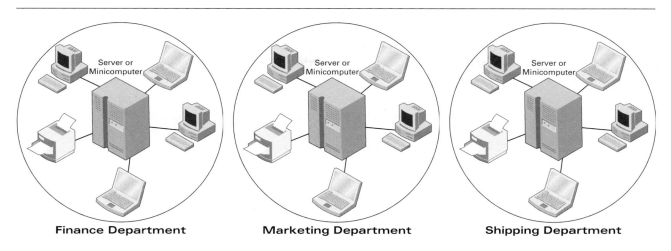

Finance Department   Marketing Department   Shipping Department

Figure 7.6

Decentralized Infrastructure

arises from users or departments developing their own systems or applications, without any central control (see Figure 7.6).

The decentralized infrastructure gives users the liberty to develop applications that meet their needs and maintain control over the applications they develop. However, this infrastructure generally prevents users from easily combining processing power or even comparing information between various information systems. It also encourages data duplication, frequently leading to inconsistencies. For example, Figure 7.6 illustrates a finance, a marketing, and a shipping department, each technologically isolated from the other. Decentralized infrastructures often arise in companies having a decentralized management approach and typically in companies built through acquisition. Decentralized infrastructures are almost a thing of the past.

CENTRALIZED INFRASTRUCTURE   A *centralized infrastructure* involves sharing information systems in one central area or on one central mainframe. For a long time, mainframes were the only computers available for business. By their nature, they dictated that information systems infrastructures be centralized because typically all applications and information were stored on a company's single mainframe. As an example, Figure 7.7 shows a typical layout of a centralized infrastructure. With the introduction of inexpensive desktop computers and reliable data communications technology, almost all organizations have moved away from the centralized infrastructure.

The great advantage of a centralized infrastructure is that it allows a high degree of control, making it easy to (1) maintain standards of hardware, software, procedures, and operations and (2) control access to information. The main disadvantage of a centralized infrastructure is its inflexibility. A centralized infrastructure is run so that it can be used by everyone, but that does not mean that the system is optimal for everyone. Different departments and remote sites have different information needs. As with the decentralized infrastructure, centralized infrastructures are dinosaurs from a different time.

Figure 7.7

Centralized Infrastructure

DISTRIBUTED INFRASTRUCTURE   A *distributed infrastructure* involves distributing the information and processing power of IT systems via a network. (This is the first true network infrastructure.) By connecting all the information systems via a distributed infrastructure, all locations can share information and applications (see Figure 7.8). The major benefit of this is that processing activity can be allocated to the locations(s) where it can most efficiently be done. To improve performance and reduce network traffic, a distributed infrastructure will often store the same application and/or information in two or more locations.

Distributed infrastructures are more complex than centralized infrastructures for several reasons. First, the distributed infrastructure must be able to determine the location of specific applications and information. Second, it must be more sophisticated in determining the optimal way to request the application and information. The order in which the system processes a request can make a significant difference in the amount of data transmitted over the network.

CLIENT/SERVER INFRASTRUCTURE (CLIENT/SERVER NETWORK)   A *client/server infrastructure* (or *client/server network*) has one or more computers that are *servers* that provide services to other computers, called clients. The client/server infrastructure is a form of distributed infrastructure. The basic notion of a client/server infrastructure is that application processing is divided between the client and the server. The functions of an information system are divided among connected computers (or clients) on a network while centralizing processing and storage for all information is on a server. For instance, surfing on the Internet is an example of a client/server infrastructure. Typical components of this type of infrastructure include an Internet browser, a personal computer (e.g., the client), and a Web server.

The primary advantage of the client/server infrastructure is that it offloads the application programs and information from the server. However, because processing occurs at many client locations, and the client and server interact frequently and extensively, information must flow rapidly between server and clients for adequate performance (see Figure 7.9).

Figure 7.8

Distributed Infrastructure

Vancouver Office

Montréal Office

Toronto Office

ONE VIEW FOR DEL MONTE FOODS

From its roots in the California Gold Rush era, San Francisco–headquartered Del Monte Foods has grown to become the largest producer and distributor of premium quality processed fruits, vegetables, and tomato products in the United States. With annual sales of over $3 billion, Del Monte is also one of the largest producers, distributors, and marketers of private-label food and pet products with a powerful portfolio of brands including Del Monte, StarKist, Nature's Goodness, 9Lives, and Kibbles 'n Bits.

Del Monte's acquisition of certain businesses (such as StarKist, Nature's Goodness, 9Lives, and Kibbles 'n Bits) from the H. J. Heinz Company required an integration between Del Monte's and H. J. Heinz's business processes. Del Monte needed to overhaul its IT infrastructure, migrating from multiple platforms, including UNIX and mainframe systems, and consolidating applications centrally on a single system. The work required integration of business processes across manufacturing, financial, supply chain, decision support, and transactional reporting areas.

The revamp of Del Monte's architecture stemmed from a strategic decision. Del Monte decided to implement an ERP system to support its entire U.S. operations, headquarters in San Francisco, operations in Pittsburgh, and distribution centres and manufacturing facilities across the country. The company concluded that the only way it could unite its global operations and open its system to its customers, which are mainly large retailers, was through the use of an ERP system.

Among other key factors was the need to embrace an e-business strategy. The challenge facing Del Monte was to select an ERP system to merge multiple systems quickly and cost-effectively. If financial and customer service targets were to be achieved, Del Monte needed to integrate new businesses that more than doubled the size of the company. Since implementing the ERP system, customers and trading partners are now provided with a single, consistent, and integrated view of the company.[4,5] In Canada, Del Monte's subsidiary CanGro Foods Inc. provides an umbrella for both the Del Monte and the venerable Aylmer brand.

The client/server infrastructure thereby places a heavy load on the network capacity, which can sometimes be a disadvantage. To read about how a client/server network actually works, see either Extended Learning Module B (Network Basics).

TIERED INFRASTRUCTURE   Most enterprise applications are now developed using a tiered infrastructure. In a *tiered infrastructure* (sometimes referred to as a *layered infrastructure*), the IT system is partitioned into tiers (or layers) where each tier (or layer) performs a specific type of functionality. The concept of a tiered infrastructure has evolved from 1-tier to n-tiers. A "tier" can be defined as one of two or more rows, levels, or ranks arranged one above another. Figure 7.10 (on the next page) illustrates the concept of a tiered infrastructure.

- A *1-tier infrastructure* is the most basic setup because it involves a single tier on a single machine. Think of an application that runs on your PC—everything you need to run the application (data storage, business logic, user interface, and so forth) is wrapped up together. An example of a 1-tiered application is a basic word processor or a desktop file utility program.

- A *2-tier infrastructure* is the basic client/server relationship. In essence, the client handles the display, the server handles the request (e.g., database query), and the application tier is contained on one or both of the two tiers.

Figure 7.9

Client/Server Infrastructure

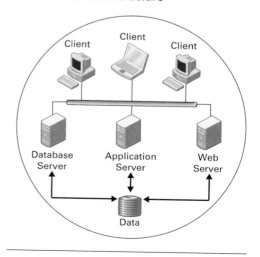

SOA + SAP: COCA-COLA'S NEW SECRET RECIPE

Coca-Cola's business model is a common one among well-known, almost market-dominant, franchisors. Coca-Cola gets the majority of its $18 billion in annual revenue from franchise fees it earns from bottlers all over the world. Bottlers, as part of the franchise agreement, license Coke's secret recipe and many others including recipes for Odwalla, Nestea, Minute Maid, and Sprite. Coca-Cola is now hoping that bottlers will also buy into adopting common business practices using a service-oriented architecture ERP system.

The target platform chosen by Coca-Cola is mySAP enterprise resource planning (ERP) by SAP. If it works, Coca-Cola and its bottlers stand to make and save a lot of money, and SAP will be able to position itself as one of the dominant players in SoA-enabled ERP.

Already, Coca-Cola and many of its bottlers use versions of SAP for finance, manufacturing, and numerous administrative functions. But Coca-Cola wants everyone to move to a "services" architecture environment. Coca-Cola hopes that this services standardization will make its supply chain more efficient and reduce costs.

In explaining why a services approach is so vitally important, Jean-Michel Ares, CIO of Coca-Cola, stated, "That will allow bottlers to converge one step at a time, one process area at a time, one module at a time, at a time that's right for the bottler. We can march across the bottling world incrementally."[6]

Figure 7.10

n-Tier Infrastructure Model

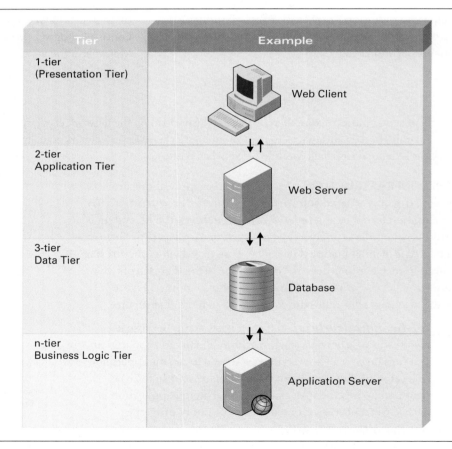

- A **3-tier infrastructure** is the most common approach used for Web applications today. A typical example of this model is the Web browser that acts as the client, an application server that handles the business logic, and a separate tier (such as a DBMS) that handles database functions.
- An **n-tier infrastructure** balances the work of the network over several different servers. The letter "n" stands for any number of tiers. Traditionally, an n-tier infrastructure starts with a basic 3-tier model and expands on it to allow for greater performance, scalability, and a host of other benefits.

IT Success Metrics

As with any organizational initiative, you must build a case for the acquisition, development, and use of technology. Technology costs money, not only for the hardware, software, and other IT–related components but also for the people involved, the changes to business processes, and the foregone opportunity to pursue other initiatives.

To justify the costs of technology, you need to be able to measure the success of technology. **Benchmarking** is the process of continuously measuring system results and comparing those results to **benchmarks**—baseline values a system seeks to attain. Benchmarks are most often industry-specific, process-specific, generated internal to your organization, or some combination of the three. An example is the Canadian high-speed Internet industry, whose members regularly benchmark network traffic throughput (upload and download speeds). They use such measurements to compare their performance against the competition. With these metrics in hand you can make a cost/benefit judgment about technology. Benchmarking can lead to identifying steps and procedures to improve system performance.

EFFICIENCY AND EFFECTIVENESS METRICS

One way to categorize *metrics* (or ways to measure something) is by *efficiency* versus effectiveness. **Efficiency** means doing something right (e.g., in the least time, at the lowest cost, with the fewest errors, etc.), while **effectiveness** is doing the right thing. While the difference may seem subtle or purely semantic, it is not—the concepts are quite distinct. Let's consider a Web development project. A success metric would be Web traffic, perhaps as measured by the number of unique visitors. We refer to that as an efficiency metric because it simply means your organization is really good at driving customers to its Web site (i.e., creating traffic volume). But if those customers don't buy anything, it doesn't matter how many customers come to your site. So, while you may be very efficient in driving customers to your Web site, your Web site is not *effective* at getting those customers to make a purchase.

Most infrastructure-centric metrics today in the IT world are *efficiency metrics*. An **infrastructure-centric metric** is typically a measure of the efficiency, speed, and/or capacity of technology. Infrastructure-centric metrics include

- **Throughput**—the amount of information that can pass through a system in a given amount of time. This is often associated with telecommunications capabilities (bandwidth) such as transmission speeds (kilobits per second, Kbps, and megabits per second, Mbps).
- **Transaction speed**—the speed at which a system can process a transaction.
- **System availability**—usually measured inversely as *downtime*, or the average amount of time a system is down and unavailable to end-users and customers. This does not include regularly scheduled maintenance.

- *Accuracy*—also usually measured inversely as *error rate*, or the number of errors per thousand (or million) that a system generates. This is analogous to defects per thousand or million in manufacturing.
- *Response time*—average time to respond to a user-generated event, such as a request for a report, a mouse click, and so on.
- *Scalability*—how well a system can adapt to increased demands. This is more of a conceptual metric that assesses your ability to upgrade the implemented infrastructure at minimal cost and service interruption.

Effectiveness metrics, on the other hand, measure results of the technology or application in some environment. For example, call centres have numerous effectiveness (success) metrics as do Web e-business applications. We'll explore several metrics for both of those in a moment. Customer relationship management and supply chain management systems have numerous associated metrics as well, including (but certainly not limited to)

- Customer relationship management (CRM)
  - Number of cross-selling successes
  - Cost-per-thousand (CPM)—sales dollars generated per dollar of advertising
  - Number of new customers generated
  - Average length of time a customer stays active (i.e., continues to buy products and services from you)
- Supply chain management (SCM)
  - Number of stockouts
  - Excess inventory
  - Distribution and warehousing costs

It's interesting to note in the above lists that you want to increase the value of all of the CRM metrics (e.g., the more cross-selling successes you have the better). This is a common characteristic of metrics that measure top-line initiatives. Conversely, you want to reduce the value of all the SCM metrics (e.g., have as little excess inventory as possible). This is a common characteristic of metrics that measure bottom-line initiatives.

If you consider the graph in Figure 7.11, you can begin to understand the relationship between efficiency and effectiveness metrics. Bottom-line initiatives, such as supply chain management, seek to optimize efficiency metrics while not negatively affecting effectiveness metrics, and top-line initiatives, such as customer relationship management, seek to optimize effectiveness metrics while not negatively affecting efficiency metrics.

Figure 7.11

Efficiency and Effectiveness Metrics

(It might appear in Figure 7.11 that the optimal area of operation is the upper-right area, but that's simply not true and seldom achievable except when undertaking extraordinary transformational activities. An excellent example here is that of Apple iTunes, which created both tremendous efficiency and effectiveness.)

WEB-CENTRIC METRICS

A *Web-centric metric* is a measure of the success of your Web and e-business initiatives. There are literally hundreds of Web-centric metrics you can use, with some being general to almost any Web or e-business initiative and others being very dependent on the particular initiative. Common Web-centric metrics include

- *Unique visitors*—the number of unique visitors to your sites in a given time. This is commonly used by Nielsen/Net ratings to rank the most popular Web sites.
- *Total hits*—number of visits to your Web site, many of which may be by the same visitor.
- *Page exposures*—average number of page exposures to an individual visitor.
- *Conversion rate*—percentage of potential customers who visit your site who actually buy something.
- *Click-through*—count of the number of people who visit a site, click on an ad, and are taken to the site of the advertiser.
- *Cost-per-thousand (CPM)*—sales dollars generated per dollar of advertising. This is commonly used to make the case for spending money to appear on a search engine.
- *Abandoned registrations*—number of visitors who start the process of completing a registration page and then abandon the activity.
- *Abandoned shopping carts*—the number of visitors who create a shopping cart and start shopping and then abandon the activity before paying for the merchandise.

CALL CENTRE METRICS

Call centre metrics measure the success of call centre efforts. Typical call centre metrics include

- *Abandon rate*—the percentage number of callers who hang up while waiting for their call to be answered.
- *Average speed to answer (ASA)*—the average time, usually in seconds, that it takes for a call to be answered by an person.
- *Time service factor (TSF)*—the percentage of calls answered within a specific time frame, such as 30 or 90 seconds.
- *First call resolution (FCR)*—the percentage of calls that can be resolved without having to call back.

If your call centre operations are partly automated in the hope of helping people with common questions, then you have additional metrics such as the percentage of people who use the automated system and then request also to speak to a service representative.

FINANCIAL METRICS

Ultimately, you must make sense of all your other metrics by comparing them to or incorporating them into financial metrics, or what is more commonly referred to as *capital analysis financial models*. Organizations must be able to express the success of their IT

Figure 7.12

Capital Analysis
Financial Models

Financial Model	Formula	Type of Result
Payback method (in years)	$\dfrac{\text{Original investment}}{\text{Annual net cash flow}}$	= time to pay back
Cost-benefit ratio (as a factor)	$\dfrac{\text{Benefits}}{\text{Costs}}$	= cost-benefit ratio
Return on investment (ROI, as a percent)	$\dfrac{\text{(Benefits – cost – depreciation)}}{\text{useful system life}}$	= net benefit
Net present value (NPV, in \$)	Total net present value of all cash flows[*]	= value today of return in future
Internal rate of return (IRR, as a percent)	The NPV represented as a percentage return[*]	= expected return

[*]The net present value and internal rate of return calculation are too complex to summarize above. So both are defined completely below:

Net present value   = sum of the present value of all future payments less the initial cost
                      $= -CF_0 + \Sigma[CF_t/(1 + r)^t]$ where CF_0 = the initial cost
                                              CF_t = each future payment
                                              r = the discount rate
                                              t = the number of the time payment

Internal rate of return = the rate that completes the following summation equation
Cost $= \Sigma[CF_t/(1 + IRR)^t]$ where CF_t = the future payments
                                              IRR = the internal rate of return
                                              t = the number of the payment

initiatives in terms of dollars and cents. How to compute and interpret all the various financial metrics is certainly beyond the scope of this book. You will, however, explore and work with these types of metrics in your finance, accounting, and business strategies. Here, we simply define each. Figure 7.12 provides more detail.

- *Payback method*—number of years to recoup the cost of an initiative based on projected annual net cash flow
- *Cost-benefit ratio*—a ratio comparing the benefits to the costs
- *Return on investment (ROI)*—the overall value of an initiative (total benefits minus total costs and depreciation) as compared to the useful life of the initiative, expressed as a percentage
- *Net present value (NPV)*—the total net present value of all cash flows over the life of an initiative
- *Internal rate of return (IRR)*—the net present value (from above) expressed as a percentage return.

SERVICE LEVEL AGREEMENTS REVISITED

To close our discussion of metrics, let's revisit the service level agreement. As we defined it in Chapter 6, a ***service level agreement (SLA)*** is a formal, contractually obligated agreement between two parties. We further described an SLA by saying that, within different environments, it takes on different meanings.

THE LONDON BRIDGE MAY FALL DOWN BUT THE EXCHANGE WON'T

The London Stock Exchange is among the most admired equity exchanges in the world, not only for its long-standing position in the financial community but also for its technology deployment and infrastructure. And when you process 15 million real-time messages per day (with peaks of 2,000 messages per second), your infrastructure had better be good.

In choosing a new technology infrastructure on which to ride into the future, the London Stock Exchange focused a great deal of its efforts on requiring vendors to meet benchmarks across a broad range of metrics. Below are just a few.

- *Guaranteed performance*: in financial trading, information is valuable only if it reaches traders within the first second.

- *Development costs*: reduced development costs and development cycle times means more productivity. Ian Homan, head of Technology for the London Exchange, estimates that implementation of the new infrastructure occurred in one-fifth to one-third the time it would have taken to implement other vendor infrastructures.

- *Scalability*: according to David Lester, CIO for the London Stock Exchange, "We want to be able to extend it and make it richer. Investment decisions of this kind aren't made carelessly and the ability to scale to our future needs was a critical factor."[7, 8]

An important aspect of any SLA is a definition of the metrics that will be used to measure the success of the interactions between the two parties. Suppose, for example, that your organization decided to outsource its call centre operations. The SLA would cover in great detail the financial agreement, such as how much money your organization will pay the call centre outsourcing organization. It would also include key metrics and benchmarks that the outsourcing organization must meet to stay in compliance with the SLA. These metrics would include many of those we listed above, including average speed to answer, abandon rate, and time service factor.

Many organizations today also outsource their Web development and e-business activities. In that case, your SLA would include key metrics and benchmarks around such areas as those we discussed within the context of Web-centric metrics. The definitions of these metrics and benchmarks are usually not present in the SLA, which is more business oriented and void of detailed technical specifications. They would, instead, appear in a supporting document (similar to a contract addendum) called a *service level specification (SLS)* or *service level objective (SLO)*.

Another important business relationship in which you find the use of a service level agreement is that between an organization and an application service provider. An *application service provider (ASP)* supplies software applications (and often related services such as maintenance, technical support, information storage, and the like) over the Internet that would otherwise reside on customers' computers. The ASP model is very popular with businesses. For example, many businesses use CRM software provided by Salesforce.com, which hosts its CRM software on its Internet servers. Businesses subscribing to Salesforce.com's CRM software access it over the Internet, thus eliminating the need to buy, store, and maintain the software on their own computers. A service level agreement is vitally important and includes application-specific metrics (such as those associated with CRM software if you use Salesforce.com's CRM software) and infrastructure-centric metrics such as system availability, transaction speed, response time, and throughput. Greyhound Canada's success with Saleforce improved the visibility of its customer information throughout the organization.

LO4

Business Continuity Planning

Business continuity planning (BCP) is a rigorous and well-informed organizational methodology for developing a ***business continuity plan***, a step-by-step guideline defining how the organization will recover from a disaster or extended disruption of its business processes. In past years, with respect to IT systems and information, the business continuity plan went by other names: *disaster recovery plan* and *contingency plan*. Given the number of natural disasters and terrorist attacks worldwide, along with businesses' increasing dependency on all their processes and resources (not just IT and information), however, the general trend has been to develop a more all-encompassing *business continuity plan* that includes all aspects of the organization.

The BCP methodology looks very similar to the systems development life cycle (see Figure 7.13). It starts with the organization's strategic plan and moves through various phases including analysis, design, implementation, testing, and maintenance. We'll focus our discussion of BCP on information technology and IT–related issues.

PHASE 1: ORGANIZATIONAL STRATEGIC PLAN

Business continuity planning starts with your organization's strategic plan, which informs you of the relative importance of resources, processes, systems, and other organizational assets. It's important to understand and develop a ranking of the importance of these assets because you cannot (and should not) develop a business continuity plan that enables you to recover every asset within minutes of some sort of disaster. That would be prohibitively expensive and unnecessary. Your organization can afford to live without some assets (i.e., systems and information) for several days or even weeks. Payroll software may be an example here. For other assets, such as customer ordering and supply chain applications, it may critical that your organization gets those up and running with minimal interruption. Data centres are also typically identified as high priorities for most organizations. According to CPM Research, "improved business continuity" was cited 70 percent of the time by respondents as being a key data centre issue.[9]

PHASE 2: ANALYSIS

In the BCP analysis phase, you perform impact analysis, threat analysis, and impact scenario analysis, and then build a requirement recovery document.

Figure 7.13

Business Continuity Planning (BCP)

- *Impact analysis*: Here you seek to truly differentiate between critical, core IT applications and information and those that are non-critical. Key factors supporting your analysis include the financial impact to the organization for the loss of IT applications and information over time, implications for stakeholders (e.g., customer loss of power if you provide utilities), and cost estimates of recovery. Impact analysis is often called ***risk assessment***, the process of evaluating IT assets, their importance of the organization, and their susceptibility to threats.

- *Threat analysis*: In step 2 of BCP analysis, you document the possible threats to your organization and its assets. These can and often do include disease, earthquakes (depending on the geographical location of your organization), fire, flood, cyber attack, terrorism, and utility outages. An assessment of these helps you develop an understanding of the magnitude of threats and how you should choose to recover from them. Note that in the case of e-business activities threats can include greatly increased shopping traffic. For example, on the day after Thanksgiving in 2006 Wal-Mart's Web site went down because so many people visited its site in the hope of buying the hard-to-find T.M.X. Elmo.[10]

- *Impact scenario analysis*: In step 3, you consider each threat (from step 2) and build a worst-case scenario for each (as opposed to smaller impact scenarios such as 10 percent of the workforce out due to a flu outbreak). An impact scenario analysis provides further definition and detail concerning the scope and magnitude of each possible disaster.

- *Requirement recovery document*: Armed with the information from steps 1 through 3, you finally build a ***requirement recovery document***, a detailed document that describes (1) the distinction between critical and non-critical IT systems and information, (2) each possible threat, and (3) the possible worst-case scenarios that can result from each disaster. This document becomes the basis for the design phase that follows.

PHASE 3: DESIGN

Using the requirement recovery document, in the design phase, you design a formal, technical, and detailed plan for recovering from a disaster—***a disaster recovery plan***. A good disaster recovery plan takes into consideration the location of the backup information. Many organizations choose to store backup information in an off-site storage facility, or a place that is located separate from the company and often owned by another company, such as a collocation facility. A ***collocation facility*** is available to a company that rents space and telecommunications equipment from another company. One such company is StorageTek, which specializes in providing off-site data storage and disaster recovery solutions.

A good disaster recovery plan also considers the actual facility where employees will work. A ***hot site*** is a separate and fully equipped facility where the company can move immediately after a disaster and resume business. A ***cold site*** is a separate facility where employees can move after the disaster but does not have any computer equipment.

A disaster recovery plan should be based on a *disaster recovery cost curve* (see Figure 7.14 on the next page). A ***disaster recovery cost curve*** charts (1) the cost to your organization of the unavailability of information and technology and (2) the cost to your organization of recovering from a disaster over time. Where the two curves intersect is the best recovery plan in terms of cost and time. Being able to restore information and IT systems quickly in the event of a disaster is obviously a crucial aspect of an IT infrastructure.

Consider an example. You are in a lecture theatre at your school listening to a captivating talk on information systems. Midsentence, all power to the campus is lost, and the lecture theatre is plunged into complete darkness, save for a couple of emergency lights over

Figure 7.14

Deciding How
Much to Spend on
Disaster Recovery

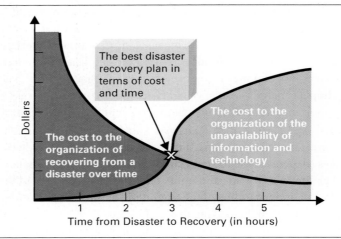

the exits. No audio, no video, no computer to demo systems. After a reasonable amount of time has passed with no restoration of power, the class is cancelled and everyone files through the exits, obviously very unhappy about having to miss a captivating lecture. Well, maybe not so much the latter, but what's important is that you are not receiving, at the moment you expected to receive it, the service that you have paid for—a lecture.

Let's pose a couple of questions, and then compare this experience with that in some other industry. What if power is not restored that day? Will your school have to close its doors? Within a week? A month? How long will it take for the university to feel the effects on its bottom line? Now let's consider if the same blackout scenario were to play out in the online retail market for fashion accessories, where competition is intense and every minute spent offline means competitors are picking up your customers, many of whom will never return. How long before the pain is felt? The time frame will be considerably shorter, you will probably agree.

So what does this mean for disaster recovery and business resumption? It means that universities aren't nearly as sensitive to this kind of disaster, and thus are not likely to spend the money required to have a completely redundant power supply allowing them to resume business immediately in the event of a blackout. It just wouldn't pay to build and keep their own mini nuclear plant on line in case of such an eventuality. But in the case of the very time- and price-sensitive fashion industry, companies would likely be willing to spend more in order to guarantee their recovery and resumption in a more timely fashion.

Figure 7.14 provides a generic picture of the outcome of a process. Organizations need to examine their resources in light of their vulnerability to disaster and spend just enough to maximize their ability to recover while simultaneously minimizing their outlay for redundant systems. Immediate recovery carries a high cost. Inability to function costs more every minute. It will be different for every organization in every industry, but the process of finding that sweet spot defined by the intersection of the two curves is the same.

PHASE 4: IMPLEMENTATION

At this point, business continuity planning diverges somewhat from the SDLC. In the SDLC, you would develop and test the solution before implementing it. In business continuity planning, you must begin to implement your disaster recovery plan before testing it. That is, you need to engage any businesses that will be providing collocation facilities, hot sites, and/or cold sites, and implement the necessary procedures for recovering from a disaster. You train your employees concerning what to do in case of any of the disasters. You also evaluate each IT system and ensure that it is configured optimally for recovering from a disaster. You can now test the disaster recovery plan.

ENTERGY SURVIVES KATRINA

Based in New Orleans, Entergy Corp. employs 14,500 people to provide electricity to 2.6 million utility consumers in Arkansas, Louisiana, Texas, and Mississippi. In late August 2005, Hurricane Katrina tested the resolve of all of Entergy's employees and the preparedness of its disaster recovery plan.

Employees rose to the occasion and the disaster recovery plan was executed well. Although returning all utilities to every customer in the region took several months (because of factors well beyond Entergy's control), it was Entergy's dedication to building a successful disaster recovery plan that paid dividends.

Located in the Gulf of Mexico in the heart of hurricane country in the southern part of the United States, the energy company had an effective disaster recovery plan well in place. Entergy tested its disaster recovery plan at least once a year. The previous year that test had come in the form of preparing for Hurricane Ivan, which ultimately made landfall to the east in Florida. Just five months before Hurricane Katrina hit, the company conducted a massive storm drill that simulated what everyone thought was the worst-case scenario—a major hurricane followed by extreme flooding.

Entergy's disaster recovery plan included several key elements, including

- Start the execution of the disaster recovery plan at least 72 hours in advance of the predicted landfall of a hurricane.
- Activate Entergy's disaster recovery site in Little Rock, Arkansas.
- Activate Entergy's storm command centre (also called *The Power House*) in Jackson, Mississippi.
- Still in advance of the predicted landfall of a hurricane, prepare the company's systems that would be most critical in restoring electricity to utility consumers.

According to everyone, the disaster recovery plan worked well, but Ray Johnson, CIO of Entergy, thought some changes needed to be made. As he explained it, "We never follow the plan to the letter. In the IT space, the plan is very solid in terms of what we have to do. But we're always working—our core IT staff in conjunction with representatives from the business areas—to see if we need to change priorities."[11]

PHASE 5: TESTING

Testing in business continuity planning involves executing simulated scenarios of disasters and having employees execute on the disaster recovery plan to ensure that the solution satisfies your organization's recovery requirements. If noticeable deficiencies are identified, your organization should return to steps 3 and 4 (design and implementation) and reconfigure and re-implement the disaster recovery plan accordingly.

This sort of testing does not stop once you believe you have developed an optimal plan. The environment in which your organization operates changes almost daily. You should test your disaster recovery plan on at least an annual basis, and, more realistically, several times a year.

PHASE 6: MAINTENANCE

Finally, you need to continually assess new threats and re-evaluate your IT systems and related assets to determine their changing importance to the organization. As with the SDLC, no "system" is ever complete; it needs constant monitoring, support, and maintenance.

Summary: STUDENT LEARNING OUTCOMES *REVISITED*

LO1 Describe how a service-oriented architecture can be used as a philosophical approach to help the organization of the future meet all its IT-related needs. A service-oriented architecture can be applied to help your organization respond to

- *Customers*—through multichannel service delivery and the provision of customizable products and services
- *End-users*—through fully integrated ERP systems supporting interoperability and mobile computing
- *Software development*—as a framework for supporting development methodologies such as RAD, XP, and agile that lead to exciting new deployments such as Web 2.0
- *Information needs*—including access to all types of integrated information (and business intelligence and knowledge), standard information formats, integrity controls, and the elimination of redundant information
- *Hardware requirements*—through the integration of different technologies, providing large storage capacities, and maintaining safe and secure telecommunications platforms.

LO2 Define and describe the various hardware and software infrastructure considerations in an organization. Hardware and software infrastructure considerations include

- Enterprise resource planning (ERP) systems provide interoperability within an ERP vendor and among modules of different ERP vendors and also hide the underlying IT infrastructure of information and hardware from end-users and customers.
- Network infrastructures include *decentralized*—little or no sharing of IT and other resources such as information; *centralized*—sharing of information systems in one central area or one central mainframe; *distributed*—distributing the information and processing power of IT systems via a network; *client/server*—one or more computers are servers that provide services to other computers, called clients;

and *tiered (layer)*—the IT system is partitioned into tiers where each tier performs a specific type of functionality.

LO3 Compare and contrast commonly used metrics for assessing the success of IT systems and IT-related initiatives. Metrics are simply ways to measure something. Common IT metrics can be categorized as

- *Infrastructure-centric metrics*—Measures of efficiency, speed, and/or capacity of technology, including *throughput*, *transaction speed*, *system availability*, *accuracy*, *response time*, and *scalability*
- *Web-centric metrics*—Measures of the success of your Web and e-business initiatives, including *unique visitors*, *total hits*, *page exposures*, *conversion rate*, *click-through*, *cost-per-thousand (CPM)*, *abandoned registrations*, and *abandoned shopping carts*
- *Call centre metrics*—Measures of the success of call centre efforts, including *abandon rate*, *average speed to answer (ASA)*, *time service factor (TSF)*, and *first call resolution (FCR)*
- *Financial metrics*—Also called *capital analysis financial models*, including *payback method*, *cost-benefit ratio*, *return on investment (ROI)*, *net present value (NPV)*, and *internal rate of return (IRR)*.

LO4 Describe business continuity planning (BCP) and its phases. *Business continuity planning (BCP)* is a rigorous and well-informed organizational methodology for developing a *business continuity plan*, a step-by-step guideline defining how the organization will recover from a disaster or extended disruption of its business processes. The phases of business continuity planning include

- *Phase 1: Organizational strategic plan*—it all starts here with understanding the relative importance of resources, systems, processes, and other organizational assets.
- *Phase 2: Analysis*—perform impact analysis, threat analysis, and impact scenario analysis,

and build a **_requirement recovery document_**, a detailed document that describes (1) the distinction between critical and non-critical IT systems and information, (2) each possible threat, and (3) the possible worst-case scenarios that can result from each disaster.

- *Phase 3: Design*—using the requirement recovery document, create a **_disaster recovery plan_**, which identifies collocation facilities, hot sites, and cold sites and illustrates a disaster recovery cost curve (the cost to your organization of the unavailability of information and technology as compared to the cost to your organization of recovering from a disaster over time).

- *Phase 4: Implementation*—engage businesses that will provide collocation facilities, hot sites, and cold sites; implement necessary procedures for recovering from a disaster; train employees; and evaluate each IT system to ensure its configuration is optimal for recovering from a disaster.

- *Phase 5: Testing*—execute simulated scenarios of disasters and have employees execute on the disaster recovery plan.

- *Phase 6: Maintenance*—continually assess new threats and re-evaluate your IT systems and related assets to determine their changing importance to the organization.

CLOSING CASE STUDY 1
International Truck Makes a Huge Bet on a Service-Oriented Architecture

www.mcgrawhill.ca/olc/haag

Service-oriented architecture (SoA) does seem to be the future for integrated IT systems within an organization, bringing together both applications and information in a seamless fashion. But SoA is still in its infancy, and some companies don't want to wait until SoAs mature. They are willing to bet on a service-oriented architecture right now. One such company is International Truck and Engine Corporation.

International Truck's SoA resulted from needing more timely information so it could identify assembly-plant problems sooner. Its current IT systems, all legacy information systems, didn't share information easily, and that led to bottlenecks in production, excessive defects and returns, shortfalls in inventory, and a host of other problems that can spell doom for a manufacturing-intensive company like International Truck.

So, the company forged ahead in embracing an SoA, knowing that it would be able to buy many of the software components that it needed and that others would have to be written from scratch by in-house IT specialists. The first focus for International Truck was the Common Vehicle Tracking system, a system that tracks production according to a specific vehicle or vehicle type. International Truck produces everything from RV motor homes to military transports.

The Common Vehicle Tracking system was a high-profile, high-payoff project with a tight deadline. The company expected the system to save it at least $3 million annually. The system, now complete and installed in one factory, tracks in near real time all information relating to works-in-progress and finished inventory. Prior to its implementation, Art Data, vice president of information technology at International Truck, succinctly explained, "We weren't doing it very well." International Truck's legacy systems stored isolated data and information in applications such as computer-aided manufacturing, in-house-developed order management, and even commercial ERP software.

The new system uses a combination of many different types of software, one of the primary goals of an SoA. For example, it uses a data integration tool from SSA Global to extract information from International Truck's Baan ERP system. From there, in-house-developed software bridges to the order management system.

International Truck is also working on an SoA extension to interface with the systems of its dealers. The company already has a centralized server that its 400 dealers use to access parts catalogues and sales tools. However, dealers can choose their own internal dealer management software systems. This makes communicating information in a common format problematic, at best. International Truck is currently working with automotive industry software vendors to create common services (i.e., software modules) that will communicate information in a standard format.

In the future, International Truck will even extend its SoA architecture perspective into the vehicles themselves. Using the vehicles' electronics system, GPS, and cellular technology, owners of the trucks will be able to track the location of their vehicles.[12]

Questions

1. With respect to its customers (dealers in this case), how is International Truck using a service-oriented architecture to meet their needs? How does using an SoA further help International Truck erect an entry barrier (from Chapter 1)?

2. With respect to information needs, what advantages and efficiencies is International Truck hoping to gain by using a service-oriented architecture? Why are these advantages and efficiencies not possible with its current legacy systems?

3. Recalling our discussion of software development methodologies in Chapter 6 that focused on component-based development (i.e., RAD, XP, and agile), how is International Truck able to integrate new software modules with existing ones?

4. What key infrastructure-centric metrics could International Truck use to justify its movement toward a service-oriented architecture? For each that you identify, provide a short description of why the metric is important.

5. How important is it for International Truck to have a good business continuity plan in place? What key IT systems and other IT resources do you believe would be at the top of the list for quick recovery? Why?

CLOSING CASE STUDY 2
Many Ontario Physicians Still Allergic to Electronic Records

E-health in Ontario has certainly made great strides from where it was just a few years ago. But industry experts are not ready to celebrate yet. They note that, despite undeniable advances, resistance to digitized patient information still remains quite high among the province's health care practitioners.

Such resistance is one of the problems Smart Systems for Health Agency (SSHA) has had to overcome in its quest to deploy a province-wide e-health infrastructure. This agency of the Ontario Ministry of Health is now five years into its mandate. So far, SSHA has connected more than 5,000 locations to its ONE Network that enables health care providers to securely store, access, and share patient data on-line, and collaborate with one another. However, many physicians operating in individual offices remain hesitant to commit their records to the system.

The agency has had its own issues. It has been criticized for being behind schedule and being secretive, and brought in a new CEO to head its turnaround strategy. Despite the difficulties they encounter, organizations such as the SSHA have a pivotal role to

play as they herald the wave of the future, says Ross Armstrong, technology analyst at Info-Tech Research Group Inc. in London, Ontario. On-line collaboration and sharing patient records and lab results delivers extraordinary benefits, says Armstrong, who has extensively researched electronic health systems in North America. "If you can transmit X-ray images or lab results from one location to another, that saves the patient from going through the same procedure again when he or she transfers to a different hospital."

And yet, though the benefits are evident, challenges to adoption remain, Armstrong said. He believes use of the technology might take off if hospitals start offering patients free access to their medical records. Workplace culture and the cost of migrating existing data to digital format also impede widespread adoption, said Armstrong. An SSHA executive agrees. About 1,500 physicians or just 8 percent of the province's doctors are connected to the agency's network, noted Paul Kilbertus, director of communications at SSHA. He says technology issues and their perceived impact on business processes are holding back most doctors and smaller organizations from taking the plunge. "The products and services are free but individual technical issues can be a considerable problem."

For instance, he said, some health clinics may be tied to legacy systems that present compatibility problems or may have limited resources that prevent them from establishing and maintaining interfaces to the SSHA network. Physicians are also considering whether moving over their records to the network makes good business sense, Kilbertus said. "For doctors used to communicating by phone and transmitting medical records by fax, the question is what value [exists] in switching to digital." Armstrong said some clinics are likely worried about the time and resources that would have to be expended in transferring hard-copy patient files on to digital media and training staff in the use of new devices and business practices.

"This would mean a considerable downtime. Most clinics are too busy already and any minute away from the practice means money going out."[13]

Questions

1. In this chapter, we noted that many effectiveness metrics depend on the application under scrutiny, such as supply chain management and customer relationship management. What sort of effectiveness metrics would the SSHA likely use to evaluate the success of this IT system?

2. How might an SoA assist in the creation and deployment of the SSHA system?

3. According to the network infrastructures we discussed in this chapter, how would you characterize the SSHA's new IT infrastructure? Justify your answer.

4. As a part of a business continuity plan, many businesses identify cold sites or hot sites to which they can move to carry on their business activities. What about a system such as SSHA? What if its location suffered a disaster such as a flood or hurricane? Sketch out a basic Business Continuity Plan for SSHA.

www.mcgrawhill.ca/olc/haag

Key Terms and Concepts

Short-Answer Questions

1. How can a service-oriented architecture (SoA) be used to guide the organization of the future?
2. How have ERP systems evolved over the last 30 years?
3. Why is interoperability important?
4. What are the main differences between a decentralized infrastructure and a centralized infrastructure?
5. How does a client/server infrastructure work?
6. What are the four types of a tiered infrastructure?
7. How do efficiency and effectiveness metrics differ?
8. What are some commonly used infrastructure-centric metrics?
9. What are some commonly used Web-centric metrics?
10. Why are service level agreements important when contracting the services of an application service provider (ASP)?
11. What is a business continuity plan?
12. Why do organizations implement a disaster recovery plan before testing it?

Assignments and Exercises

1. **SECURITY METRICS** In this chapter, we focused on metrics for measuring the success of your IT systems including infrastructure-centric metrics, Web-centric metrics, call centre metrics, and financial metrics. Another important area of metrics is security metrics, or how well you are stopping viruses from coming in, protecting against identify theft, and the like. Do some research on the Web and develop a list of commonly used metrics in the area of security. Be sure to define each metric.

2. **CREATING A CAMPUS IT INFRASTRUCTURE** You have been assigned the role of student IT infrastructure manager. Your first assignment is to approve the designs for the new on-campus Internet infrastructure. You're having a meeting at 9:00 a.m. tomorrow morning to review the designs with the student IT employees. To prepare for the meeting, you must understand the student requirements and their current use of the Internet, along with future requirements. The following is a list of questions you must answer before attending the meeting. Provide an answer to each question.

   - Do you need to have a disaster recovery plan? If so, what might it include?
   - Does the system require backup equipment?
   - When will the system need to be available to the students?
   - What types of access levels will the students need?

   - How will you ensure the system is reliable?
   - How will you build scalability into the system?
   - What are the minimum performance requirements for the system?
   - How will the system handle future growth?

3. **EFFICIENCY AND EFFECTIVENESS METRICS** Choose any of the Perspective boxes in this chapter or the opening case and identify and describe at least seven metrics that could be used to measure the success of the IT systems in your chosen example. For each metric, categorize it as either an efficiency or effectiveness metric. Justify your categorizations.

4. **APPLICATION SERVICE PROVIDERS** There are numerous application service providers that enable organizations to access and use Web-based application software. In the chapter we identified Salesforce.com as one such ASP. Search the Web and find at least five other ASPs. What are the names of the companies? What application software do they provide over the Web? What additional services do they provide, if any?

5. **PERSONAL BENCHMARKS AND BENCHMARKING** How do you use benchmarks and benchmarking in your personal life? Think about grades, making money, supporting charities, and the like. Choose one significant way in which you use benchmarks and benchmarking in your personal life and describe it. What are your benchmark values? How were you able to derive your benchmark values? Where did they come from?

Discussion Questions

1. On page 211, we listed and defined numerous Web-centric metrics. Which of those are efficiency metrics and which of those are effectiveness metrics? For each, provide justification for your answer and an illustration using a real-life or hypothetical Web business example.

2. IT infrastructures often mimic organizational hierarchies and the philosophical approach organizations take to the placement of the IT function (see Chapter 2). Describe which common network infrastructure (decentralized, centralized, distributed, client/server, or tiered) would best support the three structural placements of the IT function we listed on page 48.

3. What type of IT infrastructure does your school have? If it uses a client/server infrastructure, how does your school's client/server network increase student productivity? What recommendations, based on the contents of this chapter, could you recommend to the IT people who manage the infrastructure?

4. How is the concept of interoperability an important aspect that you rely on in your daily life? Think about the many devices, appliances, modes of transportation, and so on that you use every day. Which of these support the concept of interoperability? How would your life change if they didn't support interoperability?

5. Many people say that efficiency and effectiveness metrics are interrelated and that you can't really have one without the other or that no organization can truly be successful without both. How are efficiency and effectiveness metrics interrelated? Must you succeed in one set before addressing the other? If so, which is first and why?

6. Consider an e-business like Amazon.com. Which Web-centric metrics on page 211 would be most important to it? Justify your answers. Now consider a content provider like CNN (www.cnn.com). Which Web-centric metrics would be most important to it? Justify your answers. Why would two e-businesses have such a different focus on Web-centric metrics?

Chapter 8

Protecting People and Information

Threats and Safeguards

STUDENT LEARNING OUTCOMES

LO1 Define ethics and describe factors that affect how you make a decision concerning an ethical issue.

LO2 Define and describe intellectual property, copyright, Fair Dealing Doctrine, and pirated software.

LO3 Define privacy and describe ways in which it can be threatened.

LO4 Describe the ways in which information on your computer or network is vulnerable, and list measures you can take to protect it.

OPENING CASE STUDY
How Much Is Too Much?

Ever wonder why some people are inundated with proposals to buy this or that new and improved gadget or service? Perhaps they are on a list; a list of those who are more likely to be receptive to such purchases. This is not such a far-fetched notion. Consider the large and growing service of selling consumer information—information about you that you might not even suspect is being collected.

Acxiom is a global leader in interactive marketing services. The company stores and analyzes information, both proprietary and that of its clients, in order to deliver customer and information management solutions for many of the largest, most respected companies in the world. Acxiom gets the information it sells from many sources, including the three major credit bureaus (TransUnion, Equifax Inc., and Experian Inc.). Acxiom has a presence in the United States, Canada, Europe, and Asia-Pacific and is the global leader in real-time, multi-channel customer data integration, enabling businesses to develop and deepen customer relationships by creating a single, accurate view of their customers across the enterprise. Acxiom works with many of the world's leading companies, including

- 12 of the top 15 credit card issuers
- 7 of the top 10 retail banks
- 9 of the top 10 telecom/media companies
- 7 of the top 10 retailers
- 9 of the top 10 automotive manufacturers
- 6 of the top 8 brokerage firms
- 3 of the top 5 pharmaceutical manufacturers
- 2 of the top 5 life/health insurance providers
- 8 of the top 10 property and casualty insurers
- 2 of the top 3 lodging companies
- 2 of the top 3 gaming companies.

Forty percent of Acxiom's revenue comes from the banking sector alone. Large accounts include Canadian Tire Acceptance and Capital One Financial Corp.

Acxiom and Canadian Tire

In 2001, Acxiom announced an agreement with Canadian Tire Acceptance Limited (CTAL), a division of Canadian Tire Corporation, to provide the financial organization with a broad range of database marketing, data management, and customer relationship management (CRM) services. CTAL currently provides a variety of credit and other financial services to more than 6 million Canadian Tire customers.

Acxiom complements the CTAL team with its experts in marketing campaign strategies and tactics, analysis, decision support, postal services, data acquisition, and management. In 2006, Canadian Tire Financial Services Inc. renewed its contract with Acxiom.

Acxiom and Capital One

To help clients react quickly to changing market conditions, Acxiom offers hundreds of lists. One such list is a "pre-movers file," which lists people who are about to change residences. The list is updated every 24 hours. Another important list is of people who use credit cards, sorted in order of frequency of use.

One potential client for such lists is Capital One Financial Corporation, a financial services company based in Virginia, which spent $290 million (about 14 percent of its revenue) on marketing for the last quarter of 2003. The company sends out about one billion pieces of mail every year,

including millions in Canada, mainly in the form of advertising intended to entice consumers to sign up for credit cards. Acxiom's information and analysis helps Capital One send credit card solicitations only to those who are likely to want another credit card.

Acxiom Grows in Canada

Acxiom announced in 2006 its intention to make a significant investment in the Canadian marketplace to support new and existing clients' customer information management initiatives. The first step was the opening of a data centre in the greater Toronto area.

Acxiom also merges huge databases. U.S. and Canadian residential and business telephone listings are compiled from over 5,000 public telephone books. In Canada there are 11 million residential listings and 1.2 million business listings. Files are updated monthly from the base source of 500 printed telephone directories. Acxiom has both a marketing database and a reference database of residential listings. The reference file is a "mixed use" file and can be used for marketing and reference applications.

Lists are first cleaned, a process involving the identification and deletion of duplicate records (called "data hygiene" in the industry). Acxiom then supplements its lists with data from its own database before merging them with its clients' lists, complementing and completing the clients' customer information.

Acxiom is only one of many companies that collect and sell data on consumers.[1,2]

Questions

1. Do you feel comfortable about so many people collecting information about you and distributing it freely?

2. Is such practice an invasion of your privacy or is it just good business?

3. What are the implications of data on Canadians being held by a U.S. company? Is your information subject to being provided to U.S. authorities under the auspices of the *Patriot Act*? What are the privacy implications of this for Canadians?

Introduction

As you know, the three components of an IT system are people, information, and information technology. Most of what you've seen in previous chapters has dealt with IT and how it stores and processes information. In this chapter we're going to concentrate on information—its use, ownership, and protection. The best environment for handling information is one that has stability without stagnation and change without chaos.

To handle information in a responsible way you must understand

- The importance of ethics in the ownership and use of information
- The importance to people of personal privacy and the ways in which it can be compromised
- Threats to information and how to protect against them (security).

The most important part of any IT system consists of the people who use it and are affected by it. How people treat each other has always been important, but in this information-based and digital age, with huge computing power at our fingertips, we can affect more people's lives in more ways than ever before. How we act toward each other, including how we view and handle information, is largely determined by our ethics.

You don't have to look far to see examples of computer use that is ethically questionable. For example,

- People copy, use, and distribute software they have no right to.
- Employees search organizational databases for information on celebrities and friends.
- Organizations collect, buy, and use information and don't check the validity or accuracy of that information.
- Misguided people create and spread viruses that cause trouble for those using and maintaining IT systems.
- Information system developers put systems on the market before they're completely tested. (A few years ago, the developers of an incubator thermostat control program didn't test it fully, and two infants died as a result.)[3]
- Unethical people break into computer systems and steal passwords, information, and proprietary information.
- Employees destroy or steal proprietary schematics, sketches, customer lists, and reports from their employers.
- People read each other's e-mail and other private documents.

LO1

Ethics

Ethical people have integrity. They're people who are just as careful of the rights of others as they are of their own. They have a strong sense of what's fair and right, and what isn't. But even the most ethical people sometimes face difficult choices.

Ethics are the principles and standards that guide our behaviour toward other people. Acting ethically means behaving in a principled fashion and treating other people with respect and dignity. It's simple to say, but not so simple to do since some situations are complex or ambiguous. The important role of ethics in our lives has long been recognized. As far back as 44 B.C., Cicero said that ethics are indispensable to anyone who wants to have a good career. Having said that, Cicero, along with some of the greatest minds over the centuries, struggled with what the rules of ethics should be.

Our ethics are rooted in our history, culture, and religion, and may stay the same or shift over time. In this electronic age there's a new dimension in the ethics debate—the amount of personal information that we can collect and store, and the speed with which we can access and process that information.

TWO FACTORS THAT DETERMINE HOW YOU DECIDE ETHICAL ISSUES

How you collect, store, access, and use information depends to a large extent on your sense of ethics—what you perceive as right and wrong. Two factors affect how you make your decision when you're faced with an ethical dilemma. The first is your basic ethical structure, which you developed as you grew up. The second is the set of practical circumstances inevitably involved in the decision that you're trying to make, that is, all the shades of grey in what are rarely black or white decisions.

Your ethical structure and the ethical challenges you'll face exist at several levels (see Figure 8.1).[4] At the outside level are things that most people wouldn't consider bad, such as taking a couple of paper clips or sending an occasional personal e-mail on company time. Do these things really matter? At the middle level are more significant ethical challenges. One example might be accessing personnel records for personal reasons. Could there ever be a personal reason so compelling that you would not feel ethical discomfort doing this? Reading someone else's e-mail might be another middle-level example. At the innermost ethical level are violations that you'd surely consider very serious, such as embezzling funds or selling company records to a competitor. And yet, over time, your ethical structure can change so that even such acts as these could seem more or less acceptable. For example, if everyone around you is accessing confidential records for their own purposes, in time you might come to think such an act is no big deal. And this might spell big trouble for you.

It would be nice if every decision were crystal clear, such as in the innermost circle in Figure 8.1, but ethical decisions are seldom so easy. Ideally, your personal ethics should tell you what to do. But the practical circumstances of a decision inevitably also influence you in an ethical dilemma.[5]

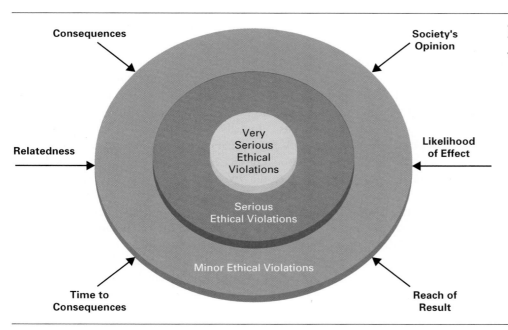

Figure 8.1

Your Ethical Structure

1. *Consequences.* How much or how little benefit or harm will come from a particular decision?
2. *Society's opinion.* What is your perception of what society really thinks of your intended action?
3. *Likelihood of effect.* What is the probability of the harm or benefit that will occur if you take the action?
4. *Time to consequences.* How long will it take for the benefit or harm to take effect?
5. *Relatedness.* How much do you identify with the person or persons who will receive the benefit or suffer the harm?
6. *Reach of result.* How many people will be affected by your action?

No matter how strong your sense of ethics, these practical aspects of the situation may affect you as you make your decision—perhaps unduly, perhaps quite justifiably. Thus, ethical dilemmas usually arise not out of simple situations but from a clash between competing goals, responsibilities, and loyalties. Ethical decisions are complex judgments that balance rewards for yourself and others against responsibilities to yourself and others. Inevitably, your decision process is influenced by uncertainty about the magnitude of the outcome, by your estimate of the importance of the situation, sometimes by your perception of conflicting "right reactions," and by more than one socially acceptable "correct" decision.

LO2

Intellectual Property

An ethical issue you will almost certainly encounter is one related to the use or copying of proprietary software. Software is a type of intellectual property. ***Intellectual property*** is intangible creative work that is embodied in physical form.[6] Music, novels, paintings, and sculptures are all examples of intellectual property. So also are your company's product sketches, schematics, and other proprietary documents. These documents—along with music, novels, and so on—are worth much more than the physical form in which they are delivered. For example, a single U2 song is worth far more than the CD on which it's purchased. The song is also an example of intellectual property that is covered by copyright law.

Copyright law protects the authorship of literary and dramatic works, musical and theatrical compositions, and works of art. ***Copyright*** is the legal protection afforded an expression of an idea, such as a song, video game, and some types of proprietary documents. Having a copyright means that no one can use your song or video game without your permission. As a form of intellectual property, software is usually protected by copyright law, although sometimes it falls under patent law, which protects an idea, such as the design of a sewing machine or an industrial pump valve.

Copyright law doesn't forbid the use of intellectual property completely; it has some notable exceptions. For example, a TV news program could show a video game you created without your permission. This would be an example of the use of copyrighted material for the creation of new material, i.e., the TV news program. And that's legal; it falls under the Fair Dealing Doctrine. Canada's ***Fair Dealing Doctrine*** (distinguished from the U.S.-style Fair Use Doctrine) says that you may use copyrighted material in certain situations, for example, in the creation of new work or, within certain limits, for teaching purposes. One of those limits is on the amount of the copyrighted material you may use.

Generally, the determining factor in legal decisions on copyright disputes is whether the copyright holder has been or is likely to be denied income because of the infringement. Courts will consider factors such as how much of the work was used and how, and when and on what basis the decision was made to use it.

Remember that copyright infringement is *illegal*. That means it's against the law, outside a fair dealing situation, to simply copy a copyrighted picture, text, or anything else without permission, whether the copyrighted material is on the Internet or not. In particular, it's illegal to copy copyrighted software. But there's one exception to that rule: In Canada (as in most countries), you may copy copyrighted software for backup purposes. When you buy copyrighted software, what you're paying for is the right to use it—and that's all.

How many more copies you may make depends on the copyright agreement that comes with the software package. Some software companies state emphatically that you may not even put the software on a second computer, even if they're both yours and no one else uses either one. Other companies are less restrictive, and agree to let you put a copy of software on multiple machines—as long as only one person is using that software package at any given time. In this instance, the company considers software to be like a book in that you can have it in different places and you can loan it out, but only one person at a time may use it. Music companies often allow three copies of a CD or individual music track to be played on different platforms, like your computer, your stereo system, and your MP3 player.

If you copy copyrighted software and give it to another person or persons, you're pirating the software. ***Pirated software*** is the unauthorized use, duplication, distribution, or sale of copyrighted software.[7] The Fourth Annual BSA and IDC Global Software Piracy Study reveals that 35 percent of the software installed in 2006 on personal computers worldwide was obtained illegally, amounting to nearly $40 billion in global losses due to software piracy. Progress was seen in a number of emerging markets, most notably in China, where the piracy rate dropped ten percentage points in three years, and in Russia, where piracy fell seven percentage points over three years. One in three business applications in Canada is thought to be pirated.[8] In some parts of the world, more than 90 percent of business software is pirated. The Software and Information Industry Association (SIIA) and the Business Software Alliance (BSA) say that pirated software means lost jobs, wages, and tax revenues, and is a potential barrier to success for software start-ups around the globe.[9]

Privacy

Privacy is the right to be left alone when you want to be, to have control over your own personal possessions, and not to be observed without your consent. It's the right to be free of unwanted intrusion into your private life. Privacy has several dimensions. Psychologically, it's a need for personal space. All of us, to a greater or lesser extent, need to feel in control of our most personal possessions, and personal information belongs on that list. Legally, privacy is necessary for self-protection.[10] If you put the key to your house in a special hiding place in your yard, you want to keep that information private. This information could be abused and cause you grief. In this section, we'll examine some specific areas of privacy: individuals snooping on each other; employers' collection of information about employees; businesses' collection of information about consumers; government collection of personal information; and the issue of privacy in international trade.

PRIVACY AND OTHER INDIVIDUALS

Other individuals, like family members, associates, fellow employees, and hackers, could be electronically invading your privacy. Their motives might be simple curiosity, or an attempt to get your password or to access something they have no right to. Obviously, there are situations in which you're well within your rights, and would be well advised to see what's going on. Examples may be if you suspect that your child is in electronic contact with someone or something undesirable, or if you think that someone is using your computer without permission. Many Web sites offer programs, collectively referred to as snoopware, to help people monitor what's happening on a computer.

For general snooping you can get key logger software and install it on the computer you want to monitor. ***Key logger***, or ***key trapper, software***, is a program that, when installed on a computer, records every keystroke and mouse click. It records all e-mail (whether you're using Eudora or Microsoft Outlook), instant messages, chat room exchanges, Web sites you visit, applications you run, and passwords you type in on that computer.

Also available for monitoring computer use are screen capture programs that periodically record what's on the screen. (They get the information straight from the video card.) These programs don't trap every single screen, just whatever is on the screen when the capturing program activates. But they still give whoever is doing the monitoring a pretty good idea of what the computer user is up to. Other tools for monitoring include packet sniffers (that examine the information passing by) on switches, hubs, or routers (the devices on networks that connect computers to each other), and log analysis tools that keep track of logons, deletions, and so forth.

As you're probably already aware, e-mail is completely insecure. E-mail content might as well be written on a postcard for all the privacy it has. Also, each e-mail you send results in at least three or four copies being stored on different computers (see Figure 8.2). It's stored first in the computer you're using. Second, it's stored by the e-mail server, the computer through which it gets onto the Internet. Third, it's stored on the recipient's computer, and may also be archived on the recipient's e-mail server.

While you probably realize that your e-mail is not totally private, do you realize that other electronic output leaves its mark too? For example, if you use a colour laser printer, your printouts have patterns of yellow dots on the back that are not visible unless you have a blue light and a microscope. These dots identify the model and serial number of your printer and the time the printout was made. Printer manufacturers introduced this feature at the request of the U.S. Secret Service, which is the agency responsible for investigating counterfeit currency.

Another example is those photos you take with your digital camera. With the right software you can load the photo and see a whole block of information like the date the photo was taken, the camera type and serial number, whether the owner of the camera signed up for a warranty, and various other details. Your CD burner leaves a distinct signature on the CDs you burn. That is, any CD that your computer burns can be traced back to your CD drive. Of course, it stands to reason that your cell phone, when it's on, can tell people where you are by virtue of the fact that it registers itself with the towers it uses to send and receive calls.

EDRs, or Event Data Recorders, are now becoming a standard feature on new vehicles. The EDR is part of the airbag control module and was originally included to improve the performance of airbags. When the airbag is deployed, data for the five seconds prior to impact is transferred to a computer chip. About seven pages of information can be downloaded from the chip. This information includes the car's speed at the time

Figure 8.2

The E-Mail You Send Is Stored on Many Computers

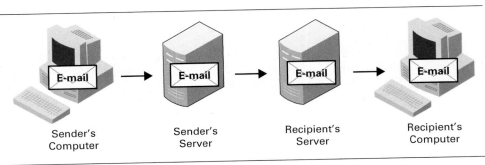

Sender's Computer   Sender's Server   Recipient's Server   Recipient's Computer

of impact, the engine's RPMs, the percent throttle, whether the brakes were applied, and whether the driver's seat belt was buckled. The system is even designed to record a second impact, which frequently happens in a collision. This is invaluable information to have about an accident, and many reckless and inebriated drivers have been taken off the roads because of it.

IDENTITY THEFT

About 10 million adults in the United States were victims of identity theft in 2006, according to a survey released by the National Association of Certified Fraud Examiners. Public Safety Canada states that the PhoneBusters National Call Centre took 7,629 identity theft complaints from Canadians in 2002, reporting total losses of more than CAN$8.5 million. In 2003, the number of complaints doubled, while the reported losses nearly tripled to more than CAN$21.8 million.[11]

The two most frequent activities related to identity theft are credit cards or application for credit cards, and cell phones and false application for cell phone service. Together, these two causes accounted for more than 40 percent of total complaints to PhoneBusters in late 2003 and 2004. A sobering thought is that law enforcement agencies in both Canada and the United States estimate that actual instances of such activity are in fact higher than reported, and particularly in the case of credit card "takeover." This is due to challenges in the way the statistics are categorized.[12]

Identity theft is the forging of someone's identity for the purpose of fraud. The fraud is often for financial gain, and the stolen identity is used to apply for and use credit cards in the victim's name or to apply for a loan. But it can also be simply to disguise a real identity, particularly if the thief is hiding from law enforcement or is running some sort of scam. Figure 8.3 shows a breakdown of identity theft by age. The list of companies and organizations in the United States whose data on individuals has been breached is long. It includes DSW, MCI, Time Warner, the Department of Justice, CitiGroup, Boeing, Ford Motor Company, and the Marines, to name just a few. In 2006, 36 million people were at risk for compromised personal information from breaches in the computer systems of organizations by hackers, lax security, or theft of notebook computers. In 300 separate breaches, more than 97 million records were put at risk of identity theft.[13] Following are examples of what happened when people became the victims of identity theft.

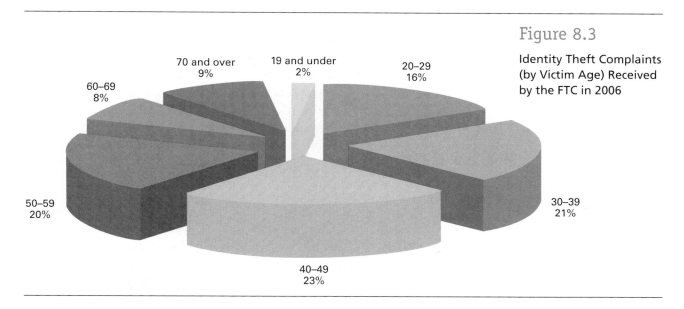

Figure 8.3

Identity Theft Complaints (by Victim Age) Received by the FTC in 2006

A 15-year-old Brandon, Manitoba, high school student was charged in May 2008 with the crime of "personating" after allegedly posing as a teacher on Facebook. The *Winnipeg Sun* reported that Brandon police charged a boy (who could face up to 10 years in prison if charged as an adult) after he allegedly created a Facebook profile using his teacher's name rather than his own. The profile also contained a photo. David Deutscher, who teaches criminal law at the University of Manitoba, said a *personation* charge is appropriate when the alleged perpetrator stands to benefit or can potentially cause harm as the result of pretending to be someone else.[14]

- Thieves stole the mail of a Canadian victim and got access to critical information such as credit card numbers. Using those numbers, thieves extended the victim's credit lines, applied for credit cards and opened fraudulent accounts. The thieves also robbed the victim of about $15,000.

- An 82-year-old woman in Fort Worth, Texas, discovered that her identity had been stolen when the woman using her name was involved in a four-car collision. For 18 months, the victim kept getting notices of lawsuits and overdue medical bills that were really meant for someone else. It took seven years for her to get her financial good name restored after the identity thief charged over $100,000 on her 12 fraudulently acquired credit cards.

- In New York, members of a pickpocket ring forged the driver's licenses of their victims within hours of snatching the women's purses. If you steal someone's cash only, your haul usually won't be more than $200, probably much less. On the other hand, if you steal the person's identity, you can net on average between $4,000 and $10,000.

- A study undertaken by the DeGroote School of Business at McMaster University in Hamilton in late 2006 reported, among other interesting statistics, that "… there are over one million victims of IDF [identity theft fraud] each year and the amount that perpetrators gain from IDF victims in Canada is over $3 billion. Dealing with identity frauds costs Canadian victims $164 million of their own money and they collectively spend over 18 million hours a year to resolve these problems."[15]

A common way to steal identities on-line is called phishing. **Phishing** (also called ***carding*** or ***brand spoofing***) is a technique to gain personal information for the purpose of identity theft, usually by means of fraudulent e-mail. One way this is done is to send out e-mail messages that look as though they came from legitimate businesses like AOL, MSN, eBay, PayPal, insurance companies, or on-line retailers like Amazon.ca. The messages look genuine with official-looking formats and logos. These e-mails typically ask for verification of important information like passwords and account numbers. The reason given is often that this personal information is needed for accounting or auditing purposes or because some fraudulent activity appears to have taken place with the account. Since the e-mails look authentic, up to one in five recipients responds with the information, and subsequently becomes a victim of identity theft and other fraud.

Legitimate businesses don't send out such e-mails. If you get such an e-mail, **don't** provide any information without checking further. For example, you could call the company and ask about it. Another clue is bad grammar and misspellings. More than one typo in an official communication is a warning sign.

A second kind of phishing is to persuade people by e-mail to click on a Web site included in the message and provide personal information. Favourite targets of this type of scheme are eBay and PayPal. You get an e-mail that purports to come from eBay and tells you that your account has been compromised or one pretending to come from PayPal saying that your PayPal account is about to pay out on merchandise worth hundreds of dollars that you didn't order. The idea is to get you to go to a site that will steal information like your eBay or PayPal password and then ask for other information, like credit card numbers.

A more sophisticated variation on this is **pharming**, which is the rerouting of your request for a legitimate Web site. You may type in the correct address for your bank and be redirected to a fake site that collects information from you. You may even get to the legitimate site and then be linked to the fake site after you have put in identifying information. You don't notice this because the fake site address is very slightly different from the real one, perhaps just one letter off or different. Make sure to look for the padlock—in the browser, not the site—to let you know that you are at a secure site before entering data (see Chapter 5 on Web e-commerce security).

Pharming is accomplished by getting access to the giant databases that Internet providers use to route Web traffic. Once they have access, they can make little changes so that you are diverted to the fake site either before or after you access the real one. It works so well because it's very hard to spot the fake site.

See Figure 8.4 for some advice from the US Federal Trade Commission regarding identity theft.

PRIVACY AND EMPLOYEES

Companies need information about their employees and customers to be effective in the marketplace. But people often object to having so many details about their lives available to others. If you're applying for a job, you'll most likely fill out a job application,

Figure 8.4

Phishing Facts and What to Do If You're at Risk

Some Facts on Phishing . . .

- In January 2004 there were 198 phishing sites, but by February 2005 that number had risen to 2,625, according to the Anti-Phishing Working Group.

- The same group says that the number of unique phishing e-mails reached 13,141 in February 2004.

- Symantec says that its Brightmail spam filters blocked an average of 33 million phishing attempts per week in December 2004, compared to an average of only 9 million during the previous July.

- The Phemon Institute says consumers lost $500 million to phishers in 2004.

- Also from the Phemon Institute: Of 1,335 people surveyed, about 70 percent visited a fake site, and as many as 15 percent said they had provided personal information to the fake site.

. . . And What to Do If You Suspect You're at Risk

The FTC says that if you believe your personal information may have been compromised, you should:

- Close your credit card accounts (using an ID Theft Affidavit form) and change all your passwords.

- Place a fraud alert on your credit reports with one of the major credit bureaus (Equifax, Experian, and TransUnion).

- Ask government agencies like the Department of Motor Vehicles to flag your file so that no one can get documents in your name.

but that's not the only information a potential employer can get about you. For a small fee, employers, or anyone else, can find out about your credit standing, your telephone usage, your insurance coverage, and many other interesting things. From companies that collect and collate chat room exchanges, an employer can also get information on what you said on the Internet. And an employer can ask job applicants to take drug and psychological tests, the results of which are the property of the company.

All such activities are quite legal. Whether or not they shade into unethical territory is definitely a topic of much debate. But consider the fairly recent and exponentially growing phenomenon of social networking sites, made possible by the advent of Web 2.0 technology. Sites such as Facebook, MySpace, Flickr, Bebo, and LinkedIn hold a wealth of personal information about their subscribers/contributors. Depending on permissions and privacy settings, more or less of this information is exposed to the general public—a general public that includes potential employers or even marriage partners. How much of what is shared in such sites is suitable for general consumption? How much of the content of your chats and IMs would you want your next boss or mother-in-law to see? Chances are the answer would be precious little. But technology is allowing and even encouraging the sharing of increasingly personal information. We all need to participate in a privacy audit regarding our exposure on such sites. It might mean the difference between getting that dream job or not.

After you're hired, your employer can monitor where you go, what you do, what you say, and what you write in e-mails—at least during working hours. The American Management Association says that as of March 2005, 60 percent of employers monitored employee e-mails, both incoming and outgoing. That figure is up from 47 percent in 2001.[16] One reason that companies monitor employees' e-mail is that they can be sued for what their employees send to each other and to people outside the company.

Chevron Corporation and Microsoft settled sexual harassment lawsuits for $2.2 million each because employees sent offensive e-mail to other employees and management didn't intervene. Other companies such as Dow Chemical Company, Xerox, the New York Times Company, and Edward Jones took pre-emptive action by firing people who sent or stored pornographic or violent e-mail messages.[17]

About 70 percent of Web traffic occurs during work hours, and this is reason enough for companies to monitor what, and for how long, employees are surfing the Web. The FBI reports that 78 percent of surveyed companies indicated that employees had abused Internet privileges by downloading pornography, pirating software, or some other activity that wasn't work related. Also, 60 percent of employees said that they visit Web sites or surf for personal use at work. Again, various software packages are available to keep track of people's Web surfing. Some software blocks access to certain sites.

Businesses have good reasons for seeking and storing personal information on employees. They

- Want to hire the best people possible and to avoid being sued for failing to adequately investigate the backgrounds of employees.
- Want to ensure that staff members are conducting themselves appropriately and not wasting or misusing company resources. (Financial institutions are even required by law to monitor all communications including e-mail and telephone conversations.)
- Can be held liable for the actions of employees.

MONITORING TECHNOLOGY   Numerous vendors sell software products that scan e-mail, both incoming and outgoing. The software can look for specific words or phrases in the subject lines or in the body of the text. An e-mail-scanning program can sneak

THE CASINO CHIPS ARE WATCHING YOU

Everyone knows that the casinos in Las Vegas have numerous cameras that track all activity on the floor. But the Hard Rock Hotel and Casino has gone one better by keeping track of individual betting tokens in its high-limit blackjack room where minimum bets are $100. Managers know where each high-denomination token is at all times and can better guard against token theft and counterfeiting.

The casino fits the plastic tokens, which are about the size of a toonie, with RFID (radio frequency identification) chips like the ones that Wal-Mart uses to track its products all the way from the factory to the store shelves. It's also the same technology that's used to keep track of health care supplies, aerospace parts, and many other products.

Up until now, casinos have been able to track slot-machine players by means of "frequent player" cards that players insert into the machines. Table games,

however, were more difficult since the only objective option was video cameras, and otherwise it was up to dealers and pit bosses to estimate how much money gamblers were wagering. The level of betting by customers determines the type and number of freebies and/or discounts customers are entitled to.

With RFID chips embedded into the gambling tokens, pit bosses can keep track of players, their average bets, the denomination of chips they're using, and a wealth of other information.

It works like this: The gambling chips with RFID are sold to a gambler, and when the chips hit the table, sensors below the surface of the table read the data and send it to the computer system. The pit boss then just has to watch the monitor to keep track of how the players are betting and how much they're winning or losing.[19] This is a form of surveillance.

into your computer in Trojan-horse software. That is, it can hide in an innocent-looking e-mail or some other file or software.

Some companies use an approach less invasive than actually reading employees' e-mail. Their e-mail inspection programs just check for a certain level of e-mail to and from the same address. When this indicates that there may be a problem, the employee is informed of the situation and asked to remedy it. No intrusive supervisory snooping is necessary.[18]

An employer can track your keyboard and mouse activity with the type of key logger software described in the previous section. An alternative that's sometimes harder to detect is a **hardware key logger**. A hardware key logger is a hardware device that captures keystrokes on their journey from the keyboard to the motherboard. These devices can be in the form of a connector on the system-unit end of the cable between the keyboard and the system unit. There's another type of hardware key logger that companies can install into the keyboard. Both have enough memory to store about a year's worth of typing. These devices can't capture anything that's not typed, but they do capture every keystroke, including backspace, delete, insert, and all the others. To defeat them you'd have to copy the password (or whatever you want kept secret) and paste it into its new location. The key logger keeps a record of the keystrokes you use, if any, in your copy-and-paste operation, but not what you copied and pasted.

There is little sympathy in the legal system for the estimated 27 million employees whom the American Management Association says are under surveillance. Employers have the legal right to monitor the use of their resources and that includes the time they're paying you for. In contrast to your home, you have no expectation of privacy when using the company's resources.

Some U.S. state laws address the issue of how far employers can go and what they can do to monitor employees. Connecticut's 1999 law requires employers in the private sector to notify employees in writing of electronic monitoring. A year earlier, Pennsylvania permitted telephone marketers to listen in on calls for quality control purposes as long as at least one of the parties is aware of the action.[20]

This issue has been the subject of a recent ruling from Alberta's Privacy Commissioner. In this case, a public-sector employer installed a key logger on the computer of one if its employees because there were concerns about the employee's productivity. The employee was unaware of the installation.

Section 33(c) of Alberta's *Freedom of Information and Protection of Privacy Act* permits collection of information (meaning the employees' activity on the computer) if such collection is necessary for a program or activity of a public body. The employer carried out the collection activity based on this belief.

However, the Alberta Privacy Commissioner stated in his ruling that the methods used were overly invasive and were not necessary for managing the employee. Of particular note was the fact that the information collected by the keystroke logger encompassed everything the employee did on his computer and this was overkill, according to the Commissioner.[21]

PRIVACY AND CONSUMERS

Businesses face a dilemma.

- Customers want businesses to know who they are, but, at the same time, they want them to leave them alone.
- Customers want businesses to provide what they want, but, at the same time, they don't want businesses knowing too much about their habits and preferences.
- Customers want businesses to tell them about products and services they might like to have, but they don't want to be inundated with ads.

Like it or not, massive amounts of personal information are available to businesses from various sources. A relatively large Web site may get about 100 million hits per day, which means that the site gets about 200 bytes of information for each hit. That's about 20 gigabytes of information per day.[22] This level of information load has helped to make customer relationship management (CRM) systems one of the fastest growing areas of software development. Part of managing customer relationships is personalization. Web sites that greet you by name and Amazon.ca's encouragement that "Customers who bought this item also bought …" are examples of personalization, which is made possible by the Web site's knowledge of you.[23]

Apart from being able to collect its own information about you, a company can readily access consumer information elsewhere. Credit card companies sell information, as do Statistics Canada and mailing list companies. Web traffic tracking companies such as DoubleClick follow you (and other surfers) around the Web and then sell the information about where you went and for how long. DoubleClick can collect information about you over time and provide its customers with a highly refined profile of you. DoubleClick is also an intermediary for companies that want to advertise to Web surfers. When hired by a company wanting to sell something, DoubleClick identifies people who might be receptive and sends the ad to them as a banner or pop-up ad. Proponents of this practice claim that it's good for the surfers because they get targeted advertising and less unwanted advertising. You can judge for yourself how true this claim is. DoubleClick, at first, undertook to track consumers without attaching their identity to the information. Then, in 1999, DoubleClick changed its policy and announced that it would attach consumer names to personal information and e-mail addresses. However, in response to negative consumer reaction, DoubleClick withdrew its proposed change. Interestingly, DoubleClick didn't state it would never resume the abandoned policy, but agreed only to wait until standards for such activity are in place.[24]

COOKIES   The basic tool of consumer Web monitoring is the cookie. A *cookie* is a small file that contains information about you and your Web activities, which a Web site you visit places on your computer. A cookie has many uses. For example, it's used to keep ID and password information so that you don't have to go through the whole verification process every time you log onto a Web site. It's also used to store the contents of electronic shopping carts, so that the next time you log on, the Web site will be able to see your wish list (which is stored on your computer in a cookie).

A cookie can also be used to track your Web activity. It can monitor and record what sites you visit, how long you stay there, what Web pages you visited, what site you came from, and the next site you went to. This type of cookie is called a *unique cookie*. Some cookies are temporary and some stay on your computer indefinitely.

Third-party or *common cookies* are the ones that have many privacy advocates disturbed. These are different from the unique cookies that a Web site you visit puts onto your hard disk. A common cookie is one that started out as a unique cookie, but the original site sold access to it to a third party, like DoubleClick, that can then change the cookie so that the third party can track the surfer's activity across many sites. The third party collects information about surfers without names or other identifiable personal information. This third party usually collect an IP address, which it then links to a random identifying ID so that the surfer can be identified at other sites. Surveys have shown that the vast majority of people (91 percent) don't like the idea of unknown companies gathering information about them that they have provided to sites with which they chose to interact.[25]

You have two options if you want to block cookies. First, you can set your browser to accept or reject all cookies. Or you can get it to warn you when a site wants to put a cookie on your computer. Second, you can get cookie management software with additional options that are not available on your browser. For example, CookieCop 2, from *PC Magazine*, will let you accept or reject cookies on a per-site basis. It also allows you to replace banner ads with the image of your choice and to block ads for sites you find offensive. With this or other cookie-stopper software, you can disable pop-up windows, and stipulate that certain cookies can stay on your hard drive for the duration of one session only.

SPAM   *Spam* is unsolicited e-mail (electronic junk mail) from businesses that advertise goods and services. Often spam mass mailings advertise pornography, get-rich-quick schemes, and miracle cures. If you haven't been inundated with spam, you're either very lucky or you don't use the Internet much. Spam has become a major irritant to consumers and a costly matter for businesses, which must sort through hundreds of e-mail messages every day deleting spam and hoping that they don't delete e-mail messages that are actually legitimate customer orders.

You can get spam filters to block out spam, but spammers are clever about including nonprinting characters in their subject lines and addresses that fool the filters into letting them pass. For example, say a spammer wanted to send out a message about a new weight loss drug called *Off*. The spammer would alter the spelling of the word or add invisible HTML tags so that the subject line would be: O*F*F or O<i/i>F<u/u>F. The HTML tags <i> and <u> would normally italicize and underline text, respectively, and the </i> and </u> would undo the italicizing and bolding, but since there's no text in between the tags do nothing except evade the filter.

Experts estimate that up to 70 percent of e-mail traffic in 2004 was spam and in June and July of 2004 spam reached the staggering figure of over 85 percent of messages sent.[26] And now it's at more than 86 percent with no end in sight, according to experts. In Europe, it's not quite as bad at 62 percent, which amounts to 16 billion messages per day. An individual spammer can send out 80 million or so spams per day. AOL and Microsoft say that their servers block a billion spam messages every day.[27] Many states have passed laws to regulate spam and the Canadian government passed an anti-spam law in 2003 called the *CAN-Spam Act*, which was widely criticized by anti-spam activists as legitimizing spam, since it set out rules for spamming rather than banning it altogether.

Most experts doubt that the *CAN-Spam Act* hurts the spammers who are the source of most of the spam; they say that it just costs legitimate businesses time and money since they have to maintain do-not-spam lists and follow the legal guidelines when sending e-mails to customers. Since the bulk of spam comes from spammers who spoof (disguise) the origin of the e-mail, they can usually operate for a long time in defiance of the law. Irate spam trackers, some of whom have become cyber vigilantes, have gone so far as to "out" spammers and publicize information about them on the Web in an effort to stop them.

Canada does not yet have a specific anti-spam law, but the Personal Information Protection and Electronic Documents Act (PIPEDA—see below and www.pipedainfo.com) covers on-line privacy and embodies several provisions relevant to the area of email marketing, under which umbrella spamming falls. Although a federal task force recommended specific anti-spam legislation in a 2005 report ("Stopping Spam: Creating a Stronger, Safer Internet"), no law has yet emanated from the recommendation at the time of writing.

One trick that spammers use to collect addresses for spamming is to send out e-mail purporting to add you to a general do-not-spam list if you reply. In fact, it adds your e-mail address to the list of "live" ones.

ADWARE AND SPYWARE   If you've downloaded a game or other software from the Web for free, you may have noticed that it came with banner ads. These ads are collectively known as adware. *Adware* is software to generate ads that installs itself on your computer when you download some other (usually free) program from the Web (see Figure 8.5). Adware is a type of *Trojan horse software*, meaning that it's software you don't want hidden inside software you do want. There's usually a disclaimer, buried somewhere in the multiple "I agree" screens, saying that the software includes this adware. At the bottom of several small-print screens you're asked to agree to the terms. Very few people read the whole agreement, and advertisers count on that. This sort of product is sometimes called *click-wrap* because it's like commercial software that has an agreement that you agree to by breaking the shrink-wrap.

Most people don't get upset about pure adware, since they feel it's worth having to view ads to get software for free. However, there's a more insidious extra that's often bundled with free downloadable software called spyware. *Spyware* (also called *sneakware* or *stealthware*) is malicious software that collects information about you and your computer and reports it to someone without your permission. It usually comes hidden in downloadable software and tracks your on-line movements and/or mines the information stored on your computer. The first release of RealNetworks' RealJukebox sent information back to the company about what CDs the people who downloaded the software were playing on that computer. This information collection was going on when the customer wasn't even on the Web.[28]

Spyware is fast becoming the hidden cost of free software. Software such as Kazaa Media Desktop and Audiogalaxy, the successors to Napster for sharing music and other files on-line, includes spyware. If you download free software and it has banner ads, it's quite possible that it has spyware, too. There's usually something in the "I agree" screens

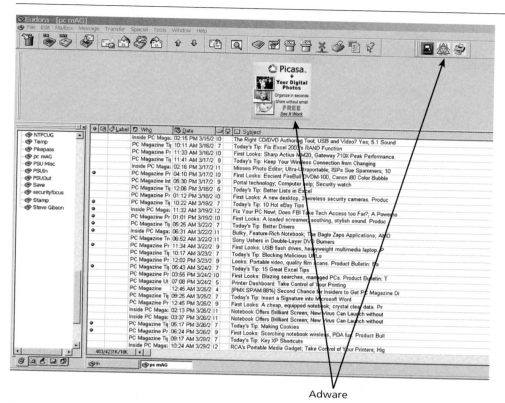

Figure 8.5

Adware in a Free
Version of Eudora,
an E-Mail Application
from Qualcomm

telling you about spyware, but it can be hard to find. Spyware can stay on your computer long after you've uninstalled the original software.

You can detect various kinds of Trojan horse software with The Cleaner from www. moosoft.com. Also check out www.wilders.org for Trojan First Aid Kit (TFAK). The best-known spyware detection programs, also called stealthware blockers, are Ad-Aware (free from www.lavasoftUSA.com) and PestPatrol. The software scans your whole computer, identifies spyware programs, and offers to delete them. If you want to check out free software for spyware before you download it, go on-line to www.spychecker.com, a site that will tell you if particular free software includes adware or spyware.

Even without spyware, a Web site can tell a lot about its Web visitors from its ***Web log***. A Web log consists of one line of information for every visitor to a Web site and is usually stored on a Web server. At the very least, a Web log can provide a Web site company with a record of your clickstream.

A ***clickstream*** records information about you during a Web surfing session such as what Web sites you visited, how long you were there, what ads you looked at, and what you bought. If, as a consumer, you want to protect information about your surfing habits, you can use various software packages to do so. Apart from cookie management software you can avail yourself of ***anonymous Web browsing (AWB)*** services, which, in effect, hide your identity from the Web sites you visit. An example is Anonymizer at www.anonymizer.com. This site, and others like it, sends your Web browsing through its server and removes all identifying information. Some of the ABW services that are available include disabling pop-up promotions, defeating tracking programs, and erasing browsing history files. If you don't want to go through an outside server, you can download software to do the job. SurfSecret is a shareware anti-tracking package available from www.surfsecret.com.

IS YOUR MUSIC CD HIJACKING YOUR COMPUTER?

When you buy a shrink-wrapped CD at a reputable music store, you don't expect it to open up your computer to hackers. That's exactly what happened to a lot of people in 2005 when Sony BMG, as part of a copy protection scheme, embedded a rootkit in its music CDs. A *rootkit* is software that gives you administrator rights to a computer or network and its purpose is to allow you to conceal processes, files, or system data from the operating system. You can read more about rootkits in *Extended Learning Module C, (Computer Crime and Digital Forensics)*.

Sony's rootkit was designed to transfer itself to your computer surreptitiously. The CD would play only from the player included on the CD. Other players didn't recognize it as an audio CD, and instead opened the CD as a data CD.

The original intent was twofold: first, to allow consumers to make up to three copies to play on different platforms, as well as to prevent P2P distribution and large-scale copying; and, second, to relay back to Sony what people were doing with Sony's CDs. It also opened up a back door for anyone who knew about it to get into your system and do whatever they wanted, like using it to send out millions of spam messages or to spread viruses.

The fallout from this scheme was a nightmare for Sony. The company lost millions of dollars when it had to pull an estimated 15 million music CDs from North America that represented 52 titles including Van Zant, Celine Dion, Neil Diamond, and Bette Midler. Lawsuits rained down on Sony. There were several class action suits and a large number of small claims court actions; states filed lawsuits, as did the provinces of Quebec, Ontario, and BC—as well as various countries in Europe. A Sony spokesman, questioned about the rootkit shortly after it was first discovered, said that since no one even knows what a rootkit is, he didn't think it would be a problem. Well, a lot more people know about it now!

As a final note on the subject, remember that even if a company promises, and fully intends, to keep its customer information protected, it may not be possible. When faced with a subpoena, the company will have to relinquish customer records.

PRIVACY AND GOVERNMENT AGENCIES

Government agencies have about numerous databases containing personal information on individuals.[29] The various branches of government need information to administer entitlement programs, such as Old Age Security (OAS), Canada Pension Plan (CPP), welfare, student loans, law enforcement, and so on.

LAW ENFORCEMENT You've often heard about someone being apprehended for a grievous crime after a routine traffic stop for something like a broken taillight. The arrest most likely ensued because the arresting officer ran a check on the license plate and driver's license. The officer might have consulted the National Integrated Interagency Information System (N-III) database operated by the RCMP and found the outstanding warrant there. The U.S. equivalent (NCIC) was used in this way to catch Timothy McVeigh and others responsible for the 1995 bombing of a federal building in Oklahoma City.

Given the wealth of information available and their broad accessibility, it's not surprising that such database systems have been abused. In the United States, several police departments have found that a significant number of employees illegally snooped for criminal records on people they knew or wanted to know more about.

The U.S. Federal Bureau of Investigation (FBI) caused a stir recently because of its electronic surveillance methods. First there was Carnivore, a rather unfortunate name, which has since been changed to DCS-1000. DCS-1000 connects hardware to an ISP to trap all e-mail sent to or received by the target of the investigation. It takes a court order to use DCS-1000, and, of course, the target is typically unaware of the surveillance. Intercepting communications is not new: The FBI put the first tap on a phone in 1885, just four years after the invention of the telephone.[30] DCS-1000 traps all communications involving the individual named in the court order. In Canada, federal law requires that at least one party to the phone conversation be aware of the recording.

Moreover, the FBI wants Canada to make Internet and phone tapping easier. In 2004, the assistant director in charge of the FBI's Criminal Justice Information Services Division, said in Ottawa that American law and spy agencies would appreciate an effort by Canada to provide Canadian agencies with the legal mandate to tap private e-mail and Internet-driven (VoIP) phone calls. This would be facilitated, moreover, by compelling cell phone and Internet service providers (ISPs) to make their equipment easier to tap.[31]

Because it can be hard to identify the data packets of one individual's e-mail among all the other Internet traffic, it's entirely possible that other people's e-mail might be scooped up in the net. And this is what happened in March 2000 when FBI agents were legally intercepting messages of a suspect, but someone else was caught in the trap. The information on the innocent party was obtained under the *Freedom of Information Act*. The FBI said the incident was an honest mistake and a result of miscommunication between it and the ISP.[32] But this is the sort of mistake that scares people. Most people want law enforcement to be able to watch the bad guys—that's necessary for our collective safety. But the prospect of information being collected on law-abiding citizens who are minding their own business worries a lot of people.

Many Canadians also worry about being caught in the intricate web of information sharing between Canada and the United States. According to a 2004 statement by the RCMP's deputy commissioner, Gary Loeppky, information about innocent people caught in police investigations ends up in a system named SCIS—the security criminal intelligence system—which is maintained jointly by the RCMP, CSIS, border and immigration officials, and local law enforcement agencies. Particularly important about this national security database is that its contents are available to U.S. authorities upon request.[33]

In 2001, the FBI acknowledged an enhancement to DCS-1000 called Magic Lantern, which is key logger software. The FBI installs it by sending the target an innocent-looking Trojan-horse e-mail, which contains the key logger software. The hidden software then sends information back to the FBI periodically.[34]

Another U.S. federal agency, the National Security Agency (NSA), uses a system called Echelon that uses a global network of satellites and surveillance stations to trap phone, e-mail, and fax transmissions. The system then screens all this information looking for certain keywords and phrases and analyzes the messages that fit the search criteria.

At the local level, the actions of the Tampa Police Department at the 2001 Super Bowl caused an outcry from privacy advocates in the United States. Police, with the agreement of the NFL, focused video cameras on the faces of tens of thousands of spectators as they entered the stadium. The images were sent to computers that used facial recognition software to compare the images to a database of pictures of suspected criminals and terrorists. The police spokesperson said that the action was legal since it's permissible to take pictures of people in public places. That's true in so far as you have no expectation of privacy in a public place. Indeed surveillance of people has been going on for years without much protest in gambling casinos, Wal-Mart stores, and other businesses in the private sector. But the American Civil Liberties Union (ACLU) protested the surveillance of Super Bowl spectators on the grounds that it was surveillance by a government agency without court-ordered authorization. The fact that the state was involved made it unacceptable to the ACLU.

OTHER FEDERAL AGENCIES   Canada Revenue Agency (CRA) gets income information from taxpayers. But the agency potentially has access to other information as well. For example CRA might be interested in vehicle registration information so that it can check up on people buying expensive cars and boats to ensure they're reporting an income level that corresponds to their purchases. CRA can go to outside government databases as well. In the United States, Verizon says that it gets 22,000 requests for phone records from the IRS, FBI, and other government agencies per year. It seldom informs the customer of the request. America Online (AOL) has a special fax number reserved just for subpoenas.

Statistics Canada collects information on all the Canadian inhabitants it can find every five years. All citizens are required to fill out a census form, and some households get a very long and detailed form requiring them to disclose a lot of personal information. The information that StatCan collects is available to other government agencies and even to commercial enterprises. The agency doesn't link the information to respondents' names but sells summarized information about geographic regions. Some of these regions are relatively small. Statistics Canada is well known, however, for its almost fanatical protection of the privacy of the data it collects on Canadians.

Nonetheless, it's fairly safe to assume that any time you have contact with any branch of government, information about you will be subsequently stored somewhere. For example, if you get a government-backed student loan, you provide personal information such as your name, address, income, parents' income, and so on. Some of the information nuggets attached to the loan would be the school you're attending, the bank dispersing the loan, your repayment schedule, and later, your repayment pattern.

LAWS ON PRIVACY

In terms of government legislation and regulation, Canada lies somewhere between the European Union on one extreme and the United States on the other, though markedly closer to the EU than to the United States. Despite some recent legislation in the United States, such as the *Health Insurance Portability and Accountability Act* (HIPAA, enacted in 1996) and the *Financial Service Modernization Act*, the United States doesn't have a comprehensive or consistent set of laws governing the use of information. The EU, on the other hand, has very strong rules and expectations regarding the use of personal information by both the public and the private sectors.

Canada's *Personal Information Protection and Electronic Documents Act* (PIPEDA) was passed into law in the late 1990s with the dual purpose of promoting trust in electronic commerce and also reassuring the EU that the personal information of European citizens was being protected in Canada.

Under PIPEDA, individuals have the right to

- Know why an organization collects, uses, or discloses their personal information
- Expect an organization to collect, use, or disclose their personal information reasonably and appropriately, and not use the information for any purpose other than that to which they have consented
- Know who in the organization is responsible for protecting their personal information.
- Expect an organization to protect their personal information by taking appropriate security measures
- Expect the personal information an organization holds about them to be accurate, complete, and up to date
- Obtain access to their personal information and ask for corrections if necessary
- Complain about how an organization handles their personal information if they feel their privacy rights have not been respected.

The law requires that organizations

- Obtain consent when they collect, use, or disclose their customers' personal information
- Supply an individual with a product or a service even if he or she refuses consent for the collection, use, or disclosure of personal information unless that information is essential to the transaction
- Collect information by fair and lawful means
- Have personal information policies that are clear, understandable, and readily available.

PIPEDA came into force in three stages. Starting in 2001, the law was applied to federally regulated industries such as airlines, banking, and broadcasting. In 2002 the health sector came under the legislation. In 2004, all organizations that collect personal information for commercial purposes were subject to the law, with the notable exception of any province having "substantially similar" privacy laws. There are four such cases:

- An *Act Respecting the Protection of Personal Information in the Private Sector* (Quebec)
- The *Personal Information Protection Act* (British Columbia)
- The *Personal Information Protection Act* (Alberta)
- The *Personal Health Information Protection Act* (Ontario).

Under PIPEDA, complaints are filed at the Office of the Privacy Commissioner of Canada, where the Commissioner investigates and produces a report regarding the complaint. The Commissioner has no powers to order compliance, award damages, or levy penalties. The final arbiter in these cases is the Federal Court of Canada, and such action can be initiated only by the complainant as PIPEDA does not explicitly grant the organization against which the claim is being made the right to do so.[35, 36, 37, 38]

Figure 8.6 outlines some important recent initiatives from our U.S. neighbours. Some (such as the *Patriot Act and Homeland Security Act*) have direct bearing on Canadians as our economies, intelligence, and defence are so intertwined. Furthermore the *Sarbanes-Oxley Act* (SOX for short) has special significance owing to our rights and obligations under NAFTA.

Figure 8.6

Recent U.S. Information-Related Laws that Impact Canadians

- *Patriot Act*, 2001 and 2003, allows law enforcement to access almost any information, including library records, video rentals, bookstore purchases, and business records when investigating any act of terrorism or hostile intelligence activities. In 2003 Patriot II broadened the original law.

- *Homeland Security Act*, 2002, provided new authority to government agencies to mine data on individuals and groups including e-mails and Web site visits; put limits on the information available under the *Freedom of Information Act*; and gave new powers to government agencies to declare national heath emergencies.

- *Sarbanes-Oxley Act*, 2002, sought to protect investors by improving the accuracy and reliability of corporate disclosures and requires companies to (1) implement extensive and detailed policies to prevent illegal activity within the company and (2) respond in a timely manner to investigate illegal activity. (You'll find more about the business implications of *Sarbanes-Oxley* in *Extended Learning Module C [Computer Crime and Digital Forensics]*.)

LO4

Security

So, what can put your important information resource in jeopardy? Well, countless things. Hard disks can crash, computer parts can fail, hackers and crackers (see below) can gain access and do mischief, thieves engaged in industrial espionage can steal your information, and disgruntled employees or associates can cause damage. The FBI estimates that computer sabotage costs businesses somewhere close to $10 billion every year. Companies are increasing their spending on Internet security software, a fact to which Symantec Corp. can attest. Symantec is the largest exclusive developer of computer security software and has a market value of $19 billion, making it one of the most valuable software companies in the world.[39] The company's most recognizable brand is the Norton Anti-Virus and Internet Security line.

SECURITY AND EMPLOYEES

Most of the press reports are about outside attacks on computer systems, but actually, companies are in far more danger of losing money from employee misconduct than they are from outsiders. It's estimated that 75 percent of computer crime is perpetrated by insiders, although this is not a problem that's restricted to computer misuse.

All too often the culprit inside the organization is the "super user"—someone who is either a network or systems administrator and, by virtue of such status, has privileges that others don't enjoy. Moreover, sometimes a special status is created and conferred on someone who possesses specific or deep knowledge of certain processes or systems. Such users, with their ability to circumvent permission-based access to data and systems, are more likely to be implicated in security issues than are other, less privileged, users. This is not to say that such persons are inherently less trustworthy. Far from it. The issue is that increased permission leads to increased risk. Organizations would do well to carefully audit such individuals and processes with an eye to assessing the risk based on "super user" status.

But white-collar crime is where the big bucks are lost (see Figure 8.7). White-collar crime in general, from multinational firms to video stores to construction companies, accounts for at least $20 billion in losses among Canadian businesses every year—and information technology makes it much easier to accomplish and conceal the crime.[40] Of all white-collar fraud, the biggest losses are those incurred by management misconduct. The following figures report U.S. statistics, but Canada has the unenviable reputation of being quite soft on white-collar criminals. Thus the normal "take the U.S. figure and divide by 10" might, in this case, produce an underestimate.[41] Manager theft of various kinds is about four times that of other employees. Take embezzlement, for example. The average cost of a non-managerial employee's theft is $60,000, while that for managerial employees is $250,000. The most astonishing aspect of this is that most insider fraud (up to two-thirds) is never reported to the legal authorities, according to the Association of Certified Fraud Examiners (ACFE).

Computer-aided fraud includes the old standby crimes like vendor fraud (sending payment to a nonexistent vendor or payment for goods not delivered), writing payroll cheques to fictitious employees, claiming expense reimbursements for costs never incurred, and so on. In addition, there are newer crimes such as stealing security codes, credit card numbers, and proprietary files. Intellectual property is one of the favourite targets of theft by insiders. In fact, the companies that make surveillance software say that employers are buying and installing the software not so much to monitor employees as to track how intellectual property, like product design sketches, schematics, and so on, is moving around the network.

Figure 8.7

Figures on Fraud

Source: 2006 ACFE Report to the Nation on Occupational Fraud and Abuse.

	Who's Committing Fraud
61%	Fraud committed by men
39%	Fraud committed by women
$250,000	Median loss from fraud committed by men
$102,000	Median loss from fraud committed by women
41.2%	Fraud committed by managers
39.5%	Fraud committed by employees
19.3%	Fraud committed by owners/executives

Fraud examiners have a rule of thumb that in any group of employees, about 10 percent are completely honest, 10 percent will steal, and, for the remaining 80 percent, it will depend on circumstances. Most theft is committed by people who are strapped for cash, have access to funds that are poorly protected, and perceive a low risk of getting caught.

SECURITY AND OUTSIDE THREATS

In 2006 in the United States, companies spent, on average, $5 million each to recover corporate data that was lost or stolen. That's 30 percent more than in 2005. The losses are the result of many problems such as someone breaking into their systems, malicious insider activity, malware like spyware and viruses, and the theft of USB devices, notebook computers, and flash memory cards. The average cost per record that was compromised was $140.[42]

The threats from outside are many and varied. Competitors could try to get your customer lists or the prototype for your new project. Cyber vandals could be joyriding in cyberspace looking for something interesting to see, steal, or destroy. You could become the victim of a generalized attack from a virus or worm, or could suffer a targeted attack like a denial-of-service attack. If you have something worth stealing or manipulating on your system, there could be people after that, too. For example, the on-line gambling industry is plagued by attacks where hackers have illicitly gained access to the servers that control the gambling, corrupting games to win millions of dollars. Exploiting well-known system weaknesses accounts for a large part of hacker damage, while only 5 percent results from breaking into systems in new ways.[43]

The people who break into the computer systems of others are "hackers" (see Figure 8.8 on the next page). *Hackers* are generally knowledgeable computer users who use their knowledge to invade other people's computers. They have varying motives. Some just do it for the fun of it. Others (called hacktivists) have a philosophical or political message they want to share, and still others (called crackers) are hired guns who illegally break in, usually to steal information, for a fee. The latter can be a very lucrative undertaking. Some highly skilled crackers charge up to $1 million per job. There are also "good guys," called white-hat hackers, who test the vulnerability of systems so that protective measures may be taken.

TYPES OF CYBERCRIME   Cybercrimes range from electronically breaking and entering to cyberstalking and murder. In October 1999, a 21-year-old woman was shot and killed outside the building where she worked. Her killer had been electronically stalking her for two years. He became obsessed with the woman and had even posted a Web site dedicated to her on which he announced his intention to kill her. He got her Social Security Number on-line, found out where she worked, tracked her down, and shot her, after which he shot himself.

Figure 8.8

Hacker Types

- White-hat hackers find vulnerabilities in systems and plug the holes. They work at the request of the owners of the computer systems.
- Black-hat hackers break into other people's computer systems and may just look around, or they may steal credit card numbers or destroy information, or otherwise do damage.
- Hacktivists have philosophical and political reasons for breaking into systems. They often deface a Web site as a protest.
- Script kiddies, or script bunnies, find hacking code on the Internet and click-and-point their way into systems, to cause damage or spread viruses.
- Crackers are hackers for hire and are the hackers who engage in corporate espionage.
- Cyberterrorists are those who seek to cause harm to people or to destroy critical systems or information. They try to use the Internet as a weapon of mass destruction.

Most cybercrimes are not as tragic, but they can be serious nonetheless. Computer viruses and denial-of-service attacks are the two most common types of cybercrime against which companies need to protect themselves.

A *computer virus* (or simply a *virus*) is software that is written with malicious intent to cause annoyance or damage. A virus can be benign or malicious. The benign ones just display a message on the screen or slow the computer, but don't do any damage. The malicious kind targets a specific application or set of file types, and corrupts or destroys them.

Today, worms are the most prevalent type of virus. A *worm* is a type of virus that spreads itself, not only from file to file, but also from computer to computer via e-mail and other Internet traffic. It finds your e-mail address book and helps itself to the addresses and sends itself to your contacts, using your e-mail address as the return address. The Love Bug worm was one of the early worms that did a lot of damage and got major press coverage. It's estimated that the Love Bug and its variants affected 300,000 Internet host computers and millions of individual PC users, causing file damage, lost time, and high-cost emergency repairs costing about $8.7 billion.[44, 45] Ford Motor Company, H. J. Heinz, Merrill Lynch, AT&T, Capitol Hill, and the British Parliament all fell victim to the Love Bug worm. Newer versions of worms include Klez, a very rapidly spreading worm; Nimda; and Sircam.

A *denial-of-service attack (DoS)* floods a server or network with so many requests for service that it slows down or crashes. The objective is to prevent legitimate customers from accessing the target site. E*Trade, Yahoo!, and Amazon.com have all been victims of this type of attack. For more information about viruses and hackers and DoSs, see Extended Learning Module C (Computer Crime and Digital Forensics).

As well as knowing what viruses can do, you need to know what they can't do. Computer viruses can't

- Hurt your hardware, such as your monitor, or processor
- Hurt any files they weren't designed to attack. A virus designed for Microsoft's Outlook, for example, generally doesn't infect Qualcomm's Eudora, or any other e-mail application.

ON-LINE BLACKMAIL

"You can ignore this e-mail and try to keep your site up, which will cost you tens of thousands of dollars in lost customers, or you can send us $10K bank wire to make sure that your site experiences no problems + we will give you our protection for a year."

Above is the message that the managers of Protx, an on-line-payment processing firm in London, England, received by e-mail. The incident was the third time the company had been attacked within the year, and it was the most savage attack. At one point, the Protx network was bombarded by a blitz of traffic, to the tune of 500 megabits per second (that's about five times more traffic per second than a large ISP would handle). This barrage came from thousands of computers whose power had been commandeered by the attackers in what's called a distributed denial-of-service attack, and it knocked the company offline.

As is often the case, the attacks were conducted with bot viruses. A bot virus is a program that attackers plant in someone else's computer that allows the perpetrator to use the resources—the CPU or hard disk, for example—for their own purposes.

In the case of Protx, computer security experts were called in to stop the attacks and prevent the same sort of thing from happening in the future. They found that as soon as they shut down one stream of attacks, another one would start from a different hijacked network. It cost Protx about $500,000 to secure its network against future attacks. Such costs are usually annual expenses and don't include the cost of shutting down the original attacks or the cost of the business lost by the victim company.[46]

SECURITY PRECAUTIONS

In Chapter 7, you learned about business contingency plans and in Extended Learning Module B (Network Basics) you read about intrusion detection. These are both very important components of any company's computer system security. There are also standard precautions that a company, and any individual who wants protection from the computer-based attacks, should take.

The most basic protection is to have anti-virus software running on your computer. ***Anti-virus software*** detects and removes or quarantines computer viruses. New viruses are created every day and each new generation is more deadly (or potentially more deadly) than the previous one. You should update your anti-virus software regularly and make sure it's running all the time so that it kicks in when you download e-mail and other files.

Many of the anti-virus software packages on the market also protect you against other cyber evils, like spyware and adware. They will also block cookies, pop-up ads, and embedded objects and scripts such as you get if you download a Flash file, for instance.

Spam protection is theoretically good to have, although it may let some spam through and may mark as spam something that isn't. You can usually choose to have the spam deleted, quarantined (in its own folder), or marked so that it stands out when you look in your Inbox. *Anti-phishing software* is also available to protect you from identity theft. The MyVault feature of ZoneAlarm, for example, will block data such as social insurance numbers, credit card numbers, and passwords from leaving your computer. Anti-phishing toolbars warn you when you arrive at a known phishing site. Symantec's anti-phishing software places a toolbar beneath the Address Bar that turns red if you land at a phishing site.

ZoneAlarm, a firewall program with additional features, will let you know if a program is trying to access the Internet for whatever reason, as spyware on your computer may be attempting to do. It also offers protection from ads and cookies. A *firewall* is hardware and/or software that protects a computer or network from intruders. The firewall examines each message as it seeks entrance to the network, like a border guard checking passports. Unless the message has the "right" markings, the firewall will block it from entering. You can set your firewall so that it identifies certain programs that are always allowed to visit a Web site. Your e-mail program would be an example. Any competent network administrator will have at least one firewall on the network to keep out unwelcome guests, such as protection against rootkits, for example, which we discussed in the Perspectives box, "Is Your Music CD Hijacking Your Computer?" on page 240.

Rootkit finders are available from Kaspersky's and F-Secure security software. There are also free programs available. Removing rootkits is tricky, and different software packages meet with varying degrees of success.

There are also programs that will block certain sites, which is useful if you have underage children. Some people suggest using FireFox or Opera as your default browser since Microsoft's Internet Explorer has long been a favourite target of hackers.

ACCESS AUTHENTICATION   While firewalls keep outsiders out, they don't necessarily keep insiders out. In other words, unauthorized employees may try to access computers or files. One of the ways that companies try to protect computer systems is with authentication systems that check who you are before they permit access.

There are three basic ways of proving your access rights: (1) what you know, like a password; (2) what you have, like an ATM card; (3) what you look like (more specifically what your fingerprint or some other physical characteristic looks like).

Passwords are very popular and have been used since computers were created. You can password-protect the whole network, a single computer, a folder, or a file. But passwords are not by any means a perfect way to protect a computer system. People forget their passwords, so someone may have to get them new passwords or find the old one. Banks spend $15 per call to help customers who forget their passwords. Then if a hacker breaks into the system and steals a password list, everyone has to get a new password. One bank had to change 5,000 passwords in the course of a single month at a cost of $12.50 each.[47]

Which brings us to biometrics, or what you look like. *Biometrics* is the use of physiological characteristics—such as your fingerprint, the blood vessels in the iris of your eye, the sound of your voice, or perhaps even your breath—to provide identification. Roughly a dozen different types of biometric devices are available at the moment, with fingerprint readers being the most popular. About 44 percent of the biometric systems sold are fingerprint systems. They work just like the law enforcement system where your fingerprint is stored in the database, and when you come along, your finger is scanned, and the scan is compared to the entry in the database. If they match, you're in. See Chapter 9 for more information on biometrics.

ENCRYPTION   If you want to protect your messages and files and hide them from prying eyes, you can encrypt them. *Encryption* scrambles the contents of a file so that you can't read it without having the right decryption key. There are various ways of encrypting messages. You can switch the order of the characters, replace characters with other characters, or insert or remove characters. All of these methods alter the look of the message, but used alone, each one is fairly simple to figure out. So most encryption methods use a combination.

PROTECTING PERSONAL RFID–STORED INFORMATION

Radio frequency ID chips are very small, almost paper-thin, in some instances, that store and wirelessly transmit and receive information. For example, Wal-Mart has for several years been implementing RFID for inventory control. The company will eventually require all its suppliers to implement RFID technology. The tags will be on crates and pallets so that they can be tracked through the supply chain. Other applications of RFID include

- Shell Canada's EasyPay and Imperial Oil's (Esso) Speedpass
- Embedding RFID chips in passports
- Monitoring the temperature of perishable items (DHL)
- Tagging consumer products with RFID instead of bar codes (many companies including Best Buy)
- Tagging overseas shipments of suppliers (Australian Department of Defence)
- Tracking cattle and domestic pets.

The most controversial use of RFID technology is when people wear it or have it implanted into their bodies. These chips have information, often medical, that can be read via radio signal in case the person becomes incapacitated. VeriChip was a pioneer creator of microchips to be implanted in humans. In 2008, Xmark (a Canadian company) bought VeriChip and now sells products that address infant protection, wander prevention, staff safety, and asset tracking to over 5,000 health care institutions worldwide. As of 2008, the company has an estimated 600 chips embedded in humans. The challenge then becomes one of protecting your personal RFID information. It can be read wirelessly, meaning that people can build reading devices and obtain your medical information by coming within three feet of you. You'll learn more about RFID in Chapter 9.[48, 49, 50, 51]

Companies that get sensitive information from customers, such as credit card numbers, need some way of allowing all their customers to use encryption to send the information. But they don't want everyone to be able to decrypt the message, so they might use public key encryption. ***Public key encryption (PKE)*** is an encryption system that uses two keys: a public key that everyone can have and a private key for only the recipient. So if you do on-line banking, the bank will give you the public key to encrypt the information you send the bank, but only the bank has the key to decrypt your information. It works rather like a wall safe, where anyone can lock it (just shut the door and twirl the knob), but only the person with the right combination can open it again.

Summary: STUDENT LEARNING OUTCOMES *REVISITED*

LO1 **Define ethics and describe factors that affect how you make a decision concerning an ethical issue.** *Ethics* are the principles and standards that guide our behaviour toward other people. How you decide ethical issues must depend especially on your basic ethical structure but also for better or worse on the practical circumstances. Your basic ethics you probably acquired growing up. The practical circumstances that you might allow to affect you include

- *Consequences:* How much or how little benefit or harm will come from a particular decision?
- *Society's opinion:* What do you perceive society thinks of your intended action?
- *Likelihood of effect:* What is the probability of the harm or benefit if you take the action?
- *Time to consequences:* How long will it take for the benefit or harm to take effect?
- *Relatedness:* How much do you identify with the person or persons who will receive the benefit or suffer the harm?
- *Reach of result.* How many people will be affected by your action?

LO2 **Define and describe intellectual property, copyright, Fair Dealing Doctrine, and pirated software.** *Intellectual property* is intangible creative work that is embodied in physical form. *Copyright* is the legal protection afforded an expression of an idea, such as a song or a video game and some types of proprietary documents. The *Fair Dealing Doctrine* says that you may use copyrighted material in certain situations. *Pirated software* is the unauthorized use, duplication, distribution, or sale of copyrighted software.

LO3 **Define privacy and describe ways in which it can be threatened.** *Privacy* is the right to be left alone when you want to be, to have control over your own personal possessions, and not to be observed without your consent. Your privacy can be compromised by other individuals snooping on you; by employers monitoring your actions; by businesses that collect information on your needs, preferences, and surfing practices; and by the various government agencies that collect information on citizens.

LO4 **Describe the ways in which information on your computer or network is vulnerable, and list measures you can take to protect it.**

- Employees can embezzle and perpetrate fraud of other types. Most of the financial losses due to computer fraud suffered by companies are caused by employees.
- Hackers and crackers try to break into computers and steal, destroy, or compromise information.
- Hackers can spread *computer viruses* or launch *denial-of-service attacks (DoS)* that can cost millions in prevention and cleanup.

Measures you can take are to install

- Anti-virus software to find and delete or quarantine viruses
- Anti-spyware and anti-adware software
- Spam protection software
- Anti-phishing toolbar
- Firewalls
- Anti-rootkit software
- Encryption
- Biometrics.

www.mcgrawhill.ca/olc/haag

CLOSING CASE STUDY 1
Cautionary Tales of Indiscreet E-Mail

Wrongdoing at Computer Associates and at Enron, once giants in their respective industries, was brought to light by forgotten and/or deleted e-mails. The recovered e-mails brought down guilty individuals, but caused some innocents to suffer as well.

COMPUTER ASSOCIATES

In 2000, Charles Wang, chairman of Computer Associates (CA), a business software development giant, was number one on *Forbes's* list of wealthiest people with earnings of $650 million, $649 million of which was performance-based. However, early in 2002, U.S. federal investigators began investigating Computer Associates for improperly booking more than $2 billion in revenue. It had apparently become common practice for executives to keep quarterly reports open so that later deals could be backdated, making the quarterlies look better. By the end of 2002, Wang had been retired to an honorary, uncompensated position, largely because of the accounting discrepancies being investigated.

Hoping to avoid the sort of disaster that killed Arthur Andersen, Computer Associates' board of directors hired experienced criminal lawyers to conduct an investigation to get to the truth. After searching hundreds of employee computers, the investigation turned up e-mails, deleted and saved, that provided evidence of fraud. These e-mails were not on the main system, but rather were stored on individual machines (see Figure 8.2 on page 230).

By April 2004, three former executives of the company had pled guilty to obstruction of justice charges and by September that number had risen to seven who had pled guilty or been indicted. The obstruction of justice charges came from the top executives' misleading the independent lawyers about the facts of their actions, knowing that the falsehoods would be passed on to federal investigators. Attorney–client privilege did not apply since the outside lawyers were hired to do an independent investigation and did not represent individual executives. By the time the main part of the investigation was over, most of the top-level executives of CA had been fired.

ENRON

When the U.S. Federal Energy Regulatory Commission (FERC), which was investigating Enron, unearthed and published confiscated e-mails, not only Enron's employees got a nasty shock when their old e-mails turned up on the Web. Everyone who had sent e-mails to Enron e-mail addresses found themselves caught in the federal net. So, people who were never accused of wrong-doing and didn't even work at Enron suddenly found their e-mail messages displayed for all the world to see, even if the message was as innocent as the confirmation of a golfing date.

FERC gathered a boatload of records, paper and electronic, during its investigation of Enron's alleged energy-market manipulations. In March 2003, FERC posted 1.6 million e-mail messages and other documents on the Web in a searchable database. The e-mails are from the period 2000–03. So anyone can go to the Web site and view the e-mails and calendars of 176 current and former Enron employees. The e-mails appear in full—including sender and receiver names.

Among the e-mail messages are lots of personal communications like executives discussing employees and vice versa; romantic messages; discussions of breakups (liaisons and marriages); in-law problems; personal photos, and so on.

FERC said that, since Enron owned the messages, it was incumbent on the company to identify personal communications and request their exclusion.

A couple of days after the e-mail database appeared on the Web, FERC agreed to take off the most sensitive documents, like a document that listed the Social Security Number of every employee. In early April, on the order of a U.S. Court of Appeals, the database was shut down for 10 days to allow Enron to examine all the documents and make up a list of documents it wanted removed.

About 100 Enron volunteers spent 350 hours going through hundreds of thousands of e-mails looking for specific terms like "social security number," "credit card number," "kids," and "divorce." FERC removed about 8 percent of the database, which amounted to about 141,000 documents.[52, 53]

Questions

1. If you were to give advice to someone who had just started using e-mail, or even someone who's been using e-mail for a while, what would you tell that person should be the one guiding principle in all his or her e-mail communications? Put your advice into one sentence.

2. Now expand on your one guiding principle in question 1, and offer 10 rules for writing e-mails.

3. Imagine you're a manager in a lawn care business and you have an office staff of five people. Your lawyer suggests that you issue guidelines or rules to your staff about storing e-mail on the company's server and on the computers they use in their work for you. What should those guidelines be? What would the rules be? Be sure to explain your rationale.

4. Do you think there should be Canadian federal guidelines governing a business's e-mail traffic just as there are regarding a business's financial records? If so, what should they be? If not, why not?

CLOSING CASE STUDY 2
The Problem of Information Protection

The theft of consumer information—particularly financial information—is causing huge headaches for financial and data companies. This case highlights recent incidents at ChoicePoint, Equifax, and Polo Ralph Lauren.

CHOICEPOINT

The opening case study in this chapter highlighted the Acxiom Corporation, a company that gathers, packages, and sells information about consumers. A direct competitor to Acxiom is ChoicePoint, a spinoff of Equifax, which is one of the three major credit bureaus in Canada (the others being TransUnion and Northern Credit Bureaus).

ChoicePoint has 19 billion records that include information on almost every adult in the United States, and sells this information to customers such as potential employers, who use it for purposes of verification, among others.

ChoicePoint was spotlighted when personal financial information on 145,000 customers was stolen in a very high-profile identity fraud theft. And this time there was no sophisticated electronic attack or break-in; rather the theft was accomplished through old-fashioned "social engineering." Social engineering is getting information that you have no right to by conning people who have access to it. The identity thieves posed as fake companies buying information on people in every state and the District of Columbia. So far, 750 confirmed cases of identity theft have surfaced from the ChoicePoint security breach.

The U.S. Attorney's Office in Los Angeles charged that ChoicePoint had been scammed previously in 2002, resulting in fraud to the tune of $1 million.

Such cases are by no means restricted to the United States. Canada has seen its share of high-profile security breaches, including one at ChoicePoint's parent company— a consumer credit rating agency that collects personal information on millions of Canadians.

EQUIFAX

Equifax confirmed in March 2004 that someone had hacked into its database and stolen hundreds of credit reports. The company collects detailed personal information about consumers, including home addresses, social insurance numbers, bank account balances, and credit card and payment histories, which in turn is used by banks, retailers and insurers to determine whether applicants should be granted credit cards, car leases, loans, and insurance.

The company revealed that criminals, posing as legitimate credit grantors, were accessing Equifax's database and obtained credit reports on 1,400 consumers, primarily in B.C. and Alberta.

It's not clear how Equifax discovered the security breach or how the criminals were using the personal information. Equifax contacted the affected consumers and alerted other credit service providers of the breach.

This was the third security breach for Equifax Canada in as many years. The company maintains more than 30 million consumer files in Canada and says it is reviewing its hiring procedures.

POLO RALPH LAUREN

Between June 2002 and December 2004, Polo Ralph Lauren was storing credit card information on its point-of-sale system instead of deleting it immediately after transactions had been completed. The realization that this data had been compromised led HSBC North America—the issuer of some of the credit cards whose numbers had been stolen—to notify 180,000 consumers of the possibility of identity theft. MasterCard, Visa U.S.A., and Discover Financial Services customers were affected. American Express said it had not seen any activity that looked suspicious.[54, 55, 56]

Questions

1. If you were the manager of a company where it was discovered that credit card information had been stolen, what responsibility would you have to the people whose personal information was compromised? What are the pros and cons of notifying and of not notifying possible victims?

2. E*Trade, a leader in on-line brokerage services, is the first company to go to a two-factor authentication system optionally available to its customers with accounts of $50,000 or more. The first factor is the ID and password that customers have always needed; the second is a security token or, as E*Trade calls it, a *digital security ID*. This is a little device that you can carry on your key chain that displays a new random six-digit number every minute. E*Trade's host system must, of course, synchronize with the device.

When you log in, you have to type in this number after your ID and password. Since the number changes so often it's virtually impossible to hack an account with this two-pronged protection. From a consumer's point of view, do you think this is a good idea? What are the advantages and disadvantages of the system to businesses and customers? With which on-line transactions would you consider it worthwhile to enforce this level of security? Remember that you might have a lot of these tokens if you use a lot of on-line services.

3. In this case study you saw how personal information can be stolen from huge databases and data warehouses. What other ways can thieves obtain personal information about you that would allow them to steal your identity and run up debts in your name? To what extent would you be liable for these debts? What would you have to do (what steps would you take) to re-establish your financial identity if you discovered your identity had been stolen?

4. Acxiom acquired ChoicePoint's Database Marketing Solutions division in July 2008, adding several more clients from multiple industries, including the financial sector. Further to the opening case's first question "Do you feel comfortable about so many people collecting information about you?" how do you feel about only a few companies having all this information about you?

Key Terms and Concepts

Adware, 238

Anonymous Web browsing (AWB), 239

Anti-virus software, 247

Biometrics, 248

Clickstream, 239

Computer virus (virus), 246

Cookie, 237

Copyright, 228

Denial-of-service attack (DoS), 246

Encryption, 248

Ethics, 226

Fair Dealing Doctrine, 228

Firewall, 248

Hacker, 245

Hardware key logger, 235

Identity theft, 231

Intellectual property, 228

Key logger software (key trapper software), 230

Pharming, 233

Phishing (carding or brand spoofing), 232

Pirated software, 229

Privacy, 229

Public key encryption (PKE), 249

Spam, 237

Spyware (sneakware or stealthware), 238

Trojan horse software, 238

Web log, 239

Worm, 246

Short-Answer Questions

1. What are ethics, and how do ethics apply to business?
2. What situation would qualify as an exception to the copyright law?
3. What is privacy?
4. What is pirated software?
5. What is identity theft?
6. What does a key logger do?
7. What is spyware?
8. What is a denial-of-service attack?
9. What is public key encryption?

Assignments and Exercises

1. **HELPING A FRIEND** Suppose you fully intend to spend the evening working on an Excel assignment that's due the next day. Then a friend calls. Your friend is stranded miles from home and desperately needs your help. It will take most of the evening to pick up your friend, bring him home, and return to your studying. Not only that, but you're very tired when you get home and just fall into bed. The next day your friend, who completed his assignment earlier, suggests you just make a copy, put your own name on the cover, and hand it in as your own work. Should you do it? Isn't it only fair that, since you helped your friend, the friend should do something about making sure you don't lose points because of your generosity? What if your friend promises not to hand in his or her own work so that you can't be accused of copying? Your friend wrote the assignment and gave it to you, so there's no question of copyright infringement.

2. **FIND OUT WHAT HAPPENED** In December 2001, British Telecom (BT) filed a lawsuit against Prodigy in New York federal court, claiming it owns the hyperlinking process. If BT wins this lawsuit then the company will be able to collect licensing revenue from the 100 billion or so links on the Web. BT has a patent that it says amounts to ownership of the hyperlinking process. Prodigy (and every other Web site in the world) stores Web pages with a displayed part, which the browser shows, and a hidden part that the viewer doesn't see, and which contains hidden information including the addresses that are used by the displayed portion.

This, BT said, is the essence of its U.S. patent No. 4873662. In reference to this case, answer the following questions:

A. Has a ruling been handed down on this matter yet? If so, what was the result?
B. If any kind of hyperlinking is, in fact, the essence of the patent held by BT, what about library card catalogues; are they infringements, too? Why or why not? What else could be?

3. **INVESTIGATE MONITORING SYSTEMS** The text listed several monitoring systems, other systems that defeat them, and an e-mail encryption program. Find two more of the following:

A. Programs that monitor keyboard activity
B. Programs that find keyboard monitoring programs
C. E-mail encryption programs

4. **CHECK OUT THE COMPUTER ETHICS INSTITUTE'S ADVICE** The Computer Ethics Institute's Web site at http://cpsr.org/issues/ethics/cei offers the "Ten Commandments of Computer Ethics" to guide you in ethical computer use. The first two are

- *Thou shalt not use a computer to harm other people.* This one is the bedrock for all the others.
- *Thou shalt not interfere with other people's computer work.* This one stems from the first and includes small sins like sending frivolous e-mail and crimes like spreading viruses and electronic stalking.

Look up the other eight and give at least two examples of acts that would be in violation of these guidelines.

Discussion Questions

1. When selling antiques, you can usually obtain a higher price for those that have a *provenance*, which is information detailing the origin and history of the object. For example, property owned by Jacqueline Kennedy Onassis and Princess Diana sold for much more than face value. What kinds of products have value over and above a comparable product because of such information? What kind of information makes products valuable? Consider both tangible (resale value) and intangible value (sentimental appeal).

2. Personal cheques that you use to buy merchandise have a standard format. Cheques have very few different sizes, and almost no variation in format. Consider what would happen if everyone could create his or her own size, shape, and layout of personal cheque. What would the costs and benefits be to business and the consumer in terms of buying cheques, exchanging them for merchandise, and bank cheque processing?

3. Consider society as a business that takes steps to protect itself from the harm of illegal acts. Discuss the mechanisms and costs that are involved. Examine ways in which our society would be different if no one ever broke a law. Are there ever benefits to our society when people break the law, for example, when they claim that the law itself is unethical or unjust?

4. Can you access all the IT systems at your college or university? What about payroll or grade information on yourself or others? What kinds of controls has your college or university implemented to prevent the misuse of information?

5. You know that you generally can't use a PC to access the information stored on a Macintosh-formatted disk. What other instances of difficulty in accessing information have you experienced personally or heard of? For example, have you used different versions of MS PowerPoint or MS Access that won't work on all the PCs that you have access to?

6. Have you, or someone you know, experienced computer problems caused by a virus? What did the virus do? Where do you think you got it? How did you fix the problem? What was the cost to you in time, trouble, and stress?

7. What laws, if any, do you think the United States should pass to protect personal information? Why? Should some personal information be more protected than other information? Why or why not?

8. The issue of pirated software is one that the software industry fights on a daily basis. The major centres of software piracy are in places like Russia and China where salaries and disposable income are comparatively low. Given that people in developing and economically depressed countries will fall behind the industrialized world technologically if they can't afford access to new generations of software, is it reasonable to blame someone for using pirated software when it costs two months' salary to buy a legal copy of MS Office? If you answered no, specify at what income level it's okay to make or buy illegal copies of software. What approach could software companies use to combat the problem apart from punitive measures, like pressuring the government to impose sanctions on transgressors?

Chapter 9

Emerging Trends and Technologies

Business, People, and Technology Tomorrow

STUDENT LEARNING OUTCOMES

LO1 Describe the emerging trends and technologies that will have an impact on the changing Internet.

LO2 Define the various types of technologies that are emerging as we move toward physiological interaction with technology.

LO3 Define the emerging trends of near field communication, Bluetooth, WiFi, cell phones, and RFID, as they relate to the wireless environment.

LO4 Define and describe emerging technologies that, while purely technology, can and will impact the future.

OPENING CASE STUDY
BlackBerry vs. iPhone: Battle of the Titans

There is no agreement in the industry about exactly what constitutes a "smartphone." For some, it's a device that runs a complete operating system and provides a proprietary, standardized interface and a platform upon which developers can deliver applications to users. Others are happy to call a phone that provides features such as e-mail and Internet browsing a *smart-enough* device.

By either definition, Waterloo Ontario's Research in Motion (RIM) makes the grade with its BlackBerry, a device RIM says is unrivalled in its e-mail and messaging capabilities, its feature-rich voice capabilities, and its extraordinary multimedia experience.

Founded in 1984, RIM operates offices in North America, Europe, and Asia-Pacific, and is a leading designer, manufacturer, and marketer of innovative wireless solutions for the worldwide mobile communications market. The company is also an important Canadian success story. The summer of 2008 saw RIM ship its 40 millionth BlackBerry. *Forty million!* One for each Canadian and a few million to spare.

RIM's BlackBerry targets the corporate and government segments, where the company is unmatched in market penetration.

Enter the iPhone. Apple's innovative and edgy design changed the cell phone environment when it was released in 2006. Four million iPhones were sold in the first 200 days on the market. Individuals, rather than corporate and government types, flocked to the iPhone in droves.

When iPhone G3 was introduced in July 2008 (including for the first time in Canada) it took direct aim at the BlackBerry's hegemony in the corporate sphere by offering the capability to sync with Microsoft Exchange servers. This allowed *push e-mail*, a critical make-it-or-break-it issue with business customers who must be able to easily retrieve their e-mail on their phone and on the fly. This made the iPhone a serious contender to the BlackBerry for corporate and government users.

RIM's application programming interface (APIs allow third-party developers to create applications that run on a device) implementation stands in stark contrast to that of Apple, where third-party developers are provided with a feature-rich toolset enabling the rapid delivery of eye-catching and fully functional applications. Net result? Apple iPhone applications come to market significantly faster than those from RIM, whose API appears outdated and not fully specified (RIM holds some details back), thus making it difficult to create exciting applications.

Although, at the time of writing (only a few months after the release of the G3) the iPhone SDK (software development kit) had been downloaded more than 100,000 times, it is apparent that RIM has been quietly helping its partners develop better tools. Not only that, but RIM has quietly amassed an arsenal of widgets and applications designed to take direct aim at the individual user.

And as a further hook, RIM is adding Facebook and MySpace to Microsoft's Live Search technology, giving its new offering an aggressive little footprint into which potential BlackBerry users can step.

The final arrow in RIM's quiver might well be the company's strategic alliance with German ERP maker SAP. SAP and RIM will bring SAP enterprise applications to the BlackBerry platform in a robust and user-friendly manner. RIM's implementation will allow workers to break their tether to the desktop. In balance, SAP has announced a version of its customer relationship management software that will run on the iPhone—so the battle rages on.

From our vantage point, it appears that RIM and Apple will slug it out over the next few years, each trying to gain inroads into the other's territory. Whatever the outcome, it will be interesting to watch a true Canadian icon at work.[1, 2, 3, 4, 5, 6]

Questions

1. Does the *Canadian factor* play into your consideration of whether or not to choose a particular brand? Why or why not?

2. Are you rooting for RIM or Apple or neither? With the escalating disappearance of manufacturing jobs in Canada, should Canadian taxpayers support Canadian high tech industries?

3. What features are most important for you in choosing a cell phone? Is safety of the technology a factor for you?

Introduction

Technology is changing every day. More important than simply staying up with the changes in technology is considering how those changes will affect your life. It's fun to read and learn about "leading- and bleeding-edge" technologies, and we encourage you to do so. The consequences of those technology changes, however, may have an impact on all our lives more far reaching than you can imagine.

In this final chapter, we will take a look at several leading- and bleeding-edge technologies, including speech recognition, biometrics, implant chips, and chipless RFID, among others. These new technologies can and will impact your personal and business life. Technology for the sake of technology (though fun) is never necessarily a good thing, and can even be counter-productive. Using technology appropriately to enhance your personal life and to move your organization toward its strategic goals, on the other hand, is *always* a good thing.

This has been both an exciting and a challenging chapter for us to write. The excitement is in the opportunity to showcase some emerging technological innovations. The challenge has been to not spotlight the technologies themselves overmuch, so as to help you focus on how those technologies will affect your life.

So, as you read this chapter, have fun but don't get caught up exclusively in the technology advances themselves. Instead, try to envision how those new technologies will change the things that you do and the way you do them, both from a personal and an organizational perspective. As throughout this book, we remind you always to consider how to make new technology relevant and productive for you, as well as be respectful of the health, safety, and rights of others.

To introduce you to just a few of the many new technologies on the horizon, we've chosen those that we believe will have the greatest impact. We present those emerging technologies within the context of four important trends (see Figure 9.1). If you want more information on these or any technology, a great reference resource is http://whatis.techtarget.com.

Figure 9.1

Emerging Trends and Technologies

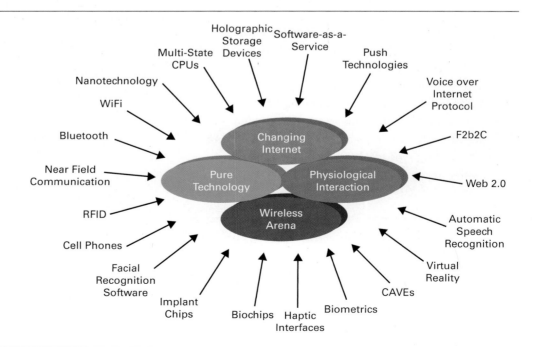

The Changing Internet

LO1

Few technologies have grown to widespread use and changed as fast as the Internet. Over the next several years, you will witness many new Internet-based trends and technologies. Among those will be software-as-a-service; push technologies and personalization; F2b2C (which also enables personalization); Internet telephony (i.e., Voice over Internet Protocol, VoIP); and Web 2.0. All of these trends and technologies are fostering the concept of an e-society.

SOFTWARE-AS-A-SERVICE

Software-as-a-service (SaaS) is a delivery model for software in which you pay for software on a pay-per-use basis instead of buying the software outright. As more technology choices become available to you (smart phones, PDAs, tablet PCs) and your need to be mobile using them also increases, these devices may not have the capacity necessary to store all your software needs. For that matter, you may need a given piece of software—photo and video editing software, for instance—perhaps only a couple of times a year. It makes sense then to rent software.

In the SaaS model you pay for software on a pay-per-use basis using a personal application service provider. An *application service provider (ASP)* supplies software applications (and often related services such as maintenance, technical support, information storage, and the like) over the Internet that would otherwise reside on customers' computers. We discussed ASPs in Chapter 7 and how the business world is already using them.

Let's focus for a moment on your personal use of an ASP (see Figure 9.2). In the future, ASPs will provide personal productivity software for you to use (for a pay-per-use fee or monthly subscription fee using the SaaS model) and storage so you can store your files on their Web servers as opposed to on your own personal devices.

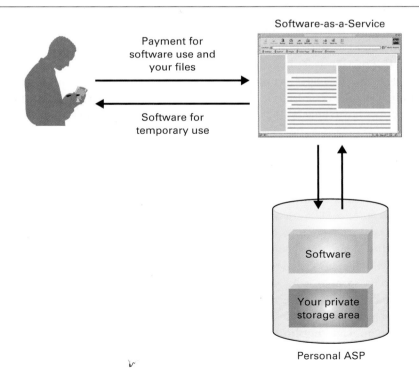

Payment for software use and your files

Software for temporary use

Software-as-a-Service

Software

Your private storage area

Personal ASP

Figure 9.2

The Software-as-a-Service Model and a Personal Application Service Provider (ASP)

For example, you might be in an airport and need to build a workbook with your Smart device, which might not have a complete version of Excel. So, you would use your device to connect to the Internet and a personal ASP. With your device, you would use the personal ASP's Excel software to create your workbook and save it on the ASP's Web server. When you got back to the office, you would use your computer there, connect to the same ASP, and retrieve your workbook and save it on your computer.

In 2007, the total sales of software as a service (SaaS) exceeded US$5.1 billion, and Gartner Group estimates it will reach $11.5 billion by 2011. This translates to 1 in 4 of all dollars spent on corporate software—a 25% market share—which is impressive indeed. This kind of prediction has led mammoth Microsoft Corp. to enter the market with the launch of Office Live, a suite of software available by subscription.[7]

There are many issues you'll have to consider when determining whether or not to use a personal ASP, with privacy and reliability definitely being important ones. If all your information is on a Web-based server, it will be easier for someone to gain access to it (for the wrong reasons) than if you stored all your information on your home or office computer. When considering reliability, you need to think about what happens if the personal ASP's Web site goes down. How will you perform your work? These are important issues that will be addressed by you're the personal service level agreement into which you would enter with the ASP. In spite of potential drawbacks, we believe personal ASPs and the SaaS model will become a part of your everyday life in the future.

PUSH TECHNOLOGIES AND PERSONALIZATION

We live in a *pull* technology environment. That is, you look for, request, and find what you want. On the Internet, for example, you visit a specific site and request information, services, and products. So, you're literally "pulling" what you want. Future emphasis will be on *push* technologies. In a **push technology** environment, businesses and organizations come to you via technology with information, services, and product offerings based on your profile. This isn't spam or mass e-mailings We briefly discussed the concept of push technology in Chapter 5 within the concepts of mobile computing and m-commerce.

For example, in some parts of the United States you can subscribe to a cell service that pushes information to you in the form of DVD rental information. Whenever you pass near a DVD store, your cell phone (which is GPS-enabled) triggers a computer within the DVD store that evaluates your rental history to see if any new DVDs have arrived that you might be interested in viewing. In this case, the system generates a personal data warehouse of rental history—including dimensions for the day of the week, the time of the day, and DVD categories—concerning you and then evaluates information in the smaller cubes (see Figure 9.3). The evaluation seeks to affirm that (1) you usually rent DVDs on that particular day, (2) you usually rent DVDs during that time of that day, and (3) there is a distinct DVD category from which you rent DVDs during that time of the day. If so, the system then checks to see if there are any movies in that category that you haven't rented and that it hasn't previously contacted you about.

If so, the DVD store computer will call your cell phone with a message concerning a new release. It will also give you street-by-street directions to the DVD store and hold the DVD for you. If the DVD store doesn't have any new releases that might interest you, you won't receive a phone call.

You might also someday receive a personalized pizza delivery message on your television as you start to watch a hockey game. The message might say, "We'll deliver your favourite pepperoni and mushroom pizza to your doorstep before the game begins. On your remote control, press the ORDER NOW button."

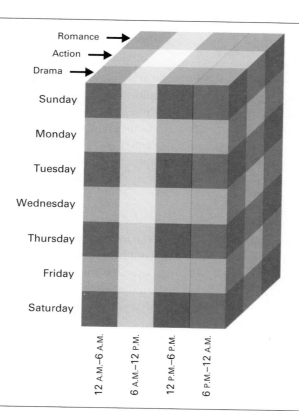

Of course, situations such as these rely on IT's ability to store vast amounts of information about you. Technologies such as databases and data warehouses will definitely play an important role in the development of push technologies that do more than just push spam and mass e-mail. In the instance of the pizza delivery message on your television, a local pizza store would have determined that you like pepperoni and mushroom pizza and that you order it most often while watching a hockey game. The pizza company and the cable/satellite company would also need to cooperate in sharing your personal data, obviously with your consent.

F2B2C: A NEW E-COMMERCE BUSINESS MODEL

In the e-commerce world, business models are identified by the players such as B2B (business-to-business) and G2C (government-to-consumer). We now have the notion of introducing a third player to create an entirely new e-commerce business model. The first of these new business models to surface is *F2b2C (factory-to-business-to-consumer)*, an e-commerce business model in which a consumer communicates through a business on the Internet and directly provides product specifications to a factory that makes the customized and personalized product to the consumer's specifications and then ships it directly to the consumer.[8]

You should notice in F2b2C that the "F" and "C" are capitalized while the "b" (for business) is not. In this model, the business is simply an Internet intermediary that provides a communication conduit between the factory and the consumer. When this happens, a form of disintermediation occurs. Broadly defined, *disintermediation* is the use of the Internet as a delivery vehicle, whereby intermediate players in a distribution channel can be bypassed. The travel agent industry is a good example of where disintermediation has occurred. Now, you can connect directly to an airline and purchase tickets, often receiving bonus mileage if you do. The Internet has disintermediated travel agents, since you need them less.

Think about connecting to a site on the Internet and custom-ordering something like a pair of pants. You would specify your exact size, inseam or leg length, waist, hip, and thigh measurements, and so on, and other information such as colour, style of pockets, how many belt loops (if any) ... the list could grow quite long. The Web site would immediately pass along your information to a factory that would create a customized and personalized pair of pants for you and ship them to your door. Is this possible? Well, it already exists to some extent. Later in the chapter, you'll read about how companies are using biometrics to create custom-fitting clothing and shoes.

VOICE OVER INTERNET PROTOCOL (VOIP)

VoIP, or *Voice over Internet Protocol*, allows you to send voice communications over the Internet and avoid the toll charges that you would normally receive from your long distance carrier. Simply put, VoIP allows you to use your Internet connection (which must be broadband such as DSL or cable) to make phone calls. This is different from today's DSL model which splits your phone line so that you can make phone calls and surf the Web at the same time. In today's model, your telephone calls are still routed through your traditional telephone service provider to which you must pay charges for long distance phone calls. Using VoIP, your telephone calls are routed through a VoIP provider (which may be your ISP) and you pay only a flat monthly fee—usually in the neighbourhood of $20 to $40 per month—to make unlimited long distance calls.

For home use, you can already use the VoIP services offered by the likes of Vonage, Primus, and Rogers. You can keep your existing phone number and you do have access to a number of value-added features such as call waiting, caller ID, and so on. Most VoIP providers offer you free unlimited long distance calling only within your country; international long distance calls may still incur an additional fee.

This certainly speaks to the growing importance of the Internet. Most of you probably cannot imagine life without the Internet already. That will be even more true once the Internet becomes the technological infrastructure that also supports all your phone calls. You can read more about VoIP in Extended Learning Module B (Network Basics).

WEB 2.0

As discussed in Extended Learning Module E (The World Wide Web and the Internet), the *Web 2.0* is the so-called second generation of the Web and focuses on on-line collaboration, users as both creators and modifiers of content, dynamic and customized information feeds, and many other engaging Web-based services. To be sure, "2.0" has caught on as a hot buzz term, for example, the Family 2.0 (family members living on and communicating through the Internet), Company 2.0 (the complete Web-enabled company), and TV 2.0 (TV-type broadcast shows delivered via the Web). Some of the exciting applications of Web 2.0 include

- *Wiki*—a Web site that allows you—as a visitor—to create, edit, change, and often eliminate content. Wikipedia (www.wikipedia.org) is the most popular. Wikis are actually an interesting implementation of sourcing, called *crowdsourcing*, when businesses provide enabling technologies that allow people (i.e., crowds)—instead of a designated paid employee—to create, modify, and oversee the development of a product or service. In the case of a Wiki, that product is information.

- *Social networking site*—a site on which you post information about yourself, create a network of friends, share content such as photos and videos, and

OFFSHORE OUTSOURCING TUTORING

In Chapter 6 we introduced you to the three major geo-political forms of outsourcing—onshore, nearshore, and offshore. Each brings with it some distinct advantages and disadvantages when outsourcing the development of IT systems.

But what about education? Many university and college students go overseas to study—perhaps for a term or semester and sometimes for a complete program. That's a form of nearshore or offshore outsourcing. Even earlier in the education process, many K-12 students are turning to offshore outsourcing for tutoring support.

One company providing this is Educomp (www. educomp.com), which provides one-on-one tutoring via the Internet in the areas of math and science. Using Educomp would be considered offshore outsourcing

tutoring because it is based in New Delhi, India. Armed with only a personal computer and a webcam, students here in Canada can get private, real-time tutoring from an Educomp employee.

Most Indian tutoring companies charge in the neighbourhood of $100 per month for unlimited, interactive tutoring over the Internet. Compare that to typical tutoring services in the Canada, which usually charge around $100 per hour for individual face-to-face tutoring. Moreover, most Indian tutoring service companies guarantee that their tutors have—at a minimum—an undergraduate degree in the discipline they teach.

Many of these technologies, and the Web 2.0 in general, will forever change how you live your personal life and how you conduct business.[9]

communicate with other people. There are several prominent social networking sites including MySpace, Facebook, Facebox, orkut, and Cyworld.

- *Blog*—a Web site in the form of a journal in which you post entries in chronological order; it often includes the capabilities for other viewers to add comments to your journal entries.

- *RSS feed*—a technology that provides frequently published and updated digital content on the Web.

- *Podcasting*—generally refers to your ability at any time to download audio and video files for viewing and listening using portable listening devices and personal computers.

E-SOCIETY The general and strong trend today in society is toward becoming an e-society. Although we provide no formal definition for an e-society, you can quickly grasp that it is all about living life in, on, and through technology, with the Internet being at the epicentre. People are finding life-long soul mates on Match.com and numerous other dating-related sites; others (especially young people) are flocking to, spending a great deal of time on, and developing friendships on sites such as MySpace, Facebook, and YouTube; people are building very successful home-based e-businesses on eBay; children are receiving tutoring via the Web (see the nearby Perspective); just as we wrote this section, PokerStars.net was dealing hand number 9,738,225,821—90 minutes later it dealt hand number 9,739,309,711, meaning that on-line poker enthusiasts had played over 1 million hands in 90 minutes (roughly 11,000 hands per minute); also at the time we wrote this section, eBay was posting its 60 billionth lot for auction (yes, that is 60,000,000,000).

The simple fact of the matter is that we live in a digital world, with technology not only for the sake of doing business but also pervading our personal lives so much so that many people cannot imagine a world without technology. That technology-based world is enabling the growth of an e-society.

LO2

Physiological Interaction

Right now, your primary physical interfaces to your computer include a keyboard, mouse, monitor, and printer (basically, your input and output devices). These are physical devices, not physiological. Physiological interfaces capture and utilize your real body characteristics, such as your breath, your voice, your height and weight, and even your iris. Physiological innovations include automatic speech recognition, virtual reality, CAVE automatic virtual environments, biometrics, and haptic interfaces, along with many others.

AUTOMATIC SPEECH RECOGNITION

An *automatic speech recognition (ASR)* system not only captures spoken words but also distinguishes word groupings to form sentences. To perform this, an ASR system follows three steps:

1. *Feature analysis*—The system captures your words as you speak into a microphone, eliminates any background noise, and converts the digital signals of your speech into phonemes (syllables).

2. *Pattern classification*—The system matches your spoken phonemes to a phoneme sequence stored in an acoustic model database. For example, if your phoneme was *dü*, the system would match it to the words do and due.

3. *Language processing*—The system attempts to make sense of what you're saying by comparing the word phonemes generated in step 2 with a language model database. For example, if you were asking a question and started with the phoneme *dü*, the system would determine that the appropriate word is much more likely to be do as opposed to due.

ASR is certainly now taking its place in computing environments. The important point is that ASR allows you to speak in a normal voice; thus it supports physiological interaction.

VIRTUAL REALITY

On the horizon (and in some instances here today) is a new technology that will virtually place you in any experience you desire. That new technology is *virtual reality*, a three-dimensional computer simulation in which you actively and physically participate. In a virtual reality system, you make use of special input and output devices that capture your physiological movements and send physiological responses back to you. These devices include

- *Glove*—An input device that captures and records the shape and movement of your hand and fingers and the strength of your hand and finger movements.

- *Headset (head-mounted display)*—A combined input and output device that (1) captures and records the movement of your head and (2) contains a screen that covers your entire field of vision and displays various views of an environment based on your movements.

- *Walker*—An input device that captures and records the movement of your feet as you walk or turn in different directions.

APPLICATIONS OF VIRTUAL REALITY   Virtual reality applications are popping up everywhere, sometimes in odd places. The most common applications are found in the entertainment industry. There are a number of virtual reality games on the market, including downhill Olympic skiing, race-car driving, golf, air combat, and marksmanship. Other applications include

- Matsushita Electric Works—Allows you to design your kitchen in virtual reality and then choose the appliances you want and even request colour changes.
- Volvo—Demonstrates the safety features of its cars.
- Airlines—Trains pilots how to handle adverse weather conditions.
- Motorola—Trains assembly-line workers in the steps of manufacturing a new product.[10]
- Health care—Train doctors how to perform surgery using virtual cadavers.[11]

Let's consider the potential ramifications of virtual reality and how you might someday interact with your computer. New virtual reality systems include aroma-producing devices and devices that secrete fluid through a mouthpiece that you have in your mouth. So, you could virtually experience a Hawaiian *luau*. The aroma-producing device would generate various smells and the mouthpiece would secrete a fluid that tastes like pineapple or roasted pig. If you were using virtual reality to surf big waves, the mouthpiece would secrete a fluid that tastes like salt water.

CAVE AUTOMATIC VIRTUAL ENVIRONMENTS

A **CAVE (cave automatic virtual environment)** is a special 3-D virtual reality room that can display images of other people and objects located in other CAVEs all over the world. CAVEs are **holographic devices** that create, capture, and/or display images in true three-dimensional form. If you watch any of the *Star Trek* movies, you'll see an example of a holographic device called the *holodeck*.

A CAVE is a "room" with only three walls, a floor, and a ceiling. Onto each of these surfaces are projected three-dimensional images from four video projectors. With appropriate eyewear, users are engaged in a three-dimensional space in which they can virtually manipulate projected images by using a wand connected to the CAVE computer.

In working form, you would enter a CAVE room. At the same time, someone else would enter another CAVE room in another location (see Figure 9.4 on the next page). Numerous digital video cameras would capture the likenesses of both participants and re-create and send those images to the other CAVE. Then, you and the other person could see and carry on a normal conversation with each other, and you would feel as if that other person were in the same room with you.

Current CAVE research is also working on the challenges of having other physical objects in the room. For example, if you sat on a couch in your CAVE, the couch would capture the indentation you made in it and pass it to the couch in the other CAVE. That couch would respond by constricting a mesh of rubber inside it so that your indentation would also appear there. And what about playing catch? Which person would have the virtual ball and which person would have the real ball? The answer is that both would have a virtual ball. When throwing it, the CAVE would capture your arm movement to determine the speed, arc, and direction of the ball. That information would be transmitted to the other CAVE, and it would use that information to make the virtual ball fly through the air accordingly.

Unlike virtual reality, in some CAVEs you don't need any special gear. Let your imagination run wild and think about the potential applications of CAVEs. An unhappy customer could call a business to complain. Within seconds, a customer service representative would not answer the phone but rather appear in the room with the unhappy customer. That would be an example of great customer service. Your teacher might never attend your class. Instead the teacher would enter a CAVE and have his or her image broadcast into the classroom. You might not really be in class either but rather a holographic likeness of you. Are CAVEs a realistic possibility? The answer is definitely yes. We believe that CAVEs are the successor to virtual reality. So, virtual reality may not be a long-term technological innovation but rather a stepping stone to the more advanced

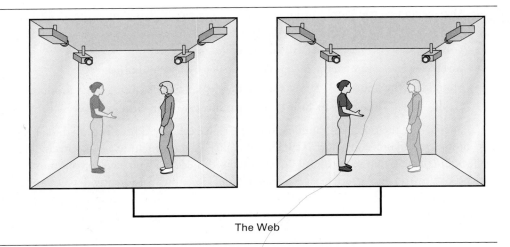

The Web

CAVE. Whatever the case, CAVEs will not only significantly alter how you interact with your computer (can you imagine the thrill of video games in a CAVE?), but also even more significantly alter how you interact with other people. With CAVE technologies, you can visit your friends and relatives on a daily basis no matter where they live. You may even have television shows and movies piped into your home CAVE.

CAVEs are being used in interesting and even critical research in various places, including the Université du Québec en Outaouais, in Gatineau, Quebec, where research into cyber psychology is using virtual reality as provided by CAVEs in innovative ways. At the University of Calgary, a CAVE developed in Kitchener, Ontario, by Fakespace Systems will enable scientists and researchers to study intimate details of biological systems, including cells, tissues, and entire organisms.[12, 13]

HAPTIC INTERFACES

A *haptic interface* uses technology to add the sense of touch to an environment that previously had only visual and textual elements. Applications of virtual reality we discussed previously that incorporate the use of gloves and walkers use implementations of haptic interfaces.

Many arcade games include haptic interfaces. For example, when you get on a stationary jet ski and control its movement (on screen) by adjusting your weight side-to-side and leaning backward and forward, you are interfacing with the arcade game via a haptic interface. Many joysticks and game controllers provide feedback to the user through vibrations, which is another form of a haptic interface.

Interacting with an arcade game via a haptic interface is a "fun" application of the technology and one that is making companies a lot of money. But consider this: With a haptic interface, sight-challenged people can feel and read text with their fingers while interacting with a computer. The fact is anyone can use technology to make money. Perhaps the most exciting thing about new technologies is the potential benefits for people. Can you envision ways to use technology to help people less fortunate than yourself? Does the potential to do harm also exist in these technologies?

BIOMETRICS

Biometrics is the use of physiological characteristics—such as your fingerprint, the blood vessels in the iris of your eye, the sound of your voice, or perhaps even your breath—to provide identification. That's the strict and narrow definition, but biometrics is begin-

Figure 9.5

Custom-Fit Clothes
through Biometrics

ning to encompass more than just identification. Consider these real-world applications
in place today (see Figure 9.5):

- *Custom shoes*—Several shoe stores, especially those that offer fine Italian leather
  shoes, no longer carry any inventory. When you select a shoe style you like, you
  place your bare feet into a box that scans the shape of your feet. That information
  is then used to make a custom pair of shoes for you. It works extremely well if
  your feet are slightly different from each other in size or shape (as is the case with
  most people). To see this, visit www.digitoe.com.

- *Custom wedding gowns*—Following the custom-fit shoe idea, many bridal boutiques
  now do the same thing for wedding dresses. Once the bride chooses the style she
  likes, she steps into a small room that scans her entire body. That information is
  used to create a wedding dress that fits perfectly. Both custom shoes and custom
  wedding dresses are examples of the future implementation of F2b2C.

- *Custom bathrobes*—Some high-end spa resorts now actually have patrons walk
  through a body-scanning device upon check-in. The scanning device measures
  the patron's body characteristics and then sends that information to a sewing
  and fabricating facility that automatically creates a custom-fit bathrobe.

BIOMETRIC SECURITY   The best form of security for personal identification encompasses
three aspects:

1. What you know
2. What you have
3. Who you are.

The first—*what you know*—is something like a password, something that everyone
can create and has. The second—*what you have*—is something like a card such as an
ATM card you use at an ATM (in conjunction with your password, what you know).
Unfortunately, most personal identification security systems stop there. That is, they do
not include *who you are*, which is some form of a biometric.

It's no wonder crimes like identity theft are spiralling out of control. Without much
effort, a thief can steal your password (often through social engineering) and steal what

you have. For the latter, the thief doesn't actually have to steal your physical card; he or she simply has to copy the information on it. However, stealing a biometric—such as your fingerprint or iris scan—is much more difficult.

Many banks are currently converting ATMs to the use of biometrics, specifically an iris scan, as the third level of personal identification security. When you open an account and request ATM use, the bank will issue you an ATM card (you pick the password). The bank will also scan your iris and create a unique 512-byte representation of the scan. To use an ATM, you must insert your card, type in your password, and allow the machine to scan your iris. The ATM uses all three forms of identification to match you to your account. You can then perform whatever transaction you wish.

Some private schools for young children now require parents and guardians to submit to iris scans. Once the scan is captured and the person is verified as a parent or guardian, the information is entered into a security database. Then, when the parent or guardian comes to the school to pick up a child, his or her iris scan is compared to the one stored in the database. Parents and guardians cannot, under any circumstances, take a child from the school without first going through verification via an iris scan.

INTEGRATING BIOMETRIC PROCESSING AND TRANSACTION PROCESSING

Once society accepts the use of biometrics for security and identification purposes, organizations of all types will be able to add another dimension of business intelligence to their data warehouses—that dimension will capture and record changes in physiological characteristics (see Figure 9.6).

Consider, as a hypothetical example, a woman using an ATM—equipped with iris scanning capabilities—to withdraw cash. Current research suggests that it might be possible to use an iris scan to determine not only that a woman is pregnant but also the sex of the unborn child. (That is a true statement.) When the woman has her iris scanned, the bank might be able to tell that she is pregnant and expecting a boy. When the woman receives her cash and receipt, the receipt would have a coupon printed on the back for 10 percent off any purchase at Babies Я Us. Furthermore, the ATM would generate another receipt that says "buy blue."

The key here is for you to consider that transaction processing systems (TPSs) of the future will be integrated with biometric processing systems (BPSs). The TPS will capture and process the "events" of the transaction—when, by whom, where, and so on. The BPS will capture and process the physiological characteristics of the person performing the transaction. Those physiological characteristics may include the presence of alcohol or illegal drugs, hair loss, weight gain, low blood sugar, vitamin deficiencies, cataracts, and yes—even pregnancy.

Figure 9.6

Integrating Biometric and Transaction Processing to Create Business Intelligence

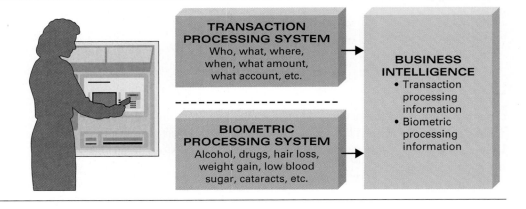

WII—REVOLUTIONIZING VIDEO GAMES THROUGH HAPTIC INTERFACES

Just a few short months after its debut, Nintendo's Wii outsold Microsoft's Xbox 360 and Sony's PlayStation 3, its primary competitors. Wii isn't a game but rather a video game console that allows you to play many different video games. Some of the games include *The Legend of Zelda: Twilight Princess*, *WarioWare: Smooth Moves*, and *Super Paper Mario*.

What is so revolutionary about Wii is that it incorporates *haptic* interfaces. Using a wireless controller, you can point at objects on the screen and the game console can also detect your motions and rotations in three dimensions.

When you bowl, for example (a very simple example at that), you see the bowling lane on the screen. You hold the wireless controller in your hand, press a button and hold it, and then go through the actual motion of bowling, releasing the button when you want to release the virtual bowling ball. You see the result of your actions on screen as the ball rolls down the lane and (hopefully) knocks down the pins.

Other video game publishers have since worked feverishly to add haptic interfaces to their games, including Electronic Arts (*The Godfather*) and Ubisoft (*Princess of Persia: Two Thrones*). As you read this text, you can probably name many more, as we suspect that haptic interface–based video games are here to stay and quickly becoming the mainstay.[14]

When businesses start to gather this type of intelligence, you can leave it to your imagination to envision what will happen. For example, because of the noted pregnancy in our previous example of the woman using an ATM, the bank might offer financing for a minivan, evaluate the size of the family's home and perhaps offer special financing for a second mortgage so another room can be added, or establish a tuition account for the child and place $25 in it. These possibilities will further intensify competition in almost all industries.

OTHER BIOMETRICS AND BIOMETRIC DEVICES   Biometrics is a hot topic in research circles right now. Although we haven't the space to discuss them all, you might want to watch for the following.

Biochip
- A *biochip* is a technology chip that can perform a variety of physiological functions when inserted into the human body. Biochips have been proven in some cases to block pain for people who suffer severe spinal injuries, help paralyzed people regain some portion of their motor skills, and help visually impaired people see better.

Implant Chip
- An *implant chip* is a technology-enabled microchip implanted into the human body that stores important information about you (such as your identification and medical history) and that may be GPS–enabled to offer a method of tracking. This is already available for tracking pets.

Facial Recognition Software
- *Facial recognition software* provides identification by evaluating facial characteristics.

Whatever becomes a reality in the field of biometrics promises to forever change your life and how you interact with technology.

LO3

The Wireless Arena

Throughout this text, we've discussed the technologies that make wireless communications possible and applications of wireless technologies in which companies have gained a significant competitive advantage. We've discussed such wireless technologies as Bluetooth and WiFi—both of which were designed to activate wireless communication via technology devices such as cell phones, printers, network hubs, and—of course—computers.

- ***Bluetooth*** is a standard for transmitting information in the form of short-range radio waves over distances of up to 10 metres.
- ***WiFi (wireless fidelity)*** is a standard for transmitting information in the form of radio waves over distances up to about several miles.

Bluetooth has become very popular for the wireless headsets (actually more like ear pieces) for cell phones. You may own one of these for your cell phone, and you've undoubtedly seen people using them. WiFi is usually the type of wireless communication used in a network environment. Verizon in the United States, for example, offers the BroadbandAccess PC Card, which you can use to wirelessly connect your computer or laptop to Verizon's wireless broadband network. Many businesses have private, firewalled wireless networks that use WiFi for their employees.

Let's now turn our attention to (1) cell phones and (2) RFID (radio frequency identification). Cell phones are a significant "disruptive technology" now and will be more so in the future. RFID, while still emerging as a technology, will definitely be around for many years and dramatically change your personal life and the way the business world works.

THE NEXT GENERATION OF CELL PHONE TECHNOLOGY

For most people, a cell phone is a necessary part of life. Even today's most basic cell phones support phone calls (that's obvious) and also real-time text messaging, photos (taking, sending, and receiving), games, and many other features. Tomorrow's cell phones may very well become the only technology you need.

Among the many innovations you'll see in cell phones over the next couple of years will be storage (in the form of a hard disk), processor capability, music enhancements, and video support. Already, new cell phones are being demonstrated that have 2 gigabytes of storage and processor speeds up to 500 Mhz. As these capacities and speeds increase, you may be able to wirelessly connect a keyboard, monitor, mouse, and printer to your cell phone. Your cell phone will essentially become your notebook computer.

Tomorrow's cell phones may spell the end for dedicated MP3 players like Apple's iPod. With enough battery life and storage capacity, many people will opt to use their cell phones for music and eliminate the other piece of equipment they have to carry around to listen to music. Video on demand will also become a reality through your cell phone. Apple's iPhone, for example, combines three technologies: (1) cell phone, (2) iPod, and (3) wireless Internet communication.

But there is a downside. Cell phones are the next great and uncharted space for hackers and viruses. The even worse news is that the development of antivirus cell phone software is very much in its infancy, far behind the capabilities of the people wanting to hack into your cell phone and unleash deadly cell phone viruses. Think about your ISP. It has antivirus software (and many more types of "anti" software such as spam blocker software and anti-spyware software) on its servers to stop a lot of malware from making it to your computer via e-mail. But that doesn't stop all malware from getting to you. You still need all types of "anti" software loaded onto and running on your computer at all times.

When was the last time your cell phone service provider contacted you about new types of "anti" software you can download onto your cell phone for added protection? That has probably never happened, and it should concern you. Do you download ring tones from the Internet? If so, your cell phone is susceptible to getting a virus. Some cell phone viruses, created in a laboratory environment, can make international calls and run your battery dead and your bill into thousands of dollars.

As your cell phone becomes increasingly more important to you—and it will—and becomes increasingly more supportive of complex computer tasks, your challenge will be to protect yourself.

RFID (RADIO FREQUENCY IDENTIFICATION)

RFID (radio frequency identification) uses a microchip (chip) in a tag or label to store information, and information is transmitted from, or written to, the tag or label when the microchip is exposed to the correct frequency of radio waves. You're probably already familiar with some implementations of RFID. For example, toll roads have lanes through which drivers can move if they have an RFID device that automatically charges an account as they drive down the road. Exxon/Mobil (ESSO in Canada) provides an RFID-enabled key ring (called Speedpass) to its customers. The Speedpass key ring contains customer account information. When making a purchase, a customer simply waves the key ring at a reader (as opposed to swiping a credit card). The reader communicates with the RFID chip on the key ring, reads the customer's account information, and proceeds with the account charge.

The most common implementation of RFID is the passive RFID chip (see Figure 9.7). A passive RFID chip has no power source itself and sits idle until passed near a reader that emits radio waves. The antenna surrounding the RFID chip picks up the radio waves and the RFID chip stores those waves as a form of energy until it has enough to literally "jolt" itself to life. The RFID chip then sends its information to the reader, which is connected to some sort of computer system containing account information and the like. After sending its information, the RFID chip goes back into passive mode. This is exactly how Esso's Speedpass RFID key ring works.

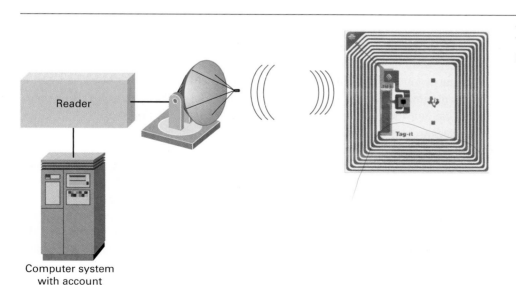

Figure 9.7

How Passive RFID Works

RFID IN USE TODAY   The current applications of RFID technologies are many, including

- *Anti-theft car keys*—inside the casing of the car key is an RFID chip. When you insert the key into the ignition, the RFID chip must communicate with the reader in your ignition system (and pass the equivalent of a password) for the car to start. So, it does criminals no good to make a copy of your car key. Of course, if you lose your car keys, it often costs in excess of $300 to get them replaced.
- *Library book tracking*—instead of a bar code on which the ISBN is stored, the RFID chip contains that information. Books are much easier to check in and check out. Even the Vatican library now uses RFID chips in its books. The old inventory process took over 30 days. Using wireless handheld RFID readers, the new inventory process takes only a day.
- *Livestock tracking*—livestock of all kinds is now tagged with RFID chips upon entering the country. The system can then track where the livestock has been on its journey throughout Canada and the United States. In the case of a biological outbreak, the system can easily identify which livestock were at the location where the outbreak is believed to have occurred.
- *Supply chain*—almost every major participant in the supply chain process is now mandating that the other participants tag merchandise, trays of merchandise, boxes and skids of merchandise, and so on with RFID chips. These major participants include Wal-Mart Canada, the U.S. Department of Defense (DOD), the U.S. Food and Drug Administration (FDA), discount retailer Target, U.S. grocery chain Albertson's, TESCO (United Kingdom retailer), and Carrefour (France retailer). Canadian supermarket giant Loblaw Companies Ltd. completed a pilot project in 2006 but declined to commit to the technology at that time.
- *Passports*—implemented in the United States in 2007, all newly issued U.S. passports now contain an RFID chip in the cover of the passport. The RFID chip contains all your passport information. RFIDs in Canadian passports are being explored. As of the time of writing, the technology had not been implemented.

The above list is just a few of the thousands of implementations of RFID in the business world.

THE FUTURE OF RFID   Today, almost every product is identified uniquely by a UPC (universal product code). However, every like product has the same UPC. So, two cans of Diet Coke, for example, have identical UPCs. This makes them indistinguishable. With RFID technologies, each individual piece of merchandise will have a unique EPC (electronic product code). The EPC will include the UPC designation as well as provide a unique number for each different can of Diet Coke that can be tied to expiration dates, supply chain movements, and just about anything else you can imagine.

Once again, use your imagination. If every product in a grocery store can wirelessly communicate with the checkout system, there will be no need to go through that process. While you shop, you'll bag your items when placing them in your cart. When you walk out the front door, an RFID system will wirelessly communicate with your credit card in your wallet, wirelessly communicate with every product in your grocery cart, tally up your bill, and charge your credit card account appropriately.

And think about washing clothes. Suppose you load your washer full of "whites" like socks and towels. Accidentally, you throw in a red shirt but don't see it. Fortunately, each piece of clothing will have an RFID chip that will include washing instructions. Your washing machine will wirelessly communicate with each piece of clothing and determine that one piece does not belong. The washing machine will not work and will notify you that you are mixing clothes.

WHEN RFID GETS "INKED" AND GOES CHIPLESS

If you look carefully at Figure 9.7 on page 271 and the RFID chip on the right, you can see the actual "chip" as a very small black rectangle surrounded by numerous red lines. (The red lines are the antenna structure.) Somark Innovation's latest innovation aims to eliminate the chip itself, creating a *chipless RFID chip.*

It is doing so with a biocompatible chipless RFID ink "tattoo." The ink is injected into the skin of animals. The chipless RFID, then, can be read as any other traditional RFID chip, that is, while not being in line of sight. According to Ramos Mays, chief scientist at Somark Innovations, "This is a true proof-of-principle [similar to a proof-of-concept prototype we discussed in Chapter 6]

and mitigates most of the technological risk. This proves the ability to create a synthetic biometric or *fake fingerprint* with Biocompatible Chipless RFID Ink and read it through hair."

Somark plans to use this first in the livestock industry to help identify and track cattle. This will certainly help in the case of an outbreak of BSE (Mad Cow Disease). But don't stop with chipless RFID ink for animals. What about tattoos for people?

If you get a tattoo using the chipless RFID ink, you could be tracked unknowingly by literally anyone with an RFID reader. How does that make you feel? Do you still want to get a tattoo?[15]

Are these all realities destined for the future? We believe so. What the future holds for RFID is limited only by imagination.

According to the NFC Forum (an industry group formed to promote the understanding and use of **near field communication**), NFC is a short-range wireless connectivity technology standard designed for intuitive, simple, and safe communication between electronic devices. NFC is possible when two NFC–enabled devices come within a few centimetres (typically fewer than four) of one another, such as when waving an NFC–enabled cell phone in front of a reader. Applications of NFC technology include contactless transactions such as payment (as discussed elsewhere in this text), transit ticketing, parking payment, calendar synchronization, exchange of contact information or other data between devices, as well as access to online digital content.

The NFC Forum also predicts that in the near term a wide range of devices and machines will likely become NFC–enabled, including but not limited to the following:

- Mobile phones
- Turnstiles at events or transit stations
- Vending machines
- Parking meters
- Check-out cash registers or "point-of-sale" equipment
- ATMs
- Office, house, and garage doors
- Personal computers
- Posters, street signs, bus stops, and local points of interest (with NFC-readable tags only)
- Product packaging.

NFC technology will allow us to "read" information stored in "tags" on everyday objects in the environment. Such tags can be affixed to such things as movie posters, transit stops and maps, street signs, medicines, certificates, food packaging and much more, allowing us to read information and act on it immediately. Moreover, NFC tags can be used on documents such as parking permits, membership and credit cards, and money to prove authenticity.

The Forum also provides a comprehensive definition of other wireless/radio frequency technologies including how they are related to NFC. Thus they define near field communication (NFC) as "... a standards-based, short-range (a few centimetres) wireless connectivity technology that enables simple and safe two-way interactions among electronic devices ..." This is in contrast to the longer-range (wider coverage area) provided by:

- Bluetooth wireless technology, which was designed to operate within a 10 metre range and to obviate the need to cables between communication devices.
- WiFi (wireless fidelity) technology was designed and optimized for Local Area Networks (LAN) as a replacement for wired networks. WiFi operates within a 100-metre or wider range.
- And finally, RFID (Radio Frequency Identification) is an automatic identification method using RFID tags. An RFID tag is a small, sometimes pliable object that can be affixed to or incorporated into a product and can receive and respond to queries from an RFID reader/writer.[16]

LO4

Pure Technology

Let's close our look at emerging technologies with a few that have broad applicability in numerous ways. These include nanotechnology, multistate CPUs, and holographic storage devices.

NANOTECHNOLOGY

One of the single greatest drawbacks to technological advances is size. The best chip manufacturers can do is to make circuit elements with a width of 130 nanometres. A nanometre is one-hundred-thousandth the width of a human hair. That may seem very, very small, but current manufacturing technologies are beginning to limit the size of computer chips, and thus their speed and capacity.

Nanotechnologies aim to change all that. As a greatly simplified definition, we would say that *nanotechnology* is a discipline that seeks to control matter at the atomic and sub-atomic levels for the purpose of building devices on the same small scale. So, nanotechnology is the exact opposite of traditional manufacturing. In the latter, for example, you would cut down a tree and whittle it down until it becomes a toothpick. That is, traditional manufacturing starts with something large and continually compresses and slices it until it becomes the desired small size. In nanotechnology, you start with the smallest unit and build up. That is, you start working with atoms and build what you want.

In nanotechnology, everything is simply atoms. Nanotechnology researchers are attempting to move atoms and encourage them to "self-assemble" into new forms. Nanotechnology is a bleeding-edge technology worth watching. The changes it will bring about will be unbelievable. Consider these:

Change the molecular structure of the materials used to make computer chips, for instance, and electronics could become as cheap and plentiful as bar codes on packaging. Lightweight vests enmeshed with sensors could measure a person's vital signs. Analysis of a patient's DNA could be done so quickly and precisely that designer drugs would be fabricated on the fly. A computer the size of your library card could store everything you ever saw or read.[17, 18]

TRACKING YOUR CHILDREN

You may not have children yet, but chances are that you will someday. Given the publicity regarding predators, parents today are more concerned for the safety of their children than ever before.

CELL PHONES FOR THE PARENTS OF CHILDREN

Most adults have cell phones; now children are quickly becoming the largest group of purchasers of cell phones and cell phone services. A 2005 survey of Canadian students indicated that 49 percent of grade 11 students owned a cellular phone. More striking is that 6 percent of grade 4 children reported ownership.

For these young children, many cell phone manufacturers provide cell phones with only four (very large) buttons. The parents of these youngsters program the cell phone by providing a different phone number for each large button. That way children don't even have to remember a phone number, just which button to push.

Moreover, new cell phone services are available that allow parents to track the location of a child using global positioning system (GPS) technology. Such a service, called *Family Finder*, is offered by Bell Canada (and others). The service is for families with multiple phones on the same service plan. When signing up, parents can specify which of the individual phones they would like to track via GPS technology.

Then, using the system functionality, a parent can view on-screen (or at a secure Web site) the location of a particular phone, and thus the location of the child using the phone. If GPS capability isn't available at the location of the child, the system can still determine location based on the nearest cell phone tower.

Parents can also program a child's phone to immediately send a text message upon safe arrival to school, a day care centre, or any other location. The child doesn't have to take any action to send the text message. Using GPS technology, when the location of the cell phone matches the pre-assigned text messaging location, the phone automatically sends the message.[19, 20]

MULTI-STATE CPUS

Right now, CPUs are binary-state, capable of working only with information represented by a 1 or a 0. That greatly slows processing. What we really need to increase speed are CPUs that are multi-state. **Multi-state CPUs** work with information represented in more than just two states; probably 10 states, with each state representing a digit between 0 and 9. When multi-state CPUs do become a reality, your computer will no longer have to go through many of the processes associated with translating characters into binary and then reversing the translation process later. (We covered this process in Extended Learning Module A [Computer Hardware and Software].) This will make them much faster. Of course, the true goal is to create multi-state CPUs that can also handle letters and special characters without converting them to their binary equivalents.

HOLOGRAPHIC STORAGE DEVICES

Storage devices currently store information on a two-dimensional surface, but research in the holographic realm will change that, creating **holographic storage devices** with many sides or faces (see Figure 9.8 on the next page). This is similar in concept to cards that you may have seen that change the picture or image as you view the cards from different angles.

If and when holographic storage devices do become a reality, you may be able to store an entire set of encyclopaedias on a single crystal that may have as many as several hundred faces. Think how small technology will become then.

Figure 9.8

3-D Crystal-Like Objects in a Holographic Storage Device

Most Important Considerations

Throughout this chapter, we've discussed some key emerging trends and technologies. They certainly are exciting and promise that the future will be different and dynamic, to say the least. We have suggested that you anticipate these changes and how they will affect you personally and in your career.

As we close this chapter (and perhaps your studies in this course), let's take a close look at five key topics. Each is a culmination in some way of the material you've learned in this course. Each is inescapable in that it will happen and you must deal with it. Finally, each is vitally important and reaches far beyond the technologies that either necessitate or support it. For you, these last few pages are a chance to reflect on what you've learned and to place that knowledge within the bigger picture.

1. THE NECESSITY OF TECHNOLOGY

Like it or not, technology is a necessity today. It's hard to imagine a world without it. Just as we need electricity to function on an everyday basis, we need technology as well.

Of course, that doesn't mean you should adopt technology just for the sake of the technology or only because it sounds fun. Rather, you need to carefully evaluate each technology and determine if it will make you more productive, enhance your personal life, enrich your learning, or move your organization in the direction of its strategic goals and initiatives.

Technology is not a panacea. If you throw technology at a business process that doesn't work correctly, the result will be that you'll perform that process incorrectly millions of times faster per second. At the same time, you can ill afford to ignore technology when it really will help you and your organization become more efficient, effective, and innovative.

2. CLOSING THE GREAT DIGITAL DIVIDE

We must, as a human race, completely eliminate the great digital divide. The *great digital divide* refers to the fact that the world is becoming one marked by "have's" and "have not's" with respect to technology. That is, the traditional notion of a third world economy is now being defined by the extent to which a country has only limited access to and use of technology.

The power of technology needs to be realized on a worldwide scale. We cannot afford to have any technology-challenged nation or culture (within reason). The great digital divide only adds to global instability. If you live and work in a technology-rich country, don't keep it to yourself. When possible, take technology to other countries by creating international business partnerships and strategic alliances. Join in a non-profit program to spread computer literacy and access in a developing country, or in this country. This may afford you great satisfaction, and the world will benefit greatly from your efforts.

3. TECHNOLOGY FOR THE BETTERMENT OF SOCIETY

Life isn't just about making money. As you approach the development and use of technological innovations (or even standard technologies), think in terms of the betterment of people and society in general. (Making money and helping people often go hand in hand, in fact.)

Medical research is performing marvellous work in the use of technology to treat ailments and cure diseases. But if these efforts are purely profit-driven, we may never wholly realize the fruits of them. For example, therapists are using virtual reality to teach autistic people to cope with increasingly complex situations. We know for a fact that this use of technology isn't making anyone a lot of money. But it isn't always about making money. It's about helping people who face daily challenges far greater than ours. You're fortunate to be in an environment of learning. Give back when you have the chance.

4. EXCHANGING PRIVACY FOR CONVENIENCE

On a personal level, you need to consider how much of your personal privacy you're giving up in exchange for convenience. The extreme example is GPS-enabled implant chips. The convenience is knowing where you are and being able to get directions to your destination. But you're obviously giving up some privacy. Is this okay? Convenience takes on many forms. When you use a discount card at a grocery store to take advantage of sales, that grocery store then tracks your purchasing history in great detail. You can bet that the grocery store will use that information to sell you more tailored products.

It really is a trade-off. In today's technology-based world, you give up privacy when you register for sweepstakes on certain Web sites. You give up privacy just surfing the Web because tracking software monitors your activities. Even when you click on a banner ad, the Web site you go to knows where you came from. Although such trade-offs may seem insignificant, small trade-offs can add up to a big trade-off over time.

Because you are very much a part of this trend, it's often hard to see the big picture and understand that every day you're giving up just a little more privacy in exchange for a little more convenience. Don't ever think that organizations won't use the information they're capturing about you. They're capturing it so they can use it. Of course, much of it will be used to better serve you as a customer, but some of it may not.

5. ETHICS, ETHICS, ETHICS

As our final note to you, we cannot stress enough again the importance of ethics as they guide your behaviour toward other people in your career. We realize that business is business and that businesses need to make money to survive. But the recent scandals involving Enron and others in the corporate world should be a reminder of how important your personal ethical compass is to you. Success shouldn't come to the detriment of other people. It's quite possible to be very ethical and very successful. That's our challenge to you.

Summary: STUDENT LEARNING OUTCOMES *REVISITED*

LO1   Describe the emerging trends and technologies that will have an impact on the changing Internet. Emerging trends and technologies that will have an impact on the changing Internet include

- *Software-as-a-service (SaaS)*—delivery model for software in which you pay for software on a pay-per-use basis instead of buying the software outright.
- *Push*—technology environment in which businesses and organizations come to you via technology with information, services, and product offerings based on your profile.
- *F2b2C (factory-to-business-to-consumer)*—an e-commerce business model in which a consumer communicates through a business on the Internet and directly provides product specifications to a factory that makes the customized and personalized product to the consumer's specifications and then ships it directly to the consumer.
- *VoIP (Voice over Internet Protocol)*—allows you to send voice communications over the Internet and avoid the toll charges that you would normally receive from your long distance carrier.
- *Web 2.0*—second generation of the Web focusing on on-line collaboration, users as both creators and modifiers of content, dynamic and customized information feeds, and many other services.

LO2   Define the various types of technologies that are emerging as we move toward physiological interaction with technology. Emerging technologies in the area of physiological interaction include

- *Automatic speech recognition (ASR)*—a system that not only captures spoken words but also distinguishes word groupings to form sentences.
- *Virtual reality*—three-dimensional computer simulation in which you actively and physically participate.
- *CAVE (cave automatic virtual environment)*—special 3-D virtual reality room that can display images of other people and objects located in other CAVEs all over the world.
- *Haptic interface*—uses technology to add the sense of touch to an environment that previously had only visual and textual elements.

- *Biometrics*—use of physiological characteristics—such as your fingerprint, the blood vessels in the iris of your eye, the sound of your voice, or perhaps even your breath—to provide identification.

LO3   Define the emerging trends of near field communication, Bluetooth, WiFi, cell phones, and RFID, as they relate to the wireless environment. Emerging trends related to the wireless environment include

- *Near field communication (NFC)*—short-range wireless technology developed mainly for use in mobile phones.
- *Bluetooth*—standard for transmitting information in the form of short-range radio waves over distances of up to 30 feet.
- *WiFi*—standard for transmitting information in the form of radio waves over distances up to about several miles.
- *Cell phones*—advances in storage capacity, processor capability, music enhancements, and video support—and threats such as viruses and hackers.
- *RFID (radio frequency identification)*—the use of a chip or label to store information, by which information is transmitted from, or written to, the tag or label when the chip is exposed to the correct frequency of radio waves.

LO4   Define and describe emerging technologies that, while purely technology, can and will impact the future. These technologies include

- *Nanotechnology*—a discipline that seeks to control matter at the atomic and sub-atomic levels for the purpose of building devices on the same small scale.
- *Multi-state CPU*—works with information represented in more than just two states, probably 10 states with each state representing a digit between 0 and 9.
- *Holographic storage device*—a device that stores information on a storage medium that is composed of 3-D crystal-like objects with many sides or faces.

CLOSING CASE STUDY 1
The NBA Goes NFC

You might hold a future technological innovation in your hand right now if you attended an Atlanta Hawks basketball game during the 2006–2007 season. The Atlanta hawks distributed some 250 Nokia 3220 phones to season tickets holders who also have Chase Visa cards and are Cingular Wireless subscribers.

The phones are NFC–enabled. NFC, or near field communication, is a wireless transmission technology being developed primarily for cell phones to support mobile commerce (m-commerce) and other cell phone activities. NFC—unlike other wireless technologies such as Bluetooth and Wifi, which use radio waves for communication—works on magnetic field induction.

Atlanta Hawk season ticket holders lucky enough to be given one of these phones could use them for many purposes including

- Buying food, drinks, merchandise, and other concessions
- Downloading player animations, ring tones, and wallpaper (of the Atlanta Hawks team, of course)

For buying merchandise, the phones contained electronic wallet (e-wallet) software that acted as an intermediary between the concession reader device that contained the total for the purchase amount and the user's Chase Visa card. Without fumbling around to find cash or a credit card, the user simply waved his or her phone within four centimetres of the reader device. The person's Chase Visa account was then automatically charged the appropriate amount. This is quite similar to how RFID works, which we covered in this chapter. However, unlike many RFID implementations, which require you to carry a special RFID–enabled card or other device, NFC technology is embedded into your cell phone, something that most people carry around with them all the time.

For downloading content to the cell phone, the Atlanta Hawks created 60 smart posters. These smart posters—although seemingly just paper posters on the wall—contained electronic content such as ring tones and images. Using the phone, a season ticket holder could select the content he or she wanted, and then—again—wave the phone within four centimetres of the

poster. The selected content was then downloaded to the cell phone. Player animations were free, but other content such as ring tones cost about $2 to $3 each, with the billing being handled by Cingular.

Near field communication is a technology endorsed by just about every mobile network operator. Further, most payment service providers (e.g., banks, credit card issuers, debit card issuers, and prepaid card issuers) have also endorsed NFC as the short-range communications media of the future for mobile phones. Big companies like Motorola and MasterCard are among the many endorsing the use of NFC.

The goal is to allow you to keep your account and card information on your cell phone. Most people now have cell phones and carry them with them wherever they go. In the case of bank and credit card accounts, the e-wallet software interacts with very little private financial information stored on the cell phone. The cell phone typically contains only an account number. The e-wallet software uses that account number to connect to the issuer's infrastructure via the cell phone network. On the back end on the issuer's side, account information is accessed and updated. The only communication back to the e-wallet software on the cell phone is that the transaction was either successful or denied.

When fully implemented, NFC–enabled financial transactions via your cell phone will enable you to buy a variety of goods and services. Some of these purchases can be extremely small (called micropayments), even less than $1. These types of purchases will be extremely fast, enabling retailers to move people more quickly through lines.

You will probably even be able to buy some types of merchandise, store it on your cell phone, and save it for later "consumption" or use. For example, at a movie theatre you could buy tickets early in the day for an evening show time and save them on your cell phone. When you get to the movie theatre in the evening, you could walk directly through the line where tickets are taken, stopping only long enough for a reader device to determine that your cell phone has the appropriate tickets.[21, 22]

www.mcgrawhill.ca/olc/haag

Questions

1. Do a little research on the Web. To what extent has near field communication and these types of contactless payments become a reality? Which cell phone service providers offer electronic wallet capabilities?

2. How might NFC–enabled financial transactions support the software-as-a-service model? How might NFC–enabled financial transactions support the push technology concept?

3. What about security? If someone steals your NFC–enabled phone, they may have access to your accounts. What are providers doing in the area of security?

4. How are NFC–enabled financial transactions further evidence that we are moving toward an e-society? Can you foresee a time when physical cards (credit, debit, and the like) will no longer be needed? What other cards do you carry in your wallet that could become a part of your e-wallet in your phone?

5. How can NFC-enabled financial transactions be used to support the notion of the Long Tail we discussed in Chapter 5?

CLOSING CASE STUDY 2
Can an E-Society Replace our Real Society?

If you step back and view our world and society, you'll notice some very interesting changes and trends. People are spending more and more time on-line. On the average, people now spend more time on-line than watching TV. The average child under the age of 12 spends only 45 minutes outdoors per week in unstructured activities, with much of the rest of the time spent in structured outdoor activities (mainly sport leagues) or indoors in front of a computer. We are definitely moving in the direction of becoming an e-society, supported and enabled by the many technological advances of today and the promises of the capabilities of technology tomorrow.

Second Life (http://secondlife.com) is a virtual world in 3D and is a form of an e-society on the Internet. There, you can create an avatar of yourself, becoming whoever you want to be. You can even buy land on which to build a home or business. Of course, you need to carefully pick the location of your virtual business, based on the location of competitors around you and the amount of traffic that moves through the virtual neighbourhood.

Like many social networking sites (Second Life is definitely a form of one of these), you can connect with people with common interests. You can form groups focusing on such topics as movies, music, and hobbies. At all times of the day and night, you can meet people at nightclubs, fashion shows, and art gallery openings.

Second Life supports a fully running economy. You can take risks and be entrepreneurial. If no one likes what you are doing, you'll go out of business and be forced to sell off assets to pay your debts. If people do like what you're doing, you can become a millionaire in Second Life. And while the money on Second Life is in the currency of Linden dollars (named after Second Life's creator) you can exchange your Linden dollars for real currency and have them transferred to your bank account. Likewise, you can transfer real dollars from your bank account and buy Linden dollars in Second Life, enabling you to expand your business, buy more property, and so on.

A basic account to start your virtual life in Second Life is free. You get avatar capabilities but you can't do certain things like own land. If you want those types of privileges, you have to purchase a membership.

Second Life boasts of a population over 6 million worldwide. Do you have a virtual life on Second Life?[23, 24]

Questions

1. How many social networking sites do you belong to? How much time per week, on the average, would you say that you spend on those social networking sites?

2. Beyond social networking sites, how much time in total do you spend on-line per week? What are the major activities you perform on-line?

3. Although we are reaching more people on-line, are we becoming a society that is disassociated with the real environment around us? Is being on-line so much (often in fantasy environments) good or bad?

Key Terms And Concepts

Application service provider
(ASP), 259
Automatic speech recognition
(ASR), 264
Biochip, 269
Biometrics, 266
Blog, 263
Bluetooth, 270
Cave automatic virtual
environment (CAVE), 265
Crowdsourcing, 262
Disintermediation, 261
Facial recognition software, 269
Factory-to-business-to-Consumer
(F2b2C), 261

Feature analysis, 264
Glove, 264
Haptic interface, 266
Headset (head-mounted display),
264
Holographic device, 265
Holographic storage device, 275
Implant chip, 269
Language processing, 264
Multi-state CPU, 275
Nanotechnology, 274
Near field communication
(NFC), 273
Pattern classification, 264
Podcasting, 263

Push technology, 260
Radio frequency identification
(RFID), 271
RSS feed, 263
Social networking site, 262
Software-as-a-service (SaaS), 259
Virtual reality, 264
Voice over Internet Protocol
(VoIP), 262
Walker, 264
Web 2.0, 262
WiFI (wireless fidelity), 270
Wiki, 262

Short-Answer Questions

1. How will software-as-a-service (SaaS) make use of a personal application service provider?
2. How does push technology differ from spam?
3. What is disintermediation? How does the F2b2C e-commerce model support disintermediation?
4. What exciting applications are associated with the Web 2.0?
5. How does automatic speech recognition work?
6. What are the devices commonly associated with virtual reality?

7. What role do haptic interfaces play?
8. What is the best form of personal identification?
9. How can you expect cell phones to change in the future?
10. What is RFID?
11. How does nanotechnology differ from traditional manufacturing?

Assignments and Exercises

1. **SELLING THE IDEA OF IMPLANT CHIPS AT YOUR SCHOOL** Let's assume for a moment that your team is in favour of using implant chips that contain vitally important information such as identification and medical information. Your task is to put together a sales presentation to your school that would require all students to obtain implant chips. In your presentation, include the following:

   A. The school-related information that each implant chip would contain
   B. The non-school-related information that each implant chip would contain
   C. The processes within your school that would use the information on the implant chips
   D. The benefits your school would realize by requiring implant chips
   E. The benefits students would realize by having implant chips

   Your presentation should be no more than five minutes, so it must be a powerful selling presentation.

2. **FINDING A GOOD AUTOMATIC SPEECH RECOGNITION SYSTEM** Research the Web for automatic speech recognition (ASR) systems. Make a list of the ones you find. What are the prices of each? Are they speaker-independent or speaker-dependent? Do they support continuous speech recognition or discrete speech recognition? What sort of add-on vocabularies can you purchase? How comfortable would you feel speaking the contents of a term paper as opposed to typing it? Would you have to be more or less organized to use speech recognition as opposed to typing? Why?

3. **UNDERSTANDING THE RELATIONSHIPS BETWEEN TRENDS AND TECHNOLOGICAL INNOVATIONS** In this chapter, we presented you with numerous key technologies and how they relate to four important trends. (See Figure 9.1 on page XXX for the list of technologies and trends.) For each trend, identify all the technologies presented in this chapter that can have an impact. For each technology that you do identify, provide a short discussion of how it might have an impact.

4. **RESEARCHING APPLICATIONS OF RFID** Visit the Web and perform a search on RFID for applications that we didn't discuss in this chapter. Prepare a short PowerPoint presentation highlighting each. Also, search the Web for the leading providers of RFID technologies. What companies did you find? Does one seem to stand out above the rest? If so, which is it?

5. **RESEARCHING INTELLIGENT HOME APPLIANCES** Visit a local appliance store in your area and find three home appliances that contain some sort of intelligence (i.e., an embedded computer chip that takes over some of the functionality and decision making). For each appliance, prepare a short report that includes the following information:

   - A description and price for the intelligent home appliance
   - The "intelligent" features of the appliance
   - How those features make the appliance better than the nonintelligent version

Discussion Questions

1. There is currently much legislation pending (and in force) in many provinces that would make it illegal for people to use a cell phone while driving a car. The reason is that society has already noticed a significant increase in the number of traffic accidents in which one of the drivers involved in the accident was using a cell phone. Think beyond that for a moment and include wearable computers. As this new technology becomes more widely available, isn't it possible for someone to be driving a car while using a computer? Should the government enact legislation to prevent it? Why or why not?

2. In a push technology environment, businesses and organizations will come to you with information, services, and product offerings based on your profile. How is a push technology environment different from mass mailings and spam? Is it an invasion of your privacy to have organizations calling you on your cell phone every time you come near a store? Why or why not? Should you be able to "opt in" or "opt out" of these offerings? Is this really any different from someone leaving a flyer at your house or on your car while it's parked in a parking lot?

3. There are three steps in automatic speech recognition (ASR): feature analysis, pattern classification, and language processing. Which of those three steps is the most challenging for a computer to perform? Why? Which of those three steps is the least challenging for a computer to perform? Why? If ASR systems are to become automatic speech understanding systems, which step must undergo the greatest improvement in its capabilities? Why?

4. Much debate surrounds the use of biometrics. Many people like it because biometrics can provide identification and increase security. Other people see it as a tremendous invasion of your privacy. Just as you read in this chapter, a bank—by using biometric identification—may be able to tell if a woman is pregnant. So, the greatest challenge to overcome is not technological but rather societal. What do you think needs to happen for society to accept the use of biometrics? Should society accept the use of biometrics? How long do you think it will be before society accepts the use of biometrics? In what year do you believe the U.S. federal government will begin requiring a biometric of every newborn child?

5. What are the ethical dilemmas associated with using facial recognition software? Is the use of this type of software really any different from a store asking to see your driver's license when you use your credit card? Why or why not? Should the government be able to place digital video cameras on every street corner and use facial recognition software to monitor your movements? Why or why not?

6. When (and if) CAVEs become a common reality, you'll be able to visit your family and friends anytime you want no matter where they live. What sort of impact will this have on the travel industry? If you can see your relatives in a CAVE as often as you want, will you be more or less inclined to buy a plane ticket and visit them in person? Why or why not?

www.mcgrawhill.ca/olc/haag

Extended Learning Module A

Computer Hardware and Software

STUDENT LEARNING OUTCOMES

LO1 Define information technology (IT) and its two basic categories: hardware and software.

LO2 Describe the categories of computers based on size.

LO3 Compare the roles of personal productivity, vertical market, and horizontal market software.

LO4 Describe the roles of operating system and utility software as components of system software.

LO5 Define the purpose of each of the six major categories of hardware.

LO1

A Quick Tour of Technology

Information technology (IT) is any computer-based tool that people use to work with information and support the information and information-processing needs of an organization. IT includes the Internet, spreadsheet software, a satellite, a gamepad for playing video games … the list of the technology you can find in your immediate life is almost endless (see Figure A.1). There are two basic categories of information technology: hardware and software. *Hardware* consists of the physical devices that make up a computer, for instance, keyboard, mouse, modem, flash memory drive (also called a thumb drive), and printer. *Software* is the set of instructions your hardware executes to carry out a specific task for you such as creating a graph (spreadsheet software, for example) and surfing the Web (Internet Explorer, for example). Hardware and software in aggregate are what people refer to as a *computer*, and even that term is becoming more blurred each day with digital media players, cell phones, and the like.

PC video camera

Tablet PC

Haptic gaming controller

iPhone

Information Technology (IT) Includes Many Tools

Smart watch

iPod

Digital camera picture printer

All hardware falls into one or another of six categories. Here's a quick summary.

1. Input: **Input devices** are tools you use to enter information and commands.
2. Output: **Output devices** are tools you use to see, hear, or otherwise recognize the results of your information-processing requests.
3. Storage: **Storage devices** are tools you use to store information for use at a later time.
4. Processing: The **central processing unit (CPU)** is the actual hardware that interprets and executes the software instructions and coordinates the operation of all other hardware. **RAM**, or **random access memory**, is a temporary holding area for the information you're working with, as well as the system and application software instructions that the CPU currently needs.
5. Telecommunications: A **telecommunications device** is a tool you use to exchange information with another person or computer in a network. Telecommunications, as a field, and its associated devices, is so broad that we've devoted an entire module to the topic. Please read *Extended Learning Module B (Network Basics)* to learn about cable and DSL modems, home networks, fibre optics, and much more.
6. Connecting: *Connecting devices* include such things as USB ports into which you connect a printer and connector cords.

The two main types of software are application and system software. **Application software** is the software that enables you to solve specific problems or perform specific tasks. Microsoft PowerPoint, for example, can help you create slides for a presentation, so it's application software. Microsoft SharePoint Designer is an example of application software because it helps you create and publish a Web page or Web site. A business might use payroll software, collaborative software such as videoconferencing, and inventory management software.

System software handles tasks specific to technology management and coordinates the interaction of all technology devices. System software includes both operating system software and utility software. **Operating system software** is system software that controls your application software and manages how your hardware devices work together. Popular personal operating system software includes Microsoft Windows, Mac OS X (for Apple computers), and Linux (an open-source operating system). There are also operating systems for networks (Microsoft Windows Server is an example), operating systems for personal digital assistants (Windows Mobile is an example), and operating systems for just about every other type of technology configuration, even for refrigerators.

Utility software is software that provides additional functionality to your operating system software. Utility software includes anti-virus software, screen savers, spam blocker software, uninstaller software (for properly removing unwanted software), and a host of other types. Some types of utility software are nice to have, like screen savers, while others are essential. For example, anti-virus software protects you from computer viruses that can be deadly for your computer. You definitely need anti-virus software.

This ends our quick tour of technology. In the remainder of this module we'll explore categories of computers by size, software in more detail, and hardware in more detail.

LO2

Categories of Computers by Size

Computers come in different shapes, sizes, and colours. Some are small enough that you can carry them around with you, while others are the size of a family refrigerator. Size is usually related to power and speed, and thus price.

SMARTPHONES

A *smartphone* is a mobile device offering capabilities previously available in a *personal digital assistant (PDA)* combined with the ability to use a mobile telephone network, connect to the internet via WiFi and perhaps even the availability of global positioning (GPS). One might think of a smartphone as having PC-like functionality. Competition in this area is fierce, with the two biggest players (Waterloo, Ontario's RIM and Apple) slugging it out in the market. Despite this high-profile battle, smartphones lack an industry standard definition. One often-cited characteristic is the ability to run operating system software that provides a platform for software developers to write applications to run on the device. Others are satisfied if, in addition to functioning as a telephone, the device offers features such as e-mail and Internet access, with or without a full QWERTY keyboard.

TABLET PCS

A *tablet PC* is a pen-based computer that provides the screen capabilities of a PDA with the functional capabilities of a notebook or desktop computer. Similar to PDAs, tablet PCs allow you to use a writing pen or *stylus* to write notes on the screen and touch the screen to perform functions such as clicking on a link while visiting a Web site. Tablet PCs come in two designs—convertibles and slates. Convertible tablet PCs look like notebook computers, including a screen that you lift up and set in position with a full keyboard and touch pad underneath. Using a convertible PC, you can swivel the screen and lay it flat on the keyboard, converting it into a topless notebook that closes.

Figure A.2

Smartphones, Tablet PCs, and Notebooks

Slate tablet PCs come without an integrated physical keyboard, making the tablet the entire computer. You can buy a docking station for a slate tablet PC, giving you the ability to connect a keyboard and mouse.

NOTEBOOK COMPUTERS

A *notebook computer* is a small, portable, fully functional, battery-powered computer. Notebooks come equipped with all the technology to meet your personal needs, and weigh not much more than a kilogram. If you need a fully functional computer in a variety of places—home, work, school, and/or on the road—then a notebook computer may be just the answer. Notebook computers range in price from about $600 to several thousand dollars depending on the selected configuration.

DESKTOP COMPUTERS

A *desktop computer* is the most popular choice for personal computing needs. You can choose a desktop computer with a horizontal system box (the box is where the CPU, RAM, and storage devices are held) or choose a desktop computer with a vertical system box (called a tower) that you usually place on the floor near your work area. Desktop computers range in price from a little less than $500 to several thousand dollars. Dollar for dollar with comparable characteristics, a desktop computer is faster and more powerful than a notebook computer. Some desktops are built especially for gaming (see Figure A.3).

Figure A.3

Desktop for Gaming

Which one you need—PDA, tablet PC, notebook, or desktop computer—is a function of your unique individual needs. PDAs offer great portability and allow you to keep a calendar, send and receive e-mail, take short notes, and even access the Web. But they're not designed to help you write a term paper, build a Web site, or create a complex graph with statistical software. For these and more complex tasks, you need a notebook, tablet PC, or desktop computer.

So, the next question is, should you buy a notebook or a tablet PC? Most likely, you need a computer that supports full word processing, spreadsheet, presentation, Web site development, and some other capabilities. You need to decide where you'll need your computer. If you need to use your computer both at home and at school (or perhaps at work), then you should buy one of these because they are, in fact, portable. So, if you'd like to be able to surf the Web and get e-mail in your hotel room while on a business or vacation trip, a notebook computer or a tablet PC may be what you need.

Smartphones already allow users to perform "complex" tasks such as creating an elaborate spreadsheet or graph, and even integrating speech recognition. Many offer Global positioning, access to secure corporate networks, and even interfaces to enterprise software such as SAP. As network capacity and availability (through WiFi) increase, the sky is the limit for smartphone technology.

MINICOMPUTERS, MAINFRAME COMPUTERS, AND SUPERCOMPUTERS

PDAs, notebooks, and desktop computers are designed to meet your personal information-processing needs. In business, however, many people often need to access and use the same computer simultaneously. In this case, businesses need computing technologies that multiple people (perhaps hundreds or even thousands) can access and use at the same time. Computers of this type include minicomputers, mainframe computers, and supercomputers (see Figure A.4).

A *minicomputer* (sometimes called a *mid-range computer*) is designed to meet the computing needs of several people simultaneously in a small to medium-size business environment. Minicomputers are more powerful than desktop computers but also cost more, ranging in price from $5,000 to several hundred thousand dollars. Businesses often use minicomputers as servers, either for hosting a Web site or as an internal computer on which shared information and software is placed. For this reason, minicomputers are well suited for business environments in which people need to share common information, processing power, and/or certain peripheral devices such as high-quality, fast laser printers.

A *mainframe computer* (sometimes just called a *mainframe*) is a computer designed to meet the computing needs of hundreds of people in a large business environment. So mainframe computers are a step up in size, power, capability, and cost from minicomputers. Mainframes can easily cost in excess of $1 million. With processing speeds greater than 1 trillion instructions per second (compared to a typical desktop that can process approximately 3 billion instructions per second), mainframes can easily handle the processing requests of hundreds (or thousands) of people simultaneously.

A *supercomputer* is the fastest, most powerful, and most expensive type of computer. Universities that are heavily involved in research and "number crunching," such as University of Montreal, University of Alberta, and University of New Brunswick, employ supercomputers because of the speed with which they can process information. Very large, customer-oriented businesses such as General Motors and AT&T also employ supercomputers just to handle customer information and transaction processing. Their business needs require the high level of support and the powerful processing power provided by supercomputers.

How much do you really need to know about the technical specifics (CPU speed, storage disk capacity, and so on), prices, and capabilities of minicomputers, mainframe computers, and supercomputers? Probably not much, unless you plan to major in information technology. What you should concentrate on is the technical specifics, prices, and capabilities of PDAs, tablet PCs, notebooks, and desktop computers. These tools will be your companions for your entire business career. Learn about them and know them well—on an ongoing basis.

Figure A.4

Minicomputers, Mainframes, and Supercomputers

LO3

Software: Your Intellectual Interface

The most important tool in your technology tool set is software. Software contains the instructions that your hardware executes to perform an information-processing task for you. So, software is really your *intellectual interface*, designed to automate processing tasks. Without software, your computer is little more than a very expensive doorstop. As we've stated, there are two categories of software: application software and system software.

APPLICATION SOFTWARE

Application software is the software you use to meet your specific information-processing needs, including payroll, customer relationship management, project management, training, word processing, and many, many others. Application software can be categorized as either personal productivity software or vertical and horizontal market software.

PERSONAL PRODUCTIVITY SOFTWARE   *Personal productivity software* helps you perform personal tasks—such as writing a memo, creating a graph, and creating a slide presentation—that you can usually do even if you don't own a computer. You're probably already familiar with some personal productivity software tools including Microsoft Word, Microsoft Excel, Firefox, and Quicken (personal finance software).

Three modules in this text help you learn how to use some of these tools—*Extended Learning Module H* (for Microsoft Excel, spreadsheet software), and *Extended Learning Module G* (for Microsoft Access, database management system). Figure A.5 describes the 10 major categories of personal productivity software and some of the better known packages within each category.

VERTICAL AND HORIZONTAL MARKET SOFTWARE   While performing organizational processes in your career, you'll also frequently use two other categories of application software: vertical market software and horizontal market software.

Vertical market software is application software that is unique to a particular industry. For example, the health care industry has a variety of application software unique to that market segment, including radiology software, patient-scheduling software, nursing allocation software, and pharmaceutical software. Vertical market software is written specifically for an industry. Health care industry patient-scheduling software wouldn't work well for scheduling hair styling and manicure appointments in a beauty salon.

Category	Examples*
Word processing—Helps you create papers, letters, memos, and other basic documents	• Microsoft Word • Corel WordPerfect
Spreadsheet—Helps you work primarily with numbers, including performing calculations and creating graphs	• Microsoft Excel • Corel Quattro Pro
Presentation—Helps you create and edit information that will appear in electronic slides	• Microsoft PowerPoint • Corel Presentations
Desktop publishing—Extends word processing software by including design and formatting techniques to enhance the layout and appearance of a document	• Microsoft Publisher • Quark QuarkXPress
Personal information management (PIM)—Helps you create and maintain (1) to-do lists, (2) appointments and calendars, and (3) points of contact	• Microsoft Outlook • Corel Central
Personal finance—Helps you maintain your cheque book, prepare a budget, track investments, monitor your credit card balances, and pay bills electronically	• Quicken Quicken • Microsoft Money
Web authoring—Helps you design and develop Web sites and pages that you publish on the Web	• Microsoft SharePoint Designer • Macromedia Dreamweaver
Graphics—Helps you create and edit photos and art	• Microsoft PhotoDraw • Adobe PhotoShop
Communications—Helps you communicate with other people	• Microsoft Outlook • Internet Explorer
Database management system (DBMS)—Helps you specify the logical organization for a database and access and use the information within a database	• Microsoft Access • FileMaker FileMaker Pro

* Publisher name given first.

Figure A.5

Categories of Personal Productivity Software

Horizontal market software, on the other hand, is application software that is general enough to be suitable for use in a variety of industries. Examples of horizontal market software include

- Inventory management
- Payroll
- Accounts receivable
- Billing
- Invoice processing
- Human resource management

The preceding functions (and many others) are very similar, if not identical, across many different industries, enabling software publishers to develop one particular piece of software (e.g., accounts receivable) that can be used by many different industries.

Personal productivity software is actually a type of horizontal market software in that it is general enough to be suitable for use in a variety of industries. No matter what industry you work in, you need basic word processing software for creating memos, business plans, and other basic documents.

There are, however, some key differences between personal productivity software and horizontal (and vertical) market software. First is the issue of price. You can buy a full suite of personal productivity software for less than $400. In contrast, some individual horizontal and vertical market software packages may cost $500,000 or more. Second is the issue of customizability. When you purchase personal productivity software, you cannot change the way it works. That is, you're buying the right to use it but not to change how it operates. With horizontal and vertical market software you may be able to purchase the right to change the way the software works. So, if you find a payroll software package that fits most of your organizational needs, you can buy the software and the right to change the operation of the software so that it meets your needs precisely. This is a very common business practice when purchasing and using horizontal and vertical market software.

In Chapter 6, we discuss how organizations go about the process of developing software for their particular needs, including how organizations can and do purchase vertical and horizontal market software and then customize that software.

LO4

System Software

System software controls how your various technology tools work together as you use your application software to perform specific information-processing tasks. System software includes two basic categories: operating system software and utility software.

OPERATING SYSTEM SOFTWARE   Operating system software is system software that controls your application software and manages how your hardware devices work together. For example, after using Excel to create a graph, if you choose to print the graph, your operating system software takes over, ensures that you have a printer attached and that the printer has paper (and tells you if it doesn't), and sends your graph to the printer along with instructions on how to print it.

Your operating system software supports a variety of useful features, one of which is multitasking. *Multitasking* allows you to work with more than one piece of software at a time. Suppose you wanted to create a graph in Excel and insert it into a word processing document. With multitasking, you can have both pieces of application software open at the same time, and even see both on the screen. So, when you complete the creation of your graph, you can easily copy and paste it into your word processing document without having to exit the spreadsheet software and then start your word processing software.

There are different types of operating system software for personal environments and for organizational environments that support many users simultaneously. The latter, called *network operating systems or NOSs*, we explore in *Extended Learning Module B (Network Basics)*. Popular *personal* operating systems include

- ***Microsoft Windows Vista***—Microsoft's latest personal computer operating system in a wide range of editions including Vista Home Basic, Vista Home Premium, Vista Business, and Vista Ultimate.
- ***Microsoft Windows XP Home*** and ***XP Professional*** (Windows XP Pro)—Microsoft's predecessor to the Vista personal computer operating system. Versions are available for home and, with enhanced features, for business users.
- ***Mac OS X***—Apple's newest operating system.
- ***Linux***—An open-source operating system that provides a rich operating environment for high-end workstations and network servers.

Open-source software is software for which the source code (how the software was actually written) is publicly available and free of charge. Unlike commercial software, open-source software is created and maintained by a distributed network of engineers, software developers, and users, each making contributions to the software.

The advantages of open-source software are numerous. Because the source code is available, users of the software may modify it to suit their needs and take comfort in the fact that changes they wish to make are fully under their control. You can compare this with commercial, or closed-source, software, for which the customer must go to the vendor and pay for changes to be made and wait until the vendor has made those changes.

There are many examples of open-source software, including

- OpenOffice.org (office suite, including word processor, spreadsheet, and presentation software)
- Apache HTTP Server (Web server)
- Linux (operating system)
- MySQL (open-source DBMS with commercial support).

If you're considering purchasing a notebook computer that you'll use extensively at school connected to a network there, we recommend that you contact your school's technology support department to determine which operating system is best for you.

UTILITY SOFTWARE Utility software adds functionality to your operating system software. Sometimes it is crucial. A simple example is screen saver software (which is probably also a part of your operating system). The most important utility software is anti-virus software. ***Anti-virus software*** is utility software that detects and removes or quarantines computer viruses. Viruses are everywhere today, with more than 100 new ones surfacing each month. Some viruses are benign: they do something annoying like causing your screen to go blank but do not corrupt your information. Other viruses are deadly, perhaps reformatting your ***hard disk*** or altering the contents of your files. You definitely need anti-virus software to protect your computer. We talk much more about this vitally important topic and guarding against possible attacks that can be launched against your computer from cyberspace in Chapter 8 and *Extended Learning Module C (Computer Crime and Digital Forensics)*.

Other types of utility software include

- ***Crash-proof software***—Utility software that helps you save information if your system crashes and you're forced to turn it off and then back on again.

- *Uninstaller software*—Utility software that you can use to remove software from your hard disk that you no longer want.
- *Disk optimization software*—Utility software that organizes the information on your hard disk in the most efficient way.
- *Spam-blocker software*—Utility software that filters unwanted e-mail from your inbox. Spam is roughly equivalent to unsolicited telephone marketing calls. The term spam is said to derive from a famous Monty Python sketch ("Well, we have Spam; tomato and Spam; egg and Spam; egg, bacon, and Spam ...") that is still popular.
- *Anti-spyware software*—Utility software that detects and removes spyware and other unwanted software that can track every electronic move you make.

You definitely need utility software. Don't think of utility software as "optional" software just because it "adds" functionality to your computer. The above examples are just a few of the many types of utility software you'll find in a utility software suite, and all are helpful.

LO5

Hardware: Your Physical Interface

To properly understand the significant role of your hardware (the physical components of your computer), it helps to know something about how your computer works. You work with information in the form of characters (A–Z, a–z, and special ones such as an asterisk, a question mark, etc.) and numbers (0–9). Computers, on the other hand, work only with 1s and 0s in terms of what we call bits and bytes. Computers use electricity to function, and electrical pulses have two states: on and off, which are assigned the values of 1 and 0, respectively.

What are bits and bytes? A *binary digit (bit)* is the smallest unit of information that your computer can process. A bit can either be a 1 (on) or a 0 (off). The technical challenge is to be able to represent all our natural language characters, special symbols, and numbers in binary form. ASCII is one agreed-upon standard to do this. *ASCII (American Standard Code for Information Interchange)* is the coding system that most personal computers use to represent, process, and store information. In ASCII, a group of eight bits represents one natural language character and is called a *byte*.

For example, if you were to type the word *cool* on the keyboard, your keyboard (a hardware device) would change it into four bytes—one byte for each character—that would look like the following to be used by your computer:

01100011	01001111	01001111	1001100
c	o	o	l

This grouping of 1s and 0s would be used for "cool" as it moves around or is stored on your computer—as it travels from one device to another, is stored on a storage device, and is processed by your CPU.

There are three important conclusions that you should draw from this discussion so far. First, your hardware works with information in a different form (although with the same meaning) than you do. Second, the term *byte* is the bridge between people and a computer. A computer can store one character, special symbol, or number in a byte.

ASCII is but one scheme for interfacing between people and machines. A newer standard is Unicode. The Unicode Consortium spearheads a drive to adopt Unicode and its 100,000 character set, with support for character properties, rules for normalization, decomposition, collation, rendering and bidirectional display order (for the correct display of text containing both right-to-left scripts, such as Arabic or Hebrew, and left-to-right scripts such as English, French and German.)[1]

Third, the primary role of your input and output devices is to convert information from one form to another. Input devices convert information from human-readable form into bits and bytes, while output devices convert the 1s and 0s to something people can recognize. All other hardware works with bits and bytes.

COMMON INPUT DEVICES

An input device is a tool you use to enter information and commands. You can use a ***keyboard*** to type in information, for example, and use a mouse to point and click on buttons and icons. As you saw in the previous section, input devices are responsible for converting information in human-readable form to the binary code that computers use. The newest input system is radio frequency ID or RFID for short. Warehouse and logistics applications are now quite common, but a novel and critical application had its start right here, when Canada became the first country to mandate RFID tags for cattle. The program allows federal food inspection teams to more effectively monitor and detect the path of animal diseases such as Bovine Spongiform Encephalopathy (BSE), commonly known as Mad-Cow Disease.[2, 3]

Below are the principal types of input devices being used today (see Figures A.6 and A.7).

- Keyboards are the most often used input devices for desktop and notebook computers, while styluses are the most frequently used input devices for PDAs and tablet PCs. A stylus is a pen-like device used to write or draw on a PDA or tablet PC. Keyboards and styluses allow you to input both information and commands, and both are used in business and personal settings.

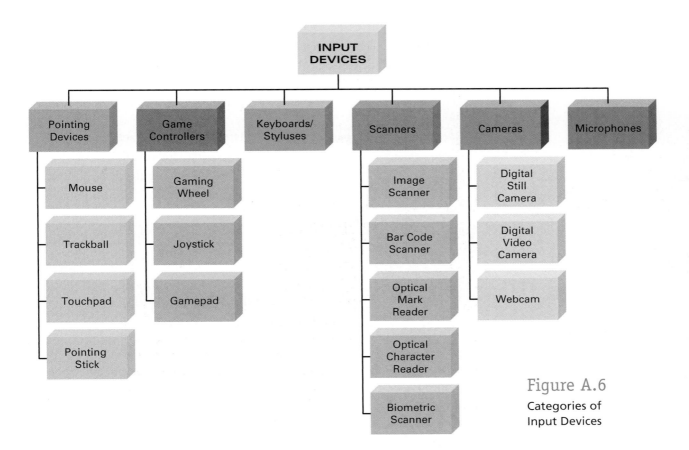

Figure A.6

Categories of Input Devices

Figure A.7

Common Input Devices

- *Pointing devices* are devices that are used to navigate and select objects on a display screen.
- A *mouse* is a pointing device that you use to click on icons or buttons. The three types are mechanical (using a ball), optical (using red light), and wireless (using waves).
- A *trackball* is similar to a mechanical mouse, but it has the ball on top.
- A *touchpad* is a little rectangle that you use to move the cursor with your finger; it is often found on notebook computers.
- A *pointing stick* is a little rod (like a pencil-top eraser) used almost exclusively on notebook computers.
- *Game controllers* are used for gaming to better control screen action.
  - A *gaming wheel* is a steering wheel and foot pedals for virtual driving.
  - A *joystick* is a vertical handle with programmable buttons that control action.
  - A *gamepad* is a multifunctional input device with programmable buttons, thumb sticks, and a directional pad.
- *Scanners* are used to convert information that exists in visible form into electronic form.
  - An *image scanner* captures images, photos, text, and artwork that already exist on paper.
  - A *bar code scanner* reads information that is in the form of vertical bars, where their width and spacing represent digits (often used in point-of-sale [POS] systems in retail environments).
  - An *optical mark reader* detects the presence or absence of a mark in a predetermined spot on the page (often used for true/false and multiple-choice exam answers).
  - An *optical character reader* reads characters that appear on a page or sales tag (often used in point-of-sale [POS] systems in retail environments).

– A *biometric scanner* scans some human physical attribute like your fingerprint or iris for security purposes.

• *Digital cameras* capture still images or video as a series of 1s and 0s. Some will capture only stills, others do both.

– *Digital still camera*—digitally captures still images in varying resolutions.

– *Digital video camera*—captures video digitally.

– *Webcam*—captures digital video to upload to the web.

– *Microphones* capture audio for conversion into electronic form.

COMMON OUTPUT DEVICES

An output device is a tool you use to see, hear, or otherwise recognize the results of your information-processing requests. The most common output devices for both business and personal computing environments are monitors and printers, but speakers and plotters (printers that generate drawings) are also output devices (see Figure A.8). Any device that converts the digital form of information in a computer to something that you can see, read, or hear is an output device.

MONITORS Monitors come in two varieties: CRT or flat-panel displays (see Figure A.9). *CRTs* are the monitors that look like traditional television sets, while flat-panel displays are thin, lightweight monitors that take up much less space than CRTs. *Flat-panel displays* are either liquid crystal display or gas plasma display. *Liquid crystal display (LCD) monitors* make the screen image by sending electricity through crystallized liquid trapped between two layers of glass or plastic. *Gas plasma displays* send electricity through gas trapped between two layers of glass or plastic to create a screen image. A gas plasma display usually provides a better image, but is more expensive than a comparably sized LCD monitor.

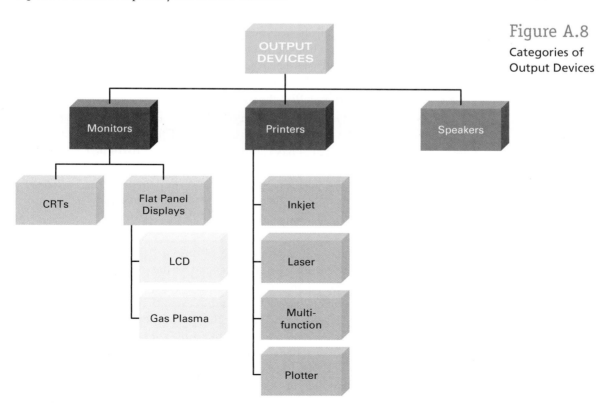

Figure A.8

Categories of Output Devices

Figure A.9
Monitors Are Common
Output Devices

When selecting a monitor, the important features to consider, besides its price and physical size, are the monitor's (1) viewable image size, (2) resolution, and (3) dot pitch.

1. The *viewable image size (VIS)* is the size of the image. The quoted size (17", 19", etc.) is measured diagonally from corner to corner. In a flat-panel display, this size is the same as the distance from corner to opposite corner of the monitor's frame, while in a CRT it's slightly less since the image doesn't completely fill the screen area on a CRT. The physical size of a CRT, for a comparable image size, is usually larger since it's much deeper than the flat-panel displays.

2. The *resolution of a screen* is the number of pixels it has. *Pixels* (picture elements) are the dots that make up the image on your screen. For example, a monitor with a resolution of 1,280 × 1,024 has 1,280 pixels across and 1,024 pixels down the screen. The higher the resolution, the better the image.

3. *Dot pitch* is the distance between the centres of a pair of like-coloured pixels. So, a monitor with .24 mm dot pitch is better than one with .28 mm dot pitch because the dots are smaller and closer together, giving a better quality image.

PRINTERS   Printers are another common type of output device (see Figure A.10). The sharpness and clarity of a printer's output depend on the printer's resolution. The *resolution of a printer* is the number of dots per inch (dpi) it produces. This is the same principle as the resolution in monitors. As is the case with monitors, the more dots per inch, the better the image, and consequently, the more costly the printer. High-end personal printers usually have a resolution of 1,600 × 1,600 or better. Multiplying these numbers gives you 2,560,000 dots per square inch. Some printers, especially those that advertise high-quality photo output, achieve resolutions of 5,760 × 1,440 by making multiple passes across the image to produce the clarity needed.

Figure A.10

Printers Are Also Common Output Devices

- ***Inkjet printers*** make images by forcing ink droplets through nozzles. Standard inkjet printers use four colours: black, cyan (blue), magenta (purplish pink), and yellow. Some inkjet printers produce high-quality images and are often advertised as photo printers. These have two shades each of magenta and cyan for a total of six colours.

- ***Laser printers*** form images using the same sort of electrostatic process that photocopiers use. Laser printers are usually more expensive than inkjets, but they have become dramatically cheaper lately. They usually provide better quality images than inkjets. They come in black and white and in colour versions.

- ***Multifunction printers*** scan, copy, and fax, as well as print. These devices are very popular in homes and small offices since they offer so many features in one unit. Multifunction printers can be either inkjet or laser.

- ***Plotters*** form their output by moving a pen across the surface of a piece of paper. Plotters were the first type of printer that could print with colours and render graphics and full-size engineering drawings. As a rule, plotters are much more expensive than printers. They are most frequently used for CAE (computer-aided engineering) applications, such as CAD (computer-aided design) and CAM (computer-aided manufacturing).

COMMON STORAGE DEVICES

As opposed to RAM, which is temporary memory, storage media don't lose their contents when you turn off your computer. The main issues to consider when choosing a storage medium are (1) whether you want portability, (2) how much storage space you need, and (3) whether you need to change the information on the medium.

Some storage devices, such as hard disks, offer easy update capabilities and high storage capacity, but may not be portable. Others, like flash memory devices, while they are portable and updateable, have less storage space. Still others like DVD-ROMs are portable with high capacity, but the information that comes on them can't be changed (see Figure A.11).

Capacities of storage media are measured in megabytes, gigabytes, and terabytes. A ***megabyte*** (MB or M or Meg) is roughly 1 million bytes; a ***gigabyte*** (GB or Gig) is roughly 1 billion bytes; and a ***terabyte*** (TB) is roughly 1 trillion bytes. A consumer hard disk would have a capacity of between 1 and 250 gigabytes while a hard disk for a large organization (also called a hard disk pack) can hold in excess of 100 TB of information. Common storage devices include

- Magnetic storage media
  - A hard disk is a magnetic storage device with one or more thin metal platters or disks that store information sealed inside the disk drive. You usually get one installed in your system unit (the computer box) when you buy a computer.

Figure A.11

Categories of
Storage Media

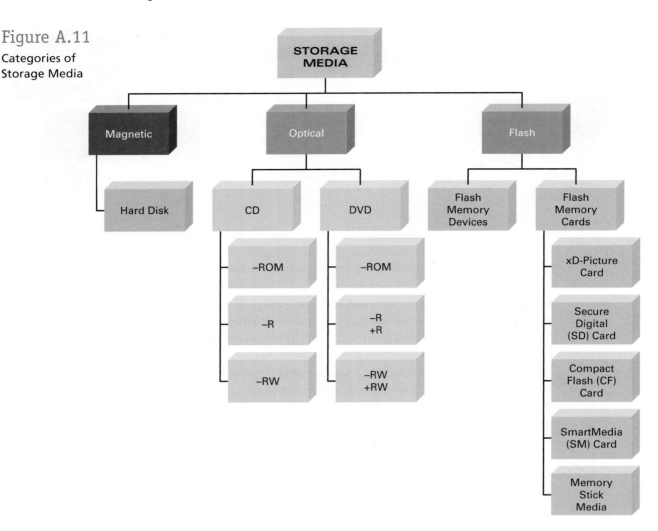

If you need more hard disk space or want portability, you can get an external
unit that you can plug into a USB port. (We'll discuss USB ports in a later
section.) A hard disk offers ease of updating and large storage capacity.

- *Optical storage media* are plastic discs on which information is stored, deleted,
  and/or changed using laser light, and include CDs and DVDs, of which there are
  several types:
  - A *CD-ROM (compact disc—read-only memory)* is an optical or laser disc on
    which information cannot be changed. A CD stores up to 800 MB of information.
  - A *CD-R (compact disc—recordable)* is an optical or laser disc that you can
    write to one time only.
  - A *CD-RW (compact disc—rewritable)* is an optical or laser disc on which you
    can save, change, and delete files as often as you like.
  - A *DVD-ROM* is a high-capacity optical or laser disc upon which information
    cannot be changed. The capacity of a DVD, unlike that of a CD, varies
    according to type.
  - A *DVD-R or DVD+R (DVD—recordable)* is a high-capacity optical or laser
    disc to which you can write one time only.
  - A *DVD-RW or DVD+RW* is a high-capacity optical or laser disc on which you
    can save, change, and delete files.

Figure A.12
Common Types
of Flash Memory

- Flash memory comes in two varieties: flash memory device and flash memory cards (see Figure A.12). A *flash memory device* (also called a jump drive, a memory key, or thumb drive) is a flash memory storage device that is small enough to fit on a key ring and plugs directly into the USB port on your computer. A *flash memory card*, on the other hand, has to be inserted into a reader, which in turn plugs into the USB port. Flash memory cards have high-capacity storage units laminated inside a small piece of plastic. There are several different types.

  - An *xD-Picture (xD) card* is a flash memory card that looks like a rectangular piece of plastic smaller than a penny and about as thick, with one edge slightly curved. xD cards have capacities ranging from 32 to 512 megabytes.

  - A *secure digital (SD) card* and a *MultiMediaCard (MMC)* are flash memory cards that look identical to each other (but SD cards have copy protection built in), are a little larger than a quarter, and are slightly thicker than a credit card.

  - A *CompactFlash (CF) card* is a flash memory card slightly larger than a toonie with capacity of up to 6 gigabytes.

  - A *SmartMedia (SM) card* is a flash memory card a little longer than a CF card and about as thick as a credit card with a capacity of up to 512 megabytes.

  - A *memory stick media card* is an elongated flash memory card about the width of a penny developed by Sony with a capacity up to 1 gigabyte.

CPU AND RAM

Together, your CPU and RAM make up the real brains of your computer (see Figure A.13). Your CPU largely determines the power (and also the price) of your computer. The central processing unit (CPU) is the hardware that interprets and executes the system and application software instructions and coordinates the operation of all other hardware. Random access memory (RAM) is a temporary holding area for the information you're working with as well as the system and application software instructions that the CPU currently needs.

Figure A.13
CPU and RAM

You'll often hear the CPU referred to as a microprocessor or a CPU chip. The dominant manufacturers of CPUs include Intel (with its Celeron, Pentium, and Xeon series for personal computers) and AMD (with its Athlon and Opteron series). As a consumer, you'll probably find the most useful information about CPUs is their relative speeds.

Today's CPU speed is usually quoted in gigahertz. *Gigahertz (GHz)* is the number of billions of CPU cycles per second that the CPU can handle. The more cycles per second, the faster the processing and the more powerful the computer. Gigahertz refers to how quickly the CPU can carry out the steps it takes to execute software instructions—a process sometimes called the *CPU cycle* or *machine cycle*. A CPU cycle (machine cycle) consists of retrieving, decoding, and executing the instruction, then returning the result to RAM. When you load (or open) a program, you're telling your computer to send a copy of the program from the storage device (hard disk or CD) into RAM. In carrying out the software instructions, the CPU repeatedly performs machine cycles as follows:

1. Retrieve an instruction: The *control unit*, which is the component of the CPU that directs what happens in your computer, sends to RAM for instructions and the information it needs. If the instruction says to add 4 and 6, for example, the two numbers travel as information with the add instruction. The instruction travels from RAM on the system bus. The *system bus* consists of electrical pathways that move information between basic components of the motherboard, including between RAM and the CPU. When the instruction reaches the CPU it waits temporarily in *CPU cache*, which is a type of memory on the CPU where instructions called up by the CPU wait until the CPU is ready to use them. It takes much less time to get the instruction from CPU cache to the control unit than from RAM, so CPU cache speeds processing.

2. Decode the instruction: The CPU gets the instruction out of cache and examines it to see what needs to be done, in this case, add 4 and 6.

3. Execute the instruction: The CPU then does what the instruction says to do. In our example, it sends the two numbers to the *arithmetic logic unit* to be added. The arithmetic logic unit (ALU) is a component of the CPU that performs arithmetic, as well as comparison and logic operations.

4. Store the result in RAM: The CPU then sends the result of the addition, 10, to RAM. There's not always a result to send back to RAM. Sometimes the CPU does intermediate calculations that don't get saved.

You'll sometimes hear the CPU speed referred to as the "clock speed." This refers to the *CPU clock*. Every CPU has its own CPU clock, which is simply a sliver of quartz that beats at regular intervals in response to an electrical charge. The beat of the CPU clock is like the drummer in a marching band. Just as the drummer keeps everyone marching in time, the CPU clock keeps all your computer's operations synchronized. Each beat or tick of the CPU clock is called a clock cycle and is equivalent to a CPU cycle (machine cycle). The CPU uses the CPU clock to keep instructions and information marching through your CPU at a fixed rate.

RAM is a sort of whiteboard that your CPU uses while it processes information and software instructions. When you turn off your computer, everything in RAM disappears—that's why we call it "temporary." When you first start your computer, system instructions that are necessary to keep your computer running get written into RAM. Then, as you open applications, like Microsoft Word or Excel, the instructions to make those programs run join the operating system in RAM. As you type in your document or enter information into your workbook, that too is stored in RAM. When you've finished your work and save it, a copy is transferred from RAM to your disk or CD.

The most important thing you need to know about RAM is its capacity for storing instructions and information. RAM capacity is expressed in megabytes or gigabytes. You'll remember that a megabyte is roughly 1 million bytes. A byte is equivalent to a character. So RAM with a capacity of 256 megabytes can hold 256 million characters—that includes operating system instructions as well as the applications and information that you're currently using.

NOTEBOOK COMPUTER CPUS AND RAM   A notebook computer is to a desktop computer as a recreational vehicle is to a traditional home—everything is smaller, and power to run devices is limited since you have to carry the power sources with you. A *mobile CPU* is a special type of CPU for a notebook computer that changes speed, and therefore power consumption, in response to fluctuation in use. A desktop CPU, running at 1 GHz, uses between 75 and 1,090 watts of power whereas a mobile CPU might run at a much smaller 34 watts. RAM modules for notebook computers are smaller than those for desktop computers.

CONNECTING THE HARDWARE OUTSIDE TO THE HARDWARE INSIDE

Since the CPU controls all computer hardware, all hardware devices must be connected to the CPU, just as your limbs are connected to your brain through your spinal cord.

The CPU, along with RAM, is located on the large circuit board (called the mother-board) inside your system unit. The connector (or plug) on the end of the cable coming out of your printer connects it to the motherboard, which then carries information between the CPU and the printer.

WIRED CONNECTIONS   All devices that are not wireless have connectors on the ends of cables that plug into ports on the computer. A *port* is the place on your system unit, monitor, or keyboard through which information and instructions flow to and from your computer system. For wired connections it's the opening or socket where you insert the connector, and for wireless devices a port is where the wave information goes in and out.

The ports are accessible on the outside of the system unit, which means that you don't have to open up the system unit to plug in your scanner. There are various types of connectors/ports (see Figure A.14) including

- *USB (universal serial bus) ports*, which fit small, flat plug-and-play, hot-swap USB connectors. Using USB hubs, you can connect up to 127 devices to a single USB port on your computer. *Hot swap* is an operating system feature that allows you—while your computer is running—to unplug a device and plug in a new one (without first shutting down your computer). *Plug and play* is an operating feature that finds and installs the device driver for a device that you plug into your computer. USB connectors/ports come in two speeds: USB 1.1 and USB 2.0 (which is faster), and in two physical shapes called Type A and Type B, respectively. Type A USB connectors/ports are all the same size and shape, but Type B USB connectors are smaller, squarer, and come in several different sizes. Type B connectors are usually on the end of the cable that plugs into the device (like a digital camera).
- *Firewire ports* (also called IEEE 1394 or I-Link) fit hot-swap, plug-and-play Firewire connectors, and you can connect up to 63 Firewire devices to a single Firewire port by daisy-chaining the devices together.
  - Serial connectors/ports are gradually being replaced by USB and Firewire.
- *PS/2 ports* fit PS/2 connectors, which you often find on keyboards and mice. PS/2 is a special type of serial connector/port.

Figure A.14

Categories of Connectors
and Ports

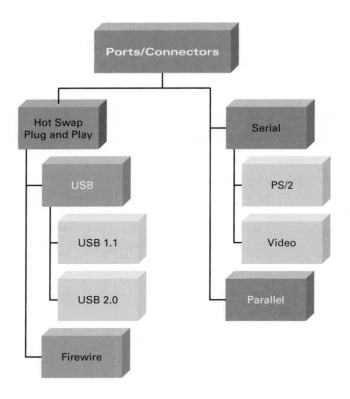

   – A standard video-out conenctor is included with all PCs and laptops to drive
     an external display. However, video cards now often include two connectors to
     allow dual monitor viewing. Several standards exist.

 • *Parallel ports* fit parallel connectors, which are large, flat connectors found almost
   exclusively on printer cables, but that are losing popularity in favour of USB.

   Figure A.15 provides photo illustration of many of the ports and connectors we've
just described.

WIRELESS CONNECTIONS   Wireless devices transfer and receive information in
the form of waves, either infrared or radio. Different types of waves have different
frequencies. The three types most frequently used in personal and business computer
environments are infrared, Bluetooth, and WiFi.

 • *Infrared*, also called IR or IrDA (infrared data association), uses red light to
   send and receive information. Infrared light has a frequency that's below what the
   eye can see. It's used for TV remotes and other devices that operate over short
   distances (the effective distance is about one mile) that are free of obstacles.

 • *Bluetooth* is a standard for transmitting information in the form of short-range
   radio waves over distances of up to 30 feet and is used for purposes such as
   wirelessly connecting a cell phone or a PDA to a computer.

 • *WiFi (wireless fidelity)* is a standard for transmitting information in the form of
   radio waves over distances up to about several miles. WiFi has several forms. For
   example, WiFi is also called IEEE 802.11a, b, or g, each of which is a unique type.
   WiFi is usually the type of wireless communication used in a network environment.

EXPANSION CARDS AND SLOTS   Whether wired or wireless, ports are sometimes
directly on the motherboard and sometimes on expansion cards. An *expansion card* (or
board) is a circuit board that you insert into the *expansion slot* (a long skinny socket)

Serial connector

Parallel connector

USB connector

Firewire connector

Ethernet connector

Figure A.15
Ports and Connectors to Connect Devices to the CPU on the Motherboard

on the motherboard and to which you connect a peripheral device. Information coming from and going to expansion slots and ports moves along wires (called a "bus") to the CPU. The *expansion bus* is the set of pathways along which information moves between devices outside the motherboard and the CPU. We have already discussed the system bus that moves information between basic motherboard components, including RAM and the CPU.

To add devices to your notebook computer, you slide a *PC card* into the *PC card slot* on the notebook, and connect the device to the PC card. A PC card (which is an updated version of the traditional PCMCIA card) is the expansion card you use to add devices to your notebook computer. PC cards look like thick credit cards. PC card slots are the openings, one on top of the other, on the side or front of a notebook, where you connect external devices with a PC card. For example, if you wanted to add a CD-ROM drive, you'd slide a PC card into the slot and then connect the CD-ROM drive to the connector on the PC card. One of the great things about PC cards is that you can hot-swap devices.

Summary: STUDENT LEARNING OUTCOMES *REVISITED*

LO1 Define information technology (IT) and its two basic categories: hardware and software. *Information technology (IT)* is any computer-based tool that people use to work with information and support the information and information-processing needs of an organization. For example, IT includes cell phones, PDAs, software such as *spreadsheet software*, and output devices such as printers. Hardware consists of the physical devices that make up a computer (often referred to as a computer system). Software is the set of instructions that your hardware executes to carry out a specific task for you.

LO2 Describe the categories of computers based on size. Categories of computers by size include personal digital assistants, tablet PCs, notebook computers, desktop computers, minicomputers, mainframe computers, and supercomputers. A *personal digital assistant (PDA)* is a small handheld computer that helps you surf the Web and perform simple tasks such as note taking, calendaring, appointment scheduling, and maintaining an address book. A *tablet PC* is a pen-based computer that provides the screen capabilities of a PDA with the functional capabilities of a notebook or desktop computer. A *notebook computer* is a small, portable, fully functional battery-powered computer designed to carry around. A *desktop computer* is the most popular choice for personal computing needs. These four are all computers designed for use by one person. A *minicomputer* (mid-range computer) is designed to meet the computing needs of several people simultaneously in a small to medium-size business environment. A *mainframe computer* (mainframe) is a computer designed to meet the computing needs of hundreds of people in a large business environment. A *supercomputer* is the fastest, most powerful, and most expensive type of computer. In the order given, PDAs are the smallest, least powerful, and least expensive while supercomputers are the largest, most powerful, and most expensive.

LO3 Compare the roles of personal productivity, vertical market, and horizontal market software. *Application software* executes your specific programs and tasks. *Personal productivity* software helps you perform personal tasks—such as writing a memo, creating a graph, and creating a slide presentation—that you can usually do even if you don't own a computer. *Vertical market software* is application software that is unique to a particular industry. *Horizontal market software* is application software that is general enough to be suitable for use in a variety of industries. *Personal productivity software* is very inexpensive when compared to both vertical market and horizontal market software. With personal productivity software, you do not obtain the right to change the way the software works. If you buy vertical market or horizontal market software, you can often buy the right to change the way the software works.

LO4 Describe the roles of operating system software and utility software as components of system software. *System software* handles technology management tasks and coordinates the interaction of all your technology devices. *Operating system software* controls your application software and manages how your hardware devices work together. So operating system software really enables you to run application software. *Utility software* adds additional functionality to your operating system, including such utilities as *anti-virus software*, screen savers, *crash-proof software*, *uninstaller software*, *disk optimization software*, *spam blocking software*, and *anti-spyware software*. Although these "add" functionality, you definitely need utility software, especially anti-virus software.

LO5 Define the purpose of each of the six major categories of hardware. The six major categories of hardware are

- *Input devices*, which convert information and commands from a form that you understand into a form your computer can understand.

- *Output devices*, which help you see, hear, or otherwise accept the results of your information-processing requests, that is, convert information from a form your computer understands into a form you can understand.
- *CPU* and RAM, which are the real brains of your computer; they execute software instructions (CPU) and hold the information, application software, and operating system software you're working with (RAM).

- *Storage devices*, which store information for use at a later time.
- *Telecommunications devices*, which send information to and from persons and locations.
- Connecting devices, which connect all your hardware devices to each other.

Key Terms and Concepts

Anti-spyware software, 294
Anti-virus software, 293
Application software, 286
Arithmetic logic unit (ALU), 302
ASCII (American Standard Code for Information Interchange), 294
Bar code scanner, 296
Binary digit (bit), 294
Biometric scanner, 297
Bluetooth, 304
Byte, 294
CD-R (compact disc—recordable), 300
CD-ROM (compact disc—read-only memory), 300
CD-RW (compact disc—rewritable), 300
Central processing unit (CPU), 286
Communications software, 291
CompactFlash (CF) card, 301
Control unit, 302
CPU cache, 302
CPU clock, 302
CPU (machine) cycle, 302
Crash-proof software, 293
CRT, 297
Database management system (DBMS), 291
Desktop computer, 288
Desktop publishing software, 291
Digital camera, 297
Digital still camera, 297
Digital video camera, 297
Disk optimization software, 294
Dot pitch, 298
DVD-R or DVD+R (DVD—recordable), 300
DVD-ROM, 300

DVD-RW or DVD+RW, 300
Expansion bus, 305
Expansion card (board), 304
Expansion slot, 304
Firewire port (IEEE 1394 or I-Link), 303
Flash memory card, 301
Flash memory device, 301
Flat-panel display, 297
Game controller, 296
Gamepad, 296
Gaming wheel, 296
Gas plasma display, 297
Gigabyte (GB or Gig), 299
Gigahertz (GHz), 302
Graphics software, 291
Hard disk, 293
Hardware, 284
Horizontal market software, 292
Hot swap, 303
Image scanner, 296
Information technology (IT), 284
Infrared, IR, or IrDA (infrared data association), 304
Inkjet printer, 299
Input device, 286
Joystick, 296
Keyboard, 295
Laser printer, 299
Linux, 293
Liquid crystal display (LCD) monitor, 297
Mac OS, 293
Mainframe computer (mainframe), 289
Megabyte (MB or M or Meg), 299
Memory stick media card, 301
Microphone, 297
Microsoft Windows XP Home, 293

Microsoft Windows XP Professional (Windows XP Pro), 293
Microsoft Windows Vista, 293
Minicomputer (mid-range computer), 289
Mobile CPU, 303
Mouse, 296
Multifunction printer, 299
MultiMediaCard (MMC), 301
Multitasking, 292
Notebook computer, 288
Open-source software, 293
Operating system software, 286
Optical character reader, 296
Optical mark reader, 296
Optical storage media, 300
Output device, 286
Parallel port, 304
PC card, 305
PC card slot, 305
Personal digital assistant (PDA), 287
Personal finance software, 291
Personal information management software (PIM), 291
Personal productivity software, 290
Pixels (picture elements), 298
Plotter, 299
Plug and Play, 303
Pointing device, 296
Pointing stick, 296
Port, 303
Presentation software, 291
PS/2 port, 302
Random access memory (RAM), 286
Resolution of a printer, 298
Resolution of a screen, 298
Scanner, 296
Secure Digital (SD) card, 301

Short-Answer Questions

1. What are the two categories of information technology (IT)?
2. What are the six categories of hardware?
3. What is the difference between application software and system software?
4. Dollar for dollar with comparable characteristics, which is faster and more powerful—a desktop computer or a notebook computer?
5. What is the difference between vertical and horizontal market software?
6. What do the terms *bit* and *byte* mean?
7. What is a gaming wheel and how does it differ from a gamepad?
8. What is the difference between a CRT and a flat-panel display?
9. How would you measure the size of a screen?
10. How is the resolution of a printer comparable to the resolution of a screen?
11. How does a CD differ from a floppy disk?
12. What are three types of flash memory cards?
13. What is a mobile CPU?
14. Which wireless standard is used by networks?

Assignments and Exercises

1. **COMPARING DIFFERENT TYPES OF COMPUTER SYSTEMS** Computers come in varying sizes and levels of power and performance. Use the Web to find out about computer system configurations. Do some comparison shopping for three types of computers: desktops, notebooks, and tablet PCs. Choose three Web sites that sell computer systems. From each of these sites, choose the most expensive and least expensive computer systems you can find for each of the three types of computers. Create a table for each of the three types of computers and compare them based on the following criteria:

   • Type and speed of CPU
   • Type and speed of RAM
   • Amount of CPU cache
   • System bus speed
   • Hard disk capacity and speed (revolutions per minute or rpm)
   • Number and type of ports.

2. **CUSTOMIZING A COMPUTER PURCHASE** One of the great things about the Web is the number of e-tailers offering a variety of products and services. One such e-tailer is Dell, which allows you to customize and buy a computer. Connect to Dell's site at www.dell.ca. Go to the portion of Dell's site that allows you to customize either a notebook or desktop computer. First, choose an already-prepared system and note its price and capability in terms of CPU speed, RAM size, monitor quality, and storage capacity. Now, customize that system to increase CPU speed, add more RAM, increase monitor size and quality, and add more storage capacity. What's the difference in price between the two? Which system is more in your price range? Which system has the speed and capacity you need?

3. **UNDERSTANDING THE COMPLEXITY OF SOFTWARE** Software instructions on how to open Microsoft Word or send information to a printer must be provided to a computer in great detail and with excruciating accuracy. Writing code to make the computer execute these instructions properly and in the right order is not a simple task. To understand how detailed you must be, pick a partner for this project and envision that you are standing in a kitchen. The task for one of you is to write down all the instructions that are necessary to make a peanut butter and jelly sandwich. When the instructions are complete, have the other person follow those instructions exactly. How successful was the second person in making the sandwich? Did your instructions include every single step? If not, what did you leave out?

4. **ADDING MEDIA TO A PRESENTATION** We certainly live in a "multimedia" society, in which it's often easy to present and receive information using a variety of (multi) media. Presentation tools such as Microsoft's PowerPoint can help you easily build presentations that include audio, animation, and video. And this may help you get a better grade in school. Using your preferred presentation software, document the steps necessary to add a short audio or video clip to a presentation. How does the representation of the clip appear on a slide? How can you initiate it? Does your presentation software include any clips that you can insert or do you have to record your own? Now, try recording a short audio clip. What steps must you perform?

5. **SMARTPHONE CAPABILITIES** The smartphone market is a ferocious, dynamic, and uncertain one. One of the uncertainties is what operating system for smartphones will become the dominant one (if any). For notebooks and desktops right now, you're pretty well limited to the Microsoft family unless you buy an Apple computer (in which case your operating system is Mac OS X) or want to venture into using Linux (which we wouldn't recommend for most people). Do some research on the more popular smartphones available today. What are the different operating systems? What different functionality do they offer? Are they compatible with each other? Take a guess—which one will come out on top?

Extended Learning Module B

Network Basics

STUDENT LEARNING OUTCOMES

LO1 Identify and describe the four basic concepts on which networks are built.

LO2 Describe what is needed to set up a small peer-to-peer network at home.

LO3 Describe the components used to build large business networks.

LO4 Define and compare local area networks (LANs), wide area networks (WANs), and metropolitan area networks (MANs).

LO5 Compare and contrast various Internet connection possibilities.

LO6 Compare and contrast types of communications media.

LO7 State the four principles of computer security and describe how different network security devices reflect those principles.

LO8 Describe client/server business networks from a business and physical point of view.

LO1

Introduction

When you're surfing the Web, accessing software on your school's server, sending e-mail, or letting your roommate use his or her computer to access the files on your computer, your computer is part of a network. A ***computer network*** (which we simply refer to as a network) is two or more computers connected so that they can communicate with each other and share information, software, peripheral devices, and/or processing power. Many networks have dozens, hundreds, or even thousands of computers.

BASIC PRINCIPLES OF NETWORKS

Networks come in all sizes, from two computers connected to share a printer, to the Internet, which is the largest network on the planet, joining millions of computers of all kinds all over the world. In between are business networks, which vary in size from a dozen or fewer computers to many thousands.

Some basic principles apply to all networks, large or small.

1. Each computer on a network must have a network interface (either as an expansion card or integrated into the motherboard, or even through software for a modem) that provides the entrance or doorway in that computer for information traffic to and from other computers.

2. A network usually has at least one connecting device (like a hub, switch, or home/broadband router) that ties the computers on the network together and acts as a switchboard for passing information.

3. There must be communications media like cables or radio waves connecting network hardware devices. The communications media transport information around the network between computers and the connecting device(s).

4. Each computer must have software that supports the movement of information in and out of the computer. This could be modem software and/or a network operating system.

First, we'll examine the smallest networks—a few computers connected in a home or dorm room—and then move on to larger business networks. We'll discuss network devices, LANs, WANs, MANs, and communications media. Finally, we'll describe network security and illustrate the client/server software model.

Home Networks

LO2

If you have a computer at home with cable or DSL Internet access, you may already be familiar with several network components. A typical home setup has

- An Ethernet network card in each computer, and/or a wireless Ethernet card in each laptop computer
- Network cables to transmit signals, or no cables if you're using wireless
- A DSL or cable line from your ISP, and a broadband or home router to pass messages and files back and forth.

Figure B.1
Typical Home Network

Coaxial Cable
or
Phone Line

Cable Modem
or
DSL Modem   Air

T1
1.5Mbps

ISP
Regional
or
National

Internet

Home Router /Firewall/
Wireless Access Point

Printer Cable

NETWORK CARDS IN EACH COMPUTER

First, each computer needs a network interface. A **network interface card (NIC)** is an expansion card for a desktop computer or a PC card for a notebook computer that connects your computer to a network and provides the doorway for information to flow in and out. The network interface card has a jack (or port) for a network cable that connects your computer to a network. Some computers have network interfaces built into their motherboards, referred to as integrated network interfaces.

An **Ethernet card** is the most common type of network interface card. It has a jack, usually an RJ-45 that looks like a telephone jack, only a little larger. You run a network cable from your Ethernet card to a hub or switch, or you can use a cable with different wiring called a *crossover cable* to plug straight into another computer or printer if you have only two devices to connect.

WIRED AND WIRELESS TRANSMISSION MEDIA

The most common transmission medium for a home network is Cat 5 cable, which is similar to phone cable (ordinary twisted-pair cable). **Cat 5**, or **Category 5**, cable is a better-constructed version of the phone twisted-pair cable. Each end of the Cat 5 cable has an RJ-45 connector. One end plugs into the Ethernet card in your computer and the other end into a network switch or broadband router (which we'll discuss in a moment).

If you'd like to access your home network wirelessly with your computer, you'll need another device on the network. A **wireless access point (WAP)** is a device that allows a computer to use radio waves to access a network. A wireless access point has a transmitter and a receiver for the bidirectional flow of information. It also has an antenna to capture the radio waves out of the air.

If your wireless access point is a separate device, it connects to a wired network with a cable to the hub or switch the same way wired computers do (see Figure B.1). Many new broadband routers (described in the next section) come with a wireless access point built in, so you may not need any extra cables.

Your notebook and any other device that accesses the network wirelessly must have a wireless adapter. Wireless adapters are available as PC Cards for notebook computers, or sometimes come built into notebooks. The wireless adapter incorporates a transmitter, receiver, and antenna, just like the wireless access point. If all your devices have wireless adapters, you can create a completely wireless network, in which the only cable used is the one connecting to the cable or DSL service.

HOME INTERNET SERVICE AND BROADBAND ROUTERS

A home network with no outside connections can still be used to share files and printers. But in order to access any services or sites outside your home, you need Internet service and equipment to connect it to your home network. Two common types of home Internet service are DSL, available through your telephone company, and cable Internet connection, available from your cable company.

A DSL or cable modem connection is designed to support only one computer, so if you want to connect more computers, you need another device, commonly called a ***broadband router*** or ***home router***. A broadband router or home router is a device to connect several computers together to share a DSL or cable Internet connection in a home or small office. It has one port to plug in your Internet connection, and usually has several ports to plug in home computers or printers.

Broadband routers are a rapidly changing part of the home network marketplace. Early models required an external DSL or cable modem, but some newer models include that built in. Early models had only one port for a computer and required a separate device to interconnect multiple computers. Many broadband routers today even include a built-in wireless access point.

NETWORK SOFTWARE

As always, when you have hardware you need software to make it work. For a small network, Windows will do fine (use version Windows 98 SE or newer) and must be installed on each network computer. To make the files on your computer available to the other computers on the network, you have to turn on the file-sharing option in Windows and indicate which drives, directories, or files to share. When you do this, the files on one computer will appear as additional folders on the other computer.

Network Components

LO3

Large networks are built in much the same way as small networks, using the same types of components. One difference is that home network devices often perform several different functions that are separated onto separate devices in large networks. Let's take a closer look at these different network components, and also look at how they're used in larger networks at corporations and universities.

HUBS

A ***hub*** is a device that connects computers and passes messages by repeating all network transmissions to all the other computers. Because of this, only one computer on a hub can transmit at a time. A network built on a hub is also called a *shared* network, because all the computers share the entire network and have to take turns using it.

Imagine a building that has several offices, a manufacturing floor, and no telephones—only a public-address system. When the ordering clerk needs to check inventory, he or she pushes the button on the microphone, and the PA system broadcasts his or her voice over all the speakers in the building. Someone on the shop floor counts the supplies, goes to his or her microphone, and his or her voice is transmitted over every speaker in the building.

This is how hubs work, and you can see several problems with this approach. Only one computer can transmit at a time, because every message is sent to every computer, tying up every communications line. For the same reason, information transmitted over hubs isn't private—you wouldn't want your boss discussing your raise request with the Human Resources department over a set of loudspeakers that are heard throughout the entire building.

Hubs are also inefficient for the computers on the network to use, because every time a message comes across, they have to interrupt what they're doing to determine whether the message pertains to them. And finally, hubs can have *collisions*, when two computers decide to start sending at the same time. This garbles both of their messages, and they would have to stop sending and try again later. In fact, the more computers connected to a hub, the more frequently collisions happen, sometimes to the point that very little actual data gets transmitted.

Historically, hubs were very inexpensive compared to other types of network devices. They've been largely replaced by switches, but in spite of their shortcomings, they're still used in some home and small offices and in older business networks.

SWITCHES

A *switch* is a network device that connects computers and passes messages by repeating each computer's transmissions only to the intended recipient, not to all the computers connected. Several computers can have different conversations at the same time through a switch, and such a network is called a *switched* network.

A switch works like a small business telephone system. When the marketing director needs to check on the status of a brochure, she calls the graphic artist to ask about it. At the same time, the shop supervisor can be giving a delivery date to the shipping manager. And the telephones all have speakers, so the operator can still get everyone's attention all at once if necessary.

You can see several advantages over hubs. Many data transmissions can happen at the same time, so a switch gives better support to a busy network. Information transmitted over switches is generally private, unless it's specifically meant to be broadcast to all the computers on the network. Likewise, computers on switches are more efficient than computers on hubs, because they have to process only messages actually meant for them, plus occasional broadcasts. And finally, switches don't have collisions, because different transmissions don't interfere with each other.

The advantages of switches are so great that switches have almost completely replaced hubs in new installations. Switches are the most commonly used components in networks today, and range in size from four- and eight-port models (connecting four or eight computers or printers) in home networks, to 24- and 48-port models (connecting 24 or 48 devices) common in business networks, to very large switches with hundreds of ports used to connect large call centres or run entire floors of office buildings.

ROUTERS

Routers connect separate networks of computers, unlike hubs and switches that connect individual computers. A *router* is a device that passes network traffic between smaller *subnetworks* (or *subnets*) of a larger network.

Think of a large business with a warehouse in one building, management offices in another, and manufacturing in yet another. Long ago, each building had its own telephone system with its own extensions—the warehouse had numbers 100–199; management had extensions 200–299; and manufacturing had numbers 400–699.

At first, the telephone systems weren't connected, and the telephones would call only within the same building. But then the business ran telephone cables from each building to a central phone system to tie them all together. Now the warehouse phone system "knows" that if it gets a call for any extension other than 100–199, it routes the call to the central system to direct to the proper building. And the central system knows to route any call starting with 1 to the warehouse phone system, any call starting with 2 to management, and any call starting with 4, 5, or 6 to manufacturing.

Routers work the same way. When a computer wants to send a message to another computer on a different subnet (like in a different building), it actually sends the message to the router on its subnet. The router then looks at the message's destination address—where the message is going—and figures out how to get it there. Medium-sized networks may have only one router at the centre, in which case it can always deliver messages directly. Larger networks may have many routers connected together, in which case messages may pass through several routers on their way from one computer to another (see Figure B.2). From each pictured hub/switch in Figure B.2 we can picture multiple connected PCs (network clients). Similarly from each router, there could be multiple connected hubs/switches. Thus the configuration pictured could support hundreds of client PCs. Figure B.2 simplifies this schema into single branches from multiple trees but there is nothing to preclude multiple branches from each.

It's important to understand that even though you have a router, you still need a hub or a switch to plug the computers into. Because large routers are expensive, it's not practical to build them with enough ports to directly support all the computers on a network. Home routers that run your Internet connection usually have both a router and a hub or switch built into the same box. But even though they may be labelled routers, remember that switching and routing are really two separate functions.

Hubs and switches can often be taken out of the box, hooked up to computers, and used without any configuration. But routers need to be programmed with information about which computer addresses are on which subnets, so installing a router generally requires someone with knowledge of network administration. Adding to or reconfiguring the network generally requires reconfiguring the router.

Figure B.2
Routers

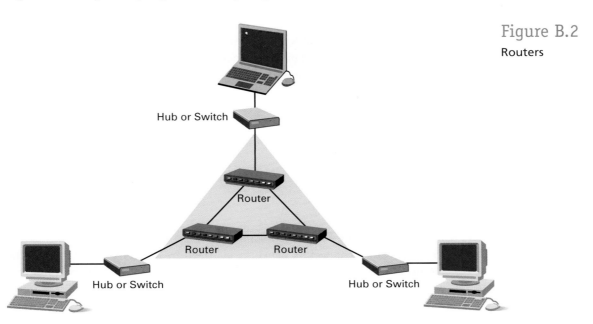

LO4

Classifying Networks by Distance

We've discussed the different devices used to build networks, and next we'll talk about ways networks are connected together. One way of describing large networks is in terms of the geographic area they cover. The size of a network can also impact whether an organization owns the communications lines or leases them from an independent provider.

LANS, WANS, AND MANS

A *local area network (LAN)* is a network that covers a building or buildings in close proximity, such as one campus of a university or corporation. The defining characteristic of a LAN isn't the actual size, but rather that the geographic area it serves is continuous. So the large network on a two-square mile campus of an aircraft manufacturer would be considered all one LAN, but the small networks of a daycare centre with two buildings a city block apart would be considered separate LANs.

A *wide area network (WAN)*, then, is a set of connected networks serving areas or buildings not in immediate proximity to each other. Another way to think of a WAN is as a network of networks. WANs generally use routers to connect LANs together, just as LANs can use routers to connect different subnets together.

Imagine a business that's large enough to have a production plant near a railroad and trucking depot, and separate corporate headquarters in a downtown office park. It has separate telephone systems on each site—in fact, the production plant has separate telephone systems in the warehouse, the manufacturing building, and the packing and shipping plant. But there are also telephone lines connecting the production plant and the headquarters, and the telephone systems know how to send calls from one to the other. In fact, except for using a different type of telephone line, sending calls from one site to the other is set up exactly the same as sending calls from one building to another.

WANs work the same way to connect networks (LANs) on different sites. WANs may connect networks at different locations around a city, or in different cities across a province, a country, or even the entire world.

Because WANs connect areas that are some distance apart, organizations don't usually own the communications lines that WANs run over. Instead, the lines are usually leased, often from a telephone or cable television company, or other commercial communications provider. Some types of WAN circuits are 56 kilobits per second (56 Kbps) leased lines; T1, running at 1.544 megabits per second (1.544 Mbps); and DS3, running at 44.736 Mbps. (T1 and DS3 are described in more detail in this module under Internet Connection Types.)

A metropolitan area network is a relatively recent term for a specific type of WAN. A *metropolitan area network* or *municipal area network (MAN)* is a set of connected networks all within the same city or metropolitan area, but not in immediate proximity to each other.

LO5

Internet

The word *internet*, with a lowercase i, comes from the word internetworking, and is a network of networks, connecting networks managed by different organizations. The largest internet of all is the *Internet* (with a capital *I*) which is a vast network of computers that connects millions of people all over the world.

To understand how computers send network communications across the Internet, consider the business described earlier that has telephone systems in separate buildings and on separate sites. When employees place calls to other buildings, each building's phone system directs the calls through a central system that knows how to route the calls to their destinations.

Besides the connections to the different buildings, the company also has connections to the public telephone system, so employees can make phone calls to place materials orders, and receive calls to accept orders for products. The company's outside telephone lines don't run directly to each building, but rather to the central system that knows how to route calls among all the buildings.

When employees at this company want to make outside calls, they dial a code starting with 9 (a digit different from the first digit of any of their local extensions), and the central system knows to route their calls over the outside lines to the public telephone system. And when customers call, they dial one of the company's telephone numbers, and the public telephone system sends the calls over the company's outside phone lines to the central system, which routes the calls to the correct departments. If customers don't know the right phone numbers to call, they can look up the company's name in a telephone directory and find the numbers they need.

This is much the way the Internet works. When a computer needs to send a message to another computer somewhere else on the Internet, it sends the message to its local router. If the router doesn't recognize the recipient as being attached to one of its LAN, MAN, or WAN connections, it sends the message over the connection to its Internet service provider (ISP). The ISP has bigger routers that learn paths to get to even more networks. Even if they're not connected directly to the receiving network, the ISP's routers send the message to another router, which may send the message to still *another*, and so forth, until the message finally gets to the receiving network. There, the receiving router will at last deliver the message to the computer at the ultimate destination or, if the destination cannot be found or does not reply, an appropriate message is returned to the sender.

Computers and routers refer to each other using network addresses, commonly Internet Protocol (IP) addresses, like *192.168.1.1*. This is similar to the way telephone systems use telephone numbers, like *+1 (414) 555-1212*, to route calls. You probably remember the phone numbers of some of your friends and family, but no one knows all the different phone numbers in the world.

Similarly, you don't have to remember the low-level network address of every computer you send network messages to. Instead, you can use names for computers, like www.mcgrawhill.ca, and your computer looks up the receiving computer's address for you in a directory called the Domain Name System, or DNS. Without DNS, the Internet would be virtually impossible to use.

BANDWIDTH

The most common measurement used when comparing different types of communications media is bandwidth, which refers to capacity. ***Bandwidth***, or capacity of the communications medium, is the amount of information that a communications medium can transfer in a given amount of time. You can think of bandwidth as the thickness of a drinking straw: the thicker the straw, the more quickly you can move the liquid from the cup into your mouth. In fact, in the communications industry, bandwidth is sometimes referenced informally as what size "pipe" you have between two locations.

Bandwidth is described as a quantity of data transferred in an amount of time, most commonly as a number of bits per second. A *bit* is the smallest possible amount of data, representing a single 1 or 0, and is abbreviated as the letter b. A *byte* is eight bits, and is used to store one letter or symbol of text, so the number of bits divided by eight gives you the approximate number of text characters. (See *Extended Learning Module A (Computer Hardware and Software)* for more information about bits, bytes, and characters.)

Bandwidth is sometimes represented in bits per second, abbreviated *bps*. Because a single bit is such a small quantity, and communications media speeds are constantly increasing, the bandwidth of different media is more likely to be represented in thousands of bits per second (kilobits per second—Kbps), millions of bits per second (megabits per second—Mbps), or billions of bits per second (gigabits per second—Gbps).

For example, if a particular communications medium has a bandwidth of 16 Mbps, then 16 million bits can be transferred in a single second. This module has about 70,000 characters in it, which is approximately 560,000 bits, so it could be transferred in less than half a second across a 16 Mbps channel.

INTERNET CONNECTION TYPES

Like the circuits used to make wide-area connections, Internet circuits aren't usually owned by individual companies. Instead, the circuits are supplied by an Internet service provider. Types of Internet circuits include

- Dial-up circuits, using an ordinary telephone line and a modem
- Digital Subscriber Line (DSL), which runs a high-speed connection over a telephone line without interfering with the voice telephone service
- Cable modem, which runs a high-speed connection over a cable television line without interfering with television reception
- Satellite modem, which runs a high-speed connection through your TV satellite without interfering with television reception
- Dedicated high-speed lines such as T1 and DS3, which run on separate circuits and are generally used for business connections.

DSL, cable modem, and dedicated lines are classified as broadband connections. A ***broadband*** connection is a high-bandwidth (high-capacity) telecommunications line capable of providing high-speed Internet service. The U.S. Federal Communications Commission defines broadband as a capacity of 200 Kbps (200 kilobits, or thousands of bits, per second) both upstream (to the Internet) and downstream (from the Internet). Other industry experts believe that broadband implies a speed of at least 750 Kbps.

Figure B.3

Digital and Analog Signals

DIAL-UP CONNECTIONS   To make a telephone or dial-up connection, you need a computer, a phone line, a modem, and, of course, an Internet service provider. Just as people use telephones to talk over telephone lines, a ***telephone modem (modem)*** is a device that connects a computer to your phone line so that you can access another computer or network. And as it is with people and telephones, the computer at the other end needs a modem, too.

A modem converts the digital signals from your computer into an analog form (by modulating the signal) that can be transmitted over a phone line, and then converts the analog signal back to digital signals (by demodulating the signal) for the computer at the receiving end of the transmission (see Figures B.3 and B.4). The word *modem* is a contraction of the modem's function of **mo**dulating outgoing and **dem**odulating incoming transmissions.

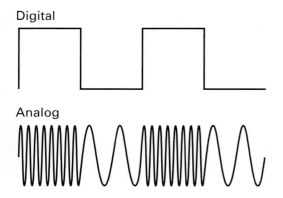

Digital

Analog

Digital	Digital-to-Analog Conversion	Analog	Analog-to-Digital Conversion	Digital
Digital uses discrete electronic pulses to represent information		Analog uses a continuous electronic stream to represent information		

Telephone Line

Figure B.4

The Role of a Telephone Modem

Modems are sometimes integrated into the motherboards of new computers, particularly laptops and notebooks. If your computer doesn't have a built-in modem, you can buy a card to plug into an expansion slot of your desktop, or a PC card for your notebook. A modem is the slowest type of Internet connection you can get. The fastest possible transmission speed using a modem over a normal telephone line is 56 Kbps, or about 56,000 bits per second.

DIGITAL SUBSCRIBER LINE   A *Digital Subscriber Line (DSL)* is a high-speed Internet connection using phone lines, which allows you to use your telephone for voice communication at the same time. There are different kinds of DSL systems, including ADSL or asymmetric DSL, SDSL or symmetric DSL, and HDSL or high-bit-rate DSL, that offer different combinations of speeds from the Internet provider to the customer and from the customer to the provider.

DSL works similarly to a traditional modem, modulating and demodulating the computer's digital signal into an analog form for transmission over the telephone line. However, unlike traditional modems, which modulate into audible sounds (the screech you hear if you pick up a telephone while your computer is connected to the Internet through its modem), DSL modems use frequencies too high for you to hear; this is how they can allow telephone conversations to happen at the same time. Even so, DSL modems sometimes cause clicks, pops, or buzzing on telephone lines, so many DSL connections use a splitter or filter to make sure that only voice calls go to the telephone and only DSL signals go to the DSL modem (see Figure B.5).

Figure B.5

DSL Internet Access

DSL Access Module

PHONE COMPANY

Splitter

YOUR HOME   DSL Modem

Because the high frequencies used by DSL are outside the range that telephone lines were originally designed to carry, only telephone lines that meet certain criteria can deliver DSL service. You need to live within about 5 kilometres of the phone company. (In larger cities, phone companies have branch offices that can connect you throughout the metropolitan area.) The phone company may have restrictions about the type of equipment it uses to provide your phone line—a relatively recent central system, and a direct line to your house without any signal-processing devices along the way. And the speed of your connection may depend on the distance to the phone company and the quality of your line. Speeds may vary from 144 Kbps to 1.5 Mbps, or even up to 6 Mbps for a business-class DSL connection.

DSL circuits—the physical cabling to your house—are always provided by the phone company. The phone company usually provides the Internet service that you use over the DSL connection, too. However, in some areas, you may be able to buy your Internet service from an independent service provider instead. To connect to a DSL circuit, you need the filter or splitter provided by the phone company (to keep noise out of your telephone conversations) and the DSL modem. The cable from the DSL modem connects to your computer in one of two ways: either to an Ethernet card, or to a USB port.

DSL service has three big advantages over dial-up connections:

1. DSL is much faster—up to 30 times faster than a traditional modem.
2. You can use the line for voice calls at the same time.
3. DSL can be an always-on connection—because it doesn't interfere with voice calls, you can leave it connected all the time, instead of having to wait for your modem to connect each time you want to use the Internet.

CABLE MODEM   If you have wired cable television, you know it comes into your home on a coaxial cable that connects to your television set. This same cable can connect you to the Internet, too. Both cable TV signals and your Internet connection travel from the cable company on one wire.

A splitter at your home splits the signals on the incoming cable, sending one part to the TV and the other to your cable modem. A ***cable modem*** is a device that uses your TV cable to deliver an Internet connection (see Figure B.6). The cable from the cable modem attaches to either an Ethernet card (an expansion card that connects your computer to a network) or to a USB port in your computer. Like DSL, cable modems provide an always-on connection. However, unlike DSL, cable modems don't use a phone line at all.

Figure B.6
Cable Internet Access

The speed of transmission with a cable modem is much faster than a phone modem, running at about 10 Mbps (10 million bits per second). While the speed of a DSL connection is guaranteed, though, the speed of a cable Internet connection depends on how many users are on-line, because the connection to the cable company is shared throughout a neighbourhood. If all your neighbours are surfing the Web with a cable connection at the same time you are, you may notice a reduction in your access speed.

SATELLITE MODEM   If you have wireless cable television, that is, if you receive your cable programming via a satellite, you can often also obtain your Internet service through the same provider. A *satellite modem* allows you to get Internet access from your satellite dish. In certain instances, you may not be receiving your cable programming via satellite, but you may be able to receive your Internet service via a dedicated satellite dish. It all depends on where you live and what types of services are offered for cable programming and Internet service.

The concept and implementation of receiving your Internet service from your satellite cable programming provider are the same as for using a cable modem. You would have a splitter with wiring for your cable programming going to your television and wiring for your Internet service going to your computer or a connecting device such as a hub or router.

T1, DS3, FRAME RELAY, AND ATM   A *T1* is a high-speed circuit typically used for business connections, running at speeds up to 1.544 Mbps (1.544 million bits per second), and a *DS3* is a high-speed business network circuit running at 44.736 Mbps. T1s were originally designed to carry 24 telephone conversations on phone companies' long-distance lines between cities. Later, equipment was developed to connect computer networks over T1 and DS3 lines. A T1's speed of 1.544 Mbps is about 24 times the speed of an analog telephone modem. A DS3 line is equivalent to 28 T1 lines bundled together, and its total speed of 44.736 Mbps is about 672 times the speed of an analog modem.

With some providers, a portion of the price of T1 and DS3 lines depends on the distance they run. Because of this distance-based pricing and their overall higher cost than some other connection types, T1 and DS3 lines are most commonly used for metropolitan area network connections—between two branches of a business within the same city. One advantage of T1 lines is that, because of their origin in voice telephony, it's possible to split their 24 channels between voice and computer communications, using the same T1 circuit to connect both telephone systems and computer networks at two offices.

Frame Relay and Asynchronous Transfer Mode (ATM) are services that the phone company or other telecommunications providers can set up over high-speed lines like T1s and DS3s to create "virtual circuits" connecting multiple offices. These virtual circuits can provide network connections from each office to every other one without having to run physical lines directly between each pair.

For example, if a business had four offices that all needed to be connected to each other, it would take six T1 lines to hook them all up (see Figure B.7). With Frame Relay or ATM, each office has a single T1 line going to the communications provider (for a total of four), and the provider makes it work the same as it would if the six direct lines actually existed.

Remember that the price of T1 and DS3 lines can depend on the distance they run. With Frame Relay or ATM, the T1 or DS3 lines actually run from each office to the telecommunications provider, rather than from office to office, so the distance and price can both be lower than when T1 lines are run directly from office to office.

Figure B.7

Frame Relay/ATM Virtual
Circuits

T1 Lines without Frame Relay/ATM

T1 Lines for Frame Relay/ATM

Virtual Circuits

Branch Office Connections without Frame Relay/ATM

Branch Office Connections Using Frame Relay/ATM

Because of this, Frame Relay and ATM are also used to connect many branch offices to a single main office. If a business had six branch offices, it would take six T1 lines to connect all the branches back to the headquarters (see Figure B.8)—each potentially running a great distance. With Frame Relay or ATM, the business can instead install a DS3 from its headquarters to the communications provider and a T1 to each branch office. The provider makes it work as it would if the headquarters had a direct connection to each branch office, and the business potentially spends less money than if it ran all of the T1 lines directly between offices. The company has a single DS3 connection at its headquarters instead of six separate T1 connections, simplifying circuit management and potentially increasing reliability.

VOICE OVER IP

We've just talked about different types of communications lines that can carry network information, but now it's time to turn that inside out. Several types of communications lines—telephone lines, T1s, and DS3s—were originally developed to transmit voice telephone calls, and later adapted to carry computer data. Voice over IP (VoIP) does the opposite—it's a means of transmitting a voice telephone call over a computer data network. *Voice over IP (VoIP)* allows you to send voice communications over the Internet and avoid the toll charges that you would normally receive from your long-distance carrier.

Why go to the trouble of sending voice calls over a computer network when they can already be sent directly through existing telephone systems and services? The answer has everything to do with overhead and with metered billing, meaning you pay an additional amount for each call and/or for each minute of the call.

Offices in most businesses and universities today have at least two different cables run to them—one that goes back to a telephone system, and one that goes back to a network hub or switch. On many telephone systems, the telephone extension number is assigned to a particular port on the central equipment. So when an employee moves from one office to another, making his or her telephone extension work in the new office involves either changing wiring or reprogramming the phone system.

In contrast, network addresses are assigned directly to the computer or other device, regardless of which switch or hub port it's connected to. So moving a VoIP extension from one office to another is as easy as unplugging the network phone from one location, carrying it to another, and plugging it back in. This reduction of maintenance effort can dramatically reduce the overhead of telephone system operation during office expansions and moves. Additionally, office technicians no longer have to maintain two sets of wiring to two different systems, which can also reduce overhead.

Network companies like Cisco Systems and telephone companies like Nortel are producing VoIP telephones that look like any other business phone, except they plug into a network jack instead of a telephone jack. Many even have an extra network jack on them for your PC, so your phone and computer can share a single connection back to the building's hub or switch.

Voice over IP is also starting to gain popularity with home users across the Internet. In most parts of the world, traditional telephone calls made from one local dialing area to another have metered billing, and some large U.S. cities even have metered billing for local calls.

Network access is often unmetered, though, particularly for broadband home access (cable modem and DSL). If you already have an Internet connection, you can use a network telephone or network phone software for your PC to make calls to other VoIP users anywhere in the world at no additional cost per call or per minute—for the moment, anyway. Telephone billing rates in Canada are set by the Canadian Radio-television and Telecommunications Commission (CRTC), a federal government agency that regulates rates by exercising tariffs. The CRTC has taken somewhat of a "wait-and-see" approach to tariffs on VoIP. The big telecom providers (Bell, Canada, Telus, and Aliant, along with provincially owned SaskTel) are required to file tariffs, whereas new-to-market and local providers, thus far, are not. It remains to be seen what will happen in this emerging area in Canada.[1]

Network Communications Media

LO6

The objective of networks and telecommunications is to move information from one place to another. This may be as simple as sending information to the office next door, or as far-reaching as sending a message to the other side of the world. Whatever the case, information must travel over some path from its source to its destination. *Communications media* are the paths, or physical channels, in a network over which information travels.

All communications are either wired or wireless. *Wired communications media* transmit information over a closed, connected path. *Wireless communications media* transmit information through the air. Forms of wired and wireless communications media include

Wired
- Twisted-Pair Cable
- Coaxial Cable
- Optical Fibre

Wireless
- Infrared
- Microwave
- Satellite

WIRED COMMUNICATIONS MEDIA

Wired communications media are those that tie devices together using cables of some kind. Twisted-pair, coaxial cable, and optical fibre are the types of cabling you'd find in computer networks.

TWISTED-PAIR   *Twisted-pair cable* is a bundle of copper wires used for transmitting voice or data communications and comes in several varieties. The Cat 5 that you already read about in connection with home networks earlier in this module is one type. Most of the world's phone system is twisted-pair and since it's already in place, it's an obvious choice for networks.

The simplest type of twisted-pair phone cabling (Cat 1) provides a slow, fairly reliable path for information at up to 64 Kbps, while a better type (Cat 3) provides up to 10 Mbps. However, distance, noise on the line, and interference tend to limit reliability for most types of twisted-pair cabling. For example, a crackle that changes a credit card number from 5244 0811 2643 741 to 5244 0810 2643 741 is more than a nuisance; in business it means retransmitting the information or applying a charge to the wrong person's credit card.

Cat 5 or Category 5 provides a much higher bandwidth than ordinary phone cable, meaning it carries more information in a given time period, at least for distances up to 100 metres. It's commonly used for connections at 100 Mbps, and an enhanced version called Category 5e is capable of carrying 1 Gbps. Cat 5 is relatively inexpensive and is fairly easy to install and maintain. Because of these advantages, it's the most widely used cabling for data transfer in today's LANs. Note, however, that twisted-pair of any kind is relatively easy to tap into and so it's not very secure. It's even possible to access the information by simply detecting the signals that "leak" out.

COAXIAL CABLE   An alternative to twisted-pair cable is *coaxial cable (coax)*, which is one central wire surrounded by insulation, a metallic shield, and a final case of insulating material. (Coax is the kind of cable that delivers cable television transmissions and also carries satellite TV from the dish to your house.) While coaxial cable was once the cable of choice for internal LAN wiring, it has been almost completely replaced by twisted-pair cable. Coaxial cable is capable of carrying at least 500 Mbps, or the equivalent of 15,000 voice calls, simultaneously. Because of its shielded construction, coaxial cable is much less susceptible to outside interference and information damage than twisted-pair cable. However, coaxial cable is generally more expensive than twisted-pair and is more difficult to install and maintain. Security is about the same with coaxial cable as with twisted-pair, except that the radiation, or leaking, of information is much less. Coax is commonly used for leased line private networks.

OPTICAL FIBRE   The fastest and most efficient medium for wired communication is *optical fibre*, which uses a very thin and flexible glass or plastic fibre through which pulses of light travel. Information transmission through optical fibre works rather like flashing code with a light through a hollow tube.

Optical fibre's advantages are size (one fibre has the diameter of a human hair); capacity (easily hundreds of Gbps, and getting faster every year); much greater security; and no leakage of information. It's very hard to "tap" into optical fibre. Attempts are pretty easy to detect since installing a tap disrupts service on the line—and that's noticeable. Optical fibre is also used for nearly all connections between different buildings, as it doesn't conduct electricity and so is immune to damage from lightning strikes. Optical fibre is more expensive than twisted-pair cable, however, and requires highly skilled technicians to install and maintain.

WIRELESS COMMUNICATIONS MEDIA

For many networks, wired communications media are simply not feasible, especially for telecommunication across rugged terrain, great distances, or when one or more parties may be in motion. For whatever reason, if wired communications media don't fit your needs, wireless may be the answer. Wireless communications radiate information into the air, either very narrowly beamed or in many directions like ripples from a pebble tossed into a pond. Since they radiate through the air, they don't require direct cable connections of any kind. Obviously, security is a big problem since the information is available to anyone in the radiation's path. However, wireless encryption methods are good, and getting better.

INFRARED AND BLUETOOTH FOR VERY SHORT DISTANCES   *Infrared* is the oldest type of wireless communication. Infrared uses red light to send and receive information. The light is invisible to humans, but snakes and some other animals can see it. Your TV remote control uses infrared. You can use infrared to connect handheld devices, such as pocket PCs, to peripheral devices such as printers. Wireless keyboards and mice usually connect to your PC with an infrared link. Infrared communication is totally line-of-sight, meaning that you can't have anything blocking the path of the signal, or it won't work. Infrared transmission has very limited bandwidth (typically 1 Mbps).

A relatively new and competing wireless technology is called **Bluetooth**. Named for a Viking king, Bluetooth is a standard for transmitting information in the form of short-range radio waves over distances of up to 30 feet and is used for purposes such as wirelessly connecting a cell phone or PDA to a computer. Virtually all digital devices, like keyboards, joysticks, printers, and so on, can be part of a Bluetooth system. Bluetooth is also adaptable for home appliances like refrigerators and microwave ovens.

OMNIDIRECTIONAL MICROWAVE (WIFI) FOR SHORT DISTANCES   Another method of short-distance wireless communications is omnidirectional (all directions) microwave transmission. **Microwave transmission** is a type of radio transmission. Microwaves occupy a portion of the electromagnetic spectrum between television signals and visible light. Microwave ovens use high-powered microwaves to heat food and can interfere with some types of microwave wireless transmissions.

The most common types of wireless networking used today—802.11b and 802.11g (known to most people as WiFi)—use microwave transmissions. **WiFi (wireless fidelity)** is a standard for transmitting information in the form of radio waves over distances up to about several kilometres. WiFi is actually a wireless industry alliance that provides testing and certification that 802.11 devices communicate with each other properly. IEEE 802.11b and 802.11g are two versions that run at 11 Mbps and 54 Mbps, respectively.

DIRECTIONAL MICROWAVE FOR MEDIUM DISTANCES   Microwaves may be transmitted very directionally with a parabolic dish antenna or can be radiated in a wide curved path for broader use. Microwave transmission is a line-of-sight medium. That is, the microwave signal cannot follow the curved surface of the earth. So to send the information over a distance of more than about 32 kilometres you'd have to use repeaters (see Figure B.9). A **repeater** is a device that receives a radio signal, strengthens it, and sends it on. (You've probably seen microwave towers—they're the tall towers with lots of little dishes on them that stand near an industrial complex.) Microwave signals have difficulty getting through walls or trees or other solid objects, so there must be a clear path from sender to receiver.

Figure B.9
Microwave

Satellite

Sending
Location

Receiving
Locations

SATELLITES FOR LONG DISTANCES   *Communications satellites* are microwave repeaters in space. They solve the problem of line-of-sight since the transmission shoots up into the sky in a straight line, bounces off, and shoots back down to earth again (see Figure B.10). Since satellites are so high, an array of them can cover essentially the whole earth (as the two dozen or so GPS satellites do). As with land-based repeaters, satellites receive information from one location and relay it to another. You'd usually use satellite communications to connect land-based networks in far-flung locations or to connect moving vehicles to each other or to the organizational network.

Satellite communications are cost-effective for moving large amounts of information, especially given a large number of receiving sites. For example, Walmart and other retailers place very small aperture terminal (VSAT) satellite dishes on the roofs of their stores. The VSATs allow individual stores to transmit information to the home office, and the home office, in turn, can transmit information to all the stores simultaneously. Satellite radio is another example of far-flung satellite transmission. If you have satellite radio in your car, you'll never be completely out of range of your favourite satellite radio station.

Network Security

LO7

Thinking about network security may call to mind images from movies of computer rooms criss-crossed by laser beams, voice and handprint recognition, security cameras, and CDs or DVDs full of top-secret blueprints. Or it may make you think of jumpsuit- wearing technicians clipping wires onto someone else's connection, greasy-haired teenagers illuminated only by the green glow of their computer monitors, or an investigator frantically trying to guess the criminal's password as the footsteps in the hallway get ever closer.

These images, although dramatic, don't give you much of an idea of the real threats to computer and network security and how to guard against them. In reality, connecting computers can make it easier to take advantage of existing security weaknesses—attacks can be performed from any distance away instead of only from within the same room—and introduces some new weaknesses.

PRINCIPLES OF COMPUTER SECURITY

The best way to understand network security is to look at the components of computer security, evaluate different threats in terms of these components, and then figure out how to reduce the effectiveness or damage of those threats. The basic principles of computer and network security are confidentiality, authenticity, integrity, and availability. Within the context of computer and network security:

- *Confidentiality* means that information can be obtained only by those authorized to access it. In even simpler terms, it means keeping secrets secret. Confidential information includes things like bank statements, business plans, credit card reports, and employee evaluations. Threats to confidentiality include network transmissions that can be captured or monitored by unauthorized individuals, passwords that are easily guessed, and even printouts left lying out in plain sight. In the world outside computers, confidentiality is protected by sealing envelopes and locking doors and file cabinets.

- *Authenticity* means that information really comes from the source it claims to come from. It's important to be sure of the authenticity of things like military orders, medical diagnoses, and buy/sell directions to your stockbroker. Threats to authenticity include fraudulent e-mail messages claiming to be from your bank (probably spoofing), Web sites registered at names that are common misspellings of popular sites, and Web browsers that can be manipulated into making it look as though you're at a different site than you really are. Nonelectronic authenticity is provided by signatures (although they can be forged), or by trusting only people you know personally.

- *Integrity* means that information has not been altered. This is closely related to authenticity. You would be concerned about the integrity of your bank balance, contents of your corporate Web site, medical prescriptions, and credit card charges. Threats to integrity include network transmissions that can be forged or taken over by unauthorized individuals and Web servers with flaws that allow their content to be replaced. Integrity is hard to guarantee in the physical world— how can you really be sure that no one has changed even a single word of your mortgage contract?—and is generally dependent on a certain degree of trust that's much harder to apply to electronic communications.

- *Availability* means simply that a service or resource is available when it's supposed to be. If a mail-order Web site is unavailable during the Christmas season, a retailer could lose millions of dollars in sales. If a corporate e-mail server is frequently unavailable, the company may lose some of the trust of its business partners. Threats to availability include unintentional network failures, poorly written server software that stops working when presented with unusual inputs, and deliberate attempts to send so much traffic to a company's network that legitimate communications are unable to get through. Noncomputer-related availability is provided by designing buildings with multiple exits in case one is blocked by fire, making photocopies of important documents, and installing electrical generators in hospitals to keep life-critical equipment operating if the city power fails.

FIREWALLS AND INTRUSION DETECTION SYSTEMS

Networks are designed to connect computers together and move information between them. But what if attackers are trying to break into your computers through your network connection? Just as a company may install card readers or hire a guard to admit only staff wearing employee badges, a *firewall* is software and/or hardware that protects a computer or network from intruders (see Figure B.11). As hardware, a firewall is a device that permits or denies network traffic based on security policy. Firewalls provide protection against threats to confidentiality, authenticity, and integrity by blocking traffic that doesn't look like legitimate access to networked computers.

Some firewalls make their policy decisions based entirely on network addresses. For example, if you have caller ID on your telephone, you may choose to answer calls only if they come from your friends or family. Likewise, a simple firewall can examine network traffic and permit only the traffic coming from a known source.

Other firewalls may permit traffic from an unknown source if it appears to be a response to a request that was made by a computer on the protected network. For example, if you call a friend at the office but she's in a meeting, you might leave a message for her to call you back. When she does, you may recognize the phone number of her office as a number you just called and answer the call, even though the office number isn't on the list of phone numbers you'd normally answer.

Even more advanced firewalls make decisions based on the content of the network traffic. Thinking back to the company with a security guard in the lobby, the guard may allow a delivery person to enter the building if he's carrying envelopes or pizza, but not if he's carrying dynamite or bottles of acid. Of course, acid may be a regular delivery item in a chemical plant; not every company will want the same firewall policies.

While a firewall typically has a predefined policy about the network traffic it will allow, an ***intrusion detection system (IDS)*** is a device that watches network traffic for intrusion attempts and reports them. An ***intrusion prevention system (IPS)*** is a type of IDS that also takes action against intrusion attempts, for example, by creating new policies in a firewall to block the source of the attack. Intrusion detection and prevention systems work by having information about many different types of network attacks and matching the current network traffic against their lists of attack characteristics. When they sense an attack in progress, they can e-mail or page network administrators about the attack, so they can take appropriate action.

Figure B.11

Firewall, Intrusion Detection System, and Virtual Private Network

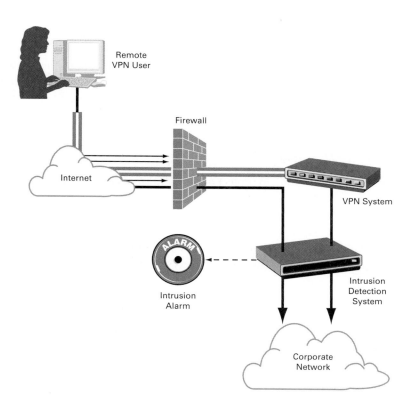

Denial-of-service attacks simply interfere with network availability. A ***denial-of-service (DoS)*** attack floods a server or network with so many requests for service that it slows down or crashes. (See *Extended Learning Module C [Computer Crime and Digital Forensics]*, for more details about denial-of-service attacks.) Imagine if someone called every pizza delivery service in town and ordered 20 pizzas delivered to your office. Eventually you'd manage to sort out the confusion and you wouldn't have to pay for the pizzas, but meanwhile you'd be too busy dealing with the situation to get any work done.

Firewalls and intrusion detection and prevention systems can protect availability by preventing or reducing the effect of denial-of-service attacks. Some denial-of-service attacks use network capabilities that are technically permissible, but are almost never seen in legitimate network traffic; these attacks are easy to foil by denying those types of traffic. Other denial-of-service attacks send completely legitimate but useless traffic. Blocking those attacks involves recognizing an increase in network traffic beyond normal levels, determining the source or sources, and then blocking even legitimate-appearing traffic from those locations.

Most home broadband devices—for DSL and cable modem Internet connections—include a simple firewall. Home networking manufacturers have been packing more and more capabilities into their products, and even though the devices may be marketed as routers or firewalls, they generally contain a router, a firewall, and a switch or hub to connect multiple home computers. Some even include the DSL or cable modem, and some have a wireless access point, all in a device not much larger than a paperback book.

ENCRYPTED COMMUNICATIONS: SSL AND VIRTUAL PRIVATE NETWORKS

Earlier, we talked about types of network devices on which communications can be overheard—hubs and wireless access points. This is a threat to confidentiality—unauthorized individuals could be watching your communications. So if you're using wireless access, or are in a location where you don't know whether you're connected to a hub or a switch—or simply somewhere that you don't know who has access to the communications lines and equipment between you and your network destination—what can you do to protect the privacy of your communications?

The solution is encrypted communication. ***Encryption*** scrambles the contents of a file so that you can't read it without having the right decryption key. It means scrambling your communication in such a way that only the intended recipient can unscramble it. If you wanted to send the message, "Reschedule the grand opening for April 10," the encrypted version might look like

V'9:P)9@A1,||>[D:J_sepnvIf.Xj2FAs_[Dhud+'.

One way of using encryption to protect network transmissions is called Secure Sockets Layer (SSL), or somewhat less commonly, by the name of its successor, Transfer Layer Security (TLS). SSL is a security technology that encrypts each network conversation—between one network client and one server—individually. Web traffic using SSL is called https, instead of just http. When you browse to a secure Web site and see the padlock icon, it's telling you that your browser is using SSL/TLS to encrypt your communications with the Web server. We cover more on SSL and other types of security technologies with respect to electronic commerce in Chapter 5.

In contrast, a ***virtual private network (VPN)*** uses encryption to protect the confidentiality of all network transmissions between two endpoints. Typically, one endpoint is a large office or headquarters, and the other endpoint may be a single computer, or it may be another office. All network communications between the two locations are routed through the VPN to be encrypted. This makes it look as though they have a dedicated network connection between them, even though they may really be communicating over public network links, hence the name, virtual private network.

OTHER SECURITY THREATS: MALWARE

You've probably heard of computer worms, viruses, and spyware, collectively known as malware. *Malware* is a contraction of malicious software, and refers to software designed to harm your computer or computer security. Malware existed even before most computers were connected to networks, but increased connectivity between computers has made it dramatically easier for malware to transfer to new victims.

A *virus* is software that is written with malicious intent to cause annoyance or damage. The virus software is activated unintentionally by the computer user. A *worm* is a type of virus that replicates and spreads itself, not just from file to file, but from computer to computer via e-mail and other Internet traffic. Viruses spread by tricking users into running them, for instance, by pretending to be an interesting program or e-mail message; worms spread by taking advantage of errors or weaknesses in computer programs. Viruses and worms most commonly threaten availability, by damaging or removing files, or by tying up a computer doing so much unauthorized work that it can't get its real job done.

Viruses and worms can be countered by running anti-virus software. Anti-virus software works very similarly to the intrusion detection systems described earlier. It has a long list of characteristics of known worms and viruses, and when it sees files being transferred or software running on the computer that has those characteristics, it alerts the user and often "quarantines" the file to part of the hard drive where it can't do any harm. Some anti-virus software can remove the malicious instructions from computer files so that they are still useful once they're disinfected.

Anti-virus software can be run at different places in the network. Some viruses are transferred from computer to computer in e-mail messages, and anti-virus software on the e-mail server will help protect against them. It's very important to run anti-virus software on every PC, to protect against worms and viruses trying to attack the computer directly. And some companies have servers where customers can upload purchase orders or problem reports; they may run anti-virus software on those servers to screen all incoming files.

Spyware is a more recent type of malware than viruses and worms. Spyware (also called sneakware or stealthware) is malicious software that collects information about you and your computer, and reports it to someone else without your permission. Therefore, spyware is a threat to confidentiality. Spyware most often gets installed on your computer secretly along with a piece of software you knew you were getting; for example, some peer-to-peer file sharing programs are notorious for including spyware.

The best defence against spyware is to install software only from trustworthy sources, but that can be hard to determine. Anti-spyware software is available that works just like anti-virus software, recognizing patterns of known spyware and removing them from your computer. Two popular anti-spyware programs are Ad-Aware (www.lavasoftusa. com) and Spybot Search & Destroy (www.safer-networking.org).

Another category of malware is servers and bots. Sometimes after breaking into a computer, attackers will set up unauthorized servers. These servers are often used to distribute illegal copies of movies, music, and software, or may even be used to distribute kits for breaking into other computers.

In the context of malware, bots are programs designed to be controlled by an attacker to perform unauthorized work over a period of time. Some bots are used to send spam, making it look like it's coming from the victim's computer instead of from the attacker's. Other bots try to break into computers or perform denial-of-service (DoS) attacks against other networks or systems.

Bots and unauthorized servers can sometimes be detected by anti-virus or anti-spyware software—but they may be indistinguishable from legitimate servers. They can also sometimes be discovered by network intrusion detection systems. Sometimes they're even discovered by network administrators, noticing an unusual amount of network traffic coming from a single computer.

LO8

The Client/Server Software Model

So far, we've talked about how computers are connected together on networks without discussing the roles of the computers themselves. In the peer-to-peer home networks described at the beginning of the chapter, the computers were all equal. Each one had its own files and devices, which it could share with the other computers. But unless you're a business with very few computers, you'd probably use a client/server network instead of a peer-to-peer network.

A *client/server network* is a network in which one or more computers are servers and provide services to the other computers, which are called clients. The server or servers have hardware, software, and/or information that the client computers can access. Servers are usually powerful computers with large storage systems. Depending on the network, the server could be a high-end PC or a minicomputer. Large companies often have several servers, each of which may provide services to different parts of the company. It's usually cheaper and more efficient to have software on a server where everyone can access it:

- A network license allowing a fixed number of people or everyone on the network to use a software package is usually cheaper than buying separate copies of software for each computer.
- It's easier to update one server copy of software than to update hundreds or even thousands of separate copies.
- Control and security of software and information are easier if they're on the server.

The parts of the network that connect the servers are usually built with stricter specifications than the parts that connect the clients. The servers' network equipment may have

- Higher-bandwidth connections, to carry the traffic from many clients across the company accessing the servers simultaneously
- Higher-powered network processors, to route the greater traffic loads
- Duplicate connections to the rest of the network, to provide continued service if one connection is accidentally or maliciously cut
- Uninterruptible power supplies, which use batteries to keep the network running even when the power fails.

CLIENT/SERVER—A BUSINESS VIEW

The term *client/server* network can mean a network structure, that is, one or more computers providing services to other computers. However, client/server is a term that also describes a business model. As a business model, client/server describes distributed processing. That is, it describes where processing takes place. Different companies have different processing needs. For example, if your school has an on-line system on which you can check your grades, you'll probably find that you can't change grades at your end—access to that kind of processing is severely restricted. On the other hand, a bank employee would need to be able to process a loan at his or her computer.

You can use one of five basic client/server implementation models. Which one you use depends on your business environment and where you want processing implemented. Client/server networks differ according to three factors:

1. Where the processing for the presentation of information occurs, that is, where the information that you see on the screen or printout is formatted, and the editing of information as you enter it.

2. Where the processing of logic or business rules occurs. Logic deals with the processing that the software implements. For example, in a payroll application, the logic would dictate how to handle overtime, sick leave, and vacation time.

3. Where the data management component (DBMS) and information (database) are located. Or, put another way, how the information in the database is stored and retrieved.

Here's an example of the concept. Say you have a data warehouse with information on sales over the past five years. Your client workstation gets its information from your company's OLTP (online transaction processing) server or servers. Software on the servers extracts the information you need and transfers it to your client workstation. Your client workstation then builds the data warehouse according to your requirements and you can use your data warehouse for the OLAP (online analytical processing) you need.

In this example, you see a separation of duties to suit particular business needs. The servers process companywide OLTP software on transaction information and copy to your workstation the information you want to have. Your client computer has, and processes, only the information that you need. This is called a distributed data management

Figure B.12

Model 5: A Personal Data Warehouse in a Client/Server Implementation model where the server's only duty is to help with data management; the client does everything else (see Figure B.12). This is one way of assigning the processing, logic, and data management. In the set of models that you'll see next, this is Model 5.

Each of the five business client/server models that follows has a different way of parcelling out the three tasks of presentation processing, logic processing, and data management.

CLIENT/SERVER MODEL 1: DISTRIBUTED PRESENTATION   In this first model, the server handles almost all functions, including a major portion of the presentation. The only processing that the client does is to help with formatting the information you see on the screen or printout.

CLIENT/SERVER MODEL 2: REMOTE PRESENTATION   In the second model, the client handles all presentation functions. The processing of business rules happens on the server, as does data management.

CLIENT/SERVER MODEL 3: DISTRIBUTED LOGIC   In this model, the server handles all data management and the client handles all presentation formatting, but the logic processing is shared between the server and the client.

CLIENT/SERVER MODEL 4: REMOTE DATA MANAGEMENT   In the fourth model, duties are fully separated again. The server handles data management only, and the client processes business rules and formats the presentation of results.

CLIENT/SERVER MODEL 5: DISTRIBUTED DATA MANAGEMENT   In this final model, the client handles all presentation formatting and business rule processing, and both the server and client share data management duties.

Which model you choose depends on the organization of your business and where you want processing to occur. We have already looked at Model 5, so now let's examine a more complicated case—Model 3, distributed logic.

CLIENT/SERVER IMPLEMENTATION: MODEL 3   In model 3 (distributed logic) the server handles the entire data management function, the client handles the entire presentation function, and server and client share in the processing or application of business rules (see Figure B.13).

Suppose you're the manager of the manufacturing division of an organization and need to give pay raises to each of your employees. You use the following divisional and organizational rules for determining pay raises.

Divisional Rules

1. Each manufacturing employee begins with a base raise of $2,500.
2. No manufacturing employee can receive less than a $2,000 raise.
3. If loss of time because of injury is longer than three days, then deduct $500 from the pay raise.
4. If the employee worked fewer than five days of overtime, then deduct $500 from the pay raise.

Organizational Rules

1. No employee with fewer than five years of experience can receive a pay raise that exceeds $2,500.
2. Each employee's pay raise must be within 20 percent of last year's raise.
3. Each employee who has taken three or more business-related trips in the last year gets an extra $500 raise.

The following process would then determine the exact pay raise for each employee.

1. You would request information for the employee.
2. Your client workstation would send that request to the server.
3. The server would retrieve the employee information from the employee database.
4. The server would return the employee information to your client workstation.
5. Your client workstation would execute the divisional manufacturing business rules (or logic) that apply to pay raises for manufacturing employees.
6. Your client workstation would format and present the information pertaining to the employee and the appropriate pay raise.
7. You would submit the proposed pay raise for processing.
8. Your client workstation would send that information to the server.
9. The server would execute the organizational business rules or logic relating to pay raises for all employees.
10. The server would return the employee's pay raise (modified according to the organizational business rules) to your work station.
11. Your client workstation would format and present the modified pay raise.
12. You would submit the finalized pay raise for final processing.
13. Your client workstation would send that information to the server.
14. The server would update the employee database to reflect the employee's pay raise.

In this example the server was responsible for data management (retrieving and updating employee information) and executing the business rules or logic that apply to all employees for pay raises. Your client workstation is responsible for editing your entry of information, formatting the presentation of information to you, and executing the business rules or logic that apply to pay raises for manufacturing employees.

When you take the process of distributed logic apart as we did in this example, it seems very complex and tedious. And if you're writing the software to do it, it is. However, as a knowledge worker, the process is completely transparent, meaning that you don't know (or care) how data management, logic, and presentation are handled.

From a management point of view, client/server is a very tidy, organized, and flexible way to make information that all managers need available to them, while keeping information and processing that individual departments need local to the appropriate office.

CLIENT SIDE

SERVER SIDE

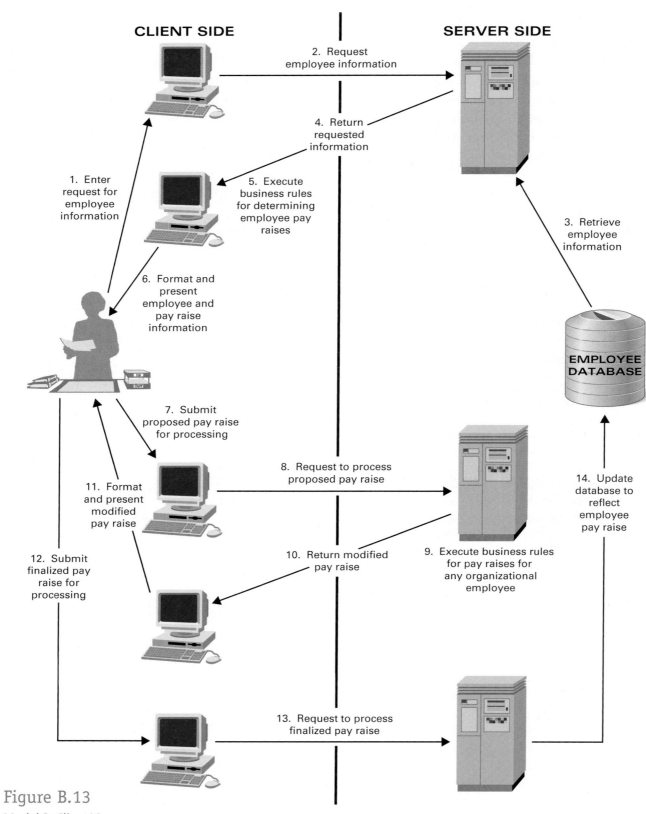

2. Request employee information

4. Return requested information

5. Execute business rules for determining employee pay raises

1. Enter request for employee information

6. Format and present employee and pay raise information

3. Retrieve employee information

EMPLOYEE DATABASE

7. Submit proposed pay raise for processing

11. Format and present modified pay raise

8. Request to process proposed pay raise

12. Submit finalized pay raise for processing

10. Return modified pay raise

9. Execute business rules for pay raises for any organizational employee

14. Update database to reflect employee pay raise

13. Request to process finalized pay raise

Figure B.13

Model 3: Client/Server Implementation for Employee Pay Raises

Summary: STUDENT LEARNING OUTCOMES *REVISITED*

LO1 Identify and describe the four basic concepts on which networks are built. There are four basic concepts on which almost all networks are built. They are

- *Network interface cards (NICs)* in each computer
- A connecting device like a *hub*, *switch*, or *home/broadband router*
- At least one communications medium
- Network operating system software.

LO2 Describe what is needed to set up a small peer-to-peer network at home. To set up a peer-to-peer network at home, you'd need

- *Ethernet cards* (as the NICs) in each computer
- A home/broadband router
- *Cat 5* cables
- A network operating system, like Windows.

LO3 Describe the components used to build large business networks. Large business networks are built using

- Network interfaces in each computer
- *Hubs* or *switches*, to connect the computers together into subnetworks
- *Routers*, to connect the subnetworks together.

LO4 Define and compare local area networks (LANs), wide area networks (WANs), and metropolitan area networks (MANs). A *local area network (LAN)* covers a geographically contiguous area. A *wide area network (WAN)* is a set of connected networks serving areas not in immediate proximity. A *metropolitan area network (MAN)* is a set of connected networks all within the same city or metropolitan area, but not geographically continuous.

LO5 Compare and contrast the various Internet connection possibilities. There are five ways described in this book to connect a computer or network to the Internet. They are

- Phone line and *modem*, which uses a phone line and prevents using the same line for voice communication at the same time. It's the slowest type of connection.

- Phone line and *Digital Subscriber Line (DSL)*, which, although it uses the phone line, does not prevent simultaneous voice communication. A DSL connection is a *broadband* connection.
- Cable TV line and *cable modem*, which brings Internet access in with your cable modem and doesn't use the phone line at all. It's also broadband.
- Cable programming via a satellite and *satellite modem*, which supports both cable television programming and Internet access.
- *T1*, a high-speed business circuit running at 1.544 Mbps, or *DS3*, a very-high-speed business circuit running at 44.736 Mbps.

LO6 Compare and contrast the types of communications media. *Communications media* are the paths, or physical channels, over which information travels in a network. There are two options: wired and wireless. Wired communications media include *twisted-pair cable*, *coaxial cable*, and *optical fibre*. Of these, optical fibre is the fastest and the most secure. Wireless communications media include *infrared*, *Bluetooth*, *WiFi*, *microwave*, and satellite. Infrared and Bluetooth are for very short distances only, Wi-Fi is for short distances, microwave has short and medium distance versions, and satellite is for long distance.

LO7 State the four principles of computer security and describe how different network security devices reflect those principles. The four principles of computer security are

- *Confidentiality*, meaning that information can be obtained only by those authorized to access it
- *Authenticity*, meaning that information really comes from the source it claims to come from
- *Integrity*, meaning that information hasn't been altered
- *Availability*, meaning that a service or resource is available when it's supposed to be.

Firewalls protect confidentiality, authenticity, and integrity by blocking traffic that doesn't look like legitimate access to networked computers. *Intrusion detection systems (IDSs)* protect all types of computer security by watching for network intrusion attempts and reporting them; intrusion prevention systems (IPSs) take action to block them. *Encryption methods*, including SSL and *virtual private networks (VPNs)*, protect confidentiality by scrambling your communication in such a way that only the intended recipient can unscramble it.

LO8 Describe client/server business networks from a business and physical point of view. A *client/server network* is a network in which one or more computers are servers and provide services to the other computers, which are called clients.

Business View: There are five different configurations based on three factors:

- Where the processing for the presentation of information occurs
- Where the processing of logic or business rules occurs
- Where the data management component (DBMS) and information (database) are located.

Physical View: The concepts on which larger networks are based are the same as those on which small networks are built. However, the network equipment for the servers may have higher-bandwidth connections and more powerful processors, duplicate connections to the rest of the network, and uninterruptible power supplies to keep the servers available during power failures.

Key Terms and Concepts

Authenticity, 328
Availability, 328
Bandwidth, 317
Bluetooth, 326
Broadband, 318
Broadband router (home router), 313
Cable modem, 320
Cat 5 (Category 5), 312
Client/server network, 332
Coaxial cable (coax), 325
Communications media, 324
Communications satellite, 327
Computer network, 310
Confidentiality, 328
Denial-of-service (DoS) attack, 330
Digital Subscriber Line (DSL), 319
DS3, 321

Encryption, 330
Ethernet card, 312
Firewall, 328
Hub, 313
Infrared, 326
Integrity, 328
Internet, 316
Intrusion detection system (IDS), 329
Intrusion prevention system (IPS), 329
Local area network (LAN), 316
Malware, 331
Metropolitan area network (municipal area network, MAN), 316
Microwave transmission, 326
Network interface card (NIC), 312
Optical fibre, 325

Repeater, 326
Router, 314
Satellite modem, 321
Spyware, 331
Switch, 314
T1, 321
Telephone modem, 318
Twisted-pair cable, 325
Virtual private network (VPN), 330
Virus, 331
Voice over IP (VoIP), 323
Wide area network (WAN), 316
WiFi (wireless fidelity), 326
Wired communications media, 324
Wireless access point (WAP), 312
Wireless communications media, 324
Worm, 321

Short-Answer Questions

1. How is a peer-to-peer network different from a client/server network?
2. What is an Ethernet card?
3. What does a network switch do?
4. What is bandwidth?
5. What do you need to have a dial-up connection to the Internet?
6. How is a DSL Internet connection different from a telephone modem connection?
7. What impact does Frame Relay have on a metropolitan area network?
8. What is Cat 5 cable used for?
9. What is Bluetooth?
10. What does WiFi do?
11. How does a VPN protect confidentiality?
12. How is client/server model 1 different from client/server model 2?

Assignments and Exercises

1. **WHAT ARE THE INTERNET ACCESS OPTIONS IN YOUR AREA?** Write a report on what sort of Internet connections are available close to you. How many ISPs offer telephone modem access? Is DSL available to you? Is it available to anyone in your area? Does your cable company offer a cable modem? If your school has residence halls, does it offer network connections? Compare each available service on price, connection speed, and extras like a help line, list of supported computers and operating systems, and people who will come out to your home and help you if you're having difficulties. What type of Internet connection do you currently use? Do you plan to upgrade in the future? If so, to what type of connection? If not, why not?

2. **INVESTIGATE BUILDING YOUR OWN HOME NETWORK** Build your own home network on paper. Assume you have the computers already and just need to link them together. Find prices for switches and routers on the Web. Also research Ethernet cards and cables. If you were to get a high-speed Internet connection like DSL or cable modem, how much would it cost? Can you buy your own, or would you have to rent the modem from the phone or cable company?

3. **DEMONSTRATE THE IMPACT OF WIRELESS TECHNOLOGY** How many devices do you own or use that transmit signals (not just computer data) wirelessly? Think of as many as you can, and make a list showing the different types of signalling used by each device. Don't forget that some devices use multiple wireless technologies, like cell phones with both cellular signals for voice transmissions and Bluetooth for syncing their address books. Hint: Don't forget cordless phones, TV and stereo remotes, radios, and portable computers and PDAs with infrared capability (look for a small, glossy black window somewhere on the edge of the case). Can any of your devices communicate with each other?

4. **INVESTIGATE SATELLITE RADIO** Do a little surfing on the Web to see how many satellite radio providers you can find.

5. **CONSIDER THE IMPORTANCE OF NETWORK SECURITY** Write a report about the importance of computer and network security in your daily life, in terms of the four principles of computer security. If you have a job in addition to being a student, write about computer security in your workplace. If you don't work outside the classroom, write about how computer security affects you at school and in your personal life. You may be surprised at how many things you do depend on some aspect of secure computer records and communications, like banking, grades, e-mail, timesheets, library and movie rental records, and many more.

6. **FIND OUT ABOUT FIREWALLS** Go to the Web and find out about software and hardware that protect your computer and home network, respectively.

   If you have only one computer connected to the Internet, then a software firewall like Zone Alarm will most likely be enough protection from intruders. Find three different firewall software packages on the Web. Start looking at sites that sell anti-virus software. Compare the firewall software on price and features. Some sites to try are

   - Symantec at www.symantec.com
   - Trend Micro at www.trendmicro.com
   - McAfee at www.mcafee.com
   - The Virus List (a virus encyclopedia) at www.viruslist.com.

   If you have a home network, look into hardware firewall options. How many different hardware firewalls can you find on the Web site of your favourite electronics retailer? (Hint: Look in the feature lists of home routers and broadband routers, even if they don't have the word *firewall* in their name.)

Extended Learning Module C

Computer Crime and Digital Forensics

STUDENT LEARNING OUTCOMES

LO1 Define computer crime and list types of computer crime that can be perpetrated from inside and from outside an organization.

LO2 Identify the seven types of hacker and explain what motivates each group.

LO3 Define digital forensics and describe the two phases of a forensic investigation.

LO4 Describe what is meant by anti-forensics and give an example of each of the three types.

LO5 Describe two ways in which businesses use digital forensics.

Introduction

Computers play a big part in crime; they are involved as targets and as weapons or tools. A computer or network is a target when someone wants to bring it down or make it malfunction, as in a denial-of-service attack or a computer virus infection. Crimes that use a computer as a weapon or tool include acts such as changing computer records to commit embezzlement, breaking into a computer system to damage information, and stealing customer lists. See Figure C.1 for examples of computer-related offences in which computers are used as weapons/tools and targets of crime.

Some crimes are clearly what we call computer crimes, like Web defacing, denial-of-service attacks, e-mail scams, and so on. But as is the case in so many parts of our modern lives, computers are so integrated in crime that it's hard to separate the two.

A member of a crime syndicate was sprayed with drive-by gunfire and was severely wounded. Believing that his services were no longer wanted by his crime gang, he switched sides, agreeing to become a witness for the state. The police secured an isolated intensive care unit room for him and guarded it heavily, allowing access only to medical staff and those on a very short list of visitors. Because the man was so badly wounded, there was a danger of infection, and since he was allergic to penicillin, the doctor prescribed a synthetic alternative.

One evening, a nurse wheeling a medicine cart went through the police cordon and into the man's room. He injected the patient with penicillin, and the patient died shortly thereafter. An investigation started immediately and the nurse was potentially in big

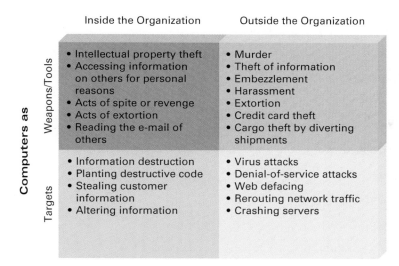

Figure C.1

Examples of Computer Crimes That Organizations Need to Defend Against

trouble. He insisted that when he looked at the patient's chart on the computer, there was an order there for penicillin. Subsequent examination of the computer records showed no such order. Eventually, it occurred to someone that perhaps a digital forensic expert should look at the computer angle more closely. Having retrieved the backup tapes (nightly backups are standard operating procedure in most places), the expert found evidence that exonerated the nurse. The patient chart had been changed in the computer to indicate penicillin and later changed back to its original form. Examination further revealed the point and time of access, and indicated that the medical record was changed by someone outside the hospital. A hacker had electronically slipped into the hospital's network unnoticed, made the change, and slipped out again—twice.

Most crimes involving a computer are not as lethal as murder, but that doesn't mean they're insignificant. Organizations want to make sure their networks' defences are strong and can prevent their computers from being used for unlawful or unethical acts. That's why so much time, money, and effort goes into security, as we discussed in Chapter 8.

This module focuses on the sort of threats that computer systems are susceptible to and the examination of electronic evidence. The latter is called *digital (or computer) forensics*.

Computer Crime

LO1

For our purposes, a **computer crime** is a crime in which a computer, or computers, play a significant part. See Figure C.2 for a list of crimes in which computers, although perhaps not essential, usually play a large part.

In this section we'll focus on crime from the organization's viewpoint. First, we'll examine some of the more high-profile types of computer crime committed against organizations that are perpetrated from the outside. Then we'll discuss the varying motivations of people who commit these acts. Last, we'll briefly discuss computer crime within the organization.

OUTSIDE THE ORGANIZATION

Computer security is a big issue in business. The concern is about people stealing electronic information, accessing systems without authorization, introducing viruses into networks, and defacing Web sites, to name just a few of the dangers. The Computer Security Institute (CSI) and the FBI's Computer Intrusion Squad have conducted studies

Figure C.2

Crimes in Which
Computers Usually
Play a Part

- Illegal gambling

- Forgery

- Money laundering

- Child pornography

- Hate message propagation

- Electronic stalking

- Racketeering

- Fencing stolen goods

- Loan sharking

- Drug trafficking

- Union infiltration

every year since 1996 to assess the extent of the security problem nationwide. In their report based on the data for 2006, virus and worm attacks continued to be the cause of the largest cost financially. That problem, together with unauthorized access; the theft of hardware like laptops, mobile phones, and PDAs; and the theft of information, accounted for about three-quarters of financial losses.

The good news was that the financial loss in 2006 decreased substantially compared to previous years, as did the average loss per company. Another good sign was that unauthorized access was down too. These trends are due to better security and better awareness on the part of employees. Another bit of good news was that more companies are reporting computer crime to law enforcement in greater numbers (25 percent) than they had in the previous two years. This may seem low compared to other types of crime, but companies are not keen on letting people know about security problems, especially when they are asking customers to trust them with credit card numbers and other important data. They are also concerned that competitors will use the information to their advantage, or don't realize it's of interest to law enforcement.

A large portion of attacks on computer systems are caused by **malware**, software designed to harm your computer or computer security.

VIRUSES   Viruses are a type of malware. The term *computer virus* is a generic term for lots of different types of destructive software. A **computer virus** (or **virus**) is software that was written with malicious intent to cause annoyance or damage. A hundred or more new viruses appear month. There are two categories of viruses. The first category comprises benign viruses that display a message or slow the computer but don't destroy any information.

Malignant viruses belong in the second category. These viruses do damage to your computer system. Some will scramble or delete your files. Others will shut your computer down, or make your Word software malfunction, or damage flash memory in your digital camera so that it won't store pictures anymore until you reformat it. Obviously, these are the viruses that cause IT staff (and everyone else) the most headaches.

Worms are the most prevalent type of malignant virus. A worm is a computer virus that replicates and spreads itself, not only from file to file, but also from computer to computer via e-mail and other Internet traffic. Worms don't need your help to spread. They find your e-mail address book and help themselves to the addresses, sending themselves to your contacts. The first worm to attract the attention of the popular press was the Love Bug worm, and permutations of it are still out there.

THE LOVE BUG WORM   Released on an unsuspecting world in 2000, the Love Bug worm caused 17 federal departments and offices to come to a standstill. It also caused problems in Parliament Hill offices and shut down e-mail in the British Parliament building. Companies as diverse as Ford Motor Company, H. J. Heinz, Merrill Lynch & Company, AT&T, and J.D. Irving Ltd. were infected.[1] All in all, the Love Bug and its variants affected 300,000 Internet host computers and millions of individual PC users, causing file damage, lost time, and high-cost emergency repairs totalling about $8.7 billion.[2,3]

A closer look at the Love Bug worm will give you a general idea of what worms do. The Love Bug arrives in your e-mail as an attachment to an e-mail message. The subject of the e-mail is "I LOVE YOU"—a very alluring message to be sure. The text says to open

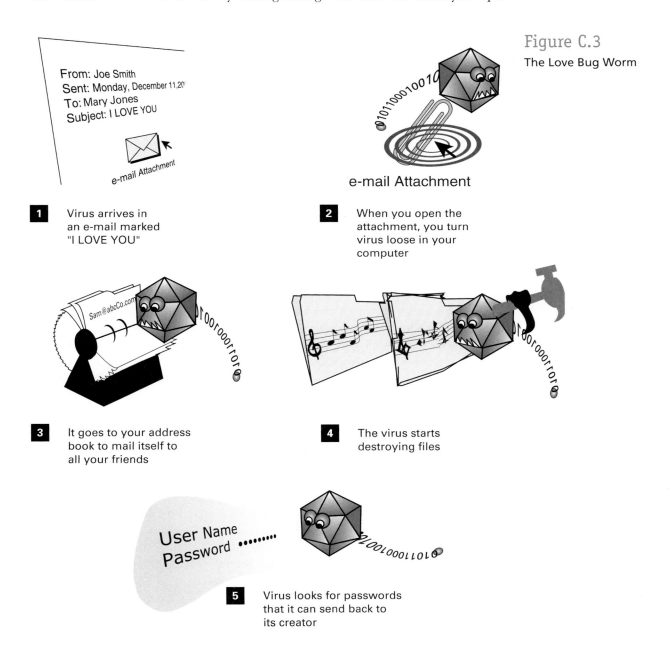

Figure C.3
The Love Bug Worm

e-mail Attachment

1 Virus arrives in an e-mail marked "I LOVE YOU"

2 When you open the attachment, you turn virus loose in your computer

3 It goes to your address book to mail itself to all your friends

4 The virus starts destroying files

5 Virus looks for passwords that it can send back to its creator the attached love letter, the name of which is, appropriately, LOVE LETTER. However, what's attached is anything but love. It's a mean piece of software that is set loose in your computer system as soon as you open the attachment.

The Love Bug has three objectives: to spread itself as far and as fast as it can, to destroy your files, and to gather passwords and other information (see Figure C.3). First, it spreads itself by mailing itself to everyone in your Outlook address book. (A previous worm of the same type named Melissa sent itself only to the first 50 people listed in Outlook's address book.) And, as if that weren't enough, it also uses your Internet chat software to spread itself to chat rooms.

Second, the Love Bug locates files on your computer that have certain extensions, .MP3 music files, .jpg picture files, .doc Word files, .xls Excel files, .wav sound files, .html browser files, and many others. Having found these files, it wipes them out and puts itself in their place, appending .vbs to the end of the filename. For example, if you had a file called MySong.wav on your hard disk drive, the Love Bug virus would change the name to MySong.wav.vbs after it had done its dirty work.

Before it's done, the Love Bug worm changes your Internet Explorer start page and downloads a program that looks for passwords and network information, sending this information off by e-mail to the virus originator.[4]

There are at least 29 versions of the Love Bug virus. After people were warned not to open the LOVE LETTER attachment, the originators of the virus changed the name of it to something else. For example, one version is MOTHER'S DAY, and the body of the text says that the receiver has been charged hundreds of dollars for a Mother's Day "diamond special." You have to open the attachment to print the invoice, and then the virus goes into action.

The moral of the story is that you should be very careful about opening an attachment if you're not sure what it is and where it came from. That won't necessarily save you from all virus attacks, but it will certainly help a great deal.

SOBIG, SLAMMER, AND BLASTER   The year 2003 was called the "worst year ever" for viruses and worms. Among the biggest, in terms of cost and name recognition, were the SoBig virus and the Slammer and Blaster worms.

There are several variations of mass-mailer viruses, but the SoBig virus is probably the best known. On Tuesday, August 19, 2003, the SoBig virus began spreading through networks generating e-mail traffic at levels never seen before. It arrived as an attachment in the victim's inbox with varying subject lines like "Your details," "Your application," and "Wicked screensaver." When the recipient opened the attachment, the virus searched through hard drives for e-mail addresses in document files, cached Web pages, and Microsoft Outlook Express databases. Then it sent out huge numbers of useless e-mail messages. At its peak, security experts estimate that 1 out of every 17 e-mail messages carried the SoBig virus, even more than the Love Bug's 1 in 20. It was estimated that SoBig sent out a mass mailing from infected computers—there were about 100,000 of those—at the rate of one every 10 minutes.

Postini Inc., an e-mail management and screening company, intercepted 1.9 million SoBig e-mails on their way to the company's customers on the first day of the virus's activation. By the next day the volume had increased to 3.5 million.

Whirlpool, a company with $11 billion a year in sales, says that about 95 percent of its sales come through the Internet and that its fast response to protect its 20,000 computers and 800 servers saved the company from suffering much damage. Others weren't so lucky. Experts say that part of the reason that SoBig was so effective was that it incorporated a line in its header that said "X-Scanner: Found to be clean," fooling a popular anti-virus application that many Internet service providers use into letting the virus through.

SoBig was pre-programmed to stop replicating itself on September 10, 2003. By that time, it had infected more than 5 million e-mails. About eight times as many private computers were infected as corporate systems, since organizations moved faster to apply the patch that blocked the destruction.

Two of the many worms that hit networks in 2003 were the Slammer worm that hit in January and the Blaster worm that arrived in August. A worm looks for some flaw, or way to enter a computer, in software (often a Microsoft network operating system product) and sneaks in to do damage. Slammer kept flooding the victim server until its buffer memory was full, then it could trick that computer into sending out thousands of new copies to other servers that were vulnerable. Slammer sent out 55 million bursts of information per second onto the Internet and at that rate it took only 10 minutes for the worm to find and invade almost all the vulnerable servers. Microsoft had a patch (a way of plugging the entry point) available on its Web site, but if the network administrators didn't download and apply it, their networks remained vulnerable.

The Blaster worm appeared only 26 days after Microsoft publicized the vulnerability that the worm utilized. Blaster spread like wildfire and among the thousands of companies that were affected were CSX, the third largest railroad company in North America; Amtrak, the commuter train company; and Air Canada. Passengers and freight in all three organizations experienced delays as their network traffic ground to a halt. Commuter trains in Washington, D.C., were delayed for two hours while IT experts worked feverishly to clean out the worm's effects while Air Canada's phone-reservation system and some check-in processes were slowed down.[5, 6, 7, 8]

STAND-ALONE VIRUSES   In any given month, between 200 and 300 viruses are travelling from system to system around the world, seeking a way in to spread mayhem.[9] And they're getting more deadly. The Love Bug worm was a Visual Basic Script (VBScript) virus and could run on any computer that can run Win32 programs (Windows 98 or later versions). More recent examples include are SirCam, Nimda, and Klez. Nimda adds JavaScript to every home page on the server it infects, then passes it on to visitors to the site. Viruses of this independent type are plentiful.

The Klez virus is actually a family of worms that introduced a new kind of confusion into the virus business. They spoof e-mail addresses. *Spoofing* is the forging of the return address on an e-mail so that the e-mail message appears to come from someone other than the actual sender. Previous worms went to the recipient from the infected sender's computer and contained the infected person's return e-mail address. The worm found recipient addresses in the infected computer's address book.

Klez goes a step further and uses the address book to randomly find a return address as well as recipient addresses. The result is that people who are not infected with the virus get e-mail from the irate recipients and spend time looking for a virus they may not have. Even worse, some of the virus-laden e-mails look as though they came from a technical support person, leading an unsuspecting victim to open them, believing them to be safe.

TROJAN HORSE VIRUSES   A type of virus that doesn't replicate is a Trojan horse virus. A *Trojan horse virus* hides inside other software, usually an attachment or download. The principle of any Trojan horse software is that there's software you don't want hidden inside software you do want. For example, Trojan horse software can carry the Ping of Death program that hides in a server until the originators are ready to launch a DoS attack to crash a Web site.

Key-logger software is usually available in Trojan horse form, so that you can hide it in e-mail or other Internet traffic. *Key logger*, or *key trapper*, software is a program that, when installed on a computer, records every keystroke and mouse click. Key logger software is used to snoop on people to find out what they're doing on a particular computer. You can find out more in Chapter 8.

MISLEADING E-MAIL   One type of misleading e-mail is a virus hoax. This is e-mail sent to frighten people about a virus threat that is, in fact, bogus. People who get such an alert will usually tell others, who react in the same way. The virus is nonexistent, but the hoax causes people to get scared and lose time and productivity. Within companies the losses can be very severe since computer professionals must spend precious time and effort looking for a nonexistent problem.

Following are some general guidelines for identifying a virus hoax:[10]

- Urges you to forward it to everyone you know, immediately
- Describes the awful consequences of not acting immediately
- Quotes a well-known authority in the computer industry.

These are signs that the e-mail is not meant to help but to cause harm. If you get such an e-mail, delete it immediately.

Another type of misleading e-mail is designed to get people to actually take action that results in setting a virus loose or to do something that will disrupt the functioning of their own computers. The first step is usually to make people believe that they have inadvertently e-mailed a virus to others. They get a message (maybe it purports to come from Microsoft) that they have sent out a virus and that they need to run an attached program or delete a file to fix the problem. They then do what the e-mail says, believing it to be genuine; furthermore, they e-mail everyone they sent messages to telling them about the problem. The recipients e-mail the people in their address books and so on. Be advised that Microsoft *never* sends out attachments in any official e-mail in a public mass mailing. It's possible that Microsoft may e-mail you warning you of a problem, but it will indicate only where you can download a file to take care of it. Before you delete a file from your computer, which may be an important system file without which your computer can't function, ask someone who knows or check out the various Web sites that keep up with the latest viruses, like www.symantec.com.

DENIAL-OF-SERVICE ATTACKS   Many organizations have been hit with denial-of-service attacks. *Denial-of-service (DoS) attacks* flood a server or network with so many requests for service that it slows down or crashes. The objective is to prevent legitimate customers from getting into the site to do business. There are several types of DoS attacks. A DoS attack can come from a lone computer that tries continuously to access the target computer, or from many, perhaps even thousands, of computers simultaneously. The latter is called a distributed denial-of-service attack and is considerably more devastating.

DISTRIBUTED DENIAL-OF-SERVICE ATTACKS   *Distributed denial-of-service (DoS) attacks* are attacks from multiple computers that flood a server or network with so many requests for service that it slows down or crashes. A common type is the Ping of Death, in which thousands of computers try to access a Web site at the same time, overloading it and shutting it down. A ping attack can also bring down the firewall server (the computer that protects the network), giving free access to the intruders. E*Trade, Amazon.com, and Yahoo!, among others, have been victims of this nasty little game. The process is actually very simple (see Figure C.4).

The plan starts with the hackers planting a program in network servers that aren't protected well enough. Then, on a signal sent to the servers from the attackers, the program activates and each server "pings" every computer. A ping is a standard operation that networks use to check that all computers are functioning properly. It's a sort of roll call for the network

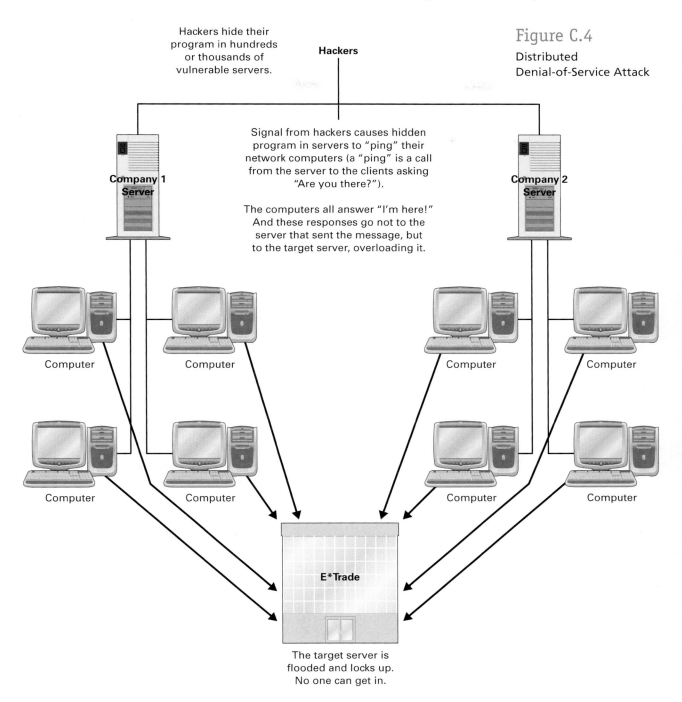

Hackers hide their program in hundreds or thousands of vulnerable servers.

Hackers

Figure C.4
Distributed
Denial-of-Service Attack

Signal from hackers causes hidden program in servers to "ping" their network computers (a "ping" is a call from the server to the clients asking "Are you there?").

The computers all answer "I'm here!" And these responses go not to the server that sent the message, but to the target server, overloading it.

Company 1 Server

Company 2 Server

Computer   Computer

Computer   Computer

Computer   Computer

Computer   Computer

E*Trade

The target server is flooded and locks up. No one can get in.

computers. The server asks, "Are you there?" and each computer in turn answers, "Yes, I'm here." But the hacker ping is different in that the return address of the are-you-there? message is not the originating server, but the intended victim's server. So on a signal from the hackers, thousands of computers try to access E*Trade or Amazon.com, to say "Yes, I'm here." The flood of calls overloads the online companies' computers and they can't conduct business.

For many companies, a forced shutdown is embarrassing and costly but for others it's much more than that. For an online stockbroker, for example, denial-of-service attacks can be disastrous. It may make a huge difference whether you buy shares of stock today or tomorrow. And since stockbrokers need a high level of trust from customers to do business, the effect of having been seen to be so vulnerable is very bad for business.

MALWARE BOTS AND ROOTKITS   A vital component of the increase in the spread of viruses and denial-of-service attacks is the use of bots. A ***bot*** is a computer program that runs automatically. Bots (the term comes from robot) can perform all sorts of tasks, both good and evil. In Chapter 4, you saw how bots take the form of intelligent agents, finding information and automatically performing computer-related tasks. Two examples are bots or intelligent agents that continuously monitor networks to find a problem before it knocks out the network, and shopping bots that find products and services on the Internet for you.

However, there's another class of bots—the kind that are used for fraud or sabotage. In *Extended Learning Module B (Network Basics)*, you learned that bots (software robots) can be used to break into computer systems. Having placed the unauthorized code into a computer, attackers set up servers that are used for such things as distributing illegal copies of movies, music, and software. These compromised machines may be used to distribute kits for breaking into other computers. Malware bots are designed to be controlled by an attacker to perform unauthorized work over some period, like sending out spam or becoming part of a denial-of-service attack. Estimates are that about three-quarters of all spam mailings come from this type of source.

A ***malware bot*** is a bot that is used for fraud, sabotage, DoS attacks, or some other malicious purpose. It allows an unauthorized user to take control of a host computer without the victim's knowledge or permission. The term *bot* is sometimes used to mean a compromised machine, i.e., a computer that has been compromised with a bot. Bot-infected computers are also called ***zombies*** or ***drones***.

Malware bot activity has become very sophisticated over the past few years and there is a whole underground society in the bad bot business. The lowest level of the underground comprises the people who find vulnerable machines and install bad bots. The next level up are bot herders. Bot herders assemble battalions of bot-infected computers and sell this network of bots or botnet to people who are called fraudsters. A ***botnet*** is a network of malware-bot-infected computers. Bot herders typically sell their networks for about $1 per machine, but the price can go up to $100 per system, per month, for access to a major organization that has lots of valuable information like customer and employee data. The fraudsters, in turn, use the botnet to steal this customer and employee data along with intellectual property, and anything else of value that they can access. Computers in organizations as varied as the U.S. Department of Defense and Colton School District in California have been compromised.

Malware bots can infect a computer in any one of a number of ways including operating system or application vulnerabilities, e-mail, instant messaging, and computer viruses. One very effective way of commandeering computers is to use a *rootkit*. It's hard to detect and even when detected, it's hard to remove. A rootkit is a Trojan-horse-type program that is activated when you start your computer. It carries code that, once inside, can do whatever it was programmed to do.

A ***rootkit*** is software that gives you administrator rights to a computer or network and its purpose is to allow you to conceal processes, files, or system data from the operating system. It can be used to carry code to perform virtually any type of malicious activity. It can take full control of a system and use that computer or network for spam, denial-of-service, or spyware, and, more chillingly, create a "backdoor" into the system for the attacker, who can then commandeer the system to be part of a botnet.

An attacker exploits an operating system vulnerability to get a rootkit onto your computer. A rootkit is hard to detect since it runs while the operating system is starting and looks to the operating system like it belongs.

Probably the most widely publicized example of a rootkit was the one that Sony put into CDs and DVDs as part of a copy protection scheme in 2005. It got onto your computer when you played the disc and was then exploited by hackers. See the Industry Perspective box in Chapter 8, "Is Your Music CD Hijacking Your Computer?"

WEB DEFACING

Web defacing is a favourite sport of some of the people who break into computer systems. They replace the site with a substitute that's neither attractive nor complimentary. Or perhaps they convert the Web site to a mostly blank screen with an abusive or obscene message, or the message may just read "So-and-so was here." In essence, Web site defacing is electronic graffiti, where a computer keyboard and mouse take the place of a paint spray can. The *USA Today* Web site was a victim in July 2002, causing the newspaper to shut down the whole site for three hours to fix the problem. The hackers replaced several news stories on the site with bogus stories that were full of spelling errors. One story said that the Pope had called Christianity "a sham." The phony stories were on the site for only 15 minutes before they were spotted and the site was taken offline.[11]

Hackers

LO2

Who's spreading all this havoc? The answer is hackers, people who break into computer systems. *Hackers* are knowledgeable computer users who use their knowledge to invade other people's computers. There are several categories of hackers, and their labels change over time. The important thing to note in the following discussion is that the motivation and reasons for hacking are as many and varied as the people who engage in it.

THRILL-SEEKER HACKERS   *Thrill-seeker hackers* break into computer systems for entertainment. Sometimes, they consider themselves to be the "good guys" since they expose vulnerabilities and some even follow a "hackers' code." Although they break into computers they have no right to access, they may report the security leaks to the victims. Their thrill is in being able to get into someone else's computer. Their reward is usually the admiration of their fellow hackers. There's plenty of information on the Web for those who want to know how to hack into a system—about 2,000 sites offer free hacking tools, according to security experts.

WHITE-HAT HACKERS   The thrill-seeker hackers used to be called white-hat hackers. But lately, the term *white-hat* is being increasingly used to describe the hackers who legitimately, with the knowledge of the owners of the IT system, try to break in to find and fix vulnerable areas of the system. These *white-hat hackers*, or *ethical hackers* are computer security professionals who are hired by a company to break into a computer system, so as to find security lapses. These hackers are also called counter hackers, or penetration testers.

BLACK-HAT HACKERS   *Black-hat hackers* are cyber vandals. They exploit or destroy the information they find, steal passwords, or otherwise cause harm. They deliberately cause trouble for people just for the fun of it. They create viruses, bring down computer systems, and steal or destroy information.

A 16-year-old black-hat hacker was sentenced to detention for six months after he hacked into military and NASA networks. He caused the systems to shut down for three weeks. He intercepted more than 3,000 e-mails and stole the names and passwords of 19 defence agency employees. He also downloaded temperature and humidity control software worth $1.7 billion that helps control the environment in the international space station's living quarters.[12]

CRACKERS   *Crackers* are hackers for hire and are the people who engage in electronic corporate espionage and other profitable ventures. This can be a pretty lucrative undertaking, paying up to $1 million per gig. Typically, an espionage job will take about three weeks and may involve unpleasant tasks like dumpster diving to find passwords and other useful information and "social engineering." *Social engineering* is conning your way into acquiring information that you have no right to. Social engineering methods include calling someone in a company and pretending to be a technical support person and getting that person to type in a login and password, sweet talking an employee to get information, and for difficult jobs, perhaps even setting up a fake office and identity.

HACKTIVISTS   *Hacktivists* are politically motivated hackers who use the Internet to send a political message of some kind. The message can be a call to end world hunger, or it can involve an alteration of a political party's Web site so that it touts another party's candidate. It can be a slogan for a particular cause or some sort of diatribe inserted into a Web site to mock a particular religious or national group.

Hacktivism, in the form of Web defacing, is becoming a common response to disagreements between nations. When a U.S. military plane made an emergency landing in China and a dispute arose about the return of the crew and plane, U.S. hackers started to attack Chinese Web sites, and Chinese hackers returned the favour, targeting government-related sites.

CYBERTERRORISTS   Since the September 11, 2001, terrorist attacks on New York and the Pentagon, officials have become increasingly worried about the threat of cyberterrorists. This group of hackers, like the hacktivists, is politically motivated, but its agenda is more sinister. A *cyberterrorist* is one who seeks to cause harm to people or destroy critical systems or information. Possible targets of violent attacks would be air traffic control systems and nuclear power plants, and anything else that could harm the infrastructure of a nation. At a less-lethal level, cyberterrorist acts would include shutting down e-mail or even part of the Internet itself, or destroying government records, say, on social security benefits or criminals.

However, the RCMP and other government agencies are very much aware of the threats they face from computer-based attacks, and have taken steps to protect the infrastructure that supports cyberspace. They can enjoy a reasonable expectation of success since a computer system is a lot easier to protect than public structures like buildings and bridges.

SCRIPT KIDDIES   *Script kiddies* or *script bunnies* are people who would like to be hackers but don't have much technical expertise. They download click-and-point software that automatically does the hacking for them. An example of this was a young man in The Netherlands who found a virus toolkit on the Web and started the Kournikova worm. It was very similar to the Love Bug worm in that it sent itself to all the people in an infected computer's Outlook address book. Tens of millions of people got the virus after opening the attachment hoping to see a picture of Anna Kournikova.[13]

The concern about script kiddies, according to the experts, apart from the fact that they can unleash viruses and denial-of-service attacks, is that they can be used by more sinister hackers. These people manipulate the script kiddies, egging them on in chat rooms, encouraging and helping them to be more destructive.

Digital Forensics

When a disturbed student at Virginia Tech went on a killing rampage in April 2007, one of the first things that law enforcement investigators did was to collect all of his information devices, like his computer system and his cell phone. They used the information they retrieved to piece together a picture of the young man and the events that preceded the tragic event.

It was not the first time electronic information was helpful in untangling criminal mysteries. Astonishingly, digital forensics solved a case that had been open for 30 years, and identified Dennis Rader as the BTK (bind, torture, kill) killer.

In 2005 Dennis Rader, a.k.a. the BTK killer, was convicted of killing 10 women over three decades. The BTK strangler had taunted police and the media over many years through letters and packages, some of which contained photos of the victims. But it was the package containing a floppy disk that he sent to a TV station on February 16, 2005, that finally led to his capture. The TV station turned the disk over to police, who in turn, called in digital forensics investigators. They found evidence of a deleted file that referenced the Christ Lutheran Church in Wichita. Police asked the church to allow them to examine its computer and found that Rader had used it to print out a church meeting agenda. Then they got a warrant to examine the computer in Rader's home and found evidence that he was, indeed, the BTK strangler whom they had been seeking for three decades.[14]

There are many more such cases. Here is a sampling:

- The case against Thomas Murray, an English professor who killed his wife, was strengthened when, during the investigation, police found e-mails he had sent to his wife and friends. The messages showed how upset he was with the fact that his wife was divorcing him and taking their daughter to California. Digital forensics experts found that he had done Yahoo! searches for "how to make a bomb," "murder for hire," "how to hire an assassin," and "how to murder someone and not get caught." He was convicted and sentenced to 25 years in prison.

- A search that ended on March 5, 2002, uncovered 339 discarded bodies on the grounds of Tri-State Funeral home in Walker County, Georgia. Ray Brent Marsh was formally charged with multiple counts of abusing a corpse and almost 200 counts of fraud for allegedly taking money for cremations that were not performed and for giving loved ones fake remains. Photos of the dead bodies arranged in lewd poses had appeared on the Internet.

- In November 2004, Scott Peterson was convicted of killing his wife Laci and the couple's unborn son, Connor. Both bodies washed ashore separately in San Francisco Bay during April 2003. While gathering evidence to solve the crime, police had searched the hard drives of four computers in the Petersons' home. On a notebook computer they found that someone had examined maps, fishing reports, and charts of water currents in the Bay Area just before Laci disappeared. Someone at the couple's home, presumably Scott, had also done searches for keywords like divorce, silencer, and shooter.

What all these news stories have in common is the investigative technique that unearthed crucial information—the process of finding, examining, and analyzing electronic information saved on computer storage media or handheld devices like cell phones. This process is called *computer* or *digital forensics*. (Since computer forensics is no longer limited to desktop and notebook computers, the term *digital forensics* is becoming the term that is widely used.) Many digital forensics investigations involve intellectual property cases, where a company believes that an employee is secretly copying and perhaps selling proprietary information such as schematics, customer lists, financial statements, product designs, or notes on private meetings. Other investigations involve child exploitation, domestic disputes, labour relations, and employee misconduct cases.

Digital forensics is the collection, authentication, preservation, and examination of electronic information (often for presentation in court). Electronic evidence can be found on any type of computer storage media, such as hard disks, CDs, flash cards, USB devices, pocket PCs, cell phones, and pagers.

There are two basic motivations for engaging in digital forensics. The first is to gather and preserve evidence to present in court. The second is to establish what activities have occurred on a computer, often for the purpose of dispute settlement. Evidentiary standards differ for criminal and civil cases. In criminal cases, the standard is "beyond a reasonable doubt." In civil cases, it's the "preponderance of evidence." For instance, you may find yourself in a situation that doesn't require the involvement of the legal system. Suppose you have an employee that you suspect has been using the company's computer system to gamble on-line. In this case your proof standard can be lower, perhaps just enough to fire the person while reducing the risk of being named in a wrongful termination lawsuit.

In a well-conducted digital forensics investigation, there are two major phases: (1) collecting, authenticating, and preserving electronic evidence; and (2) analyzing the findings.

THE COLLECTION PHASE

Step one of the collection phase is to get physical access to the computer and related items. Thus, the digital forensic team collects computers, cell phones, pocket PCs, disks, printouts, Post-it notes (see below), and so on and takes them back to the lab. This process is similar to what police do when investigating crime in the physical world: collecting hair, clothing fibres, bloodstained articles, papers, and anything else that they think might be useful. The crime investigators usually take these potential clue carriers with them and secure them under lock and key, where only authorized personnel may have access, and even they must sign in and out.

Digital forensic experts use the same kind of protocol. To conduct a thorough investigation, they first take digital photos of the surrounding environment and start developing extensive documentation. Then they start collecting anything that might store information. The hard disk is an obvious place to look, but digital forensic investigators also collect any other media where information might be stored (see Figure C.5). If they can't take a clue source with them, they secure it and create an exact copy of the contents of the original media.

As well as electronic media, investigators collect any other potentially helpful items, especially passwords, for use in case any of the files they come across are encrypted or are otherwise difficult to access. Apparently, a favourite hiding place for passwords that people write down (which you should *not* do) is under the keyboard, so that's the first place that investigators look. Then they look in desk drawers and anywhere else that passwords might be, perhaps on Post-it notes or slips of paper. Some people keep all their passwords and PINs in the My Documents folder. This certainly makes life easier for digital forensics examiners—and for thieves. Passwords don't help much since, with a password cracker program like Passware, anyone can get the password in seconds. Other helpful items might be printouts and business cards of associates or contacts of the person being investigated.

Step two of the collection process is to make a forensic image copy of all the information. A *forensic image copy* is an exact copy or snapshot of the contents of an electronic medium. It is sometimes referred to as a bit-stream image copy. To get a forensic image copy, specialized forensic software copies every fragment of information, bit-by-bit, on every storage medium—every hard disk (if there's more than one),

Figure C.5

Where You Might Find
Electronic Evidence

- Floppy disks
- CDs
- DVDs
- PDAs
- USB drives
- Flash memory cards, like an xD-Picture card, CompactFlash card, or similar storage medium for digital cameras and other devices
- Backup tapes of other media
- USB mass storage devices such as Thumb drives
- Voice mail
- Cell phones
- Electronic calendars
- MP3 players and iPods
- Scanner
- Pocket PCs
- Photocopiers
- Fax machines

every floppy disk, every CD, every USB drive and flash memory card. That's usually a lot of stuff. Remember that a CD holds about a half gigabyte of information, and a hard disk array can hold a terabyte (one trillion bytes) or more. It can take a long, long time to copy it all. And the investigator must be able to swear in court that he or she supervised the entire copying process, and that no one and nothing interfered with the evidence. This could mean sitting in the lab literally for days just copying files. Also, many experts advise that the investigator make two copies of everything in case there's a problem later with the first copy.

By the end of 2007, there were 860 cell phone networks in more than 220 countries[15] serving more than 2 billion users[16] —and that's just GSM-type cell phones (the type that Rogers and Bell use, and the one that is the most popular in Europe and China). The number of people who have personal computers is only one-third of that. Over 1 billion cell phones were sold in 2006 alone and this number is expected to keep rising. Since cell phones and other handheld devices also store important information on user activity, they're also part of the collection process.

Cell phones are simply a specialized type of computer. Since there are so many people using cell phones, it stands to reason that some of them are using the handy devices to commit crime. The list of cell phone crimes includes much of the illegal activity that's possible with computers (or without them) and some that's unique to cell phones. Some examples are

- Illegal drug deals.
- Stealing data and storing it on a cell phone.
- Stealing the cell phone to fraudulently obtain goods and services. A variation on this theme is stealing subscriber information and using it to create duplicate

accounts that are then used to purchase goods from the Internet using the original subscribers' accounts. These crimes are particularly prevalent in Europe and Japan, where people use their cell phones to buy snacks and drinks out of vending machines, pay parking tickets, make credit card payments, and engage in a host of other types of mobile commerce.

- On a vastly more serious scale, cell phones have been used by terrorists to set off explosives. This happened in Madrid in 2004 when bombs went off in commuter trains; at Hebrew University in Jerusalem in 2002, when seven people died; and in Bali outside a night club in 2002 and in the Jakarta Marriott.[17]

THE AUTHENTICATION AND PRESERVATION PROCESSES   To get a forensic image copy of hard disk and other media contents, investigators physically remove the hard disk from the computer. They never turn the suspect computer on, because when the PC is turned on, Windows or Vista performs hundreds of changes to files. Access dates change, and so do temporary files, and so on. So, once turned on, the hard drive is no longer exactly the same as it was when it was shut down. Thus, opposing counsel could argue that this is not the same hard disk that the suspect used.

Having removed the hard disk, investigators connect it to special forensic hardware that can read files but can't write or rewrite any medium. (They prefer to remove storage devices, but if that's not possible, they copy the contents in place using cables.) Then they use forensic software like EnCase to extract a forensic image copy of the original medium without changing the files in any way.

How do we know that nothing changed on any disk during the entire investigation, from the time the computer was seized up to the present time? That's the question that opposing counsel will ask the computer forensic expert on the witness stand. So, during the collection phase and later, the analysis phase, the investigators have to make absolutely sure that evidence to be used in a trial could not have been planted, eliminated, contaminated, or altered in any way. This is a basic evidentiary rule for all court proceedings. Forensic experts have to be able to document a chain of custody and be able to account for the whereabouts and protection of evidence. To help establish a complete chronology of activity, investigators also check the BIOS, which a computer uses to time and date stamp files and actions like deleting, updating, and so on.

In a digital forensic investigation, investigators use an authentication process so that they can show sometime in the future—perhaps even five or six years later—that nothing changed on the hard drive or other storage medium since seizure. They can do this with an MD5 hash value. An **_MD5 hash value_** is a mathematically generated string of 32 letters and digits that is unique for an individual storage medium at a specific point in time. The MD5 hash value is based on the contents of that medium. Any change in the content changes the MD5 hash value.

A hash value is a seemingly meaningless set of characters. It's the result of applying a mathematical algorithm to a large block of data to reduce it to a small set of characters. For example, a hash value could be the sum of the ISBNs and the number of pages in all the books on a bookstore shelf. The result, which would be a mixture of ISBN codes and quantities of pages, would be meaningless for anything except identification. If a book, or even a page, were added to or removed from the shelf, the hash total would change, so the contents of the shelf could be shown not to be the same as they were when the hash value was originally computed. Similarly, adding so much as one space in one tiny Word document on a disk will change the MD5 hash value. See Figure C.6 for an example of an MD5 hash value generated by EnCase forensic software.

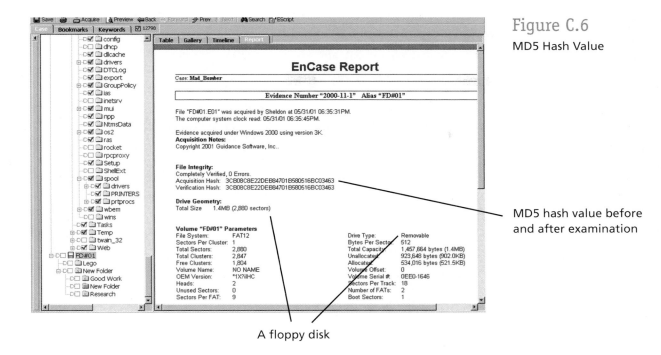

Figure C.6

MD5 Hash Value

MD5 hash value before and after examination

A floppy disk

MD5 hash values are considered very reliable and have become an industry standard accepted by the FBI, the U.S. Marshall Service, the Royal Canadian Mounted Police, and most other law enforcement authorities, as well as private professional firms, as a way of uniquely authenticating a set of contents on a particular storage medium. This confidence in MD5 hash values is based on the fact that the probability of two hard disks with different contents having the same MD5 hash value is 1 in 10 to the 38th power: that's 1 with 38 zeros behind it. This makes the MD5 hash value a sort of DNA or fingerprint for computer media contents. Actually, it's more reliable than those physiological identifiers, since the probability of two sets of hard disk contents resulting in the same MD5 hash value are less than the odds of two individuals' DNA and fingerprints being identical. As an example of this probability, consider that you would have better odds of winning the Powerball lottery 39 times in your lifetime than you would of finding two hard disks with different contents that have matching MD5 hash values.

In 2005 some researchers managed, under closely controlled circumstances and with a lot of computer power and sophisticated mathematics, to cause a collision of MD5 hash values, i.e., caused two different blocks of data to yield the same MD5 hash value. This precipitated much discussion in the digital forensics industry about the reliability of MD5. Since the chances of a collision are so very small, MD5 continues to be used. However, a new method of generating a hash value has emerged. This one is called SHA and it has an even lower probability of yielding the same value for two different blocks of data. Some software, such as FTK, which is another software package that digital forensics experts use for forensic examinations, generates SHA instead of MD5 for authentication purposes.

CELL PHONES AND OTHER HANDHELD DEVICES   When it comes to cell phones and other handheld devices, the most frequently used software is Device Seizure developed by Paraban. EnCase has recently added Nutrino, which is a similar product. The procedure is to use Device Seizure to recover the data itself and then a program that uses hex dumping to get headers, footers, dates, and so on. This kind of software also finds deleted files in unallocated space. Device Seizure is often the forensic tool of choice for investigators partly because it does not allow data to be changed on the device.

Figure C.7

Recoverable Cell Phone
Information

- Phone book
- Subscriber, equipment, and service provider identifiers
- Calendar
- To-do list
- Phone number log and most recently dialled numbers
- E-mail
- Web activity
- Text messages and multimedia messages
- Voice mail
- Electronic documents
- Last active location and other networks encountered
- Graphics, photos, and videos

This is one of the strongest features of EnCase, the forensic tool used to investigate desktop and notebook computers. Since the handheld part of the industry is not as well established as the forensic examination of desktop and notebook computers, there aren't as many tools available.

Adding to the complexity is the huge range of designs in the handheld world. What kind of data and how much of it is stored on a cell phone, for example, depends on many factors such as the manufacturer, the options chosen by the user, the software it uses, and so on. Cell phones that have PDA (Personal Digital Assistant) features are becoming more widely used and these usually have flash memory cards such as an SD card. See Figure C.7 for a partial list of the types of information that can be recovered from a cell phone.

FORENSIC HARDWARE AND SOFTWARE TOOLS   As we've already mentioned, digital forensic experts use special hardware and software to conduct investigations. Usually the computer system has more power than the standard computer on a desktop and much more RAM, as well as much more hard disk capacity. This is to speed the copying and analysis process. Digital forensic experts are also very careful not to let static electricity cause any damage or changes to magnetic media (like hard disks, Zips, and floppies). Therefore, they use nonconductive mats under all computer parts, and wear wristbands that connect by wire to the ground of an electrical outlet. And just in case they need a tool, such as a screwdriver, they have a special nonmagnetic set of tools nearby, too.

There are many kinds of software in a digital forensics toolkit, in addition to forensic software, that can help in digital forensic investigations. Quick View Plus, used by many forensic experts, is an example. This is software that will load Word, Excel, image, and many other file formats. If it comes across a file with an .xls extension, which is actually an image and not a spreadsheet file, Quick View will show the file as an image regardless of its extension. That saves the investigator having to try it in multiple programs after loading fails in Excel. Conversions Plus is a package that does the same sort of thing. Other helpful software includes Mailbag Assistant, which reads many e-mail formats, and IrfanView, which is an image viewer that will read most picture files. Gargoyle is software that identifies encrypted files and can decrypt some of them.

Ingenium is software that does latent semantic analysis also known as concept searching. This means that it can search for your *meaning* rather than just terms that match exactly. For example, if you type in "house" as a search term, the software will search for cottage, hut, domicile, home, property, estate, holdings, manor, housing, mansion, cabin, bungalow, chalet, lodge, residence, dwelling, abode, habitat, etc. It uses a neural network to find other terms that are close in meaning to your search term. You can learn more about neural networks in Chapter 4.

We have been using the EnCase forensic software for this discussion, but it's not the only package available. Helix and FTK are other examples of this kind of software. For investigations that might be headed toward litigation, digital forensic experts often use EnCase, since it's widely accepted as robust and reliable. EnCase has routinely been judged acceptable by courts in meeting the legal standard for producing reliable evidence.

As you've already seen, the most frequently used forensic software for handheld devices is Device Seizure by Paraban, which is the equivalent of EnCase, but for cell phones and Pocket PCs. Guidance Software, the company that makes EnCase, sells Nutrino—a newcomer to the industry—for handheld devices. There are other options on the market too and they, like all forensic tools, keep improving. Since handheld device investigation is still so recent, national standards have not yet evolved in this arena.

THE ANALYSIS PHASE

The second phase of the investigation is the analysis phase when the investigator follows the trail of clues and builds the evidence into a crime story. This is the phase that really tests the skill and experience of the investigators. The analysis phase consists of the recovery and interpretation of the information that's been collected and authenticated. If all the necessary files were there in plain sight with names and extensions indicating their contents, life would be much easier for the forensic investigator, but that's seldom the case. Usually, particularly if those being investigated know that they're doing something wrong, the incriminating files will have been deleted or hidden.

Investigators can recover all of a deleted file pretty easily as long as no new information has been written to the space where the file was. But they can also recover fragments—perhaps rather large fragments—of files in parts of a disk where new files have been written, but have not completely filled the space where the old file was. With the appropriate software they can recover files or fragments of files from virtually any part of any storage medium (see Figure C.8).

Digital forensic programs can pinpoint a file's location on the disk, its creator, the date it was created, the date of last access, and sometimes the date it was deleted, as well as file formatting, and notes embedded or hidden in a document (see Figure C.9).

Also stored on the hard disk is information about where the computer user went on the Web. For example, every graphic image you view on the Internet is copied to your hard disk, usually without your knowledge. In addition, web servers have information on which computer connected to the Web and when. The same server can also tell you the sites visited by the user of that computer, the date and time of the visits, and the actions of the user at the site. These attributes are useful if the suspect claims to have reached an inappropriate site by accident, since delving deeper into the site implies a deliberate action. And, of course, if a password was required to reach the material in question, you can rest your case.

LIVE ANALYSIS   The usual digital forensic examination is conducted when the computer or computers are off. However, there are situations where this may not be possible or even the best course of action. So, the forensic team has to gather the information they need while the system is still running. For such an analysis to be acceptable there has to be a good reason for not following the more traditional procedure—an examiner won't

Figure C.8

Some of the Files
Recoverable from
Storage Media

E-Mail Files
• E-mail messages
• Deleted e-mail messages
Program Files and Data Files
• Word (.doc) and backup (.wbk) files
• Excel files
• Deleted files of all kinds
• Files hidden in image and music files
• Encrypted files (with keys or passwords)
• Compressed files
Web Activity Files
• Web history
• Cache files
• Cookies
Network Server Files
• Backup e-mail files
• Other backup and archived files
• System history files
• Web log files

get away with saying that it was simply too much work to do the usual type of examination. A *live analysis* is the term used to describe an examination of a system while it is still running. It may be necessary under certain circumstances such as

- If the company hosts a Web site that takes customer orders. In this situation a complete shutdown would cost the company precious business, and a judge might consider such action as an "undue burden" on the company.
- If information is needed that is in RAM and the examiner pulls the plug, that information will be lost. So in this case it would actually be better for the forensic experts to get data from a computer that's still running. For example, if someone is caught red-handed using a computer for some illicit activity it might be much better to get a memory dump from the system rather than pull the plug, which would wipe out the contents of volatile RAM.
- With hard disk storage now in the terabyte range, it's simply too wasteful to copy all the data when only a small portion of it is relevant to the investigation. Under these circumstances, it may be acceptable to extract only certain well-defined portions.

In a live analysis, the examiner doesn't make a forensic image of the disk and, therefore, there's no MD5 hash value. This is a big disadvantage in making a case. All you have is a momentary snapshot of what's going on within that system. On the plus side, examiners can glean information from memory (RAM) and on processes and services that are

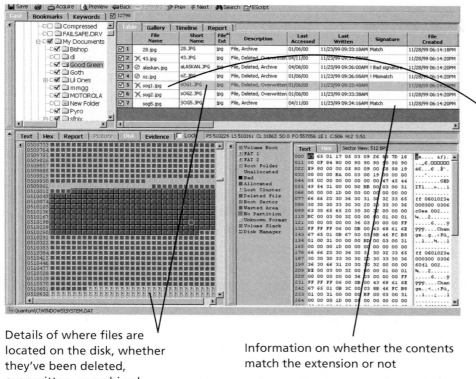

Figure C.9
History of File Activity

File marked as deleted

Details of where files are located on the disk, whether they've been deleted, overwritten, or archived

Information on whether the contents match the extension or not

running and also on open ports on the computer. Live analysis can also defeat on-the-fly encryption (OTFE) systems that encrypt drives when the system is shut down.

Helix, which is freeware, is one widely used tool for this type of analysis and has been endorsed by EnCase. This type of examination is still in the early stages of development and there are not yet many tools with good track records. Helix, which is Linux-based, provides a utility that allows examiners to download a PDF file, which is not easily changeable, detailing what the examiner did in the correct sequence and what tools were used. This provides some assurance that the examiner did what was necessary and followed proper procedure.

RECOVERY AND INTERPRETATION

As with all evidence, the analysis of the electronic clues and the assembling of the pieces into a credible and likely scenario of what happened are very important. Much of the information may come from recovered deleted files, currently unused disk space, and deliberately hidden information or files. Some people's e-mail that was recovered to their extreme embarrassment (or worse) but arguably to society's benefit is shown in Figure H.10.

Following is a discussion, not necessarily exhaustive, of places from which digital forensic experts can recover information.

PLACES TO LOOK FOR USEFUL INFORMATION

Information is written all over a disk, not only when you save a file, but also when you create folders, print documents, repartition the disk, and so on. System and application software alike continually create temporary files, resulting in space and file locations being rearranged. Leftover information stays on the disk until another file writes over it, and is often recoverable with forensic software. Next, we'll examine places where files or file remnants and other indicators of user activity can be found.

DELETED FILES AND SLACK SPACE   It's actually not very easy to get rid of electronically stored information completely. A surprising number of people think that if they delete a file it's gone. It's not—at least not immediately, and perhaps never. When you delete a file, all you're actually doing is marking it as deleted in the disk's directory. The actual file contents are not affected *at all* by a delete action.

Figure C.10
Recovered E-mail Messages

" . . . something could get screwed up enough . . . and then you are in a world of hurt . . . "

and

"I can only hope the folks . . . are listening . . . "

Excerpts of e-mail traffic that flew back and forth only two days before the February 1, 2003, *Columbia* shuttle disaster, in which an engineer discussed his misgivings about the possibility of a disaster

To:	David B. Duncan
Cc:	Michael C. Odom@ANDERSEN WO: Richard Corgci@ANDERSEN WO
BCC:	
Date:	10/16/2001 08:39 PM
From:	Nancy A. Temple
Subject:	Re: Press Release draft
Attachments:	ATT&ICIQ: 3rd qtr press release memo.doc

Dave - Here are a few suggested comments for consideration.

- I recommend deleting reference to consultation with the legal group and deleting my name on the memo. Reference to the legal group consultation arguably is a waiver of attorney-client privileged advice and if my name is mentioned it increases the chances that I might be a witness, which I prefer to avoid.

- I suggested deleting some language that might suggest we have concluded the release is misleading.

- In light of the "non-recurring" characterization, the lack of any suggestion that this characterization is not in accordance with GAAP, and the lack of income statements in accordance with GAAP, I will consult further within the legal group as to whether we should do anything more to protect ourselves from potential Section 10A issues.

One of the "smoking gun" e-mails that helped sink Andersen Consulting and Enron

From the arresting officer in the Rodney King beating

"oops I haven't beaten anyone so bad in a long time...."

" . . . do we have a clear plan on what we want Apple to do to undermine Sun . . . ?"

From Bill Gates in an intra-office e-mail about a competitor in the Microsoft antitrust action

If you delete a file from a hard disk you usually get a message asking you if you want it in the *Recycle Bin* and then you can recover it from there. In the case of a removable medium, like a USB flash drive, it's a little harder, but not much. The message you get asks whether you're sure you want to delete the file because it may not be recoverable. Actually that message should read "not as easily recoverable as files in the recycle bin," since you can get it back with utility programs such as Norton Utilities, and of course, forensic software.

When you mark a file as deleted, the space is freed for use by some other file. So, another file may shortly be written to that space. However, it's not quite that straight-forward. The operating system divides storage space into sectors of bytes or characters. The sectors are grouped into clusters. A file is assigned a whole number of clusters for storage, whether it completely fills the last cluster or not. This storage allocation method usually leaves unused portions of clusters. This is analogous to writing a three and one-half page report. You'd have to use the top half of the fourth page and leave the rest of the page blank. So, the fourth page is allocated to the report but not completely used. If the previously stored file (the deleted one) was bigger and used that last part of the space, then the remnants of the deleted file remain and can be recovered using the appropriate software. The space left over from the end of the file to the end of the cluster is called *slack space*, and information left there from previous files can be recovered by forensic software (see Figure C.11).

SYSTEM AND REGISTRY FILES   Operating system files manage the hardware and software of your computer and let your application software access hardware without having to know how all the various types of hardware function. As one of its many functions, the operating system controls virtual memory. Virtual memory is hard disk space used when RAM is full. Details of virtual memory activity are stored in system files. For example, if you have several applications running and you're instant messaging someone, that exchange may be stored on the hard disk without your knowing it simply because there wasn't room for it in RAM.

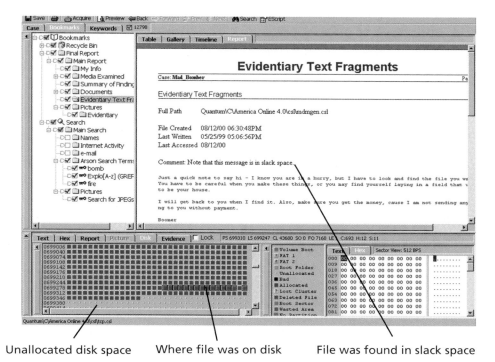

Figure C.11

Fragment of E-Mail Found in Slack Space by Encase

Unallocated disk space   Where file was on disk   File was found in slack space

The registry is the database that Windows and Vista use to store configuration information. Registry files have information such as preferences for users of the system, settings for the hardware, and system software, and installed programs. This information can be very valuable. For example, even if you uninstall a program, remnants of the install process remain in the registry file. Registry files also contain the MAC (Media Access Control) address, which is a special ID for a computer on a network. When this MAC address is contained in a file, as it is in a Word document, it links that document file to its "owner" computer.

UNALLOCATED DISK SPACE   If your hard disk gets a lot of use, it's probable that each sector has had information put into it many times. The operating system is always moving files around, and if you changed a Word file and resaved it, the previous version is marked as deleted and the space becomes unallocated. *Unallocated space* is the set of clusters that has been marked as available to store information, but has not yet received a file, or still contains some or all of a file marked as deleted. Until the new information takes up residence, the old information remains. The bigger the hard disk, the longer it usually takes for old space to be used.

UNUSED DISK SPACE   Unused space results from rearranging disk space. For example, when a hard drive is repartitioned, the new partitioning may not use all the space on the hard disk. So, again, those unused portions are not overwritten. The partition table and other operating system information are stored on their own tracks and are not visible under normal circumstances, but may have once stored a Word document. To be able to see the fragments of files tucked away in these tracks, the user needs forensic software.

ERASED INFORMATION   By now you may be asking whether it's possible to completely erase information from a storage medium. It is possible, but you need to know what you're doing. You can get disk-wiping programs that erase information from a disk by writing nonsense information over the previous contents. Utilities like Norton have this feature. However, erasing a disk takes a lot of time. A 10-gigabyte hard disk (not very big) would take several hours to clean. Even then you're not necessarily safe, for three reasons:

- A single overwrite may not erase the information completely. The U.S. Department of Justice recommends that government agencies write over old information seven times to be sure it's completely gone.
- Some programs keep track of what was deleted by whom, and that record is viewable if you know where to look.
- Disk-wiping programs vary greatly in which parts of the hard disk they clean. For most of them, you have to change the settings to reach certain parts of the disk. Some claim to go through the wipe process up to 35 times, but that still doesn't erase the areas that the software isn't set to erase. Also keep in mind that if you're trying to erase information because of some illicit activity, traces may still be left of the information you're trying to discard, and unless you are very careful, you'll leave traces of your attempt to wipe the disk. At the very least, you'll most likely leave a record in the registry that you installed the wiping program.

LO4

Anti-Forensics

Because of high-profile digital forensics cases, people nowadays understand more about how data is stored on computer storage media and how it can be accessed by forensic software. As a result, a new branch of the digital forensics industry is growing quickly—

the anti-forensics industry. Some of the tools now available that make it hard or impossible to trace user activity or access the data in files were not specifically intended to defeat law enforcement probes; rather, they are there mainly to help computer owners to protect themselves and their data. For example, encryption is a very good way to protect the data on your notebook computer so that if it's stolen, the thief can't get the data. Another is keeping deleted files out of the Recycle Bin, so that someone can't recover your files easily. However, products with names such as Evidence Eliminator, are clearly intended to keep the bad guys from getting caught.

Anti-forensic tools fall into three categories:

1. Configuration settings—included in your operating system, browser, and applications like Word and Excel
2. Third-party tools—utility software on the market that performs specific tasks
3. Forensic-defeating software developed to remove or change the sort of data that forensics experts look for.

CONFIGURATION SETTINGS   This category includes the *Shift + Delete* option that you can use instead of simple *Delete* so that the file is not listed in the Recycle Bin. However, if you use this bypass option you still leave a special signature that digital forensics experts can find. In Windows there are several options that mask user activity, like renaming the file with a different extension. This is probably the simplest, and most easily detected, way of deliberately hiding a file. Say you had an Excel file that had calculations you didn't want anyone to know about. You could name the file Calgary Tower.jpg. It would then appear in Windows Explorer in the list of files as an image file, with the name implying that it's just a vacation photo or something else equally innocuous. If you click on that file, Windows will try to load it with the default .jpg viewer, and of course, it won't load. What digital forensic experts usually do is load the file into a program that accommodates many file formats. This way, you save a lot of time trying to load the renamed file into lots of different types of software. Even more helpful is having a forensic tools like EnCase that actually flag files with extensions that don't match the contents and also show files in their true formats.

Another thing you can do would be to use the option that that clears out virtual memory so that any RAM data that was temporarily stored on the hard disk for use by the processor is removed when the system no longer needs it. Enabling this option, however, will make your system shut down much more slowly. The *Defrag* option rearranges data on your hard disk and overwrites deleted files. *Disk Cleanup*, listed as an option in the Properties of the C: drive, lets you delete ActiveX controls and Java applets (little blocks of code that generate Web page content) that you download automatically and without realizing it from Web sites you visit.

Internet Explorer has similar features like the option to clear temporary Internet files when you close the browser. Another one is the option to clear the history file so that your Internet surfing activity is not easy to find.

Word and Excel allow you to make your font *Hidden* so that it's not visible on the page. You could also use a very small font or make the characters the same colour as the background. Plug-ins are available for Word to remove hidden data and to redact a document. ***Redacting*** means blacking out portions of the document, usually to protect confidential information, so that it cannot be recovered later. The redacted portion of the document has black bars covering the selected text and the text is no longer there.

Office lets you password protect files so that when someone tries to open the file a pop-up window asks for the password. Unless you know the password, you won't be able to read the file. Forensic software can sometimes view the contents of a file without opening the file, eliminating the effectiveness of many types of password protection. And of course there are very effective third-party password-cracking programs available, although not as part of the operating system.

THIRD-PARTY TOOLS   There are lots of these utility programs. For example, some alter your registry—the file that logs installations of hardware and software. Another type hides Excel files inside Word documents and vice versa. Such alteration of hiding does not protect files from an experienced examiner. Others change the file properties in Windows, like the creation date or the extension. Still another type can split files, password protecting and encrypting parts of the file or storing parts in different places on the storage medium.

Probably the best known type of third-party tools are the wiping programs that overwrite the disk, effectively obliterating the information that was there before. They work well enough to clean a hard disk that you may be giving away to someone, but, depending on the actual software, there may be lots of fragments that digital forensics experts can still recover.

There are lots of encryption programs available that protect files so that even if someone manages to get them, it won't be any good because they're not readable without the decryption key. *Encryption* scrambles the contents of a file so that you can't read it without the right decryption key. Often investigators can find the decryption key in a password file or on a bit of paper somewhere around the keyboard. Password-cracking programs can find passwords very easily (alarmingly easily, in fact). They have dictionaries of words from multiple languages, so whole words from any widely used language are not hard to crack. Some people put a digit or two on the front or back of a word. That doesn't fool password-cracking programs at all.

Using images to hide data is another way of protecting information. This is called steganography. *Steganography* (see Figure C.12) is the hiding of information inside other information. Paper money is a good example of steganography. If you hold a Canadian 20-dollar bill up to the light you'll see a watermark of the Queen. The watermark image is hidden inside the other markings on the bill, but it can be seen if you know what you are looking for. All Canadian paper currency denominations contain watermarks.

A very useful tool, but a hardware/software combination this time, is a *U3 Smart drive*, which looks like and is a USB flash drive, but it stores and can launch and run software on any computer. You can have all the software and files you need on the U3 and plug it into any computer, and it can take over computer resources like the CPU, screen, and keyboard—nothing gets stored on the hard disk of the computer you're using, and you can have all your own programs—even your own wallpaper—on the screen. All cache and cookie items go to the U3 and it runs its own programs. This works because it appears to your computer to be a CD and so Windows AutoPlay feature automatically runs the U3 LaunchPad, which is the U3's own user interface. It works very similarly to the Windows interface. You can get a large range of software for a U3 device.

One of the most effective (but not completely foolproof) ways users try to evade detection is by using a U3 Smart device, since it can be plugged into virtually any computer and leaves no trace of the user or the user's activity.

FORENSIC-DEFEATING SOFTWARE   In addition to the utilities that could arguably be acquired for personal privacy or protection purposes, there is software that makes no secret of its purpose to fool investigators. One type removes residual data—data left when files are deleted and the space is partially overwritten. Other software is designed to erase cache memory, cookies, Internet files, the Google search history, and so forth. Some programs are aimed at specific forensic software. EnCase is the usual target because of its standing as the most popular and most accepted software in the industry.

Figure C.12
Steganography Hides a
File in an Image

You can't see the parts of the picture that were changed to encode the hidden message. You'll be able to access the hidden file only when you put the right password into a pop-up window.

Of course, if you're doing something illegal and there are records of it on your computer, for example, if you're keeping track of drug dealing, you could also use any or all of the tools provided by Windows or the utilities supplied by third parties.

Even given all these tools and more, it's not as easy as it may sound to hide your activity on a computer. First, not all programs function as advertised, or as fully as promised. Second, very few people have the knowledge and skill to completely hide their tracks. Third, the installation of third-party utilities or forensic-defeating software or even operating system settings can be detected and can indicate intent to hide something.

A final note on the use of software to evade detection by law enforcement: If you find yourself in litigation and use such tools to get rid of information you believe may be incriminating and then claim that it was never there, you might be in for a rude awakening. The law says that "any product used to circumvent discovery" may be taken as consciousness of guilt. Even though the documents are not available, during the court hearing the inference may be made that you had them and that, by destroying them, you have shown yourself to be guilty. So, being able to determine that such tools have been used is almost as good as finding the evidence itself. This line of reasoning has often been used in cases of illegal distribution of movies and music.

Who Needs Digital Forensics Investigators?

LO5

Digital forensics is widely used wherever and whenever the investigation of electronically stored files is warranted, such as

- In the military, both as part of national security intelligence gathering and analysis and for internal investigations of military personnel

Figure C.13

Professional Organizations and Standards

Professional organizations exist that support digital forensic experts in doing their jobs. The organizations below provide interaction between members who share information, experience, and methods. Such organizations also provide ethical guidelines and certification.

- IACIS (International Association of Computer Investigative Specialists) is open to law enforcement personnel and sets standards and guidelines for computer forensic investigations. On the Web: http://www.cops.org

- ACFI (Association of Certified Forensic Investigators of Canada) is the Canadian governing and accrediting organization for those specialists engaged in fraud detection, prevention, and investigation. On the Web: http://www.acfi.ca

- The HTCIA (High Technology Crime Investigation Association) is open to law enforcement and corporate investigators alike and facilitates the sharing of resources among its members. On the Web: http://www.htcia.org

The Sedona Conference Working Group Series published *The Sedona Canada Principles Addressing Electronic Document Production*. Released in February 2007, this document addresses the disclosure and discovery of electronically stored information in Canadian civil litigation. *The Sedona Canada Principles* will make similarly positive contributions to the development of Canadian law as the first U.S. public comment draft of *The Sedona Principles* in March 2003.[18]

- In law enforcement, when the RCMP, provincial forces, and local police departments need to gather electronic evidence for criminal investigations
- Inside corporations or not-for-profit organizations, when conducting internal audits, for example, or investigating internal incidents
- In consulting firms that specialize in providing digital forensic services to corporations and law enforcement.

Digital forensics experts work both proactively, educating and warning people about possible problems, and reactively, when they're called in to help in response to an incident. The need for such expertise is growing, especially considering that it is estimated that 93 percent of all information is generated in digital form. Since computing and investigative techniques are improving continuously, digital forensics experts need a forum to exchange ideas and information (see Figure C.13).

PROACTIVE DIGITAL FORENSICS EDUCATION FOR PROBLEM PREVENTION

Companies are increasingly providing proactive education for two reasons: first, to educate employees on what to do and not to do with computer resources and why; and second, to teach employees what to do if they suspect wrongdoing, and how not to make things worse by destroying evidence.

People who use computers every day are often not very knowledgeable about what, when, and how information is stored on computers. For example, many corporations have strict policies on how long e-mails will be kept on the system (or in the form of backups). Usually the period of time is about 60 days. You might decide to save your e-mails on your hard disk so that you'll have them indefinitely. This might not be wise since the reason that companies have this policy is that should the company find itself involved in litigation, all electronic information, including e-mail, may be discoverable. That is, the company may have to hand it over to opposing counsel. Also, the more there is, the more it costs to collect, organize, and deliver it.

In Chapter 8 you saw the Industry Perspective box detailing Enron's e-mail situation. Lots of personal information that was not directly related to the legal case became public information and was put on the Internet.

The second reason for providing some education in computer forensics has to do with conducting internal investigations properly. Say a company wants to file a complaint with law enforcement about the suspected illegal activity of an employee. Before law enforcement can look into the situation, however, it needs to have sufficient cause to do so. It can happen that in collecting relevant information the company inadvertently contaminates or destroys the "crime scene." The result may be that law enforcement can't prosecute after all because of lack of evidence.

REACTIVE DIGITAL FORENSICS FOR INCIDENT RESPONSE

Companies need digital forensics, in a reactive mode, to track what employees have been doing with company resources. You saw in Chapter 8 that employees may be using the Internet to such an extent during working hours that their productivity is affected, and the level of personal traffic on the company network may be such that people who are actually working are slowed down. This is just one example of misuse of the company computer system. The evidence of such misappropriation of computer resources can be found on the system itself—on individual client computers and on the servers.

A second reason for reactive digital forensics is changes in laws and government regulations and new laws passed as a consequence of corporate crime and misbehaviour, probably the most important being the U.S. *Sarbanes-Oxley Act* of 2002, signed into law by President George Bush. Known as "Sarbanes-Oxley" or simply "SOX," the law requires companies to (1) implement extensive and detailed policies to prevent illegal activity within the company and (2) respond in a timely manner to investigate illegal activity.

In Closing Case Study 1 in Chapter 8, you saw what happened to Enron's e-mail when the government filed charges against the company.

The act expressly states that executives must certify that their financial statements are accurate. They will be held criminally liable for fraudulent reporting, removing the insulation that executives previously had of being able to say that they didn't know about misstatements. *Sarbanes-Oxley* also specifically requires publicly traded companies to provide anonymous hotlines so that employees and others can report suspicious activity.

There is a Canadian version of *Sarbanes-Oxley*, now simply referred to as Bill 198. An Ontario legislative bill that protects investors by improving the accuracy and reliability of corporate disclosures, it was enacted as Chapter 22 of the Statutes of Ontario, 2002. Written purposely to be similar to SOX, Bill 198 requires that companies not only adopt internal controls over their financial reporting, but also demonstrate their effectiveness and disclose their strengths and weaknesses.

The provision that suspicious activity must be investigated in a timely manner in many instances automatically requires digital forensics. In earlier litigation, courts have determined that computer-stored evidence is crucial to the proper investigation of alleged corporate fraud. Add to that the fact that delay in investigating alleged wrongdoing meets with severe penalties and that courts impose severe sanctions on those judged guilty of destroying evidence including electronic information.

IN THE CANADIAN CONTEXT

The sections of the Criminal Code of Canada pertinent to our discussion are contained in part IX, entitled "Offences against Rights of Property," and specifically deal with "Offences Resembling Theft" and are further subdivided into the four following parts of Section 342:

- Section 342 concerns theft and/or forgery of credit cards
- Section 342.01 concerns making, having, or dealing in instruments for forging or falsifying credit cards
- Section 342.1 concerns unauthorized use of computers
- Section 342.2 concerns possession of a device(s) to obtain computer services.

Upon conviction under one or another section of the code, persons are subject to a sentence ranging from 2 to 10 years in federal prison. But information systems, the Internet, and the ingenuity of criminals has led to a proliferation of crimes where the perpetrator is in one country and the victim in another. Thus computer crime, often referred to as cybercrime, is a dynamic and growing international phenomenon. How do we define such crime? Computer crime (sometimes called cybercrime, e-crime, hi-tech crime, or electronic crime) refers to criminal activity in which a computer or network is either the origin, method, target, or location of a crime. The salient definitions are found in the Council of Europe Convention on Cybercrime, dated November 23, 2001, and entered into force on July 1, 2004. Canada participated in drafting and then signed this international treaty, which defines the following areas of criminal offence involving computer use:

- Offences against the confidentiality, integrity, and availability of computer data and systems
- Computer-related offences
- Content-related offences
- Offences related to infringements of copyright and related rights
- Ancillary liability.

In January 2008, the code was amended to include criminal offences contained in the additional protocol to the Convention on Cybercrime wherein the criminalization of acts of a racist and xenophobic nature, committed through the use of computer systems, were added. At the time of writing, Canada had not yet ratified the Convention on Cybercrime or the Additional Protocol to the Convention on cybercrime.

What is important in this taxonomy is the recognition that the commission of more traditional crimes such as theft, blackmail, fraud, embezzlement, and forgery may be facilitated by computers and networks and may not necessarily be the target or location of the criminal activity. Thus the Internet itself has become both a crime tool and a crime scene, further muddying the already murky waters of international crime.[19, 20, 21, 22, 23]

A case in point is that involving a 15-year-old boy from Montreal who gained international notoriety for engineering several DoS attacks on high-profile Web sites in February 2000. The sites included Yahoo!, Amazon.com, Dell, Inc., E*TRADE, eBay, and CNN. Due to his age, he was identified only by his online moniker, mafiaboy. Under the Criminal Code of Canada, mafiaboy could have received up to two years in detention. He was instead sentenced to eight months in a youth detention centre and to one year probation upon release. He was also ordered to donate $250 to charity.

What makes this case interesting outside of the breadth of the attacks orchestrated by mafiaboy was that the target Web sites were all outside Canada. The RCMP collaborated with the FBI in bringing mafiaboy to justice but since he was Canadian and the crimes originated in Canada, mafiaboy was tried under Canadian law. If he had been convicted of the corresponding offence In the United States, mafiaboy's sentence could have been up to 10 years in jail and double the monetary fine under Canadian law. The FBI maintained that hundreds of millions of dollars of damage resulted from the attacks. One estimate pegged the total damages at US$1.2 billion.[24, 25, 26, 27]

Of further interest in this vein is the responsibilities and pressures placed on companies that operate in the international context. An important case in point is the dispute between Waterloo, Ontario-based Research in Motion (RIM), makers of the popular BlackBerry devices and the Government of India over the high level of security RIM's systems put on the communications occurring over its network. On one side of the coin, strong encryption of messages passing between clients could be seen as an important selling feature. On the other hand, governments such as India are involved in the high-stakes fight against terrorism.

It is precisely this struggle that led India to demand that RIM give it unfettered access to all communications between individuals that pass through RIM's Blackberry network. India's Union Home Ministry was particularly concerned with terrorist activity in the Kashmir district. RIM countered that giving such access would not solve the country's problem as other smartphone vendors offered similar confidentiality features to clients. Terrorists could simply switch to another vendor to circumvent the security issue. RIM pointed to four other systems extant in India with similar encryption systems: Windows Mobile ActiveSync, Nokia Intellisync, Motorola's Good, and Seven Networks.

The debate centres around whether or not RIM should allow the Indian government security services to essentially spy on some users. India's department of Telecom (DoT) issued an ultimatum to RIM to either provide some solution to its encryption feature or cease operations in the country. At the time of writing, RIM and India were in the final stages of providing a solution to the issue but the details had not yet been made public.

This case has interesting parallels to the Canadian situation as it is impacted by the *U.S. Patriot Act* (discussed in Chapter 8). The flow of data is no longer controlled and regulated by the country in which the flow originates or terminates. Increasingly, the issue needs to be addressed at the global level. The Internet has changed everything.[28, 29, 30]

Summary: STUDENT LEARNING OUTCOMES *REVISITED*

LO1 Define computer crime and list three types of computer crime that can be perpetrated from inside and outside the organization.
Computer crime is a crime in which a computer, or computers, played a significant part in its commission. Crimes perpetrated outside the organization include

- *Computer viruses* • Web defacing
- *Denial-of-Service (DoS) attacks* • *Trojan-horse virus.*
- *Malware bots*

Crimes perpetrated inside the organization include
- Fraud
- Embezzlement
- Harassment.

LO2 Identify the seven types of hackers and explain what motivates each group. *Hackers* are knowledgeable computer users who use their knowledge to invade other people's computers. The seven types are

- *Thrill-seeker hackers*, who are motivated by the entertainment value of breaking into computers
- *White-hat hackers*, who are hired by a company to find the vulnerabilities in its network
- *Black-hat hackers*, who are cyber vandals and cause damage for fun
- *Crackers*, who are hackers for hire and are the people who engage in electronic corporate espionage
- *Hacktivists*, who are politically motivated hackers who use the Internet to send a political message of some kind

- *Cyberterrorists*, who seek to cause harm to people or destroy critical systems or information for political reasons
- *Script kiddies* or *script bunnies*, who would like to be hackers but don't have much technical expertise.

LO3 **Define digital forensics and describe the two phases of a forensic investigation.** *Digital forensics* is the collection, authentication, preservation, and examination of electronic information for presentation in court. Electronic evidence can be found on any type of computer storage medium. A computer forensic investigation has two phases: (1) collecting, authenticating, and preserving electronic evidence; and (2) analyzing the findings. The collection phase consists of

- Getting physical access to the computer and any other items that might be helpful
- Creating a *forensic image copy* of all storage media
- Authenticating the forensic image copy by generating an *MD5 hash value*, that, when recalculated at a later date, will be exactly the same number, as long as nothing at all on the storage medium has changed in any way
- Using forensic hardware that can read storage media but cannot write to them
- Using forensic software that can find deleted, hidden, and otherwise hard-to-access information.

The analysis phase consists of
- Finding all the information and deducing what it means
- Assembling a crime story that fits the information that has been discovered.

LO4 **Describe what is meant by anti-forensics and give an example of each of the three types.** Anti-forensics is a name for tools that mask or eliminate traces of user activity on a computer. The three types are

1. Configuration settings—included in your operating system, browser, and applications like Word and Excel. An example is *Shift + Delete* to bypass the Recycle Bin.
2. Third-party tools—utility software on the market that performs specific tasks. An example is encryption software.
3. Forensic defeating software developed to remove or change the sort of data that forensics experts look for. An example is software that changes creation and access dates on files.

LO5 **Describe two ways in which businesses use digital forensics.** Corporations use computer forensics for proactive education and for reactive incident response. Education serves to explain to employees what they should and should not do with computer resources and also how to conduct an internal computer forensic investigation. Incident response involves uncovering employee wrongdoing and preserving the evidence so that action can be taken.

Key Terms and Concepts

Black-hat hacker, 349
Bot, 348
Botnet, 348
Computer crime, 341
Computer virus (virus), 342
Cracker, 350
Cyberterrorist, 350
Denial-of-Service (DoS) attack, 346
Digital forensics, 352
Distributed denial-of-Service (DDoS) attack, 346
Drone, 348
Encryption, 364

Forensic image copy, 352
Hacker, 349
Hacktivist, 350
Key logger (key trapper) software, 345
Malware, 342
Malware bot, 348
MD5 hash value, 354
Redacting, 363
Rootkit, 348
Script bunny (script kiddie), 350
Slack space, 361
Social engineering, 350

Spoofing, 345
Steganography, 364
Thrill-seeker hacker, 349
Trojan horse virus, 345
U3 Smart drive, 364
Unallocated space, 362
White-hat hacker (ethical hacker), 349
Worm, 342
Zombie, 348

Short-Answer Questions

1. In what two ways are computers used in the commission of crimes or misdeeds?
2. What constitutes a computer crime?
3. What kind of software is a computer virus?
4. How does a denial-of-service attack work?
5. What is the effect of a virus hoax?
6. What is the difference between the Klez family of viruses and previous worms?
7. What is a white-hat hacker?
8. What do crackers do?
9. Is there a difference between a cyberterrorist and a hacktivist? If so, what is it?
10. What is digital forensics?
11. What is anti-forensics?
12. What is live analysis?

Assignments and Exercises

1. **FIND DIGITAL FORENSICS SOFTWARE** On the Web are many sites that offer digital forensics software. Find five such software packages and for each one answer the following questions:
   - What does the software do? List five features it advertises.
   - Is the software free? If not, how much does it cost?
   - Is there any indication of the software's target market? If so, what market is it (law enforcement, home use, or something else)?

2. **WHAT EXACTLY ARE THE *SEDONA CANADA PRINCIPLES*?**
   Write a report on the stipulations of the *Sedona Canada Principles*. Do some research and find out exactly what the *Sedona Canada Principles* suggest. Here's the first one to get you started: Electronically stored information is discoverable. Be sure to explain in your paper any legal terms, such as "discoverable," that appear in the first principle above.

3. **THE INTERNATIONAL ANTI-CYBERCRIME TREATY** Determine the provisions of the international anti-cybercrime treaty, and how they will affect Canada. One of the concerns that will have to be addressed is the issue of whether laws of one country should apply to all. For example, if certain sites are illegal in Saudi Arabia, should they be illegal for all surfers? Or if Germany has a law about hate language, should a German or a Canadian citizen be extradited to stand trial for building a neo-Nazi Web site? What do you think?

Extended Learning Module D

Careers in Business

STUDENT LEARNING OUTCOMES

LO1 Identify the career field and business specialization in which you are interested.

LO2 Provide typical job titles and descriptions for your career field.

LO3 List and describe the IT skills you need to gain while in school.

Introduction

In the business world, you need to be "a jack of all trades and a master of one." That means that you need to excel in a particular business functional area (or specialization), such as finance, accounting, marketing, or any of the other many business specializations. It also means that, although your expertise lies within one functional area, you need to be competent in all the other functional areas.

Think about majoring in marketing, for example. You need expertise in consumer behaviour, marketing strategies, branding techniques, and many other marketing-oriented concepts. But as a marketing analyst, you need other skills to be successful. You need knowledge of accounting and finance so you can put together a budget and monitor expenses. You need team and employee management skills so you can work effectively in a group and manage other people. You need knowledge of production and operations management so you can understand works-in-progress information and transportation optimization algorithms.

No matter what your career choice, you need knowledge of information technology tools that will allow you to perform your tasks more efficiently and effectively. This textbook isn't about trying to get you to major in information technology or choose MIS as a career. It's about informing you of the role of information technology and MIS in an organization and enabling you to select and use the right IT tools to carry out your tasks.

In this module, we want to explore with you many of the career specializations in business, including

- Accounting
- Finance
- Hospitality and tourism management

- Information technology
- Management
- Marketing
- Production and operations management
- Real estate and construction management.

At your school, there are probably departments devoted to providing degrees in these specializations. While titles and nomenclatures may differ (e.g., production and operations management is often called management science, operations research, statistics and operations technology, or some other variation), those specializations represent the major functional areas in a typical business.

After providing you with a brief introduction to each specialization, we include the following information:

- List of typical job titles and their descriptions
- IT tools you should focus on learning while in school
- Statistics concerning the job market.

It is our hope that, after reading this module, you will come to understand that IT and MIS are important no matter what your career choice. You may be taking this class because it's a required part of the business curriculum. It's required because, no matter what career you choose, you need knowledge of IT and MIS. It's similar to taking a human resource management class. While you may not be majoring in human resource management, you will at some time in your career probably have to manage people. Knowing how to manage them effectively is a career opportunity for you.

We believe that being able to identify the right technology tools and use them effectively is also a career opportunity for you. We encourage you to take some time to critically evaluate the many specializations in business, select the one you're most interested in, and then identify what information technology tools you need to learn in school to make your business career a success.

Accounting

Accounting is the language of business. All businesses, for-profit and not-for-profit, need accountants to communicate financial information. Accountants must understand all aspects of business in order to properly communicate the financial information.

There are five broad areas of accounting—public practice, industry, government, non-profit, and education. The first three are the most common and are discussed here. In public accounting, the accountant serves as an outside adviser to business organizations. The primary areas of responsibility are auditing, which involves examining the financial statements of a company to assure compliance with generally accepted accounting principles; and tax advisory services, which involve helping businesses plan the most beneficial structure and practices for applying tax rules and regulations, as well as preparing the actual tax returns.

Industry accounting involves working within a company to manage investor relations, banking relations, and daily financial affairs, as well as plan new products or services. Since almost all activities in a company involve either cash inflow or outflow, the accounting function is involved in almost every business decision of an organization.

Government accounting can range from working at the city level to working at the federal level. Typical positions are auditors, revenue managers, and budget analysts. There are also many government agent positions with organizations such as the CSIS,

CRA, and RCMP. These positions involve enforcement of federal laws and regulations. Any accounting position requires knowledge of broad business concepts, government regulations, and the financial implications of both.

TYPICAL JOB TITLES AND DESCRIPTIONS

The typical job titles found in accounting and their descriptions are listed below.

Chief Financial Officer—Corporate officer primarily responsible for managing the financial risks of the business or agency. This officer is also responsible for financial planning and record keeping, as well as financial reporting to higher management. Additional duties involve investor relations, banking relations, and long-term financial planning.

Management Accountant—Also called cost, managerial, industrial, corporate, or private accountant—records and analyzes the financial information of the companies for which he or she works. Other responsibilities are budgeting, performance evaluation, cost management, and asset management. Management accountants usually are part of executive teams involved in strategic planning or new product development. They analyze and interpret financial information needed by corporate executives in order to make sound business decisions. They also prepare financial reports for other groups, including stockholders, creditors, regulatory agencies, and tax authorities. Within accounting departments, management accountants may work in various areas, including financial analysis, planning and budgeting, and cost accounting.

Environmental Accountant—Helps businesses understand their environmental costs and factor these costs into their financial and other decision-making processes. Helps businesses find ways to save money through environmental protection measures. Using special environmental cost assessment systems, environmental accountants help companies improve their decisions regarding product mixing, manufacturing, waste management options, and other areas.

Government Accountant and Auditor—Works in the public sector, maintaining and examining the records of government agencies and auditing private businesses and individuals whose activities are subject to government regulations or taxation. Accountants employed by federal, provincial, and local governments guarantee that revenues are received and expenditures are made in accordance with laws and regulations. Those employed by the federal government may work in financial management, financial institution examination, or budget analysis and administration.

Internal Auditor—Verifies the accuracy of the organization's internal records and checks for mismanagement, waste, or fraud. Internal auditors examine and evaluate their firms' financial and information systems, management procedures, and internal controls to ensure that records are accurate and controls are adequate to protect against fraud and waste. They also review company operations, evaluating their efficiency, effectiveness, and compliance with corporate policies and procedures, laws, and government regulations. Internal auditors also may recommend controls for their organization's computer system, to ensure the reliability of the system and the integrity of the data.

Public Accountant—Performs a broad range of accounting, auditing, tax, and consulting activities for clients, which may be corporations, governments, non-profit organizations, or individuals. Some public accountants concentrate on tax matters, such as advising companies about the tax advantages and disadvantages of certain business decisions and preparing individual income tax returns. Others offer advice in areas such as compensation or employee health care benefits, the design of accounting and data-processing systems, and the selection of controls to safeguard assets. Still others audit clients' financial statements and inform investors and authorities that the statements have been correctly prepared and reported. Public accountants, many of whom are Chartered Accountants (CA) or Certified Management Accountants (CMA), generally have their own businesses or work for public accounting firms.

Tax Accountant—Responsible for tax planning and tax return preparation. Requires an understanding of tax laws and other regulations for individuals, estates, trusts, and businesses (both large and small). Tax accountants are frequently consulted for the legal/tax structuring of new business ventures to ensure the most beneficial application of tax regulations.

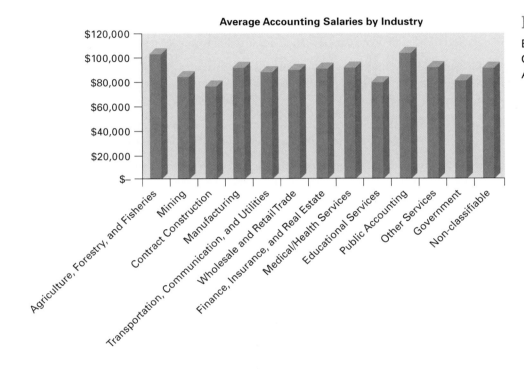

Figure D.1

Employment and Other Information in Accounting (US Data) [1]

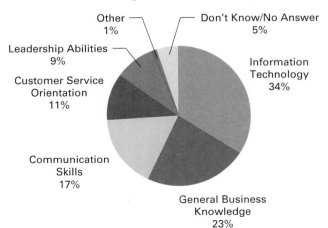

INFORMATION TECHNOLOGY SKILLS YOU SHOULD PURSUE

To be effective in accounting, we recommend that you gain knowledge in the IT tools and concepts listed below and on the next page.

Accounting Information Systems—Almost all accounting systems are computerized. The accountant must know how to operate the software and be able to quickly learn new software as the technology changes.

Database Management—Many accounting systems require ad hoc reports and structural changes to keep up with changes to the company. The accountant is responsible for keeping the accounting system current. This requires knowledge of database management systems as accounting information is stored in a database.

Database Design—To properly audit an accounting system, the accountant must understand the design of the database and be able to follow transactions through the system.

Web Research—Accountants must frequently consult rules and regulations available on the Internet. The ability to rapidly search and apply information is a necessity for any accounting position.

Spreadsheet Modelling—Financial projections and analyses require extensive use of electronic spreadsheets. Accountants must be expert at these skills to be productive.

Network Security—The accountant is responsible for the security of the assets of a company. Knowledge of the computer systems and networks is required to assure the security of the company's information.

Finance

Finance plays an integral part in the decision-making process at most companies. There are several distinct areas of study in finance that lead to very different professional job tracks. These tracks, broadly described, are corporate finance, banking, and investments. However, a common thread to each of these tracks is the basic tools that you use to aid in decision making. In addition, finance professionals need to have strong interpersonal skills to aid others in making the correct decisions for their companies or their personal finances.

The study of finance draws heavily from three different academic disciplines: accounting, economics (especially microeconomics), and statistics. These disciplines provide the informational and analytical frameworks with which a decision maker works on a day-to-day basis. Thus, a finance professional must have a background in each of these areas of study. The finance professional can work at a company, aiding in the allocation of resources; in the banking industry, providing funds for businesses and individuals; or in the investments industry, aiding individuals or institutions with the investment of their resources. In all of these roles, the decision maker must rely on information technology to support the analysis and decisions being made, and in many situations the IT function in a company will be integral to the implementation of the decisions made. Of growing importance is the maintenance of large databases containing information regarding clients, customers, projects, and other areas that are a focus of research by the finance professional. These databases can be either provided by third-party vendors or created by the finance professional.

TYPICAL JOB TITLES AND DESCRIPTIONS

The typical job titles found in finance and their descriptions are listed below.

Corporate Treasurer—Responsible for controlling the cash needs of the corporation. The cash-budgeting process will identify whether the corporation has a cash surplus or deficit. Any surplus will be invested in short-term, safe investment securities. Any deficit will need to be provided for with bank loans or issues of commercial paper.

Corporate Financial Analyst—Aids in the investment of corporate resources. Prepares project reports for the capital budgeting process and helps the various operating units control spending and manage their investment in both short-term and long-term assets. Includes management of inventory investment, accounts receivable investment, and cash management.

Bank Loan Officer—Works with individuals, small businesses, and large corporations to provide funds for their spending needs. This can range from the purchase of a car to the financing of a fleet of airplanes. Strong analytical skills as well as interpersonal skills are a requirement in this field.

Trust Officer—Works at a commercial bank primarily with two very different groups. First are individuals who establish trusts for estate planning and other reasons. Second are business and municipal issuers of bonds. In this second role, the trust officer serves to ensure that the interests of the investors are met by the issuer.

Security Analyst—Works in the markets to provide investment information and sometimes advice to individual and institutional investors. Can work either for a brokerage firm or for an institutional investment company.

Portfolio Manager—Typically works for institutions such as mutual funds or insurance companies. Directs the investment decisions for these institutions, choosing which stocks, bonds, and other investments are appropriate. Directs the efforts of several security analysts in this process.

Stock Broker—Works primarily with individuals to aid in investment in stocks and bonds. Purchases and sells stocks at the direction of the client. In some circumstances is also responsible for providing information and even an investment strategy for the client.

INFORMATION TECHNOLOGY SKILLS YOU SHOULD PURSUE

To be effective in finance, we recommend that you gain knowledge in the IT tools and concepts listed below.

Spreadsheet Modelling—An advanced knowledge of spreadsheet modelling is essential to most careers in finance. Forecasting future cash flows and evaluating changes in assumptions will aid the decision maker.

Statistical Packages—Statistical analysis helps the decision maker identify and measure the risk inherent in a project. The advanced statistical packages available support this analysis.

Database Management—The ability to create, maintain, and manipulate databases is essential to the decision-making tools in finance. Information such as returns, credit risk measures, and so on are used by investors.

Figure D.2

Employment and Other Information in Finance (US Data)

Internet and Web Portals—Corporations use Web sites to provide investors with information regarding the company. Automated bill payment is a means of controlling accounts receivable and accounts payable, both for individuals and businesses.

Search Engines—Information is the lifeblood of decision making. Being able to accurately and efficiently gather information is a critical skill.

Technology Strategy and Innovation—Banks are innovating new ways to efficiently process customer deposits/withdrawals. Businesses are creating new payment systems via intranets. An understanding of how this innovation affects the company is critical to the finance professional.

Hospitality and Tourism Management

If you dream about exotic vacations, travelling to alluring destinations, and having fun, a career in hospitality and tourism management (HTM) might be for you. HTM is one of the world's largest, most diverse, and exciting industries. According to the World Travel and Tourism Council (www.wttc.org), by the end of 2007, the industry is expected to generate US$7.1 trillion in economic activity (or 10.4 percent of the world's total Gross Domestic Product) and account for 8.3 percent of the world's total employment. That is in excess of 231 million jobs—or one out of every 12 jobs. With a projected 4.3 percent per annum real growth rate for the next 10 years, the industry outlook is extremely favourable. By 2017, the industry is expected to reach US$13.2 trillion and employ nearly 263 million people. Careers can range from hotel general managers and controllers to restaurant operators and event planners to technology developers and electronic commerce specialists. In fact, you can find positions associated with every academic business discipline somewhere in the hospitality and tourism field.

Hospitality and tourism businesses make money by serving guests and creating for their guests unique, personable, and memorable experiences. These businesses are especially challenging to operate because of the intangible nature of what consumers purchase and the perishability of the services or products sold (for example, revenue from rooms not sold today or cruise ships that sail not filled can never be recouped). Adding to the challenge are the heterogeneity of the customers (each customer has different needs and expectations), the simultaneous production and consumption of the services, the dependence on labour, and the ease with which products and services can be copied.

TYPICAL JOB TITLES AND DESCRIPTIONS

A sampling of typical job titles found in hospitality and tourism management and their descriptions are listed below. Increasingly, to be effective in any hospitality business role, one must have a solid grounding in concepts related to information technology (IT) because of its pervasiveness throughout and impact on every aspect of the business. It is not enough to understand only one business discipline (e.g., marketing, finance, accounting, human resources, etc.) but rather at least one, if not more, business disciplines and the roles technology plays to enable (or sometimes constrain) activities, service, customer loyalty, business strategies, etc. IT has become an indispensable tool for any business and such an integral part of the business that practically every business decision affects IT, and every IT decision impacts the business. And this is especially so in hospitality and tourism. IT can help organizations drive revenues and cut costs (thereby improving profitability), enhance guest service and experiences (thereby improving loyalty), improve managerial controls (thereby reducing loss or theft), and enhance communications and reporting (thereby improving information flows so that employees are empowered to make informed decisions and perform their jobs to help the organization operate effectively and efficiently and to help "wow" guests and create outstanding and memorable experiences).

General Manager—Responsible for overseeing an entire operation (e.g., hotel, restaurant, casino, theme park, etc.). Typically works his or her way through the various departments of the operation to understand it from the ground up. Sets strategy, oversees the financial aspects of the business, interfaces with the community, helps market the operation, manages people, and is accountable to the owner of the operation. Relies on operational systems and reports to manage, control, and direct the business. Uses technology to track and communicate with customers, suppliers, and employees.

Controller—Responsible for the accounting and financial aspects of the operation. Establishes and manages budgets, maintains the books, prepares financial reports, acquires funding for capital projects, and controls against theft and waste. Typically a heavy spreadsheet user; maintains the back-office accounting systems.

Director of Sales and Marketing—Oversees the sales and marketing activities of the operation and is typically responsible for group business (i.e., corporate accounts, meetings, and conventions). In charge of all the operation's marketing collateral, promotions, and electronic commerce initiatives. Also responsible for the sales and catering system, lead tracking system, and sales force automation.

Director of Human Resources—Responsible for all aspects of staffing and team building. Responsibilities include hiring and termination decisions, benefits administration, payroll, policy compliance, training, promotions, special programs, and succession planning. Uses time and attendance systems, payroll systems, and human resource information systems.

Director of Room Operations—Responsible for all guest service functions in a hotel. These include front desk, bell staff, housekeeping, concierge, and reservations. Responsible in part for managing several key systems, including the property management system, the reservation system, the telephone accounting systems, the guest lock system, and in-room guest amenities (e.g., movies, high-speed Internet access, mini bars, etc.).

Revenue Manager—Responsible for setting rates, restrictions, and selling strategies for hotel rooms and managing room inventory allocated to the various distribution channels used by the hotel. Relies on the hotel's revenue (yield) management system, reservation system, and property management system to perform his or her daily tasks.

Food and Beverage Director—Oversees all food and beverage operations. Manages day-to-day operations, purchasing, and inventory management. Key systems maintained and used include point-of-sale, inventory management, and purchasing and receiving systems. Culinary expertise is helpful to complement strong business acumen.

IT Manager—Oversees, maintains, and secures the various computer systems used throughout the organization, provides support to end users, and assists with the selection, procurement, and implementation of computer applications and hardware.

INFORMATION TECHNOLOGY SKILLS YOU SHOULD PURSUE

To be effective in hospitality and tourism management, we recommend that you gain knowledge in the IT tools and concepts listed below.

Personal Computer (PC) Applications—Proficiencies in Microsoft Office applications, electronic mail, and the Internet are essential to every professional position in the hospitality and tourism industry.

Hospitality-Specific Applications—Numerous systems are required to run a hospitality and tourism operation. Some of the core systems include the hotel property management system (to manage hotel room inventory and check in/out guests), the central reservations system (for hotel bookings), the point-of-sale system (for food, beverage, and gift shop sales), the revenue (yield) management system (for managing hotel rates, restrictions, and selling strategies), the accounting system (for maintaining the books), and the guest history/loyalty system (for guest preferences, past purchases, frequent travel program management, and CRM).

Database Management—The underlying technology behind most hospitality applications is a database management system. This allows information to be collected, stored, managed, and reported.

Project Management—Hospitality businesses are complex entities with many variables that must be carefully managed, especially when technology applications are involved. Important responsibilities of any manager (not just an IT manager) are to be able to simultaneously manage many activities (tasks or projects) and multiple personnel, budget for and allocate resources, and deliver results by holding people accountable and managing scope. To do this, strong project management skills are essential.

Business Analysis—Because the impacts of technology are far-reaching within the organization and impact job skills/duties, business processes, and information flows, it is important to have a strong analytical mind to understand how and where to use technology, the potential implications (both good and bad), and the resource needs. A large part of any business person's role is to be able to see problems and opportunities and to match technology where appropriate to solve problems and capitalize on opportunities.

Decision Support Systems/Executive Information Systems—Hospitality and tourism operations are fast paced and information intensive. Managers must be able to use software applications to analyze and interpret information, model the business under different scenarios, and make informed and timely decisions.

Computer/Network Security—Given our dependence upon technology, both as individuals and as business organizations, and the many potential threats that come with using technology and conducting business digitally (e.g., exposure to viruses and worms, hacking, computer outages, etc.), managers must be well versed (at least from a macro level) about these vulnerabilities, educate their employees, and be prepared to take pre-emptive action (that is, develop and implement strategies, practices, and policies to protect the organization so that systems, data, identities, and assets are not compromised).

Electronic Commerce—Electronic commerce goes beyond hotel and restaurant bookings and merchandise or gift certificate purchases, etc. Hospitality and tourism professionals must know how to use the Internet to effectively and cost-efficiently reach consumers, serve them, and gain their loyalty. It is important to understand Web site design principles, interactive or electronic marketing, Web positioning strategies, and search engine optimization. Increasingly important is tapping into Travel 2.0, a term coined to reflect the next generation of Internet developments occurring in the travel space. Adapted from the concept of Web 2.0, Travel 2.0 reflects the growing interactive, multimedia experience of the Web and increased consumer empowerment as a result of the democratization of information, consumer-generated content, social networking, comparison-shopping tools, mashups (the combining of content from multiple Web sites into a single display), and more.

Distribution Channel Management—One of the most complex aspects of the hospitality and tourism business today is distribution channel management. Having the ability to build and manage channel relationships, synchronize channel information, track channel productivity, integrate the various technologies, and maintain the technology infrastructure required to support the many available distribution channels is a competitive necessity.

Revenue Management—One of the greatest career growth areas is revenue management, which involves analyzing and forecasting supply and demand patterns and trends and setting appropriate room rates, sell strategies, and room inventory allotments to maximize hotel revenues. This area brings together statistics, marketing, and finance.

Customer Relationship Management (CRM)—At the heart of any hospitality and tourism firm is the guest, the primary reason for being in business. Taking a guest-centric view of the business to provide unique and personalized experiences is fundamental to building guest loyalty and maintaining a competitive edge.

IT Strategy—It is important for business executives to understand how to align IT with the business strategy and allocate resources appropriately to achieve business goals and create competitive advantage. One must be able to assess risk factors, evaluate costs versus benefits, and build convincing business cases to win the necessary approval, support, and resources to launch IT project initiatives.

Figure D.3

Median Salaries for Hotel Positions (by Hotel Size, US Data)

Position	Nationwide	150–350 Rooms	>800 Rooms
Banquet Director	$ 42,436	$ 35,019	$ 65,740
Catering Sales Manager	37,795	35,824	48,225
Controller	68,541	59,707	95,532
Director of HR	59,717	53,073	82,202
Director of MIS	54,636	53,045	60,972
Director of Sales	68,269	N/A	99,495
Director of Rooms	63,688	59,685	73,607
Executive Chef	67,505	61,665	95,532
General Manager	85,616	102,625	165,970
Restaurant Manager	37,151	37,131	42,436

Information Technology

Information technology (IT) tools and management information systems (MIS) are now so pervasive in business environments and every aspect of your life that it's hard to imagine how the world would operate without them.

As this book is about IT and MIS, we have often discussed the varied careers in this specialization. Careers in this field range from the very managerial—such as the chief information officer (CIO) who oversees the use of information as an important organizational resource—to the very technical such as network security specialists who develop security and encryption algorithms and fight the never-ending battle protecting network resources from viruses and worms. Regardless, all IT people need to possess a solid understanding of the business environment as well as possess people-oriented and communications skills. IT specialists work daily with business colleagues in other functional areas to develop IT systems that meet business needs. IT people must, therefore, be able to communicate clearly and articulately and understand how the IT system serves the greater good of the organization.

TYPICAL JOB TITLES AND DESCRIPTIONS

The typical job titles found in information technology and their descriptions are listed below.

Programmer—Responsible for taking technical design documents concerning a new IT system and writing the software. Requires tremendous expertise in any of the many popular software programming languages such as Java, ASP, and C++. May also require expertise in development tools such as Rational Rose.

Business Analyst—Responsible for working with end users to determine the logical requirements for a new IT system and then building the technical design documents that a programmer will use to write the software. Requires tremendous people skills for soliciting and understanding end-user requirements. May also require expertise in development tools, which can create a repository of design documents for an IT system.

Database Designer/Developer—Responsible for working with end users to determine information requirements for a new IT system and then designing and implementing a database solution. Requires expertise in data modelling (such as E-R diagramming) and the use of popular DBMS tools such as Oracle and DB/2.

Web Services Expert—Facilitates the development of network-based IT systems that support e-commerce activities for an organization. Requires expertise in a number of IT tools and concepts including databases, security, and Web Services programming languages and tools such as ASP, XML, ASP.Net, XML.Net, C#, and Visual Studio.Net.

Network Engineer—Responsible for a wide range of activities associated with the design, development, implementation, and maintenance of IT networks. May include expertise in security and encryption methodologies. Usually requires expertise in the development of methodologies to stop, eliminate, and/or quarantine viruses and worms.

Data Warehouse Analyst/Developer—Responsible for working with end users to determine information requirements for new IT systems and then designing and implementing a data warehouse solution. Requires expertise in both database modelling and data warehouse information modelling. Requires expertise in the use of popular data warehousing platforms such as IBM's Cognos and Informatica.

INFORMATION TECHNOLOGY SKILLS YOU SHOULD PURSUE

To be effective in information technology, we recommend that you gain knowledge in the IT tools and concepts listed below.

Programming Languages—Programming languages are special-purpose languages that programmers use to write software code. While you may not be a programmer, you must understand both basic and advanced programming constructs to understand what a proposed system can and cannot do.

Development Platforms—Development platforms are support software tools for logical and technical modelling and writing software. They not only provide a repository of project information, but also often support the automated translation of logical requirements into technical requirements and/or technical requirements into various platforms of implementation.

Databases—Databases are central to the information management activities of any organization. Databases support the design and implementation of logically related information. Database-stored information can then be used, manipulated, and massaged according to the needs of the end user without regard to the physical storage characteristics of information.

Data Warehouses—These support the management and assimilation of information for decision making and important business analysis activities. Data warehouses summarize and aggregate information in multiple dimensions or perspectives, giving end users the ability to "slice and dice" their way through the information to see patterns, identify problems, and identify competitive advantage opportunities.

Networks and Security—These include a vast array of technologies including communications protocols, telecommunications hardware such as routers, and architectures such as 2-tier and 3-tier (i.e., client/server networks).

Multimedia Tools—This tool set includes a variety of hardware and software associated with the capturing, creating, and manipulating of information in forms other than text and numbers. Such information includes audio, video, still photos, art, and so on.

Figure D.4

Employment and
Other Information in
Information Technology

Job Type	2008 Range	% change 2007
CIO	$125,250–182,250	2.5
Director of IS	84,000–122,500	2.2
IT Manager	84,000–122,500	2.2
Project Manager	74,250–108,250	6.1
Lead Applications Developer	67,250–94,250	3.2
Applications Architect	78,250–100,500	1.9
Web Developer	54,500–77,250	4.2
Applications Manager	87,000–110,750	7.6

Search Term	Hits on Monster.ca
Programming	1,000+
Visual Basic	400+
Chief Information Officer	40+
Database (Administrator)	150+
Network (numerous terms included)	~2,000
Web Services	1,250++
Data Architect	160+

Management

Managers play a critical role in shaping the future of Canadian businesses. Managers must be well educated, creative, and effective. Managers hold over 300,000 jobs in Canada and are in every industry. Managers plan, organize, direct, control, and coordinate the operations of organizations and major departments or programs. Organizations today operate in an increasingly complex and fast-changing environment, and managers depend increasingly on the use of technology to carry out their responsibilities. Successful managers possess a broad range of interpersonal and analytical skills.

The management major is one of the most eclectic disciplines in all of academia. *Administrative services managers* perform a broad range of duties in virtually every sector of the economy. They coordinate and direct support services to organizations as diverse as insurance companies, computer manufacturers, and government offices. *Marketing managers* develop the firm's detailed marketing strategy. Along with *product development managers* and *market research managers*, they determine the demand for products and services offered by the firm and its competitors. *Public relations managers* direct publicity programs to targeted audiences. They sometimes specialize in a specific area, such as crisis management, or in a specific industry, such as health care. *Sales managers* direct the firm's sales program. They assign sales territories, set goals, and establish training programs for the sales representatives. As computers are increasingly used to record and organize data, *financial managers* are spending more time developing strategies and implementing the long-term goals of their organization. *Human resources managers* handle all aspects of human resources work, including employment, compensation, benefits, and employee relations. *Management analysts*, or *management consultants*, analyze and propose ways to improve an organization's structure, efficiency, or profits.

TYPICAL JOB TITLES AND DESCRIPTIONS

The typical job titles found in management and their descriptions are listed below.

Business Development Manager—Is a team leader. The team is responsible for developing meaningful and profitable relationships with business partners. The manager recruits, trains, and enables subordinates to identify and exploit revenue opportunities with business partners. The manager coordinates and updates all ongoing relationships using the company's information technology system.

Entrepreneur—Begins businesses and becomes his or her own boss. Entrepreneurs usually start by creating and operating a small business. Sometimes they purchase a franchise as a way to start. Increasingly, entrepreneurs are starting their first business on the Internet using e-commerce applications. Successful entrepreneurs face many options, including selling their business for large profits or equity in larger corporations (for example, the owners of Ben & Jerry's Ice Cream).

Human Resources Manager—Serves as a link between management and employees. The HR manager provides specialized services to members of the organization. The manager's goal is to foster positive relationships, increase job satisfaction, and make sure all customers' or clients' needs are met. The HR manager's responsibilities include administration, recruitment, compensation and benefits, training and development, health and safety, and employee relations.

Management Analyst—Defines the nature and extent of problems and develops solutions. Management analysts analyze relevant data including annual revenues, employment, and expenditures. They interview managers and employees while observing operations. In recent years, information technology and e-commerce have provided new opportunities for management analysts. Companies hire management analysts to develop strategies for entering and remaining competitive in the new electronic marketplace.

Project Manager—Has direct accountability for all aspects of assigned projects including development of strategy and tactical plans. The project manager creates timelines for implementation, identifies resources required for the project, and oversees actual execution through to the final analysis. This position typically requires a master's degree; however, a bachelor's degree in business, with certification, is often sufficient.

Retail Manager—Are responsible for day-to-day management of a department or store. A major responsibility is to make sure that sales targets are met by ensuring that products and services are available and finding the best ways to sell them quickly and profitably. Primary goals of retail managers are to improve the economic performance of the company, increase customer satisfaction, and provide for continued growth.

Supply Chain Manager—Is responsible for managing and improving the supply chain of products and information flow. The individual builds relationships and linkages with customers and integrates them throughout the organization. The manager also assesses financial feasibility and impacts on businesses processes. The supply chain manager develops metrics for assessing supply chain value and links them with corporate revenue management. Managers use relevant feedback to improve the supply chain processes.

INFORMATION TECHNOLOGY SKILLS YOU SHOULD PURSUE

To be effective in management, we recommend that you gain knowledge in the IT tools and concepts listed below.

Database Management and Integration—Project managers use IT to develop various requirements, budgets, and schedules for projects. They schedule and coordinate projects using IT. Project managers develop projects that upgrade the firm's information security and other resources.

Internet and Web Portals—IT tools are invaluable resources for managers. They are able to access information critical to organizational success. HR managers use the Internet to link with employees, recruiters, and other organizations.

Spreadsheets—Spreadsheets help managers to organize work, calculate value, develop bar graphs or pie charts to display financial and other data, and determine the comparative cost of employee benefit programs and selected projects under consideration.

Enterprise Systems (ES)—In many corporations, managers recognize the need for a corporate-wide system for communicating and sharing information. ES provides an IT–based approach for creating and managing such a system.

Database Management—Managers create a centralized database relating to customers and the nature of contacts. The database includes client information, concerns, and resolutions. The database is available to relevant organization members.

Geographical Information Systems (GIS)—Managers who depend on natural resources such as fisheries for their business use GIS to identify, protect, and manage these resources. GIS is used to determine the habitats and migration patterns of various species, for instance.

Electronic Commerce (E-Commerce)—Business-to-business and business-to-customer transactions via the Internet have accelerated the need for business managers to understand the potential of IT. Managers need the skills required for success in e-commerce.

Figure D.5

Employment and Other Information in Management

Median Salaries for Selected Positions in Management*	
Human Resources Manager	$111,487
Marketing Manager	88,411
Retail Store Manager	46,984
Sales Manager	71,395
Arts & Entertainment Technical Director	109,052
Purchasing Manager	74,001
Telecommunications Manager	83,889
Administrative Services Manager	61,602
Public Relations Manager	73,767
Industrial Engineering Manager	84,175

"Salary Wizard-Canada from Salary.com" http://swz.salary.com/csalarywizard/layoutscripts/cswzl_newsearch.asp, accessed August 15, 2008.

*These are base median salaries for a select few positions. The salaries do not include other benefits usually reflected in total compensation.

Marketing

Marketing as a career field and business specialization encompasses a broad range of activities including marketing, product development, advertising, public relations, promotions, and sales. Combined, these activities are undertaken to market and sell a company's products and services in a profitable way and give the company a competitive advantage in the marketplace.

Marketing programs in a business school often have the largest number of student majors because of the vast array of marketing positions and because of the perceived glamour of the field. While the field may be glamorous, it is also highly competitive, requiring a unique blend of people skills and technical skills. Marketing professionals work extensively with technology in many ways. They use statistical and data-mining tools to better understand consumer buying behaviours and make decisions regarding target marketing. They often interface with supply chain management (SCM) and customer relationship management (CRM) systems to enable the company to integrate and capitalize on what can be a vast chain of suppliers and customers. Many marketing professionals use sophisticated personal computer applications to develop marketing and promotional material such as flyers and other forms of advertisements. Marketing is most often the primary mechanism of contact with an organization's clients as marketing includes sales, promotions, advertising, and even customer service.

TYPICAL JOB TITLES AND DESCRIPTIONS

The typical job titles found in marketing and their descriptions are listed below.

Creative Marketing Specialist—Designs creative marketing solutions for all forms of advertising including print, Web-based, radio, and television. Possesses a tremendous knowledge of how people perceive and react to different types of advertising and promotional campaigns.

Marketing Coordinator—Manages and directs all marketing and advertising campaigns. Works closely with brand managers to uniquely identify and describe each brand within a company.

Account Manager—Develops, coordinates, and executes marketing strategies aimed at a select number of customers, with some account managers being responsible for only one customer. Develops very personal one-to-one relationships with key executives within the account.

Market Research Analyst—Designs, implements, and analyzes the information gathered from market research surveys and other instruments. Analyzes a variety of customer and consumer demographic information to determine competitive advantages in new marketing and advertising campaigns and new product development.

Market Development Manager—Contributes to the definition and development of new market opportunities for the company. May focus on products, geographical regions, and/or customer segments. Responsible for determining how the company can best launch into a new area.

Brand Manager—Drives branding strategies and ensures that all external communications convey the message of the brand. Works closely with marketing communications and market development professionals to help the company achieve a competitive advantage through its branding efforts.

Title	Median Salary
Advertising Manager	$ 81,484
Marketing Manager	88,411
Top Marketing Executive	136,664
Top Public Relations Executive	130,455
Public Relations Manager	73,767

Salary Information for Public Relations Managers		
City	Median Base Pay	Median Base + Incentive
Vancouver	$ 81,711	$ 87,686
Calgary	76,298	81,887
Toronto	82,364	88,387
Montreal	78,999	84,776
Charlottetown	66,297	71,144

Product Development Manager—Responsible for acquiring insight into customer wants and needs and translating that insight into product specifications and quality. Works extensively in the field with focus groups of customers and often with product engineers in product design.

Product Manager—Charged with a product line and its contribution to the total sales of the company. Works to increase the profitability of existing products and to develop new products. Manages the entire product line life cycle from strategic planning to tactical and implementation activities.

INFORMATION TECHNOLOGY SKILLS YOU SHOULD PURSUE

To be effective in marketing, we recommend that you gain knowledge in the IT tools and concepts listed below.

Customer Relationship Management (CRM) Systems—Marketing professionals are the primary interface to a company's customers. Knowledge of CRM software is essential for managing the relationships established with customers.

Budget Analysis/Impact Software—Marketing professionals spend much of their time evaluating the financial feasibility of new products and services, advertising campaigns, promotional strategies, and the like. Budget analysis/impact software allows marketing professionals to explore a variety of "what if" scenarios for a given situation or campaign.

Database Management—Marketing professionals work with vast amounts of information stored in the form of a database. Knowledge of the logical organization of a database and how the information can be accessed is essential.

Data Warehouses and Data-Mining Tools—These tools offer marketing professionals a way of summarizing large amounts of information and viewing it from different perspectives. This is often the first step in understanding the relationships inherent (but often hidden) in large amounts of information. Although marketing professionals usually do not design and build the actual data warehouse, they must understand the process and must also be well versed in using the data-mining tools for extracting information from a data warehouse.

Communications Support Software—This may include simple e-mail software but also extends to contact management software that enables marketing professionals to track their contacts with customers.

Desktop Publishing Software—Many marketing professionals are responsible for the development of "copy" material that will eventually become some form of paper-based advertisement such as a flyer or an insert in a newspaper. These documents must be developed using desktop publishing software to yield the highest quality.

Production and Operations Management

In general terms, production and operations management is a specialization that deals with the production, manufacturing, warehousing, and transportation of physical products and also the operations of some business environments such as how to schedule nurses in a hospital. So, production and operations management encompasses such aspects as inventory management, production design and control, logistics and transportation, raw materials acquisition and storage, employee scheduling, and so on. Along with finance and accounting, production and operations management is one of the most analytical and technical specializations in business.

Production and operations management touches on many major business initiatives. For example, to determine the right levels of inventory and timing of shipments, people in production and operations management must understand the needs and desires of customers, so customer relationship management is very much a part of production and operations management. People in production and operations management are often in charge of creating a tight supply chain with suppliers and customers, as well, so supply chain management is essential to effective production and operations management. Statistical and data-mining tools are also very important to a person in production and operations management. Many initiatives in this specialization focus on the "bottom line," that is, increasing bottom-line net profits by reducing costs. For this reason, people in production and operations management use highly sophisticated statistical and data-mining tools to explore every opportunity to drive costs out of the production, manufacturing, warehousing, and transportation functions.

TYPICAL JOB TITLES AND DESCRIPTIONS

The typical job titles found in production and operations management and their descriptions are listed below.

Production Scheduler—Usually found in a manufacturing environment focusing on preparing production schedules. Generates late-order reports, prioritizes operations and materials flow, and determines human resource allocations within a manufacturing environment. A knowledge of ERP (enterprise resource planning) systems is usually required.

Inventory Manager—Facilitates the planning for and procurement of inventory items including indirect materials and direct materials. Maintains accurate inventory counts and determines the optimal inventory levels to keep. Monitors inventory for potential stock-outs, oversupplies, and inventory obsolescence. Often helps to determine master schedule for production and manufacturing processes.

Figure D.7

Employment and
Other Information
in Production and
Operations Management

Salary Range	25th percentile	Median	75th percentile
Product Fulfillment Manager	$58,667	$60,016	$72,467
Warehouse Manager	$54,668	$63,442	$74,860
Inventory Control Manager	$57,556	$71,049	$81,981

Quality Assurance Analyst—Works with all departments to ensure that QA/QC (quality assurance/quality control) guidelines are followed and metrics are met. Manages and oversees quality specifications for raw materials, processing, and packaging. Performs quality audits periodically to help the organization maintain its desired quality levels.

Purchasing Manager—Works directly with suppliers to develop programs that result in the low-cost acquisition of high-quality materials. Negotiates terms of contracts with suppliers.

Operations Analyst—Analyzes a variety of business operation segments including marketing, sales, purchasing, distribution, and warehousing. Makes recommendations concerning how to optimize business operations by reducing costs. Often works with sales and marketing groups to make recommendations on product performance, price adjustments, and product eliminations.

Statistical/Research Analyst—Analyzes a variety of business operation segments using sophisticated statistical and data-mining tools to determine how best to improve a company's operations. May include determining market segments for new or existing products, setting prices, and a variety of other business issues that require significant statistical analysis.

Logistics Analyst—Focuses on the development of optimal solutions for logistical issues including cargo weight solutions, locations for distribution centres, and routing schedules for transportation modes such as trains and fleet trucks. Works extensively with supply chain management (SCM) systems to integrate logistics solutions within the company's supply chain activities.

INFORMATION TECHNOLOGY SKILLS YOU SHOULD PURSUE

To be effective in production and operations management, we recommend that you gain knowledge in the IT tools and concepts listed below.

Statistical Tools—For most careers in production and operations management, a detailed knowledge of statistics is essential, including the use of popular statistical software tools such as SAS and STATISTA.

Advanced Decision Support Spreadsheet Functions—Spreadsheet decision-support functions such as goal seeking, optimization, and statistical tools provide support for the many careers in production and operations management.

Supply Chain Management (SCM) Systems—A knowledge of supply chain management (SCM) systems allows individuals in this specialization to work with every department in a company, integrating solutions to maximize customer value.

Production and Inventory Control Software—There are many types of vertical market software relating to production and inventory control. These are essential for this career as most jobs require the use of such tools.

Material Requirements Planning Software—This is often called enterprise resource planning (ERP) software and allows a production and operations manager to understand the operations of a business from beginning to end and to optimally model those operations.

Data-Mining Tools—As data warehouses are becoming more widespread, production and operations managers can use data-mining tools to find new relationships in data warehouse information and employ a variety of statistical techniques to explore data warehouse information.

Scheduling Software—Scheduling software facilitates the optimal scheduling of a variety of resources within a business environment including people, plant equipment, transportation modes, and manufacturing operations.

Real Estate and Construction Management

Often when people think of the real estate industry, they think only of residential real estate agents selling homes. In fact, real estate is an approximately $3 trillion annually worldwide industry encompassing residential, office, retail, industrial, and many other property types. People in the real estate industry are developers, brokers, investors, Bay Street analysts, pension fund advisers, and many others.

The field of real estate and construction management (RECM) is inherently interdisciplinary. Feasibility and development analysts must understand urban economics, consumer behaviour, and finance and regulatory issues. Appraisers estimate the value of property using systematic procedures, judgment, and statistics, and may also be called on to provide expert testimony in legal proceedings. Construction lenders need to understand money and credit, certainly, but also construction project scheduling, estimating, and contracts. A corporate real estate professional must understand the corporation's core business and how real estate assets can contribute to both the "top line" and "bottom line." Real estate developers epitomize this interdisciplinary approach. They coordinate and direct the activities of many professionals and consultants, from the time the development project is simply a concept, through construction, occupancy, and the eventual disposition of the property.

TYPICAL JOB TITLES AND DESCRIPTIONS

The typical job titles found in real estate and construction management and their descriptions are listed below.

Commercial Real Estate Loan Officer—Responsible for soliciting and servicing a variety of commercial real estate loans, including large and complex transactions for real estate investments, development, and construction. Requires familiarity with financial analysis and modelling as well as other concepts, practices, and procedures in the field.

Commercial Real Estate Appraiser—Examines and evaluates commercial property to estimate a fair market value for loan collateral. Analyzes local and national market trends and investment valuation using a variety of techniques. Prepares very complex and detailed reports and is called upon to testify in court proceedings and act as a consultant.

Property Manager—Responsible for the financial and physical maintenance of commercial, industrial, or residential properties including oversight of leasing of properties in the portfolio. Responsible for analyzing information on operating costs as well as preparation of the annual budget for the properties.

Real Estate Development Manager—Directs the activities of firms that acquire real property for development or redevelopment. Leads the company in these endeavours as the head of the development team.

Real Estate Development Representative—May acquire land for new development or older properties for redevelopment. Assists the company in these endeavours as a part of the development team.

Construction Manager—Responsible for the overall management of construction projects and may oversee multiple projects. Ensures construction projects are completed on time, within budget, and to the client's satisfaction. Performs a variety of tasks and leads and directs the work of others.

Construction Field Superintendent—Oversees the daily construction activities at the work site, including project scheduling, delivery of equipment and materials, and progress of the project. Resolves contract disputes and arranges any necessary order changes. Requires a familiarity with a variety of construction management concepts, practices, and procedures.

Real Estate Financial Analyst—Responsible for building and maintaining complex financial models. Prepares look-back analyses of acquisitions and developments, draws conclusions, and makes recommendations. Analyzes capital markets alternatives and derivatives, as well as their impact on the company's financial position and earnings outlook. Examines capital investments and their impact on the company's financial position and earnings outlook as well as key expenses for potential cost savings.

INFORMATION TECHNOLOGY SKILLS YOU SHOULD PURSUE

To be effective in real estate and construction management, we recommend that you gain knowledge in the IT tools and concepts listed below.

The Internet and Web Portals—The use of Web portals, or virtual project sites, allows professionals to store and share project documents, schedules, and other information 24 × 7 in a real-time environment.

Geographic Information Systems (GIS)—GIS aids in site selection, feasibility analysis, and investment strategy by combining spatial and tabular information, allowing real estate professionals to use maps that are near real-time and relevant.

Database Management and Integration—Supports the varied needs of accounting, lease administration, finance, and property management, allowing the entire project team to share information and support the client's needs.

Spreadsheet Modelling—Allows the real estate analyst to efficiently perform discounted cash flow analysis, ratio analysis, and underwriting analysis, and to measure the sensitivity of various assumptions.

Computer Aided Design (CAD)—CAD provides for digital imaging of architectural designs, allowing users to test the results of changes in layout and design on the functionality and efficiency of the building.

Project Scheduling—Construction project scheduling involves estimates of timing, precedence, and critical path essential to the completion and success of development projects.

Automated Valuation—An Automated Valuation System (AVS) uses statistical and other analyses to automate the loan underwriting process, loan origination, collateral scoring, and appraisal.

Customer Relationship Management (CRM) Systems—Combines contact management, calendars, schedules, and client information into a database providing a centralized repository of contacts in which all team members share one contact record and subsequent relationship activity.

Specialty Software—ARGUS is the industry standard commercial real estate cash flow projection, transaction analysis, and asset valuation solution. CircleDeveloper™ is real estate development pro forma software in use by thousands of owners, developers, brokers, advisers, and financial institutions involved in property development. DYNA is a versatile forecasting and portfolio management solution used by many asset managers, REITs, and other institutional investors around the globe.

Executive Positions ($100,000 plus)	Ascendant Positions ($80,000–$100,000)
Chief Commercial Real Estate Executive	Senior Construction Manager
Chief Construction Executive	Commercial Real Estate Appraiser
Level V Construction Cost Engineer	Leasing Administration Manager
Chief Mortgage Executive	Construction Project Manager
Chief Property Acquisition Officer	Commercial Real Estate Loan Officer
Commercial Real Estate Manager	Mortgage Credit Supervisor
Director of Construction Management	Loss Prevention and Construction Safety Manager
Facilities Maintenance Manager	General Manager
Mortgage Loan Area Manager	Mortgage Loan Processing Supervisor
Mortgage Operations Manager	Property Manager
Real Estate and Relocation Director	Retail Real Estate Representative
Real Estate Attorney	
Retail Real Estate Manager	
Trust Director—Real Estate	

Figure D.8

Employment Information in Real Estate and Construction Management

Figure D.8
(cont'd)

Employment
Information in
Real Estate and
Construction
Management

Ascendant Positions ($50,000–$80,000)	Starting Positions ($30,000–$50,000)
Chief Mortgage Credit Manager	Leasing Manager
Lead Construction Representative	Community Development Representative
Estimating Manager	Construction Inspection Services Manager
Facilities Planner	Mortgage Collector
Development Manager	Mortgage Credit Analyst
Level II Commercial Real Estate Loan Officer	Construction Estimator
Mortgage Collections Manager	Mortgage Loan Processor
Construction Field Superintendent	Apprentice Real Estate Appraiser
Mortgage Credit Manager	Associate Real Estate Sales Agent
Real Estate Appraisal Manager	Assistant Construction Supervisor
Facilities Maintenance Supervisor	
Real Estate Property Acquisition Associate	
Regional Property Operations Manager	
Trust Manager—Real Estate	

Assignments and Exercises

There is only one assignment and exercise for this module, and it's all about you. What you've just read is a summary and broad overview of the many career opportunities in the business world. It's now your turn to think seriously about your future career and perform some research.

Business Specialization	Job Title
•	
•	
•	
•	
•	

Classes Offered by Your School	IT Skills You Need to Acquire
•	
•	
•	
•	
•	

Locations You Would Consider	Companies You Would Consider
•	
•	
•	
•	
•	
•	
•	

Jobs on Monster.ca		
Job Title	Location	Salary
•		
•		
•		
•		
•		
•		
•		
•		
•		
•		
•		
•		

GLOSSARY

1-tier infrastructure the most basic setup because it involves a single tier on a single machine.

2-tier infrastructure the basic client/server relationship.

3-tier infrastructure the most common approach used for Web applications today.

A

Abandoned registrations number of visitors who start the process of completing a registration page and then abandon the activity.

Abandoned shopping carts the number of visitors who create a shopping cart, start shopping, and then abandon the activity before paying for the merchandise.

Abandon rate the percentage of callers who hang up while waiting for their call to be answered.

Accuracy usually measured inversely as *error rate*, or the number of errors per thousand (or million) that a system generates.

Ad hoc (nonrecurring) decision decision you make infrequently (perhaps only once) and for which you may even have different criteria for determining the best solution for each time.

Ad-supported derives revenue by selling advertising space, much like the concept of an affiliate program.

Adware software to generate ads that installs itself on your computer when you download some other (usually free) program from the Web.

Affiliate program an arrangement made between two e-commerce sites that directs viewers from one site to the other.

Agent-based modelling way of simulating human organizations using multiple intelligent agents, each of which follows a set of simple rules and can adapt to changing conditions.

Agile methodology a form of extreme programming that aims for customer satisfaction through early and continuous delivery of useful software components.

Analysis phase of the systems development life cycle involves end users and IT specialists working together to gather, understand, and document the business requirements for the proposed system.

Anonymous Web browsing (AWB) service hides your identity from the Web sites you visit.

Anti-spyware software utility software that detects and removes spyware and other unwanted software that can track every electronic move you make.

Antivirus software detects, removes, or quarantines computer viruses.

Application generation subsystem of a DBMS contains facilities to help you develop transaction-intensive applications.

Application service provider (ASP) supplies software applications (and often related services such as maintenance, technical support, and the like) over the Internet that would otherwise reside on its customers' in-house computers.

Application software the software that enables you to solve specific problems or perform specific tasks.

Arithmetic logic unit (ALU) a component of the CPU that performs arithmetic, as well as comparison and logic operations.

Artificial intelligence (AI) the science of making machines imitate human thinking and behaviour.

ASCII (American Standard Code for Information Interchange) the coding system that most personal computers use to represent, process, and store information.

Automatic speech recognition (ASR) a system that not only captures spoken words but also distinguishes word groupings to form sentences.

Average speed to answer (ASA) the average time, usually in seconds, that it takes for a call to be answered by an actual person.

B

Back-office system used to fulfill and support customer orders.

Backup the process of making a copy of the information stored on a computer.

Bandwidth capacity of the communications medium; refers to the amount of information that a communications medium can transfer in a given amount of time.

Bar code scanner reads information that is in the form of vertical bars, where their width and spacing represent digits (often used in point-of-sale [POS] systems in retail environments).

Basic formatting tag HTML tag that allows you to specify formatting for text.

Benchmarking a process of continuously measuring system results, comparing those results to optimal system performance (benchmark values), and identifying steps and procedures to improve system performance.

Benchmarks baseline values a system seeks to attain.

Binary digit (bit) the smallest unit of information that your computer can process.

Biochip a technology chip that can perform a variety of physiological functions when inserted into the human body.

Biometrics the use of physiological characteristics—such as your fingerprint, the blood vessels in the iris of your eye, the sound of your voice, or perhaps even your breath—to provide identification.

Biometric scanner scans some human physical attribute, like your fingerprint or iris, for security purposes.

Biomimicry learning from ecosystems and adapting their characteristics to human and organizational situations.

Black-hat hacker a cyber vandal.

Blog a Web site in the form of a journal in which you post entries in chronological order; often includes the capabilities for other viewers to add comments to your journal entries.

Bluetooth a standard for transmitting information in the form of short-range radio waves over distances of up to 30 feet, used for purposes such as wirelessly connecting a cell phone or a PDA to a computer.

Bot computer program that runs automatically.

Botnet   network of malware-bot-infected computers.

Broadband   connection that is a high-bandwidth (high-capacity) telecommunications line capable of providing high-speed Internet service.

Broadband (home) router   a device to connect several computers together to share a DSL or cable Internet connection in a home or small office.

Browser-safe colours   215 colours that can be viewed by all browsers and computers.

Business continuity plan   a step-by-step guideline defining how the organization will recover from a disaster or extended disruption of its business processes.

Business intelligence (BI)   collective information about your customers, your competitors, your business partners, your competitive environment, and your own internal operations that gives you the ability to make effective, important, and often strategic business decisions.

Business process   standardized set of activities that accomplishes a specific task, such as processing a customer's order.

Business requirement   a detailed set of knowledge worker requests that the system must meet to be successful.

Business-to-business (B2B) e-commerce   when a business sells products and services to customers that are primarily other businesses.

Business-to-consumer (B2C) e-commerce   when a business sells products and services to customers who are primarily individuals.

Business-to-government (B2G) e-commerce   occurs when a business sells products and services to a government entity.

Buyer agent or shopping bot   an intelligent agent on a Web site that helps you, the customer, find the products and services you want.

Buyer power   in Porter's Forces Model it is high when buyers have many choices from whom to buy, and low when their choices are few.

Byte   a group of eight bits that represents one natural language character.

C

Cable modem   a device that uses your TV cable to deliver an Internet connection.

Call centre metrics   measure the success of call centre efforts.

Capacity planning   determines your projected future IT infrastructure requirements for new equipment and additional network capacity.

Cat 5 (Category 5) cable   a better-constructed version of twisted-pair phone cable.

CAVE (cave automatic virtual environment)   a special 3-D virtual reality room that can display images of other people and objects located in other CAVEs all over the world.

CD-R (compact disc—recordable)   an optical or laser disc that you can write to one time only.

CD-ROM (compact disc—read-only memory)   an optical or laser disc whose information cannot be changed. A CD stores up to 800 Mg of information.

CD-RW (compact disc—rewritable)   an optical or laser disc on which you can save, change, and delete files as often as you like.

Centralized infrastructure   involves sharing of information systems in one central area or one central mainframe.

Central processing unit (CPU)   the hardware that interprets and executes the system and application software instructions, and coordinates the operation of all the hardware.

Chief information officer (CIO)   responsible for overseeing every aspect of an organization's information resource.

Chief privacy officer (CPO)   responsible for ensuring that information is used in an ethical way and that only the right people have access to certain types of information such as financial records and payroll.

Chief security officer (CSO)   responsible for the technical aspects of ensuring the security of information such as the development and use of firewalls, intranets, extranets, and antivirus software.

Chief technology officer (CTO)   responsible for overseeing both the underlying IT infrastructure within an organization and the user-facing technologies (such as CRM systems).

Choice   the third step in the decision-making process where you decide on a plan to address the problem or opportunity.

Class   contains information and procedures, and acts as a template to create objects.

Click-and-mortar   refers to those organizations that have a presence in the physical world such as a building you can visit and also a presence in the virtual world of the Internet.

Click-and-order (pure play)   an organization that has a presence in the virtual world but no presence in the physical world.

Clickstream   a stored record about your Web surfing session, such as which Web sites you visited, how long you were there, what ads you looked at, and what you bought.

Click-through   a count of the number of people who visit one site, click on an ad, and are taken to the site of the advertiser.

Client/server infrastructure (client/server network)   a network in which one or more computers are servers and provide services to the other computers, called clients.

Coaxial cable (coax)   one central wire surrounded by insulation, a metallic shield, and a final case of insulating material.

Cold site   a separate facility that does not have any computer equipment but is a place where the knowledge workers can move after the disaster.

Collocation facility   available to a company that rents space and telecommunications equipment from another company.

Communications medium   the path, or physical channel, in a network over which information travels.

Communications protocol (protocol)   a set of rules that every computer follows to transfer information.

Communications satellite   microwave repeater in space.

Communications software   helps you communicate with other people.

CompactFlash (CF) card   a flash memory card that is slightly larger than a toonie, with a capacity of up to 6 gigabytes.

Competitive advantage   providing a product or service in a way that customers value more than the competition's.

Competitive intelligence (CI)   business intelligence focused on the external competitive environment.

Component-based development (CBD)   a general approach to systems development that focuses on building small self-contained blocks of code (components) that can be reused across a variety of applications within an organization.

Composite primary key   consists of the primary key fields from the two intersecting relations.

Computer crime   a crime in which a computer, or computers, plays a significant part.

Computer network (network)   two or more computers connected so that they can communicate with each other and share information, software, peripheral devices, and/or processing power.

Computer virus (virus)   software that is written with malicious intent to cause annoyance or damage.

Conditional formatting   highlights information in a cell that meets some criteria you specify.

Connectivity software   enables you to use your computer to dial up or connect to another computer.

Constant   a named element whose value doesn't change.

Consumer-to-business (C2B) e-commerce   when an individual sells products and services to a business.

Consumer-to-consumer (C2C) e-commerce   when an individual sells products and services to other individuals.

Consumer-to-government (C2G) e-commerce   when an individual sells products and services to a government entity.

Control unit   the component of the CPU that directs what happens in your computer, then sends to RAM for instructions and the information it needs.

Conversion rate   the percentage of potential customers who visit your site who buy something.

Cookie   a small record deposited on your hard disk by a Web site containing information about you.

Copyright   the legal protection afforded an expression of an idea, such as a song, video game, and some types of proprietary documents.

Cost-per-thousand (CPM)   sales dollars generated per dollar of advertising, commonly used to make the case for spending money to appear on a search engine.

CPU cache   a type of memory on the CPU where instructions called up by the CPU wait until the CPU is ready to use them.

CPU clock   a sliver of quartz that beats at regular intervals in response to an electrical charge.

CPU (machine) cycle   consists of retrieving, decoding, and executing the instruction, then returning the result to RAM, if necessary.

Cracker   a hacker for hire; a person who engages in electronic corporate espionage.

Crash-proof software   utility software that helps you save information if your system crashes and you're forced to turn it off and then back on again.

Critical success factor (CSF)   a factor simply critical to your organization's success.

Crossover   the process within a genetic algorithm where portions of good outcomes are combined in the hope of creating an even better outcome.

Crowdsourcing   when businesses provide technologies that enable people (i.e., crowds)—instead of a designated paid employee—to create, modify, and oversee the development of a product or service.

CRT   a monitor that looks like a traditional television set.

CRUD (Create, Read, Update, Delete)   the four procedures, or ways, a system can manipulate information.

Customer relationship management (CRM) system   uses information about customers to gain insights into their needs, wants, and behaviours in order to serve them better.

Customer self-service system   an extension of a TPS that places technology in the hands of an organization's customers and allows them to process their own transactions.

Custom filter function   allows you to hide all the rows in a list except those that match criteria, besides "is equal to," that you specify.

Cyberterrorist   one who seeks to cause harm to people or destroy critical systems or information.

D

Data   raw facts that describe a particular phenomenon.

Data administration   the function in an organization that plans for, oversees the development of, and monitors the information resource.

Data administration subsystem   of a DBMS helps you manage the overall database environment by providing facilities for backup and recovery, security management, query optimization, concurrency control, and change management.

Database   a collection of information that you organize and access according to the logical structure of that information.

Database administration   the function in an organization that is responsible for the more technical and operational aspects of managing the information contained in organizational information repositories (databases, data warehouses, and data marts).

Database management system (DBMS)   helps you specify the logical organization for a database, and access and use the information within a database.

Data definition subsystem   of a DBMS helps you create and maintain the data dictionary, and define the structure of the files in a database.

Data dictionary   contains the logical structure for the information in a database.

Data management   component of a DSS that performs the function of storing and maintaining the information that you want your DSS to use.

Data manipulation subsystem   of a DBMS helps you add, change, and delete information in a database and query it for valuable information.

Data mart   a subset of a data warehouse in which only a focused portion of the data warehouse information is kept.

Data-mining agent   an intelligent agent that operates in a data warehouse discovering information.

Data-mining tool   a software tool you use to query information in a data warehouse.

Data warehouse   a logical collection of information—gathered from many different operational databases—used to create business intelligence that supports business analysis activities and decision-making tasks.

DBMS engine   accepts logical requests from the various other DBMS subsystems, converts them into their physical equivalent, and actually accesses the database and data dictionary as they exist on a storage device.

Decentralized infrastructure   involves little or no sharing of information systems.

Decision support system (DSS)   a highly flexible and interactive IT system that is designed to support decision making when the problem is not structured.

Demand aggregation   the combining of purchase requests from multiple buyers into a single larger order, which justifies a discount from the business.

Denial-of-service (DoS) attack   floods a server or network with so many requests for service that it slows down or crashes.

Design   the second step in the decision-making process, where you consider possible ways of solving the problem, filling the need, or taking advantage of the opportunity.

Design phase   of the systems development life cycle builds a technical blueprint of how the proposed system will work.

Desktop computer   the type of computer that is the most popular choice for personal computing needs.

Desktop publishing software   extends word processing software by including design and formatting techniques to enhance the layout and appearance of a document.

Development phase   of the systems development life cycle takes all your detailed design documents from the design phase and transforms them into an actual system.

Differentiation   (in Porter's three generic strategies) offering a product or service that is perceived as being "unique" in the marketplace.

Digital camera   captures still images or video as a series of 1s and 0s.

Digital dashboard   displays key information gathered from several sources on a computer screen in a format tailored to the needs and wants of an individual knowledge worker.

Digital forensics   the gathering, authentication, examination, and analysis of electronic information for presentation in court.

Digital immigrants   people who were born and raised in a time prior to the digital society in which we now live.

Digital natives   generation of people ushered into this world in the midst of the digital revolution.

Digital still camera   digitally captures still images in varying resolutions.

Digital Subscriber Line (DSL)   a high-speed Internet connection using phone lines, which allows you to use your phone for voice communications at the same time.

Digital video camera   captures video digitally.

Digital wallet   both software and information—the software provides security for the transaction and the information includes payment information (for example, the credit card number and expiration date) and delivery information.

Direct materials   materials that are used in production in a manufacturing company or are placed on the shelf for sale in a retail environment.

Disaster recovery cost curve   charts (1) the cost to your organization of the unavailability of information and technology and (2) the cost to your organization of recovering from a disaster over time.

Disaster recovery plan   a detailed process for recovering information or an IT system in the event of a catastrophic disaster such as a fire or flood.

Disintermediation   use of the Internet as a delivery vehicle, whereby intermediate players in a distribution channel can be bypassed.

Disk optimization software   utility software that organizes your information on your hard disk in the most efficient way.

Distributed denial-of-service (DDoS) attack   attack from multiple computers that floods a server or network with so many requests for service that it slows down or crashes.

Distributed infrastructure   involves distributing the information and processing power of IT systems via a network.

Distribution chain   the path followed from the originator of a product or service to the end consumer.

Document management system   manages a document through all the stages of its processing—similar to a workflow system except that the focus is more on document storage and retrieval.

Domain name   (technical name for a Web site address) identifies a specific computer on the Web and the main page of the entire site.

Dot pitch   the distance between the centres of a pair of like-coloured pixels.

Drone   bot-infected computer.

DS3   a high-speed business network circuit running at 44.736 Mbps.

DVD-R or DVD+R (DVD—recordable)   a high-capacity optical or laser disc to which you can write one time only.

DVD-ROM   a high-capacity optical or laser disc whose information cannot be changed.

DVD-RW or DVD+RW   (depending on the manufacturer) a high-capacity optical or laser disc on which you can save, change, and delete files.

E

E-collaboration   the use of technology to support work activities with integrated collaboration environments, knowledge management with knowledge management systems, social networking with social networking systems, learning with e-learning tools, and informal collaboration to support open-source information.

Effectiveness   refers to doing the right thing.

Efficiency   doing something right (e.g., in the least time, at the lowest cost, with the fewest errors, etc.).

E-gallery   electronic gallery of works that demonstrates your skills.

Electronic Bill Presentment and Payment (EBPP)   a system that sends bills (usually to end consumers) over the Internet and provides an easy-to-use mechanism (such as clicking on a button) to pay them if the amount looks correct.

Electronic cheque   a mechanism for sending money from your chequing or savings account to another person or organization.

Electronic commerce (e-commerce)   commerce, but it is commerce accelerated and enhanced by IT, in particular the Internet.

Electronic data interchange (EDI)   the direct computer-to-computer transfer of transaction information contained in standard business documents, such as invoices and purchase orders, in a standard format.

Electronic government (e-government)   the use of digital technologies to transform government operations in order to improve efficiency, effectiveness, and service delivery.

Electronic job market   consists of employers using Internet technologies to advertise and screen potential employees.

Electronic marketplace (e-marketplace)   an interactive business providing a central space where multiple buyers and sellers can engage in e-commerce and/or other e-commerce business activities.

Electronic portfolio (e-portfolio)   collection of Web documents used to support a stated purpose such as demonstrating writing, photography, or job skills.

E-mail (electronic mail) software   enables you to electronically communicate with other people by sending and receiving e-mail.

Encapsulation   information hiding.

Encryption   scrambles the contents of a file so that you can't read it without having the right decryption key.

Enterprise resource planning (ERP) system   software system for business management, supporting areas such as planning, manufacturing, sales, marketing, distribution, accounting, finance, human resource management, project management, inventory management, service and maintenance, transportation, and e-business.

Entity class   a concept—typically people, places, or things—about which you wish to store information and that you can identify with a unique key (called a primary key).

Entity-relationship (E-R) diagram   a graphic method of representing entity classes and their relationships.

Entry barrier   a product or service feature that customers have come to expect from organizations in a particular industry and that must be offered by an entering organization to compete and survive.

Ethernet card   the most common type of network interface card.

Ethical (white-hat) hacker   a computer security professional who is hired by a company to break into its computer system, so as to find security lapses.

Ethics   the principles and standards that guide our behaviour toward other people.

Expandability   refers to how easy it is to add features and functions to a system.

Expansion bus   the set of pathways along which information moves between devices outside the motherboard and the CPU.

Expansion card (board)   a circuit board that you insert into the expansion slot on the motherboard and to which you connect a peripheral device.

Expansion slot   a long skinny socket on the motherboard into which you insert an expansion card.

Expert system (knowledge-based system)   an artificial intelligence system that applies reasoning capabilities to reach a conclusion.

External information   describes the environment surrounding the organization.

Extranet   an intranet that is restricted to an organization and certain outsiders, such as customers and suppliers.

Extreme programming (XP) methodology   breaks a project into tiny phases and developers cannot continue on to the next phase until the first phase is complete.

F

F2b2C (Factory to business to Consumer)   e-commerce business model in which a consumer communicates through a business on the Internet that directly provides product specifications to a factory that makes the customized and personalized product to the consumer's specifications and then ships it directly to the consumer.

Facial recognition software   software that provides identification by evaluating facial characteristics.

Fair Use Doctrine   allows you to use copyrighted material in certain situations.

Feature analysis   captures your words as you speak into a microphone, eliminates any background noise, and converts the digital signals of your speech into phonemes (syllables).

Feature creep   occurs when developers add extra features that were not part of the initial requirements.

File transfer protocol (ftp)   communications protocol that allows you to transfer files of information from one computer to another.

Filter function   filters a list and allows you to hide all the rows in a list except those that match criteria you specify.

Financial cybermediary   an Internet-based company that makes it easy for one person to pay another person or organization over the Internet.

Financial EDI (financial electronic data interchange)   an electronic process used primarily within the business-to-business e-commerce model for the payment of purchases.

Firewall   software and/or hardware that protects a computer or network from intruders.

Firewire (IEEE 1394 or I-Link) port   fits hot-swap, plug-and-play Firewire connectors and you can connect up to 63 Firewire devices to a single Firewire port by daisy-chaining the devices together.

First-call resolution (FCR)   the percentage of calls that can be resolved without having to call back.

First-mover advantage   being the first to market with a competitive advantage and thus having a significant impact on gaining market share.

Five Forces Model   helps business people understand the relative attractiveness of an industry and the industry's competitive pressures.

Flash memory card   has high-capacity storage units laminated inside a small piece of plastic.

Flash memory device (jump drive, thumb drive)   a flash memory storage device that is small enough to fit on a key ring and plugs directly into the USB port on your computer.

Flat-panel display thin, lightweight monitor that takes up much less space than a CRT.

Focus (in Porter's three generic strategies) focusing on offering products and services (1) to a particular market segment or buyer group, (2) within a segment of a product line, and/or (3) to a specific geographic market.

Foreign key a primary key of one file (relation) that appears in another file (relation).

Forensic image copy an exact copy or snapshot of the contents of an electronic medium.

Front office system the primary interface to customers and sales channels.

FrontPage Web authoring software.

Ftp (file transfer protocol) server maintains a collection of files that you can download.

Function procedure a VBA macro that returns a single value.

Fuzzy logic mathematical method of handling imprecise or subjective information.

G

Game controller used for gaming to better control screen action.

Gamepad a multifunctional input device with programmable buttons, thumb sticks, and a directional pad.

Gaming wheel a steering wheel and foot pedals for virtual driving.

Garbage-in garbage-out (GIGO) if the information coming into your decision-making process is in bad form (i.e., garbage in), you'll more than likely make a poor decision (garbage out).

Gas plasma display sends electricity through gas trapped between two layers of glass or plastic to create a screen image.

Genetic algorithm an artificial intelligence system that mimics the evolutionary, survival-of-the-fittest process to generate increasingly better solutions to a problem.

Geographic information system (GIS) a decision support system designed specifically to analyze spatial information.

Gigabyte (GB or Gig) roughly 1 billion bytes.

Gigahertz (GHz) the number of billions of CPU cycles per second that the CPU can handle.

Glove an input device that captures and records the shape and movement of your hand and fingers and the strength of your hand and finger movements.

Government-to-business (G2B) e-commerce when a government entity sells products and services to businesses.

Government-to-consumer (G2C) e-commerce the electronic commerce activities performed between a government and its citizens or consumers including paying taxes, registering vehicles, and providing information and services.

Government-to-government (G2G) e-commerce either (1) the electronic commerce activities performed within a single nation's government or (2) the electronic commerce activities performed between two or more nations' governments including providing foreign aid.

Graphics software helps you create and edit photos and art.

H

Hacker a knowledgeable computer user who uses his or her knowledge to invade other people's computers.

Hacktivist a politically motivated hacker who uses the Internet to send a political message of some kind.

Haptic interface uses technology to add the sense of touch to an environment that previously had only visual and auditory elements.

Hard disk magnetic storage device with one or more thin metal platters or disks that store information sealed inside the disk drive.

Hardware the physical devices that make up a computer (often referred to as a computer system).

Hardware key logger a hardware device that captures keystrokes on their journey from the keyboard to the motherboard.

Heading tag HTML tag that makes certain information, such as titles, stand out on your Web site.

Headset (head-mounted display) a combined input and output device that (1) captures and records the movement of your head, and (2) contains a screen that covers your entire field of vision.

Help desk a group of people who respond to knowledge workers' questions.

Hidden job market the collective term used to describe jobs that are not advertised.

Holographic device a device that creates, captures, and/or displays images in true three-dimensional form.

Holographic storage device stores information on a storage medium that is composed of 3-D crystal-like objects with many sides or faces.

Horizontal e-marketplace an electronic marketplace that connects buyers and sellers across many industries, primarily for MRO materials commerce.

Horizontal government integration the electronic integration of agencies, activities, and processes across a specific level of government.

Horizontal market software application software that is general enough to be suitable for use in a variety of industries.

Hot site a separate and fully equipped facility where the company can move immediately after the disaster and resume business.

Hot swap an operating system feature that allows you—while your computer is running—to unplug a device and plug in a new one without first shutting down your computer.

HTML document a file that contains your Web site content and HTML formatting instructions.

HTML tag specifies the formatting and presentation of information on a Web site.

Hub a device that connects computers together and passes messages by repeating all network transmissions to all the other computers.

Hypertext markup language (HTML) the language you use to create a Web site.

Hypertext transfer protocol (http) the communications protocol that supports the movement of information over the Web.

I

Identity theft the forging of someone's identity for the purpose of fraud.

Image scanner   captures images, photos, text, and artwork that already exist on paper.

Implant chip   a technology-enabled microchip implanted into the human body that stores important information about you (such as your identification and medical history) and that may be GPS–enabled to offer a method of tracking.

Implementation   the final step in the decision-making process where you put your plan into action.

Implementation phase   of the systems development life cycle distributes the system to all the knowledge workers so they can begin using the system to perform their everyday jobs.

Information   data that have a particular meaning within a specific context.

Information agent   intelligent agent that searches for information of some kind and brings it back.

Information decomposition   breaking down the information and procedures for ease of use and understandability.

Information granularity   the extent of detail within the information.

Information-literate knowledge workers   can define what information they need, know how and where to obtain that information, understand the information once they receive it, and can act appropriately based on the information to help the organization achieve the greatest advantage.

Information partnership   two or more companies cooperating by integrating their IT systems, thereby providing customers with the best of what each can offer.

Information technology (IT)   any computer-based tool that people use to work with information and support the information and information-processing needs of an organization.

Information view   includes all of the information stored within a system.

Infrared, IR, or IrDA (infrared data association)   uses red light to send and receive information.

Infrastructure   a relative term meaning "the structure beneath a structure."

Infrastructure-centric metric   is typically a measure of the efficiency, speed, and/or capacity of technology.

Inheritance   the ability to define superclass and subclass relationships among classes.

Inkjet printer   makes images by forcing ink droplets through nozzles.

Input device   tool you use to enter information and commands.

Insourcing   using IT specialists within your organization to develop the system.

Instance   an occurrence of an entity class that can be uniquely described with a primary key.

Integrated collaboration environment (ICE)   the environment in which virtual teams do their work.

Integration testing   verifies that separate systems can work together.

Integrity constraint   rule that helps ensure the quality of the information.

Intellectual property   intangible creative work that is embodied in physical form.

Intelligence   the first step in the decision-making process where you find or recognize a problem, need, or opportunity (also called the diagnostic phase of decision making).

Intelligent agent   software that assists you, or acts on your behalf, in performing repetitive computer-related tasks.

Interface   any device that calls procedures and can include such things as a keyboard, mouse, and touch screen.

Inter-modal transportation   the use of multiple channels of transportation—railway, truck, boat, and so on—to move products from origin to destination.

Internal information   describes specific operational aspects of an organization.

Internet   a vast network of computers that connects millions of people all over the world.

Internet backbone   the major set of connections for computers on the Internet.

Internet server computer   computer that provides information and services on the Internet.

Internet service provider (ISP)   a company that provides individuals, organizations, and businesses access to the Internet.

Interoperability   the capability of two or more computing components to share information and other resources, even if they are made by different manufacturers.

Intersection relation (composite relation)   a relation you create to eliminate a many-to-many relationship.

Intranet   an internal organizational Internet that is guarded against outside access by a special security feature called a firewall (which can be software, hardware, or a combination of the two).

Intrusion-detection software   looks for people on the network who shouldn't be there or who are acting suspiciously.

Intrusion detection system (IDS)   a device that watches network traffic for intrusion attempts and reports them.

Intrusion prevention system (IPS)   type of intrusion detection system (IDS) that also takes action against intrusion attempts, for example, by creating new policies in a firewall to block the source of the attack.

Invisible backlog   the list of all systems that an organization needs to develop but—because of the prioritization of systems development needs—never get funded because of the lack of organizational resources.

IRC (Internet Relay Chat) server   supports your use of discussion groups and chat rooms.

IT culture   affects the placement structurally of the IT function within an organization and manifests the philosophical approach to the development, deployment, and use of IT within an organization.

J

Joint application development (JAD)   occurs when knowledge workers and IT specialists meet, sometimes for several days, to define and review the business requirements for the system.

Joystick   vertical handle with programmable buttons that controls action.

Just-in-time (JIT)   an approach that produces or delivers a product or service just at the time the customer wants it.

K

Keyboard   the most often used input device for desktop and notebook computers.

Key logger (key trapper) software   a program that, when installed on a computer, records every keystroke and mouse click.

Knowledge   (1) provides contextual explanation for business intelligence; (2) points toward actions to take to affect business intelligence; (3) includes intellectual assets such as patents and trademarks; and (4) includes organizational know-how for things such as best practices.

Knowledge-based system (expert system)   an artificial intelligence system that applies reasoning capabilities to reach a conclusion.

Knowledge management (KM) system   an IT system that supports the capturing, organization, and dissemination of knowledge (i.e., know-how) throughout an organization.

L

Language processing   attempts to make sense of what you're saying by comparing the word phonemes generated in step 2 with a language model database.

Laser printer   forms images using the same sort of electrostatic process that photocopiers use.

Legacy information system (LIS)   represents a massive, long-term business investment; such systems are often brittle, slow, and nonextensible.

Link (hyperlink)   clickable text or an image that takes you to another site or page on the Web.

Linux   an open-source operating system that provides a rich operating environment for high-end workstations and network servers.

Liquid crystal display (LCD)   makes the screen image by sending electricity through crystallized liquid trapped between two layers of glass or plastic.

List   a collection of information arranged in columns and rows in which each column displays one particular type of information.

List definition table   a description of a list by column.

Local area network (LAN)   a network that covers a building or buildings in close proximity, such as one campus of a university or corporation.

Location mashup   a geographic information system (GIS) that displays a particular geographic area and then overlays content according to the user's desires.

Logical view   focuses on how you as a knowledge worker need to arrange and access information to meet your particular business needs.

Long Tail   refers to the tail of a sales curve—first offered by Chris Anderson, editor-in-chief of *Wired Magazine,* as a way of explaining e-commerce profitability.

Looping   repeating a block of statements or code numerous times.

Loss leader   product sold at or below cost to entice customers into a store in the hope that they will also buy more profitable products.

Loyalty program   rewards customers based on the amount of business they do with a particular organization.

M

Mac OS   Apple's operating system.

Macro   a set of actions recorded or written by a user.

Macro language   a programming language that includes built-in commands that mimic the functionality available from menus and dialogue boxes within an application.

Mailing list   discussion groups organized by area of interest.

Mail server   provides e-mail services and accounts.

Mainframe computer (mainframe)   a computer designed to meet the computing needs of hundreds of people in a large business environment.

Maintenance phase   of the systems development life cycle; monitors and supports the new system to ensure it continues to meet the business requirements.

Maintenance, repair, and operations (MRO) materials (indirect materials)   materials that are necessary for running a modern corporation, but do not relate to the company's primary business activities.

Malware   software designed to harm your computer or computer security.

Malware bot   bot that is used for fraud, sabotage, DoS attacks, or some other malicious purpose.

Management information systems (MIS)   deals with the planning for, development, management, and use of information technology tools to help people perform all tasks related to information processing and management.

Marketing mix   the set of marketing tools that your organization will use to pursue its marketing objectives in reaching and attracting potential customers.

Mashup   a combination of content from more than one source.

Mass customization   the ability of an organization to give its customers the opportunity to tailor its product or service to the customers' specifications.

M-commerce   the term used to describe electronic commerce conducted over a wireless device such as a cell phone, PDA, or notebook.

MD5 hash value   a mathematically generated string of 32 letters and digits that is unique for an individual storage medium at a specific point in time.

Megabyte (MB or M or Meg)   roughly 1 million bytes.

Memory Stick Media card   elongated flash memory card about the width of a penny developed by Sony with capacities up to 512 megabytes.

Message   how objects communicate with each other.

Metropolitan (municipal) area network (MAN)   a set of connected networks all within the same city or metropolitan area, but not in immediate proximity to each other.

Microphone   captures audio for conversion into electronic form.

Microsoft Windows Vista   Microsoft's latest personal computer operating system in a wide range of editions including Vista Home Basic, Vista Home Premium, Vista Business, and Vista Ultimate.

Microsoft Windows XP Home   Microsoft's predecessor to Vista designed specifically for home users.

Microsoft Windows XP Professional (Windows XP Pro) Microsoft's predecessor to Vista with enhanced features to support home users and business users.

Microwave transmission a type of radio transmission.

Minicomputer (mid-range computer) a computer designed to meet the computing needs of several people simultaneously in a small to medium-size business environment.

Mobile computing broad general term describing your ability to use technology to wirelessly connect to and use centrally located information and/or application software.

Mobile CPU a special type of CPU for a notebook computer that changes speed, and therefore power consumption, in response to fluctuation in use.

Mobisode short one-minute video clips of TV shows designed for viewing on a small cell phone screen.

Model management component of a DSS that consists of both the DSS models and the DSS model management system.

Monitoring-and-surveillance agent (predictive agent) intelligent agent that constantly observes and reports on some entity of interest, that could, for example, be a network or manufacturing equipment.

Mouse a pointing device that you use to click on icons or buttons.

Multi-agent system system in which groups of intelligent agents have the ability to work independently and interact with each other.

Multi-channel service delivery the term that describes a company's offering of multiple ways in which customers can interact with it.

Multidimensional analysis (MDA) tool slice-and-dice technique that allows you to view multidimensional information from different perspectives.

Multifunction printer a printer that can scan, copy, and fax, as well as print.

MultiMediaCard (MMC) flash memory card that looks identical to an SD card (but SD cards have copy protection built-in), is a little larger than a quarter, and is slightly thicker than a credit card.

Multimedia (HTML) résumé a multimedia format displayed on the Web for employers to explore at their convenience.

Multi-state CPU works with information represented in more than just two states, probably 10 states with each state representing a digit between 0 and 9.

Multitasking allows you to work with more than one piece of software at a time.

Mutation the process within a genetic algorithm of randomly trying combinations and evaluating the success (or failure) of the outcomes.

N

Nanotechnology a discipline that seeks to control matter at the atomic and sub-atomic levels for the purpose of building devices on the same small scale.

Near Field Communication (NFC) a wireless transmission technology being developed primarily for cell phones to support mobile commerce (m-commerce) and other cell phone activities.

Nearshore outsourcing contracting an outsourcing arrangement with a company in a nearby country.

Network access point (NAP) a point on the Internet where several connections converge.

Network hub a device that connects multiple computers into a network.

Network interface card (NIC) an expansion card for a desktop computer or a PC card for a notebook computer that connects your computer to a network and provides the doorway for information to flow in and out.

Network service provider (NSP) such as MCI or AT&T, owns and maintains routing computers at NAPs and even the lines that connect the NAPs to each other.

Neural network (artificial neural network or ANN) an artificial intelligence system that is capable of finding and differentiating patterns.

Nonrecurring (ad hoc) decision one that you make infrequently (perhaps only once); you may have different criteria for determining the best solution each time.

Nonstructured decision a decision for which there may be several "right" answers and there is no precise way to get a right answer.

Normalization process of assuring that a relational database structure can be implemented as a series of two-dimensional tables.

Notebook computer a small, portable, fully functional, battery-operated computer.

N-tier infrastructure balances the work of the network over several different servers.

O

Object an instance of a class.

Objective information quantifiably describes something that is known.

Object-oriented approach combines information and procedures into a single view.

Object-oriented database works with traditional database information and also complex data types such as diagrams, schematic drawings, video, and sound and text documents.

Object-oriented programming language a programming language used to develop object-oriented systems.

Offshore outsourcing contracting with a company that is geographically far away.

Online ad (banner ad) small advertisement that appears on other sites.

Online analytical processing (OLAP) the manipulation of information to support decision making.

Online training runs over the Internet or off a CD or DVD.

Online transaction processing (OLTP) the gathering of input information, processing that information, and updating existing information to reflect the gathered and processed information.

Onshore outsourcing the process of engaging another company in the same country for services.

Open-source information content that is publicly available (in a broad sense), free of charge, and most often updatable by anyone.

Open-source software software for which the source code (how the software was actually written) is publicly available and free of charge.

Operating system software   system software that controls your application software and manages how your hardware devices work together.

Operational database   a database that supports OLTP.

Optical character reader   reads characters that appear on a page or sales tag (often used in point-of-sale [POS] systems in retail environments).

Optical fibre   uses a very thin and flexible glass or plastic fibre through which pulses of light travel.

Optical mark reader   detects the presence or absence of a mark in a predetermined spot on the page (often used for true/false and multiple-choice exam answers).

Optical storage media   plastic discs on which information is stored, deleted, and/or changed using laser light.

Output device   a tool you use to see, hear, or otherwise recognize the results of your information-processing requests.

Outsourcing   the delegation of specific work to a third party for a specified length of time, at a specified cost, and at a specified level of service.

Overall cost leadership   (in Porter's three generic strategies) offering the same or better quality product or service at a price that is less than any of the competition.

P

Page exposures   average number of page exposures to an individual visitor.

Parallel implementation   using both the old and new system until you're sure that the new system performs correctly.

Parallel port   fits parallel connectors, which are large flat connectors found almost exclusively on printer cables.

Path-to-profitability (P2P)   a formal business plan that outlines key business issues such as customer targets (by demographic, industry, etc.), marketing strategies, operations strategies (e.g., production, transportation, and logistics), and projected targets for income-statement and balance-sheet items.

Pattern classification   matches your spoken phonemes to a phoneme sequence stored in an acoustic model database.

PC card   the expansion card you use to add devices to your notebook computer.

PC card slot   the opening on the side or front of a notebook, where you connect an external device with a PC Card.

Peer-to-peer collaboration software   permits users to communicate in real time and share files without going through a central server.

Personal digital assistant (PDA)   a small handheld computer that helps you surf the Web and perform simple tasks such as note taking, calendaring, appointment scheduling, and maintaining an address book.

Personal finance software   helps you maintain your chequebook, prepare a budget, track investments, monitor your credit card balances, and pay bills electronically.

Personal information management software (PIM)   helps you create and maintain (1) to-do lists, (2) appointments and calendars, and (3) points of contact.

Personal productivity software   helps you perform personal tasks—such as writing a memo, creating a graph, and creating a slide presentation—that you can usually do even if you don't own a computer.

Pharming   the rerouting of your request for a legitimate Web site, that is, you type in the correct address for your bank and are redirected to a fake site that collects information from you.

Phased implementation   implementing the new system in phases (e.g., accounts receivables, then accounts payable) until you're sure it works correctly and then implementing the remaining phases of the new system.

Phishing (carding or brand spoofing)   technique to gain personal information for the purpose of identity theft, usually by means of fraudulent e-mail.

Physical view   deals with how information is physically arranged, stored, and accessed on some type of storage device such as a hard disk.

Pilot implementation   having only a small group of people use the new system until you know it works correctly and then adding the remaining people to the system.

Pirated software   the unauthorized use, duplication, distribution, or sale of copyrighted software.

Pivot table   enables you to group and summarize information.

Pixels (picture elements)   the dots that make up the image on your screen.

Planning phase   of the systems development life cycle, in which you create a solid plan for developing your information system.

Plotter   form output by moving a pen across the surface of a piece of paper.

Plug and play   an operating feature that finds and installs the device driver for a device that you plug into your computer.

Plunge implementation   discarding the old system completely and immediately using the new system.

Podcasting   your ability at any time to download audio and video files for viewing and listening using portable listening devices and personal computers.

Pointing device   a device that is used to navigate and select objects on a display screen.

Pointing stick   a little rod (like a pencil-top eraser) used almost exclusively on notebook computers.

Polymorphism   to have many forms.

Pop-under ad   a form of a pop-up ad that you do not see until you close your current browser window.

Pop-up ad   small Web page containing an advertisement that appears on your screen outside the current Web site loaded into your browser.

Port   a place on your system unit, monitor, or keyboard through which information and instructions flow to and from your computer system.

Portable document format (PDF)   standard electronic distribution file format.

Portable document format (PDF) résumé   a standard electronic distribution format typically used for e-mailing.

Predictive analytics   uses a variety of decision tools and techniques—such as neural networks, data mining, decision trees, and Bayesian networks—to analyze current and historical data and make predictions about the likelihood of the occurrence of future events.

Presentation software   helps you create and edit information that will appear in electronic slides.

Primary key   a field (or group of fields in some cases) that uniquely describes each record.

Primary value processes   (in value-chain analysis) the chain of processes that takes in the raw materials and makes, delivers, markets, sells, and services your organization's products or services.

Privacy   the right to be left alone when you want to be, to have control over your own personal possessions, and not to be observed without your consent.

Procedure   manipulates or changes information.

Procedure view   contains all of the procedures within a system.

Program   a set of instructions that, when executed, cause a computer to behave in a specific manner.

Programming language   the tool developers use to write a program.

Project manager   an individual who is an expert in project planning and management, defines and develops the project plan, and tracks the plan to ensure all key project milestones are completed on time.

Project milestone   represents a key date by which you need a certain group of activities performed.

Project plan   defines the what, when, and who questions of systems development including all activities to be performed, the individuals, who will perform the activities, and the time required to complete each activity.

Project scope document   a written definition of the project scope, usually no longer than a paragraph.

Proof-of-concept prototype   a prototype you use to prove the technical feasibility of a proposed system.

Prototype   a smaller-scale representation or working model of the user's requirements or a proposed design for an information system.

Prototyping   the process of building a model that demonstrates the features of a proposed product, service, or system.

PS/2 port   fits PS/2 connectors, which you often find on keyboards and mice.

Public key encryption (PKE)   an encryption system that uses two keys: a public key that everyone can have and a private key for only the recipient.

Push technology   an environment in which businesses and organizations come to you via technology with information, services, and product offerings based on your profile.

Q

Query-and-reporting tool   similar to a QBE tool, SQL, and a report generator in the typical database environment.

Query-by-example (QBE) tool   helps you graphically design the answer to a question.

R

Random access memory (RAM)   a temporary holding area for the information you're working with as well as the system and application software instructions that the CPU currently needs.

Rapid application development methodology (RAD, rapid prototyping)   emphasizes extensive user involvement in the rapid and evolutionary construction of working prototypes of a system to accelerate the systems development process.

Recovery   the process of reinstalling the backup information in the event the information was lost.

Recurring decision   a decision that you have to make repeatedly and often periodically, whether weekly, monthly, quarterly, or yearly.

Redacting   blacking out portions of a document, usually to protect confidential information, so that it cannot be recovered later.

Regression testing   catching re-emergence of errors that have already been fixed but then reappear later in the design process.

Relation   describes each two-dimensional table or file in the relational model (hence its name relational database model).

Relational database   uses a series of logically related two-dimensional tables or files to store information in the form of a database.

Repeater   a device that receives a radio signal, strengthens it, and sends it on.

Report generator   helps you quickly define formats of reports and what information you want to see in a report.

Request for proposal (RFP)   a formal document that describes in detail your logical requirements for a proposed system and invites outsourcing organizations (or "vendors") to submit bids for its development.

Requirement recovery document   a detailed document that describes (1) the distinction between critical and noncritical IT systems and information, (2) each possible threat, and (3) the possible worst-case scenarios that can result from each disaster.

Requirements definition document   defines all the business requirements and prioritizes them in order of business importance.

Resolution of a printer   the number of dots per inch (dpi) it produces.

Resolution of a screen   the number of pixels it has.

Response time   average time to respond to a user-generated event, such as a request for a report, a mouse click, and so on.

Résumé   summary of your qualifications.

Reverse auction   the process in which a buyer posts its interest in buying a certain quantity of items with notations concerning quality, specification, and delivery timing, and sellers compete for the business by submitting successively lower bids until there is only one seller left.

RFID (radio frequency identification)   uses a microchip (chip) in a tag or label to store information, and information is transmitted from, or written to, the tag or label when the microchip is exposed to the correct frequency of radio waves.

Risk assessment   the process of evaluating IT assets, their importance to the organization, and their susceptibility to threats to measure the risk exposure of these assets.

Risk-based testing   ranks the functions or features of a system that are most prone to failure, and tests them first.

Rivalry among existing competitors   in the Five Forces Model is high when competition is fierce in a market, and low when competition is more complacent.

Rootkit   software that gives you administrator rights to a computer or network whose purpose is to allow you to conceal processes, files, or system data from the operating system.

Router   a device that passes network traffic between smaller subnetworks (or subnets) of a larger network.

RSS feed   a technology that provides frequently published and updated digital content on the Web.

Run-grow-transform (RGT) framework   an approach in which you allocate in terms of percentages how you will spend your IT dollars on various types of business strategies.

S

Sales force automation (SFA) system   automatically tracks all of the steps in the sales process.

Satellite modem   modem that allows you to get Internet access from your satellite dish.

Satisficing   the process of making a choice that meets your needs and is satisfactory, without necessarily being the best possible choice available.

Scalability   refers to how well your system can adapt to increased demands.

Scannable (or ASCII) résumé   a paper résumé without any formatting that becomes electronic when it is scanned into a computer.

Scanner   used to convert information that exists in visible form into electronic form.

Scope creep   occurs when the scope of the project increases beyond its original intentions.

Screenagers   the term applied to the current generation of young people because they spend so much time in front of a screen.

Script bunny (script kiddie)   someone who would like to be a hacker but doesn't have much technical expertise.

Search engine   a facility on the Web that helps you find sites with the information and/or services you want.

Secure Digital (SD) card   flash memory card that looks identical to an MMC card (but SD cards have copy protection built-in), is a little larger than a quarter, and is slightly thicker than a credit card.

Secure Electronic Transaction (SET)   a transmission security method that ensures transactions are legitimate as well as secure.

Secure Sockets Layer (SSL)   creates a secure and private connection between a Web client computer and a Web server computer, encrypts the information, and then sends the information over the Internet.

Selection   the process within a genetic algorithm that gives preference to better outcomes.

Self-sourcing (also called end-user development)   the development and support of IT systems by end users (knowledge workers) with little or no help from IT specialists.

Selling prototype   a prototype you use to convince people of the worth of a proposed system.

Service level agreement (SLA)   a formal contractually obligated agreement between two parties; within different environments, an SLA takes on different meanings.

Service level specification (SLS) or service level objective (SLO)   supporting document to a service level agreement that clearly defines key metrics for success regarding the SLA.

Service-oriented architecture (SOA or SoA)   a software architecture perspective that focuses on the development, use, and reuse of small self-contained blocks of code (called services) to meet all the application software needs of an organization.

Sign-off   the knowledge workers' signatures indicating they approve all the business requirements.

Skill words   nouns and adjectives used by organizations to describe job skills that should be woven into the text of an applicant's résumé.

Slack space   the space left over from the end of the file to the end of the cluster.

Smart card   a plastic card the size of a credit card that contains an embedded chip on which digital information can be stored and updated.

SmartMedia (SM) card   flash memory card that's a little longer than a CF card and about as thick as a credit card with capacities of up to 512 megabytes.

Social engineering   conning your way into acquiring information that you have no right to.

Social networking site   a site on which you post information about yourself, create a network of friends, share content such as photos and videos, and communicate with other people.

Social network system   an IT system that links you to people you know and, from there, to people your contacts know.

Software   the set of instructions that your hardware executes to carry out a specific task for you.

Software-as-a-service (SaaS)   delivery model for software in which you would pay for software on a pay-per-use basis instead of buying the software outright.

Software suite   bundled software that comes from the same publisher and costs less than buying all the software pieces individually.

Spam   unsolicited e-mail (electronic junk mail) from businesses that advertises goods and services.

Spam blocker software   utility software that filters unwanted e-mail from your inbox.

Spoofing   the forging of the return address on an e-mail so that the e-mail message appears to come from someone other than the actual sender.

Spreadsheet software   helps you work primarily with numbers, including performing calculations and creating graphs.

Spyware (sneakware, stealthware)   malicious software that collects information about you and your computer and reports it to someone else without your permission.

Steganography   the hiding of information inside other information.

Storage area network (SAN)   an infrastructure for building special, dedicated networks that allow rapid and reliable access to storage devices by multiple servers.

Storage device   a tool you use to store information for use at a later time.

Storyboard   a visual representation illustrating relationships of objects on a Web page.

Stress (or load) testing   the ability of a system to maintain a certain level of performance under unusual (unfavourable) circumstances.

Structured decision   a decision where processing a certain kind of information in a specified way will always get you the right answer.

Structured query language (SQL)   a standardized fourth-generation query language found in most DBMSs.

Structure tag   HTML tag that sets up the necessary sections and specifies that the document is indeed an HTML document.

Stylus   penlike device used to write or draw on a PDA or tablet PC.

Subjective information   attempts to describe something that is unknown.

Sub procedure   computer code that performs some action on or with objects.

Supercomputer   the fastest, most powerful, and most expensive type of computer.

Supplier power   in the Five Forces Model is high when buyers have few choices from whom to buy, and low when their choices are many.

Supply chain management (SCM)   tracks inventory and information among business processes and across companies.

Supply chain management (SCM) system   an IT system that supports supply chain management activities by automating the tracking of inventory and information among business processes and across companies.

Support value processes   (in value-chain analysis) including infrastructure, human resource management, technology development, and procurement that ensure the smooth operations of the primary value processes.

Swarm (collective) intelligence   collective behaviour of groups of simple agents that are capable of devising solutions to problems as they arise, eventually leading to coherent global patterns.

Switch   a network device that connects computers and passes messages by repeating each computer's transmissions only to the intended recipient, not to all the computers connected.

Switching cost   a cost that makes customers reluctant to switch to another product or service supplier.

System availability   usually measured inversely as *downtime*, or the average amount of time a system is down and unavailable to end users and customers.

System bus   electrical pathways that move information between basic components of the motherboard, including between RAM and the CPU.

Systems development life cycle (SDLC)   a structured step-by-step approach for developing information systems.

System software   handles tasks specific to technology management and coordinates the interaction of all technology devices.

System testing   verifies that the units or pieces of code written for a system function correctly when integrated into the total system.

T

T1   a high-speed business network circuit typically used for business connections, running at speeds up to 1.544 Mbps (1.544 million bits per second).

Tablet PC   a pen-based computer that provides the screen capabilities of a PDA with the functional capabilities of a notebook or desktop computer.

TCP/IP (Transport control protocol/Internet protocol)   the primary protocol for transmitting information over the Internet.

Technical architecture   defines the hardware, software, and telecommunications equipment required to run the system.

Technology innovation failure   a reward system for trying new technologies even if they prove to be unsuccessful.

Technology-literate knowledge worker   person who knows how and when to apply technology.

Telecommunications device   tool you use to send information to and receive it from another person or computer in a network.

Telephone modem (modem)   a device that connects your computer to your phone line so that you can access another computer or network.

Terabyte (TB)   roughly 1 trillion bytes.

Test conditions   the detailed steps the system must perform along with the expected results of each step.

Testing phase   of the systems development life cycle verifies that the system works and meets all the business requirements defined in the analysis phase.

Threat of new entrants   in the Five Forces Model is high when it is easy for new competitors to enter a market, and low when there are significant entry barriers to entering a market.

Threat of substitute products or services   in the Five Forces Model is high when there are many alternatives to a product or service, and low when there are few alternatives from which to choose.

Thrill-seeker hacker   a hacker who breaks into computer systems for entertainment.

Throughput   the amount of information that can pass through a system in a given amount of time.

Tiered infrastructure (layer infrastructure)   the IT system is partitioned into tiers (or layers) where each tier (or layer) performs a specific type of functionality.

Time service factor (TSF)   the percentage of calls answered within a specific time frame, such as 30 or 90 seconds.

Top-level domain (TLD)   extension of a Web site address that identifies its type.

Total hits   number of visits to your Web site, many of which may be by the same visitor.

Touchpad   the little dark rectangle that you use to move the cursor with your finger, often found on notebook computers.

Trackball   similar to a mechanical mouse, but it has a ball on the top.

Traditional technology approach   has two primary views of any computer-based system—information and procedures—and it keeps these two views separate and distinct at all times.

Transaction processing system (TPS)   a system that processes transactions within an organization.

Transaction speed   the speed at which a system can process a transaction.

Trojan horse software   software you don't want hidden inside software you do want.

Trojan horse virus   hides inside other software, usually an attachment or download.

Twisted-pair cable   a bundle of copper wires used for transmitting voice or data communications; it comes in several varieties.

U

U3 Smart drive   looks like and is a USB flash drive, but it stores and can launch and run software on any computer.

Ubiquitous computing   computing and technology support anytime, anywhere with access to all needed information and access to all business partners, both internal and external to the organization.

Unallocated space   the set of clusters that have been set aside to store information, but have not yet received a file, or still contain some or all of a file marked as deleted.

Uniform resource locator (URL)   an address for a specific Web page or document within a Web site.

Uninstaller software   utility software that you can use to remove software from your hard disk that you no longer want.

Unique visitors   the number of unique visitors to your site in a given time.

Unit testing   tests individual units or pieces of code for a system.

USB (universal serial bus) port   fits small flat plug-and-play, hot-swap USB connectors, and, using USB hubs, you can connect up to 127 devices to a single USB port on your computer.

User acceptance testing (UAT)   determines if the system satisfies the business requirements and enables knowledge workers to perform their jobs correctly.

User agent (personal agent)   an intelligent agent that takes action on your behalf.

User documentation   highlights how to use the system.

User interface management   component of a DSS that allows you to communicate with the DSS.

Utility software   software that provides additional functionality to your operating system software.

V

Value chain   the chain or series of business processes, each of which adds value to your organization's products or services for customers.

Value-chain analysis   a systematic approach to assessing and improving the value of business processes within your organization to further increase its competitive strengths.

Variable   a place to store a piece of information.

Vertical e-marketplace   an electronic marketplace that connects buyers and sellers in a given industry (e.g., oil and gas, textiles, and retail).

Vertical government integration   electronic integration of agencies, activities, and processes up and down federal, state, and local government levels.

Vertical market software   application software that is unique to a particular industry.

View   allows you to see the contents of a database file, make whatever changes you want, perform simple sorting, and query to find the location of specific information.

Viewable image size (VIS)   the size of the image on a monitor.

Viral marketing   encourages users of a product or service supplied by a B2C e-commerce business to encourage friends to join in as well.

Virtual private network (VPN)   uses encryption to protect the confidentiality of *all* network transmissions between two endpoints.

Virtual reality   a three-dimensional computer simulation in which you actively and physically participate.

Virtual team   a team whose members are located in varied geographic locations and whose work is supported by specialized ICE software or by more basic collaboration systems.

Virus (computer virus)   software that is written with malicious intent to cause annoyance or damage.

Visual Basic Editor (VBE)   a separate application where you write and edit your Visual Basic macros.

VoIP (Voice over Internet Protocol)   allows you to send voice communications over the Internet and avoid the toll charges that you would normally receive from your long distance carrier.

Volume testing   involves testing a system to determine whether it can do a large volume of calculations in the time required.

W

Walker   an input device that captures and records the movement of your feet as you walk or turn in different directions.

Waterfall methodology   a sequential, activity-based process in which one phase in the SDLC is followed by another from planning through implementation.

Web 2.0   so-called second generation of the Web, which focuses on online collaboration, users as both creators and modifiers of content, dynamic and customized information feeds, and many other engaging Web-based services.

Web authoring software   helps you design and develop Web sites and pages that you publish on the Web.

Web browser software   enables you to surf the Web.

Webcam   captures digital video to upload to the Web.

Web-centric metric   a measure of the success of your Web and e-business initiatives.

Web log   consists of one line of information for every visitor to a Web site and is usually stored on a Web server.

Web page   a specific portion of a Web site that deals with a certain topic.

Web portal   a site that provides a wide range of services, including search engines, free e-mail, chat rooms, discussion boards, and links to hundreds of different sites.

Web server   provides information and services to Web surfers.

Web site   a specific location on the Web where you visit, gather information, and perhaps even order products.

Web site address   a unique name that identifies a specific site on the Web.

Web space   storage area where you keep your Web site.

White-hat (ethical) hacker   a computer security professional who is hired by a company to break into its computer system, so as to find security lapses.

Wide area network (WAN)   a set of connected networks serving areas or buildings not in immediate proximity to each other.

WiFi (wireless fidelity or IEEE 802.11a, b, or g)   a standard for transmitting information in the form of radio waves over distances up to about 300 feet.

Wiki   a Web site that allows you—as a visitor—to create, edit, change, and often eliminate content.

Wired communications media   transmit information over a closed, connected path.

Wireless access point (WAP)   a device that allows a computer to use radio waves to access a network.

Wireless communications media   transmit information through the air.

Word processing software   helps you create papers, letters, memos, and other basic documents.

Workflow   defines all of the steps or business rules, from beginning to end, required for a business process.

Workflow system   facilitates the automation and management of business processes.

Workshop training   held in a classroom environment and is led by an instructor.

World Wide Web (Web)   a multimedia-based collection of information, services, and Web sites supported by the Internet.

Worm   a type of virus that replicates and spreads itself, not just from file to file, but from computer to computer via e-mail and other Internet traffic.

X

xD-Picture (xD) card   flash memory card that looks like a rectangular piece of plastic smaller than a penny and about as thick, with one edge slightly curved.

Z

Zombie   bot-infected computer.

CHAPTER 1

1. PhoneBusters, year-end statistics, www.phonebusters.com/english/documents/Yearlyen0001_000.pdf, retrieved January 23, 2008.

2. Greenemeier, Larry, and Nicholas Hoover, "The Hacker Economy," *InformationWeek*, February 12, 2007, pp. 32–39.

3. "Sexcerpts," *Rocky Mountain News*, March 25, 2006, p. 2E.

4. America's Largest Corporations, Fortune 2006 500, *Fortune*, April 17, 2006.

5. Christensen, Clayton M. and Michael E. Raynor, *The Innovator's Solution: Creating and Sustaining Successful Growth*, HBS Press, 2003.

6. www.systransoft.com.

7. Kallman, Ernest, and John Grillo, *Ethical Decision Making and Information Technology* (San Francisco: McGraw-Hill, 1993).

8. Kontzer, Tony, "Brink's Gets Smarter about Learning," *InformationWeek*, December 15, 2003, www.informationweek.com/story/showArticle.jhtml?articleID16700281, accessed December 20, 2003.

9. Porter, Michael, "How Competitive Forces Shape Strategy," *Harvard Business Review*, March/April 1979.

10. "Accenture: Customer Satisfaction Driving Egovernment," from www.nua.com/surveys/index.cgi?f5VS&art_id5905358759&rel5true, accessed December 2, 2003.

11. Greenspan, Robyn, "U.S. Web Usage and Traffic, August 2004," ClickZ Network, Jupitermedia Corporation, September 21, 2004, www.clickz.com/stats/sectors/traffic_patterns/print.php/3410151, accessed October 30, 2008.

12. "Benchmarking E-Government: A Global Perspective," United Nations Division for Public Economics and Public Administration, released May 2002, www.unpan.org.

13. "NRDC Equity Partners Announces the Acquisition of Hudson's Bay Company," www.hbc.com/hbc/mediacentre/press/hbc/press.asp?prId=335, accessed October 30, 2008.

14. www.commercialware.com/public/customers/testimonialsContent.asp, accessed January 26, 2008.

15. "Why Do Americans Still Write Checks?", www.frbsf.org/publications/economics/letter/2002/el2002-27.html, accessed October 30, 2008.

16. Edwards, Own, "Bow Tech: ASAP Case Study," *Forbes ASAP*, June 3, 1996, pp. 54–58.

17. "Social Network Stats: Facebook, MySpace, Reunion," January 2008, www.web-strategist.com/blog/2008/01/09/social-network-stats-facebook-myspace-reunion-jan-2008, accessed October 30, 2008.

18. Rodgers, Zachary, "What MySpace Means for Marketers," ClickZ Network, May 6, 2005, Jupitermedia Corporation, www.clickz.com/features/article.php/3565776 , accessed October 30, 2008.

19. www.myspace.com, accessed March 28, 2006.

20. McGee, Marianne, "The Useless Hunt for Data," *InformationWeek*, January 1/8, 2007, p. 19.

21. Ibid.

CHAPTER 2

1. Claburn, Thomas, "Let's Make a Deal Online," *InformationWeek*, March 5, 2007, p. 52.

2. "Dell: Coming Soon to Best Buy Stores in U.S." December 6, 2007, www.dell.com/content/topics/global.aspx/corp/pressoffice/en/2007/2007_12_06_rr_000?c=us&cs=19&l=en&s=dhs, accessed October 30, 2008.

3. "Configuring 9 500 Percent ROI for Dell," i2 White Paper, www.i2.com/customer/hightech_consumer.cfm, accessed May 5, 2004.

4. James P. Farrell, "What Is the Extended Enterprise?" April 9, 2008, jpfarrell.blogspot.com/2008/04/extended-enterprise.html, accessed October 30, 2008.

5. Malykhina, Elena, "Retailers Take Stock," *InformationWeek*, February 7, 2005, www.informationweek.com/shared/printableArticleSrc.jhtml?ArticleID559301319, accessed March 3, 2005.

6. "Websmart," *BusinessWeek*, November 24, 2003, p. 96.

7. Koudal, Peter, et al., "General Motors: Building a Digital Loyal Network through Demand and Supply Chain Integration," Stanford Graduate School of Business, Case GS-29, March 17, 2003.

8. McGee, Marianne Kolbasuk, "APC Wants to Know You a Whole Lot Better," *InformationWeek*, September 11, 2006, pp. 55–57.

9. American Power Conversion Corporation, *APC—Corporate Profile*, www.apc.com/corporate/profile.cfm, accessed April 21, 2007.

10. Surmacz, Jon, "Collaborate and Save: Collaboration Technology Can Save Big Money for the Oil and Gas Industry," *CIO Magazine*, November 5, 2003, www2.cio.com/metrics/2003/metric625.html, accessed June 19, 2004.

11. Davenport, Thomas, and Laurence Prusak, *What's the Big Idea? Creating and Capitalizing on the Best Management Thinking* (Boston: Harvard Business School Press, 2003).

12. McGee, Marianne Kolbusak, "Let's Talk: Constellation Gets Collaborative," *InformationWeek*, September 11, 2006, pp. 98–102.

13. Rashid, Mohammad, et al., "The Evolution of ERP Systems: A Historical Perspective," www.ideagroup.com, accessed May 11, 2004.

14. Babcock, Charles, "FedEx Integration Wins Customers for Keeps," *InformationWeek*, September 11, 2006, pp. 112–14.

15. Whiting, Rick, "Sun Raises the Bar on Build to Order," *Information-Week*, September 11, 2006, pp. 106–8.

16. Adapted with permission from www.maximizer.com/company/success_stories/crm/scotia.html.

CHAPTER 3

1. McGee, Marianne Kolbasuk, "High Cost of Data Loss," *Information-Week*, March 20, 2006, pp. 34–46.

2. Lemos, Robert, "TJX Theft Tops 45.6 Million Card Numbers," Security Focus, March 30, 2007, www.securityfocus.com/news/11455, accessed October 30, 2008.

3. Watterson, Karen, "A Data Miner's Tools," BYTE, October 1995, pp. 170–72.

4. "Britannia Airways—Keeping the Crews Flying High," Customer Success Stories from Open Text Corp., www.opentext.com/customers/ success-stories.html (Britannia Airways), accessed May 5, 2005.

5. Cash, James, "Gaining Customer Loyalty," *InformationWeek*, April 10, 1995, p. 88.

6. versaterm.com, accessed August 28, 2008.

7. Maselli, Jennifer, "Insurers Look to CRM for Profits," *InformationWeek*, May 6, 2002, www.informationweek.com/story/IWK200220502 50007, accessed March 1, 2005.

8. "Laurentian Bank Creates Online Scoring Models for Dealer Financing," Customer Success Story from SAS Corporation, www.sas.com/success/laurentian.html, accessed April 21, 2005.

9. Kling, Julia, "OLAP Gains Fans among Data-Hungry Firms," *Computerworld*, January 8, 1996, pp. 43, 48.

10. Hutheesing, Nikhil, "Surfing with Sega," *Forbes*, November 4, 1996, pp. 350–51.

11. LaPlante, Alice, "Big Things Come in Smaller Packages," *Computerworld*, June 24, 1996, pp. DW/6–7.

12. Weier, Mary Hayes, "QUERY: What's Next in BI?" *InformationWeek*, March 5, 2007, pp. 27–29.

13. Dragoon, Alice, "Business Intelligence Gets Smart(er)," *CIO Magazine*, September 15, 2003, www.cio.com/archive/091503/smart.html, accessed October 30, 2008.

14. Gray, Paul, "Business Intelligence: A New Name or the Future of DSS?" in T. Bui, H. Sroka, S. Stanek, and J. Goluchowski (eds.), *DSS in the Uncertainty of the Internet Age* (Katowice, Poland: University of Economics in Katowice, 2003).

15. Willen, Claudia, "Airborne Opportunities," *Intelligent Enterprise 5*, no. 2 (January 14, 2002).

16. Bosavage, Jennifer, "BI Helps H&B Hit Business Targets," *Information-Week* Business Intelligence Pipeline, February 22, 2005, www.bizintel-ligencepipeline.com/ showArticle.jhtml?articleID=60402524, accessed March 1, 2005.

17. Canada Health Infoway, www.infoway-inforoute.ca/en/Home/home.aspx, October 30, 2008.

18. Hoover, J. Nicholas, "Get Well Soon," *InformationWeek*, December 4, 2006, pp. 26–28.

19. Schlosser, Julie, "Tech@Work," *Fortune*, March 3, 2003, www.fortune.com/fortune/subs/print/0,15935,427294,00.html?cookie=11073974157, accessed January 10, 2004.

20. Whiting, Rick, "Analysis Gap," *InformationWeek*, April 22, 2002, www.informationweek.com/story/IWK20020418S0007, accessed October 30, 2008.

21. "Bigelow Teas," Customer Spotlight from Business Objects, at www.businessobjects.com/company/customers/spotlight/bigelow.asp, accessed May 17, 2005.

22. "Caffe Nero Customer Success," www.cognos.com/pdfs/success_stories/ss_caffe-nero.pdf, accessed January 12, 2008.

23. "Red Robin International," company success story from Cognos at www.cognos.com/company/success/ss_entertainment.html, accessed January 13, 2004.

24. "Mining the Data of Dining," *Nation's Restaurant News*, May 22, 2000, pp. S22–S24.

25. Brown, Erika, "Analyze This," *Forbes*, April 1, 2002, pp. 96–98.

26. Levinson, Meredith, "The Brain Behind the Big, Bad Burger and Other Tales of Business Intelligence, *CIO Magazine*, March 15, 2005, at www.cio.com/archive/031505/intelligence.html, accessed May 1, 2005.

CHAPTER 4

1. "Navigating Arctic Waterways Using GIS," Summer 2002, www.esri.com/news/arcnews/summer-02articles/navigating-arctic.html, accessed October 30, 2008.

2. Gambon, Jill, "A Database That 'Ads' Up," *InformationWeek*, August 7, 1995, pp. 68–69.

3. Simon, Herbert, *The New Science of Management Decisions*, rev. ed. (Englewood Cliffs, NJ: Prentice Hall, 1977).

4. Kauderer, Steven, and Amy Kuehl, "Adding Value with Technology," *Best's Review*, October 2001, p. 130.

5. "M/W Planning: It's All in the Data," *Railway Age*, January 2001, pp. 60–61.

6. Marlin, Steven, Cristina McEachern, and Anthony O'Donnell, "Cross Selling Starts with CRM System," *Wall Street & Technology*, December 2001, pp. A8–A10.

7. "Software Integration from Down on the Farm," *Fleet Equipment*, April 2004, pp. 8–10.

8. "GIS Hall of Fame: Roger Tomlinson," www.urisa.org/node/395, accessed October 30, 2008.

9. Greiner, Lynn, "Putting Canada on the Map," December 17, 2007, www.theglobeandmail.com/servlet/story/RTGAM.20071217.wgt-GIS1214/BNStory/PersonalTech/home, accessed October 30, 2008.

10. Stewart, Mary Ann, "Tracking Cattle in the Heartland," *Geospatial Solutions*, September 2005, pp. 20–25.

11. Malykhina, Elena, "Maps Meet Mashups," *InformationWeek*, March 17, 2007, www.information-week.com/showArticle.jhtml;jsessionid=F4CSRST1GWTH0QSNDLPSKHSCJUNN2JVN?articleID=198001255&queryText=%22geographic+information%22, accessed April 27, 2007.

12. Kay, Alexx, "Artificial Neural Networks," *Computerworld*, February 12, 2001, p. 60.

13. Ibid.

14. Perry, William, "What Is Neural Network Software?" *Journal of Systems Management*, September 1994, pp. 12–15.

15. Port, Otis, "Diagnoses That Cast a Wider Net," *BusinessWeek*, May 22, 1995, p. 130.

16. Baxt, William G., and Joyce Skora, "Prospective Validation of Artificial Neural Network Trained to Identify Acute Myocardial Infarction," *The Lancet*, January 6, 1997, pp. 12–15.

17. McCartney, Laton, "Technology for a Better Bottom Line," *InformationWeek*, February 26, 1996, p. 40.

18. Wu, D., Yang, Z., Liang, L. (2006). "Using DEA-neural Network Approach to Evaluate Branch Efficiency of a Large Canadian Bank," *Expert Systems with Applications* 31 108–15.

19. Whiting, Rick, "Companies Boost Sales Efforts with Predictive Analysis," *InformationWeek*, February 25, 2002.

20. Ibid.

21. Punch, Linda, "Battling Credit Card Fraud," *Bank Management*, March 1993, pp. 18–22.

22. "Cigna, IBM Tech Tool Targets Health Care Fraud," *National Underwriter Property & Casualty—Risk & Benefits*, October 1994, p. 5.

23. Anthes, Gary H., "Picking Winners and Losers," *Computerworld*, February 18, 2002, p. 34.

24. "Weblining," *BusinessWeek Online*, April 3, 2000, www.businessweek.com, accessed May 29, 2005.

25. Llewellyn, Mike, "Check One, Two," *Dealerscope*, March 2005, p. 82.

26. Johnson, Colin, "Breeding Programs," *Financial Management*, February 2001, pp. 18–20.

27. Ruggiero, Murray, "Enhancing Trading with Technology," *Futures*, June 2000, pp. 56–59.

28. Patrick, C., L. Hui, S. F. Frency, Keith Ng, and C. C. Chan, "A Study of the Roll Planning of Fabric Spreading Using Genetic Algorithms," *International Journal of Clothing Science & Technology*, 2000, pp. 50–62.

29. Begley, S., "Software au Naturel," *Newsweek*, May 8, 1995, pp. 70–71.

30. Goldbert, David E., "Genetic and Evolutionary Algorithms Come of Age," *Communications of the ACM*, March 1994, pp. n113–119.

31. Hill, Alice, "Google Inside Out," *Maximum PC*, April 2004, pp. 44–48.

32. Thibodeau, Patrick, "Agents of Change," *Computerworld*, September 6, 2004, p. 24.

33. Dobbs, Sarah Boehle Kevin, Donna Gordon Goldwasser, and Jack Stamps, "The Return of Artificial Intelligence," *Training*, November 2000, p. 26.

34. Totty, Patrick, "Pinpoint Members with New Data-Mining Tools," *Credit Union Magazine*, April 2002, pp. 32–34.

35. Wolinsky, Howard, "Advisa Helps Companies Get More from Their Data: Helps Managers to Understand Market," *Chicago Sun-Times*, December 20, 2000, p. 81.

36. Anthes, Gary H., "Agents of Change," *Computerworld*, January 27, 2003, pp. 26–27.

37. Bonabeau, Eric, "Swarm Intelligence," O'Reilly Emerging Technology Conference, April 22–25, 2003, Santa Clara, CA.

38. Bonabeau, Eric, and Christopher Meyer, "Swarm Intelligence: A Whole New Way to Think about Business," *Harvard Business Review*, May 2001, pp. 107–14.

39. Bonabeau, "Swarm Intelligence."

40. Patrick, Ryan, "SaskTel Soups up CRM Efforts," June 10, 2005, www.itworldcanada.com/a/search/6b886ee9-709e-4544-889b-790b1a274c5a.html, accessed October 30, 2008.

41. Himmelsbach, Vawn, "Why Do Analytics on the Back of an Envelope?" October 25, 2005, www.itbusiness.ca/it/client/en/Home/News.asp?id=37227&bSearch=True, accessed October 30, 2008.

42. Lucas, Peter, "Behavior Forecast," 2005, www.cbcollections.com/crm.html, accessed October 30, 2008.

43. Whiting, Rick, "Businesses Mine Data to Predict What Happens Next," *InformationWeek*, May 29, 2006, www.informationweek.com/shared/printableArticleSrc.jhtml?ArticleID=188500520, accessed April 27, 2007.

44. McGee, Marianne Kolbasuk, "Mayo Builds toward Customized Medicine," *InformationWeek*, August 9, 2004, www.information-week.com/shared/printableArticleSrc.jhtml?articleID=26806448, accessed April 25, 2007.

45. McGee, Marianne Kolbasuk, "Mayo and IBM Search for Personalized Medicine," *InformationWeek*, August 4, 2004, www.information-week.com/shared/printable/ArticleSrc.jhtml?articleID=26805830, accessed April 25, 2007.

46. McGee, Marianne Kolbasuk, "IBM Partners with Cleveland Clinic for Better Medical Data Access," *InformationWeek*, September 30, 2004, www.informationweek.com/shared/printableArticle.Src.jhtml?articleID=48800505, accessed April 25, 2007.

CHAPTER 5

1. Gordon, Sheldon, "Major Credit-Card Issuers Go 'Contactless'" *Business Edge*, September 19, 2008, www.businessedge.ca/article.cfm/newsID/18581.cfm, accessed October 20, 2008.

2. Roseman, Ellen, "Credit Card Companies Open New Retail Horizons," *Toronto Star*, www.thestar.com/Business/article/503109, accessed October 30, 2008.

3. Perkins, Tara, *The Globe and Mail*, November 2, 2007.

4. "Cellphones as Wallets?" Know It or Not, http://knowitornot.blogspot.com/2007/11/cellphones-as-wallets-rbc-visa-test.html accessed October 30, 2008.

5. "Canada Is Not Only Moving to Chip and PIN but Also NFC," November 2, 2007, www.contactlessnews.com/2007/11/02/canada-is-not-only-moving-to-chip-and-pin-but-also-nfc?tag=Retail, accessed October 30, 2008.

6. "Pourquoi Paypal est promu a un bel avenir? The C2B Revolution: Consumer Empowerment," August 27, 2005, http://c2b.typepad.com, accessed October 30, 2008.

7. The Lockheed Martin Corporation, About Us, www.lockheedmartin.com/wms/findPage.do?dsp5fec&ci54&sc5400, accessed April 22, 2007.

8. "Global eXchange Services and ChinaECNet Establish B2B Exchange for China's $80 Billion Electronics Industry," Global eXchange Services, Inc., www.gxs.com.gxs/press/release/press20040318, accessed April 4, 2004.

9. "Introduction to China eHub System," ChinaECNet Organization, www.chinaecnet.com/eng/eHub/int.asp, accessed May 30, 2005.

10. "eBags.com Celebrates Five Years of Helping Customers Find the Perfect Bag Online," eBags.com, www.ebags.com/info/aboutebags/index.cfm?Fuseaction5pressitem&release_ID5102, accessed April 6, 2004.

11. "Awards," eBags.com, www.ebags.com/info/aboutebags/index.cfm?Fuseaction5awards, accessed May 30, 2005.

12. Home Page, www.epost.ca/main/en/home.shtml, accessed February 1, 2008.

13. *Young Canadians in a Wired World—Phase II* (YCWW II) www.media-awareness.ca/english/research/YCWW/phaseII/key_findings.cfm, accessed October 30, 2008.

14. Burns, Enid, "Wi-Fi Increases Time Spent Online," Incisive Interactive Marketing LLC, February 26, 2007, www.clickz.com/showPage.html?page5clickz_print&id536 25105, accessed April 23, 2007.

15. Burns, Enid, "Mobile Internet Population Grows," Incisive Interactive Marketing LLC, August 14, 2006, www.clickz.com/showPage.html?page5clickz_print&id 53623146, accessed April 23, 2007.

16. Staff Writer "Mobile Gaming Revenue Set for a Boom—Analysts," June 2007, www.tectonic.co.za/view.php?id=1600 19, accessed December 20 2007.

17. Houle, David, "Another Cell Phone Milestone," www.evolutionshift.com/blog/2008/02/13/another-cell-phone-milestone, accessed October 30, 2008.

18. Anderson, Chris, "The Long Tail," *Wired Magazine*, October 2004, www.wired.com/wired/archive/12.10/tail.html, accessed October 30, 2008.

19. Anderson, Chris, *The Long Tail* (New York: Hyperion, 2006).

20. "Cellphone Use Potentially Risky for Kids, Teens: Health Agency, www.cbc.ca/canada/story/2008/07/12/cellphones-kids.html July 12, 2008, accessed October 30, 2008.

21. Hoffman, Martin, "VW Revs Its B2B Engine," *Optimize*, March 2004, pp. 22–30.

22. Hansen, Meike-Uta, "Volkswagen Drives Supply-Chain Innovation," *Optimize*, April 2005, www.optimizemag.com/showArticle.jhtml;jesssionid5AWFT0BGTAWLIQQSNDBCSKHSCJUMEKJVN?articleID51599 04448, accessed May 29, 2005.

23. Burns, Enid, "Mobile Content Usage Is Higher in Developing Countries," Interactive Marketing LLC, March 2, 2007, www.clickz.com/showPage.html?page5clickz_print&id536 25143, accessed April 23, 2007.

24. Heilemann, John, "Unlocking the Middle Kingdom," *Business 2.0*, April 2006, pp. 44–46.

25. Schonfeld, Erick, "Cyworld Attacks," *Business 2.0*, April 2006, pp. 84–89.

CHAPTER 6

1. Mitchell, Robert, "This Integration Project Could Be a Lifesaver," *Computerworld*, January 22, 2007, www.computerworld.com/action/article.do?command5viewArticleBasic&taxonomyName5web_services&articleId5278040&taxonomyId561&intsrc5kc_feat, accessed April 24, 2007.

2. Krill, Paul, "FedEx Seeks Improved Software Testing," *Computerworld*, December 20, 2006, www.computerworld.com/action/article.do?command5viewArticleBasic&articleId 59006342, accessed April 24, 2007.

3. Roth, Sabine, "Profile of CAS Software AG," March 29, 2005, www.cas.de/English/Home.asp, accessed June 9, 2005.

4. Barnes, Cecily, "More Programmers Going 'Extreme,'" April 9, 2001, www.news.com, accessed June 1, 2005.

5. "Who We Are," www.agilealliance.org, accessed June 2, 2005.

6. www.cgi.com, accessed October 30, 2008

7. www.tpsgc-pwgsc.gc.ca/recgen/txt/index-eng.html, accessed October 30, 2008

8. "Government of Canada Service Oriented Architecture Series—Primer," Treasury Board Secretariat, March 30, 2006, www.tbs-sct.gc.ca/cio-dpi/webapps/architecture/p-gi/p-gi03-eng.asp, accessed October 30, 2008.

9. Government of Canada Service Oriented Architecture Series—Statement of Direction," Treasury Board Secretariat, March 30, 2006, www.tbs-sct.gc.ca/cio-dpi/webapps/architecture/sd-eo/sd-eo03-eng.asp. accessed October 30, 2008.

10. Gilhooly, Kym, "Visualization Tools for Requirements Definition," *Computerworld*, November 6, 2006, www.computerworld.com/action/article.do?command5viewArticleBasic&taxonomyId51&articleId5269 197&intsrc5hm_topic, accessed April 24, 2007.

11. "Industry Associations," http://connextions.net/IndustryAssoc.asp, accessed June 1, 2005.

12. "Outsourcing's Next Wave," *Fortune*, July 15, 2004, www.fortune.com, accessed June 2, 2005.

13. Cohen, Peter, "Twelve Technical and Business Trends Shaping the Year Ahead," May 6, 2004, www.babsoninsight.com, accessed June 2, 2005.

14. "Calling out Bangalore," Financial Post section of the *National Post*, September 6, 2008, page FP3.

15. Babcock, Charles. "In-Stock Parts Lead to Loyalty," *InformationWeek*, March 27, 2006, pp. 60-62.

16. "Count to 10 and Be Secure," *InformationWeek*, December 4, 2006, pp. 53–55.

17. Greenemeier, Larry, "A Not-So-Desperate Measure," *Information-Week*, December 18/25, 2006, pp. 57–58.

CHAPTER 7

1. Webb, Dave, "Offsite Backup a Snug Fit for Adidas," January 9, 2008, www.itworldcanada.com/a/Network-World/48363f78-046e-4357-b6f0-af2cdf7d7439.html, accessed October 30, 2008.

2. "President Bush's Proposed FY06 Budget Represents Growth in IT Spending for Federal Government," February 8, 2005, www.bitpipe.com, accessed May 19, 2005.

3. "ERP Outsourcing Picks Up and Takes Off," www.outsourcing.com, accessed May 19, 2005.

4. "Company Profile," www.delmonte.com, accessed May 16, 2005.

5. "Industry Implementations," www.dmreview.com, accessed May 16, 2005.

6. Weier, Mary Hayes, "Coca-Cola Launches Ambitious Technology Project with Bottlers," *Information-Week*, April 23, 2007, www.informationweek.com/shared/printableArticleSrc.jhtml?articleID5 199200834, accessed April 30, 2007.

7. "London Stock Exchange," Case Study at Microsoft.com, www.microsoft.com/casestudies/casestudy.aspx?casestudyid551828, accessed April 30, 2007.

8. Bettendorf, Michael, "London Stock Exchange Chooses Windows over Linux for Reliability," *Information-Week*, December 18/25, 2006, p. 7.

9. "The State of the Data Center," *InformationWeek*, December 18/25, 2006, p. 9.

10. Murphy, Chris, and Antone Gonsalves, "Elmo's at It Again," *InformationWeek*, December 18/25, 2006, p. 21.

11. Overby, Stephanie, "It Pays to Have a Disaster Recovery Plan in Place," *CIO Magazine*, September 16, 2005, www.cio.com/article/print/11931 , accessed October 30, 2008.

12. Murphy, Chris, "SOA Isn't Perfect, But It Solves a Problem," *Informa-tionWeek*, September 11, 2006, pp. 60–61.

13. Arellano, Nester, "Many Ontario Physicians Still Allergic to Electronic Records," www.itbusiness.ca/it/client/en/Home/News.asp?id=47385&bSearch=True, accessed October 30, 2008.

CHAPTER 8

1. "Canadian Tire Acceptance Limited Chooses Acxiom to Enhance Marketing Database Capabilities," January 26, 2001, http://findarticles.com/p/articles/mi_m0EIN/is_2001_Jan_26/ai_69534127, accessed October 30, 2008.

2. "Acxiom Announces New Canadian Data Centre," October 31, 2006, http://findarticles.com/p/articles/mi_m0EIN/is_2006_Oct_31/ai_n27060995, accessed October 30, 2008.

3. Pliagas, Linda, "Learning IT Right from Wrong," *InfoWorld*, October 2, 2000, pp. 39–40.

4. Fogliasso, Christine, and Donald Baack, "The Personal Impact of Ethical Decisions: A Social Penetration Theory Model," Second Annual Conference on Business Ethics Sponsored by the Vincentian Universities in the United States, New York, 1995.

5. Jones, T. M., "Ethical Decision-Making by Individuals in Organizations: An Issue-Contingent Model," *Academy of Management Review*, 1991, pp. 366–95.

6. Baase, Sara, *The Gift of Fire: Social, Legal and Ethical Issues in Computing* (Upper Saddle River, NJ: Prentice Hall, 1997).

7. Moores, Trevor, "Software Piracy: A View from Hong Kong," *Communications of the ACM*, December 2000, pp. 88–93.

8. Software and Information Industry of America, www.siaa.net/shared-content/press/.2000/5-24-00.html, accessed May 31, 2005.

9. "2007 Global Piracy Survey," http://w3.bsa.org/globalstudy/ accessed October 30, 2008.

10. Rittenhouse, David, "Privacy and Security on Your PC," *ExtremeTech*, May 28, 2002, www.extremetech.com, accessed May 31, 2005.

11. "Identity Theft," Public Safety Canada, October 2004, http://ww2.ps-sp.gc.ca/publications/Policing/identity_theft_e.asp#_Toc86053404 accessed October 30, 2008.

12. Ibid.

13. Vanbokkelen, James, "2006: The Year of the Breach," *Federal Computer Week*, December 18, 2006. p. 1.

14. Romaniuk, Ross, "Posed as Teacher?" May 5, 2008, http://winnipegsun.com/News/Manitoba/2008/05/05/5471331-sun.html, accessed October 30, 2008.

15. Sproule, Susan, and Norm Archer, *Measuring Identity Theft in Canada: 2006*, www.merc-mcmaster.ca/working-papers/meauring-identity-theft-in-canada-2006-consumer-survey, accessed May 8, 2008.

16. Tam, Pui-Wang, Erin White, Nick Wingfield, and Kris Maker, "Snooping E-Mail by Software Is Now a Workplace Norm," *The Wall Street Journal*, March 9, 2005, pp. B1, B3.

17. Corbin, Dana, "Keeping a Virtual Eye on Employees," *Occupational Health & Safety*, November 2000, pp. 24–28.

18. Pliagas, "Learning IT Right from Wrong."

19. Sanders, Peter, "Casinos Bet on Radio-ID Gambling Chips," *The Wall Street Journal*, May 13, 2005, pp. B1, B7.

20. Vaught, Bobby, Raymond Taylor, and Steven Vaught, "The Attitudes of Managers Regarding the Electronic Monitoring of Employee Behavior: Procedural and Ethical Considerations," *American Business Review*, January 2000, pp. 107–14.

21. Heydary, Javad, "Companies Step Up Electronic Monitoring of Employees," www.heydary.com/publications/employee-monitoring.html, accessed October 30, 2008.

22. Parker, Laura, "Medical-Privacy Law Creates Wide Confusion," *USA Today*, October 17–19, 2003, pp. 1A, 2A.

23. Medford, Cassimir, "Know Who I Am," *PC Magazine*, February 7, 2000, pp. 58–64.

24. Charters, Darren, "Electronic Monitoring and Privacy Issues in Business-Marketing: The Ethics of the DoubleClick Experience," *Journal of Business Ethics*, February 2002, pp. 243–54.

25. Naples, Mark, "Privacy and Cookies," *Target Marketing*, April 2002, pp. 28–30.

26. Forelle, Charles, "IBM Embraces Bold Method to Trap Spam," *The Wall Street Journal*, March 22, 2005, pp. B1, B2.

27. Angwin, Julia, "Elusive Spammer Sends Web Service on a Long Chase," *The Wall Street Journal*, May 7, 2003, pp. A1, A10.

28. Graven, Matthew P., "Leave Me Alone," *PC Magazine*, January 16, 2001, pp. 151–52.

29. Baase, *The Gift of Fire*.

30. Rittenhouse, "Privacy and Security on Your PC."

31. Staples, Sarah, "FBI Wants Canada to Make Internet and Phone Tapping Easier," April 2004, http://72.14.205.104/search?q=cache:PaXpUsPBt_MJ:www.fipa.bc.ca/library/News_Archive/FBI_wants_Canada_to_make_Internet_%26_phone_tapping_easier_April_27_04.doc, accessed October 30, 2008.

32. Soat, John, "IT Confidential," *InformationWeek*, June 3, 2002, p. 98.

33. "RCMP Official at Arar Inquiry Says Innocent People Placed in National Database," June 30, 2004, www.cbc.ca/canada/story/2004/06/30/ArarRCMP_040630.html, accessed October 30, 2008.

34. Salkever, Alex, "A Dark Side to the FBI's Magic Lantern," *BusinessWeek Online*, November 27, 2001, www.businessweek.com, accessed May 14, 2005.

35. "Privacy Legislation," January 6, 2004 www.privcom.gc.ca/legislation/02_06_01_01_e.asp, accessed October 30. 2008.

36. "The Digital Economy in Canada," June 24, 2008, Industry Canada, www.ic.gc.ca/epic/site/ecic-ceac.nsf/en/h_gv00464e.html, accessed October 30, 2008.

37. Fraser, David, www.privacylawyer.ca/blog/index.html.

38. http://en.wikipedia.org/wiki/Personal_Information_Protection_and_Electronic_Documents_Act, accessed May 13, 2008.

39. Bank, David, "Keeping Information Safe," *The Wall Street Journal*, November 11, 2004, pp. B1, B2.

40. Puri, Poonam, "Judges Require Better Corporate Crime Education: Judicial Training Has Historically Keyed on Blue-Collar Wrongdoing," *Financial Post*, November 10, 2004, http://osgoode.yorku.ca/media2.nsf/83303ffe5af03ed585256ae6005379c9/0e5667533a46214285256f48005623de!OpenDocument, accessed November 30, 2008.

41. Gray, John, "A Good Country for Crooks: Canada's Losing War against White-Collar Crime," *Canadian Business*, www.canadianbusiness.com/managing/strategy/article.jsp?content=20070918_19904_19904 October 30, 2008.

42. Fontana, John, "Average Data Breach Costs Companies $5 Million," *Network World*, November 6, 2006, p. 20.

43. "Europe Plans to Jail Hackers," April 23, 2002, zdnet.com/2100-11105-889332.html, accessed May 31, 2005.

44. Meyer, Lisa, "Security You Can Live With," *Fortune*, Winter 2002, pp. 94–99.

45. "Fast Times," *Fortune*, Summer 2000, pp. 35–36.

46. "Tech-Savvy Blackmailers Hone a New Form of Extortion," *The Wall Street Journal*, May 5, 2005, pp. B1, B3.

47. Graafstra, Amal, "How Radio-Frequency Identification and I Got Personal,' *IEEE Spectrum*, March 2007, pp. 18–23.

48. "Chase Brings 'Blink' Technology to Tiger," www.LSUsports.net, accessed May 2, 2007.

49. "Australia Sends First Active RFID Tag System to Middle East," *Defense Daily International*, April 20, 2007.

50. Roybal, Joe, "All Tagged Up," *Beef*, April 2007, p. 34.

51. Radcliff, Deborah, "Beyond Passwords," *Computerworld*, January 21, 2002, pp. 52–53.

52. Eyres, Patricia, "Legal Traps for Unwary Managers during Corporate Criminal Investigations," *Business Credit*, February 2005, pp. 62–63.

53. Berman, Dennis, "Online Laundry: Government Posts Enron's E-Mail," *The Wall Street Journal*, October 6, 2003, pp. A1, A12.

54. "Personal Info Stolen from Equifax Database," March 15, 2004, www.ctv.ca/servlet/articlenews/story/ctvnews/20040315/equifax040315/20040315, accessed October 30, 2008.

55. Jaikumar, Vijayan, "Breach of Credit Data May Have Broad Scope," *ComputerWorld*, April 18, 2005, p. 6.

56. "Data Security Breaches Lead to Calls for Legislation," *ABA Bank Compliance*, March 2005, p. 7.

CHAPTER 9

1. "Research in Motion Reports First-Quarter Results," June 25, 2008, http://press.rim.com/financial/release.jsp?id=1684, accessed October 30, 2008.

2. "Apple Reports Record Second Quarter Results, April 23, 2008, www.apple.com/pr/library/2008/04/23results.html, accessed October 30, 2008.

3. "HSBC May Ditch BlackBerry for iPhone: Report," August 13, 2008, www.cbc.ca/technology/story/2008/08/13/tech-rim.html, accessed October 30, 2008.

4. "BlackBerry Losing Business Customers to iPhone?" www.cellphones.ca/news/post003642, accessed October 30, 2008.

5. "Blackberry vs. iPhone—Which Device Will Business Users Back," March 24, 2008. www.itbusiness.ca/it/client/en/home/News.asp?id=47656, accessed November 22, 2008.

6. Hoover, Lisa, "BlackBerry vs. iPhone: Which Device Will Business Users Back?" March 24, 2008, www.theglobeandmail.com/servlet/story/RTGAM.20080305.wgtsaasTECH-POINT06/BNStory/Technology/home, accessed October 30, 2008.

7. "SaaS Gives Small Business a Big Engine," March 5, 2008, www.theglobeandmail.com/servlet/story/RTGAM.20080305.wgtsaasTECH-POINT06/BNStory/Technology/home, accessed October 1, 2008.

8. Lu, Stephen C-Y, "Process Planning as Negotiation—A Step toward F2B2C Ecommerce," STC/O CAPP Working Group, January 24, 2001, www.3s.hmg.inpg.fr/ci/GAMA/01Lu.pdf, accessed June 6, 2005.

9. Overdorf, Jason, "Tutors Get Outsourced." *Business 2.0*, August 2006, p. 32.

10. Adams, Nina, "Lessons from the Virtual World," *Training*, June 1995, pp. 45–47.

11. Flynn, Laurie, "VR and Virtual Spaces Find a Niche in Real Medicine," *The New York Times*, June 5, 1995, p. C3.

12. Collier, Roger, "Virtually Better," CMAJ, August 26, 2008, www.cmaj.ca/cgi/content/full/179/5/410, accessed October 30, 2008.

13. Hilson, Gary, "Medical Holodeck Opens in Calgary," www.itbusiness.ca/it/client/en/home/News.asp?id=21682, accessed October 30, 2008.

14. Kesten, Lou, "'Paper Mario' Leads the Latest Wii Wave," *Kansas City Star*, May 3, 2007, www.kansascity.com/211/v-print/story/91776.html, accessed May 5, 2007.

15. "Somark Innovations Announces Successful Live Animal Testing of Biocompatible Chipless RFID Ink in Cattle and Laboratory Rats," Somark Innovations, January 9, 2007, www.somarkinnovations.com/Files/SomarkBiocompatibleChipless-RFIDInk.pdf, accessed May 5, 2007.

16. "NFC Forum News," www.nfc-forum.org/home, accessed November 9, 2008.

17. Corcoran, Elizabeth, "The Next Small Thing," *Forbes*, July 23, 2001, pp. 96–106.

18. Center to Integrate Nanotechnologies, United States Department of Energy, http://cint.lanl.gov, accessed June 1, 2005.

19. "The Expansion of Cellphone Services," Canada's Office of Consumer Affairs, January 22, 2008, www.ic.gc.ca/epic/site/oca-bc.nsf/en/ca02267e.html, accessed October 30, 2008.

20. "Family Finder," Wavemarket, www.wavemarket.com/products_page.php?product=1, accessed October 30, 2008.

21. "Atlanta NFC Pilot, and Others, Will Lead to Late '06 Commercialization," Digital Transactions, December 14, 2005, www.digitaltransactions.net/newsstory.cfm?newsID5800, accessed May 6, 2007.

22. "Motorola Looks to Start Commercial M-Wallet Service by Summer," Digital Transactions, February 9, 2006, www.digitaltransactions.net/newsstory.cfm?newsID5852, accessed May 6, 2007.

23. Hof, Robert, "My Virtual Life," *BusinessWeek*, May 1, 2006, www.businessweek.com/magazine/content/06_18/b3982001.htm, accessed May 4, 2007.

24. "What Is Second Life," Linden Research, Inc., http://secondlife.com/whatis/, accessed May 4, 2007.

ELM A

1. http://unicode.org, retrieved October 10, 2008.

2. "Canada's Cattle Go High-Tech Using RFID," March 8, 2005, www.itbusiness.ca/it/client/en/home/News.asp?id=123571., accessed October 5, 2008

3. Canadian Cattle Identification Agency, www.canadaid.com/About/FAQs.shtml, accessed October 5, 2008.

ELM B

1. CBC.ca. (September 1, 2006). "CRTC Reaffirms VoIP Decision, Will Review Regulations," www.cbc.ca/news/story/2006/09/01/crtc-voip.html, accessed November 15, 2007.

ELM C

1. Pack, Thomas, "Virus Protection," *Link-Up*, January/February 2002, p. 25.

2. Meserve, Jason, "People around the World Bitten by 'Love Bug,'" *Network World*, May 8, 2000, pp. 14, 28.

3. Zemke, Ron, "Tech-Savvy and People-Stupid," *Training*, July 2000, pp. 16–18.

4. York, Thomas, "Invasion of Privacy? E-Mail Monitoring Is on the Rise," *InformationWeek*, February 21, 2000, pp. 142–46.

5. Meserve, "People around the World Bitten by 'Love Bug.'"

6. Harris, Shane, "SoBig: A Look Back," *Government Executive*, November 2003, p. 72.

7. Babcock, Charles, "Fast-Moving Virus Slams E-Mail Systems," *InformationWeek*, August 2003, p. 22.

8. Roberts, Paul, "The Year Ahead in Security," *InfoWorld*, January 2004, p. 17.

9. Kirkpatrick, David, "Taking Back the Net," *Fortune*, September 29, 2003, pp. 117–22.

10. Luhn, Robert, "Eliminate Viruses," *PC World*, July 2002, p. 94.

11. Landolt, Sara Cox, "Why the Sky Isn't Falling," *Credit Union Management*, October 2000, pp. 52–54.

12. "Hackers Attack *USA Today* Website," *Morning Sun* (Pittsburgh, KS), July 13, 2002, p. 6.

13. Hulme, George, "Vulnerabilities Beckon Some with a License to Hack," *InformationWeek*, October 23, 2000, pp. 186–92.

14. Kornblum, Janet, "Kournikova Virus Maker: No Harm Meant," *USA Today*, February 14, 2001, p. 3D.

15. Lefler, Dion, "'Erasing' Data Often Does No Such Thing," www.kansas.com/mid/kansas/news/special_packages/bkt/11037867.htm, accessed May 1, 2007.

16. GSM World, "GSM Operators, Coverage Maps and Roaming Information," www.gsmworld.com/roaming/gsminfo/index.shtml, accessed November 15, 2007.

17. GSM World, "Security Advice for Mobile Phone Users," www.gsmworld.com/using/security/advice.shtml accessed November 15, 2007.

18. CNN.com, www.cnn.com/2004/TECH/04/04/mobile.terror, accessed May 1, 2007.

19. The Sedona Conference® Working Group 7 ("Sedona Canada"). The Sedona Canada Principles, Addressing Electronic Document Production [Public Comment Draft] (February 2007) www.lexum.umontreal.ca/e-discovery/2_07WG7pubcomment.pdf, accessed November 17, 2007.

20. http://en.wikipedia.org/wiki/Computer_Crime_in_Canada#Laws_and_Bills, accessed October 13, 2008.

21. Bill C-27, www2.parl.gc.ca/HousePublications/Publication.aspx?Docid=3125690&file=4, accessed October 13, 2008.

22 Criminal Code, www.thecanadianencyclopedia.com/index.cfm?PgNm=TCE&Params=A1ARTA0002020, accessed October 13, 2008.

23. Criminal Code C-46, http://laws.justice.gc.ca/en/ShowFullDoc/cs/C-46///en, accessed October 13, 2008.

24. "Computer crime," http://en.wikipedia.org/wiki/Cybercrime, accessed October 13, 2008.

25. "'Mafiaboy' Sentenced to 8 Months," September 13, 2001, www.wired.com/techbiz/media/news/2001/09/46791, accessed October 13, 2008,

26. "MafiaBoy," http://en.wikipedia.org/wiki/MafiaBoy, accessed October 13, 2008.

27 "'Mafiaboy' Faces up to 3 years in Prison," April 19, 2000, http://archives.cnn.com/2000/TECH/computing/04/19/dos.charges/index.html, accessed October 13, 2008.

28. "Analyst Puts Hacker Damage at $1.2 Billion and Rising," February 10, 2000, www.infoworld.com/articles/ic/xml/00/02/10/000210icyankees.html, accessed October 13, 2008.

29. "Rumors Fly as RIM, India Talk BlackBerry Snooping, Privacy," May 27, 2008 http://arstechnica.com/news.ars/post/20080527-rumors-fly-as-rim-india-talk-blackberry-snooping-privacy.html, accessed October 13, 2008.

30. "RIM India's Blackberry Encryption Worries," June 2, 2008 www.informationweek.com/news/security/encryption/showArticle.jhtml?articleID=208401643, accessed October 13, 2008.

31. "Will RIM Let India Spy on Users? Or Won't It?," May 31, 2008 www.p2pnet.net/story/16103, accessed October 13, 2008.

ELM D

1. "ITWorld.com Salary Calculator" www.itworldcanada.com/salarycalculator/result.aspx, accessed August 15, 2008.

CHAPTER 9

p. 267 (left): © Euan Myles / Getty Images;

p. 267 (middle): Andersen Ross / PhotoDisc / Getty Images;

p. 267 (right): © Stockbyte / Getty Images;

p. 271: Courtesy Texas Instruments

MODULE A

p. 285 (top left): Courtesy of Veo;

p. 285: (top middle): Courtesy of Fossil;

p. 285 (middle left): Gateway, Inc.;

p. 285 (bottom left): Photo Courtesy of Kensington Technology Group (www.kensington.com);

p. 285 (bottom middle): Used with permission of Eastman Kodak Company;

p. 285 (bottom left): Photo by Apple

p. 285 (middle right): Photo by Apple via Getty Images;

p. 287 (left): Treo 650 smartphone by palmOne;

p. 287 (top right): Courtesy of Dell Inc.;

p. 287 (bottom right): Image reprinted with permission from ViewSonic Corporation;

p. 287 (bottom right) Photo by BlackBerry

p. 288: Photo courtesy of Overdrive PC;

p. 289 (top left): Hewlett-Packard Company;

p. 289 (bottom left): Photo Courtesy of Cray Inc.;

p. 289 (right): Courtesy of International Business Machines Corporation. Unauthorized use not permitted.;

p. 296 (left): Hewlett-Packard Company;

p. 296 (middle): Courtesy of Microsoft Hardware;

p. 296 (right): Photo used with permission from Plantronics, Inc.;

p. 298 (top left): Image reprinted with permission from ViewSonic Corporation;

p. 298 (top right): © Copyright 2005 Samsung Electronics America. All Rights Reserved.;

p. 298 (top bottom): Copyright © 2007 Apple Inc. All rights reserved;

p. 299 (top left): Courtesy of Epson America, Inc.;

p. 299 (top middle): Hewlett-Packard Company;

p. 299 (top right): Courtesy of Epson America, Inc.;

p. 301 (top left): Courtesy of SanDisk Corporation;

p. 301 (top right): Image courtesy of Kingston Technology;

p. 301 (bottom left): Photo Courtesy of Intel Corporation;

p. 301 (bottom right): Image courtesy of Kingston Technology;

p. 305 (top left): Courtesy of Belkin International, Inc.;

p. 305 (middle left): Courtesy of Belkin International, Inc.;

p. 305 (bottom left): © Crutchfield Corporation;

p. 305 (center): Hewlett-Packard Company;

p. 305 (top right): Photo by R.D. Cummings, Pittsburg State University;

p. 305 (bottom right): © Crutchfield Corporation;

MODULE B

p. 312 (top): Courtesy of NETGEAR Inc.;

p. 312: Photo courtesy of 3M Corporation;

p. 312: Photo courtesy of 3com Corporation;

p. 312: Photo by R.D. Cummings, Pittsburg State University;

p. 312 (bottom): Courtesy of Linksys;

p. 312: Microsoft product box shot reprinted with permission from Microsoft Corporation;

p. 325 (top): © Spencer Grant / Photo Edit;

p. 325 (middle): © Mark Antman / The Image Works;

p. 325 (bottom): PhotoDisc / Getty Images

MODULE E

p. 99: © Anthony Redpath / Corbis

MODULE I

Figure I.5 (left): PRNewsFoto / Cambridge SoundWorks / AP / Wide World Photos;

Figure I.5 (middle): Weinberg-Clark;

Figure I.5 (right): © Nance S. Trueworthy;

Figure I.8 (left): © David Madison 2005;

Figure I.8 (right): © David Madison 2005